Sarvāstivāda Abhidharma

Sarvāstivāda Abhidharma

Bhikkhu KL Dhammajoti
法光

Centre of Buddhist Studies
The University of Hong Kong
2007

First Edition: Colombo, 2002
Second Revised Edition: Colombo, 2004
Third Revised Edition: Hong Kong, 2007

Published in Hong Kong by
Centre of Buddhist Studies
The University of Hong Kong
2007

This publication is sponsored by
the Li Chong Yuet Ming Buddhist Studies Fund
of the Li Ka Shing Foundation

ISBN: 978-988-99296-1-9

CONTENTS

PREFACE TO THE SECOND EDITION

As stated in my preface to the first edition published in 2002, this book was originally intended as an outline of the Sarvāstivāda doctrines. It mainly grew out of the outlines and notes that I have given in the past years to my students at the Postgraduate Institute of Pali and Buddhist Studies, University of Kelaniya. Some of these outlines were also distributed to students at the Department of Religious Studies, University of Calgary when I served there as the Numata Professor of Buddhist Thought in winter, 2002. In response to the need of my students, I had also been elaborating on different parts of these outlines and notes at different times. The result was this book which now comes to be entitled "Sarvāstivāda Abhidharma".

Chapter Five on "*Sarvāstitva* and Temporality" was adapted from an essay of mine which was first included in the appendix of my *Entrance to the Supreme Doctrine* (Colombo, 1998) as "The Theory of Sarvāstitva", and subsequently slightly revised and published as "*Sarvāstitva* and Temporality: The Vaibhāṣika Defence" in the *Journal of the Postgraduate of Pali and Buddhist Studies*, vol. I, 1999.

If some chapters appear more terse and succinct compared to others, it was because the original outlines were used at different times with somewhat different emphases for the different classes, and were not planned as a single project from the beginning. I would have liked to postpone and elaborate further on these outlines in the little leisure that I have, to improve on the material presented herein. However, in view of the fact that there is hardly any book available in English dealing comprehensively with the doctrines of the Sarvāstivāda, I have decided to bring out this publication at this juncture, in spite of its many imperfections. I look forward to the not too distant future when I shall be able to find sufficient time to offer a more carefully revised edition for the students of Abhidharma who I hope will find this book useful for their studies. In the past several years of my teaching, I have also discussed various Abhidharma controversies; and some of these discussions have been published in academic journals. It is my belief that these controversies can offer us much insight into the abhidharma thought system as a whole, and help us importantly to gain a proper perspective of the development in Buddhist thought in general – the period of the Abhidharma schools being one of the most creative phases of this development in India. I have, however, with one or two limited exception, refrained from incorporating these discussions into this book as most of them are rather lengthy. It is my intention to have them summarized and integrated in a book form to be published as a sequel to the present book on another occasion.

I suggest that this book be used together with my *Entrance to the Supreme Doctrine* to which I have referred quite frequently. However, readers should take note that I have in this present publication changed some of my earlier rendering of the Sanskrit technical terms; a notable example is 'activity'(作用 *zuo yong*) for *kārita* and funtion (功能 *gong neng*) for *vṛtti, vyāpāra*, etc.

I would like to take this opportunity to express my deep gratitude to Professor Y. Karunadasa for his constant encouragement to my Abhidharma studies, and moral support in my times of difficulties in Sri Lanka. I am also grateful to Venerable Bhikṣuṇī Chun Yi for spending several sleepless night carefully going through the entire proof of this book excepting the last chapter; to Venerable Dhammapāla for proof-reading part of the book; and to Venerable Bangladesh Bhaddiya Tanchangya for generating the index, and checking through again part of the final proof. Venerable Bangladesh Assaji Tanchangya and Mr. W. Sugath Chandra must also be thanked for helping at the final stage of the preparatory work.

In this second edition, I have added a chapter (10) on the theories of knowledge of the Sarvāstivāda and the Sautrāntika. Some minor adjustments have also been made in a few places. I must thank my disciples, Ven. Bhaddiya Tanchangya, Ven. Dhammadīpa (Joyadip Tanchangya) and Ven. Dhammarakkhita Barua, for their devoted effort in proof-reading and generating the index of this new edition.

KL Dhammajoti (法光)
22nd July 2004, Mulleriyawa

PREFACE TO THE THIRD EDITION

This edition is a substantial revision of the second edition published in 2004. I have elaborated on numerous points in the chapters, and incorporated relevant material from several papers I have published in journals. In addition, I have prepared a glossary of the Sanskrit terms occurring in the book, which may otherwise scare away those readers unfamiliar with the Sanskrit language. The whole revision process, however, was constrained within the time frame of some two and a half months during this summer vacation, and there is no doubt that further revision and addition is to be desired.

I believe that this edition is stylistically much more presentable and free from typological and English errors compared to the previous two editions. This is largely due to the tireless proofreading effort — with numerous suggestions and criticism — of Ven. Gelong Lodrö Sangpo and Gelongma Migme Chödrön, both members of the Chökyi Gyatso Translation Committee at the Gampo Abbey Monastery, Canada. I must therefore record my deep appreciation for these two venerables. Whatever stylistic imperfection still remains is due to my own obstinacy and oversight.

My special thanks are also due to my student, Liza Cheung, for her equally tireless effort in the proof-reading process. At the Centre, she has been overseeing the various aspects of the whole revision process, working from early morning till late night. She was also responsible for extracting the Sanskrit terms for inclusion in the glossary. My thanks are also due to my students, Ven. Huifeng, Alan Mok and Aosi Mak; the former two, especially for the difficult task of generating the index, the latter, especially for drawing and revising the charts throughout the whole book. Other students who had helped in one respect or another of the publication project include Sandra Lam, Ven. Chandaratana,

Ven. Zhen Jue and Francis Kwan. I am also grateful to Sandra for looking after me in various ways, in spite of her engagement with our Abhidharma Dictionary project.

My thanks are also due to Professor CF Lee, Ven. Dr. Jing Yin, Ven. Hin Hung and other members of the Li Chong Yuet Ming Buddhist Studies Fund of the Li Ka Shing Foundation, for accepting this book as the first English book of the publication series of the Centre of Buddhist Studies, University of Hong Kong.

Finally, and most importantly, I'd like to express my deep gratitude for Venerable Dr. Yin Shun and Professor Y. Karunadasa for encouraging me to embark on my Abhidharma studies, and the profound inspiration that I have derived from them.

KL Dhammajoti 法光
August 2007, Hong Kong

ABBREVIATIONS

Note:

(i) All references of Chinese Tripiṭaka texts are to the Taishō edition, unless otherwise stated.

(ii) All references of Pāli texts are to the PTS edition, unless otherwise stated.

(iii) All references of Pāli *ṭīkā* and *anuṭīkā* are those of the *Chaṭṭha Saṅgāyana* edition of the *Tipiṭaka* published electronically by the Vipassanā Research Institute, Dhammagiri, Maharastra, India.

A	*Aṅguttara Nikāya.*
ADV	*Abhidharmadīpa* (*with Vibhāṣāprabhāvṛtti*) = Bib. no. 3.
AH	**Abhidharma-hṛdaya*, T no. 1550.
AHS	**Abhidharma-hṛdaya Sūtra*, T no. 1551.
AKB	*Abhidharmakośabhāṣya* = Bib. no. 4.
AKB(C)	Chinese tr. of AKB by Xuan Zang, T no. 1558.
AKB(E)	English tr. of AKB(F) = Bib. no. 197.
AKB(F)	*L'Abhidharmakośa de Vasubandhu*, by La Vallée Poussin = Bib. no. 166.
AmRŚ	**Abhidharmāmṛta-rasa-śāstra.* Chinese tr. (Translator unknown), T no 1553.
Asm	*Abhidharmasamuccaya* of Asaṅga = Bib. no. 11.
AsmB	*Abhidharmasamuccayabhāṣya* = Bib. no. 12.
Avatāra	**Abhidharmāvatāra* by Skandhila.
Avatāra(T)	Tibetan tr. of *Avatāra* = Bib. no. 27.
BAM	*Buddhist Analysis of Matter* = Bib. no. 149.
D	*Dīgha Nikāya.*
DhsA	*Dhammasaṅgani Aṭṭhakathā* (=*Atthasālinī*).
DKŚ	**Dhātu-kāya-śāstra,* 阿毗達磨界身足論, T no. 1540.
DSŚ	**Dharma-skandha-śāstra,* 阿毗達磨法蘊足論, T no. 1537.
EnB	*Encyclopaedia of Buddhism.* Ed., Malalasekera, GP (Colombo, 1961).
Entrance	*Entrance into the Supreme Dharma* = Bib. no. 107.
Frauwallner	Frauwallner (1995) = Bib. no. 124.
HVy	**Abhidharma-hṛdaya-vyākhyā*, T no. 1552.

IAKB	*Index to the Abhidharmakośabhāṣya* = Bib. nos. 133, 134, 135.
ISVm	Bib. no. 244.
JCBSSL	*Journal of the Centre for Buddhist Studies*, Sri Lanka.
JPŚ	*Jñānaprasthāna-śāstra,* 阿毗達磨發智論, T no. 1544.
JRAS	*Journal of the Royal Asiatic Society of Great Britain and Ireland*
Katō	Bib. no. 154.
Kvu	*Kathāvatthu.*
M	*Majjhima Nikāya.*
MA	*Majjhimanikāya Aṭṭhakathā.*
MCB	*Mélanges Chinois et Bouddhiques,* l'Institute Belge des Hautes Etudes Chinoises, Bruxelles
MPPU	**Mahāprajñāpāramitā-upadeśa,* 大智度論, T no. 1509.
MVŚ	**Abhidharma-mahā-vibhāṣa-śāstra,* 阿毗達磨大毗婆沙論, T no. 1545.
Ny	**Abhidharma-nyāyānusāra,* 阿毗達磨順正理論, T no. 1562.
Perception	Bib. no. 112.
PjŚ	*Prajñapti-śāstra,* 施設論, T no. 1538.
PrŚ	*Abhidharmaprakaraṇa-śāstra,* 阿毗達磨品類足論, T no. 1542.
PTS	The Pāli Text Society, London.
PVV	*Pañcavastuka-vibhāṣā-śāstra,* T no. 1555.
S	*Saṃyutta Nikāya.*
SĀ	*Saṃyuktagāma,* 雜阿含, T no. 98.
SatŚ	**Satyasiddhi-śāstra,* 成實論, Chinese tr. by Kumārajīva. = Bib. no. 81.
SDS	*Sarva-darśana-saṃgraha* = Bib. no. 31.
SgPŚ	*Abhidharma-saṅgīti-paryāya-śāstra,* 阿毗達磨異門足論, T no. 1536.
Siddhi(C)	**Vijñaptimātratā-siddhi,* 成唯識論, compiled by Xuan Zang, T no. 1585. = Bib. no. 75.
Siddhi(F)	Bib. no. 170.
Siddhi(S)	Sanskrit text of Sthiramati's *Triṃśikā Vijñaptimātratā* (*-siddhi*) (= *Siddhi*) = Bib. no. 40.
Siddhi(T)	Bib. no. 33.
SPrŚ	**Abhidharma-samaya-pradīpikā-śāstra,* 阿毗達磨顯宗論, T no. 1563.
Study	Bib. no. 242.
T	*Taishō Shinshu Daizokyo*, 大正大藏經. Ed., Takakusu, J. 1924—1932.

Tatia	Bib. no. 230.
TA(U-J)	Bib. no. 218.
TSP	*Tattvasaṃgraha-pañjikā* = Bib. no. 36.
ZY	*Selected Chinese Tripiṭaka Texts*, 藏要. Ed., Ou Yang Jian. (Nanking, 1930—1945).
UdA	*Udāna Aṭṭhakathā* (*Paramatthadīpanī*).
Viṃś	*Viṃśatikā Vijñaptimātratāsiddhi* = Bib. no. 40.
Vism	*Visuddhimagga*. Ed., Kosambi, D (Bombay, 1940).
VKŚ	*Abhidharma-vijñāna-kāya-śāstra,* 阿毗達磨識身足論, T no. 1539.
Vy	*Sphuṭārthā Abhidharmakośa-vyākhyā* of Yaśomitra (= *Vyākhyā*) Bib. no. 9.
YBŚ	*Yogācārabhūmi śāstra of Asaṅga,* 瑜伽師地論, T no. 1579.
ZW	藏外佛教文獻, Vol. I (Bejing, 1995).

1. Abhidharma

Its Origin, Meaning and Function

1.1. Origin of the *abhidharma*

1.1.1. Origin according to tradition

Traditionally, the *abhidharma-piṭaka* is given as the last of the *tripiṭaka*-s whose order is: *vinaya*, *sūtra*, *abhidharma* — or *sūtra*, *vinaya*, *abhidharma* in the northern tradition. This very probably reflects the historical fact that the *abhidharma* texts were evolved and compiled as a *piṭaka* later than the other two. This same fact is also discernible in the ancient triple designations given to the specialists of the Buddhist Canon — *vinaya-dhara*, *sūtra-dhara*, *mātṛkā-dhara*. Significantly, the third term in the list has, instead of *abhidharma*, the term *mātṛkā* (Pāli: *mātikā*), meaning a matrix in the form of a list summarily enumerating topics to be elaborated upon. This suggests that at the earlier stage, the study of these *mātṛkā*-s had served as a major basis for the development of the *abhidharma-piṭaka*. (See below).

It is possible that most of the so-called Hīnayāna schools in India possessed their own sets of *tripiṭaka*. Unfortunately, most of these *tripiṭaka* texts are no longer extant. As far as the canonical *abhidharma* texts are concerned, we are now in possession of only two complete sets: the seven texts of the Theravāda preserved in Pāli, and the seven Sarvāstivāda texts in Chinese translation. Of the latter, however, the *Prajñapti-śāstra* (PjŚ) is only a partial translation; a fuller version is preserved in the Tibetan (see *infra*, § 4.1.1.3). It is in the *abhidharma* treatises — comprising commentaries, sub-commentaries and compendia besides the canonical texts — that these Hīnayāna schools gradually defined and articulated their distinctive doctrinal positions. While it is a fact that the extant *vinaya*- and *sūtra-piṭaka*-s can no longer claim to be the pristine words of the Buddha, much as we would like, the sectarian coloring within these two collections are by and large marginal compared to that in the *abhidharma* texts — a well-known fact borne out by comparative studies of the extant Pāli *nikāya* and the Chinese *āgama* texts.

According to the Theravāda tradition, Śāriputra transmitted the *abhidhamma* to the disciples. All of the seven canonical *abhidhamma* texts are said to be by the Buddha, the first *ābhidhammika*.[1] The Buddha first taught it to the gods in the Thirty-three (*tāva-tiṃsa*)-Heaven; and it was studied and transmitted through Śāriputra by a succession of teachers.[2]

The Sarvāstivāda tradition, on the other hand, accepts that their canonical *abhidharma* works were compiled by the disciples. Nevertheless, like the Theravāda, it too maintains that the Buddha is the real author; the compilers simply gathered up and re-arranged His dispersed teachings:

> Without the exposition of the *abhidharma*, the pupil is unable to examine the *dharma*-s. However, it was spoken by the Fortunate One in a dispersed manner. The Venerable Kātyāyanīputra and others, having collected it, established it [as the *abhidharma*] — just as the Venerable Dharmatrāta made the *Udāna-varga* [by collecting the scattered sayings of the Buddha]. (*na hi vinābhidharmopadeśena śiṣyaḥ śakto dharmān pravicetum iti / sa tu prakīrṇa ukto bhagavatā / bhadantakātyāyanīputraprabhṛtibhiḥ piṇḍīkṛtya sthāpito bhadanta-dharmatrātodāna-vargīya-karaṇavat //*)[3]

The *Abhidharma-mahāvibhāṣā* (MVŚ) likewise speaks of Kātyāyanīputra compiling what the Buddha had spoken in the *sūtra*-s.

It further declares:

> The *abhidharma* was originally the words of the Buddha; it is only the compilation of the Venerable [Kātyāyanīputra]. Moreover, whether they are the Buddha's or the disciples' words, [so long as] they do not contradict *dharmatā*, the Bhagavat allowed all of them to be studied (lit: upheld) by the *bhikṣu*-s. Accordingly, the Venerable made the compilation from what he had heard from the line of tradition or from his examination through the power of his resolution-knowledge (*praṇidhi-jñāna*).

The 5th century C.E. orthodox Vaibhāṣika master, Saṃghabhadra, speaks in the same vein:

> ...the Buddha first expounded the *abhidharma* Himself. Without the Buddha's exposition, the great disciples, Śāriputra and others, would not have been capable of the proper investigation into the characteristics of the *dharma*-s. ... [The compilation of the Buddha's dispersed *abhidharma* teachings] by Venerable Kātyāyanīputra and others ... was like the collective compilation (*saṃgīti*) of the *vinaya* and the *sūtra*-s by the Venerable Mahākāśyapa and others. The two *piṭaka*-s, *sūtra* and *vinaya*, were compiled in accordance with the words; it was only the *abhidharma-piṭaka* that was compiled in accordance with the meanings. ... The compilation of the *abhidharma* in accordance with the Buddha's noble teachings was permitted by the Buddha and can therefore be called the Buddha's words.[4]

1.1.2. Historical origin

In all probability, the *abhidharma* has its origin in the *sūtra*-s. However, the term *abhidharma* — although occurring, often alongside *abhivinaya,* in the *sūtra*-s — does not refer to the *abhidharma* texts constituting the third *piṭaka*, for in the *sūtra*-s the meaning of *abhidharma* seems to be 'about the *dhamma*', or 'the profound doctrines' (of the Buddha).

The following types of *sūtra*-s are particularly noteworthy as having features which contributed to the development of the *abhidhamma*/*abhidharma* in the later specialized sense, all aiming at unfolding and clarifying the Buddha's profound teachings:

(a) Those featuring ***abhidharma-kathā*** — a solemn dialogue between two *bhikṣu*-s concerning the spiritual path; others listening are not permitted to interrupt. An example is the *Mahāgosinga-sutta*:[5] Sāriputta asks Ānanda, Anuruddha, Revata, Mahā Kassapa and finally Mahā Moggallāna in turn what kind of *bhikkhu* could enhance the brilliance of the Gosiṅga-sālavana-dāya which is delightful in the moon-lit night. Moggallāna replies: "Here, friend Sāriputta, two *bhikkhu*-s engage in an *abhidhamma-kathā*, and each, being questioned by the other, answers without floundering, and their discussion proceeds in accordance with the Dhamma. Such kind of *bhikkhu*-s could illuminate this Gosinga-sālavana-dāya." The 6th century Theravāda commentator, Buddhaghoṣa, in fact, links *dhammakathika* with *abhidhamma*. (*Atthasālinī*, 25)

(b) Those featuring ***vedalla*** (Skt. *vaidalya*): Derived from √*dal* meaning to 'crack'/'open', this feature signifies the extensive unraveling of the profound doctrinal meanings that have been hidden. In form, it consists of a question and answer session on doctrinal matters with a scope apparently broader than that in *abhidhamma-kathā* — either between the Buddha and the fourfold disciples (with others listening) or among the disciples themselves. *Vedalla-kathā* is also sometimes juxtaposed to *abhidhamma-kathā*;[6] e.g., the *Mahā-vedalla-sutta*[7] where Mahā-koṭṭhila questions and Sāriputta answers; the *Cūḷavedalla-sutta*[8] where Visākha questions, Dhammadinnā answers.

In the Theravāda classificatory scheme of the Buddha's nine-fold teachings (*navaṅga-satthu-sāsana*), *vedalla* occurs as the last member, which may suggest that it came to be incorporated into the scheme at the time of the evolution of *abhidharma* into the genre of which it was considered to correspond. Both the Sarvāstivāda and the Yogācāra equate it with *vaitulya* and *vaipulya*. Saṃghabhadra's explanation is as follows:

> *Vaipulya* refers to the extensive analytical clarification of *dharma*-s by means of logical reasoning (正理; **yukti*, **nyāya*); for, all *dharma*-s have numerous natures and characteristics which cannot be analytically clarified without extensive discussion. It is also known as extensive bursting (廣破; *vaidalya* < *vi* + *dal*), for this extensive discussion is capable of bursting the extremely strong darkness of nescience (*ajñāna*). It is also known as unmatchability (無比; *vaitulya* < *vi* + *tul*), for this extensive discussion has subtle and profound principles which cannot be matched.[9]

The same equation of the three terms is also seen in the *Abhidharma-samuccaya* (under *Dharma-viniścaya*) and its *bhāṣya* which noteworthily gives a Mahāyānic stress in this context.[10] It may well be that by Asaṅga's time, if not earlier, this had become a common northern Buddhist tradition.[11]

(c) Those featuring the ***vibhaṅga*** ('analysis/exposition') style — a brief, summarized teaching is elaborated by the Buddha or a competent disciple. The *vibhaṅga* methodology, however, is to be understood as originally representing a distinctive characteristic of the Buddha's teachings, and not just a feature characterizing an exposition on the brief teachings. The two terms, *abhidharma* and *abhivinaya* ('concerning the *dharma*', 'concerning the *vinaya*'), often juxtaposed in the *sūtra*-s, are indicative of the earliest development. The significance of being the elaboration on brief teachings, however, came to predominate at least by the time of formation of the *nikāya/āgama* collections. In the *Madhyamāgama*, we find some 35 *sūtra*-s grouped as **vibhaṅga* recitations (分別誦). Likewise, there are some 12 *sutta*-s grouped under the Pāli *Vibhaṅga-vagga*. Like *vedalla*, then, it also came to signify the explication of the profound meanings intended in the Buddha's words, and the *vibhaṅga* method is to effect this through an analytical elaboration. Such a development was obviously connected with the emergence of the *abhidharma*. Indeed, the earliest *abhidharma* texts, such as the *Dharma-skandha-śāstra*, exhibit the feature of being a technical commentary on the *sūtra*-s, and one of the early Pāli canonical *abhidhamma* texts is noticeably named a *Vibhaṅgappakaraṇa*.

(d) Those featuring ***mātṛkā/mātikā*** — originally meaning a matrix or list of headings purporting to systematically summarize the Buddha's teaching (see above), e.g., the list of 37 doctrinal topics often known as *bodhipakṣya-dharma*[12] — four *smṛtyupasthāna*-s, four *samyak pradhāna*-s, four *ṛddhipāda*-s, five *indriya*-s, five *bala*-s, seven *bodhyaṅga*-s, eight *āryāṣṭāṅgika-mārga*-s. In the *Kinti-sutta*[13] these are given as the *dhamma* taught by the Buddha who has realized them directly (*ye vo mayā dhammā abhiññā desitā*), and the *bhikkhu*-s are exhorted to train themselves in them concordantly. It is noteworthy that, in this context, the term *abhidhamma* occurs: *tesañ ca vo bhikkhave samaggānaṃ … sikhataṃ, siyaṃsu dve bhikkhū abhidhamme nānāvādā…* ("O *bhikkhu*-s, while you are training concordantly…, two *bhikkhu*-s might dispute as regards the *abhidhamma*…"). The same list of 37 are given in the *Mahāparinibbāna-suttanta* as a summary of the Dhamma taught by the Buddha throughout His whole career. The *Abhidharmakośabhāṣya* (AKB) refers to them as constituting the Buddha's *Saddharma* pertaining to realization (*adhigama*); that pertaining to teaching (*āgama*; lit. 'tradition') is said to comprise the *sūtra*, *vinaya* and *abhidharma*.[14] In the northern tradition, however, it came to include as well the fundamental *abhidharma* texts and the truthful abhidharmic commentaries on the Buddha's words. (See below).

This feature represents a tendency toward organization and systematization which is the essential characteristic of *abhidharma*. Many scholars believe that *abhidharma* evolved from *mātṛkā*. The whole of the *Saṅgīti-suttanta* of the *Dīgha-nikāya* may be considered as a *mātṛkā*, which in the Sarvāstivāda evolved into a fundamental *abhidharma* text entitled the *Saṅgīti-paryāya*. It is noteworthy that, as late as the 5th century C.E., we find Saṃghabhadra mentioning *mātṛkā* unambiguously as being synonymous with *abhidharma* and *upadeśa* (see below), and cites as *mātṛkā* the early Sarvāstivāda canonical texts: the *Saṅgītiparyāya*, the *Dharma-skandha* and the *Prajñapti-śāstra*. Similarly, in explaining the *abhidharma-piṭaka*, the *Mūla-sarvāstivāda-vinaya-kṣudraka-vastu* also says, "the four *smṛtyupasthāna*-s, the four *samyak-prahāṇa*-s, … the *Dharma-saṃgīti* (= SgPŚ), the *Dharma-skandha* — these are collectively known as *mātṛkā*-s".[15] The *Aśokāvadāna*, too, speaks of the *mātṛkā-piṭaka*, giving similar contents.[16]

(e) Those featuring ***upadeśa*** — an expository or exegetical discourse. This is explained by Saṃghabhadra as follows, equating it with *mātṛkā* and *abhidharma*:

> *Upadeśa* refers to the non-erroneous (*aparyasta*, *aviparīta*) revealing, answering of objections and ascertainment, of the preceding [eleven] members. According to some, *upadeśa* also refers to analytical explanations, in accordance with reasoning, given by those who have seen the truth of the profound meanings of the *sūtra*-s, or by other wise ones.[17] It is none other than what is called *mātṛkā*, for, when the meaning of other *sūtra*-s is to be explained, this serves as the *mātṛkā*. It is also called *abhidharma*, on account of its being face to face (*abhi*) with the characteristics of *dharma*-s, and of its being a non-erroneous unraveling of the characteristics of *dharma*-s.[18]

The Yogācāra tradition also equates likewise:

> What is *upadeśa*? It refers to all the *mātṛkā*-s, *abhidharma*-s. The investigation into the profound *sūtra-piṭaka* and the proclamation of all the essential tenets of the *sūtra*-s — this is known as *upadeśa*.[19]

Such equation points clearly to the definite connection that this last member (*aṅga*) of the *dvādaśāṅga* has with the evolution of the *abhidharma*. The 12 *aṅga*-s, as given by Saṃghabhadra,[20] are: 1. *sūtra*, 2. *geya*, 3. *vyākaraṇa*, 4. *gāthā*, 5. *udāna*, 6. *nidāna*, 7. *avadāna*, 8. *itivṛttaka*/*ityuktaka*, 9. *jātaka*, 10. *vaipula*/*vaitulya* (which also seems to be connected with *vaidalya* = Pāli *vedalla*), 11. *adbhuta-dharma*, 12. *upadeśa*.[21] As we have seen above, Saṃghabhadra asserts that *upadeśa* is the non-erroneous revealing, unraveling of difficulties and ascertainment, of the meaning of all the preceding 11 parts of the *dvādaśāṅga*. This is in fact a Sarvāstivāda description of the nature and function of *abhidharma*.

Saṃghabhadra's assertion of *upadeśa* being the true criterion for the Buddha's words (*buddha-vacana*) is quite in line with the definition in the MVŚ:

> What is *upadeśa* (議論)? It refers to those teachings within the *sūtra*-s which serve as criteria for the black-teachings (黑[22]說), the great-teachings (大說), etc.
>
> Furthermore, it is as in the case where once the Buddha, having briefly expounded on a *sūtra,* entered into his room remaining silent for a long time, [whereupon] the great disciples assembled together, each explaining the Buddha's words with different words and meanings.[23]

In brief, three basic meanings of *upadeśa* are discernible in the northern tradition:

(i) Those teachings within the *sūtra-piṭaka*, given by the Buddha Himself, which serve to ascertain what may or may not be accepted as the Buddha's true teachings. In Saṃghabhadra's terms, they are represented by the last of the Buddha's twelve-fold teachings, serving to ascertain the authenticity of all the other *aṅga*-s as *buddha-vacana*.

(ii) The collective elaborate discussion by the great disciples on the brief discourses of the Buddha.[24]

(iii) Since, as Saṃghabhadra states, *upadeśa* also refers to truthful expositions by "those who have seen the truth" of the *sūtra*-s or "other wise ones", it can then subsume not only the canonical *abhidharma* texts but also certain authoritative post-canonical commentaries satisfying the Sarvāstivādin conditions.[25]

1.2. Definitions of *abhidharma*

In the Pāli tradition, two main meanings are given: (i) supplementary (*atireka*) doctrines, (ii) special/superior (*visesa/visiṭṭha*) doctrines.[26] There are also other meanings, notably 'supreme (*uttama*) doctrines'.[27] These meanings are based on the interpretation of the prefix, *abhi*, as 'supreme' or 'excellent', and of *dhamma* as 'doctrine'. The other interpretation of *abhi*, which seems to be historically earlier,[28] is 'pertaining to', or 'facing/envisaging'; *abhidhamma* accordingly means 'pertaining to the doctrine' or 'concerning the doctrine'.

In the northern tradition, the second foregoing interpretation is the predominant one, and Xuan Zang consistently renders *abhidharma* as 'facing/envisaging *dharma*' (對法). However, the two components, 'facing/pertaining' and '*dharma*', are further elaborated differently. Thus, the MVŚ gives numerous explanatory definitions of the term *abhidharma* as follows:

(I) According to the Ābhidharmikas, it is so called because (1) it can properly and utterly determine (*vi-niś-√ci*) the characteristics of all *dharma*-s; (2) it can properly examine and penetrate the *dharma*-s, (3) it can directly realize (*abhi-sam-√i*) and realize (*sākṣāt-√kṛ*) with regard to all *dharma*-s; (4) it can get to the very bottom of the profound nature of *dharma*-s; (5) through it, the wisdom-eye of the noble ones comes to be purified; (6) it is only through it that the nature of the *dharma*-s, subtle from beginningless time, comes to be revealed; (7) what it expounds is not contradictory to the nature of the *dharma*-s — one who is extremely well-versed with regard to the specific and common characteristics in the *abhidharma* cannot be faulted in any way and made to contradict the nature of the *dharma*-s; (8) it can refute and defeat all the heretical views.

(II) According to the Venerable Vasumitra, it is so called because (9) it can always ascertain the nature of the *dharma*-s given in the *sūtra*-s; (10) it can properly understand the nature of the twelve-link conditioned co-arising (*pratītya-samutpāda*); (11) it can directly realize the *dharma*-s of the four noble truths; (12) it skillfully expounds on the practice of the noble eightfold path; (13) it can realize *nirvāṇa*; (14) it repeatedly analyses the *dharma*-s from innumerable doctrinal perspectives.

(III) According to the Bhadanta (Dharmatrāta), it is so called because (15) — by means of words, phrases and sentences — it systematically compiles, organizes and analyses the *dharma*-s pertaining to defilement, purification, bondage, liberation, and to the saṃsāric process (*pravṛtti*) and its cessation (*nivṛtti*).

(IV) According to Venerable Parśva, because (16) it is the final, judgmental, absolute and non-erroneous *prajñā*.

(V) According to Venerable Ghoṣaka, because (17) it can properly explain, to a seeker of liberation engaged in the proper practice, what he has not understood: "this is *duḥkha*; this is the cause of *duḥkha*; this is the cessation of *duḥkha*; this is the path leading to the cessation; this is the preparatory path (*prayoga-mārga*); this is the unhindered path (*ānantarya-mārga*); this is the path of liberation (*vimokṣa-mārga*); this is the path of progress/advancement/distinction (*viśeṣa-mārga*);[29] this is the path of the candidate (*pratipannaka*); this is the acquisition of the spiritual fruit."

(VI) According to the Dharmaguptas, because this *dharma* is predominant.

(VII) According to the Mahīśāsakas, because (18) *prajñā* can illuminate the *dharma*-s.

(VIII) According to the Dārṣṭāntikas, because (19) it is next to *nirvāṇa*, the supreme among all *dharma*-s.

(IX) According to the Grammarians (Śābdika, Śābdavāda), because (20) it can abandon the fetters, bondages, proclivities, secondary defilements and envelopments; and it can ascertain the aggregates (*skandha*), abodes (*āyatana*), elements (*dhātu*), conditioned co-arising (*pratītya-samutpāda*), truths (*satya*), foods (*āhāra*), spiritual fruits (*śrāmaṇya-phala*), factors conducive to enlightenment (*bodhipakṣya-dharma*), etc. — *a* means to abandon, and *bhi* means to ascertain.

(X) According to Venerable Buddhapālita, because (21) the prefix *abhi* means 'face to face', and this *dharma* can induce all the skillful *dharma*-s — the *bodhi-pakṣya-dharma*-s, etc. — to appear face to face.

(XI) According to Venerable Buddhadeva, because (22) *abhi* means 'predominant', and this *dharma* is predominant.

(XII) According to Vāmalabdha, because (23) *abhi* means 'veneration', and this *dharma* is honorable and venerable.[30]

Among the various meanings given above, some are more or less overlapping, and some find correspondence in the Theravāda. They may be subsumed into two broad senses: (i) that of clear, decisive discernment and ascertainment; (ii) that of being direct, face to face.[31] The first, while bringing out the characteristic concern of *abhidharma* articulated by the Ābhidharmika tradition, emphasizes its intellectual function; the second, the spiritual or soteriological function. In these explanations, *dharma* is explicitly interpreted as either the fundamental constituents of existence or as *nirvāṇa* qua the supreme Dharma, and implicitly, in some cases, as doctrine.

Both aspects — the traditional understanding of *abhi* as 'excellent' and 'pertaining', on the one hand, and the essential characteristic of the ābhidharmic exegesis, on the other — are brought out in the following definition of Saṃghabhadra:

> All those profound (*gambhīra*) exegetical discourses (論道) associated with the nature and characteristics of *dharma*-s are called *abhidharma* on account of the fact that they are capable of being face to face with the nature and characteristics of *dharma*-s.[32]

AKB explains the term as follows:

> A *dharma* is so called because it sustains its own characteristic. This *dharma* faces (*abhi*) toward the *dharma* in the highest sense, i.e., *nirvāṇa*, or toward the characteristics of *dharma*-s,[33] thus it is *abhidharma*.[34]

Abhidharma in the highest, real, sense is none other than the pure *prajñā* defined as the examination of *dharma*-s (*dharma-pravicaya*). Secondarily or conventionally, it also refers to the with-outflow (*sāsrava*) *prajñā* — derived from listening, reflection and cultivation (*śruta-cintā-bhāvanā-mayī prajñā*) — innate or acquired, which helps to bring about the pure (i.e., outflow-free) *prajñā*. The *abhidharma śāstra*-s, too, inasmuch as they serve as a means or as requisites (*saṃbhāra*) to its acquisition, are also to be considered as *abhidharma*.[35] Saṃghabhadra states:

> All the best discourses associated with *adhiśīla* are called *abhivinaya*, as they are capable of being face to face with the *vinaya*. All the profound discourses associated with the characteristics of *dharma*-s are called *abhidharma*, as they are capable of being face to face with the nature and characteristics of *dharma*-s.[36]

The characteristics of the *abhidharma* are distinguished from those of the other two *piṭaka*-s as follows:

The *sūtra-piṭaka* is the emanation (*niṣyanda*) of the Buddha's power (*bala*), for none can refute the doctrines therein.

The *vinaya-piṭaka* is the emanation of great compassion (*mahā-karuṇā*), for it advocates morality (*śīla*) for the salvation of those in the unfortunate planes of existence (*durgati*).

The *abhidharma* is the emanation of fearlessness, for it properly establishes the true characteristics of *dharma*-s, answering questions and ascertaining fearlessly.[37]

1.3. The soteriological function of the *abhidharma*

The above discussion (§ 1.1.2, § 1.2) should suffice to indicate that *abhidharma* originated with a spiritual motivation: It developed in the process of the disciples desiring to properly, fully, and systematically understand the profound teachings of the Buddha. In the AKB (*ca.* 5th century C.E.) and *abhidharma* works subsequent to it, we can still clearly discern the firm conviction in the soteriological function of *abhidharma*. Thus, in the AKB the Ābhidharmika declares that *abhidharma* has been taught by the Buddha because it is the only excellent means for the appeasement of defilements enabling worldlings to get out of *saṃsāra*:

> Since apart from the examination of *dharma*-s (= *prajñā* = *abhidharma*), there is no excellent means for the appeasement of the defilements; And it is on account of the defilements that beings wander in the existence-ocean. For this reason, therefore, it is said, the [*abhidharma*] is taught is taught by the Master.[38]

The Ābhidharmika distinction in terms of the functions of the three *piṭaka*-s is also indicative of the spiritual function of the *abhidharma*: the *sūtra-piṭaka* is taught so that those who have not planted the roots of skillfulness (*kuśala-mūla*) and become delighted therein will plant them and be delighted; the *vinaya*, so that those who have planted and become delighted in the roots of skillfulness will mature their series, practicing what should be practiced; the *abhidharma*, so that those who have so matured and practiced will have the proper means to be enlightened and liberated.[39]

Intellectual studies and Ābhidharmika analysis must serve the sole purpose of spiritual realization. This soteriological function is also brought out in the following explanation in the MVŚ regarding the practitioners of insight meditation (*vipaśyanā-bhāvanā*):

> Those who mostly cultivate the requisites (*saṃbhāra*) of insight are those who, at the stage of preparatory effort, always delight in studying and reflecting on the *tripiṭaka*. They repeatedly examine the specific and general characteristics of all *dharma*-s, [— topics of fundamental importance for *abhidharma*]. When they enter into the noble path, they are called the *vipaśyanā*-type of practitioners (*vipaśyanā-carita*).[40]

The same text further explains the ultimate purpose of abhidharmic analysis which is to proceed from our deluded state and reach absolute quiescence through a gradual progression from intellectual to spiritual insight:

> One wishing to examine all *dharma*-s should first examine their subsumption (*saṃgraha*) in terms of intrinsic nature.
>
> What are the benefits and merits to be derived from the examination of the subsumption in terms of the intrinsic nature of *dharma*-s?
>
> It removes the notions of Self and unity and trains in the notion of *dharma*-s … which intensify defilements…. When the notions of Self and unity are removed, one is then able to gain the insight that material *dharma*-s … will soon be dispersed and immaterial *dharma*-s … will soon perish. …
>
> In this way, one will come to acquire the seeds similar to the gateway of liberation of emptiness (*śūnyatā*).

Examining that conditioned *dharma*-s are empty and not-Self, one will come to be deeply averse to *saṃsāra*, thus further acquiring the seeds similar to the gateway of liberation of the signless (*animitta*).

Not delighting in *saṃsāra*, one then comes to take deep delight in *nirvāṇa*, thus further acquiring the seeds similar to the gateway of liberation of non-aspiring (*apraṇihita*).

With regard to these three *samādhi*-s [of liberation], one generates the medium with the support of the lower, and the higher with the support of the medium, bringing forth *prajñā*, becoming detached from the triple spheres, attaining perfect enlightenment and realizing absolute quiescence.[41]

NOTES

[1] DhsA, 17.

[2] DhsA, 3, 5, 21.

[3] AKB, 3.

[4] Ny, 779c.

[5] M, i, 212 ff.

[6] E.g., A, ii, 107.

[7] M, i, 293 ff.

[8] M, i, 299 ff.

[9] T 29, 595a–b.

[10] AsmB, 96: *vaipulyaṃ vaidalyaṃ vaitulyam ity ete mahāyānasya paryāyāḥ / tad etat saptavidha-mahattva-yogān mahattva-yānam ity ucyate / saptavidhaṃ mahattvam ālaṃbana-mahattvaṃ ... pratipatti-mahattvaṃ ... jñāna-mahattvaṃ ... vīrya-mahattvaṃ ... upāyakauśalya-mahattvaṃ ... prāpti-mahattvaṃ ... karma-mahattvaṃ ...*

[11] See also: Dhammajoti, KL, 'Abhidharma and *Upadeśa*', in *Journal of Buddhist Studies*, Vol. 3, 112 f., (Colombo, 2005).

[12] MVŚ, 496, equates *bodhi* here with the knowledge of exhaustion (*kṣaya-jñāna*) and the knowledge of non-arising (*anutpāda-jñāna*).

[13] M, ii, 238 f.

[14] AKB, 459. Also *cf.* MVŚ, 917c, where the *Saddharma* is subdivided into the conventional and the absolute (*paramārtha*) ones. The former comprises the verbal teachings of the *tripiṭaka*; the latter is the noble path, i.e., the outflow-free *indriya*, *bala*, *bodhyaṅga* and the *mārgāṅga*.

[15] T 24, 408b.

[16] T 50, 113c.

[17] See also **Satyasiddhi-śāstra*, T 32, 245b.

[18] T 29, 595b.

[19] T 30, 419a.

[20] Ny, 595a–b.

[21] This enumeration agrees with that in the MVŚ, 2a.

[22] 默 in MVŚ. But as Yin Shun (*Study*, 24) points out, it clearly is an error for 黑.

[23] MVŚ, 660b.

[24] MVŚ, 660b. See Yin Shun, 原始佛教聖典之集成 (*Compilation of the Canon of Primitive Buddhism*), (Taipei, 1971), 617 ff.

[25] See also, Dhammajoti, KL, *op. cit.*, 113 ff.

[26] DhsA, 2: *kenaṭṭhena abhidhammo / dhammātireka-dhamma-visesaṭṭhena / atireka-visesaṭṭhadīpako hi ettha abhisaddo //*

[27] *Aṅguttara-nikāya Aṭṭhakathā*, iii, 271.

[28] See Sakurabe, H, 倶舍論の研究 (Kyoto, 1969), 14 ff.

[29] For these paths, see *infra*, § 15.

[30] MVŚ, 4a–c.

[31] *Cf. Study*, 38.

[32] Ny, 330b.

[33] TA(U-J), 139, states more specifically that the *dharma*-s here exclude *ākāśa* and *apratisaṃkhyā-nirodha*.

[34] AKB, 2: *svalakṣaṇa-dhāraṇād dharmaḥ / tad ayaṃ paramārtha-dharmaṃ vā nirvāṇaṃ dharma-lakṣaṇaṃ vā praty abhimukho dharma ity abhidharmaḥ //*

[35] MVŚ, 3b–4a; AKB, 2.

[36] Ny, 330b.

[37] MVŚ, 1c; Ny, 595b.

[38] AKB, 2: *dharmāṇāṃ pravicayam antareṇa nāsti kleśānāṃ yata upaśāntaye 'bhyupāyaḥ / kleśaiś ca bhramati bhavārṇave 'tra lokas taddhetor ata uditaḥ kilaiṣa śāstrā //*

[39] MVŚ, 2a; Ny, 595b.

[40] MVŚ, 148b.

[41] MVŚ, 307a.

2. The Ābhidharmika
Standpoint, Scope and Methodology

2.1. Fundamental standpoint of the Ābhidharmikas

2.2. Arguments for *abhidharma* being *buddha-vacana*

2.3. Scope of study of the Ābhidharmikas

- 2.3.1. Intrinsic/unique characteristic (*svalakṣaṇa*)
- 2.3.2. Common characteristic (*sāmānya-lakṣaṇa*)
- 2.3.3. Subsumption/inclusion (*saṃgraha*)
- 2.3.4. Association/conjunction (*saṃprayoga*)
- 2.3.5. Cause (*hetu*), condition (*pratyaya*) and fruit (*phala*)
- 2.3.6. Endowment, non-endowment (*samanvāgama, asamanvāgama*)

2.4. Ābhidharmika methodology for *dharma-pravicaya*

- 2.4.1. Taxonomy of *skandha* (aggregate), *āyatana* (abode/entrance), *dhātu* (element)
- 2.4.2. Five-group taxonomy
- 2.4.3. Doctrinal perspectives
  - 2.4.3.1. *Saṃskṛta* (conditioned), *asaṃskṛta* (unconditioned)
  - 2.4.3.2 *Kuśala* (wholesome/skillful), *akuśala* (unwholesome), *avyākṛta* (non-defined)
  - 2.4.3.3. *Sāsrava* (with-outflow) and *anāsrava* (outflow-free)
  - 2.4.3.4. *Darśana-heya* (abandonable by insight), *bhāvanā-heya* (abandonable by cultivation), *aheya* (not to be abandoned)
  - 2.4.3.5. Other taxonomical categories
- 2.4.4. Method of catechism

2.1. Fundamental standpoint of the Ābhidharmikas

Succinctly, an Ābhidharmika is one who specializes in the *abhidharma* and takes the *abhidharma* as the final authority. For him, the *abhidharma* is definitive (*lākṣaṇika*) and represents the true intention of the Buddha, taught at the level of absolute truth (*paramārtha-satya*), with fully drawn out meanings (*nītārtha*). In contrast, the *sūtra*-s do not represent the Buddha's true intention (*ābhiprāyika*).[1] They generally represent the expedient (*aupacārika*) teachings whose meanings are yet to be fully drawn out (*neyārtha*).

This fundamental standpoint may be contrasted with that of the Sautrāntika, a school that was evolved from the Dārṣṭāntika and which came into prominence in the process of constantly repudiating and criticizing the Ābhidharmikas. A Sautrāntika takes the *sūtra*-s as the final authority and rejects the *abhidharma* texts as representing the Buddha's teachings. For him, *abhidharma* refers only to certain types of *sūtra*-s characterized by the concern with properly determining the meaning (*arthaviniścaya*) of what the Buddha has taught.[2]

The AKB represents the standpoint of the Vaibhāṣika Ābhidharmikas, the most established Ābhidharmikas, as follows: "Without the expositions in the *abhidharma*, a student is unable to discern the *dharma*."[3]

In exact contrast to this, the author of *Arthaviniścaya-sūtra-nibandhana*, who often favors the Sautrāntika standpoint, states — as if correcting the Vaibhāṣika claim — "Without the expositions in the *sūtra*-s, the student is unable to discern the *dharma*."[4]

Contradicting the Vaibhāṣika, the Sautrāntika master, Sthavira Śrīlāta, asserts:

> Those noble teachings elaborated by the Buddha Himself are called *nītārtha-sūtra*-s; all the other *sūtra*-s are said to be *neyārtha*.[5]

Besides the Sautrāntika, there are other schools, particularly those belonging to the Mahāsāṃghika lineage, who also contradict the Vaibhāṣika standpoint. For the Mahāsāṃghika, "all the *sūtra*-s discoursed by the Buddha are *nītārtha*".[6]

2.2. Arguments for *abhidharma* being *buddha-vacana*

For the Ābhidharmikas, the *abhidharma* doctrines are not speculative philosophy or intellectual inventions; they are the *buddha-vacana par excellence*. Their opponents, the Sautrāntikas, repudiate this claim. Saṃghabhadra analyses the Sautrāntika disagreement as being threefold:

(a) They were said to be composed by Kātyāyanīputra and others.
(b) The Buddha never mentioned that *abhidharma* is a reliance (*pratiśaraṇa*).
(c) The tenets of the different *abhidharma* schools vary.[7]

Saṃghabhadra[8] replies:

a. As the *abhidharma* [texts] were compiled by the great disciples on the basis of the Buddha's teaching, they are approved by the Buddha; they are also *buddha-vacana*. As they are in accord with the knowledge which knows fully (*pari-√jñā*) the causes and effects of defilement and purification, they are like the *sūtra*-s. If what has been approved by the Buddha is not called *buddha-vacana*, then innumerable *sūtra*-s would have to be abandoned!

b. If you say that what the Buddha has not mentioned as a *pratiśaraṇa* is not *buddha-vacana*, then the *vinaya* would not be *buddha-vacana*. … Moreover, the *abhidharma* should definitely be accepted as *sūtraviśeṣa*, and thus constituting a *pratiśaraṇa*. Or, it should be the case that the *gāthā*-s, etc., do not constitute *pratiśaraṇa*, for the Buddha only exhorted us to take the *sūtra*-s as *pratiśaraṇa*…. Furthermore, when the Buddha exhorted Ānanda to take the *sūtra*-s as *pratiśaraṇa*, He was in actual fact exhorting him to take the *abhidharma* as *pratiśaraṇa*; for the latter is the authority (*pramāṇa*) of the *sūtra*-s, hence it is the *sūtra-pramāṇa*, that is, it comprises the definitive meanings of the *sūtra*-s; for the *abhidharma* can ascertain as to which *sūtra*-s are *nītārtha*, which ones are *neyārtha*. The name, '*abhidharma*', can subsume all words which do not contradict any of the noble doctrines; based on this principle, it is known as a *nītārtha-sūtra*. Whatever contradicts this principle is said to be *neyārtha*.

c. As to your assertion that the *abhidharma* is not *buddha-vacana* on account of the fact that the tenets of the different *abhidharma* schools vary — in that case, the same should apply to the *sūtra*-s, for differences in wording and meaning do exist in the extant *sūtra*-s of the various schools; on account of these differences, their tenets become different.

Thus, as Saṃghabhadra argues, the *abhidharma* is not only *sūtra* in the highest sense, it is the ultimate criterion or authority for ascertaining the genuine *sūtra*-s (*sūtra-pramāṇa*). (*Cf.* nature and function of *upadeśa* as *abhidharma* — § 1.1.2.*e*). In that sense, the Ābhidharmikas would argue, it is they themselves who properly take the *sūtra*-s as the final authority. The claim that the *abhidharma* represents the real words of the Buddha is also reflected in Saṃghabhadra's definition of *sūtra* as the first of the *dvādaśāṅga-dharma-pravacana* (= *buddha-vacana*): "By *sūtra* is meant that which subsumes and contains all the words which accord with the firm principles of both the *saṃvṛti*- and *paramārtha-satya*-s. *Sūtra*-s in this sense are either discoursed by the Buddha or the disciples, for [the latter] discoursed because [the content was] approved by the Buddha."[9]

2.3. Scope of study of the Ābhidharmikas

Like the Theravādins, the Sarvāstivādins too claim that the Buddha Himself was the supreme Ābhidharmika.[10] One way to define an Ābhidharmika is to locate his scope of study. The MVŚ speaks of the scope of the *abhidharma-piṭaka* as follows:

> The meanings of the *abhidharma-piṭaka* should be understood by means of 14 things: (1-6) the six causes (*hetu*), (7-10) the four conditions (*pratyaya*),

(11) subsumption/inclusion (*saṃgraha*), (12) conjunction (*saṃprayoga*), (13) endowment (*samanvāgama*), (14) non-endowment (*asamanvāgama*). Those who, by means of these 14 things, understand the *abhidharma* unerringly, are called Ābhidharmikas, not [those who] merely recite and memorize the words.

Other masters say that the meanings of the *abhidharma-piṭaka* should be understood by means of seven things: (1) skillfulness with regard to causes (*hetu-kauśalya*), (2) skillfulness with regard to conditions (*pratyaya-kauśalya*), (3) skillfulness with regard to intrinsic characteristic (*svalakṣaṇa-kauśalya*), (4) skillfulness with regard to common characteristic (*sāmānyalakṣaṇa-kauśalya*), (5) skillfulness with regard to subsumption and non-subsumption (*saṃgraha-asaṃgraha-kauśalya*), (6) skillfulness with regard to conjunction and disjunction (*saṃprayoga-viprayoga-kauśalya*), (7) skillfulness with regard to endowment and non-endowment (*samanvāgama-asamanvāgama-kauśalya*). Those who, by means of these seven things understand the *abhidharma* unerringly, are called Ābhidharmikas, not [those who] merely recite and memorize the words.[11]

Skandhila's **Abhidharmāvatāra* (T no. 1554) too explains the *caitasika prajñā* as "the examination (*upalakṣaṇa*) — as the case may be — of the following eight kinds of *dharma*-s: *saṃgraha*, *saṃprayoga*, *samanvāgama*, *hetu*, *pratyaya*, *phala*, *svalakṣaṇa*, *sāmānya-lakṣaṇa*."[12] Since *abhidharma* in the highest sense is none other than the pure (*amalā*) *prajñā*, this definition too constitutes a statement of the scope of *abhidharma* itself and hence a definition of an Ābhidharmika. In brief then, an Ābhidharmika as a specialist is one devoted to the study of these doctrinal categories.

Among these topics, some, like *svalakṣaṇa* and *sāmānya-lakṣaṇa*, are used in conjunction with the application of Ābhidharmika methodological devices (more in § 2.4) for Abhidharma investigation, while others — like *saṃgraha* and *saṃprayoga* — themselves constitute methodological devices of fundamental importance. Thus, the application of *saṃgraha* is indispensable for the study of *svabhāva/ svalakṣaṇa* of all *dharma*-s and of the *saṃprayoga* of mental activities.

2.3.1. Intrinsic/unique characteristic (*svalakṣaṇa*)

By determining the intrinsic or unique characteristic of each constituent in the complex of human experience, sensory and suprasensory, and of the whole universe — either through direct experience or inference — a list of discrete, real, entities (*dravya*) called *dharma*-s is derived.

A *dharma* is defined as that which holds its intrinsic characteristic (*svalakṣaṇa-dhāraṇād dharmaḥ* — § 1.2). The intrinsic characteristic of *rūpa*, for example, is the susceptibility of being molested (*rūpyate*), obstructability and visibility; that of *vedanā* is sensation, etc. And for a *dharma* to be a *dharma*, its characteristic must be sustainable throughout time: A *rūpa* remains as a *rūpa* irrespective of its various modalities. It can never be transformed into another different *dharma* (such as *vedanā*). Thus, a uniquely characterizable entity is a uniquely real (in the absolute sense) entity, having a unique intrinsic nature (*svabhāva*): "To be existent as an absolute entity is to be existent as an intrinsic characteristic (*paramārthena sat svalakṣaṇena sad ityarthaḥ*)."[13]

As the MVŚ explains, this is on account of the fact that "the entity itself is [its] characteristic, and the characteristic is the entity itself; for it is the case for all *dharma*-s that the characteristic cannot be predicated apart from the *dharma* itself."[14] This is no doubt quite in keeping with the fundamental Buddhist stance which consistently rejects any substance-attribute dichotomy. By accounting for the *svalakṣaṇa* of a *dharma* — its phenomenologically cognizable aspect — its very ontological existence as a *svabhāva/dravya* is established. Ultimately these two are one.[15]

The general Sarvāstivāda tradition recognizes a list of 75 *dharma*-s (see *infra*).

2.3.2. Common characteristic (*sāmānya-lakṣaṇa*)

The MVŚ[16] distinguishes *svalakṣaṇa* from *sāmānya-lakṣaṇa* as follows: "The analysis of the *lakṣaṇa* of a single entity (*dravya*) is the analysis of *svalakṣaṇa*. The analysis of the *lakṣaṇa* of numerous entities is the analysis of *sāmānya-lakṣaṇa.*" Further: "The *svabhāva* of *dharma*-s is the *svalakṣaṇa* of *dharma*-s. Homogeneity in nature is *sāmānya-lakṣaṇa*." Thus, all *rūpa*-s, *vedanā*-s, *saṃjñā*-s, etc., have the nature of being impermanent. This impermanent nature is a *sāmānya-lakṣaṇa*.

Whereas a sensory consciousness cognizes only the *svalakṣaṇa* of a *dharma*, the mental consciousness with its ability of abstraction can cognize *sāmānya-lakṣaṇa*. Thus, the latter pertains to the domain of inference (*anumāna*), the former to direct perception (*pratyakṣa*). However, distinguishing the understanding (*prajñā*) that examines *svalakṣaṇa* from that which examines *sāmānya-lakṣaṇa*, the MVŚ states:

> The understanding not subsumed under the 16 modes of understanding (*cf. infra*, § 15.2.2.1) mostly discerns *svalakṣaṇa*; the understanding subsumed under the 16 modes of understanding discerns only *sāmānya-lakṣaṇa*.
>
> Furthermore, the understanding that perceives (行; √*car*, lit: 'courses') the [four] truths mostly discerns *svalakṣaṇa*; the understanding at the time of direct realization (*abhisamaya*) discerns only *sāmānya-lakṣaṇa*.[17]

This statement is to be understood as follows: The 16 modes of understanding (*ākāra*) are those pertaining to the four truths (four each): unsatisfactoriness, impermanent, etc., for the truth of unsatisfactoriness, etc. These are no doubt the *sāmānya-lakṣaṇa*-s of *dharma*-s. But they are the non-erroneous universal characteristics discernible only by spiritual insight as direct perception *par excellence* in direct realization.

2.3.2.1. Of all the Ābhidharmika studies, the examination of *svalakṣaṇa* and *sāmānya-lakṣaṇa* may be considered as the most important. In fact, the MVŚ goes so far as to declare that "*abhidharma* is [precisely] the analysis of the *svalakṣaṇa* and *sāmānya-lakṣaṇa* of *dharma*-s".[18] It appears that at first, the Ābhidharmika analysis of *svalakṣaṇa* was that of the individual doctrinal topics found in the *sūtra*-s — *skandha, āyatana, dhātu, satya, indriya*, etc. Later, various taxonomical topics were utilized for the analysis in terms of *sāmānya-lakṣaṇa*. In the course of development, the Sarvāstivāda Ābhidharmikas tended to regard the 16 modes of understanding (*ākāra*) pertaining to the four noble truths as *sāmānya-lakṣaṇa*-s in the highest sense.

In this connection, the relativity as regards the notions of *svalakṣaṇa* and *sāmānya-lakṣaṇa* is to be noted. Thus, among various *rūpa*-s — different colors, different shapes — there is the common nature of being resistant and subject to deterioration. Accordingly, this *svalakṣaṇa* of a *rūpa* is distinct from a *vedanā*, etc. But, at the same time, it is also the *sāmānya-lakṣaṇa* of these various types of *rūpa*-s. Similarly, the Great Element, Earth (*pṛthivī*), is both *svalakṣaṇa* and *sāmānya-lakṣaṇa* — it is said to be a *svalakṣaṇa* in contrast to the other three Great Elements; and a *sāmānya-lakṣaṇa*, since all Earth Elements have the characteristic of firmness. In this way, the MVŚ declares, "there are infinite distinctions [that can be made] between *svalakṣaṇa* and *sāmānya-lakṣaṇa*".[19]

The Sarvāstivada Ābhidharmikas distinguish two kinds of *svalakṣaṇa*: The first, *dravya-svalakṣaṇa*, is the intrinsic characteristic of the *dharma* as a unique entity in itself, for instance: that of a particular color, say, blue. The second, *āyatana-svalakṣaṇa*, refers to the intrinsic characteristic of the *dharma* as a member of a unique class — an *āyatana* — of which it is a member, for instance: the particular blue color as a unique class of *dharma*-s known as "visibles" (*rūpa*), i.e., the *rūpa-āyatana*. We can see from this example that, in this context, the *āyatana-svalakṣaṇa* is, in a sense, a common characteristic in relation to the *dravya-svalakṣaṇa*. It is for this reason that the MVŚ states:

> From the point of view of *dravya-svalakṣaṇa*, the five sensory consciousnesses (*pañca-vijñāna-kāya*) also take *sāmānya-lakṣaṇa* as their object (*ālambana*). But from the point of view of *āyatana-svalakṣaṇa*, the five sensory consciousnesses take *svalakṣaṇa* alone as their object.[20]

It is probably in consideration of the relativity in the notions of the *svalakṣaṇa* and *sāmānya-lakṣaṇa* of a given *dharma* that the Sarvāstivāda master, Skandhila, prefers to speak in terms of different degrees of *sāmānya-lakṣaṇa* only, giving a threefold classification of the characteristics of *dharma*-s — (i) specifically common, (ii) partially common, (iii) universally-common.[21] These three characteristics represent three ascending degrees of generality or universality. The examples he gives make this point evident: (i) an example of the specifically-common characteristic is the *rūpaṇa* of all *rūpa*-s; (ii) examples of the partially-common characteristic are *anityatā* and *duḥkhatā*; (iii) examples of the universally-common characteristic are *nairātmya* and *śūnyatā*.

2.3.3. Subsumption/inclusion (*saṃgraha*)

This is an important methodological device through which the Ābhidharmikas arrive at a final list of unique *dharma*-s. The MVŚ, disputing the view that *dharma*-s having different intrinsic natures — *para-bhāva* as opposed to *svabhāva* — are mutually subsumable, declares that "all *dharma*-s are subsumable with respect to *svabhāva*; this is subsumption with respect to *paramārtha*".[22] Put differently, the study of subsumption in terms of *svabhāva* is none other than the study of the *svalakṣaṇa*-s of all *dharma*-s. This analysis may be made between one single *dharma* and another *dharma*, or between one *dharma* and several other *dharma*-s, or between one category of *dharma*-s and another category, or between one category and several other categories.

The Sarvāstivādin conception of both the phenomenal existence and the domain of the unconditioned (*asaṃskṛta*) is a pluralistic one in each case. There are innumerable real entities — *dharma*-s — in either domain. The uniquely characterized types are designated by different names, often on account of the fact that the Buddha Himself speaks of the same thing or phenomenon in different terms.

Thus, from the Ābhidharmika perspective, the *dharma* 'understanding' (*prajñā*) subsumes what are given as various synonymous terms in the *sūtra*-s: light (*āloka*), illumination (*prabhā*), faculty of understanding (*prajñā-indriya*), power of understanding (*prajñā-bala*), investigation of *dharma*-s (*dharma-pravicaya*), etc. Through the process of *saṃgraha*, then, they can reduce all of them to one unique *dharma*, with the realization that they are all just different modalities of the same category of *dharma*. The Ābhidharmikas in fact arrive at further modalities of *prajñā* such as knowledge (*jñāna*), receptivity (*kṣānti*), view (*dṛṣṭi*), non-defiled ignorance (*akliṣṭājñāna*), etc. In brief, two entities having two distinctly different *svabhāva/svalakṣaṇa* are established as two distinct *dharma*-s since each *dharma* is unique. The abhidharmic classification of these *dharma*-s into *skandha, āyatana* and *dhātu* (see below) is an application of this methodology of *saṃgraha* in respect to *svabhāva/svalakṣaṇa*.

2.3.4. Association/conjunction (*saṃprayoga*)

Conjunction is another important methodological device for *abhidharma* studies, employed in the mental domain. The understanding of mental processes is of paramount importance for the Buddhist practitioners, Ābhidharmikas included. Through the investigation of *saṃprayoga*, the Ābhidharmikas derive an understanding of which mental factors are conascent, and which factors affect the mind and other thought concomitants, and in what ways. In other words, it is an investigation into the dynamic interaction among simultaneously existing mental elements.

The Sarvāstivāda eventually arrived at a set of five conditions — a fivefold sameness or equality (*pañcadhā samatā*) — for the mental constituents said to be in conjunction [by the Sarvāstivāda/Vaibhāṣika]:

1. they must be supported by the same sense organ (*āśraya-samatā*);
2. they must take the same object (*ālambana-samatā*);
3. they must have the same mode of understanding (*ākāra-samatā*);
4. they must be simultaneous (*kāla-samatā*);
5. they must, in each case, be of a singular substance (*dravya-samatā*): only one sensation (*vedanā*), one ideation (*saṃjñā*), etc., is conjoined in one *citta,* though there can be various types of sensation and ideation.

2.3.5. Cause (*hetu*), condition (*pratyaya*) and fruit (*phala*)

All *dharma*-s in phenomenal existence are *pratītya-samutpanna* — dependently originated from an assemblage of conditions. In this respect, they are often called *saṃskṛta*-s, 'the compounded/conditioned'.

In the Sarvāstivāda conception, *dharma*-s are distinct ontological entities which, in their intrinsic nature, abide throughout time, totally unrelated to one another and totally devoid of any activities.[23] Given such a theory, it is of fundamental importance that the school has an articulated causal doctrine capable of accounting for the arising of *dharma*-s as phenomena and their dynamic inter-relatedness in accordance with the Buddha's teaching of *pratītya-samutpāda*. Moreover, for the establishment of each of the *dharma*-s as a real entity, a conditioning force (*saṃskāra*), its causal function in each case must be demonstrated. It is probably for this reason that the Sarvāstivāda was also known as Hetuvāda — a school specifically concerned with the theory of causation.[24] In this connection, we may also note that in the definition of an Ābhidharmika quoted above from the MVŚ (§ 2.3), *hetu/hetu-kauśalya* and *pratyaya/ pratyaya-kauśalya* top the lists in each case.

The Sarvāstivādins eventually articulated a doctrine of four conditions, six causes and five fruits (see *infra*, § 6 and § 7). Significant portions of the Sarvāstivāda canonical *abhidharma* treatises are devoted specifically to these topics. Thus, the *Vijñāna-kāya-śāstra* discusses the four conditions (*pratyaya*) at length; the *Jñāna-prasthāna-śāstra* expounds on the six causes; the chapter 'On *saṃgraha*, etc.' of the *Prakaraṇa-pāda-śāstra* contains a total of 20 doctrinal perspectives connected with *hetu-pratyaya*. (See *infra*, § 4.1.2)

2.3.6. Endowment, non-endowment (*samanvāgama, asamanvāgama*)

Acquisition (*prāpti*) became a topic of increasing importance in the establishment and defense of the thesis of *sarvāstitva*. A *dharma* — e.g., a defilement like *rāga* — though past, can continue to belong to a personal stream (*santāna*) by virtue of the fact that a corresponding force — in nature neither material nor mental (*cf. infra*, § 11.3.1), i.e., its *prāpti* — continues to link it to the person. When the defilement is abandoned (*prahīṇa*), it is not that the defilement (a *dharma*) loses any existential status — *dharma*-s are existent always (*sarvadā asti*). What happens is that its *prāpti* is rendered inoperative and, at the same time its corresponding non-acquisition (*aprāpti*), another force also neither material nor mental, comes into play, continuously preventing it from being associated with the person.

Endowment (*samanvāgama*) seems to be a relatively late doctrinal concern (that is, late compared to the other topics above). But at least by the time of the MVŚ, the doctrine had already been well articulated. When a person first acquires a *dharma*, he is said to have the *prāpti* of that *dharma*. Having acquired the *dharma*, when he continues to possess it, he is said to have the endowment of that *dharma*. Thus, what is *samanvāgata* (endowed) is *prāpta* (acquired); but not *vice versa*, as what is acquired may be lost subsequently.

2.4. Ābhidharmika methodology for *dharma-pravicaya*

As we have seen, *abhidharma* in the real sense is *amalā prajñā*, and *prajñā* is *dharmapravicaya* — discernment or examination of *dharma*-s (*supra*, § 1.2). For the Ābhidharmikas, it is only by a thorough and systematic examination of the true nature of all *dharma*-s that the true import of the Buddha's Dharma can be ascertained and liberation assured. The *Jñāna-prasthāna-śāstra* quotes the following stanza to emphasize the fundamental importance of examining the *dharma*-s:

> The forest is the sphere (*gati*) proper to the beasts; the sky is the sphere proper to the birds; *nirvāṇa* is the sphere proper to the noble ones; distinction is the sphere proper to the *dharma*-s.[25]

The MVŚ[26] comments:

> With regard to the *sūtra*-s, one should skillfully distinguish between the explicit (*nītārtha*) and implicit (*neyārtha*) [teachings]. … The wise should skillfully distinguish the meanings in the *sūtra*-s and not simply explain in the manner that the words are uttered [therein]. If one simply explains in the manner that the words are uttered, one will create contradictions among

> the noble teachings and also give rise to topsy-turvy attachment in one's own mind.

This just-mentioned principle is apparently put into practice without apologies by the Sarvāstivāda Ābhidharmikas. Here we may illustrate this with the example of their doctrine on the life-principle (*āyus*) which they identify with the category known as *jīvitendriya*. The Sarvāstivāda doctrine is that this *viprayukta-saṃskāra-dharma* operates on both material as well as mental *dharma*-s. A sentient being in a thoughtless (*acittaka*) state of meditation (see *infra*, § 11.3.3) is alive thanks to the function of this force, despite the absence of all mental activities. The Vibhajyavāda, however, asserts that *āyus* is *cittānuvartin*; i.e., it operates necessarily with thought. They cite the *sūtra* which speaks of *āyus*, *ūṣma* and *vijñāna* as always going together. The Sarvāstivāda, of course, cannot deny the statement in the *sūtra*. Instead, they argue that the statement must be properly discerned and not taken literally:

> If these three *dharma*-s necessarily go together, there ought to be *ūṣma* in the *ārūpya-dhātu*, and [likewise] the manifestation of *vijñāna* in the ideationless meditational state, etc. If this were to be conceded, the noble teachings and logical reasoning will be contradicted. Hence, one must not take the literal meanings of the statement rigidly. One must understand that the statement here refers to the possible case when it speaks of the going together [of the three].[27]

It is in accordance with the aforementioned principle that the Ābhidharmikas proceeded to systematize and classify the Buddha's discourses. In this process, they created many new doctrinal categories which they believed to be doctrinally justifiable and eventually finalized a list of the ultimate reals — the unique *dharma*-s. The methodological devices we have discussed above (§§ 2.3.3, 2.3.4), are used by the Ābhidharmikas to study the dynamic interaction among them. We will examine below some of the other more important methodological devices employing these Abhidharma doctrinal categories — some taken over from the *sūtra*-s — which serve as doctrinal perspectives (*paryāya*) with which they study and classify these *dharma*-s so derived.

2.4.1. Taxonomy of *skandha* (aggregate), *āyatana* (abode/entrance), *dhātu* (element)

At first, the taxonomies of the five-*skandha*, twelve-*āyatana* and eighteen-*dhātu* were taken over from the *sūtra*-s by the Ābhidharmikas for the examination of *dharma*-s in terms of *svabhāva*, by applying the methodological device of *saṃgraha*. The five-*skandha* taxonomy is seen in the earlier canonical *abhidharma* texts such as the **Dharma-skandha-śāstra* (DSŚ), the *Prakaraṇaśāstra* (PrŚ), and also later texts which conform to the *sūtra* tradition, such as the *Abidharmāmṛta-rasa-śāstra* (AmRŚ). In the post-AKB works such as the *Abhidharmadīpa* (ADV) and the *Abhidharmāvatāra* (*Avatāra*), the three *asaṃskṛta*-s are added to form the apparently more popular eight-category (*padārtha*) scheme.[28]

2.4.1.1. The five *skandha*-s (aggregate) constitute the totality of phenomenal existence: 1. *rūpa* (matter), 2. *vedanā* (sensation/ feeling), 3. *saṃjñā* (ideation), 4. *saṃskāra* (conditionings), 5. *vijñāna* (consciousness). The analysis in terms of the five *skandha*-s is often employed in the *sūtra*-s to explain the Buddhist doctrine of no-Self (*nairātmya*). This fundamental Buddhist doctrine continues to be the central concern of *abhidharma*, and accordingly, the five-*skandha* scheme continues to be an important Ābhidharmika taxonomy.

Skandha is explained as 'heap' (*rāśi*): Each of these five forms a heap of its own category which may be past, present or future. The import of this taxonomy is the emphasis that phenomena are all dependently arisen, without any ontological status; they are all reducible to these five *skandha*-s which alone are the ultimate reals forming the basis of our conceptual superimposition.

The *saṃskāra-skandha* includes the conjoined (*saṃprayukta*) *dharma*-s, i.e., *caitta*-s, as well as the disjoined (*viprayukta*) *dharma*-s. The *rūpa-skandha* includes a peculiar matter called *avijñapti* (*infra*, § 8.1.3) and special types of subtle matter such as those of the sensory faculties called 'clear matter' (*rūpa-prasāda*) and that of a being in the intermediate existence (*antarābhava*).

In the *abhidharma* conception, all *dharma*-s are *saṃskāra*-s — conditioning forces. These forces themselves are conditioned; hence the term is also synonymous with *saṃskṛta*. This is quite in keeping with the notion in early Buddhism which declares that "all *saṃskāra*-s are impermanent" (*sarve saṃskārā anityāḥ*). However, in the five-*skandha* scheme, the *saṃskāra-skandha* refers to all other *dharma*-s excluding the other four *skandha*-s.[29] This taxonomy does not include the unconditioned *dharma*-s, as the latter, being beyond space and time, do not form such heaps.

Five *skandha*-s

rūpa	11	5 *indriya*-s, 5 *viśaya*-s, *avijñapti*
vedanā	1	*vedanā* (a *caitta*)
saṃjñā	1	*saṃjñā* (a *caitta*)
saṃskāra	44	*saṃprayukta* (*caitta-s* excluding *vedanā*, *saṃjñā*)
	14	*viprayukta-saṃskāra* (# not absolutely fixed)
vijñāna	1	*vijñāna*

Total: **72** *dharma*-s

2.4.1.2. The 12 *āyatana*-s (abode) comprise the six sense faculties (*indriya*) — eye, ear, nose, tongue, body, mind; and the six corresponding objects — the visible, sound, smell, taste and the tangible. The meaning of *āyatana* is 'gate of arising' (*āyadvāra*):[30] They are the gateways through which the *citta* and the *caitta*-s originate. That is to say, they serve the functions of being the supporting basis (*āśraya*, i.e., the faculties) and the perceptual objects (*ālambana*) — the two requisites — for the arising of consciousness (*vijñāna*) and the mental factors associated with it. In *abhidharma*, as in early Buddhism, *citta*, *manas* and *vijñāna* refer to the same reality, though with different functional stresses.

Āyatana is etymologically explained in the AKB[31] as "that which extends the arising of *citta-caitta*-s" (*cittacaittānām āyaṃ tanvantīti āyatanāni /*). The MVŚ provides more elaboration on this meaning:

> The meaning of *āyatana* is 'gate of arising': Just as various things arise within a city on account of which the bodies of sentient beings are nourished, so, within the supporting bases (*āśraya*) and object-supports (*ālambana*) — [the two constituent components of the *āyatana*-s] — various *citta-caitta-dharma*-s arise on account of which the defiled and pure serial continuities (*santati*) are nourished.[32]

12 *āyatana*-s

1. eye (*cakṣus*)	7. visible (*rūpa*)	
2. ear (*śrotra*)	8. sound (*śabda*)	
3. nose (*ghrāṇa*)	9. smell (*gandha*)	
4. tongue (*jihvā*)	10. taste (*rasa*)	
5. body (*kāya*)	11. tangible (*spraṣṭavya*)	
6. mind (*manas*)	12. mental objects (*dharma*) (68)	*caitta* (46) *viprayukta-saṃskāra* (14) *avijñapti* (1) *asaṃskṛta* (3)

The Sautrāntika objects to the doctrine that *dharma*-s exist tri-temporarily. For them, *sarvāstivāda* can only be accepted in the sense given in the *sūtra*: 'All' refers to the 12 *āyatana*-s.[33] Nothing exists outside what is empirically verifiable through the six senses. It must, however, be noted that the orthodox Sarvāstivādin Saṃghabhadra sees no difficulty in accepting this *sūtra* statement. For him, the 12 *āyatana*-s indeed subsume all the *dharma*-s recognized by the Sarvāstivāda. In fact, all *dharma*-s, including the *asaṃskṛta*-s, are *ālambana*-s — objects contributing to the arising of consciousness and its associated *caittas*-s in a cognitive process.[34] Even *nirvāṇa* is verifiable — by the saints.

2.4.1.3. The 18 *dhātu*-s (element) comprise the six sense faculties, the six corresponding objects and the six corresponding consciousnesses. The meaning of *dhātu* is *gotra*, 'family/kin': There are these 18 families or species of *dharma*-s in the human series.[35] It also has the sense of being the source or origin or cause; in this sense it is explained as a 'mine' (*ākara*), such as a gold-mine from which the metal gold can be extracted.[36]

2.4.1.3.1. In this scheme, the *mano-dhātu* is not an entity ontologically distinct from the mind itself. It is simply the mind in a preceding moment of the series serving as the 'similar and immediate condition' (*samanantara-pratyaya*) for the arising of the succeeding moment.

As for the *dharma-dhātu,* the MVŚ gives the following definition:

> What is *dharmadhātu*? *Dharma*-s that have been, are being, and will be cognized by the mind are called *dharmadhātu*. 'Those that have been cognized by the mind' refers to the *dharmadhātu* that has been cognized by the past mind. 'Those that are being cognized by the mind' refers to the *dharmadhātu* that is being cognized by the present mind. 'Those that will

be cognized by the mind' refers to *dharmadhātu* that will be cognized by the future mind.[37]

The same definition is also found in the earlier PrŚ.[38] Accordingly, as far as the definition goes, *dharmadhātu* clearly refers to the tritemporal mental objects, and these should include all possible "categories" of *dharma*-s. This is explicitly indicated in the following passage from the VKŚ which specifies the objects of each type of consciousness. In the description, the objects of mental consciousness clearly amount to all possible types of *dharma*-s — all the types of *dharma*-s constituting the 12 *āyatana*-s:

> There is the group of six consciousnesses: visual, auditory, olfactory, gustatory, bodily and mental.
>
> What does visual consciousness cognize? Visual consciousness cognizes the visibles.
>
> What does it not cognize? The [remaining] 11 *āyatana*-s.
>
> [Likewise for the next four consciousnesses] …
>
> What does mental consciousness cognize? Mental consciousness cognizes: eye, visibles and visual consciousness; ear, sounds and auditory consciousness; nose, odors and olfactory consciousness; tongue, tastes and gustatory consciousness; body, tangibles and bodily consciousness; mind, *dharma*-s (mental objects) and mental consciousness. …
>
> There are 12 abodes (*āyatana*): the eye-abode, the visible-abode, […] *dharma*-abode.
>
> By how many consciousnesses is the eye-abode cognized? …. By how many consciousnesses is the *dharma*-abode cognized? The visible abode is cognized by two consciousnesses: visual and mental consciousnesses. [Likewise up to] the tangible-abode is cognized by two consciousnesses:

bodily and mental consciousnesses. The remaining seven abodes are cognized by mental consciousness alone.[39]

Since the *dharmāyatana* in the 12-*āyatana* scheme corresponds to the *dharma-dhātu* in the 18-*dhātu* scheme, the above passage has also specified the nature and scope of the *dharmāyatana*. It is clear that the objects of mental consciousness include even the mind, objects of the mind, and mental consciousness. As for thought, it is true that the present thought cannot know itself or its concomitants and co-existents (such as the co-existent conditionings disjoined from thoughts). But it can know past and future thoughts and other's thoughts/the thought of others, etc. As for *rūpa*, the subtle *rūpa* of the faculties[40] and the non-information matter (*avijñapti*) can, in fact, be cognized only by thought.

We must remember that originally in the *sūtra*-s, the 18-*dhātu* taxonomy was a pragmatic classificatory scheme, mainly employed to underscore the Buddha's no-Self doctrine. This scheme was intended to show the correlation between the six faculties of a human being with their corresponding objects and the consciousnesses generated. It is essentially an epistemological consideration without any explicit ontological commitment. In this scheme, *dharma-dhātu* corresponded to the objects of the mind and mental consciousness just as the visibles corresponded to those of the eye and visual consciousness. When this scheme (together with those of the *skandha*- and *āyatana*-taxonomies) came to be adopted as a methodology of *dharma-pravicaya*, what is the Abhidharmic principle that it was made to represent? We have seen above that it is essentially a method for the understanding of *dharma*-s in terms of their intrinsic characteristics. In the words of the MVŚ, "these 18 *dhātu*-s are established on the basis of (intrinsic) characteristic".[41] While the Abhidharmic application of the scheme too — in keeping with the characteristically Buddhist emphasis — is also primarily from an epistemological perspective, the consideration in terms of intrinsic characteristic would mean, among other things, that the specific items assigned to each of the 18 *dhātu*-s must represent ultimate real existents (i.e., *dharma*-s in the proper Abhidharmic sense). Accordingly, even though the mind can think of all kinds of things, the *dharma-dhātu* cannot be said to comprise objects that are relatively real. This is clear from the items enumerated in the VKŚ and PrŚ as objects cognized by mental consciousness (eye … mental consciousness).

In this context, the MVŚ elaborates further on the principles involved in the *dhātu* taxonomy:

> How are the 18 *dhātu*-s established?
>
> The 18 are established on the basis of three things: 1. the supporting basis, 2. that which is supported, 3. the objects (*viṣaya*). On the basis of being supporting bases, the eye element up to the mind element are established as the six internal elements. On the basis of being the supported, the visual consciousness element up to the mental consciousness element are established as the six consciousness elements. On the basis of being objects, the matter element up to the *dharma* element (*dharma-dhātu*) are established as the six external elements.[42]

The two explanations above on *dharmadhātu* — from the VKŚ and MVŚ — may be said to be still in keeping with the *sūtra*-s. Both speak of *dharma-dhātu* as referring to objects of the mind and mental consciousness.

But when we examine further the Vaibhāṣika position, at least starting from the JPŚ,[43] we find that the content of *dharmadhātu* refers not to mental objects *per se*, but specifically to "seven *dharma*-s":

> Herein, we have analyzed the essential nature of the three aggregates, i.e., sensation, ideation and the conditionings. They should also be established as *āyatana*-s and *dhātu*-s. That is, these three aggregates, together with the non-information matter and the three unconditioned — these seven *dharma*-s — are established as *dharmāyatana* in the *āyatana* scheme and *dharma-dhātu* in the *dhātu* scheme.[44]

2.4.1.3.2. Incongruities concerning the Sarvāstivāda explanations on *dharmāyatana/dharma-dhātu*

The foregoing discussions should suffice to highlight certain incongruities in the Sarvāstivāda position concerning the *dharmāyatana/ dharma-dhātu*. While on the one hand, influenced by the intention in the *sūtra*, the Sarvāstivādins speak of the 'mental objects', as including all possible types of *dharma*-s, at the same time they would not state that *dharmadhātu* subsumes the "totality" of real existents — even though some Sarvāstivāda masters apparently maintain precisely that.[45]

One reason for this is that the Vaibhāṣikas must maintain their ontology which includes *dharma*-s other than those seven mental objects specified by the tradition as being *dharmadhātu*, as real existents.

Another reason is that, since the PrŚ, the five-group taxonomy was gradually becoming the standard classification of *dharma*-s better suited for subsuming the totality of *dharma*-s among which the *avijñapti rūpa* and the three unconditioned had come to be decisively upheld by the orthodox Vaibhāṣikas as being an integral part. The older classification in terms of *skandha*, *āyatana* and *dhātu* must now be reformulated to incorporate all these *dharma*-s and to correlate them with the new taxonomy as a whole.

Saṃghabhadra, repudiating the Sautrāntika master Śrīlāta's position that all *dharma*-s are subsumed under the *dharmāyatana* in-as-much as all *dharma*-s are the domain of activity of the mind, argues as follows:

> If this is the case, then only one single [*āyatana*] — *dharmāyatana* — ought to be established, since all *dharma*-s without exception would be the objects of the mind.[46]

In this connection, the JPŚ[47] (likewise the first chapter of the AKB) states that the totality of *dharma*-s is subsumed by one aggregate (i.e., *rūpa-skandha*), one abode (i.e., *mana-āyatana*) and one element (i.e., *dharma-dhātu*).[48] The MVŚ, citing this statement, goes on to explain as follows:

> Why is that? The totality of *dharma*-s is comprised of the five categories (*pañca-vastu*): matter, thought, thought-concomitant, conditionings disjoined from thought, and the unconditioned. The *rūpa-skandha* (matter-aggregate) subsumes matter; the *manāyatana* (mind-abode) subsumes thought; the *dharmāyatana* subsumes all the rest. Thus, the totality of *dharma*-s comes to be subsumed.
>
> Furthermore, all *dharma*-s are comprised of the 18 *dhātu*-s. Among them, the *rūpa-skandha* subsumes the ten *rūpa-dhātu*-s; the *manāyatana* subsumes the seven *citta-dhātu*-s; the *dharma-dhātu* subsumes the *dharma-dhātu*. Thus, the totality of *dharma*-s comes to be subsumed.
>
> Furthermore, all *dharma*-s are included in the aggregates, elements and abodes, and these three are mutually subsumed: the *rūpa-skandha* subsumes the ten matter-elements, the ten matter-abodes, and one part of the *dharma*-element and *dharma*-abode; the *manāyatana* subsumes the seven thought-elements and the consciousness-aggregate; the *dharma-dhātu* subsumes the *dharma*-abode, the aggregates of sensation, ideation and the conditionings, and one part of the matter-aggregate. Thus, these three subsume the totality of *dharma*-s.[49]

But apparently, even Saṃghabhadra, while upholding the same orthodox Vaibhāṣika position, ostensibly under the shadow of the *sūtra* tradition, at times speaks of the *dharmāyatana* explicitly as the cognitive objects corresponding to mental consciousness:

> The totality of *dharma*-s is just the twelve *āyatana*-s, i.e., the visual, auditory, olfactory, gustatory and mental consciousness, with their corresponding cognitive objects, the visibles, sound, odors, tastes tangibles and *dharma*-s.[50]

In this same context, it is noteworthy that he states, just as the MVŚ does, that the condition qua objects (see § 7.1.3) comprises the totality of *dharma*-s. This means, among other things, that all *dharma*-s can serve as the cognitive objects of the mental consciousness.

Another incongruity concerns the case of the faculties. According to the Ābhidharmikas, these faculties are objects cognized exclusively by mental consciousness — the first five sensory faculties, determined to be a subtle form of matter, are said to be invisible to the eye. Yet they are not subsumed as part of the *dharmāyatana* and *dharma-dhātu*. The reason for this, however, is not far to seek. In keeping with the classification in the *sūtra*, the six faculties must be retained as the corresponding supporting bases (*āśraya*) of the six types of consciousness generated by the six corresponding types of object. This means that the *dharma*-s, constituting the *dharmāyatana* and *dharma-dhātu*, must not be comingled with the five sensory faculties or the mental faculty (the mind). The five sensory faculties must be retained as five of the ten traditional subdivisions of matter. The mental faculty likewise has to be separated from the mental objects. The result is that the *dharma-dhātu* then came to subsume all the remaining *dharma*-s qua mental objects excluding the five sensory objects, the six faculties and the six consciousnesses. It must of course further take in the non-information matter, the conditionings disjoined from thought and the three unconditioned which were newly established as real entities by the orthodoxy.

Correlation between the 5 categories, 5 *skandha*-s, 12 *āyatana*-s and 18 *dhātu*-s

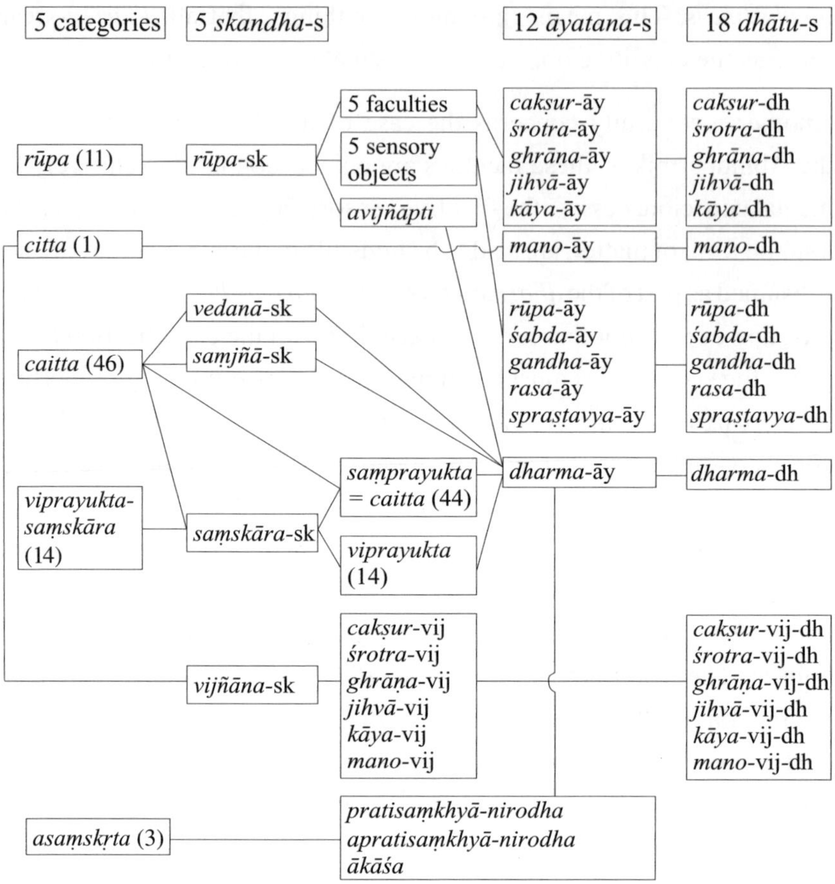

Diagram Text Abbreviations

sk = *skandha* ām āy = *āyatana* dh = *dhātu*

vij = *vijñāna*

2.4.1.4. Of the three — *skandha, āyatana* and *dhātu* — the Vaibhāṣika regards all as real. The Sautrāntika argues that *skandha* is unreal as it signifies a heap. As for the *āyatana*-s, some Sautrāntikas, as well as Vasubandhu, the Kośakāra, accept them as real.

But for Śrīlāta, they too are unreal. This, however, is not a new proposition, as the *Samayabhedoparacaṇa* also records the Prajñaptivāda view that "the 12 *āyatana*-s are not real".[51] Śrīlāta's contention is that neither a visual faculty nor an object can function as such (as *āśraya* and *ālambana* respectively) in the cognitive process except as a conglomeration of atoms. In fact, each individual atom is devoid of the function of seeing, and a conglomeration of them is likewise devoid of such a function, as in the case of a group of blind men who cannot see. The *dhātu*-s alone, he declares, are real,[52] in the sense of being causally efficacious factors of existence (*dharma*-s) existing only in the present moment of a *dharma*-series. In this sense, as Saṃghabhadra argues, *dhātu* would have essentially the same significance as the Sautrāntika notion of seeds (*bīja*),[53] the causal efficacy that is passed down in the series. This significance is brought out well by the term *anudhātu* or **pūrvānudhātu*, proposed by Śrīlāta, which is said to subsume all the karmic efficacies hitherto accumulated in a given moment of a series.

Saṃghabhadra, however, points out the difficulty in the *bīja* doctrine, since the Sautrāntika does not consider *bīja* — though real as a causal efficacy — as being an ontological entity. This causal efficacy — the *dharma* — is neither identical with nor different from the series itself; the series is considered unreal and yet, at the culminating moment of the serial transmission of the causal efficacy, is productive of a fruit![54]

2.4.2. Five-group taxonomy

Starting from the *Pañcavastuka* of Vasumitra's PrŚ, the five-group classification into *rūpa, citta, caitta*-s, *viprayukta-saṃskāra*-s and *asaṃskṛta*-s came into vogue. Group IV, the conditionings disjoined from thought, represents a distinctive doctrinal development in Sarvāstivāda Abhidharma, not to be found in the Theravāda.

The Five-group-Seventy-five-*dharma* classification of the Sarvāstivāda

I. ***rūpa*** (matter, 11)

1. *cakṣur-indriya* (visual faculty)
2. *śrotra-indriya* (auditory fac)
3. *ghrāṇa-indriya* (olfactory fac)
4. *jihvā-indriya* (gustatory fac)
5. *kāya-indriya* (tangible fac)
6. *rūpa-artha* (visual object)
7. *śabda-artha* (auditory obj)
8. *gandha-artha* (olfactory obj)
9. *rasa-artha* (gustatory obj)
10. *spraṣṭavya-artha* (tangible obj)
11. *avijñapti-rūpa* (non-informative matter)

II. ***citta*** (thought)

III. ***caitasika dharma*-s** (thought-concomitants, 46)

1) *mahābhūmika dharma*-s (universal *dharma*-s, 10)

1. *vedanā* (sensation)
2. *cetanā* (volition)
3. *saṃjñā* (ideation)
4. *chanda* (predilection)
5. *sparśa* (contact)
6. *prajñā* (understanding)
7. *smṛti* (memory)
8. *manaskāra* (mental application)
9. *adhimokṣa* (resolve)
10. *samādhi* (concentration)

2) *kuśala-mahābhūmika dharma*-s (skillful universal *dharma*-s, 10)

1. *śraddhā* (faith)
2. *apramāda* (diligence)
3. *praśrabdhi* (calm)
4. *upekṣā* (equanimity)
5. *hrī* (modesty)
6. *apatrāpya* (shame)
7. *alobha* (non-greed)
8. *adveṣa* (non-hatred)
9. *avihiṃsā* (harmlessness)
10. *vīrya* (vigor)

3) *kleśa-mahābhūmika dharma*-s (universal *dharma*-s of defilement, 6)

1. *moha* (delusion)
2. *pramāda* (non-diligence)
3. *kauśīdya* (slackness)
4. *āśraddhya* (lack of faith)
5. *styāna* (torpor)
6. *auddhatya* (restlessness)

4) *akuśala-mahābhūmika dharma*-s (unskillful universal *dharma*-s, 2)

1. *āhrīkya* (non-modesty)
2. *anapatrāpya* (shamelessness)

5) *parīttakleśa-bhūmika dharma*-s (subsidiary universal *dharma*-s of defilement, 10)

1. *krodha* (anger)
2. *upanāha* (enmity)
3. *śāṭhya* (dissimulation)
4. *īrṣyā* (jealousy)
5. *pradāśa* (depravity)
6. *mrakṣa* (concealment)
7. *mātsarya* (avarice)
8. *māyā* (deceptiveness)
9. *mada* (pride)
10. *vihiṃsā* (harmfulness)

6) *aniyata dharma*-s (indeterminate *dharma*-s, 8)

1. *kaukṛtya* (remorse)
2. *middha* (drowsiness)
3. *vitarka* (reasoning)
4. *vicāra* (investigation)
5. *rāga* (greed)
6. *pratigha* (hostility)
7. *māna* (conceit)
8. *vicikitsā* (doubt)

IV. ***cittaviprayukta saṃskāra dharma*-s**
(conditionings disjoined from thought, 14)

1. *prāpti* (acquisition)
2. *aprāpti* (non-acquisition)
3. *nikāyasabhāga* (group homogeneity)
4. *āsaṃjñika* (ideationlessness)
5. *āsaṃjñi-samāpatti* (ideationless attainment)
6. *nirodha-samāpatti* (cessation attainment)
7. *jīvitendriya* (vital faculty)
8. *jāti-lakṣaṇa* (production-characteristic)
9. *sthiti-lakṣaṇa* (duration-characteristic)
10. *jarā-lakṣaṇa* (deterioration-characteristic)
11. *anityatā-lakṣaṇa* (impermanence-characteristic)
12. *nāma-kāya* (words)

13. *pada-kāya* (phrases)
14. *vyañjana-kāya* (syllables)

V. ***asaṃskṛta dharma*-s** (unconditioned *dharma*-s, 3)

1. *ākāśa*
2. *pratisaṃkhyā-nirodha* (cessation through deliberation)
3. *apratisaṃkhyā-nirodha* (cessation independent of deliberation)

2.4.3. Doctrinal perspectives

The examination of *dharma*-s is also commonly made through various doctrinal perspectives — taxonomical categories in the form of dyads, triads, etc. Some of these were taken over from the *sūtra*-s, others innovated by the Ābhidharmikas. The methodological devices described above are applied in juxtaposition with these categories. This method of taxonomical investigation is essentially the *dharma-pravicaya* in terms of *sāmānya-lakṣaṇa*. It is already evident among the oldest of the extant *abhidharma* texts such as the **Śāriputra-abhidharma*,[55] and was undoubtedly instrumental in bringing about a characteristically abhidharmic feature of these texts marking an important development in *abhidharma* methodology.

The investigation may be done with regard to all *dharma*-s, e.g.:

> "How many are visible (*sanidarśana*)? How many are invisible (*anidarśana*)?" — a dyad.
>
> "How many are skillful (*kuśala*)? How many are unskillful (*akuśala*)? How many are non-defined (*avyākṛta*)?" — a triad.

It may also be done with one particular doctrinal category as the focus — a methodology which is essentially one of collecting scattered data and their analysis. Thus, in the chapter on *karma* in **Śāriputra-abhidharma*, the various types of *karma* mentioned in the *sūtra*-s — from the group of two *karma*-s to the group of 40 *karma*-s — are incrementally classified.

The following are among the most important doctrinal perspectives employed by the Ābhidharmikas:

1. *saṃskṛta, asaṃskṛta*;
2. *kuśala, akuśala, avyākṛta*;
3. *sāsrava, anāsrava*;
4. *darśana-heya*, *bhāvanā-heya*, *aheya*.

The discussion of these major topics, with their various subdivisions, cover the whole scope of *abhidharma* analysis.

2.4.3.1. *Saṃskṛta* (conditioned), *asaṃskṛta* (unconditioned)

The MVŚ gives various distinctions between the *saṃskṛta*- and *asaṃskṛta*- *dharma*-s, the first of which — the most comprehensive one — is as follows:

> A *dharma* is said to be conditioned if it has arising and ceasing, cause and effect, and acquires the characteristics of the conditioned.
>
> A *dharma* is said to be unconditioned if it has no arising and ceasing, no cause and effect, and acquires the characteristics of the unconditioned.[56]

It is explained that the conditioned *dharma*-s have causes and conditions because they are weak in nature and must therefore depend on causes and conditions for their activities. The unconditioned *dharma*-s, on the other hand, are strong and therefore not dependent on them. Moreover, the unconditioned *dharma*-s have no activities at all, hence no use of causes and conditions.[57]

The AKB defines *saṃskṛta* as follows: "Conditioned — because they are made (*kṛta*) by conditions co-existing in assemblage — there is nothing that is produced by a single condition."[58] What is conditioned is what is dependently originated (*pratītya-samutpanna*) and characterized by the four characteristics of the conditioned (*saṃskṛta-lakṣaṇāni*: *jāti, sthiti, jarā/anyathātva, anityatā/vyaya*). These four — each a distinct force — are real entities belonging to the class of *viprayukta-saṃskāra* which together cause a so-called conditioned *dharma* to be impermanent, nay, momentary (*kṣaṇika*). (See *infra*, § 11.3.5).

All of the five *skandha*-s are conditioned. In terms of the five-group (*pañca-vastu*) classification, they comprise: *rūpa*-s, *citta, caitta*-s, *viprayukta-saṃskāra*-s and *asaṃskṛta*-s. This fivefold taxonomy was first articulated by Vasumitra in the *Pañca-vastuka* of his *Abhidharma-prakaraṇa-śāstra*.

> The unconditioned *dharma*-s are permanent, non-arising, non-ceasing — totally beyond the temporal process. They comprise three types of *dharma*-s: (i) *pratisaṃkhyā-nirodha* — cessation obtained through discriminative effort; (ii) *apratisaṃkhyā-nirodha* — cessation obtained without any selective effort, but simply due to the deficiency in the conditions for arising; (these cessations also serve as real obstructive forces making it impossible for the *dharma*-s concerned to arise again); and (iii) *ākāśa* — not to be confounded with *ākāśa-dhātu* which is empty space that is visible in between objects occupying space — that by virtue of which things can be accommodated and have their activities in space. (*Cf. infra*, § 16).

2.4.3.2 *Kuśala* (wholesome/skillful), *akuśala* (unwholesome/unskillful), *avyākṛta* (non-defined)

This classification concerns the moral causal order. The MVŚ explains the triad as follows:

> A *dharma* which is to be subsumed as being skillful, which effects a desirable fruit, and which is by nature secure (*kṣema*) is said to be *kuśala*.

> … Some say: A *dharma* which can produce the germs of a desirable existence and of liberation is said to be *kuśala*.
>
> A *dharma* which cannot produce the germs of a desirable existence and of liberation is said to be *akuśala*.
>
> That which is opposed to these two classes is said to be *avyākṛta*.[59]

Various additional definitions are given elsewhere in the MVŚ: A *kuśala dharma* is that which is sustained by skillfulness, which induces the sprouts of desirable existence and liberation, which causes rebirth in the desirable plane of existence (*sugati*), which pertains to regression (*nivṛtti*) from *saṃsāra*, etc. Those which are opposed in nature to these are *akuśala*; those which are neither are *avyākṛta*.[60] Saṃghabhadra explains thus: A non-defined *dharma* is that which cannot be defined as being either skillful or unskillful, its nature being indistinct. A *dharma* is said to be (morally) defined (*vyākṛta*) if it is praise-worthy or contemptible, and definable as pertaining to the 'black' or 'white' (i.e., good or bad) species. A skillful *dharma* is that which is opposed to the unskillful, or that which sustains or is sustained by *prajñā*, or that which brings about the auspicious. The opposite to this is unskillful.[61] Of the 18 *dhātu*-s, ten can be skillful, unskillful or non-defined — the seven mental *dhātu*-s, *rūpa*-, *śabda*-, and *dharma-dhātu*-s. The remaining eight are non-defined.

2.4.3.2.1. *Dharma*-s are said to be *kuśala* in four ways:

(i) absolutely (*paramārthatas*) — this refers to *nirvāṇa* which completely transcends *duḥkha*;

(ii) in their intrinsic nature (*svabhāvatas*) — this refers to moral shame (*hrī*) and moral fear (*apatrāpya*) and the three roots of skillfulness (*kuśala-mūla*-s);

(iii) through conjunction (*saṃprayogatas*) — this refers to mental factors which become *kuśala* through conjunctions with the *dharma*-s which are *kuśala* in their intrinsic nature;

(iv) through their originating cause (*samutthānatas*) — this refers to bodily and vocal *karma*-s, and to the *citta-viprayukta-saṃskāra*-s which become good through their originating cause.[62]

Saṃghabhadra gives an additional explanation on *nirvāṇa* as *paramārthataḥ kuśala*: it is *parama* because it is supreme and without an equal. It is an *artha* because it exists as a real entity. Hence it is *paramārtha*. It is *kuśala* in the sense of being secure, for it is *kuśala* and permanent (*nitya*).[63] In the MVŚ, this fourfold distinction is attributed to Venerable Vāṣpa. According to the Vibhajyavādins, *jñāna* is *kuśala* in its intrinsic nature; *vijñāna* is *kuśala* through conjunction with *jñāna*; the bodily and vocal *karma*-s and the *citta-viprayukta-saṃskāra*-s — *jāti*, etc., *prāpti*, the *asaṃjñi*- and *nirodha-samāpatti*-s — originated by it, are *kuśala* through origination; *nirvāṇa* is absolutely *kuśala*.[64]

2.4.3.2.2. Likewise, *dharma*-s are said to be *akuśala* in the same four ways:

(i) *saṃsāra* is *paramārthaḥ akuśala*;

(ii) moral shamelessness (*āhrīkya*) and moral fearlessness (*anapatrāpya*) and the three roots of unskillfulness are *akuśala* in their intrinsic nature;

(iii) the mental factors conjoined with the previous [i.e., (ii)] are *akuśala* through conjunction;

(iv) the bodily and vocal *karma*-s and the *citta-viprayukta-saṃskāra*-s originated by the same are *akuśala* through their originating cause.

According to the Vibhajyavādins: (i) is *saṃsāra*; (ii) is *moha*; (iii) is *vijñāna* conjoined with *moha*; (iv) are the *citta-viprayukta-saṃskāra*-s originated by the same.[65]

2.4.3.2.3. The *avyākṛta*-s are further divisible as (i) *nivṛta-avyākṛta* (veiled-non-defined) and (ii) *anivṛta-avyākṛta* (non-veiled-non-defined).

(i) A *nivṛta-avyākṛta* — being weak in nature — is that which, though incapable of inducing an undesirable fruit, is obstructive to the arising of the *anāsrava prajñā* or the noble path. An example of this is the 'Self-view', *satkāya-dṛṣṭi*, which is a defiled *prajñā*. The MVŚ[66] explains why *satkāya-dṛṣṭi* is not *akuśala*, but *avyākṛta* (i.e., *nivṛta-avyākṛta*):

> Question: Why is *satkāya-dṛṣṭi avyākṛta*?
>
> Answer: That *dharma* which is, in its intrinsic nature (*svabhāva*), moral shamelessness (*āhrīkya*) and moral fearlessness (*anapatrāpya*), which is conjoined with moral shamelessness and moral fearlessness, and which is the emanation (*niṣyanda*) of moral shamelessness and moral fearlessness — that is *akuśala*. *Satkāya-dṛṣṭi* is not moral shamelessness or moral fearlessness in its intrinsic nature, not conjoined with moral shamelessness and moral fearlessness, not an emanation from moral shamelessness and moral fearlessness; hence it is not *akuśala*.
>
> Furthermore, this *satkāya-dṛṣṭi* is not always (*ekaṃśena*) of evil intention (*āśaya-vipanna*), hence not *akuśala*. It is not always of evil intention because it is not conjoined with moral shamelessness and moral fearlessness.
>
> Furthermore, it is because this *dṛṣṭi* is not opposed to the practice of giving and ethical conduct (*dāna-śīla-aviruddha*). One who is attached to the Self holds thus: "By giving, I shall become rich and happy; by observing ethical rules, I shall be reborn in heaven; by practicing meditation, I shall be liberated." Hence it is *avyākṛta*.

> Furthermore, this *satkāyadṛṣṭi* is merely a delusion with regard to a person's own Self; it is not an oppression of others; hence *avyākṛta* …
>
> Furthermore, this *satkāyadṛṣṭi* does not have a retribution-fruit (*vipāka-phala*); hence *avyākṛta* …

However, the Dārṣṭāntikas deny this veiled-non-defined category of *dharma*-s.[67]

(ii) An *anivṛta-avyākṛta dharma* is that which is neither capable of inducing a retribution-fruit — desirable or undesirable — nor obstructing the arising of the noble path. Examples of this category are: the knowledge (a *prajñā*) of a particular art and craft (*śailpasthānika*), or the mind associated with a supernormal power (*abhijñā-phala*) or with deportment (*īryāpatha*). (a) Karmic retribution and (b) physical matter — *rūpa, gandha, rasa* and *spraṣṭavya* — are also *anivṛta-avyākṛta*. The latter are in fact *avyākṛta* in their intrinsic nature (*svabhāvataḥ*). The two *asaṃskṛta*-s — *apratisaṃkhyā-nirodha* and *ākāśa* — which are *paramārthato'vyākṛta*, also belong to this category. The following chart summarizes the whole classification:

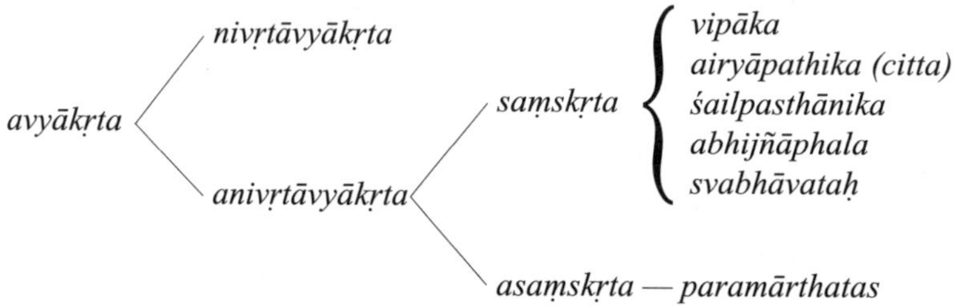

2.4.3.3. *Sāsrava* (with-outflow) and *anāsrava* (outflow-free)

Āsrava (lit. 'flowing out/toward') is a synonym for *kleśa* (defilement). *Avatāra*: "The outflows are so named because they keep (*āsayanti*) beings for a long time in the three spheres of existence, [thus] hindering their progress toward liberation. Or, because they cause beings to flow around (*āsravanti*) from the highest plane of existence (*bhavāgra*) to [the lowest], the Avīci hell. Or, because they incessantly discharge (√*kṣar*) inexhaustible impurities through the six wound-like entrances [— the six sense faculties —] of beings (*ṣadbhir āyatanavranāiḥ*)."[68] Even acts which are *kuśala* may also be *sāsrava*. For instance, one may practice generosity in the hope of having a favorable rebirth in the future. Thus the scope of the '*sāsrava*' is greater than that of the *akuśala*.[69]

The AKB discusses this classification with respect to the four noble truths and explains the meaning of *sāsrava*:

> *Dharma*-s are either with-outflow or outflow-free. The conditioned, with the exception of the noble path, are with-outflow, for therein the outflows grow concordantly (*sam-anu-√śī*; 等隨增).[70] It is true that the outflows are born taking the *nirodha*- and *mārga-satya* as objects, but they do not grow concordantly therein; thus it does not follow that the two are of the nature of being with-outflow.[71]

Thus, although an *anāsrava dharma* may serve as an object for a defilement, it does not accord with or conduce to its growth; or — more in conformity with the Sanskrit *anu-√śī* — it does not adhere therein.

A defilement can grow concordantly with the conascent defiled *citta-caitta* associated with it, through the fact of being conjoined with them (*saṃprayogato 'nuśete;* 相應隨增). It can also grow concordantly by taking a *sāsrava* object (*ālambanato 'nuśete;* 所緣隨增). (See *infra*, § 12.8.2).

2.4.3.4. *Darśana-heya* (abandonable by insight), *bhāvanā-heya* (abandonable by cultivation), *aheya* (not to be abandoned)

The first two categories pertain to the with-outflow *dharma*-s; the third, to outflow-free *dharma*-s.

The *darśana-heya dharma*-s are the defilements abandonable by insight into the four noble truths. The *bhāvanā-heya dharma*-s are those defilements abandonable by the path of cultivation which may be mundane (*laukika*; i.e., with-outflow) or transcendental (*lokottara*; i.e., outflow-free). (See *infra*, § 15.3). The third category refers to the outflow-free *dharma*-s — they are not to be abandoned.

Among the with-outflow *dharma*-s, the *kuśala* and *avyākṛta* ones, not being defilements, are not really abandonable in the proper sense. However, when the defilement which takes a *kuśala* or an *avyākṛta dharma* as its object is destroyed, this *dharma* is said to be abandoned (*tadālambana-kleśa-prahāṇāt*); for at that time the *dharma* comes to be disconnected. In fact, having been 'abandoned', a *kuśala dharma* can still re-arise. Thus, this is not a case of abandonment in terms of the *dharma*'s intrinsic nature (*svabhāva-prahāṇa*).[72]

2.4.3.5. Other taxonomical categories

There are various other such taxonomical categories employed as doctrinal perspectives. The AKB discusses the 18 *dhātu*-s in terms of a total of 22 such doctrinal perspectives.[73] The more important among these other perspectives are: *rūpin* (material), *arūpin* (immaterial); *sanidarśana* ('visible'), *anidarśana* ('not visible'); *sapratigha* ('resistant'), *apratigha* ('non-resistant'); *sālambana* (which take objects), *anālambana* (which do not take objects); *ādhyātmika* (internal), *bāhya* (external); *indriya* (of the nature of a faculty), *nendriya* (not of the nature of a faculty); *śaikṣa* ('pertaining to the trainee'), *aśaikṣa* ('pertaining to the non-trainee'), *naiva-śaikṣa-naśaikṣa* (pertaining neither to the trainee nor the non-trainee); *kāmāvacara-pratisaṃyukta* (pertaining to the sphere of sensuality), *rūpāvacara-pratisaṃyukta* (pertaining to the fine-material sphere), *ārūpyāvacara-pratisaṃyukta* (pertaining to the immaterial sphere), *apratisaṃyukta* (not pertaining to any sphere); etc.

2.4.4. Method of catechism

In the oldest canonical *abhidharma* texts, such as the Sarvāstivādin *Dharma-skandha-śāstra* (DSŚ) and the Theravādin *Vibhaṅgappakaraṇa*, the simpler method of defining a doctrinal category by answering a question constitutes a dominant feature. In the DSŚ, the series of questions and answers is usually preceded by a brief *sūtra* quotation of each important doctrinal term which is then commented on in the form of question and answer in the abhidharmic style. This is an analysis of *svabhāva* with a methodology derived from a combination of the catechetical format of the sūtric *abhidhamma-kathā*, *vedalla-kathā* and *uddesa-vibhaṅga*; e.g.: the DSŚ:[74]

> What is *cakṣur-indriya*?
>
> The *cakṣus* which has seen, is seeing, and will see *rūpa*; as well as its facsimile (*tatsabhāga*). Further, the *ādhipateya* of *cakṣus* induces *cakṣur-vijñāna* which has cognized (*vi-√jñā*), is cognizing and will cognize *rūpa* — [this *cakṣus*] and its facsimile are the *cakṣur-indriya*....

This catechetical format also predominates in the MVŚ which purports to comment on the *Jñānaprasthāna-śāstra* (JPŚ), and continues to be used in the later commentaries such as the AKB. Often, a question may lead to another which again leads to others (called *anuṣaṅga/prasaṅga*).

Another important methodology adopted in the *abhidharma* texts is that of answering a propositional question in alternatives (*pāda*):

The simplest is an answer in either "yes" (*evam*) or "no" (*na evam*) to the question: "Is *p* true?". This is called an ***evaṃ-pādaka***, e.g.: Question: "Those *dharma*-s which are conjoined with the vigor Enlightenment-factor (*bodhyaṅga*), are they also conjoined with Proper Exertion (*samyak-pradhāna*)?" Answer: "Yes (or 'It is so')."[75] This is a straightforward type of answer. In this example, it is clear that the vigor Enlightenment-factor is none other than the Exertion. The answer, although simple, helps to systematize and organize knowledge.

The question may also be in the form: "If *p* is true, is *q* also true?". The answer then may be either: "*p* is true, but not *q*" — a ***pūrva-pādaka*** (an answer which affirms only the former part of the question); or "*q* is true, but not *p*"— a ***paścāt-pādaka*** (an answer which affirms only the latter part of the question).

This same question may have an answer in four alternatives, a **tetralemma (*catuṣ-koṭi*)**:

(i) *p* is true, not *q*
(ii) *q* is true, not *p*
(iii) both *p* and *q* are true
(iv) neither *p* nor *q* is true

An example of such a tetralemma regarding the question, "Is all faith (*śraddhā*) affection (*premā*)?", is as follows:

(i) There is faith which is not affection — faith having *duḥkha-* and *samudaya-satya* as objects.

(ii) There is affection which is not faith — the defiled affection.

(iii) There is faith which is also affection — faith having *nirodha-* and *mārga-satya* as objects.

(iv) There are *dharma*-s which are neither faith nor affection — the other *dharma*-s.[76]

The catechetical investigation into the relationship *viś-à-viś* several *dharma*-s, i.e., A, B, C, D, E, etc., takes several rounds: First between A and B, A and C, A and D, A and E, … Next, between B and C, between B and D, between B and E, … . The whole process can be a rather complex one.[77] The MVŚ highlights the importance of such catechetical methodology for *abhidharma*:

> What is a *pūrva-pādaka*? What is a *paścāt-pādaka*? What is an *evaṃ-pādaka* (如是句)? What is a *naivam-pādaka* (不如是句 "not thus")? Nothing can match *abhidharma* in its ability to enlighten sentient beings with regard to such objects of knowledge.

For the Ābhidharmikas, by investigating a given *dharma* by means of such methodological devices and doctrinal perspectives, its nature and characteristic comes to be fully and accurately determined. Thus, *vijñāna* can be so determined to be: *saṃskṛta, arūpin, anirdarśana, apratigha*; either *sāsrava* or *anāsrava*; either *kuśala, akuśala* or *avyākṛta*; either past, present, or future; etc.

NOTES

[1] *Cf.* AKB, 133: *abhiprāyikaḥ sūtre lākṣaṇiko 'bhidharmaḥ /*

[2] Vy, 11: *kaḥ sautrāntikārthaḥ / ye sūtra-prāmāṇikā na śāstra-prāmāṇikāḥ ... sūtra-viseṣā eva hy arthaviniścayādayo 'bhidharma-saṃjñāḥ* / *Cf.* AKB, 146: *sūtra-pramāṇakā vayaṃ naśāstra-pramāṇkāḥ /*

[3] AKB, 3: *na hi vinā abhidharmopadeśena śiṣyaḥ śakto dharmān pravicetuṃ*

[4] *Arthaviniścaya-sūtra-nibandhana: na hi vinā sūtropadeśena śiṣyaḥ śakto dharmaṃ pravicetuṃ /*

This contrast is pointed out by Samtani, NH, in his edition of the *Arthaviniścaya-sūtra* and its Commentary (*nibandhana*) (Patna, 1971), 140 f., in a discussion on the Sautrāntika leaning of the commentator.

[5] Ny, 495b.

[6] T 49, 16c.

[7] Ny, 329c.

[8] Ny, *loc. cit.*

[9] Ny, 595a.

[10] MVŚ, 542c.

[11] MVŚ, 116b.

[12] *Entrance*, 93.

[13] Vy, 889 f.

[14] MVŚ, 777a. *Cf.* Ny, 432b: *lakṣaṇa = svarūpa/svabhāva.*

[15] MVŚ, 196c.

[16] MVŚ, 217a.

[17] MVŚ, 217a.

[18] MVŚ, 1c.

[19] MVŚ, 405c.

[20] MVŚ, 65a.

[21] *Cf. Entrance*, 62 ff.

[22] MVŚ, 306b–c.

[23] *Cf.* MVŚ, 105c, 108c, 283b, 396a, etc.

[24] T 49, 15b.

[25] For the various versions of this stanza, see La Vallée Poussin, L de (1930), 'Documents d'Abhidharma', 249, n. 1.

[26] MVŚ, 145c.

[27] MVŚ, 770c–771a; cf. *infra*, § 1.3.4.

[28] *Cf. Entrance*, 15 ff.

[29] *Cf.* AKB, 10.

[30] AKB, 13.

[31] AKB, *loc. cit.*

[32] MVŚ, 379a. Some 14 meanings for *āyatana* are given herein.

[33] AKB, 301. *Cf.* S, iv, 13; M, i, 3; *Mahāniddesa*, 133: *sabbaṃ vuccati dvādasāyatanāni.*

[34] Ny, 477b.

[35] AKB, 13.

[36] AKB, *loc. cit.*; Ny, 343c (which indicates a preference for the meaning of *gotra*); SPrŚ, 782a.

[37] MVŚ, 370c.

[38] T 26, 699a.

[39] VKŚ, T 26, 546c.

[40] *Cf.* AKB, i, under stanza 48. SPrŚ, 823b: "The six faculties are the exclusive objects of mental consciousness". Also, Ny, 377a: "Among the 18 *dhātu*-s, the five *dhātu*-s, visibles, etc, … each is cognized by two among the six consciousnesses. By this, it is known that the remaining 13 *dhātu*-s are all cognized by mental consciousness alone, as they are not the objects of the five sensory consciousnesses."

The Theravāda in fact speaks of them as *dhammāyatana-rūpa*-s. See Karunadasa, Y, BAM, 35.

[41] MVŚ, 367b.

[42] MVŚ, 367b.

[43] JPŚ does not enumerate the seven, but the implication in the assertion "one *skandha*, one *āyatana* and one *dhātu*" is clear enough.

[44] MVŚ, 783b; AKB 11.

[45] MVŚ, 370c: 有餘師說, 法界總攝一切法盡. MVŚ, 985b: … 或說法處攝一切法.

[46] Ny, 344b.

[47] T 26, 1027b.

[48] MVŚ, 987b.

[49] MVŚ, 987b.

[50] Ny, 447b.

[51] T 49, 16a.

[52] Ny, 350c.

[53] Ny, 398b. Also *cf.* MVŚ, 367c (種種因義). In Sthiramati's commentary on the *Abhidharma-samuccaya*, *dhātu* is explicitly glossed as *bīja* (T 31, no. 1606, 704b: 一切法種子義).

[54] Ny, 633a; TSP, 509.

[55] *Cf. Study*, 73 ff., for a good discussion of this feature in this text.

[56] MVŚ, 392c–393a.

[57] MVŚ, 711a–b – various other explanations are also given.

[58] AKB, 4 f: *sametya saṃbhūya pratyayaiḥ kṛtā iti saṃskṛtāḥ / na hy ekapratyayajanitaṃ kiṃcid astīdi //*

[59] MVŚ, 741a.

[60] MVŚ, 263a–c, 740c–741a.

[61] Ny, 348c.

[62] *Cf.* AKB, 202.

[63] SPrŚ, 863c–864a.

[64] MVŚ, 263a, 741a.

[65] MVŚ, 263b, 741a.

[66] MVŚ, 259c–260a.

[67] MVŚ, 269c

[68] *Entrance*, 112.

[69] Theravāda has essentially the same notions. *Cf.* Lamotte, E, in Balasooriya, S., *et. al.*, ed., *Buddhist Studies in Honour of Walpola Rahula* (London, 1980), 127.

[70] *Cf. Entrance*, 104 & note; AKB(E), 133, n. 19.

[71] AKB, 3: *sāsravānāsravā dharmāḥ / saṃskṛtā mārgavarjitāḥ sāsravāḥ / āsravās teṣu yasmāt samanuśerate // kāmaṃ nirodhamārga-satyālambanā apy āsravā upajāyante na tv anuśerate tatreti na tayoḥ sāsravatvaprasaṅgaḥ //*

[72] *Cf.* AKB, 236.

[73] AKB, 18 ff.

[74] DSŚ, 498b.

[75] *Cf.* MVŚ, 550b.

[76] *Cf.* AKB, 60.

[77] *Cf. Study*, 203.

3. The Sarvāstivāda School and Its Notion of the Real

3.1. History of the Sarvāstivāda

Although it is difficult to speak of the exact date of the 'founding' of the Sarvāstivāda school, its presence, as well as that of its rival — the Vibhajyavāda lineage — in the time of Emperor Aśoka is beyond doubt. Since Aśoka's reign is around 268–232 B.C.E., this means that at least by the middle of the 3rd century B.C.E., it had already developed into a distinct school. Vasumitra's **Samayabhedoparacaṇacakra*, a Sarvāstivāda treatise, places the school's establishment at the beginning of the third century after the Buddha's demise:

> The Sthaviravāda remained united for a certain period of time. At the beginning of the 3rd century, there arose some disputes, and it split into

> two schools: 1. the Sarvāstivāda, also called Hetuvāda; 2. the original Sthaviravāda which [then] changed its name to the Haimavāda.[1]

Emperor Aśoka's ascendance to the throne is established as around 270 B.C.E. Accordingly, if we follow the Sarvāstivāda tradition itself which gives this date as 116 years (or a hundred odd years)[2] after the Buddha's *parinirvāṇa*, the date given by **Samayabhedoparacaṇa-cakra* for the establishment of Sarvāstivāda would be around the first part of 2nd century B.C.E. This tallies with the date of Kātyānīputra (*ca.* 150 B.C.E.) who is credited by tradition with the effective founding of the school.[3] The earliest inscriptional evidence, however, was the Mathurā Lion Capitol which dates from the beginning of the first century C.E. This inscription mentions the giving of alms and donation of monasteries by the wife of the *mahākṣatrapa* Rājuvula to the Sarvāstivāda community. His son, Śoḍāsa, is also recorded as having given lands to two Sarvāstivādin monks, Ārya Buddhadeva and Bhikṣu Buddhila.[4]

It appears that the Sarvāstivāda as well as its rival camp, the Vibhajyavāda, at first maintained its position as the orthodox Sthaviravāda. At this initial stage, the term 'Sarvāstivāda' was perhaps not specifically insisted upon. In Devaśarman's/Devakṣema's *Vijñānakāya-śāstra* (VKŚ), one of the seven canonical Sarvāstivāda texts, the author established — for the first time in explicit terms — the *sarvāstitva* standpoint against the Vibhajyavādins represented by a certain Maudgalyāyana. If this person could be identified with the Moggaliputta-tissa who was said to have presided over the Third Council of the Theravāda in Aśoka's time and who compiled the *Kathāvatthuppakaraṇa*, then the Chinese tradition transmitted by Xuan Zang that Devaśarman lived within 100 years after the Buddha's demise would seem credible.[5] This identification is tempting when we consider the fact that the controversy that the author deals with after having established his thesis *sarvāstitva* against Maudgalyāyana, corresponds to the very first controversy taken up in Moggaliputta-tissa's *Kathāvatthuppakaraṇa*, and even some of the phrases in both texts on this controversy bear much resemblance. The fact, however, that this text exhibits highly developed polemics betraying considerable influence from the JPŚ has prevented Yin Shun from accepting the above-mentioned tradition from Xuan Zang;[6] Yin Shun proposed instead that it was composed in the early part of the 1st century C.E. However, this fact could well have been the result of subsequent revision; it may also be in part a reflection of the author's intellectual acumen. La Vallée Poussin opined that it was composed after the Pāli *Kathāvatthu*.[7]

The Sarvāstivāda remained the most powerful and influential school in north-western India from around the beginning of the Common Era to about the 7th century C.E., initially established in Mathurā and expanding in the north where Kāśmīra became its center of orthodoxy. With its highly developed *abhidharma* doctrines, it was the leading *abhidharma* school capable of repudiating the emerging Mahāyāna philosophy as well as the pro-Mahāyāna tenets upheld by other schools of Nikāya (i.e., non-Mahāyāna) Buddhism. Around the 6th or 7th century C.E., its leading position seemed to have been eventually replaced by the Sāṃmitīya which had a well developed doctrine of *karma*.[8]

It is noteworthy that in the VKŚ, the Sarvāstivādins never call themselves as such. When arguing against the Vibhajyavādins, they refer to themselves as the Yukta-vādins (應理論者); against the Pudgalavādins, as the Śūnyatā-vādins (性空論者). It was perhaps later, in the course of doctrinal confrontation with rival schools and being hard pressed to articulate their position, that the term "Sarvāstivāda" came distinctly to be insisted upon. The traditional term, Yuktavādin/ Yuktavāda, continued to be employed frequently in the MVŚ.[9] It was used by the orthodox Sarvāstivādins in even the 5th century C.E.[10] In the MVŚ, in such a context where the Sarvāstivāda standpoint is contrasted with that of another school, the Vibhajyavādins are often ridiculed as not conforming to logic and as being "the fruit of nescience (*ajñāna*), of darkness (*andha-kāra-phala*?), of ignorance (*avidyā*), of not applying effort diligently".[11]

By around the earlier part of the 2nd century C.E., the Sarvāstivādins seemed to have more or less determined what they considered to be distinctively orthodox Sarvāstivāda doctrines in contradistinction to the other contemporary schools. This is represented by the encyclopedic compilation of the *Abhidharma-mahāvibhāṣā*, the 'Great Commentary' by the Sarvāstivāda orthodoxy in Kāśmīra (see below). Subsequently, however, within the broad Sarvāstivāda lineage itself, there still appeared to be disagreement concerning many of these doctrines. This fact is reflected in the post-MVŚ works, such as the **Satyasiddhi-śāstra* (成實論), the **Abhidharmahṛdaya* (T no. 1550) and its commentaries (T no. 1551, no. 1552), the AKB and its commentaries, the ADV and the **Nyāyānusāra* (Ny). In the introductory section of the 5th century C.E. **Samayapradīpika* (顯宗論) (SprŚ), the staunch Vaibhāṣika, Saṃghabhadra, in an attempt to establish the Buddha's omniscience, cites the Sarvāstivāda version of the *Saṅgīti-sūtra* (集法契經) where the Buddha is supposed to have predicted that there will be contentious views within the Buddhist movement after Him. These views are not to be found in the extant Chinese Āgama or Pāli version of the *sūtra*, but they are doctrinal positions considered heterodox by the Vaibhāṣikas, and their contraries would *ipso facto* represent the orthodox Sarvāstivāda positions as held at the time. Many of these sectarian views, said to be predicted by the Buddha, are disputed at length in AKB and Ny. They are enumerated as follows:

(1) It is only in the *vajropama-samādhi* that defilements can be eradicated all at once.
(2) *Pratisaṃkhyā-nirodha* and *nirvāṇa* are two distinct entities.
(3) The conditionings disjoined from thought are not real entities.
(4) *Vijñapti karma*-s do not exist, not to speak of *avijñapti karma*-s.

(5) All *rūpa-dharma*-s are comprised of the Great Elements (*mahābhūta*).

(6) The homogeneous cause (*sabhāga-hetu*) consists in the preceding being similar to the succeeding.

(7) The *rūpāyatana* comprises color (*varṇa-rūpa*) alone.

(8) The *spraṣṭavyāyatana* comprises the Great Elements alone.

(9) Only the tangible *āyatana*-s are obstructive (*sapratigha*).

(10) The *spraṣṭavyāyatana* and the *kāyāyatana* are obstructive.

(11) Only the five external *āyatana*-s are obstructive.

(12) It is visual consciousness that sees.

(13) It is the assemblage that sees.

(14) The *mano-dhātu* and the *dharma-dhātu* may be both permanent and impermanent.[12]

(15) *Rūpa-dharma*-s do not perish momentarily.

(16) There exist conditionings disjoined from mind which abide for some time.

(17) *Citta* exists in the ideationless and cessation meditations.

(18) The immediate conditions (*samanantara-pratyaya*) apply to *rūpa-dharma*-s as well.

(19) No *rūpa-dharma*-s can be homogeneous cause.

(20) Retribution-born (*vipākaja*) *rūpa* can resume after having been cut off.

(21) *Prātimokṣa-śīla* can also be acquired by animals, *preta*-s and *deva*-s.

(22) Relinking (*pratisaṃdhi*, at the time of rebirth) can take place even when the *citta* is undefiled.

(23) All relinking is due to craving and hatred.

(24) Restraint (*saṃvara*) and non-restraint (*asaṃvara*) can be undertaken either partially or fully.

(25) The gravest evil *karma* (*ānantarya*) can exist among animals and *preta*-s.

(26) Defilements can be abandoned by both the *ānantarya-* and *vimukti-mārga*-s.

(27) All skillful with-outflow *prajñā* conjoined with mental consciousness (*manovijñāna-saṃprayuktā kuśala-sāsrava-prajñā*) is not views (*dṛṣṭi*).

(28) *Satkāya-dṛṣṭi* and *antagrāha-dṛṣṭi* are unskillful and take objects pertaining to other spheres (*anya-dhātv-ālambana*).

(29) All defilements are unskillful.

(30) There exists no pleasurable or neutral sensation.

(31) Only neutral sensation does not exist.

(32) *Rūpa*-s exist in *ārūpya-dhātu*.

(33) All those falling from the ideationless heaven are reborn in the evil planes of existence (*durgati*).

(34) There is no untimely death for any sentient being.

(35) All outflow-free *prajñā* is of the nature of knowledge (*jñāna*) and view.

(36) [The *dharma*-s] are to be asserted separately: past and future [*dharma*-s] do not exist; all exist in the present.[13]

(37) Matter and thought cannot become co-existent causes (*sahabhū-hetu*).

(38) At the *kalala* stage of development the embryo is already in possession of all the material faculties.

(39) All those who have acquired the *mūrdhan dharma*-s are not susceptible to rebirth in the evil planes of existence.

(40) All skillful and evil *karma*-s are capable of being transformed and ceasing.

(41) The unconditioned *dharma*-s do not exist as real entities.

(42) The mundane paths of praxis do not eradicate defilements.

(43) The vow-knowledge, the non-dispute, the non-obstruction and the [threefold] double *samādhi* can arise only in Jambudvīpa.

(44) The *citta* and *caitta*-s can also take non-existent objects (*asad-ālambana*).

3.2. Sarvāstivāda vs. Vibhajyavāda

In spite of various doctrinal disagreements — some of considerable importance — the various subgroups within the Sarvāstivāda school were united in their central tenet of Sarvāstivāda. It seems to have been a genuine belief on the part of the Sarvāstivāda that "*sarvam asti*" was what the Buddha Himself had taught. It became a problem — philosophically — only when they came to be questioned by their opponents as to the exact implication of their doctrine of *sarvāstitva*. As noted above, even after they had eventually articulated this doctrinal position sufficiently to be established as a distinct school, they seemed to have continued to assume the position of the orthodox Sthaviravāda.

The working out of the implication of this thesis was still visible even as late as the time of Ny. The whole confrontation came to be zeroed in/focused on the dispute between Sarvāstivāda versus Vibhajyavāda. We are dealing here, in this context, with these two opposing theses and not with the issue of identification of the two broad sectarian lineages. As for the identity of the Vibhajyavādins in the MVŚ, Yin Shun has made an excellent investigation. According to him:

> The Vibhajyavādins in the *Mahāvibhāṣā* were the continental schools generally referred to as the Vibhajyavāda comprising the Mahīśāsaka, the Dharmagupta, and the Kāśyapīya which prevailed in the Kāśmīra region, particularly with the Mahīśāsaka as the main stream.[14]

In the AKB, the main opponents of the Sarvāstivādins, the Sautrāntikas, belonging to the Vibhajyavāda camp, propose that the Sarvāstivādin way of understanding *sarvāstitva* is not the only possible one. Indeed, they consider it to be a bad interpretation of the notion. For the Sautrāntikas, one could say 'all exists' only in the following manner: Past *dharma*-s have existed; future *dharma*-s will come into existence; present *dharma*-s are existing. Alternatively, one could also say 'all exists' in the sense in which the *sūtra*[15] expresses itself: Everything that is within the range of perception — within the 12 *āyatana*-s (and nothing more) — can legitimately be said to exist.

In this work, the Sarvāstivāda is represented by Vasubandhu as defining their position as follows:

> Those who hold 'all exists' — the past, the present and the future — belong to the Sarvāstivāda. Those, on the other hand, who hold that some exist, viz., the present and the past *karma* that has not given fruit but not those that have given fruit or the future, are followers of the Vibhajyavāda.[16]

In Saṃghabhadra's Ny, a post-AKB polemic in defense of the Vaibhāṣika orthodoxy, an additional requirement for the definition is noticeable:

> It is only those who believe in the real existence of the three periods of time, as discussed above, as well as of the three kinds of the unconditioned, who can be considered as belonging to the Sarvāstivāda.[17]

This same requirement is also found in the ADV:[18]

> Sarvāstivāda is so called because it accepts [the reality of] the three periods of time, distinguished on account of activity, and the three reals [— the three unconditioned]...

The additional requirement seems to confirm our suggestion that even as late as the time of Ny, the orthodox Sarvāstivādins were still struggling to define themselves. According to the **Samayabhedopara caṇacakra*, most of the early Buddhist sects had accepted the doctrine of *sarvāstitva*, even though they seem to have disputed endlessly on what it really meant for them in each case. It seems possible that even as late as the time of the AKB and Ny, there were still some Buddhists, both within and without the broad Sarvāstivāda lineage — including some sections of the Sautrāntika-Dārṣṭāntika — who would accept the doctrine in a revised or different version from that adopted by the orthodox Vaibhāṣikas. It is perhaps because of this that Saṃghabhadra felt it necessary to dissociate the Vaibhāṣikas distinctly from the others whom he could not accept as real Sarvāstivādins in any sense. In Ny, he names them as follows:

Pudgalavādins, called by him "the Superimposers or Additionists (Samāropavādins)" on account of their acceptance of the reality of the *pudgala* in addition to that of the *dharma*-s in the three times;

Vibhajyavādins who accept the existence of only the present and the past *karma* that has not given fruit;

Kṣaṇikavādins who accept only the reality of the 12 *āyatana*-s of the present *kṣaṇa*;

Prajñaptivādins who deny the reality of even the *dharma*-s of the present;

Vaināśikas who hold that all *dharma*-s are without *svabhāva*, like empty flowers.

Sautrāntikas, here referred to as the Kṣaṇikavādins, are singled out by Saṃghabhadra who denies that they qualify as Sarvāstivādins, for their view "differs from the Vaināśikas by just a mere *kṣaṇa*!"[19]

3.3. Proof of the thesis of *sarvāstitva* in the VKŚ, MVŚ and AKB[20]

3.3.1. Arguments in the VKŚ

In the VKŚ, the author establishes the thesis of tri-temporal existence on the basis of four fundamental principles commonly and tacitly assumed by the Ābhidharmikas — partly on the authority of the *sūtra*-s and partly from among accepted *abhidharma* tenets:

(i) Two thoughts cannot be conascent, and a thought or thought-concomitant cannot know itself (*cf. infra*, § 9.4): It is said in the *sūtra* that a person can observe the craving in his mind, etc. When one is making the observation, the observing thought and the craving (i.e., the thought having the craving) observed cannot be simultaneous, nor can the present thought know itself. The craving observed then must be either past or future. Hence past and future *dharma*-s must be existent.

(ii) *Karma* and its retribution (*vipāka*) cannot be simultaneous (*cf. infra*, § 7.3.5): the fact that a *karma* which has become past can give rise to its retribution later proves the existence of the former as a past *dharma*, i.e., an existent in its past mode.

(iii) The Buddha has taught that consciousness necessarily has an object (*ālambana*): since we can have consciousness of what is past and future, past and future *dharma*-s must be existent.[21]

(iv) One can be endowed with (*samanvāgata*) *dharma*-s which do not arise presently: It is taught in the *sūtra* that someone in *nirodha-samāpatti* wherein no mental activity arises is still endowed with mental qualities such as moderateness in wishes (*alpecchatā*), shamefulness (*lajjā*), etc.; likewise, a trainee (*saikṣa*) is still endowed with the five spiritual faculties — faith, vigor, etc. — even when he has an enwrapped or defiled mind. Accordingly, those which are not present but can still be possessed must be existing as past or future *dharma*-s.[22]

3.3.2. Arguments in the MVŚ

The arguments for the tri-temporal existence of *dharma*-s are put forth to refute "those who are deluded with regard to the intrinsic nature of the three times (*adhvan*) — denying the past and the future, and holding that what exists in the present are the unconditioned *dharma*-s".

The first argument employs the Sarvāstivāda notion of endowment (*samanavāgama*), a notion that suggests some doctrinal development:

One is 'endowed' with a *dharma* when one, having acquired it, continues to possess it. When a *dharma* has not been acquired and one continues in the state of not possessing it, there is the 'non-endowment' of this *dharma*. For the Sarvāstivāda, this human experience presupposes the existence of past and future *dharma*-s. The other arguments employ systematic logical disputation coupled with an appeal to scriptural authority.

a. If past and future are non-existent, there would not be endowment and non-endowment of these *dharma*-s, just as there is no endowment and non-endowment of a second head, a third hand, etc., which are non-existent. Since there are in fact the endowment and non-endowment, it is known that past and future are existent.

b. The person who denies the past and the future must say in which temporal period the fruit of a present retribution-cause exists — past, present or future. If he says "past", then the past exists; if he says "future", then the future exists; if he says "present", then it amounts to the proposition that a retribution cause and its fruit exist simultaneously, which contradicts scriptural statements.[23] If he says "Its fruit is not within the three periods of time", then he is proposing that there is no fruit, since a retribution fruit is not unconditioned (*asaṃskṛta*). And if there is no fruit, then there would be no cause either.

Likewise, if the retribution fruit exists in the present, then he must say in which temporal period that corresponding cause occurs — past, present or future. If he says "past", then the past exists; if he says "future", then the future exists; if he says "present", then it amounts to the proposition that a retribution cause and its fruit exist simultaneously, which contradicts scriptural statements. If he says "Its cause is not within the three periods of time", then he is proposing that there is no cause, since a retribution cause is not unconditioned (*asaṃskṛta*). And if there is no cause, then there would be no fruit either.

c. If the past and the future were non-existent, then there would not be the facts of 'leaving home' (*pravrajyā*) and receiving 'higher ordination', in accordance with the stanza below:

> If one holds that the past does not exist, there would not be past Buddhas.
> If there were no past Buddhas, there would not be Leaving Home and receiving Higher Ordination.

d. If the past and the future were non-existent, then it must be that Saṅgha members practice false speech while possessing proper knowledge, in accordance with the stanza below:

> If [a Saṅgha member] holds that the past is non-existent and yet speaks of his [ordination] age,
> He would be increasing, day by day, [both] his proper knowledge and false speech.

e. The non-existence of the past and future implies that the present likewise does not exist, since the present is designated in relation to the past and future. The three times not existing, the conditioned would not exist. The conditioned not existing, the unconditioned too would not exist since the latter is established in relation to the former. The conditioned and the unconditioned both not existing, then there would not be any *dharma* whatsoever, which entails that there is no liberation and *nirvāṇa* — a serious false view!

3.3.3. Arguments in the AKB

The argument put forth by the Sarvāstivāda in the AKB, by way of both scriptural authority (*āgama* — *a.* and *b.*) and logical reasoning (*yukti* — *c.* and *d.*), are essentially similar:

a. For, it has been said by the Buddha: "O *bhikṣu*-s, if past *rūpa* did not exist, the learned noble disciple could not have become disgusted with regard to the past *rūpa*. It is because past *rūpa* exists that the learned noble disciple becomes disgusted with regard to the past *rūpa*. If future *rūpa* did not exist, the learned noble disciple could not have become free from delight with regard to the future *rūpa*. It is because future *rūpa* exists that..."[24]

b. It has been said by the Buddha, "Conditioned by the two [— sense organ and the object —], there is the arising of consciousness..."[25]

c. Consciousness arises when there is an object, not when there is no object. This is a fixed principle. If past and future [*dharma*-s] were non-existent, there would be a consciousness having a non-existent object. Hence, in the absence of an object, consciousness itself would not exist.[26]

d. If past [*dharma*-s] were non-existent, how could there be in the future the fruit of pure or impure *karma*? For it is not the case that at the time of the arising of the fruit a present retribution-cause exists![27]

3.4. Sautrāntika critique of the epistemological argument

The logical argument for the two requisites for the arising of consciousness — object and sense faculty — is in conformity with what the Vaibhāṣika cites in *b.* as the scriptural authority. The Vaibhāṣika insists on these twofold requisites. Accordingly, if past and future *dharma*-s are non-existent, then mental consciousness of them would not arise, since one of the requisites (object) is lacking. But this contradicts experience: We do have cognition (*buddhi*) of them, which proves that they are real.

The Sautrāntika does not accept that a *buddhi* must have a corresponding existent object. For him, objects of cognition can be either existent or non-existent. But even when an object is non-existent, the principle (*niyama*) of the two requisites is not violated. Sthavira Śrīlāta, a prominent Sautrāntika leader in Saṃghabhadra's time, explains:

> This follows in accordance with the principle of inferring from a succession of causes and effects. How?
>
> It is after having grasped a present [object] that [the mind] can swiftly infer to and fro: It can infer that such and such an effect is produced by a past cause of such and such a kind. This cause in turn arose from such and such a cause, and so on, correspondingly up to the remote [past]. It is completely from a process of inference that one has the vivid perception [of a past object] as if it were present (如現證得).
>
> Or, [the mind] infers that such and such a kind of cause in the present moment can produce such and such a kind of effect in the future. This effect in turn will induce the arising of such and such an effect, [in this way] correspondingly up to the remote [future]. …
>
> Although at this stage the object does not exist, it does not mean that the *jñāna* is without the two requisites… This is because causes and conditions exist in the particular series, at the time when a particular knowledge qua cause (*hetu-jñāna*) arises. That is: In the past there arose such a *jñāna*; through a causal transmission, a *jñāna* having such and such a form is produced in the present moment. Since the present *jñāna* has the past *jñāna* as its cause, this present *jñāna* arises with an understanding that is like the previous one, having the very past object (*viṣaya*) as its present *ālambana*. However, that *ālambana* does not exist now. Yet, although non-existent now, it nevertheless serves as the *ālambana*. Hence one cannot say [such

> and such a cognition] is devoid of the two requisites. [The same applies to the *jñāna* of a future object]. ...[28]

The Sautrāntika explains that he does not in fact object to the proposition of "All exists" (*sarvam asti*), provided it is properly understood in accordance with the *sūtra* statement:

> O brahmins, 'all exists' means no more than the 12 *āyatana*-s.[29]

Or rather, one should say: past is that which was existent; future is that which, given its cause, will exist — past and future 'exist' in this sense, not in the sense that the present *dharma*-s exist as real entities.[30] This amounts to defining the characteristic of the existent (*sallakṣaṇa*) as 'having arisen and not yet ceased'. Saṃghabhadra objects to such a notion of *sallakṣaṇa* which, for him, amounts to the *a priori* assumption that the past and the future do not exist:

> Their proposition is invalid, for what has arisen and not yet ceased is just another name for the present. [And] to say that the present time is *sallakṣaṇa* is to say that the past and the future are non-existent: One should further herein question: Why does *sallakṣaṇa* pertain to the present and not the other [times]?[31]

3.5. Notion of the real/existent

But just what precisely do the Sarvāstivādins mean when they insist that a *dharma* which has become past or one which has not yet arisen in the present is real/existent? The articulate theory of *sarvāstivāda* will be discussed in chapter 5. Here we will first examine their notion of an existent, beginning with the MVŚ.

3.5.1. Opinions of the various ancient masters in the MVŚ

In the two logical arguments above, the criterion for reality is clearly causal efficacy. The MVŚ informs us of various views on what existent/ real. The most notable and representative view of the Sarvāstivāda is that what is real is what abides uniquely in its intrinsic nature: What is real is what has a *svabhāva*. Among the various synonyms of *svabhāva* is the term *avayava*, 'part'.[32] A 'part' here refers to the smallest possible unit which cannot be further analyzed; it is the ultimate real. Whatever can be further analyzed either physically or mentally — a composite (e.g., a person) — is 'having a part' (*sāvayava*); it is a relative real, superimposed on the ultimate reals (e.g., the five *skandha*-s). This also means that what is real or what exists truly is what exists from the highest or ultimate standpoint (*paramārtha-sat*), as opposed to what exists relatively/conventionally (*saṃvṛti-sat*). MVŚ informs us of various Ābhidharmika notions of the existent:

> Regarding the existents, some say they are of two kinds: 1. Existents as real entities (*dravyataḥ sat*) — the *skandha, āyatana*, etc.; 2. Existents as concepts (*prajñaptitaḥ sat*) — male, female, etc.
>
> Some say they are of three kinds: 1. What exists relatively — a given thing exists relatively to this but does not exist relatively to that; 2. What exists by virtue of an assemblage — a given thing exists here but does not exist there; 3. What exists at some given time — a given thing exists at this time but does not exist at another time.
>
> Some say they are of five kinds: 1. what exists in name [only] — a tortoise's hair, a hare's horn, a garland of empty flowers, etc.; 2. what exists as a real entity (*dravyato'sti*) — all *dharma*-s each of which is abiding in its own-nature *(svabhāva*); 3. what exists conventionally — a vase, garment, vehicle, army, forest, house, etc.; 4. what exists as an assemblage — a *pudgala* is designated with regard to an assemblage of the *skandha*-s;

5. what exists relatively — 'this shore' [exists relatively to] 'that shore', a 'long thing' [exists relatively to] a 'short thing', etc.[33]

The MVŚ also distinguishes that which pertains to the relative truth and that which pertains to the absolute truth, with regard to the four noble truths. It enumerates various opinions on this. The position of the compilers is: the particularities of the four truths pertain to the relative truth; the 16 *ākāra*-s[34] pertain to the absolute truth, i.e., that which pertains to the absolute truth are the universal principles directly comprehended (*abhi-sam-√i*) by the *ārya*-s — that which is directly seen by them as being universally true.[35] (*Cf. supra*, § 2.3.2). It seems possible that the emphasis came to be shifted by the Ābhidharmikas from the latter (§ 2.3.2) to the former (§ 2.3.1).

The following discussion on the relationship between the conventional truth and the absolute truth shows that while these two truths as discoursed/uttered by the Buddha are to be upheld as being two perspectives of understanding, in reality — from the ontological perspective — there is ultimately only one truth, the absolute truth:

Question: Is the fact of conventionality (世俗性; **saṃvṛtitva*?) in the conventional [truth] existent from the standpoint of the absolute truth or is it non-existent from the standpoint of the absolute truth? ….

Answer: It should be said that the fact of conventionality in the conventional [truth] is existent from the standpoint of the absolute truth. If the fact of conventionality in the conventional [truth] is/would be non-existent from the standpoint of the absolute truth, then the Buddha's discourse on the two truths would be false. …

Question: If so, there should be only one truth, the absolute truth.

Answer: There indeed is only one truth, the absolute truth.

Question: If so, why are two truths established?

Answer: The two truths are established in terms of difference in perspective (差別緣; 'different reasons'), not in terms of substance: In terms of substance, there is only one truth, the absolute truth; in terms of difference in perspective, two types [of truth] are established. The absolute truth is not established from the same perspective from which the conventional truth is established. The conventional truth is not established from the same perspective as the absolute truth. …

Question: Is it also possible to designate the conventional and the absolute as being each distinct, without the two being mingled?

Answer: It can also be so designated. How is this? According to Venerable Vasumitra: The word that reveals is conventional; the *dharma* that is revealed is absolute. He states further: that which accords with conventional usage is conventional; that which accords with what the Āryas say is absolute. According to the Bhadanta: The speech generated from a thought that is not untrue, speaking of things like sentient beings, vase, garment, etc., is conventional truth. The speech generated from a thought that is not untrue, speaking of principles such as conditioned co-arising, etc., is absolute truth. …[36]

3.5.2. Relative/conventional and absolute truths as postulated in the AKB

The distinction between relative and absolute truths is explained in the AKB as follows:

That, the *buddhi* of which does not arise when it is broken into parts (*avayavaśo bhinne*), is conventionally existent; for instance, a pot. For therein, when it is broken into pieces, the *buddhi* of a pot does not arise. And therein, when the [constituent] *dharma*-s [of a thing] are mentally removed (*apohya*), the *buddhi* of it does not arise — that too is to be understood as a conventionally existent; for instance water. For therein,

> when the *dharma*, *rūpa*, etc., are removed mentally, the *buddhi* of water does not arise.
>
> A conventional notion (*saṃvṛti-saṃjñā*) is made with regard to those very things. Thus, those saying that a pot or water exists by virtue of convention speak truly and not falsely; thus this is conventional truth (*saṃvṛtisatya*).[37]
>
> Absolute truth (*paramārthasatya*) is other than this. Therein, even when [a thing] has been broken, the *buddhi* of it definitely arises and likewise, even when its [constituent] *dharma*-s are removed mentally — that is [to be understood as] an absolute existent (*paramārthasat*). For instance *rūpa*: for, therein, when the thing is broken into the atoms (*paramāṇuśaḥ*), and when the [constituent] *dharma*-s taste, etc., have been removed mentally, the *buddhi* of the intrinsic nature of *rūpa* definitely arises. *Vedanā*, etc., are also to be seen in the same way. This is called absolute truth as the existence is in the absolute sense (*etat paramārthena bhāvāt paramārthasatyamiti*).[38]

Vasubandhu also informs us of the view of the ancient masters (*pūrvācārya*) which, like the distinction made by the MVŚ compilers with regard to the four noble truths (above, § 3.5.1), has an epistemological basis: Absolute truth is that which accords with the manner in which a thing is perceived by transcendental knowledge (*lokottara-jñāna*) or the worldly knowledge (*laukikajñāna*) acquired subsequent (*pṛṣtalabhdha*) to the transcendental knowledge. Conventional truth is that which accords with the manner in which a thing is perceived by any other — defiled or non-defiled — type of knowledge.[39] Judging by Yaśomitra, these ancient masters would seem to be the masters of meditation, the Yogācāras, who speak of three kinds of reals — absolutely real, conventionally real and real as a thing in itself (*dravya-sat*). The last refers to what is real in terms of being an entity and in terms of its specific characteristic (*dravyataḥ sva-lakṣaṇataḥ sad dravya-sad iti*).[40]

3.5.3. Saṃghabhadra's characterization of the existent

In his defense of the existence of past and future *dharma*-s, Saṃghabhadra develops the epistemological argument of the real/existent:

> This is divisible into two: What exists truly (*dravyato'sti*) and what exists conceptually (*prajñaptito'sti*), the two being designated on the basis of *saṃvṛti-satya* and *paramārtha-satya*, [respectively]. If, with regard to a thing, a *buddhi* is produced without depending on anything else, this thing exists truly — e.g., *rūpa, vedanā*, etc. If it depends on other things to produce a *buddhi*, then it exists conceptually/relatively — e.g., a vase, army, etc.
>
> Those that exist truly are further divisible into two: Those that have only their essential natures (*svabhāva/svarūpa*) and those that, [in addition,] have activities (*kāritra*). Those that have *kāritra* are again of two types: with or without function (*sāmarthya/vyāpara/śakti*) ... Those that exist relatively are also of two types: having existence on the basis of something real or on something relative, like a vase and an army, respectively.[41]

3.5.3.1. Past and future *dharma*-s are not merely designations (*prajñapti*)

The Vibhajyavādins, of which the Sautrāntika is a vehement representative, maintain that only the present is real; but the totally unreal past and future objects can also be cognized by consciousness. The so-called past and future are in fact merely designations imposed on the present.[42] Saṃghabhadra repudiates this, defending *sarvāstitva*:

> Let us consider our proposition above that both real [or absolute] existents and relative existents can give rise to *buddhi*. Now since past and future objects (*ālambana*) can also give rise to *buddhi*, are the past and future [*dharma*-s] real or relative existents? Some assert that they are merely relative existents. Their assertion is untrue, for the following reasons:

[i] That on which the unreal *dharma*-s are based does not exist in the past and the future. If they say that the present constitutes their basis, this is also illogical, for they are not mutually dependent: Without depending on the present, there can also arise consciousnesses having the past and the future as objects. I have explained earlier that if *buddhi* arises with regard to something [whose existence] depends on other things, then that thing has a relative existence.

[ii] Moreover, it is observed in the world that when that on which a relative existent depends is fully exhausted, [the *buddhi* of] this relative existent no longer arises — … such as a *pudgala*, a vase, …, etc. On the other hand, it is observed that when the present *dharma*-s are completely exhausted, the past and the future can still be designated (*prajñāpyante*). …

[iii] Moreover, it is observed that that on which a relatively real depends and the relatively real are not mutually exclusive. [Now,] when *saṃskṛta-dharma*-s proceed in time, the past and the future do not co-exist. How can the past and the future be relatively established on the basis of the present? Hence, the past and the future are not mere relative existents.

[iv] Moreover, it has never been observed that in a before-after sequence, a real can turn into an unreal, and an unreal can turn into a real. Thus, [logically,] if one holds that the future is a mere relative existent, one should concede that the present too is unreal. Or, if one concedes that the present exists truly, one should concede that the past too is real and not unreal. …

[v] Moreover, the unreal cannot be objects of the *ārya-mārga*-s — relative existents such as the *pudgala*, vase, garment, etc., are not the objects [of cognition] of the *ārya-mārga*. But the *ārya-mārga*-s do have the past and future *saṃskṛta-dharma*-s as their objects as well. If it were otherwise, the past and future *saṃskṛta-dharma*-s

would not be understood by the receptivities (*kṣānti*) and knowledges (*jñāna*) in direct realization (*abhisamaya*).

[vi] Moreover, at the time of direct realization, if one does not concede that past and future *vedanā*, etc., serve as its objects, then those *dharma*-s such as *vedanā*, etc., within the person [i.e., the meditator] will never be objects of the direct realization, because they hold that it cannot have past and future objects, and because no two *vedanā*-s, etc., can arise simultaneously. Should this be the case, then the *ārya-mārga*-s cannot fully understand (*pari-jñā*) the *saṃskṛta-dharma*-s — which contradicts the *sūtra* which says: 'If one has not mastered, has not understood even a single *dharma*, I say that one cannot make an end of suffering' (*cf. nāham eka-dharmam apy anabhijñāya aparijñāya duḥkhasyānta-kriyāṃ vadāmi*). Hence the *ārya-mārga*-s necessarily have the past and the future [*dharma*-s] as their objects. Just as a consideration of the knowables proves that merely relatively existent past and future *dharma*-s cannot become objects of knowledge (*jñeya*); just so, from various other considerations — of the abandonables and the realizables — one can prove, in each case, that the past and the future cannot be mere relative existents, for unreal *dharma*-s cannot be abandoned, etc.

[vii] Moreover, the unreal [which depends on the real for its designation] and the real [on which the unreal is based] cannot be said definitely to be either identical or different.... The past, future and present times being different in their sequential positions, how can one say that the two times — past and future — are merely relative existents without their own essential natures and are [mere] designations on the basis of the present?

Thus their propositions, being contradictory to logic and disagreeing with the Noble Words, are totally unacceptable.[43]

3.5.3.2. Distinction among past, present and future *dharma*-s as existents

Saṃghabhadra further explains that, following the Ābhidharmikas, the definite existence of the past and the future should be properly understood as follows:

> On account of the fact of causality, and of defilement and freedom from defilement, their essential natures being not unreal, they are said to exist truly (*dravyataḥ sat*), [but] not in the same manner that the present [*dharma*-s] are said to exist truly: The past and the future are not absolute non-existents like a mare's horn, an empty flower, etc., nor are they merely relative existents like a vase, a garment, an army, a forest, a chariot, a room, a *pudgala*, etc., nor are they real existents in the manner of the present. Why? Neither absolute non-existents like a mare's horn or an empty flower, etc., nor relative existents like a vase, a garment, an army, a forest, a chariot, a room, a *pudgala*, etc., can be said to have the nature of causality, etc. Moreover, what has ceased and what has not arisen cannot be said to have real existence in the same manner as the present.

If a past or a future *dharma* exists truly, how can we talk about it as being past or future? Saṃghabhadra replies:

> It has been universally established (*prasiddha* — established for both parties involved in the debate) that a given real existent can have diverse modes of existence. The Sarvāstivādin can equally question you: "If both the past and the future are non-existent, how can one say 'this has gone', 'this is to come'?" On the basis of an essentially existent *dharma*, the Always-exist school can establish the variation in the modes of existence on account of the variation in the essential nature and the different causes and conditions [that obtain]. For those who assert that the past and the future are devoid of essential nature, they cannot speak in terms of variation in essential nature and in the causes and conditions — the past and the future being definitely non-existent. How can they distinguish past and future times?

3.5.3.3. Cognitive distinctiveness of the reals/existents

In Saṃghabhadra's characterization of the existent above, there is an emphasis on cognitive distinctiveness with regard to existent objects: the eye sees only forms, the ear hears only sounds, etc. A particular form is seen in its particularity, a particular sound is heard in its particularity, etc. This fact of distinctive cognition in each case is due to the distinctiveness in the object itself. It is a mark of the object's reality. The fact that a real object can be cognized in a unique way is due to the efficacy of its unique *svalakṣaṇa* which is intrinsic to it as a real. A non-existent, being without a *svalakṣaṇa*, can never give rise to cognition. In other words, the possibility of a cognition necessarily implies the true ontological status of the object cognized. For this reason, Saṃghabhadra's argument may be characterized as epistemic-ontologic. Saṃghabhadra elucidates this notion as follows:

> Cognition (*buddhi*) is *vis-à-vis* the cognized, for cognition can only be accomplished where an object of cognition exists. That is to say, a cognition is so called only when its object (*viṣaya*) can be apperceived (*upa-√labh*). If the perceived does not exist, of what is that which perceives? (I.e., it is a cognition of what?). Moreover, the intrinsic nature of consciousness is the discerning of an object; if the object of consciousness does not exist, what does consciousness discern? Hence, the consciousness of a non-existent object conceded by the [Sautrāntika] ought not to be called consciousness, since there is nothing to discern. A non-existent is an absolute non-entity and necessarily without (lit., 'going beyond' — 越) *svalakṣaṇa* and *sāmānya-lakṣaṇa*, what is it that is said to be the object of cognition or consciousness? Should one say that non-existence itself is the object of consciousness — no, for a consciousness necessarily has an object. That is: All mental elements (*citta-caitta-dharma*-s) have *svalakṣaṇa* and *sāmānya-lakṣaṇa* as their objects; it is not the case that an absolutely non-existent *dharma* arises as an object.[44]

The author of the ADV expresses an essentially similar notion:

> An objective entity having a unique form established by its intrinsic nature, whose distinctive characteristic is observed by an error-free observation of *dharma*-s, is said to be a real/existent entity.[45]

Saṃghabhadra further articulates on the real. It is characterized by its possession of efficacy which affects the way we perceive it:

> In our cognition of *rūpa*, it is only if the objects are true existents that there comes to be the possible difference between a correct and incorrect cognition on account of the difference in regard to the [state of] the faculty, light, remoteness, nearness and location, etc.[46]

We may also compare this to the logician Dharmakīrti's definition of the absolutely real: The object of direct perception (*pratyakṣa*) is the specific characteristic (*svalakṣaṇa* = particular) — a unique essence/ entity (*tattva*), the point-instant of efficiency capable of affecting our sensibility (*artha-kriyā-samartha*):

> The object of that [— direct perception —] is the specific characteristic. That of which there is a variation in the cognitive image on account of [its] nearness or remoteness, is the specific characteristic. That alone is the absolutely real, for a [real] entity (*vastu*) is characterized by its efficacy for a purposive action.[47]

3.6. The various components of the Sarvāstivāda school

In the narrower sense, as found in the MVŚ, the Ābhidharmikas often refer to 'the Sarvāstivāda theoreticians'. Sometimes, 'Sarvāstivāda theoreticians' is even used in specific reference to the Kāśmīrian Vaibhāṣikas. Thus, whereas the MVŚ ascribes the proposition that the *rūpa-dharma*-s also have *sabhāga-hetu* (see *infra*, § 6.3.2), to 'the masters of Kāśmīra',[48] the older version of this work[49] ascribes it to simply 'the Ābhidharmikas' (阿毗曇人).[50] The 'old Ābhidharmikas' are occasionally mentioned. But if the Ābhidharmikas constituted the mainstream of the Sarvāstivāda, they did not exhaust the totality of the school. In the time of the MVŚ, the early Dārṣṭāntikas who were the *sūtradhara*-s, with Dharmatrāta and Buddhadeva as the most eminent, also constituted a school of thought within the fold of the Sarvāstivāda. Even subsequent to the MVŚ, the Dārṣṭāntika leader, Kumāralāta, who was instrumental in the evolution of the Dārṣṭāntika into the Sautrāntika, was known to subscribe to the view of *sarvāstitva*.[51]

In the MVŚ, the Dārṣṭāntikas are never referred to as the Sautrāntikas, although by the time of the AKB, the two appellations were seen to be used interchangeably. The **Samayabhedoparacaṇa-cakra* never mentions the Dārṣṭāntikas as among the so-called 18 sects, and the Sautrāntika is noticeably enumerated at the very end of the list of the Sthaviravāda lineage. This suggests that the Dārṣṭāntika as a school or a movement evolved gradually into the Sautrāntika, some time after the compilation of the MVŚ. The early Dārṣṭāntika masters were known for their active effort in popularizing the Buddha's teachings, employing poetry and possibly other literary devices in the world in the process, and were particularly skilled in utilizing similes and allegories in demonstrating the Buddhist doctrines. It was most probably for this reason that they came to be known as the Dārṣṭāntikas. They were also noted as meditators and proponents of meditation.[52] At the same time, we see in the MVŚ some of their masters — such as Dharmatrāta and Buddhadeva — as being engaged in controverting the Ābhidharmika doctrines. It is therefore conceivable that, broadly speaking, there existed two sections of the early Dārṣṭāntikas — one more pre-occupied with popular preaching and meditation, the other with doctrinal disputation. It was probably from the latter section that the Sautrāntika evolved. In this process of disputation, they also seem to have contributed to the development of Buddhist logic, as the Vaibhāṣikas, themselves proud of being in conformity to logic, spoke of the Sautrāntikas as being arrogant in their logical skill (*tarkābhimāna*).[53]

Professor Przyluski, however, proposed that the two appellations, Dārṣṭāntika and Sautrāntika, referred to the same group of people — the former used derogatively by their opponents, and the latter used by the Sautrāntikas to refer to themselves.[54] La Vallée Poussin endorses Przyluski's view, quoting one passage from the MVŚ in which the Sarvāstivādins condemn the Dārṣṭāntikas for employing worldly examples to support their theory against the Ābhidharmikas whose theory is said to be *ārya-dharma*.[55] Katō also endorses Przyluski's view.[56] However, Przyluski's confounding *dṛṣṭa* with *dṛṣṭi* in this context, along with his assertion that Buddhist *sūtra*-s were considered to be the Buddha's revelation, has been convincingly repudiated by Jayatilleke.[57] Moreover, we must take note of the fact that even in such a disputatious context, the Sarvāstivādins referred to them as "the Venerable/Honorable Dārṣṭāntikas (譬喻尊者)[58]— which is hardly humiliating. Dharmatrāta was apparently so highly revered that he was simply referred to as the Bhadanta (大德). Moreover, the Dārṣṭāntikas were not the only ones condemned for "relying on conventional parlance in the world" (依世俗言論) Others, like the Mahāsāṃghika[59] and the Vibhajyavādins[60] too, were condemned in exactly the same way:

> ...If so, how is the simile given by the Mahāsāṃghika to be explained (*nīyate*)?
>
> Answer: It need not be explained, for that is not subsumed under the *sūtra, vinaya* and *abhidharma*. Moreover, one cannot employ an example (*dṛṣṭānta*) visible in the world to repudiate the noble Dharma, for the noble Dharma and the conventional Dharma are different.

Accordingly, in such a context, we have evidence only that the Sarvāstivādins objected to the manner in which worldly similes are used to controvert the Ābhidharmika doctrines — whether they are used by the Dārṣṭāntikas or others.[61]

From the beginning, divergent viewpoints within the school were found and even tolerated — as long as they did not directly contravene the thesis of Sarvāstivāda. To take just a few examples: Dharmatrāta, Buddhadeva, Vasumitra and Ghoṣaka, — the so called 'four great Ābhidharmikas of the Sarvāstivāda' — each offered a different explanation as to how, given the theory that a *dharma* exists as an everlasting *dravya*, the difference in the three periods of time can be accounted for (see *infra*, § 5.2). Ghoṣaka also did not completely go along with the orthodox Ābhidharmikas in asserting that the totality of the *abhidharma* is *buddha-vacana*. To him, "all *abhidharma* is explanations on the *sūtra*-s. Such and such an exposition is made on account of such and such a *sūtra*; whatever is not said in the *sūtra*-s must be removed".[62] With regard to the thought-concomitants, we find Buddhadeva and the Dārṣṭāntikas denying their reality apart from thought.[63] Dharmatrāta held that all thought-concomitants are subsumable under volition (*cetanā*);[64] while others acknowledged the real existence of the thought-concomitants apart from thought. With regard to the three unconditioned, Buddhadeva[65] and others acknowledged their reality; Dharmatrāta held that Space (*ākāśa*) is unreal,[66] and the Dārṣṭāntikas denied the reality of all the three.[67]

But since the compilation of the JPŚ, the Kāśmīrian Sarvāstivādins upheld the supreme authority of the JPŚ system and raised this work to the status of being the Buddha's words.[68] As time went on, they assumed the position of orthodoxy and became increasingly dogmatic and intolerant toward all other views not compatible with the JPŚ system. Partly to consolidate their position as the orthodox Sarvāstivādins, they eventually compiled the encyclopedic MVŚ which purports to be a commentary on JPŚ. In it, besides their own views, those of the following Sarvāstivāda schools of thought were also cited and usually criticized and rejected: The Dārṣṭāntikas, the western masters (*pāścātya*; also called 'the Venerables of the west' 西方尊者; and 'the western *śramaṇa*-s'), the foreign masters (*bahirdeśaka*; also called 'the masters outside Kaśmīra', and the 'Gāndhārian masters'[69]). Even the so-called 'old Kāśmīrian masters'[70] were not spared.

Subsequent to the compilation of the MVŚ, the orthodox Kāśmīrians who based themselves on it were known as the Vaibhāṣikas. We must bear in mind, however, that the views accepted by the Vaibhāṣikas were not necessarily proposed by themselves for the first time. Many of them must have been the achievement of the great Sarvāstivāda masters up to the time of the compilation of the MVŚ. The term "Vaibhāṣikas" eventually came to connote the orthodox Sarvāstivādins, based mainly — but not exclusively — in Kāśmīra. It is important to realize that not all of them necessarily subscribed to each and every view sanctioned by the MVŚ compilers. Moreover, the evolving nature of the Vaibhāṣika views must be recognized as well.

This dogmaticism and intolerance of the Vaibhāṣikas inevitably brought about a reaction from the other Sarvāstivādins. On the one hand, it resulted in the split of the Sarvāstivāda school into two major camps — the eastern one representing the Kāśmīrian school and the western one representing the Gāndhārian school — although it would seem that not all Kāśmīrian Ābhidharmikas were as orthodox or dogmatic as the professed Vaibhāṣikas. On the other hand, it compelled the *sūtra*-centered Dārṣṭāntikas to co-operate with other holders of heterodox views, including the Mahāyāna Śūnyatāvādins, prevailing around the first and second centuries C.E., and finally to change over to the 'present-only-exist' standpoint. In this connection, it may be noted that in his **Nyāyānusāra*, Saṃghabhadra repeatedly accuses the Sautrāntika of siding with the followers of the 'sky-flower' (空花; *ākāśa-puṣpa*) doctrine — apparently referring to the Śūnyatā-vāda prevailing at the time — in obstinately denying the *svabhāva* of all *dharma*-s.[71] It was in this process that, a section among their radicals, the Dārṣṭāntika, eventually evolved into the Sautrāntika.

Although the appellations 'Gāndhārian masters', 'western masters' and 'foreign masters' may suggest a considerable difference in the geographical locations of these masters, in actual fact, they refer mainly to the Sarvāstivāda masters west of Kāśmīra — the western masters — of Gāndhāra and Parthia, with Gāndhāra as the center. In the AKB,[72] Vasubandhu speaks of the Kāśmīrians and the western masters where the MVŚ[73] has "masters of this country" (此國諸師) and "foreign masters" (外國諸師), respectively. In many places in the MVŚ, a certain view said to be held by one of these groups is also said, in the same context or elsewhere, to be held by another.[74] However, we do come across one instance[75] in the MVŚ where the 'foreign masters' hold a slightly different view from the 'western masters'. It is with regard to the number of *rūpa* heavens: The Vaibhāṣikas say 16;[76] the western masters, 17;[77] the foreign masters, who hold that there are nine distinct abodes in *rūpadhātu*,[78] 18.[79] Also, where the MVŚ[80] ascribes the view that *rūpa*-s have no *sabhāga-hetu* to 'the foreign masters', the Old MVŚ[81] ascribes it to 'the Dārṣṭāntikas'. This may then suggest that the term "foreign masters" possibly has a broader connotation than the term "western masters". We must, of course, also allow for the possibility of individual differences in views even among the so-called western masters or foreign masters themselves.

The western masters too studied JPŚ, although with a more critical attitude than the Kāśmīrians. They too, being Sarvāstivādin Ābhidharmikas, were not really opposed to the Kāśmīrians in a sectarian sense. The MVŚ compilers held them in considerable regard, calling them 'the honored ones of the west'.[82] Yin Shun observes that "the doctrines of the western school are mostly the orthodox views of the MVŚ and were absorbed in this work. The views of the western masters, foreign masters and

Gāndhārian masters pointed out specifically in the MVŚ, are but a small number of heterodox views."[83]

But the work which most deeply influenced the basic attitude of these western masters was the PrŚ whose importance for the Sarvāstivādins was next only to the JPŚ. A new trend of development was inherited from the tradition of the PrŚ, tending toward organization, the essential and conciseness. It is for this reason that many views found in the PrŚ, such as 'four non-defined roots' (*avyākṛta-mūla*),[84] 'four meanings of *anuśaya*',[85] etc., were often attributed by the Vaibhāṣikas to the western or foreign masters.

NOTES

[1] T 49, 15b.

[2] T 49, no. 2033, 20a; no. 2031, 15a.

[3] *Cf.* T 45, 9b.

[4] See Lamotte, E, *Histoire du bouddhisme indien: des origines à l'ère Śaka* (Louvain, 1967), 543.

[5] T no. 1821, 8c.

[6] *Study*, 169 f.

[7] La Vallée Poussin (1925b), 344 f.

[8] See Lu Cheng, 2367 ff.

[9] E.g., MVŚ, 138c ff., 169a–171b, 222a–222c, 308b, etc.

[10] *Cf.* Ny, 469a.

[11] E.g., MVŚ, 313a, 358a, etc.

[12] 意界法界俱常非常。

[13] 無有去來, 一切現在;別別而說。

[14] *Study*, 412.

[15] *Cf. sabba-sutta* in *Saṃyutta-nikāya*.

[16] AKB, 296: *ye hi sarvamastīti vadanti atītam anāgataṃ pratyutpannaṃ ca te sarvāstivādāḥ / ye tu kecid asti yat pratyutpannam adatta-phalaṃ cātītaṃ karma kiṃcin nāsti yad datta-phalam atītam anāgataṃ ceti vibhajya vadanti te vibhajyavādinaḥ /*

[17] Ny, 630c.

[18] ADV, 259: *icchaty adhva-trayaṃ yasmāt kṛtyataś ca dhruva-trayam / sarvāstivāda ity uktas tasmād… //*

[19] Ny, 630c–631a. A similar distinction between the Sarvāstivāda and other schools is also made in the ADV, 257 f.

[20] AKB, 295 f.

[21] Maudgalyāyana, however, maintains that one can be conscious of non-existent objects.

[22] VKŚ, 531a–537a.

[23] The *Dharmapada* stanza corrresponding to *Dhammapada,* 71, *Udānavarga,* IX, 17 and the Chinese version of *Udānavarga* (T 212), 671b, etc.

[24] AKB, 295: *uktaṃ hi bhagavatā'tītaṃ ced bhikṣavo rūpaṃ nābhaviṣyan na śrutavān ārya-śrāvako'tīte rūpe'napekṣo'bhaviṣyat / yasmāttarhyastyatītaṃ rūpaṃ tasmāc chrutāvān ārya-śrāvako'tīte rūpe'napekṣo bhavati / anāgataṃ ced rūpaṃ nābhaviṣyat na śrutavān ārya-śrāvako'nāgataṃ rūpaṃ nābhyanandiṣyat / yasmāttarhyastyanāgataṃ rūpam… /*

[25] AKB, 295: *dvayaṃ pratītya vijñānasyotpāda ityuktam /* The relevant *sūtra* passage is cited in AKB, 146: *cakṣuḥ pratītya rūpāṇi cotpadyate cakṣurvijñānam / trayāṇāṃ saṃnipātaḥ sparśaḥ / sahajātā vedanā saṃjñā cetaneti / Cf.* S, ii, 72: *cakkhuṃ ca paṭicca rūpe ca uppajjati cakkhuviññāṇaṃ / tiṇṇaṃ saṅgati phasso / phassapaccayā vedanā / vedanāpaccayā taṅhā / …*; M, i, 111 ff. has, after *vedanā, "yaṃ vedeti taṃ sañjānāti / yaṃ sañjānāti taṃ vitakketi… /".* Only in *Peṭakopadesa*, 89, is the word *sahajātā* found: *cakkhuṃ ca paṭicca rūpe ca uppajjati cakkhu-viññāṇaṃ / tattha sahajātā vedanā saññā cetanā phaso manasikāro ete te dhammā eka-lakkhaṇā uppāda-lakkhaṇena //* SĀ, 72c, 87c: 緣眼色，生眼識，三事和合觸，俱生受想思).

[26] AKB, 295: *yadi cātītānāgataṃ na syād asadālambanaṃ vijñānaṃ syāt / tato vijñānam eva na syād ālambanābhāvāt /*

[27] AKB, 295 f.: *yadi cātītaṃ na syāt śubhāśubhasya karmaṇaḥ phalam āyatyāṃ kathaṃ syāt / na hi phalotpattikāle varttamāno vipāka-hetur astīti /*

[28] Ny, 628c–629a. Katō J unfortunately misunderstands this important phrase, phrase 智緣非有，亦二決定, the 'two' as referring to the past and the future (Katō J, *op. cit.*, 289, 291).

[29] AKB, 301: *evaṃ tu sādhur bhavati / yathā sūtre sarvam astīty uktaṃ tathā vadati / … "sarvamastīti brāhmaṇa yāvad eva dvādaśāyatanānī"ti — cf.* S, iv, 13; SĀ, 91a–b.

[30] AKB, 299: *atītaṃ tu yad bhūtapūrvam / anāgataṃ yatsati hetau bhaviṣyati / evaṃ ca kṛtvā 'stīty ucyate na tu punar dravyataḥ /*

[31] Ny, 621c.

[32] MVŚ, 4a.

[33] MVŚ, 42a–b. This notion of the relatively or conventionally real versus the

absolutely real continued to be found in the post-AKB Vy: *saṃvṛti-sad iti saṃvyavahāreṇa sat / paramārtha-sad iti paramārthena sat / svalakṣaṇena sad ity arthaḥ* // (Vy, 521). Note that *saṃvṛti* corresponds to Pāli *sammuti* (< √*man*, changed phonetically(?) to √*mu*). In the process of sanskritization → *sam-vṛti*. Later Sanskrit grammarians came to derive it from √*vṛ*. Already in the MVŚ (548b), we are told that the Grammarians (*śābdika*) take this to be from √*vṛ*, 'to cover': "This *saṃvṛti-satya* is concealed by *ajñāna*, like that which is inside a vessel is concealed/covered by the vessel." The Sanskrit Buddhist tradition generally interprets it in terms of *sam* + *vṛt/vṛ*.

[34] Four for each truth — for *duḥkha-satya*: *duḥkhatā, śūnyatā, anityatā, anātmatā/nairātmya*; etc. See *infra*, § 15.2.2.1.

[35] MVŚ, 399c–400a.

[36] MVŚ, 400a–b.

[37] *Cf.* Saṃghabhadra's explanation that the two truths are really two aspects of the one, absolute, truth, Ny, 666a ff.

[38] AKB, 334.

[39] AKB, 334: *yathā lokottareṇa jñānena gṛhyate tatpṛṣṭhalabdhena vā laukikena tathā paramārtha-satyam / yathā anyena tathā saṃvṛti-satyam iti pūrvācāryāḥ /*

[40] Vy, 542.

[41] Ny, 621c–622a. Saṃghabhadra's definition of the real may be said to be based on § 3.3.2 *b* & *c*.

[42] *Cf.* ADV, 278 (*vide*, ADV, *Introduction*, 125): *atra pratyavatiṣṭhante dārṣṭāntikāḥ / na brūmaḥ sarvathā'tītaṃ na vidyate / kiṃ tarhi / dravyātmanā na vidyate, prajñapty-ātmanā tu sad iti.*

[43] Ny, 624c ff.

[44] Ny, 622b.

[45] ADV, 264: *yasya khalv arthavastunaḥ svabhāvasiddha-svarūpasyā'vip arītākārayā dharmopalakṣaṇayā paricchinnaṃ lakṣaṇam upalakṣyate tat saddravyam ity ucyate*

[46] Ny, 471b.

[47] *Nyāyabindu*, 12–15: *tasya [pratyakṣasya] viṣayaḥ svalakṣaṇam / yasyārthasya*

saṃnidhānāsaṃnidhābhyāṃ jñānapratibhāsabhedastatsvalakṣaṇam / tadeva paramārthasat / arthakriyāsāmarthyalakṣaṇatvādvastunaḥ // Cf. Saṭīkaṃ Nyāyabinduprakaraṇam, 12 f.; also *cf.* Th. Stcherbatsky's translation in his *Buddhist Logic* II, 33 ff.

[48] MVŚ, 88a.

[49] Old MVŚ, 72c.

[50] Old MVŚ, 72c.

[51] *Cf.* ADV, 277.

[52] *Cf. Study*, 365 ff.

[53] See Singh, A, *The Heart of Buddhist Philosophy – Diṅnāga and Dharmakīrti* (Delhi, 1984), 21. Also *cf.* Dhammajoti, KL, *The Chinese Version of Dharmapāda* (Colombo, 1995), 22 ff.

[54] Przyluski, J, 'Dārṣṭāntika, Sautrāntika and Sarvāstivādin', in the *IHQ*, vol. XVI, 2, 1940, 246 ff.

[55] AKB(E), *Introduction*, 36; MVŚ, 782b.

[56] Katō J, *Kyōryōbu no Kenkyū*, 73 f.

[57] Jayatilleke, KN, *Early Buddhist Theory of Knowledge* (London, 1963), 381 f.

[58] E.g., MVŚ, 105a.

[59] E.g., MVŚ, 43c.

[60] E.g., MVŚ, 312b, 357a–b.

[61] See Dhammajoti, KL, 'Sarvāstivāda, Dārṣṭāntika, Sautrāntika and Yogācāra — Some Reflections on Their Interrelation', in the *JCBSSL*, Vol. IV, 185 ff.

[62] MVŚ, 326b.

[63] MVŚ, 8c, 661c, 730a, etc.

[64] MVŚ, 8c.

[65] MVŚ, 662a.

[66] MVŚ, 388c.

[67] MVŚ, 161a.

[68] MVŚ, 1a.

[69] Other schools of thought outside the Sarvāstivāda cited in the MVŚ include:

the Vibhajyavāda, Mahāsāṃghika, Dharmagupta, Mahīśāsaka, Kāśyapīya, Vātsīputrīya, Sthaviravāda, etc. The views of the following individual *ācārya*-s are also cited: Buddharakṣa, Jīvala, Ghoṣa-varman, Kṣemadatta, Vāṣpa, Vāmalabdha, Saṅghavasu, Dharadatta, Dharmanandin and Pūrṇayaśas.

[70] We also find the appellations 'the old Ābhidharmikas' and 'the old foreign masters'. In this connection, we must bear in mind that the doctrines of the Vaibhāṣikas and the western masters, etc., were constantly evolving, and that, therefore, "MVŚ views" and "Vaibhāṣika" do not always have the same connotation. See also *Entrance*, Introduction, § XI.

[71] E.g., Ny, 432b.

[72] AKB, 28.

[73] MVŚ, 368a.

[74] See examples quoted in *Study*, 306.

[75] *Study*, 307.

[76] AKB, 111; Ny, 475a.

[77] MVŚ, 85b.

[78] MVŚ, 784b.

[79] From Ny, 457a, we learn that the Sautrāntika master Śrīlāta also holds that there are 18 *rūpa* heavens.

[80] MVŚ, 87c.

[81] Old MVŚ, 72c.

[82] This regard was also given to 'the Venerable Dārṣṭāntikas' (譬喻尊者), although not to the Vibhajyavādins.

[83] *Study*, 310.

[84] PrŚ, 693a; AKB, 291 f.; ADV, 246 f.; Ny, 618b–c.

[85] PrŚ, 702a. Out of the four meanings given in our text, the Vaibhāṣika (MVŚ, 257a) gives only three for the meaning of the term *anuśaya*, i.e., without that of *anu-√sañj*. The explanation in terms of four meanings is attributed to the foreign masters (*ibid.*, 257b).

4. The *Abhidharma* Treatises of the Sarvāstivāda

4.1. Seven canonical treatises

The seven *abhidharma* works that came to be recognized as canonical treatises of the school are: 1. *Dharmaskandha*, 2. *Saṃgītiparyāya*, 3. *Prajñapti*, 4. *Vijñānakāya*, 5. *Prakaraṇa*, 6. *Dhātukāya*, 7. *Jñānaprasthāna*. Yaśomitra mentions the JPŚ as the body, in relation to the other six as its feet, enumerating in the following order: "The *śāstra* is the JPŚ; it is like a body having six feet — PrŚ, VKŚ, DSŚ, PjŚ, DKŚ, SgPŚ."[1] In a similar manner, Pu Guang explains:

> The earlier six treatises have less doctrinal topics; it is the JPŚ that contains the most extensive doctrinal perspectives. Accordingly, the *abhidharma* masters of later time spoke of the six as the feet and of the JPŚ as the body.[2]

The tradition that six of these texts constituted a group in contrast to the JPŚ, appears to have existed at least by around the early part of the 3rd century C.E., as attested in the **Mahāprajñāpāramitopadeśa* (MPPU):

> Question: The *Aṣṭagranthaka* (= JPŚ), the six-membered *abhidharma*, etc., whence were they?
>
> Answer: In the Buddha's time, the Dharma was non-erroneous. After the Buddha's demise, at the time of the first recitation (*saṅgīti*), [the Dharma] was just as when the Buddha was alive. In the subsequent century, at the time of King Aśoka, … there arose the names of the different schools. Henceforth, through a succession, it came to the time of a brahmin religieux from the clan of Kātyāyanīputra. He was intelligent and of sharp faculty and had read the whole *Tripiṭaka* and the scriptures belonging to both the Buddhist and non-Buddhist traditions. Desiring to understand the Buddha's words, he composed the *Jñānaprasthāna* comprising eight chapters (*grantha*). … Subsequently, the disciples composed the *Vibhāṣā* ([Great-]Commentary) for the sake of those who could not fully understand the eight chapters.[3]

In addition to authorship, Pu Guang further provides the size and the relative chronology of these seven treatises:

> Śāriputra composed the *Saṃgīti-paryāya* comprising 12,000 verses; the shorter version comprised 8,000 verses. Mahā-maudgalyāyana composed the *Dharma-skandha-pāda-śāstra*, comprising 6,000 verses. Mahā-kātyāyana composed the *Prajñapti-pāda-śāstra*, comprising 18,000 verses. The aforementioned three *śāstra*-s were composed in the Buddha's time. In the middle of the first century after the Buddha's demise, Devaśarman composed the *Vijñānakāya-pāda-śāstra*, comprising 7,000 verses. Coming to the beginning of the 3rd century [after the Buddha's demise], Vasumitra composed the *Prakaraṇa-pāda-śāstra*, comprising 6,000 verses. He further

composed the *Dhātu-kāya-pāda-śāstra*, whose longer version comprised 6,000 verses and shorter version comprised 700 verses.[4]

However, it is more reasonable to understand that these texts must have evolved as separate treatises, some being revised by several editors as a result of mutual influence; and it must have taken considerable time for the school to finally adopt this set of seven texts as their distinctive canonical *abhidharma*. It is possible that this canonical set came to be fixed sometime after the MVŚ, completed around the middle of 2nd century C.E. The PjŚ was probably incorporated as a canonical text around the time of the MVŚ (see below). In any case, the MVŚ does not mention the set of seven. In spite of the fact that it holds the JPŚ as the supreme authority, it never speaks of the JPŚ as the 'body' and quotes from only five of the other six *śāstra*-s — except for the DKŚ. The reference to the JPŚ as the 'body' in comparison to the other six treatises was probably the result of the Vaibhāṣika bias. The Tibetan tradition enumerates the seven texts in a different order: 1. DSŚ, 2. PjŚ, 3. DKŚ, 4. VKŚ, 5. JPŚ, 6. PrŚ, 7. SgPŚ.[5] The MPPU also speaks of "the body and meaning of *abhidharma*" (阿毘曇身及義) as one type of *abhidharma* and the "six-part [*abhidharma*]" as another.[6] Elsewhere, it also mentions the *ṣaṭpāda-abhidharma*.[7]

Given the scarcity of historical data and the fact that all seven texts seem to have been revised and interpolated subsequent to their original compilation, we must be content with only a relative chronology. Most scholars have attempted to classify these texts into three periods: early, middle and late; but their criteria are divergent.

Thus, Erich Frauwallner classified the PrŚ and JPŚ as the most recent of the three periods.[8] While observing that the PrŚ is not a systematic compilation and "consists of a number of sections, all virtually independent of each other and complete in themselves", he stated that its author, Vasumitra, "makes a purely outward attempt to unite in one work all the most important achievements that had been made up to his time". And this must have been his main reason for classifying it as one of the two most recent ones. However, this assumption of all the sections as being authored by Vasumitra alone is questionable (see below). As to the JPŚ — as the perceptive Yin Shun quite rightly remarks — its time of compilation cannot be too late considering the fact that it was this text which fundamentally established the definitive doctrines of the Sarvāstivāda school.[9]

Moreover, the question as to which text(s) had been borrowed or been influenced by which other text(s) — and also *vis-à-vis* two given texts, which had first influenced which — is disputable.

Furthermore, we cannot simply assume that a text showing more systematic or developed doctrines is necessarily later than one which shows otherwise — the difference as regards caliber and intellectual gift, personal views, etc., of the authors must be taken into consideration. An example of the developed Sarvāstivāda tenets is the three *asaṃskṛta*-s; yet it is noteworthy that whereas all the three are mentioned in the DSŚ, only two are mentioned in the JPŚ (see below).

Finally, even the three treatises — DSŚ, SgPŚ and PjŚ, commonly held to be the earliest — show clear signs of influence from the PrŚ and JPŚ in their extant versions, and to that extent cannot be regarded as the earlier sources for these two treatises in pure and simple terms. It is more likely that all seven texts, before their being properly incorporated as the Sarvāstivāda canonical texts, i.e., 'sarvāstivādized', had derived material from ancient sources of *abhidharma* investigation common to all schools.[10] Accordingly, the periodization of the relatively more developed texts must in part remain a subjective one. This being the case, we prefer to classify the seven treatises more simply into two broad groups:

I. the three texts concerning which we have more objective grounds to classify them as the earliest — and this is more or less a consensus of opinions among most scholars;

II. the other treatises which exhibit a more developed nature or which can be determined otherwise as being subsequent to the earliest three.

4.1.1. Treatises of the earliest period

Of the seven canonical texts, the DSŚ, SgPŚ and PjŚ belong to this period. They all exhibit features similar to the 'abhidharmic' discourses in the *sūtra-piṭaka* (see *supra*, § 1.1.2), and generally show little organization and doctrinal articulation. There is also the absence of explicit definition or establishment of the thesis of *sarvāstitva*. Furthermore, these three texts are noticeably attributed by tradition to the immediate disciples of the Buddha. We may note here that the Sarvāstivāda tradition enumerates these three texts by name as part of the *abhidharma-piṭaka* (see below § 4.1.1.2).

4.1.1.1. *Dharmaskandha-śāstra* (DSŚ)

According to the Chinese tradition, this *śāstra*, translated in full by Xuan Zang (T no. 1537), was authored by Maudgalyāyana, but the Sanskrit and Tibetan traditions[11] ascribe it to Śāriputra. Sanskrit fragments exist, totaling 22 numbered folios. The DSŚ begins with a *mātṛkā* — given as a summary (*uddāna*) — of the topics to be discussed. These topics are then taken up and commented upon one by one, sequentially. In each exposition, a *sūtra* passage precedes the item-wise commentary. The following is an example from "the chapter on the noble truths":[12]

> At one time, the Bhagavat was residing in Vārāṇasī (Banāras) at the Deer-park of Ṛṣipatana. At that time, the Bhagavat told the *bhikṣu*-s: "This is the

noble truth of unsatisfactoriness (*duḥkha*). If one applies the mind properly to such *dharma* unheard of before, there will definitely arise [in him] the eye, knowledge, wisdom (*vidyā*), discernment (*buddhi*). This is the noble truth of the origination of unsatisfactorines. ... With regard to these four noble truths, because I have made the threefold turning with the twelve aspects, ... At that time, Mahābrahma, having heard about this, rejoiced in it. ..."

Herein it relates the event of the turrning of the *Dharmacakra*. It is thus named the *Dharmacakrapravartana-sūtra*. At that time, the five *bhikṣu*-s and the 80,000 *devaputra*-s, having heard the discourse, rejoiced in it and accepted it with faith.

(Immediately after the *sūtra* quotation, the commentary follows:)

What is the noble truth of unsatisfactoriness? Birth is unsatisfactory ... In brief, the whole of the five aggregates of grasping is unsatisfactory.

What is birth-unsatisfactoriness? ...

For what reason is birth said to be unsatisfactory? ...

What is old-age-unsatisfactoriness? ...

(After commenting on each of the key terms concerning the first truth described in the *sūtra* passage, it goes on to expound on the other three truths in a similar manner.)

The doctrinal topics discussed in the 21 chapters of this text are divisible into the following three sections:

I. 1. *śikṣāpada*, 2. *srota-āpattyaṅga*, 3. *avetya-prasāda*, 4. *śrāmaṇya-phala*, 5. *pratipad*, 6. *ārya-vaṃśa*, 7. *samyak-pradhāna*, 8. *ṛddhi-pāda*, 9. *smṛtyupasthāna*, 10. *ārya-satya*, 11. *dhyāna*, 12. *apramāṇa*, 13. *ārūpya*, 14. *samādhi-bhāvanā*, 15. *bodhyaṅga*

II. 1. *kṣudra-vastuka*

III. 1. *indriya*, 2. *āyatana*, 3. *skandha*, 4. *bahu-dhātu*, 5. *pratītya-samutpāda*

The following features are noticeable:

(a) The topics discussed are those concerning spiritual praxis (I.) and doctrinal concepts which are the concern of the *sūtra*-s (III.). The emphasis on praxis is discernible from the fact that the treatise begins with a discussion on the practice of the five precepts (*pañca-śīla*) and ten skillful paths of action (*kuśala-karmapatha*), followed by the factors leading to stream-entry (*śrotaāpatti*), faith (*prasāda*), spiritual fruits (*śrāmanya-phala*), etc. Under the section on stream-entry, it attempts to map out the path of spiritual progress, and summarizes as follows:

> [One must begin by attending and honoring the True Men (*satpuruṣa*).] If one is able to attend and honor the True Men, one can then listen to the True Dharma. Having listened to the True Dharma, one is then able to comprehend properly (*yoniśas*) its profound meaning. Having properly comprehended its profound meaning, one can then proceed to practice the *dharmānudharma*-s. Having vigorously practiced the *dharmānudharma*-s, one is then able to enter into the perfection (*samyaktvāvakrānti*), [i.e., attain stream entry].[13]

(b) All commentaries are based on a specific *sūtra* passage, exhibiting the *vibhaṅga* style in the *sūtra-piṭaka*. (See e.g., quote above).

(c) Its classification of *dharma*-s is in terms of *āyatana*, *skandha* and (*bahu-*)*dhātu*, the discussion of each of which forms a separate chapter (i.e., chapter 18, 19, 20). But it is in the *Skandha* chapter that we see the explicit enumeration of all the conditioned *dharma*-s of the Sarvāstivāda under the five *skandha*-s, as follows:

rūpa-skandha	— *rūpa*, comprising the 4 Great Elements and the derived matter
vedanā-skandha	— *vedanā*, subdivided into various types
saṃjñā-skandha	— *saṃjñā* (briefly mentioned as to be understood similarly as the case of *vedanā*)
saṃskāra-skandha	conjoined: *cetanā*, etc. up to all *jñāna*, *dṛṣṭi* and *abhisamaya*
	disjoined: *prāpti*, etc. up to *vyañjana-kāya*
vijñāna-skandha	— *vijñāna* (briefly mentioned as to be understood similarly as the case of *vedanā*)

(d) There is little organization and systematization of its discussions.

(e) Although there is no attempt at establishing the thesis of *sarvāstitva*, its implication is sufficiently clear — all analysis is in terms of the past, the present, the future. Thus, *cakṣur-indriya* is explained as the *cakṣus* "which has seen, is seeing and will see *rūpa*, and the non-participating (*tat-sabhāga*) *cakṣus*"; etc.

(f) It enumerates the eye of intermediate existence (*antarā-bhava*) — a distinct doctrine of the Sarvāstivāda.

(g) In its discussion on *rūpa*, the *avijñapti* is not mentioned.

(h) Some relatively advanced doctrinal concepts — such as that of the 98 *anuśaya*-s innovated by the JPŚ and the classification of *citta-caitta*-s, *viprayukta-saṃskāra*-s and *asaṃskṛta*-s found in the PrŚ — are included in this text.[14] All the three *asaṃskṛta*-s are mentioned.[15] Explanations on the four *śrāmaṇya-phala*-s also seem to have been taken from the PjŚ.[16]

These features suggest that the DSŚ represents the most archaic type of *abhidharma* of the Sarvāstivāda, still visibly under the influence of the abhidharmic *sūtra*-s. The omission of *avijñapti-rūpa* suggests that the text probably belongs to the period before this topic came to be hotly debated among the *abhidharma* schools. However, (h) suggests that the present version must have been revised subsequently under the influence of the two most esteemed canonical texts — JPŚ and PrŚ[17] — and perhaps some other *pāda* treatises subsequent to it.

4.1.1.2. *Saṃgītiparyāya-śāstra* (SgPŚ)

The Chinese translation (T no. 1536) by Xuan Zang gives Śāriputra as its author, but the Sanskrit and Tibetan tradition[18] ascribe it to Mahākauṣṭhila. Only some fragments in Sanskrit exist. The text is a commentary on the *Saṃgīti-sūtra* (T no. 9, *Dīgha-nikāya,* no. 33) which is essentially a *mātṛkā* purporting to collect scattered teachings of the Buddha, presented in an enumerative format. The SgPŚ follows this format. As commentarial explanations presumably must have accompanied such concise, enumerated doctrinal topics from the Buddha's time, the SgPŚ — as a direct commentary on the *Saṃgīti-sūtra* to whose format it is confined — can be conceived as representing the result of the earliest *abhidharma* development contemporaneous with the *sūtra-piṭaka*. Yin Shun, on the following three grounds, concludes that the SgPŚ must have been composed subsequent to the DSŚ:[19]

(i) There are numerous places where the explanations are explicitly said to be "as explained in the *Dharmaskandha-śāstra*"[20] There are also some explanations — such as that on the three *akuśala-vitarka*-s[21] — which in content are the same as those in the DSŚ.

(ii) The SgPŚ is based on the *Saṃgītiparyāya-sūtra* of the *Dīrghāgama*, yet like the DSŚ, it also adopts the doctrine of 62 *dhātu*-s found in the *Bahudhātuka-sūtra* of the *Madhyamāgama* (T 1, no. 181).

(iii) This *śāstra* refers to variant explanations — "some say" (有說),[22] "some explained thus" (有作是說)[23] — suggesting that at the time of its compilation, *abhidharma* doctrines were gradually entering the stage of divergent views developed by the various *abhidharma* schools.

One might also consider the use of dyads and triads and the tetralemma analysis as further suggesting a relatively developed *abhidharma* methodology. However, such features may also have been accrued as a result of revision of the text over time. Moreover, it is to be noted in this connection that in speaking of the *mātṛkā* (= *abhidharma*), Saṃghabhadra enumerates these three texts in the following order: SgPŚ, DSŚ, PjŚ.[24] Likewise in the *Mūla-sarvāstivāda-vinaya-kṣudraka-vastu* and the *Aśokāvadāna* (see *supra*, § 1.1.2.*d*). This order of enumeration may well hint at the Sarvāstivāda tradition of the relative chronology of the three texts.

4.1.1.3. *Prajñapti-śāstra* (PjŚ)

Pu Guang ascribes this text to Mahā-kātyāyana (see above), whereas the MPPU, as well as the Sanskrit and Tibetan, to Mahā-maudgalyāyana.[25] This is the only canonical text not translated by Xuan Zang. The Chinese translation (T no. 1538) made in the early part of the 11th century by Fa-hu (Dharmarakṣita) and Wei-jing is a partial one, containing the chapter known as *kāraṇa-prajñapti*.

The Chinese translation mentions in an embedded note that the first part is named *Loka-prajñapti,* the original Sanskrit of which is not extant.[26] The MPPU records a tradition that the third part of the six-part (= six feet) *abhidharma*, entitled *Loka-prajñapti* (= PjŚ), comprises eight chapters. It seems, therefore, that the extant Tibetan version, comprising *Loka-prajñapti* (*'jig-rten bshag-pa*), *Kāraṇa-prajñapti* (*rgyu gdags-pa*) and *Karma-prajñapti* (*las gdags-pa*),[27] is also only a partial translation. The *Aśokāvadāna* explains the *mātṛkā-piṭaka* (= *abhidharma-piṭaka*) as comprising "the four *smṛtyupasthāna*-s … *praṇidhi-jñāna-samādhi*, the one-incremental (*ekottara*) *dharma*-s, the hundred-and-eight defilements, the explanation (記) of the world, the explanation of the fetters, the explanation of *karma*, the explanations of *samādhi, prajñā*, etc."[28] On the basis of all this information, Yin Shun concludes that originally the PjŚ must have taken the first chapter — its main doctrinal concern — as the general title, and that *Loka-prajñapti*, *Kāraṇa-prajñapti, Karma-prajñapti, Saṃyojana-prajñapti, Samādhi-prajñapti* and *Prajñā-prajñapti* must have constituted part of its chapter titles.[29]

The PjŚ is quoted 135 times in the MVŚ. The content of these quotations pertains mostly to cosmological doctrines, supernormal powers and — particularly — *karma* doctrines. This is in keeping with the general characteristics of the *Dīrghāgama* which, according to the Sarvāstivādin tradition, is meant for the proselytizers[30] and aims at meeting the needs of the popular mentality. Some scholars believe that it most likely derived its sources from the *shi-ji-jing* (T no. 30, 世記經; 'Explanation of the World' = *Loka-prajñapti*?[31]) of the *Dīrghāgama* and the *Li-shi-a-pi-tan-lun* (T no. 1644) which deal with Buddhist cosmology. Yin Shun, however, opines that it developed its doctrines from the various ancient sūtra sources dealing with cosmological topics which constituted a common doctrinal concern among the various Buddhist schools at the time; and depending on the school, such expositions came to be variously compiled, either as a *sūtra* or a *śāstra*. He points out, for instance, that the Theravāda too also discussed similar cosmological topics even though it does not possess a *sūtra* corresponding to the Chinese *shi-ji-jing*.[32] It appears that, besides the Sarvāstivāda, other schools/lineages such as the Vibhajyavāda and Vātsīputrīya too held the PjŚ in high esteem.[33] There are also places in the MVŚ where the explanations given by the PjŚ were accepted with difficulty or rejected, which again suggests that the text did not belong exclusively to the Sarvāstivāda. One such rejection concerns the nature of ignorance (*avidyā*):

> The *Prajñapti-śāstra* states: "What is ignorance? All the past defilements." It should not state so. Stating so would amount to the abandoning of

intrinsic nature. Rather, it should state: "What is ignorance? It is the stage of the past defilement." [34]

Yin Shun believes that it was subsequent to the MVŚ that the text came to be recognized as one of the six *pāda-śāstra*-s.[35]

4.1.2. Later, more developed texts

In contrast to the above three treatises, the remaining four are clearly more developed in terms of organization and doctrinal concepts. Moreover, some divergence not-withstanding, they all contain sectarian doctrines which can be regarded as specifically Sarvāstivādin. In addition, as regards authorship, all traditions agree in ascribing them to the *abhidharma* masters subsequent to the Buddha's time. The following enumeration reflects only a probable relative chronological of these four treatises.

4.1.2.1. *Vijñānakāya-śāstra* (VKŚ)

The Chinese translation gives its author as 提婆設摩 which agrees with the Sanskrit tradition — Devaśarman.[36] According to Pu Guang, he lived about 100 years from the Buddha's demise, which seems credible (see *supra*, § 3.1). Doctrinally, this is a highly esteemed Sarvāstivāda text, quoted 39 times by the MVŚ. It is in this text that, for the first time, the fundamental thesis of *sarvāstitva* was explicitly upheld against the Vibhajyavādins. The whole text consists of six *skandhaka*-s, the discussions being centered around the six consciousnesses:

I. *Maudgalyāyana-skandhaka*
II. *Pudgala-skandhaka*: refutation of *pudgalavāda*
III. *Hetu-pratyaya-skandhaka*
IV. *Ālambana-pratyaya-skandhaka*

V. *Kṣudraka-*(or *Saṃkīrṇa-)pratyaya-skandhaka*
VI. *Samanvāgama-skandhaka*

In repudiating the Vibhajyavādins' present-only-exist standpoint, we see the distinct employment of logical apparatus similar to that found in the Pāli *Kathāvatthu*.

I. *Maudgalyāyana-skandhaka* is the refutation of Śramaṇa Maudgalyāyana's assertion that "the past and future do not exist; the present and the unconditioned exist." Devaśarman's arguments here have been discussed above (§ 3.3.1). The only argument given by Maudgalyāyana in its defense is that there can be a thought (*citta*) without an object, so that the past and future, though non-existent, can serve as object of cognition.[37]

II. The *Pudgala-skandhaka* refutes the Pudgalavādins (Vātsīputrīya and Sāmmitīya) who assert: "In the true and absolute sense the *pudgala* is perceivable (*upalabhyate*), realizable (*sākṣātkriyate*), exists (現有; *saṃvidyate/vidyamāna/dṛśyate*?) and is well observed (等有; *saṃdṛśyate*?).[38] Hence there is definitely the *pudgala*." This phraseology is comparable to that in *Kathāvatthu* in a similar refutation of the *puggala*: *sacikaṭṭha-paramaṭṭhena puggalo upalabbhati*. The following is an illustration of the author's method of refutation with the first part of his argument:

1. The Pudgalavādin's proposition stated: In the true and absolute sense the *pudgala* is perceivable, realizable, exists and is well observed. (= *p*)

2. Śūnyatāvādin (= Sarvāstivādin) seeks confirmation with his opponent as to the latter's acceptance of the *sūtra* statements: Would you say that the *sūtra* has properly taught that the five *gati*-s — *naraka*, etc. — are definitively established without confusion, that each *gati* exists distinctly? (= *s*)

3. Pudgalavādin: Yes.

4. Śūnyatāvādin seeks further confirmation: Would you say that there is someone (i.e., your *pudgala*) who dies in the infernal plane of existence (*naraka-gati*) and is reborn into the plane of existence of the animals (*tiryag-gati*)? (= *p* 1)

5. Pudgalavādin: Yes.

6. Śūnyatāvādin: Recognize your defeat (汝聽墮負 — *cf. Kathāvatthu*: *ājānāhi niggahaṃ*)! For: $s \supset {\sim}p\ 1$, and $p\ 1 \supset {\sim}s$.

7. Pudgalavādin: We confirm *p* 1.

8. Śūnyatāvādin: Would you say that it is the very same person (彼即是彼; *sa eva saḥ*) — the one who dies and the one who is reborn? (= *p* 2)

9. Pudgalavādin: No. (~*p* 2)

10. Śūnyatāvādin: Recognize your defeat! For: $p\ 1 \supset p\ 2$; ${\sim}p\ 2 \supset {\sim}p\ 1$.

11. Śūnyatāvādin: Would you say that it is a different person in each case?

12. Pudgalavādin: It is different (= *p* 3) (given as an anticipated answer).

13. Śūnyatāvādin: Would you say that the infernal being is annihilated and a different being is born as an animal? (= *p* 4)

14. Pudgalavādin: No. (~*p* 4)

15. Śūnyatāvādin: Recognize your defeat! For: $p\ 3 \supset p\ 4$; ${\sim}p\ 4 \supset {\sim}p\ 3$.

16. Pudgalavādin: It is ineffable as to whether they are different or the same (= *p* 5) (given as an anticipated answer).

17. Śūnyatāvādin: Would you say that the same ineffability as regards identity or difference applies to the person in your *p* 1 as well? (= *p* 6)

18. Pudgalavādin: No. ($\sim p$ 6)

19. Śūnyatāvādin: Recognize your defeat! For: $p\,5 \supset p\,6$; $\sim p\,6 \supset \sim p\,5$.

The whole argument can be summarized as follows: $p \supset q$; ~q, therefore $\sim p$. Here, *p* is the opponent's proposition; *q* is its logical implications which are contradictory to either *sūtra* teachings or logic. Note that *p* 2 above is *śvāśvata-vāda* and that *p* 3 is *uccheda-vāda*, both contradicting the Buddha's teachings.

Another example of such contradictory implication is in regard to the question whether the retribution of pleasurable and unpleasurable experiences are self-caused. The Śūnyatāvādin argues that the opponent's thesis of a real person necessarily implies either that they are self-caused (*svayaṃ-kṛta*) or other-caused (*para-kṛta*). Both options, however, are extremes rejected by the *sūtra*-s, one implying *śvāśvata-vāda*, the other, *uccheda-vāda*.[39] The *pudgala* is also refuted on the ground that it is not among the objects of cognition of the six consciousnesses as taught by the Buddha — *rūpa*, *śabda*, etc. Neither can there be a seventh consciousness of which it is the object.[40]

III.–V. *Skandhaka*-s III to V deal with the Sarvāstivāda doctrine of the four *pratyaya*-s focusing on the six consciousnesses:

III. *Hetu-skandhaka* discusses *hetu-pratyaya*;
IV. *Ālambana-skandhaka* discusses *ālambana-pratyaya*;

V. *Saṃkīrṇa-skandhaka* discusses *samanantara-pratyaya* and *adhipati-pratyaya*.

VI. The *Samanvāgama-skandhaka* discusses *samanvāgama* and *asamanvāgama* — a topic which is to gain central importance in the Sarvāstivāda soteriology.

4.1.2.2. *Jñānaprasthāna-śāstra* (JPŚ)

The fundamental importance of this treatise is clear from the fact that the Sarvāstivāda tradition came to uphold this as the 'body' of their canonical *abhidharma*, in contrast to the six 'feet', although this does not necessarily in a straight forward manner imply that the JPŚ was a later compilation deriving its sources from the 'feet' texts (see above § 4.1). The definitive, encyclopedic **Abhidharma-mahāvibhāṣā* purports to be its commentary.

Two Chinese translations of the JPŚ are extant; one by Xuan Zang (T no. 1544) comprising 20 fascicles, and an earlier one translated in 383 C.E. by Saṃghadeva, Zhu-fo-nien and Dharmapriya under the title of **Aṣṭa-skandhaka-(/Aṣṭa-granthaka-)śāstra* (T no. 1543) comprising 30 fascicles. This treatise is unanimously ascribed by all traditions to Kātyāyanīputra.

As to the date of the author, Collett Cox mentioned the MPPU as suggesting that he lived 100 years after the Buddha.[41] However, what the MPPU actually says there is that 100 years after the Buddha's demise, there arose doctrinal disputes among the great masters giving rise to distinctly named schools. "Henceforth, through a succession, it came to [the time of] a brahmin religieux from the clan of Kātyāyana (= Kātyāyanīputra) … who composed the *Jñānaprasthāna-sūtra* in eight *skandhaka*-s"[42] (see above § 4.1). According to the **Samayabheda-uparacaṇacakra*, the Sarvāstivāda split from the original Sthaviravāda lineage at the beginning of the 3rd century after the Buddha (see above). If we take this to be the time when the JPŚ effectively established the Sarvāstivāda as a distinct school, then this is also the period to which Kātyāyanīputra belonged. The tradition originating from Xuan Zang also assigned him to the 3rd century after the Buddha.[43] So did Ji Zang's 三論玄義.[44] We believe Yin Shun is right that since the JPŚ decisively established the fundamental doctrines of the Sarvāstivāda, the date of its compilation cannot be too late. Xuan Zang's tradition placing Kātyāyanīputra in the 3rd century after the Buddha seems reasonable, and this would — according to the Sarvāstivāda tradition (see above, § 3.1) — place him around 150 B.C.E. Paramārtha's *Biography of Vasubandhu* places him in the 5th century after the Buddha's demise,[45] which seems to be a confounding with the time of the compilation of the MVŚ.[46]

The MVŚ explains the meaning of the title of this treatise, giving two interpretations of *prasthāna*: (i) 'setting out' or 'initiating' or 'starting point', (ii) 'base' or 'foot-hold':

> Question: Why is this treatise called *jñāna-prasthāna*?
>
> Answer: All knowledges in the absolute sense (*paramārtha-jñāna*) set out from here; this is the starting point. Hence it is called *jñāna-prasthāna*.
>
> Furthermore, this treatise should be called *The foot-hold of knowledge* — all the knowledges in the absolute sense have this as their foundation; they are established on this. Hence it is called *The foot-hold of knowledge*.
>
> Furthermore, this [treatise] is most capable of initiating the mighty knowledges; as the mighty knowledges have this as their object (*ālambana*), it is called *jñāna-prasthāna*.
>
> Furthermore, it is called *jñāna-prasthāna* because, depending on this, the knowledges reach the other shore (i.e., become perfected); there is

> none that can match this in setting forth the *sva-lakṣaṇa* and *sāmānya-lakṣaṇa* of all *dharma*-s.
>
> Furthermore, it is called *jñāna-prasthāna* because all knowledges — whether mundane (*laukika*) or transcendental (*lokottara*) — are dependent on this as their origin; it is the wonderful gate of the knowledges.[47]

The whole treatise is divided into eight major chapters called *skandhaka*-s, each with several sections called *āśvāsa* 納息 — called *varga* (跋渠) in the **Aṣṭa-skandhaka*. Each of these sections is made up of several doctrinal topics (章), each of which is then discussed in terms of various doctrinal perspectives (門). Thus, the whole treatise consists of 4 strata:

I. doctrinal topics;
II. doctrinal perspectives in terms of which a topic is analyzed;
III. a section comprising the various doctrinal topics;
IV. a *skandhaka* (chapter) comprising the various sections.

The eight major chapters are: 1. Miscellaneous; 2. The fetters; 3. The knowledges; 4. *Karma*; 5. The Great Elements; 6. The faculties; 7. The meditations; 8. The views.

The eight chapters are as follows: (1) *Saṃkīrṇaka*, with eight sections; (2) *Saṃyojana*, with four sections; (3) *Jñāna*, with five sections; (4) *Karman*, with five sections; (5) *Mahābhūta*, with four sections; (6) *Indriya*, with seven sections; (7) *Samādhi*, with five sections; (8) *Dṛṣṭi*, with six sections.

As to its order of presentation, which begins with the 'supreme worldly *dharma*-s' (*laukikāgra-dharma*), i.e., the first section of the *Saṃkīrṇaka-skandhaka*, the MVŚ cites divergent interpretations given by the various masters. The first few interpretations agree that there was no particular consideration of the order on the part of the author.[48] This seems to echo the general view of the Sarvāstivāda Ābhidharmikas, stated at the beginning of the MVŚ, that "one should seek the true nature and characteristics of *dharma*-s within the *abhidharma,* not the order [of presentation] or the introductions (*nidāna*)".[49]

The doctrinal topics which are enumerated, constituting an attribute-*mātṛkā*, are said to be established with the *sūtra*-s as the basis, for the treatises have the explanations of the *sūtra*-s as their purpose.[50] The MVŚ explains the rationale for this sub-structure of doctrinal topics being followed by doctrinal perspectives, as follows:

> Question: Why are the doctrinal topics first set up here?
>
> Answer: In order to elucidate the doctrinal perspectives. If the doctrinal topics are not set up, the doctrinal perspectives cannot be elucidated — like a painter not being able to paint space with color. …
>
> Moreover, if the doctrinal topics are not set up, it is a void and nothing can be asked — there must be a basis on which to ask a question. …
>
> Moreover, it is like the case of the Buddha explaining the Dharma — first outlining, then explaining: He first outlines, "the six *dhātu*-s, the six *sprasṭavya-āyatana*-s…, these are said to be a sentient being". Then he further explains: "These are called the six *dhātu*-s …, these are called…"[51]

This exegetical sub-structure may be illustrated with the topic of the 'supreme worldly *dharma*-s'. This is discussed in terms of seven doctrinal perspectives — each in the form of a question, followed by answer(s) and explanations:

(1) "What are the 'supreme worldly *dharma*-s'?"

(2) "Why are they called the 'supreme worldly *dharma*-s'?"

(3) "Are the 'supreme worldly *dharma*-s' to be said to pertain to the sphere of sensuality (*kāmadhātu-pratisaṃyukta*), to the sphere

of fine-materiality (*rūpadhātu-pratisaṃyukta*), or to the sphere of immateriality (*ārūpyadhātu-pratisaṃyukta*)?"

(4) "Are the 'supreme worldly *dharma*-s' to be said to be *savitarka-savicāra, avitarka-savicāra* or *avitarka-avicāra*?"

(5) "Are the 'supreme worldly *dharma*-s' to be said to be conjoined with (*saṃprayukta*) the *sukhendriya*, *prītīndriya*, or *upekṣendriya*?"

(6) "Are the 'supreme worldly *dharma*-s' to be said to consist of one thought moment (*citta*) or many thought moments?"

(7) "Are the 'supreme worldly *dharma*-s' to be said to be susceptible to retrogression or not susceptible to retrogression?"[52]

The five categories of *dharma*-s recognized as the ultimate reals in the Sarvāstivāda system — *rūpa, citta, caitasika, citta-viprayukta-saṃskāra*, and *asaṃskṛta* — are already clearly enumerated in the JPŚ,[53] although not yet properly schematized as a taxonomical doctrine as in the PrŚ:

As to *rūpa*, there is a whole *mahābhūta-skandha* elaborately discussing the *mahābhūta*-s and the *bhautika-rūpa*-s. There is a whole section on *avijñapti* under the *Karma-skandhaka*, with clear notions of *saṃvara, asaṃvara, naiva-saṃvara-nāsaṃvara*, *prātimokṣa-saṃvara*, etc.[54]

As to *citta*, various considerations of its nature are made, some of which are likely to have influenced the other canonical treatises, either by way of being inherited or by way of influencing their subsequent stage of revision. The following are some examples from the *Saṃkīrṇaka* chapter:

> Is there a single consciousness which apprehends all *dharma*-s? No.
>
> But if this consciousness generates [the understanding] that all *dharma*-s are without Self, what does this consciousness not cognize? It does not cognize

itself and those *dharma*-s conjoined with it and co-existent with it.

Are there two *citta*-s which are mutually a cause to each other? No. Because no two *citta*-s can arise simultaneously in a given person (*pudgala*)...

Why is it that no two *citta*-s arise simultaneously in any given person? Because there is no second equal-immediate condition (see § 7.1.2) and because the *citta*-s of a sentient being arise one after another.

But if no *pudgala* exists and there is no preceding *citta* that goes to the succeeding *citta*, how can it be possible for one to recollect what one has done previously? By virtue of the force of repeated practice, a sentient being acquires a particular knowledge of homogeneity with regard to a *dharma* and comes to be able to know in a corresponding way in accordance with what he has experienced. ... [55]

As to the *caitasika*-s, the ten which are later to be known as the *mahā-bhūmika*-s are clearly grouped together in the discussion on *saṃprayuktaka-hetu* as follows: *vedanā, saṃjñā, cetanā, sparśa, manaskāra, chanda, adhimokṣa, smṛti, samādhi, prajñā*.[56]

As to the *citta-viprayukta-saṃskāra*-s, there is the mention of *prāpti*, the *saṃskṛta-lakṣaṇa*-s, *nikāya-sabhāgatā*, *pṛthagjanatva*, *jīvitendriya*, etc.[57] The distinction between acquisition/non-acquisition (*prāpti/aprāpti*) and endowment/non-endowment (*samanvāgama/asamanvāgama*) is made — *samanvāgama* is the non-loss of what has been acquired (*prāpta*); *asamanvāgama* is the not having acquired or the loss of what has been acquired.[58] (See *infra,* § 11.3.1.1). As an example:

Those who have not cut off their roots of skillfulness (*kuśala-mūla*) are endowed with the five [spiritual] faculties, faith, etc., and those who have cut off their roots of skillfulness are not endowed with them. Those who have acquired and not lost the three outflow-free faculties are endowed with them; those who have not yet acquired or have lost [them] are not endowed with them.[59]

As to the *asaṃskṛta*-s, only *pratisaṃkhyā-nirodha* and *apratisaṃkhyā-nirodha* are mentioned;[60] *ākāśa* is noteworthily absent — possibly suggesting that the JPŚ was compiled earlier than the PrŚ in which this third *asaṃskṛta* is clearly mentioned and defined. (See below).

An important innovation is the theory of the six causes — *saṃprayuktaka-hetu, sahabhū-hetu, sabhāga-hetu, sarvatraga-hetu, vipāka-hetu, kāraṇa-hetu*. (See *infra,* § 6).[61] In regard to *vipāka-hetu*, the authors give a very comprehensive definition, bringing into its scope all the five conditioned *skandha*-s constituting the four categories — *rūpa* (bodily and vocal *karma*-s), *citta*, *caitasika* and *citta-viprayukta-saṃskāra*.[62] (See *infra,* § 6.3.4).

4.1.2.3. *Prakaraṇa-śāstra* (PrŚ)

All traditions unanimously ascribe this text to Vasumitra. Besides Xuan Zang's translation (T no. 1542; translated in 660 C.E.) comprising 18 fascicles, there is an earlier Chinese translation in 12 fascicles (T no. 1541), made by Guṇabhadra and Bodhiyaśas from 435–443 C.E. Its first chapter on the five classes of *dharma*-s seem to have enjoyed considerable popularity in China. It was translated as an independent text by An Shi-gao in one fascicle around 148 C.E. (T no. 1557), and later in the Tang Dynasty by Fa-cheng (T no. 1556). There is also a commentary on this first chapter, entitled **Pañca-vastuka-vibhāṣā* (T no. 1555) ascribed to Dharmatrāta, translated by Xuan Zang.

The PrŚ consists of eight chapters:

1. 'On the five groups' (*Pañcavastuka*)
2. 'On the knowledges' (*Jñāna-nirdeśa*)
3. 'On the entrances' (*Āyatana-nirdeśa*)
4. 'On the seven groups' (*Saptavastuka*)
5. 'On the proclivities' (*Anuśaya-nirdeśa*)

6. 'On subsumption, etc.' (*Saṃgrahādi-nirdeśa*)
7. 'Thousand-questions' (*Sahasra-praśnaka*)
8. 'On ascertainment' (*Viniścaya-nirdeśa*)

Frauwallner remarked that the PrŚ is a compilation of virtually independent and self-contained sections (see above, § 4.1), although he also took note of the **Mahā-prajñāpāramitā-śāstra* (MPPU) which records an opinion which — enumerating the PrŚ as the first of the 'six part' *abhidharma* — states that of its eight chapters four are authored by Vasumitra and the other four by Kaśmīrian *arhat*-s.[63] Frauwallner conjectured that chapters 1, 2, 3 and 8 are later additions, while 4–7 represent the earlier part.[64] Yin Shun, too, on the basis of this tradition in the MPPU and an analysis of its contents, ascertained that the PrŚ is indeed divisible into the following two groups:

I. four chapters which are essentially a reworking of ancient treatises — 4, 6, 7, 8;
II. four chapters which are a revision of ancient doctrines with innovations — 1, 2, 3, 5.[65]

As an example of the first group, let us look at the 4th chapter, the *Saptavastuka*. Yin Shun thinks that the *sapta-vastu*-s three *dharma*-s, i.e., *skandha, dhātu*, and *āyatana*, and four *dharma*-s, i.e., *vedanā, saṃjñā, saṃskāra* and vijñāna,[66] have their source in the ancient treatises:

The *Saptavastuka*'s enumeration of all the *saṃskṛta-dharma*-s in the five-*skandha* scheme seems to be an inheritance from the DSŚ (see above § 4.1.1.1). Likewise its discussion of what are subsumed (*saṃgṛhīta*) and what are not, and also what are conjoined (*saṃprayukta*) and what are not — all in terms of *skandha, dhātu, āyatana* — can be seen as an inheritance from an ancient source based on the *sūtra*-s. In its discussion of the *caitasika-dharma*-s, the following classes are enumerated: ten *mahā-bhūmika*-s; ten *kuśala-mahā-bhūmika*-s;

ten *kleśa-mahā-bhūmika*-s; ten *parītta-kleśa-mahā-bhūmika*-s; five *kleśa*-s, five *saṃsparśa*-s; five *dṛṣṭi*-s, five *indriya*-s, five *dharma*-s — eight classes totaling 65 *dharma*-s. However, the ten *kuśala-mahā-bhūmika*-s are not mentioned in the older translation and could have been added from the MVŚ.[67] Although Yin Shun places this text under the first group, such classification of mental elements represents an important innovative step in psychological analysis. According to some scholars, this chapter is a reworking of the first part of the *Dhātu-kāya*.[68] Its five-*skandha* scheme of enumeration seems to have had some definite and continued influence on some orthodox Sarvāstivādins even posterior to the AKB, such as Skandhila and the author of the ADV. Both masters subsumed all *dharma*-s under the *aṣṭa-padārtha* scheme — five *skandha*-s comprising all the *saṃskṛta-dharma*-s plus three *asaṃskṛta*-s.[69]

As an example of the second group, let us look at the 5th chapter, *On the proclivities*, which is the most rigorous chapter of the whole treatise. On the basis of the 98 proclivities established in the JPŚ, it discusses them in terms of seven doctrinal perspectives given as dyads, triads and pentads — e.g.: how many pertain to the *kāma-dhātu*, to *rūpa-dhātu*, to *ārūpya-dhātu*; how many are *duḥkha-darśana-heya, samudaya-darśana-heya, nirodha-darśana-heya, mārga-darśana-heya, bhāvanā-heya*; etc. Incorporated in this are the definition of proclivities and the mutual subsumption between the 98 proclivities and the seven and 12 proclivities. The 98 proclivities are also discussed in terms of the mode of their adherence and growth (*anuśayana*) — through taking an object (*ālambanataḥ*) and through conjunction (*saṃprayogataḥ*).[70]

Another example of the reworking of earlier *abhidharma* texts is the 6th chapter, *On subsumption, etc.* This chapter begins by enumerating a total of 182 doctrinal perspectives: 5 of one-perspective, 103 of two-perspectives, 31 of three-perspectives, 21 of four-perspectives, 5 of five-perspectives, 2 of six-perspectives, 3 of seven-perspectives, 3 of eight-perspectives, 2 of nine-perspectives, 2 of ten-perspectives,

1 of eleven-perspectives, 1 of twelve-perspectives, 1 of eighteen-perspectives, 1 of twenty-two-perspectives and 1 of ninety-eight-perspectives. This is followed by an item-wise explanation. The enumeration constitutes a miscellaneous *mātṛkā* after the fashion of the early *abhidharma*:

> There are [five categories of *dharma*-s comprising a single perspective—] *jñeya-dharma*-s, *vijñeya-dharma*-s, ...
>
> [There are 103 categories of *dharma*-s comprising two perspectives—] *rūpi-dharma*-s, *arūpi-dharma*-s; *sanirdarśana-dharma*-s, *anirdarśana-dharma*-s; *sapratigha-dharma*-s, *apratigha-dharma*-s; ...
>
> [There are 31 categories of *dharma*-s comprising three perspectives—] *kuśala-dharma*-s, *akuśala-dharma*-s, *avyākṛta-dharma*-s; *śaikṣa-dharma*-s, *aśaikṣa-dharma*-s, *naiva-śaikṣa-nāśaikṣa-dharma*-s; *darśana-heya-dharma*-s, *bhāvanā-heya-dharma*-s, *aheya-dharma*-s; ...[71]

As Frauwallner points out, this procedure is the same as that in the 3rd and 4th chapters of the *Dhammasaṅgaṇī*.[72] The enumeration shows that the triads (103) and dyads (31), comprising as they do the largest numbers of categories, provide the core of the attribute-*mātṛkā*. Another noteworthy point is that among the enumerated doctrinal perspectives, some 20 pertain to *hetu-pratyaya*-s, indicating the emerging emphasis by the early Sarvāstivādins on this topic. This includes: *citta-hetuka*, *acittta-hetuka*; *karma-hetuka, akarma-hetuka; saṃskṛta-hetuka, asaṃskṛta-hetuka; pratītya-samutpanna, apratītya-samutpanna; hetu, na hetu*; etc. This inheritance from archaic *abhidharma* is then appended with a new Ābhidharmika analysis: These enumerated categories are: (i) subsumed under how many *dhātu*-s, *āyatana*-s and *skandha*-s; (ii) known by how many *jñāna*-s; (iii) cognized by how many types of *vijñāna*; (iv) adhered to by how many *anuśaya*-s?

The most important innovation is made by Vasumitra in the *Pañcavastuka* (chapter 1) which systematizes all *dharma*-s into five categories

— *rūpa, citta, caitasika, citta-viprayukta-saṃskāra* and *asaṃskṛta* — already established in outline in the JPŚ (see above § 4.1.2.2). The three *asaṃskṛta*-s are mentioned and defined.[73] This fivefold classification was to become the standard classification by later Sarvāstivādins in particular and by the northern *abhidharma* tradition in general. The manner in which the *caitasika-dharma*-s are enumerated in this chapter suggests an implicit taxonomical consideration influenced by the *sūtra*-s and represents the early stage of the development of the theory of *caitasika* in which no explicit grouping was done. (See *infra,* § 9.3.2). It also initiated a tendency toward succinctness and organization (see below).

Collett Cox comments that "the **Mahāvibhāṣā* occasionally opts for interpretation of the *Prakaraṇa*, which is declared to be explicit, not in need of further interpretation (*nītārtha*), over that of *Jñānaprasthāna*, which is declared to be implicit and in need of clarification (*neyārtha*)" and gives an example in the discussion on *vipāka-hetu*.[74] However, this does not seem to suffice as an example of the MVŚ's preference of an interpretation of the PrŚ over that of the JPŚ. In those instances, the MVŚ is simply stating the difference in the two interpretations given in different perspectives — one from the *nītārtha* view-point, the other, *neyārtha*. As a matter of fact, shortly before this, in the same discussion on *vipāka-hetu*, the statement in the PrŚ that *jīvitendriya* is a karmic retribution is said to be implicit and based on conventional usage — in contrast with that in the JPŚ.[75] Nevertheless, it is certain that the compilers of the MVŚ held the PrŚ in high esteem as a doctrinal authority second only to the JPŚ, quoting it by name some 100 times. This frequency is next only to that of the PjŚ. However, the esteem accorded to a text by the MVŚ cannot be judged by the frequency of its quotation alone. In the case of the PjŚ, it is quoted many times, partly because such topics as the cosmology and supernormal phenomena, etc., were a reflection of popular demand and concern at the time.

Moreover, sometimes the PrŚ — and for that matter the other *pāda* texts — is apparently quoted by some un-named party which sees some contradiction between the interpretation given by the JPŚ or certain masters on the one hand, and that of the PrŚ on the other hand. As we have mentioned just above, the PrŚ sets the trend of development in *abhidharma* toward organization and succinctness, leading to the development of manuals culminating in the AKB. Both doctrinally and in terms of this tendency toward succinctness, the PrŚ is of especial importance for the so-called western or outside masters. (See § 3.6).

4.1.2.4. *Dhātukāya-śāstra* (DKŚ)

The only extant Chinese translation (T no. 1540) in three fascicles by Xuan Zang ascribes this to Vasumitra. The Sanskrit and Tibetan tradition, however, give its author as Pūrṇa.

The DKŚ consists of two parts:

(i) The first, called *The fundamental section* (本事分), enumerates mental elements which are divisible into 2 groups:

(a) ten *mahā-bhūmika*-s — *vedanā, saṃjñā, cetanā, sparśa, manaskāra, chanda, adhimokṣa/adhimukti, smṛti, samādhi, prajñā*; ten *kleśa-mahā-bhūmika*-s — *āśraddhya, kauśīdya, muṣita-smṛti, vikṣepa, avidyā, asaṃprajanya, ayoniśo-manaskāra, mithyādhimokṣa, auddhatya, pramāda*; ten *parītta-kleśa-bhūmika*-s — *krodha, upanāha, mrakṣa, pradāśa, īrṣyā, mātsarya, māyā, śāṭhya, mada, vihiṃsā* ;

(b) six *vijñāna-kāya*-s, six *sparśa-kāya*-s, six *vedanā-kāya*-s, six *saṃjñā-kāya*-s, six *saṃcetanā-kāya*-s, six *tṛṣṇā-kāya*-s.

Group (a) pertains to the classification of the *caitasika*-s. The correspondence between this enumeration and that in the

Saptavastuka of the PrŚ has been noted by many. (See above § 4.1.2.3). However, the beginning part of the *Saptavastuka* — 18 *dhātu*-s, 12 *āyatana*-s, five *skandha*-s, five *upādāna-skandha*-s, six *dhātu*-s — is absent in the DKŚ list. So are the ten *kuśala-mahābhūmika*-s. As this category is also absent in the older translation of PrŚ, Yin Shun suggests that it was inserted from the MVŚ.[76] The enumeration in the *Saptavastuka* of the 18 *dhātu*-s is obviously gathered from the ancient *sūtra*-s. Its absence in the DKŚ therefore could well signal that this text is chronologically later than the PrŚ, probably representing a more conscious effort to move away from the *sūtra* taxonomy. The fact that the DKŚ is not quoted even once in the MVŚ which enumerates the very same three classes of *mahābhūmika*-s[77] might also suggest that it was composed after the MVŚ. However, it must also be noted that the classification of *caitasika*-s in the MVŚ is apparently more developed, enumerating additionally the ten *kuśala-mahā-bhūmika*-s, the five *akuśala-mahā-bhūmika*-s, the three *nivṛtāvyākṛta-mahā-bhūmika*-s, the ten *anivṛtāvyākṛta-mahā-bhūmika*-s. On this basis, Yin Shun believes that it was composed before the MVŚ.[78]

(ii) The second part of the DKŚ is called *Analysis* (**Vibhaṅga*). It analyses the mental elements given in the first part employing the taxonomical devices of (a) conjunction (*saṃprayoga*) and (b) subsumption (*saṃgraha*):

(a) The analysis of conjunction is applied in relation to the *vedanendriya*, *vijñāna-kāya*, *āhrikya* and *anapatrāpya*: how many elements in the list are conjoined or not conjoined with these four?

(b) The analysis of subsumption is applied in relation to the *dhātu*-s, *āyatana*-s and *skandha*-s. The elements in the list — starting with *vedanā* and *saṃjñā* — are considered in turn in the following manner: under how many *dhātu*-s, etc., are the elements conjoined with one given member of the list and not conjoined with another subsumed? Thus, the first consideration is applied to those elements which are "conjoined with *vedanā* and not conjoined with *saṃjñā*":

(1) "Those conjoined with *vedanā*" — the *citta-caitta-dharma*-s — are subsumed under how many of the 18 *dhātu*-s, 12 *āyatana*-s and five *skandha*-s? Answer: Eight *dhātu*-s, two *āyatana*-s and three *skandha*-s.

(2) "Those not conjoined with *saṃjñā*" — *saṃjñā* itself, *rūpa*-s, *asaṃskṛta*-s and *citta-viprayukta-saṃskāra*-s — are subsumed under how many *dhātu*-s, *āyatana*-s and *skandha*-s? Answer: 11 *dhātu*-s, 11 *āyatana*-s and three *skandha*-s.

Next, the same consideration applied to those which are conjoined with *saṃjñā* and not conjoined with *vedanā*. Such an analysis — called a "one-row" (一行) analysis[79] — operates as follows: Given, say four members A, B, C, D, the analysis is first made between A and B, then A and C, then A and D; next between B and C, B and D; next between C and D.

The summary verse (*uddāna*) at the beginning of this second part states that there are in all 88 ways (門) of examining — three with respect to conjunction, 85 with respect to subsumption;[80] but only 16 ways are actually shown.

Various scholars have also noted the unmistakable relationship between the DKŚ and the Pāli *Dhātu-kathā*. The similarities are particularly conspicuous in the second part of the DKŚ. Frauwallner observes that in many points, the PrŚ corresponds to the Pāli *Dhātu-kathā* rather than to the DKŚ. He summarizes the relationship between the *Dhātu-kathā*, the DKŚ and the *Saptavastuka* of the PrŚ as follows:

> Compared to the *Dhātukāya*, the *Prakaraṇa* further developed the doctrine contained in its first part... The second part was left largely unchanged. By contrast, the second part was reworked in the *Dhātukāya*, namely, after the work had been incorporated into the *Prakaraṇa*.[81]

However, he also points out an important difference: the *mātṛkā* of the *Dhātu-kathā* and that of the DKŚ are completely different. The former is based on the *mātṛkā* of the *Vibhaṅga*, while the latter is not a *mātṛkā* of the early type. This means that the similarity observed in the two works could also simply be the result of employing the same method of writing. However, Frauwallner thinks it more likely that both are derived from a common ancestor.[82]

4.2. Development of the Sarvāstivāda manuals

4.2.1. *Abhidharma-mahāvibhāṣā* (MVŚ)

Subsequent to the definitive establishment of the Sarvāstivāda *abhidharma* doctrines by the JPŚ, there followed active and creative study, discussion, elaboration and systematization of these doctrines, the result of which was the compilation by the Kāśmīrian Sarvāstivādins of the MVŚ mention of which has been made above at various places. Xuan Zang tells us that the MVŚ was compiled at the so-called 'Third Council' sponsored by King Kaniṣka of Gāndhāra.[83] He asserts the same thing in the epilogue to his translation of the MVŚ.[84] But modern researchers have noted that Kaniṣka is referred to in the MVŚ as a past king of Gāndhāra.[85] Their view is that the MVŚ was compiled by the followers of the Kātyāyanīputra tradition. This view is supported by a statement in the MPPU.[86]

The MVŚ is now extant in three Chinese translations only. The earliest translation (T 28, no. 1547), now surviving in 14 fascicles (卷), was first made in 383 C.E. by Saṃghabhūti. Saṃghadeva revised it, producing the extant version in around 389 C.E.[87] The second translation, originally comprising 100 fascicles but now surviving in 60 fascicles, was made by Buddhavarman from 425 C.E. to 427 C.E. The third and most complete one, comprising 200 fascicles, was made by Xuan Zang from 656 C.E. to 659 C.E. The fact that the contents in the corresponding sections of these three versions often disagree to varying degrees suggests that their Sanskrit originals were probably different, and that there must have been a process of revision and emendation subsequent to the initial compilation, possibly spanning over a century. The orthodox Kāśmīrian Sarvāstivādins who upheld the supreme authority of the MVŚ came to be known as the 'Vaibhāṣikas', an adjective derived from *Vibhāṣā* (see *supra*, § 3.6).

Purporting to be the Great Commentary on the JPŚ, it structurally follows the same sequence of the eight major chapters of the latter (see § 4.1.2.2), with an additional introductory chapter. In this gigantic work — encyclopedic in scope — are found not only the JPŚ viewpoints upheld by its compilers as orthodox, but also the heterodox views of the other Sarvāstivāda *ācārya*-s, as well as those held by other early Buddhist schools and independent masters. Accordingly, it is a work of great importance, indispensable for the understanding of not only the orthodox Sarvāstivāda doctrines, but also of the historical development of all the contemporary schools, containing as it does a wealth of material largely unavailable elsewhere. The doctrinal positions and interpretations by the so-called "four great *ācārya*-s of the Sarvāstivāda" — Vasumitra, Dharmatrāta, Buddhadeva and Ghoṣaka — are frequently given side by side. Among them, those of Vasumitra are generally upheld as being the best and most acceptable.[88] Other masters mentioned in the MVŚ include: Pārśva (who, according to Xuan Zang, initially proposed the project of compilation[89]), Pūrṇayaśas, Aśvaghoṣa, Śamadatta (寂授), Saṃghavasu, Dharmanandi, Vamalabdha, etc.[90]

Besides new doctrinal categories and developed arguments, we can also see in the MVŚ the employment of articulate logical tools and format.[91]

Even a brief survey indicates a definite logical methodology emerging on the part of the Ābhidharmikas during the 1st and 2nd century C.E. The conscious logical analysis of a debate made by the compilers may be said to represent more evolved and formalized techniques and procedures of debate than what is discernible in the earlier *abhidharma* texts such as the VKŚ. The specific mention of logical treatises, some definite methods of refutation, and the three acceptable *pramāṇa*-s (*pratyakṣa*, *anumāna* and *āptāgama*) contrasting with the pre-Dignāga logical texts which acknowledged various and generally a greater number of *pramāṇa*-s, are to be noted. In addition, there is the recognition, albeit rather indirect, of the important logical function of *dṛṣṭānta*. There is also evidence of a clear understanding in this period of the nature of *pratyakṣa* and *anumāna*, despite the absence of any explicit definition. Such definitions, however, need not be expected in an *abhidharma* commentary which is not primarily a logical treatise. The lack of indication of the knowledge of such important concepts as the *trairūpya* doctrine for a valid reason (*hetu*), however, suggests possibly an earlier stage of development in Buddhist logic than that represented in such early texts as the *Fang Bian Xing Lun*.[92]

At several places, the compilers analyze in detail the debates given in the JPŚ between the Vibhajyavādins (Vv) and the Yukta-vādins (Yv = Sarvāstivādins), ending with the declaration of the latter's victory. We will illustrate one such analysis below on the proposition (*p*) by the Yv that craving for non-existence (*vibhava-tṛṣṇā* = *vt*) — defined as the craving for the impermanence of the triple sphere (*traidhātukī anityatā*),[93] i.e., saṃsāric existence — is abandonable by repeated cultivation (*bhāvanā-heya* = *bhā-h*) alone and not by insight into the four noble truths (*darśana-heya*):[94]

JPŚ	**Comments by MVŚ**
A1. [Vv:] Do you assert that *vt* is *bhā-h*, and that the stream-entrants have not abandoned it (p)? [Yv:] Yes.	**A1.** Question by Vv to confirm the Yv's proposition (p). Yv affirms indicating conformity of p to the *sūtra*.
A2. [Vv:] What do you concede: Does a stream-entrant generate the thought, "Isn't it bliss if I'm annihilated, non-existent, after death?" (q) [Yv:] No. [Vv:] Why doesn't a stream-entrant generate this craving? [Yv:] Because he sees the [true] nature of *dharma*-s — he sees the cause-effect serial continuity of the *dharma*-s, hence does not crave for annihilation … (other explanations given).	**A2.** Vv inserts this implication (q) intended to show that p contradicts the correct doctrines. Yv counteracts the question, indicating no contradiction in p.
A3. [Vv:] Accept our thesis: If *vt* is *bhā-h* alone and a stream-entrant has not abandoned this craving (i.e., p), you ought to say that he generates such a thought ($p \supset q$). [Conversely,] if he does not generate such a thought, you ought not to assert that *vt* is *bhā-h* alone and a stream-entrant has not abandoned this craving ($\sim q \supset \sim p$). Such an assertion is not logical (不應理; *na yuktam*) in either case. [Yv:] Our school does not assert that all not yet abandoned [defilements] necessarily arise; for some that are not yet abandoned do not arise, and some which have been abandoned may arise. If it is the case that all those that are not yet abandoned necessarily arise, then there would be no liberation and exit. This is because *dharma*-s that are not yet abandoned are infinite; if they [necessarily] arise, when can their arising be exhausted?	**A3.** Vv poses 2 conversely related objections — the first accords with p but is contradictory to doctrine (順宗違義); the second accords with doctrine but is contradictory to p (順義違宗). Hence conclude: "… not logical in either case". Yv explains his position (showing that p is not contradicted).

B1. [Yv:] Do you also assert that the craving for the retribution (*vipāka*) of *naraka*, *tiryañc* and *preta* is *bhā-h* alone, [and] that the stream-entrants have not abandoned this craving (*r*)? [Vv:] Yes.	Next, Yv counteracts the objections using the second method of refutation in the *sūtra*-s [mentioned above]. **B1**. Question by Yv to confirm the Vv's proposition (*r*). Answer by Vv to show the necessity of the truth concerning what is asked.
B2. [Yv:] What do you concede: Does a stream-entrant generate the thought, "I shall become the dragon king or the Yama king and govern the sentient beings in the *naraka* realm" (*s*)? [Vv:] No. [Yv:] Why doesn't a stream-entrant generate this craving?" [Vv:] Because that *gati* pertains to the *pṛthagjana*. An *ārya* [— as is a stream-entrant] — has [proper] *jñāna* [and does not aspire for it] … (other explanations given). [Yv:] Is it the case that an *ārya* does not generate craving for any of the *durgati* whatsoever? [Vv:] Although the *ārya*-s have no craving for being born there, they do have craving for objects of enjoyment (*bhoga*) [therein].… [Also,] they generate a thought of craving (= attachment) on hearing that their parent, etc., fall into such *durgati*-s.	**B2.** Yv inserts this implication intended to show that *r* contradicts the correct doctrines. Vv counteracts the question, indicating no contradiction in *r*.
B3. [Yv:] Accept our thesis: If *r*, then you ought to say that he generates such a thought (i.e., $r \supset s$). [Conversely,] if he does not generate such a thought, you should not assert *r* (i.e., $\sim s \supset \sim r$). Such an assertion is not logical in either case.	**B3.** Yv poses two conversely related objections — the first accords with *r* but is contradictory to doctrine; the second accords with doctrine but is contradictory to *r*. Hence conclude: "… not logical in either case".

But the JPŚ and MVŚ, magnificent as they are, lack sufficient unity and systematization as a whole. Besides, the MVŚ contains frequent digressions from the main point under discussion and thus adds to the complication and confusion for beginners. In fact the MVŚ itself, at the outset, states: "One should seek, in the *abhidharma*, the true characteristics of *dharma*-s and not the order [of presentation] or the introductions (*nidāna*). There is no fault if [a doctrine is presented] earlier or later, or without a *nidāna*." This nature of the *abhidharma* works is contrasted with that of the *sūtra* and the *vinaya* which are said to be concerned with order of presentation and *nidāna* respectively.[95] Thus, within such an *abhidharma* tradition, and further restricted by the absolute authority of the form and content of the JPŚ, there was little possibility for any major advance in genuine doctrinal development and especially in the systematization of the Sarvāstivāda doctrines.

4.2.2. Development of the more concise manuals

Nevertheless, such a state of affairs eventually brought about a significant reaction from some of the more progressive doctors of the Sarvāstivāda, and this led to a new line of development. These doctors deviated to varying degrees from the Kāśmīrian orthodoxy — known after the MVŚ as the Vaibhāṣika — and began to compose manuals aimed at being concise, lucid and systematic.

The earliest of such manuals that we possess in Chinese is the AmRŚ by a certain Ghoṣaka, which effectively serves as an introduction to the JPŚ and MVŚ. Its Chinese translation comprises 16 short chapters in two fascicles. There is clear evidence that while AmRŚ derives its material from the JPŚ, MVŚ, PrŚ and other sources, it is basically inclined toward PrŚ and the Gāndhāra school.[96] As Bhadanta Ghoṣaka, one of the "four great Sarvāstivāda Ābhidharmikas", was pre-MVŚ, the author of the AmRŚ must be a different Ghoṣaka whose date is probably not far from the completion of the MVŚ.[97] The title itself "*Amṛta*(*-rasa*)" suggests also a practical purport: At the end of the chapter on *dhyāna*, there is a description of the meditational practices, with *aśucyanusmṛti* and *ānāpānasmṛti* as the foundation, which are said to lead to "the end of suffering".[98] It states that "there are two paths which lead to *nirvāṇa* — (i) the contemplation of the impurity of the body; (ii) the mindfulness of breathing…"[99] Thus, we may say that there is, in the AmRŚ, an emphasis on the need to return from purely scholastic discussion to the aim of realizing *nirvāṇa* (*amṛta*).

After the AmRŚ, this emphasis on practice and realization seemed to have been lost. But the new development of a liberal attitude in regard to the selection of material with the emphasis on organization and conciseness was continued in a series of manuals, in which a given manual partly inherited the form and content of the preceding one and readjusted it with new addition of materials. The following is a list of these manuals extant in Chinese translation:

1. **Abhidharmāmṛta*(*-rasa*)*-śāstra* (T no. 1553), by Ghoṣaka, 2 fasc., translator unknown.
2. **Abhidharmahṛdaya* (T no. 1550) by Dharmaśrī, 4 fasc., tr. by Saṅghadeva *et. al.*
3. **Abhidharmahṛdaya-sūtra* (? T no. 1551) by Upaśānta, 2 fasc., tr. by Narendrayaśas.
4. **Abhidharmahṛdayavyākhyā* (? T no. 1552), by Dharmatrāta, 11 fasc., tr. by Sanghabhūti.
5. *Abhidharmakośa-mūla-kārikā* (T no. 1560) by Vasubandhu, 1 fasc., tr. by Xuan Zang.
6. *Abhidharmakośabhāṣyam* (T no. 1558) by Vasubandhu, 1 fasc., tr. by Xuan Zang; (there is also an earlier translation by Paramārtha: T no. 1559).
7. **Abhidharmakośaśāstra-tattvārthā-ṭīkā* (T no. 1561) by Sthiramati, 2 fasc., translator unknown.

8. **Abhidharma-nyāyānusāra* (T no. 1562) by Saṃghabhadra, 40 fasc., tr. by Xuan Zang.
9. **Abhidharma-samayapradīpikā* (T no. 1563) by Saṃghabhadra, 40 fasc., tr. by Xuan Zang.
10. **Abhidharmāvatāra* (T no. 1554) by Skandhila, 2 fasc., tr. by Xuan Zang.

The next manual to appear after the AmRŚ was the **Abhidharmahṛdaya* by Dharmaśrī (or Dharmaśreṣṭhī 法勝), around 200 C.E. It was basically a re-organization of the AmRŚ, with revision and addition. Its chief contribution lies in the composition of summary verses (probably added after the original prose text) which expound the *abhidharma* doctrines succinctly and serve as a great aid to memorization. Doctrinally, it not only sympathizes with the Gāndhārian views and other heterodox Sarvāstivādin views, but even adopts some of those held by the Vibhajyavādins.[100] In this respect, it may be regarded as the predecessor of the AKB.

As a result of its summary verses, the **Abhidharmahṛdaya* became very popular as a beginners' manual and triggered off several works of a similar nature purporting to be commentaries on it. The most important of these is the **Abhidharmahṛdayavyākhyā* (雜阿毗曇心論) by Dharmatrāta, which revised and supplemented the **Abhidharmahṛdaya*, with the intention of bringing the latter back in line with the orthodox Vaibhāṣika (Kāśmīrian) view points, while being also tolerant toward certain heterodox views.[101] This work shows considerable development in the Sarvāstivāda doctrines and has attained greater precision in definition. Many scholars believe that it is the immediate source of the monumental AKB.[102]

The AKB represents the culmination of this new development. Known in India also as "The Treatise of Intelligence" (聰明論),[103] it excels all the others in respect to organization, scope, and presentation of arguments, and is a treasure-house of all the essential doctrines that the early schools had hitherto developed. Besides the two Chinese translations listed above, the AKB is also extant in a Tibetan translation by Jinamitra and dPal brtsegs, entitled *Chos mngon pa'i mdzod kyi bshad pa* (Peking ed., no. 5591). Most scholars opine that Vasubandhu bases his work on the **Abhidharma-hṛdaya-vyākhyā* (or **Abhidharma-hṛdaya-bhāṣya*?; T no. 1552).[104] But it is undoubtedly a great improvement in terms of content over the latter, and Vasubandhu would have derived its additional material from other major *abhidharma* treatises, particularly the MVŚ. The AKB consists of the following nine chapters:

1. *Dhātu-nirdeśa*,
2. *Indriya-nirdeśa*,
3. *Loka-nirdeśa*,
4. *Karma-nirdeśa*,
5. *Anuśaya-nirdeśa*,
6. *Mārga-pudgala-nirdeśa*,
7. *Jñāna-nirdeśa*,
8. *Samādhi-nirdeśa*
9. *Pudgala-pratiṣedha-nirdeśa*.

However, whereas the first eight chapters contain stanzas (*kārikā*) on which the *bhāṣya* comments, the 9th chapter is purely in prose. Moreover, at the end of the 8th chapter, the author states: "This *abhidharma* established in accordance with the principles of Kāśmīrian Vaibhāṣikas has for the most part been expounded by me..."[105] Accordingly it would appear that the 9th chapter was originally an independent work which subsequently came to be appended to the AKB. In this work, Vasubandhu provides full opportunity for the Sautrāntikas and other schools to argue against the Vaibhāṣikas. His own standpoint is, for the most part, that of the Sautrāntika, and he often gives little chance for the Vaibhāṣikas to answer their opponents. But he at times does not hesitate to express his own views which happen to contradict those of the Sautrāntika. One well-known example of his deviation from the latter's position is his view that *āyatana*-s too, besides the *dhātu*-s, are real — contradicting the Sautrāntika stand that the *dhātu*-s alone are real, not the *skandha*-s or the *āyatana*-s.[106]

In reaction to this, Saṃghabhadra spent 12 years in composing the **Nyāyānusāra* to dispute with the Kośakāra, leveling his criticisms chiefly against the contemporary Sautrāntika leader Sthavira Śrīlāta and his pupil Rāma. Saṃghabhadra also composed the SPrŚ (roughly half the size of Ny in Chinese translation) which consists mainly of the expository part, *sans disputation,* of the Ny. In this work, he occasionally replaces or modifies a stanza given in the AKB in case he thinks it goes against the Vaibhāṣika tenets. An example of this is the definition of *avijñapti* given in the 4th chapter (see *infra,* § 13.4.2). Saṃghabhadra is very articulate in his exposition of the controversial doctrines and notions of the Vaibhāṣikas, so much so that many scholars regard his interpretations as 'neo-Sarvāstivāda'. However, while there are certainly developed interpretations and articulations in Ny and the SPrŚ, the term 'neo-Sarvāstivāda', if applied in a generalized manner, would seem rather unjustified.[107]

There is a partially preserved Sanskrit work, the *Abhidharma-dīpa-prabhā-vṛtti* (= ADV),[108] which is also an apologia for the Vaibhāṣika orthodoxy against the Kośakāra. Its author holds many views identical with those of Saṃghabhadra and is conjectured by Jaini PS to be his pupil Vimalamitra.[109] Professor J. W. de Jong, however, has pointed out that he could be the *śāstra* master Iśvara.[110]

Thus we witness during this period the most acute controversy between the Sarvāstivādin on the one hand and the Sautrāntika and others on the other. But with all these involved and subtle controversies comprising the greater part of these works, their pragmatic value as beginners' manuals decreases drastically. As Skandhila puts it, "the terms and meanings in the *abhidharma*, [are as bewildering as] a dense forest (*gahana*)", and beginners are apt to feel bewildered and lost. Moreover, such controversies did much damage to the Ābhidharmika tradition as a whole, especially at a time when this tradition was being greatly threatened by the challenge of both the Sautrāntikas and the Mahāyānists. It was with such considerations in mind, and perhaps also with the hope of bringing together the eastern and western camps to face this challenge, that Skandhila composed his **Abhidharmāvatāra*, aiming at beginners. In a scheme of eight *padārtha*-s — five *skandha*-s and three *asaṃskṛta*-s — he succinctly summarizes practically all the fundamental doctrines of the Sarvāstivāda. It is noteworthy that most of his definitions on the *citta-caitta*-s and the *viprayukta-saṃskāra*-s are strikingly similar to and, often enough, virtually identical with those given in the ADV. Throughout this short treatise, the author shows no hostility toward other Sarvāstivādin views differing from his own, although he does make one critical allusion to the Sautrāntika.[111] Indeed in much of the treatise, particularly the sections on the *viprayukta-saṃskāra*-s and the *asaṃskṛta*-s, we sense a definite concern of the author to defend the Sarvāstivāda against the Sautrāntika. Most probably, the author was a Kāśmīrian Vaibhāṣika who nevertheless shares certain views with the western/foreign masters.[112]

NOTES

[1] Vy, 9.

[2] T 41, 8c.

[3] T 25, 70a.

[4] T 41, 8b–c.

[5] Bu-ston, *History of Buddhism*. Tr. by Obermiller, E (Heidelberg, 1931–1932), I; 49.

[6] MPPU, 70b.

[7] MPPU, 752b. If these pieces of information in MPPU are to be considered as interpolations by the translator, Kumārajīva, as some scholars opine (e.g., Lamotte, E; *cf.* Lamotte (1970), 203 f.), then we must count the colophon — dated 379 C.E. and appended to the 24th fascicle of the older translation of the JPŚ — as the earliest mention of the set of seven texts, with the **Aṣṭa-skandhaka* (= JPŚ) as the body and the others as the six feet. (T no. 1543, 887a).

[8] *Frauwallner*, 14.

[9] *Study*, 115. See below.

[10] See *Study*, 179 f.

[11] Vy, 19; Bu-ston, I, 49.

[12] DSŚ, 479b–482a.

[13] DSŚ, 459c

[14] *Cf. Study*, 125 ff.

[15] DSŚ, 504c, 501a, etc.

[16] See 131 f.; MVŚ, 337c.

[17] See *Study*, 131 f.

[18] Vy, 11; Bu-ston, *loc. cit.*

[19] *Study*, 134 f.

[20] SgPŚ, 369c, 370a, 378b, 378c, 384a, 388a, 400b, 430b, 441a — in all, some 14 occurrences.

[21] SgPŚ, 377b–378a.

[22] SgPŚ, 379a, 380c, 383c, 426a, 426b, 430b, 443c.

[23] SgPŚ, 387c.

[24] T 29, 330b.

[25] T 25, 70a, Vy, 11.

[26] T 26, 514a.

[27] Peking no. 5587–5589.

[28] T 50, 113c.

[29] *Study*, 138 f.

[30] *Cf.* Dhammajoti, KL, "The *Mahāpadāna-suttanta* and the Buddha's spiritual lineage", in *Sri Lanka Journal of Buddhist Studies*, vol. I (Colombo, 1987), 190 ff.

[31] MPPU, 70a, in a note speaks here of the *Lou-tan-jing* (樓炭經 — *lokotthāna-sūtra/ loka-upasthāna-sūtra*?).

[32] *Study*, 140 f.

[33] *Cf.* MVŚ, 336c–337a, 612c. See *Study*, 143.

[34] MVŚ, 119a.

[35] *Study*, 144.

[36] Vy, 11.

[37] VKŚ, 535a.

[38] 諦義勝義, 補特伽羅可得可證現有等有; 故定有補特伽羅.

[39] VKŚ, 542b ff.; S, ii, 19, 23; *Kathāvatthu*, I, 1, 212; VII, 6, 1.

[40] VKŚ, 543b f.

[41] Willemen, C *et. al.*, *Sarvāstivāda Buddhist Scholasticism*, 221.

[42] T 25, 70a.

[43] T 51, 889c; T 41, 8c; T, 2b.

[44] T no 1852, 2b.

[45] T no 2049, 189a.

[46] *Cf. Study*, 115 f.

[47] MVŚ, 4c.

[48] MVŚ, 5b–7b. A rationalization of the order is attempted by some masters who assert that, in the reverse order, it first discusses the pure and then the defiled *dharma*-s of

an ordinary worldling (*pṛthagjana*). Thus it begins with the 'supreme worldly *dharma*-s', the critical stage at which one will transit from being an ordinary worldling to being an *ārya*. This is arrived at by abandoning the defilements — hence the second chapter on the fetters; etc. (MVŚ, 7a–b).

[49] MVŚ, 1c.

[50] MVŚ, 5b, 236b, etc.

[51] MVŚ, 236c–237b.

[52] JPŚ, 318a–c; T 26, 771b–772b.

[53] E.g., JPŚ, 920c, 929a (心心所法色無為心不相應行), 998c, etc.

[54] JPŚ, 977b.

[55]JPŚ, 919b.

[56] JPŚ, 920c.

[57] JPŚ, 1008a, 926a–b, 921c, 929a, 921c.

[58] E.g., JPŚ, 946c–947a, 969a–b; etc.

[59] JPŚ, 947a.

[60] JPŚ, 923b.

[61] JPŚ, 920c.

[62] JPŚ, 920c; *Study*, 188.

[63] T 20, 70a.

[64] *Frauwallner*, 36.

[65] *Study*, 150.

[66] *Study*, 151 f. However, it may also be noted that this text, having defined all the elements in the attribute-*mātṛkā*, immediately proceeds to ask the first question concerning their subsumption (*saṃgraha*) with respect to *dhātu*, *āyatana* and *skandha*, in seven ways. Thus, concerning *cakṣur-dhātu*:

(1) Under how many *dhātu*-s, *āyatana*-s and *skandha*-s is it subsumed?

(2) The *dharma*-s subsumed under the *cakṣur-dhātu* — under how many *dhātu*-s, *āyatana*-s and *skandha*-s are they subsumed?

(3) The *dharma*-s not subsumed under the *cakṣur-dhātu* — under how many *dhātu*-s, *āyatana*-s and *skandha*-s are they subsumed?

(4) The *dharma*-s subsumed, and those not subsumed, under the *cakṣur-dhātu* — under how many *dhātu*-s, *āyatana*-s and *skandha*-s are they subsumed?

(5) The *dharma*-s other than those subsumed under the *cakṣur-dhātu* — under how many *dhātu*-s, *āyatana*-s and *skandha*-s are they subsumed?

(6) The *dharma*-s other than those not subsumed under the *cakṣur-dhātu* — under how many *dhātu*-s, *āyatana*-s and *skandha*-s are they subsumed?

(7) The *dharma*-s other than those subsumed, and those not subsumed under the *cakṣur-dhātu* — under how many *dhātu*-s, *āyatana*-s and *skandha*-s are they subsumed? (T 26, 701c ff.)

Could this seven-way investigation which comes at the beginning of the chapter, be the reason for naming the chapter as *Saptavastu*?

[67] *Cf. Study*, 164; see also *infra,* § 9.3.3.

[68] E.g., *Frauwallner*, 25 f., 33 f. Fukuhara R opts for the view that the PrS was an expansion and elaboration of the DKŚ [Fukuhara R, *Ubu Abidatsumaronsho no Hattatsu* (Kyoto, 1965), 129].

[69] See *Entrance*, introduction, 15 ff.

[70] See *Study*, 149 f.

[71] PrŚ, 711b–713c.

[72] *Frauwallner*, 34.

[73] PrŚ, 692c, 694a–b (briefly defined).

[74] Willemen, C, *et. al.*, *op. cit.*, 214; MVŚ, 97b.

[75] MVŚ, 96c–97a.

[76] *Study*, 164. See also *infra,* § 9.3.3.

[77] MVŚ, 220a.

[78] *Study*, 165.

[79] This is the simplest of the four analytical procedures — 一行，歷七，小七，大七 — innovated in the JPŚ (e.g., 933c ff.).

[80] DKŚ, 616b.

[81] *Frauwallner*, 26.

[82] *Frauwallner*, 27 f.

[83] T no. 2087, 886b–887a.

[84] T 27, 1004a.

[85] MVŚ, 593a.

[86] T 25, 70a. For a discussion on the traditional views concerning its author and the date of compilation, see *Study*, 221 ff. Also cf. Fukuhara R, *op. cit.,* 220 ff.

[87] See *Study*, 205 f.

[88] E.g., see the four explanations offered by them on *sarvāstitva* discussed *infra*, § 5.2.

[89] T 51, 886c.

[90] See *Study*, chapter seven, 305 ff., for an excellent discussion on the various masters figuring in the MVŚ.

[91] For the logical notions and disputation in the text, cf. Dhammajoti, KL, 'Logic in the *Abhidharma-mahāvibhāṣā*', in the *JCBSSL*, vol. II, 180ff. See also the logical arguments for *sarvāstitva* discussed in *supra*, § 3.3.1.

[92] *Cf.* Dhammajoti, *op. cit.*

[93] MVŚ, 140a; AKB, 286. *Cf.* D, III, 216; *Visuddhimagga*, 568, 594.

[94] MVŚ, 138c–139c; the whole debate is further continued in a similar manner until the Yuktavādins are finally considered as having fully defeated the Vibhajyavādins (140a). See other similar analyses in 113c f., 169a–171b, 222a–222c, 612c–613a.

[95] MVŚ, 1c.

[96] See *Study*, 479–486.

[97] *Study*, 486.

[98] AmRŚ, 975b.

[99] AmRŚ, *loc. cit.* *Cf.* also the MVŚ, 662c, which speaks of these two meditations as "the true *amṛta-dvāra* for the entry into the *buddha-dharma*".

[100] Cf. *Study*, 493 ff.

[101] *Cf. Study*, 520 ff.

[102] E.g., Kimura T, *A Study of the Abhidharma Śāstras*, (1922), 259–324; IAKB, xxx; etc.

[103] According to Pu Guang (T 41, 1a).

[104] See IAKB, xxx.

[105] AKB, 459.

[106] AKB, 14.

[107] See *Entrance*, 23 f.; also *infra,* § 5.

[108] *Abhidharmadīpa with Vibhāṣāprabhāvṛtti*, critically edited with notes and introduction by Jaini, PS (Patna, 1977), 2nd edition.

[109] *Ibid.*, 132 f. But elsewhere (EnB, vol. 1 fas. 1, 57), Jaini says, "We therefore can ascribe this work either to Saṃghabhadra, or to one of his disciples, particularly Vimalamitra".

[110] de Jong, JW, "L'Auteur de l'Abhidharmadīpa", in *Buddhist Studies*, ed., Schopen, G (Berkeley, 1979), 116.

[111] T no. 1554, 984b.

[112] For a discussion of his date and personal affiliation, see *Entrance*, 65 ff.

5. *Sarvāstitva* and Temporality

5.1. The big debate

The Sarvāstivādin theory of *sarvāstitva* is often interpreted — both by their ancient opponents and many modern scholars — as a far cry from mainstream Buddhism. For some, it comes very close to the Sāṃkhya doctrine of *pariṇāma*. Among the extant Sarvāstivāda *abhidharma* texts, it is in the *Vijñānakāya-śāstra* that we first come across a controversy on it. (In the Pāli, it is already debated elaborately in the *Kathāvatthu*). But it is only in the much later texts, like the AKB and Ny, that we find an articulated definition offered by the Sarvāstivāda themselves. All said and done, *sarvāstitva* must imply the continuous existence of an essence in some sense. But just precisely in what sense, was something that the Ābhidharmika Buddhists — Sarvāstivādins themselves included — were unable to specify. For the Sarvāstivādins, the failure to do so is not to be considered a fault on their part. It is on account of the profound nature of *dharma*-s which, in the final analysis, transcends human conceptualization.

Once this metaphysical notion, however elusive, of an underlying essence of phenomena came to be emphasized, the debates — as to its truth or otherwise, and as to its precise implications — continued endlessly. It was to leave a lasting influence on the subsequent development of Buddhist thought. Thus, partly on account of this influence, the Vātsīputrīyas came to formulate the doctrine of the *pudgala*, and the Mahāyāna (mainly

Yogācāra) continued to speculate, giving rise to the rich philosophy of *vijñaptimātratā* and *tathāgata-garbha*. From the sources that we have examined, however, one thing seems sufficiently clear: The *svabhāva* of a *dharma*, even from the orthodox Vaibhāṣika standpoint, is not as immutable as is conceived by many scholars.

In these debates, we see the Ābhidharmikas — including the self-professed *sūtra*-based Sautrāntikas — utilizing logic as a tool to the utmost. At the end of the day, the Vaibhāṣikas had to be content with a form of identity-in-difference (*bhedābheda*) logic. In the depths of their hearts, however, it would seem that it is their religious insight and intuition — even if they happen to defy Aristotelian logic — that must be upheld at all cost.

In this chapter, we will attempt to see the extent to which the Vaibhāṣikas can articulate conceptually this doctrine of *sarvāstitva*. Our main primary sources are the MVŚ and Saṃghabhadra's **Nyāyānusāra*. The latter represents the most rigorous defense of the thesis and the former is, among other things, useful in helping us to better understand the development of this doctrine in the proper historical perspective and to ascertain whether — as claimed by many modern scholars — Saṃghabhadra's defense can justifiably be called 'neo-Sarvāstivāda'.[1]

5.2. Time and temporality

When the Sarvāstivāda asserts that the three periods of time exist (*asti*), what it actually means is that "*dharma*-s" in the three periods of time exist. For the Sarvāstivāda, time is none other than the activity of *dharma*-s, and temporality is superimposed by us on these activities. This is in fact the general Buddhist tradition since the Buddha's time. The MVŚ, however, records an exceptional view, said to be held by the "Dārṣṭāntika-Vibhajyavādins", that impermanent *dharma*-s course in permanent time:

> The "Dārṣṭāntika-Vibhajyavādins" (譬喻者分別論師) maintain that time (*adhvan*) and the conditioning forces (*saṃskāra*) are distinct entities. Time is a permanent entity; the conditioning forces are impermanent entities.[2] When the conditioning forces are coursing in time, they are like the fruits in a vessel, coming out from this vessel and turning into that vessel. … Likewise the conditioning forces: they enter into the present time from the future time, and enter into the past time from the present time.
>
> To repudiate the "Dārṣṭāntika-Vibhajyavādins" proposition, it is shown [here] that time and the conditioning forces are not different in intrinsic nature.[3]

It is not clear whether the term "Dārṣṭāntika-Vibhajyavādins" (譬喻者分別論師) in the above passage, which we have rendered here as a compound, stands for 'the Dārṣṭāntikas who are Vibhajyavādins', or 'Dārṣṭāntikas and Vibhajyavādins', i.e., as a *karmadhāraya* (descriptive compound) or a *dvandva* (co-ordinative compound). Yin Shun takes it in the former sense, although he thinks that the Dārṣṭāntikas referred to here probably represent only a section of those who were beginning to merge with the Vibhajyavādins.[4] However, we must note that in the older translation of the *Mahāvibhāṣā* (T no. 1546), the term here is simply Dārṣṭāntikas (譬喻者).[5] More importantly, however, in this context, the *Vibhāṣā* compilers begin by citing the *Jñānaprasthāna* that "there are three [categories] of *dharma*-s, viz, past, present and future"; it is only after quoting the above passage that they say:

> Furthermore, [another reason why the *Jñānaprasthāna* presents this topic is that] there are some [i.e., a second group of people] who are deluded with regard to the intrinsic nature (*svabhāva*) of [the *dharma*-s] of the three times, denying the existence of the past and future [*dharma*-s], and who maintain that the present [*dharma*-s] are unconditioned. To repudiate their proposition, it is shown [here] that the characteristic and intrinsic natures of the past and future [*dharma*-s] exist truly, and that the present [*dharma*-s] are conditioned. Why? If the past and future [*dharma*-s] were non-existent… (*loc. cit.*)

It is, therefore, clear that concerning the Dārṣṭāntika view, the point to be refuted is the independent existence of time. The impermanence of the *svabhāva* of conditioned *dharma*-s is no problem at all for the Sarvāstivādins, the Dārṣṭāntikas included. The intrinsic nature of a *dharma*, although existing throughout time (*sarvadā asti*), is not permanent; only the unconditioned *dharma*-s, transcending the temporal process, are permanent (*nitya*).[6] It is only the second group of people (probably the Mahāsāmghika) who are to be refuted concerning the unreality of the tri-temporal *dharma*-s. The same view of this second group is refuted elsewhere several more times,[7] and in each case the *Vibhāṣā* compilers argue for the reality of the tri-temporal existence of *dharma*-s. In the two occurrences of this view in the older version of the *Vibhāṣā*, the compilers' argument is also unambiguously against the unreality of the past and future *dharma*-s.

5.3. The four main theories of the Sarvāstivāda

The major question the Sarvāstivādins must answer is: Given the thesis that all *dharma*-s in the three periods of time equally exist, how do the Sarvāstivādins differentiate — how can they account for our experience of the difference — as regards 'past *dharma*-s', 'present *dharma*-s' and 'future *dharma*-s'? Each of the 'Four Great Ācarya-s' of the Sarvāstivāda offers an explanation. We now quote the relevant passage in the *Abhidharma-mahāvibhāṣā*:[8]

> The Venerable Dharmatrāta says that there is change in mode of being (*bhāva-anyathātva*). The Venerable Ghoṣaka says that there is change in characteristic (*lakṣaṇa-anyathātva*). The Venerable Vasumitra says that there is change in state (*avasthā-anyathātva*). The Venerable Buddhadeva says that there is change in [temporal] relativity (*anyathā-anyathātva*).

The advocate of difference in mode of being says that when *dharma*-s operate (*pra-√vṛt*) in time, they change on account of their modes of being (*bhāva*); there is no change in substance. This is like the case of breaking up a golden vessel to produce another thing — there is just a change in shape, not in *varṇa-rūpa*. It is also like milk, etc., turning into curds, etc. — just the taste, digestibility, etc., are given up, not the *varṇa-rūpa*. Similarly, when *dharma*-s enter into the present from the future, although they give up their future mode of existence and acquire their present mode of existence, they neither lose nor acquire their substantial essence (AKB: *dravya-bhāva*). Likewise, when they enter the past from the present, although they give up the present mode of existence and acquire the past mode of existence, they neither give up nor acquire their substantial nature.

The advocate of difference in characteristic says that when *dharma*-s operate in time, they change on account of characteristic (*lakṣaṇa*); there is no change in substance. A *dharma* in each of the temporal periods has three temporal characteristics; when one [temporal] characteristic is conjoined, the other two are not severed. This is like the case of a man being attached to one particular woman — he is not said to be detached from other women. Similarly, when *dharma*-s abide in the past, they are being conjoined with the past characteristic but are not said to be severed from the characteristics of the other two temporal characteristics. When they abide in the future, they are being conjoined with the future characteristic but are not said to be severed from the characteristics of the other two temporal characteristics. When they abide in the present, they are being conjoined with the present characteristic, but are not said to be severed from the characteristics of the other two temporal characteristics.

The advocate of difference in state says that when *dharma*-s operate in time, they change on account of state (*avasthā*); there is no change in substance. This is like the case of moving a token [into different positions]. When placed in the position (*avasthā*) of ones, it is signified as one; placed in the position of tens, ten; placed in the position of hundreds, hundred.

While there is change in the positions into which it is moved, there is no change in its substance. Similarly, when *dharma*-s pass through the three temporal states, although they acquire three different names, they do not change in substance.

In the theory proposed by this master, there is no confusion as regards substance, for the three periods are differentiated on the basis of activity (*kāritra*).

The advocate of difference in [temporal] relativity says that when *dharma*-s operate in time, they are predicated differently [as future, present, or past], relative to that which precedes and that which follows (*cf.* AKB: *pūrvāparamapekṣyānyo'nya ucyate avasthāntarato na dravyāntarataḥ*); there is no change in substance. This is like the case of one and the same woman who is called 'daughter' relative to her mother, and 'mother' relative to her daughter. Similarly, *dharma*-s are called 'past' relative to the succeeding ones, 'future' relative to the preceding ones, 'present' relative to both.

5.4. Comments on the four theories and Frauwallner's observations

As regards the above four theories, Professor Erich Frauwallner believes that their order of presentation represents the actual chronological order of the development of the theories of *sarvāstivāda*, each subsequent one attempting to avoid the mistakes in the earlier explanation.[9] He asserts further that Vasumitra's theory as given above in fact is an equation, on the part of the Sarvāstivāda masters, of two originally different theories, by two different Vasumitras:

The older Vasumitra proposed, as did the other three great *ācārya*-s mentioned above, that *dharma*-s migrate through the different stages of time, which was very similar to the subsequent theory of eternal time (*kāla*) proposed by certain Dārṣṭāntika-Vibhajyavādins,[10] but without the latter's acknowledgement of the eternality of time. When the theory of eternal time was introduced into the Sarvāstivāda system due to foreign influences, it was soon rejected by the Vaibhāṣikas who then sought to explain the difference between the times solely in terms of the *kāritra* of *dharma*-s as proposed by another Vasumitra. The older "Vasumitra's doctrine, which assumes the migration of things through the stages of time, is, although it does not have a concept of time, closely related to the doctrine of the Dārṣṭāntika and Vibhajyavādin, whereas the doctrine of efficacy, which does not recognize stages of time and denies migration through them, is no less opposed to it than to the doctrine of the Dārṣṭāntika. Indeed, the relationship between them is almost that of thesis and antithesis."

5.4.1. As regards Frauwallner's assumption of the chronological order of the development of these theories, we may concede its possibility considering, among other things, the conspicuous fact that Vasumitra's theory, although fully approved and adopted by the Vaibhāṣika, is not enumerated as the first. However, we should observe that the earliest extant source of the four theories is probably the **Vasumitra-saṃghṛhīta-śāstra*[11] by a certain Vasumitra of *ca.* 1st century C.E. This work predates the MVŚ and is very likely to have been consulted by the compilers of the latter.[12] According to Watanabe Baiyū,[13] the author of this work enumerates four theories in the following order: 1. *avasthā* (起); 2. *lakṣaṇa* (相); 3. *bhāva* (事); 4. *apekṣā* (因緣) — corresponding, though in a different order — to the four theories related by the MVŚ. The passage in question (punctuations ours) is as follows:

> ….此有為法於三世各有自相,; 得知外相, 以何等故? 或起或不起, 此之謂也, 或作是說: 相有若干. 問: 彼相本無住, 是故彼有相生? 答曰: 本有此相未生…. 或作是說: 事有若干; 此亦如本所說. 或作是說: 因緣或生或不生也…. 或作是說: 三世處或生或不生; 此之謂也. 未來處是謂未來, 過去處是謂過去, 現在處是謂現在.

Unfortunately, its Chinese translation by Saṃghabhūti (384 C.E.) is not sufficiently clear for an absolutely definite identification of the theories briefly described therein with those of the four *ācārya*-s. Nevertheless, it is fairly evident that Watanabe has misinterpreted the passage. First, clearly, "或起不起" ("may or may not arise") — identified by Watanabe as the first, equating "arise" with *avasthā* — cannot be one of the theories. The author is just explaining here how we can experience the *saṃskṛta-dharma*-s — how we know them as phenomenal existents in the different times — given that they abide in their intrinsic nature in the three times. The answer is that "they may or may not arise": When they arise in the present moment, they are cognized as present; in the past and future times, they do not arise. Immediately after this, he introduces the four theories (underlined by us) with the phrase "此之謂也" ("the explanation for this is"). This same phrase occurs again in the elaboration of the 4th theory which is not accounted for by Watanabe.

Judging by the context and style of rendering of the translator, we believe that, very probably, the four theories enumerated herein are, in the order of their enumeration ("punctuated" by the phrase "或作是說"): (1) *lakṣana-anyathātva* of Ghoṣaka; (2) *bhāva-anyathātva* of Dharmatrāta; (3) *anyathā-anyathātva* of Buddhadeva; (4) *avasthā-anyathātva* of Vasumitra.[14] In any case, the first theory does not seem to be that of Dharmatrāta. This observation would contradict Frauwallner's assumption of the chronological order. The fact that all extant accounts subsequent to the MVŚ agree with the latter's order of enumeration may simply mean that the AKB was influenced by the authority of the MVŚ as representative of the Vaibhāṣika orthodoxy; and the Ny, ADV, the *Tattvasaṃgraha-pañjikā* (TSP), etc., in turn, are either commentaries on the AKB or were influenced by it.

This also means that Dharmatrāta's theory was not the first — and least satisfactory — attempt, as Frauwallner's observation[15] implies. It seems quite clear to us that Dharmatrāta, as much as the other three *ācārya*-s, is concerned to show the integrity of the *dharma*'s *svabhāva*/*dravya*, despite Frauwallner's assertion that Dharmatrāta's explanation "was soon abandoned because no one wanted to accept a change of this type in the essence of things".[16] It is probable that there had been different Vaibhāṣika masters, responding variously to the four theories, although all indications are that Vasumitra's theory in terms of *kāritra* is the favored one. In the MVŚ, only Vasumitra's theory is fully approved of. Dharmatrāta's theory is the last of the remaining three to be criticized, in the following words:

> What is the so-called *bhāva* apart from the *svabhāva* of the *dharma*? Thus, [this theory] too is unreasonable. When *saṃskṛta-dharma*-s arrive at the present time from the future *adhvan*, their anterior *bhāva* should cease; when they arrive at the past time from the present *adhvan*, the posterior *bhāva* should arise: There is arising of the past and ceasing of the future — how can this accord with logic?

This, however, is unfair; for Dharmatrāta, *bhāva* is not meant to have any ontological status. It is our mental superimposition on the empirical aspect of the *dharma* as it is exposed to our experience: it is as arbitrary as the designation — in Vasumitra's theory — of the different positions into which the token is moved.

Vasubandhu criticizes this theory even more severely, branding it a Sāṃkhya theory of *pariṇāma*.[17] However, it is even more unfair, as the theory does not suggest a unitary eternal substance that manifests through transformation, as the Sāṃkhya theory does.[18] As a matter of fact, in the two older translations of the *Vibhāṣā*, no criticism of Dharmatrāta's theory is to be found and, in the oldest translation, only Buddhadeva's theory is criticized in general terms as being the most confusing designation of *adhvan*. Moreover, in spite of the critical comment in the MVŚ, made in the context of contrasting Vasumitra's explanations with the other three, the compilers of the MVŚ did not seem to have treated Dharmatrāta's view as being on a *par* with the *pariṇāma* theory of the Sāṃkhya.[19] (See translation of the passage below).

We will return to this important passage later. For the time being, it may be observed that here Dharmatrāta is quoted alongside Vasumitra — whose views the orthodox compilers revere most. The fact that both their views are not criticized implies that the compilers do not consider the two interpretations of *pariṇāma* as contradictory.

Saṃghabhadra[20] objects to Vasubandhu's criticism of Dharmatrāta's theory, maintaining that this theory is in part the same as Vasumitra's. As a matter of fact, Saṃghabhadra utilizes this theory as an indispensable tool for the Vaibhāṣika defense. In the AKB, the Sautrāntika ridicules the Vaibhāṣika position that the *svabhāva* of a *dharma* exists at all times but at the same time its *bhāva* is not permanent.[21] Saṃghabhadra defends this position, rather than objecting to any misrepresentation of the Vaibhāṣika doctrine on Vasubandhu's part — as he does in many other places. This may suggest that between the time of the MVŚ and AKB, Dharmatrāta's *bhāvānyathātva* theory could have been accepted by the Vaibhāṣika along with Vasumitra's theory in terms of *kāritra*. In Saṃghabhadra's defense[22] here, he actually utilizes both theories:

> The essential nature of a *dharma* remains eternally; its *bhāva* changes: When a *saṃskṛta-dharma* traverses through *adhvan*, it gives rise to its *kāritra* in accordance with the *pratyaya*-s, without abandoning its substantial nature; immediately after this, the *kāritra* produced ceases. Hence it is said that the *svabhāva* exists eternally and yet it is not permanent, since its *bhāva* changes.

Elsewhere,[23] he states in similar terms:

> There is no change in essential nature, but it is not the case that the *bhāva* of *dharma*-s do not vary. The essential nature and the *bhāva* are neither different nor identical. Thus, the *svalakṣaṇa* (= *svabhāva*) of a *saṃskṛta*-

dharma remains at all times, while its special *kāritra* arises and ceases. (For further details, see below).

As evidence for his assertion that the second Vasumitra who proposes the *kāritra* theory — unlike the earlier Vasumitra — does not teach migration of *dharma*-s in time, Frauwallner cites the following MVŚ passage:

> [Questioner:] ... Thus the Venerable Vasumitra says: 'The *saṃskāra*-s have no coming, nor do they have going; being momentary in nature, they do not stay either.' Now, since the *saṃskāra*-s do not have any characteristics of coming and going, etc., how is the differentiation of the three *adhvanaḥ* to be established?
>
> Answer: The differentiation of the three *adhvanaḥ* is established in terms of *kāritra*. It is on this very basis that they are said to have migration: That is, when a *saṃskṛta-dharma* has not yet exercised its *kāritra*, it is said to be future; when it is exercising its *kāritra*, it is said to be present; when its *kāritra* has ceased, it is said to be past. ...[24]

But Frauwallner does not account for the sentence: "It is on this very basis that they are said to have migration." In any case, even without this sentence (which does not occur in the two older translations), one cannot claim to have sufficient reason here for asserting that this supposedly second Vasumitra does not allow any sense of migration of the *dharma*. Besides, we must remember that the whole concern of all these Sarvāstivāda *ācārya*-s is precisely to account for our empirical experience of the activities of *dharma*-s, i.e., of their "passage" in time, given that their essential identities never change. By the same token, the supposedly "older Vasumitra" too surely does not preach migration in a literal sense. His example of the different designations that a token acquires in accordance with the different significations that one assigns to a given position, clearly shows that his *avasthā* is intended to be relative notions: They are distinctions that we superimpose in our perception, even though, of course, this perceptual experience is not without an objective aspect in the causal process: The distinctions are made possible by virtue of the *kāritra* of the *dharma*.

There are other places in the MVŚ where Vasumitra is represented as speaking in terms of migration. Thus, on the three *saṃskṛta-lakṣaṇa*-s, he explains:

> *jāti* causes *dharma*-s to enter from the future into the present ... *jarā* and *anityatā* cause *dharma*-s to enter from the present into the past.[25]

Elsewhere, the compilers of the MVŚ[26] explain that one can equally speak of change or non-change of *saṃskṛta-dharma*-s. One can say that they do not undergo change — which entails, among other things, that they do not "migrate" — from the point of view that *dharma*-s always remain unchanged in their individual essential nature. One can also say that they undergo change, from the point of view that they arise when potency is acquired and cease when potency is lost. The MVŚ further explains:

> There are two kinds of change — that of essential nature, and that of *kāritra*. From the view-point of essential nature, one should say that *saṃskāra*-s do not change, there being no variation in their essential nature. From the point of view of *kāritra*, one should say that *saṃskāra*-s do change: when a *dharma* is in the future it has not yet acquired its *kāritra*; when it reaches the present, it acquires its *kāritra*; when it has entered into the past, its *kāritra* has already ceased; hence there is change...[27]

Neither is it necessarily true, as Frauwallner claims, that Buddhadeva's explanation, enumerated last in the MVŚ, is a subsequent attempt to avoid the philosophical difficulties entailed in the other three. The dates of all four *ācārya*-s are still unsettled,[28] and Frauwallner himself does not offer any suggestion in this regard.

Furthermore, we disagree with Frauwallner that "finally, the last two teachers, Vasumitra and Buddhadeva, avoided not only anything that touched on the essence of things itself, but moreover derived the difference of things in the different stages of time *exclusively from external connections*" (italics ours).[29] The contrast is perhaps overdone. In Buddhadeva's example, the designations of "mother" and "daughter", while being our superimposition, is nevertheless not purely subjective. We perceive a mother or a daughter because of the different functions — biological or otherwise — in the respective cases. Moreover, the MVŚ compilers themselves also do not seem to hesitate in explaining temporality in terms of relativity:

> The conditioned *dharma*-s are designated as being future in relation to the past and the present. They are not designated as being future in relation to the future, for a fourth time period (*adhvan*) does not exist. They are designated as being past in relation to the future and the present. They are not designated as being past in relation to the past, for a fourth time period (*adhvan*) does not exist. They are designated as being present in relation to the past and the future. They are not designated as being present in relation to the present, for a fourth time period (*adhvan*) does not exist. ...[30]

In the case of Ghoṣaka's *lakṣaṇānyathātva*, as Yin Shun[31] has pointed out, his time-characteristics are quite comparable with the Vaibhāṣika doctrine of the *saṃskṛta-lakṣaṇa*-s and should, therefore, have been acceptable in principle to the Vaibhāṣikas. These time-characteristics are the temporal modes of a *dharma*, and in this respect similar to Dharmatrāta's 'mode of being'. In both cases, the characteristic or mode is neither identical with nor different from the *dharma* itself. But whereas a mode of being is either taken up or relinquished as the *dharma* courses in time, the time-characteristics are always with the *dharma* entity, though one among them comes into play at a given temporal period. In the Sarvāstivāda system, a conditioned *dharma* possesses the three *saṃskṛta-lakṣaṇa*-s in every moment, yet it is argued that since they do not exercise their function all at once, it does not amount to the absurdity that a *dharma* arises, deteriorates and vanishes at the same time. Accordingly, Ghoṣaka's time-characteristics too need not be considered to result in temporal confusion.

In brief, we may conclude from the MVŚ account that, some differences in matters of details and expressions not-withstanding, all four theories in fact agree on the following points:

(1) The substantial nature of a *dharma* remains unchanged.
(2) Temporal distinctions are superimposed by us in our experience of the *dharma*-s appearing in the phenomenal world.
(3) All explain this distinction by means of an aspect of the *dharma* which does not have any reality in itself apart from the *dharma*.

Accordingly, we can neither go along with Frauwallner that "the relationship between [the two explanations by the two supposedly different Vasumitras] is almost that of thesis and antithesis"; nor that the four theories in the order and manner in which they are enumerated in the MVŚ represent the actual historical sequence of development of the theory of *sarvāstivāda*, one superceding another.

5.5. The Vaibhāṣika theory of *kāritra*

Following Vasumitra's theory, the Vaibhāṣika argues that a *dharma* is present when it exercises its *kāritra*, future when its *kāritra* is not yet exercised, past when it has been exercised. But this leads to some philosophical difficulties both as regards the exact nature and ontological status of *kāritra* as causal *kāritra* as well as its relationship with the *dharma* itself. Many modern scholars assert that, confronted with the Sautrāntika criticism, Saṃghabhadra innovated a "neo-Vaibhāṣika" doctrine of *kāritra*. To determine the extent to which one can justifiably call Saṃghabhadra's explanations an innovation, let us begin by examining what he actually has to say in this regard. Below we present some of the major points of controversy in this connection between the Vaibhāṣika and the Sautrāntika. The dialogue given herein is, on the whole, a more or less literal translation from passages in the Ny:[32]

Sautrāntika's objection: If *kāritra* is the determining characteristic for the differentiation of past, present and future *dharma*-s, then [you have such problems as the following]:

1. A present but 'non-participating' eye (*tatsabhāga-cakṣus*) such as an eye in darkness, etc., which does not exercise its *kāritra* of seeing, cannot be called present.

2. If you say that such an eye nevertheless has the *kāritra* of both *phala-pratigrahaṇa* (acquiring causal efficiency for an effect) and *phala-dāna* (being productive of an effect), then you have to admit that a past homogeneous cause (*sabhāga-hetu*), etc., being capable of *phala-dāna*, has *kāritra*. This means that it is demi-present.

Saṃghabhadra's reply: The potencies (*śakti* of *dharma*-s are of two kinds, activity (*kāritra*) and efficacy/function/capability/capacity (*sāmarthya/ vṛtti/vyāpāra*). It is only the activity of inducing or projecting a *dharma*'s own fruit (*phalākṣepa* = *phala-pratigrahaṇa/phala-parigrahaṇa*) that is called *kāritra*. This does not exhaust the set of efficacy of a given *dharma*; it also has efficacies that are not *kāritra*. Thus, in darkness, the eye's efficacy of seeing *rūpa* is impaired by darkness. But its *kāritra* of inducing a fruit is not impaired, so that even in darkness, the eye can induce the production of itself [in the next moment]. This *kāritra* always exists in the present moment; for it is solely on the basis of *kāritra* that the present is established [i.e., designated]. Those [*dharma*-s which have arisen and] whose *kāritra*-s have ceased, do not become *asaṃskṛta*-s.[33] [As for] their capability to contribute causally (能為因性)[34] to the arising of a different entity (於餘性生; *dngos po gzhan skyes pa la*), this is not *kāritra*, but efficacy, because it is only at the present moment that a *dharma* can induce a fruit, because an *asaṃskṛta* cannot induce its own fruit, and because it is only the inducing of a *dharma*'s own fruit that is called *kāritra*. Thus, the fact that the Sūtrakāra (i.e., Vasubandhu) in his explanation includes the efficacy of *phala-dāna* as *kāritra* as well, this is very much because he has not properly understood the *abhidharma* tenets! For, although a past cause can produce a fruit (*phala-dāna*), it does not have *kāritra* and hence there is no confusion (*saṃkara*) of the times.[35]

Sautrāntika: If a *dharma* is always existent in its essential nature, it should be able to exercise its *kāritra* at all times — what obstruction is there so that this *dharma*-substance can only exercise its *kāritra* at the present and not other times: There being no difference as regards a *dharma*'s essential nature in the three periods of time, what prevents it from remaining in one identical empirical nature/modality/form (*bhāva*) at all times?

Saṃghabhadra: There are ample examples in the world where, for a given substance, there exist various forms or modalities. Thus, there are feelings (*vedanā*) which are pleasant, unpleasant and neutral; fires which appear as straw-fire, husk-fire, wood-fire, etc.

Sautrāntika: [I may phrase my objection this way:] In our school, we hold that when the necessary conditions obtain, conditioning forces arise not having existed previously. But these conditions are various and at times they assemble together and at other times do not. Accordingly, *dharma*-s do not keep arising eternally. On the other hand, your school concedes that conditioning forces and the various conditions are ever present substantially. As you do not admit that *dharma*-s come into existence without any pre-existence, what can prevent them from being always present?

Saṃghabhadra: As we have argued before, an identical substance can manifest in different forms/modes — this point is sufficient to counteract your objection. Should you be obstinate, let me ask you a counter-question:

In your doctrine of *santati-pariṇāma* (progressive change of a series), it is conceded that the conditioning forces (*saṃskāra*) and their causal conditions become different from moment to moment, even though there is no difference in essential nature between the preceding and the succeeding ones. Now, there being no modification in their causal conditions in the preceding and succeeding moments, what prevents them from arising identical from moment to moment?

That is, the conditioning forces of the previous moment arise at the same time as their conditions and, without diminution in their essential nature, cease together with the conditions. It is by the force of this cause that the fruit is produced in the subsequent moment: It should not be different in form/species from the previous cause, since the two kinds of generative conditions, of the same species or not of the same species, are not differentiated between the preceding and succeeding moments. What condition is there then that constitutes an obstruction causing the modification in the two moments? If you assert that this is so by virtue of the nature (*dharmatā*) of the conditioned *dharma*-s, then why don't you concede the same with regard to the *kāritra* of a *dharma*?

Sautrāntika: You concede that the conditions are always existent. Accordingly, the *kāritra* produced should also be always existent.

Saṃghabhadra: This objection is not reasonable. For even though there is always the assemblage of conditions, it is observed that sometimes a fruit does not result from the conditions. This is like the case of [your doctrine of] impregnation or the case of the eye, etc.: You do not concede that a fruit arises from a cause that has ceased, after a time interval. The different *bīja*-s induced by various causes exist at the same time within a *santati*, and yet their fruits do not co-arise at all times. … Now, since at all times all the causes exist, what prevents the various fruits from co-arising always? … Again, although the conditions for the eye, etc., are always present, yet visual consciousness, etc., do not always arise.

Sautrāntika: According to our school, a series undergoes a progressive transformation and can only give rise to a fruit when some specific conditions obtain.

Saṃghabhadra: Then you should also concede the same in the case of *kāritra*. A *dharma* can have the capacity for inducing or projecting (*ā-√kṣip*) a fruit only in dependence on the forces of various conditions — which may be simultaneous or otherwise, pertaining to its own species or otherwise. This capacity is called *kāritra*.

As a matter of fact, I am not clear as to what you mean by the term *kāritra* in your objection. [Let me define:] *kāritra* is the special capacity that is produced when the assemblage of conditions obtains for a given future *dharma*. That very *dharma* having the *kāritra* is said to be present. When the *kāritra* ceases, it is said to be past. It is not the case that in the previous and subsequent moments there is any difference in the *dharma*'s essential nature.

The *kāritra* of a *dharma* is neither identical with it nor different from it. The former arises in dependence on conditions and exists for only one moment (present) while the latter persists through time. This is much like the case of the series of a *dharma*: A series consists of the non-interrupted arising of a *dharma* from moment to moment. This series is not different from the *dharma* itself, being without an essential nature other than that of the *dharma*. It is also not identical with the *dharma* itself, lest there be a series which consists of just one moment. Neither can we say that it is non-existent since it is observed to produce some effect. Likewise, the distinctive *kāritra* at the present moment is neither different from the *dharma*, as it does not have an essential nature apart from the *dharma*, nor is it identical with the *dharma*, as there are times when only the essential nature exists without *kāritra*. Nor can we say that it is non-existent, for when the *kāritra* has arisen, it can project a *phala*.[36] The following stanza [summarizes] this:

> The *santati* has no distinct essence,
> [But] a distinct effect is conceded;
> *Kāritra* is to be understood likewise.
> Thus, [with it] the times are established.[37]

> We can [also] find examples in [the notions of] cause-effect relationship, of conjunction, and of the purity of *citta*, etc. Hence, although in the past, present and future, a *dharma*'s essential nature is the same, its modes of being (*bhāva*) are different. Accordingly, we have established the distinction of the three times [on the basis of *kāritra*].

We may summarize the important points made by Saṃghabhadra in the above dispute as follows:

1. Saṃghabhadra is very articulate in contrasting the term *kāritra* with the other terms expressing the various other types of causal functions or potencies of a *dharma*. These latter terms include *vyāpāra, kriyā, vṛtti, sāmarthya, śakti,* etc. In the Ny, in a similar contrasting context, Xuan Zang also very consistently renders *kāritra* as *zuo yong* (作用) and as distinct from *gong neng* (功能) used for the terms denoting activities other than *kāritra*.

   It is important to observe, however, that in other contexts, both in the AKB(C) and MVŚ, he is unfortunately not so consistent. Thus, comparing his AKB(C) and Ny with the AKB, Vy and TSP, it can be seen that his rendering of *gong neng* corresponds to *prabhāva, vṛtti, sāmarthya, śakti*, and *vyāpāra*. The last one can be adduced from the TSP:[38] *darśanādilakṣaṇo vyāpāraḥ*, in comparison to 見色功能 in the Ny;[39] and the rest from the AKB and AKB(C). However, he also renders *vyāpāra* as *zuo yong.*[40] Also, in the MVŚ,[41] we have "…The *tatsabhāga-cakṣus* … [at the present moment], although without the *zuo yong* of *rūpa-darśanādi*, definitely has the *zuo yong* of *phalākṣepa*." (Note the two *zuo yong*).

2. *kāritra* is defined as a *dharma*'s capability of inducing the production of its own next moment. This is called *phala-grahaṇa*/*phalākṣepa*. However, elsewhere[42] Saṃghabhadra also claims that although *kāritra* is in actual fact confined to *phalākṣepa* alone, sometimes when the *abhidharma śāstra*-s are referring to a function (e.g., that of *jāti*) that serves as a proximate condition, the term *kāritra* is also used expediently.[43]

3. All *dharma*-s at the present moment have the activity of *phalākṣepa*. Hence *kāritra* uniquely defines presentness, and it is in terms of *kāritra* that the differentiation of the three times can be properly defined.

4. This same temporal differentiation can be explained in other words: Each *dharma* is in a different *avasthā* (following Vasumitra) or *bhāva* (following Dharmatrāta) — future, present or past — depending on the presence or otherwise of *kāritra*. For Saṃghabhadra, *avasthānyathātva* and *bhāvānyathātva* are the same as far as this point is concerned.

5. A *dharma* acquires its mode as present when the necessary assemblage of various conditions obtains — which may be simultaneous with its arising or otherwise, belonging to its own series or otherwise.[44] When this takes place, and only when this takes place, it becomes endowed with its *kāritra*. In its past and future modes, only its intrinsic nature exists, devoid of *kāritra*. Nevertheless, it can still contribute causally to the actual production of some other *dharma*-s. This latter potency is not called an activity but rather a function or capacity.

6. *kāritra* — likewise *bhāva* — is neither different from nor completely identical with the *svabhāva*/*dravya* of a *dharma*.

In addition to what can be gathered from the above dispute, there are other important doctrinal points made by Saṃghabhadra elsewhere in his exposition on *kāritra*. These are:

7. As Frauwallner[45] has pointed out, Saṃghabhadra explains explicitly *kāritra* in terms of the theory of *hetu-pratyaya*:

   If a *saṃskṛta dharma* serves as a cause for the projection of its own fruit, it is said to be [exercising its] *kāritra*. If it serves as a condition assisting [in the producing of the fruit of] a different [series], it is said to be [exercising its] efficacy/function (功能) … All present [*dharma*-s] can serve as cause for the projection of their own fruits. [But] not all present [*dharma*-s] can serve as auxiliary conditions for [*dharma*-s] belonging to a different species: The *cakṣus* in darkness or one whose function has been impaired cannot serve as a condition that assists the arising of visual consciousness. The *kāritra* [of the *cakṣus*], on the other hand, is not impaired by darkness, as it can, without fail, serve as the cause for the projection of the future *cakṣus*. Hence, there is a difference between *kāritra* and efficacy. However, with regard to the production of a fruit within the series of its own species, there is a projecting power which may or may not be definite; it is called a *kāritra* as well as an efficacy. If [a power], with regard to the production of the fruit within a series of a different species, can serve only as a condition assisting its arising — this is an efficacy, not a *kāritra*.[46] (See also the following point).

8. In Saṃghabhadra's *kāritra* theory, the four *saṃskṛta-lakṣaṇa*-s also play an important role. He defines these *lakṣaṇa*-s in terms of a *dharma*'s *svaphalākṣepa-kāritra*. We may say that according to Saṃghabhadra, the four *lakṣaṇa*-s together completely ensure that *kāritra* can arise and, indeed, arise for just one *kṣaṇa*. This implies that they too — together with *kāritra* — are indispensable for the establishment of the difference of the three times:

   Although the *saṃskṛta-dharma*-s are assisted by various external causes and conditions, they must be assisted internally by *jāti, sthiti, jarā* and *anityatā* as proximate causes, before they can traverse through time. …[47]

> Efficacy (功能) refers to the function of serving as a direct condition…
>
> The efficacy of *jāti* is its capability to serve as the direct (*sākṣāt*) condition (親緣) enabling [a *dharma*] to give rise to its *kāritra* of projecting its own fruit…
>
> The efficacy of *sthiti* is its capability to serve as the direct condition enabling a *dharma* to stay temporarily and to project its own fruit…
>
> The efficacy of *jarā* is its capability to serve as the direct condition for impairing a *dharma*'s *kāritra* of projecting its own fruit…
>
> The efficacy of *anityatā* is its capability to serve as the direct condition for destroying a *dharma*'s *kāritra* of projecting its own fruit.[48]

5.6. Saṃghabhadra's theory — an innovation?

Having examined the important features of Saṃghabhadra's *kāritra* theory, we will now attempt to determine — within the limit of the data accessible to us — the extent to which we may consider it an innovation.

Collet Cox,[49] observing that the MVŚ uses the term *zuo yong* where, in the same context, Saṃghabhadra clearly uses *sāmarthya*, concludes:

> This would suggest that the **Mahāvibhāṣā* does not recognize the clear distinction between *kāritra* and *sāmarthya* proposed by Saṃghabhadra.

But this conclusion seems to have betted too much on Xuan Zang's consistency in rendering these terms (see § 5.5, summary-point 1). Moreover, if what Saṃghabhadra claims is true that the masters before him sometimes used the term *kāritra* expediently (see above, § 5.5, summary-point 2), we may consider the possibility that the two contrasting causal functions had already been taught by at least some of the Sarvāstivāda masters at an earlier stage, even though the usage of these terms had not been strictly observed. Besides, there are actually several places in the MVŚ[50] where *zuo yong* and *gong neng* are used side by side in the same context, although we often cannot be too certain as to the degree of contrast or the exact distinction intended. Thus, on the question as to why *dharma*-s do not arise and cease constantly, there being always the assemblage of causes and conditions — a question similar to one of the Sautrāntika's objections in the AKB and Ny (see preceding section above) — the MVŚ cites the explanations given by various masters, and Buddhadeva's explanation is:

> *Dharma*-s should have their *zuo yong* for arising and ceasing only once in each. It would be useless if they arise repeatedly and cease repeatedly. …
>
> Question: When the causes and conditions assemble for the arising of *dharma*-s, are the *gong neng*-s many or one? …
>
> Answer: One can say they are many or that they are one. … The *gong neng* of the causes and conditions can be considered as one in-as-much as they together enable the *dharma*-s to give rise to their *zuo yong*…[51]

Another instance, with regard to past and future *anuśaya*-s:

> Given that past and future *anuśaya*-s have no *zuo yong*, how can they be said to adhere and grow (*anuśerate*)?
>
> Answer: Because they can give rise to the *prāpti* [of the present *anuśaya*] which manifests at the present moment. This is like the case that, although fire does not manifest at the present moment, yet it can give rise to smoke. The Venerable Ghoṣaka explains thus: 'Although they do not have the *zuo yong* of grasping the objects, yet, with regard to the *ālambana* and the *saṃprayukta dharma*-s, they have the *gong neng* of bondage just like [when they are] present. Hence these [past and future] *anuśaya*-s can be said to adhere and grow.[52]

Regarding the relationship between the *kāritra* of a *dharma* and its *svabhāva*, as Frauwallner[53] has shown, the MVŚ already explained in the same manner as Saṃghabhadra: "It cannot be said categorically that[54] they are identical or different."

Frauwallner rightly observes that this important passage is not found in the two earlier Chinese versions of the *Mahāvibhāṣā* and is therefore possibly a later addition[55] — made somewhere after the two earlier recensions. Frauwallner proposes that in the final stage of development of the *kāritra* doctrine before Saṃghabhadra, *kāritra* came to be equated with *bhāva*, and Saṃghabhadra took over from here. However, from Saṃghabhadra's own exposition, it can be seen that the absence or presence of *kāritra* in fact constitutes a different *bhāva* in each case. No equation is asserted by him here.

In another instance, the MVŚ also speaks of the *avasthā* and the essential nature (體) of a *dharma* as being neither identical nor different:

> The *avasthā* and the essential nature [of a fruit] are neither identical nor different. Whereas its essential nature exists at all times (*sarvadā asti*), its *avasthā* does not (*na sarvadā*).[56]

The doctrine that the *kāritra* of *phalākṣepa* (= *phala-pratigrahana*) uniquely defines the present in contradistinction to the past and future times is also already found in the MVŚ:[57]

> Question: A *tatsabhāga-cakṣus*, etc., at the present moment have no activity of seeing, etc. They should therefore not be present.
>
> Answer: Although they do not have the activities of seeing, etc., they definitely have the *phala-pratigrahaṇa-kāritra*, for they are the *sabhāga-hetu* for the future *dharma*-s: all *saṃskṛta-dharma*-s at the present moment can serve as *hetu* for the *pratigrahaṇa* of *niṣyanda-phala*. As this *phala-pratigrahaṇa-kāritra* applies to all the present *dharma*-s, without any confusion (*saṃkara*), it is used as the basis for the establishment of the differentiation of past, present and future.

This important passage too is missing in the two earlier versions of the *Mahāvibhāṣā* and so was likewise possibly added after these two earlier recensions and before the MVŚ. Moreover, the doctrine that *phala-grahaṇa* of all the six *hetu*-s in each case takes place solely at the present moment is also found in the MVŚ.[58]

Saṃghabhadra protests very confidently that the Ābhidharmikas do not teach that the *kāritra* includes *phaladāna*. (See above, § 5.5). He also protests similarily elsewhere that the Vaibhāṣika never taught that *kāritra* has temporal distinction.[59] *Kāritra* in fact comes into being not having been, and vanishes in a single moment of the present.[60] Another equally confident protest is that the Sautrāntika bases his criticism on the wrong assumption that the Vaibhāṣika teaches that the past and the future exist in the same manner as the present. In fact, he says, this is a misrepresentation of the Vaibhāṣika position which is that the *dharma* exists with a different *bhāva* in each of the three times. (See above, § 5.5, summary-point 3).

Based on the representation of Vaibhāṣika views by Vasubandhu, Yaśomitra, Śāntarakṣita and Kamalaśīla — all notably Sautrāntikas or pro-Sautrāntika — some scholars seem to claim all too readily that the Vaibhāṣika views underwent radical transformation under the pressure of the Sautrāntika criticism. While understandably this could well be true in some cases, we must not ignore these unambiguous and confident protests by Saṃghabhadra in arriving at our conclusions. Thus, like Frauwallner, Tatia also expounds the theory of *sarvāstivāda* in a manner that clearly suggests that *kāritra* included *phaladāna* and *phalākṣepa*, a theory that was then revised by Saṃghabhadra to include only the latter.[61] His exposition similarly suggests that the Vaibhāṣika taught the temporality of *kāritra*.[62] Unlike the case of Frauwallner's investigation, however, Tatia's also does not have the merit of having consulted the Chinese and Tibetan sources.

Saṃghabhadra's explanation of the *saṃskṛta-lakṣaṇa*-s in terms of a *dharma*'s *phalākṣepa-kāritra* is already attested — once again — in the following MVŚ passage which, moreover, provides early evidence that the *kāritra* theory has already been explicitly linked with that of cause-effect:

> By the force of *sthiti-lakṣaṇa*, the *saṃskāra*-s — having arisen — are capable of grasping their own fruit (this is *phala-grahana* = *phalākṣepa*), and of grasping the *ālambana*. By the force of *jarā* and *anityatā*, there is no further activity after one *kṣaṇa*. If *sthiti-lakṣaṇa* were non-existent, there should not be the cause-effect series of the *saṃskāra*-s, and the *citta-caitta-dharma*-s should not have any *ālambana*.[63]

All this taken into consideration, we must dissent here from others who are fond of labeling Saṃghabhadra's explanations on *kāritra* as a neo-Sarvāstivāda/neo-Vaibhāṣika doctrine. To us, Saṃghabhadra's contribution to the Sarvāstivāda theory of *kāritra* consists essentially in his more articulate presentation and greater consistency in the use of terminologies. He has fine-tuned the theory considerably but this does not amount to a novel interpretation, since practically all the important doctrinal propositions he made in this connection were already found in the time of the MVŚ or earlier.

5.7. *Bhāva*, *svabhāva* and the *dharma*

5.7.1. We saw above (§ 5.3, § 5.4) that each of the four main theories stresses that, throughout the three periods of time, the *dravya* (= *svabhāva*) remains unchanged. This is *sarvāstivāda* or *sarvāstitva* in a nutshell: But just precisely what is meant by a *dharma*'s intrinsic nature "not changing"? One thing is certain that the theory does not amount to the Sāṃkhya doctrine of *pariṇāma*. Even Vasubandhu, the arch-critic of the Vaibhāṣika, does not allege.

But then, the MVŚ seems to be obscure and even contradictory at times on this fundamental question. The following passage is a good illustration. On the one hand, it says that the essential nature does not undergo change (see quotation in § 5.4 above); on the other, that when *dharma*-s undergo transformation — and hence are impermanent — it is their very essential nature that is involved in the transformation:[64]

> Question: Why are *rūpa*-s and *citta*-s, etc., impermanent?
>
> Answer: [Since] they are subject to *pariṇāma* and do not remain the same, how could they be considered to abide permanently?
>
> Question: When it is held that their essential natures arise and cease, how do you know that the *pariṇāma* is not the concealing and manifesting [of these essential natures]?
>
> The Venerable Vasumitra explains thus: If their *pariṇāma* is merely on account of concealing and manifesting, then a baby in the embryo would have its stages of childhood, youth, middle age and old age, all arising at once. Yet [the fact is that] they arise sequentially. Thus we know that it is not on account of the concealing and manifesting of the entities themselves (體 — *svarūpa/svabhāva*?) that there is *pariṇāma*. …
>
> The Bhadanta [Dharmatrāta] explains: It is seen in the world that when conditions assemble, a *dharma* arises; when conditions are not in concord, a *dharma* is destroyed. It is not the case that that which conceals and manifests has such a difference (*viśeṣa*). Thus we know that the *pariṇāma* is not on account of the concealing and manifesting [of the entity itself]. It is only on account of the essential mode's arising and ceasing. Furthermore, when a *dharma* is undergoing *pariṇāma*, its previous and subsequent modes (相 — *ākāra/ākṛti/bhāva*?) are different and hence the entity itself should also be different, since the mode and the entity itself are the same. [On the other hand,] if a *dharma* abides permanently, then even though there is differentiation in stage (*avasthā*) — those of concealing and manifesting

— there is no difference in its mode. Thus we know that in the *pariṇāma*, the entity itself arises and ceases.

Prima facie, this passage may seem to utterly contradict the fundamental Sarvāstivāda standpoint that essential natures never change! But it actually provides us with important clues for an answer to the question we have just raised — nay, for an understanding of the very theory of *sarvāstitva*: not only does it show that this theory differs from the Sāṃkhya concept of *pariṇāma*, it also spells out explicitly that, although the *svabhāva/dravya* is said to be *sarvadā asti*, this does not entail that it is immutable or even permanent, for a *dharma*'s mode of existence and its essential nature are not different, so that when the former is undergoing transformation, so is its *svabhāva*. This, however need not be — and should not be — a contradiction to what the MVŚ says elsewhere that "from the view-point of essential nature, one should say that *saṃskāra*-s do not change" (see above, § 5.3). The same entity, not a different one, remains throughout the times. In this sense there is no change in *svabhāva* or *svalakṣaṇa*[65] — no *anyathātva* of substance. At the same time, a *dharma* keeps having a different mode of being and each mode is actually a new — but not different in terms of essence — *dharma*. In this sense there is change or transformation of essential nature — a change, nevertheless, which does not entail the result of an ontologically different substance. To take Dharmatrāta's examples: When the same piece of gold is transformed into different entities — a golden bowl, cup, etc. — each time a brand new 'thing' or 'entity' results but the essential nature of this selfsame piece of gold which is involved in the process of transformation remains the same, i.e., the *svabhāva/svalakṣaṇa/svarūpa/dravya* remains the same in this process of change.

Saṃghabhadra's refutation of the identification of *sarvāstitva* with the Sāṃkhya theory of *pariṇāma* is even more articulate:

[This allegation] is untenable, for [the Sāṃkhya] holds that the effect is none other than the cause transformed, and that the effect again will vanish, turning back into the essential nature. The essential nature of the past, future and present is one identical substance. [On the other hand,] in our school, there is no confounding (*saṃkara*) of times (*adhvan*):

[i] activity (*kāritra*) exists only in the present moment; this [present] position (*avasthā*) definitely is not subsumable by the [other] two times;

[ii] cause and effect are completely distinct and there is no mutual operation;

[iii] *dharma*-s, once they have ceased, do not arise again;

[iv] the effect does not vanish and turn back into the essential nature;

[v] causes have no beginning;

[vi] [*dharma*-s] are produced by various causes, [not by a unitary cause];

[vii] causes and effects do not have a Person (*puruṣa*) as the arbiter.

In this way, there are innumerable differences [between the two systems].[66]

5.7.2. In regard to the Sarvāstivāda position that a *dharma* can exist in different modes without losing its *svabhāva*, Saṃghabhadra illustrates as follows: The *svabhāva* of all *vedanā*-s is sensation, yet we can speak of various types of sensations — pleasurable, etc. The various organs — visual, auditory, etc., within the same personal series (*santati*), are all of the essential nature of *prasāda rūpa*; yet among them there are different modes of existence, i.e., there are the different functions of seeing, hearing, etc. "Now, herein, it is not the case that since the function is different from the existence, that there can be the difference in the functions of seeing, hearing, etc. Rather, *the very function of seeing,* *etc., is none other than the existence of the eye, etc*. On account of the difference in function, there is definitely the difference in the mode of existence… Since it is observed that there are *dharma*-s that co-exist as essential substances and whose essential characteristics do not differ but that [nevertheless] have different modes of existence, we know that when *dharma*-s traverse the three times, their modes of existence vary while their essential characteristics do not change."[67]

Like the compilers of the MVŚ, Saṃghabhadra also insists on the impermanence of *svabhāva*.[68] But in the light of the above MVŚ passages, we can now see that this is not really that innovative either:

> [*Svabhāva* is not permanent, for] whatever is permanent does not go through time. Neither should [the Sthavira Śrīlāta] say '*svabhāva* remains constant (性恆住)',[69] for we concede that the *bhāva* (有) of an existent in the past, present and future varies.
>
> … [Our explanations] also have properly refuted the objection that [our theory of *sarvāstitva*] implies the permanence of [a *dharma*'s] essential nature, for, while the essential nature remains always [the same], its *avasthā* differs [in the stages of time] since there is change. This difference of *avasthā* is produced on account of conditions and necessarily stays no more than one *kṣaṇa*. Accordingly, the essential nature of the *dharma* too is impermanent, since it is not distinct from the difference [that arises in it]. [But] it is only in an existent *dharma* that changes can obtain; there cannot be change in a non-existent. In this way, therefore, we have properly established the times.[70]

Our examination above leads us to the belief that for the Vaibhāṣikas, the *svabhāva-bhāva* relationship is not one of essence and attribute/ quality — contrary to the representation made by the Sautrāntikas and some modern scholars. It may be true to say that Saṃghabhadra clarifies this point better than the MVŚ compilers: a *svabhāva* always exists in a specific *bhāva*; it cannot be (√*bhū*) other than in a particular mode of being (*bhāva*) which can be infinitely various[71] — but this is no innovative proposition, being part of Dharmatrāta's *bhāva-anyathātva* theory. And accordingly, the two are neither identical with nor different from each other.

From the point of view of their opponents, however, if a new *bhāva* implies a new entity, it should follow that an ontologically different entity results. The Vaibhāṣikas, while at the depth of their hearts unafraid of logical contradictions when it comes to the fundamental level of things, would not consider here that their position is untenable.[72] They appeal to a fundamental notion accepted by all Buddhist schools: the identity in difference of a series (*santāna*). The logical incongruity will dissolve — at least for the Buddhists — when a *dharma* is seen as manifesting in ever renewing forms constituting a series. A *dharma*-series (*dharma-santāna*) is not statically identical at any time; yet it retains an overall individuality or integrity. It is dynamically identical. One cannot step into the same river twice; but at the same time, one river is distinct from another. And this dynamic identity or distinctiveness is by virtue of the *dharma*'s *svabhāva* — a *dharma*-series has no *svabhāva* other than that of the *dharma* (*cf. supra*, § 5.5). It is in this sense that the *svabhāva* too may be said to undergo change — and hence be impermanent — even though ontologically it never becomes a totally different substance. As a matter of fact, the identity-in-difference (*bhedābheda*) relationship obtaining between *svabhāva* and *bhāva*/*kāritra* — indeed their whole thesis of *sarvāstitva* — can never make sense if the Vaibhāṣika conception of *dharma* is taken as one of static identity! From the standpoint of Aristotelian logic, of course, "not totally different" hardly suffices to establish that the "same" *dharma* continues to exist. This is the limit of the *bhedābheda* logic viewed from the Aristotelian standpoint.

If this way of understanding *sarvāstitva* represents a compromise on the Vaibhāṣika part on the reality of a *dharma*, it should be remembered that any *bhedhābheda* relationship is an "intrinsic compromise" of essential reality in ontological terms. But from the Vaibhāṣika standpoint, this does not so much represent an intentional, last resort, compromise, as a statement of fact. Both the Sautrāntikas and the Vaibhāṣikas would consider a series as a mental superimposition. But for the former, it has no ontological status whatsoever (Saṃghabhadra[73] points out their fallacy — see *supra*, § 5.5). For the latter, it has a relative reality inasmuch as it is based on the ever-existent *dharma* manifesting in new forms from moment to moment.

Saṃghabhadra goes so far as to claim that it is in fact only *sarvāstitva* so understood that is logically compatible with the central Buddhist doctrine of impermanence: A *dharma* undergoes transformation in its essential nature, yet without entailing a different substance.

> [For,] if the essential substance becomes different, an [ontologically] distinct *dharma* would result; then it ought not to be impermanent, there being no transformation in essence involved. That is: if one holds only that [a *dharma*] exists in the present time and [regards] past or future [*dharma*-s] as non-existent essentially, then it should follow that all *saṃskāra-dharma*-s are permanent in nature, there being no transformation involved. … An existent and a non-existent have their respective fixed natures; there is no transformation [possible]: transformation is not possible because they hold that only the momentary present *dharma*-s exist. Past and future *dharma*-s being completely without any essential nature, how can one speak of transformation of non-existent *dharma*-s? Thus, one is unable to say that all *saṃskāra*-s are impermanent. One cannot argue that transformation consists of a non-existent being transformed into an existent, or an existent into a non-existent for existence (*astitva*) and non-existence (*nāstitva*) are not mutually accomplishing in their essence, since an existent and a non-existent are essentially contradictory to each other. … If one concedes that past and future [*dharma*-s] are both existent and non-existent, [then a *dharma*], from being non-existent in [the sense of] not having yet arisen, can arise and become existent, and, from being existent [in the sense of]

> having arisen, can cease and become non-existent. This non-existence in the past and future and the existence in the present are in both cases not fixed, so that there is possibility of variation. The existence in the past and the future is the same as that in the present; there is no change in all the periods of time. It is on account of the fact that the essential nature [always] exists and the *kāritra* may or may not exist, that one can speak of a conditioned (*saṃskṛta*) having difference in state. Hence it is only the school which asserts the existence [of the essential nature] in the three periods of time that can speak of change with regard to a given *dharma*.[74]

The answer to the question that we raised at the beginning of this section now emerges more clearly: When the Vaibhāṣika says that there is no change in a *dharma*'s *svabhāva* or *dravya* when it "traverses" in time, they mean that its integrity — its *svalakṣaṇa* (= *svabhāva*) — is untouched, and the essential nature does not change from being an existent into a non-existent (*sarvadā asti*). It is not that this essential nature is — mysteriously, as it were — totally uninvolved in the temporal process: It is *sarvadā asti* and yet *anitya*; non-temporal, i.e., not temporal in the usual sense of the term and yet not atemporal, i.e., not totally transcending the temporal process. If this answer sounds ambiguous, it is on account of the fundamental ambiguity or elusiveness that is necessarily implied in the *bhedābheda* relationship that obtains between the *svabhāva* of a *dharma* on the one hand, and its *kāritra* and *bhāva* on the other. But then, for the Vaibhāṣika, and, for that matter, for all 'religious philosophers', such fundamental ambiguity — wholly or partly derived from a long tradition of experience and/or contemplation — must come first, before logic, even if the Ābhidharmikas at the same time find the logical tools indispensable for the defense of their religious insight and convictions.

NOTES

[1] For the discussion on the definition of Sarvāstivāda, see *supra*, § 3.2.

[2] 世體是常, 行體無常. But T no. 1546 has simply: 世是常, 行無常.

[3] MVŚ, 393a; also, 700a.

[4] *Study*, 303.

[5] T 26, no. 1546, 293c.

[6] T 27, 1003c–1004a; T 29, 630b.

[7] T 27, 65b, 85b, 116b, 190a, 479a, 796a–b, 919b, 919b–c; also *cf.* 74b.

[8] MVŚ, 396a–b. For the corresponding Sanskrit passages, see AKB, 296 f.

[9] *Frauwallner*, 188 ff.

[10] Frauwallner seems to understand, in this context, that the Dārṣṭāntika and Vibhajyavāda were different from the Sarvāstivāda (*op. cit.*, 191). But as we have noted above (§ 5.2), in the older version of the MVŚ, this theory is said to be held by "the Dārṣṭāntikas".

[11] T no. 1549, 724b.

[12] See *Study*, 382 ff.

[13] Watanabe Baiyū, *Ubu abidatsuma ron no kenkyū* (Tokyo, 1954), 186 f.

[14] Yin Shun (*Study*, 303) ascribes these different explanations to their advocators somewhat differently.

[15] *Frauwallner*, 188 f.

[16] *Frauwallner*, 205 f.

[17] AKB, 297.

[18] However, we do find in the MVŚ (201c–202a) some masters who speak of milk turning into curd as an exemplification of the Sāṃkhya doctrine.

[19] MVŚ, 1003c–1004a.

[20] Ny, 631b.

[21] AKB, 298: *svabhāvaḥ sarvadā cāsti bhāvo nityaśca neṣyate* /

[22] Ny, 633c.

[23] Ny, 632c.

[24] MVŚ, 393c.

[25] MVŚ, 121b.

[26] MVŚ, 200a–b.

[27] MVŚ, *loc. cit.*

[28] In one place (Tāranātha, 15) the comparatively late tradition of Tibet gives the chronological placing: Dharmatrāta → Vasumitra → Ghoṣaka → Buddhadeva. In another place (*ibid.*, 103), Dharmatrāta → Ghoṣaka → Vasumitra → Buddhadeva. But this second order is very likely influenced by the order of enumeration of their theories in the MVŚ. Yin Shun (*op. cit.*, 268, 271, 274, 285) gives the following dates:

Dharmatrāta	— around the end of 2nd century B.C.E., contemporary or slightly earlier than Vasumitra;
Buddhadeva	— 10 B.C.E.–10 C.E., junior contemporary of Dharmatrāta;
Vasumitra	— 100 B.C.E., after Kātyāyanīputra (but the MVŚ, 231c, is divided as to whether his PrŚ precedes the JPŚ or otherwise);
Ghoṣaka	— between 1st and 2nd century C.E., considerably later than Vasumitra.

[29] *Op. cit.*, 189.

[30] MVŚ, 394b. See also *Study*, 300 f.

[31] *Study*, 297 ff.

[32] *Cf.* Ny, 631c–633b. I have given here a more or less literal translation from the Chinese, with only slight paraphrasing.

[33] *Cf.* Ny, 410b: "A [*dharma*] whose *kāritra* has ceased, relinquishes only its presentness; the *dharma*'s essential nature remains."

[34] *Cf.* Tibetan in **Tattvārthā* : *rgyur gyur pa 'di dag gi nus pa nyid.*

[35] *Cf.* Ny, 409c f. We have translated this passage very literally in view of its importance. Frauwallner is not sure of a sentence here, and accordingly his rendering in this place seems unintelligible. *Cf.* Sthiramati's **Tattvārthā*: *gang yang 'gags pa skyes pa 'dus byas kyi chos rnams kyi mthu'i khyad par dngos po gzhan skyes pa la rgyur gyur pa 'di dag gi nus pa nyid bya ba ma yin pa da ltar ba'i gnas skabs kho na 'phangs pa'i phyir / 'dus ma byas rnams kyis 'bras bu 'phen pa mi 'thad pa'i phyir ro / 'bras bu 'phen pa'i bya ba ma yin no /*

[36] *Cf.* TSP, 509: *na kāritraṃ dharmād anyat, tadvyatirekeṇa svabhāvānupalabdheḥ / nā'pi dharmamātram, svabhāvāstitvepi kadācid abhāvāt / na ca na viśeṣaḥ, kāritrasya prāgabhāvāt /*

[37] *Cf.* TSP, *loc. cit.*: *santatikāryaṃ ceṣṭaṃ, na vidyate sāpi santatiḥ kācit / tadvad avagaccha yuktyā kāritreṇā'dhvasaṃsiddham //*

[38] TSP, 506.

[39] Ny, 631c.

[40] *Cf.* AKB(C), 11b: 無作用 which translates *nirvyāpāra* in the AKB, 31.

[41] MVŚ, 393c — see quotation below.

[42] Ny, 410a.

[43] Also cf. Ny, 450b: "…It is not the case that there can be *kāritra* in the past [when the corresponding retribution fruit is presently arising]. The term *kāritra* [which is employed in this case] is intended to mean a function."

[44] Ny, 632b.

[45] *Frauwallner*, 199 ff.

[46] Ny, 409c f. (also *cf. ibid.*, 409a–b, and MVŚ, 393c which is quoted above). Contra Frauwallner's translation which is very misleading: "If this acts as a cause, it produces its effect. If it acts as a condition, it fosters a difference of property (*bhāva*)." (*Frauwallner*, 201)

[47] Ny, 409a–b.

[48] SPrS, 809b–c; also *cf.* Ny, 409a–c.

[49] Cox, C, *Disputed Dharmas: Early Buddhist Theories on Existence* (Tokyo, 1995), 157, n. 75.

[50] E.g., MVŚ, 105a, 113b, 200a–b, 480a–b.

[51] MVŚ, 105a.

[52] MVŚ, 113a–b.

[53] *Frauwallner,* 197 f.

[54] Contra Frauwallner: "with any certainty that" — which is misleading.

[55] *Frauwallner,* 199. Frauwallner concedes that it is older than Vasubandhu.

[56] MVŚ, 87b.

[57] MVŚ, 393c–394a.

[58] MVŚ, 108c. An alternative opinion as regards the *kāraṇa–hetu* is also given here. This is refuted in the Ny. The MVŚ (89b) — as well as the two earlier recensions — already contains the Vaibhāṣika rule that there must first be *phalagrahaṇa* before there can be *phaladāna*: The fruit must first be causally determined or "effectualized" before it can actually be produced.

[59] Ny, 632b–c; contra *Tatia*, 104.

[60] Ny, 631a, 635a.

[61] *Tatia*, 100–102.

[62] *Ibid.*, 104.

[63] MVŚ, 201c.

[64] MVŚ, 1003c–1004a.

[65] *Cf.* Ny, 632c: "Although a *dharma*'s essential nature remains, when specific conditions obtain, or by virtue of the nature of things (*dharmatā*), a distinctive *kāritra* arises not having been, and returns nowhere after having existed. The *dharma*'s essential nature is just as before, its *svalakṣaṇa* remaining always."

[66] Ny, 635a.

[67] Ny, 625a.

[68] Ny, 630b.

[69] According to the immediate context, this 性 must be the same as 自性 — *svabhāva*. La Vallée Poussin (1936–1937) takes this to be *bhāva* ("Sarvāstivāda", 84).

[70] Ny, 633a.

[71] Ny, 633c.

[72] In the AKB, 301, Vasubandhu represents the Vaibhāṣika as finally exclaiming that the nature of *dharma* (*dharmatā*) is profound and beyond intellectual comprehension. Saṃghabhadra (Ny, 634c–635a) protests that this is a distortion: "These are not the words of the true Vaibhāṣikas." He further claims that he has properly refuted all the objections raised by Vasubandhu (Ny, 635a).

[73] Ny, 633a.

[74] Ny, 410c.

6. Theory of Causality I

The Six Causes

6.1. The 6 *hetu*-s, 4 *pratyaya*-s and 5 *phala*-s — their correlation

The investigation of causes, conditions and their effects constitutes one of the special topics of concern of the Ābhidharmikas (*supra*, § 2.3.5). In the Sarvāstivāda theory of causality, two doctrinal schemes are employed: that of the four conditions (*pratyaya*) and that of the six causes (*hetu*). Saṃghabhadra[1] maintains that the doctrine of the four conditions is found in the *sūtra*-s of their school. As for the six causes, he says that they were once in their *Ekottarāgama*, although no longer extant. He quotes *sūtra* passages to show that indications of the six causes are scattered in the various *sūtra*-s. Thus, *cakṣuḥ pratītya rūpāṇi cotpadyate cakṣurvijñānam* is supposed to indicate the doctrine of *kāraṇa-hetu*, etc. The MVŚ[2] likewise states that the *sūtra*-s speak only of the four conditions, not the six causes. But it also quotes the opinions of other masters — one identical with Saṃghabhadra's — which the compilers do not repudiate. Accordingly, the doctrine of the four conditions most probably preceded that of the six causes. At any rate, the latter are already mentioned in the *Jñānaprasthāna*.[3] The six *hetu*-s, the four *pratyaya*-s, and their corresponding *phala*-s are correlated as follows:

4 *pratyaya*-s	**6 *hetu*-s**	**5 *phala*-s**
hetu-pratyaya	*sahabhū-hetu* *saṃprayuktaka-hetu*	*puruṣakāra-phala*
	sabhāga-hetu *sarvatraga-hetu*	*niṣyanda-phala*
	vipāka-hetu →	*vipāka-phala*
samanantara-pratyaya		
ālambana-pratyaya		
adhipati-pratyaya —	*kāraṇa-hetu* →	*adhipati-phala*
		visaṃyoga-phala (not a fruit of any of the 6 causes)

It can be noticed from the above chart that the *samanantara-pratyaya* and the *ālambana-pratyaya* have no correlatives among the six causes. This suggests that the doctrine of the four *pratyaya*-s has a wider scope than that of the six *hetu*-s.

This raises an interesting question: What is the doctrinal need and significance in the subsequent elaboration of the *hetu-pratyaya* (condition *qua* cause) into the five *hetu*-s? We will show that this elaboration serves, on the one hand, to explain the dynamic arising and interaction of the distinct *dharma*-s that are totally unrelated in their *svabhāva*-s, and, on the other, to corroborate fundamentally their central doctrine of *sarvāstitva*. Moreover, in the latter context, the *sahabhū-hetu* is doctrinally of fundamental importance for the Sarvāstivāda doctrine of causality. For this reason, this category, together with its subset, the *saṃprayuktaka-hetu*, will be dealt with in comparatively greater details below.

6.2. The special importance of the doctrine of causality for the Sarvāstivāda

According to Vasumitra's **Samaya-bhedoparacaṇa-cakra*, the Sarvāstivāda school was also known as the Hetuvāda.[4] While no explanation whatsoever of this latter name is given in the treatise itself, we surmise that it was very probably derived from the special importance that the school attaches to the doctrine of causes: Real, existent *dharma*-s are real forces; at the same time, their arising into the phenomenal world — out of their *svabhāva*-s as it were — is totally dependent on specific causes.

6.2.1. *Dharma*-s as causal forces

At the outset, we must realize that for the Sarvāstivāda, causal efficacy is the central criterion for the reality/existence (*astitva*) of a *dharma*. How do the Sarvāstivādins arrive at a definite list of *dharma*-s which they claim to be real/existent throughout the three periods of time? As we have seen (§ 1.2), a *dharma* — an ultimate real — is that which sustains its unique characteristic. When such a unique characteristic is found, it is to be known that a specific or unique intrinsic nature (*svabhāva*) exists correspondingly, i.e., a *dharma* as a real distinct entity (*dravyāntara*) is discovered, and it is to be added to the recognized list of *dharma*-s.

The existence of such a unique characteristic may be perceived directly through the senses, as in the case of the objects of the five senses. Where direct sensory perception is not possible, the Sarvāstivādins argue for the existence of a *dharma* from the observation or mental analysis of the unique causal contribution that it makes in the occurrence of a given event in space-time. Thus, it is argued, the thought-concomitants must exist as real entities, for each of them contributes uniquely and necessarily to our empirical experience: *vedanā* enables sensation, *saṃjñā* enables ideation, *smṛti* enables recollection, etc. Likewise, the *viprayukta-saṃskāra*-s are also real entities on account of their being real causal forces: *jāti*, *sthiti*, *jarā/anityatā* and *vyaya* are the *sine qua non* that together cause a conditioned *dharma* to be momentary; acquisition (*prāpti*) is a force/cause for effecting the specific connection between a *dharma* and a sentient continuum (*santati*); etc.

A *dharma* then is a real on account of it being a real force — of having a causal efficacy — in other words, on account of it being a cause. It is for this reason that *dharma*-s are also called *saṃskāra*-s — conditioning forces. Failure to prove an alleged existent's causal efficacy is tantamount to failure to prove its very existence/reality. Accordingly, if *saṃskāra-dharma*-s are asserted to be existent tri-temporally, they must be established as belonging to one category or another of *hetu*. The MVŚ, citing the authority of the PrŚ, states that the causes comprise the totality of existent *dharma*-s:

> The causes, the path and 'conditioned co-arising' … completely subsume the totality of the *dhātu*, *āyatana* and *skandha dharma*-s. … The causes, the path and 'conditioned co-arising' all refer to the six causes, because

> they are all synonyms of *hetu*. According to some, the causes refer to the totality of conditioned *dharma*-s, as is stated in the PrŚ: "What are the *hetu dharma*-s? All the conditioned *dharma*-s.[5]

Similarly, the reality of the four causal conditions (*pratyaya*) must be upheld. The Dārṣṭāntika masters in the MVŚ deny them, asserting that they are no more than conventional terms designated by the various masters. The compilers repudiate this assertion:

> If the conditions (lit.: the fact of the conditions, 諸緣性; *pratyayatā*) are not real existents, then all *dharma*-s are not real existents, since the causes and conditions subsume all *dharma*-s.[6]

In the same text, a question is asked:

> Are those four Great Elements which have not yet arisen also [mutually] co-existent causes?
>
> Answer: They are also co-existent causes because they fall under the category of cause and because they have the cause-characteristic (*hetu-lakṣaṇa*).[7]

The MVŚ compilers here endorse the view that all the Great Elements, whether arisen or not, are reciprocally co-existent causes and quote in support the PrŚ which states "What are the *dharma*-s arisen through causes? Answer: All conditioned *dharma*-s." This implies that the causal nature is intrinsic to the *dharma*-s themselves. In a similar vein, Saṃghabhadra explains that the retribution cause exists in the future period as well:

> ...Although there is necessarily a before-after in the case of a retribution cause, this cause is not established from the view-point of this before-after [sequence]: ... A specific *karma* cause effects a corresponding retribution — this nature (*lakṣaṇa*) can be said to exist in the future period as well, and thus [this cause] can also be established in the future period. However,

from the view-point of the nature of a *dharma*, one speaks of the future [period] anticipatively: such a cause arises before and such an effect arises after; at the stage when the cause has arisen, the posteriority of the effect comes to be established. It is only then that one can speak of a real before-after. It is not the case that there exists any real before-after at the stage when [the *dharma*-s] are not yet arisen. That the causes can be said to exist in the future period is on account of the fact that these causes are not established in dependence on [their] coursing through time, like the case of the co-existent and conjoined causes, etc. [The necessarily conascent *dharma*-s function as co-existent causes to one another in the future period, i.e., at the time when they are co-arising].[8] (See also, *infra*, § 5.5.5).

Likewise, Saṃghabhadra asserts that the nature of *ālambana-pratyaya* being objects of perception is determined — even though they are not being perceived.[9] The *ālambana-pratyaya* comprises the totality of *dharma*-s — past, present, future, as well as the *asaṃskṛta*-s.[10] In fact, the Sarvāstivādins argue they are real because they can function as objects for the arising of *buddhi*. Indeed, it is this causal efficacy that constitutes the very mark of the existent *(sal-lakṣaṇa)*.[11] All existent *dharma*-s have such an efficacy, but only the present *dharma*-s have *kāritra* which is the efficacy of projecting their own fruits.

The same principle applies even in the case of the unconditioned *dharma*-s. Although "the way of establishing causes and effects among the conditioned is not applicable to the case of the unconditioned"[12] in-as-much as the latter transcend space-time and therefore are not directly involved in the cause-effect processes in phenomenal existence, they can, nevertheless, be regarded as causes in the sense that they too function as objects of thought. Saṃghabhadra also argues that the fact that a saint (*ārya*) in his 'direct insight' (*abhisamaya*) sees truly all the four truths — including the unconditioned *dharma* called cessation through deliberation (*pratisamkhyā-nirodha*) — proves the reality of the latter: it has the efficacy of causing the arising of the practitioner's *prajñā* that perceives it.[13] Moreover, they are dynamic forces. Thus, the cessation through deliberation acts to ensure that the acquisition of the defilements so abandoned will absolutely no longer be able to arise.[14] The causal efficacy of *nirvāṇa* is also inferable from the fact that it can have an impact on the mental stream of receptive beings so that they give rise to delight in *nirvāṇa* and disgust towards *saṃsāra*.[15] (See also, § 16.2).

6.2.2. *Dharma*-s as factors of phenomenal existence arisen through causes

The special emphasis on *hetu* on the part of the Sarvāstivādins is also to be understood as their concern to prove the realities of the tri-temporal *dharma*-s by working out a causal doctrine that suffices to account for their arising and dynamic interaction in phenomenal existence. Not only must *dharma*-s as real existents in each case be causally efficacious — hence called conditioning forces — as we have seen above, but as phenomena arisen through causes — hence said to be conditioned — their arising (and ceasing) must also in each case be causally accounted for. As stated in the AKB:

> That which exists as a real entity necessarily has a cause; or it ought to be an unconditioned.[16]

In the Sarvāstivāda perspective, all *dharma*-s have been always existing. As a matter of fact, time is an abstraction on our part derived from their activities.[17] A *dharma* exists throughout time and yet is not permanent as it "courses in time" (*adhvan-saṃcāra*). But as the MVŚ explains, "conditioned *dharma*-s are weak in their intrinsic nature, they can accomplish their activities only through mutual dependence" (cf. *infra*. § 2.4.3.1):

> We declare that the causes have the activities as their fruits, not the entities in themselves (*svabhāva/dravya*). We further declare that the effects have the activities as their causes, not the entities in themselves. The entities in themselves are without transformation throughout time, being neither causes nor effects.[18]

Moreover,

> the tri-temporal *dharma*-s exist throughout time as entities in themselves; there is neither increase nor decrease. It is only on the basis of their activities that they are said to exist or not exist [as phenomena].[19]

But, in turn, their activities necessarily depend on causes and conditions:[20]

> Being feeble in their intrinsic natures, they have no sovereignty (*aiśvarya*). They are dependent on others, they are without their own activity and are unable to do as they wish.[21]

Indeed, given the Sarvāstivāda theory of the unique entities being absolutely isolated from one another in their intrinsic natures, without a proper theory of causality which can account for the arising of and dynamic interplay among them, the Sarvāstivādins would utterly fail to present any version of the central Buddhist teaching of 'conditioned co-arising'. It may be noted in this context that in his *Mūla-madhyamaka-kārikā*, Nāgārjuna proves the non-arising (*anutpāda*) of *dharma*-s precisely by refuting each of the four *pratyaya*-s acknowledged by the Sarvāstivādins.

In brief, this aspect of a *dharma*'s very arising being conditioned by causes and conditions can be discerned in the other major doctrinal term used to describe the factors of phenomenal existence — *saṃskṛta* (see *supra*, § 2.4.3.1). If all *dharma*-s cannot arise except through causes, then the real existence of any given *dharma* must be accounted for by finding its causes of one category or another. Besides, it is only by accounting for its intrinsic characteristic — its phenomenologically cognizable aspect manifested through causes — that its very existence as a real entity can be established. Ultimately, the intrinsic characteristic and the intrinsic nature of a *dharma* are one.[22] Saṃghabhadra in fact argues for the reality of *nirvāṇa* via the experiencibility of its *lakṣaṇa*: "…the *lakṣaṇa* is none other than the *dravya*. Now, since *nirvāṇa* has the *lakṣaṇa* of being cessation (*nirodha*), calmed (*śānta*) etc., it is established that it exists as a real entity (*dravya*)".[23] (See *infra*, § 16.3.1).

6.3. Definitions of the six causes

6.3.1. Efficient cause (*kāraṇa-hetu*)

This is the most comprehensive or generic type of cause: It is any *dharma* that either directly or indirectly — by not hindering — contributes to the arising of another *dharma*. "A conditioned *dharma* has all *dharma*-s, excepting itself, as its *kāraṇa-hetu*, for, as regards its arising, [these *dharma*-s] abide in the state of non-obstructiveness."[24] The MVŚ explains this category as follows:

> What is the efficient cause?
>
> Answer: Conditioned by eye and a visible, visual consciousness arises. This visual consciousness has as its efficient cause the eye, the visible, the *dharma*-s conjoined with it, the *dharma*-s co-existent with it, as well as the ear, sound, auditory consciousness, … the mental organ (*manas*), the mental objects (*dharma*), mental consciousness, [i.e.,] all the *dharma*-s which are material (*rūpin*), immaterial (*arūpin*), visible, invisible, resistant, non-resistant, with-outflow, outflow-free, conditioned, unconditioned, etc. — all *dharma*-s excepting itself. … Efficient (*kāraṇa*) means 'being non-obstructive', 'accomplishing something' (有所辦).[25]

6.3.2. Homogeneous cause (*sabhāga-hetu*)

An exemplification of this cause is the homogeneous causality in which the moral species of the succeeding effect is the same as that of the preceding cause. Thus, in the serial continuity of a *citta* represented by *c1* → *c2* → *c3*, if *c1* is *kuśala*, it functions as the homogeneous cause to generate *c2* as the effect, which is also *kuśala*; *c2* in turn functions as a homogeneous cause to generate *c3,* which is again *kuśala*. According to the Sarvāstivādins, this type of causality obtains in the case of a mental series, and among physical matter. However, both the 'western masters' and the Dārṣṭāntikas deny that *rūpa-dharma*-s can have a homogeneous cause.[26] There are, in fact, other disagreements among the various Sarvāstivāda masters in terms of details concerning the nature and scope of this causal category.[27]

The AKB explains this cause as follows:

> The similar *dharma*-s are the homogeneous causes of *dharma*-s similar [to them], for e.g., the five *skandha*-s which are skillful, are [the homogeneous causes] of the five skillful *skandha*-s, among themselves. Likewise the defiled and the non-defined five *skandha*-s, [in each case, among themselves]...
>
> [But] *dharma*-s belonging to a given category [such as defilements abandonable by insight (*darśanaheya*)][28] and to a given stage [such as the sensual sphere] are [homogeneous causes] only of those belonging to their own category and stage. ...
>
> [Moreover, only] a previously arisen [similar *dharma*] is the homogeneous cause of a subsequent [*dharma*], arisen or not arisen. The future [*dharma*-s] are not homogeneous causes.[29]

In this context, Vasubandhu also records other views on the nature and scope of this cause:

> According to other masters: [Concerning the non-defiled non-defined aggregates —] non-defined matter is [the homogeneous cause] of [the non-defined] five [*skandha*-s]; but the other four [*skandha*-s] are not [the homogeneous cause] of matter. This is because [the matter aggregate] is inferior [in nature[30] to the other aggregates].
>
> [According to some other masters:][31] In a given group-homogeneity (i.e. within the same sentient being), *kalala* is [the homogeneous cause] of the ten states comprising *kalala*, etc.[32] The *arbuda* [state], etc., [each] successively decreasing by one, are [the homogeneous cause of from nine to one] of [the states comprising] *arbuda*, etc. [This is because a later state can serve only as a condition (not as a cause; cf. § 7.2) with regard to the earlier states].[33]
>
> [The Dārṣṭāntikas][34] deny that matter is the homogeneous cause of matter. …[35]

Saṃghabhadra cites,[36] as scriptural evidence of this cause, the following passages:

> "Such a *pudgala* is endowed with skillful and unskillful *dharma*-s. It should be known that in this *pudgala*, the skillful *dharma*-s vanish and the unskillful *dharma*-s appear; but there exists an accompanying (隨俱行; *anusahagata*) root of skillfulness (*kuśala-mūla*) which has not been cut off (*asumucchinna*). On account of its not having been cut off, there is still the possibility of the arising of another root of skillfulness from this root of skillfulness."[37]
>
> "The inclination of a *bhikṣu*'s mind is towards that about which he frequently thinks."[38]
>
> "With nescience (*avidyā*) as cause, he generates defilements; with understanding (*vidyā*) as cause, he is freed from the defilements…"

Having cited the above passage, Saṃghabhadra then explains as follows:

> The past and present homogeneous *dharma*-s, on account of their inducing their own fruits, are established as homogeneous causes.[39]

In Saṃghabhadra's commentary on the AKB explanations that we have quoted above, he does not seem to have any objections to Vasubandhu's explanations. Like Vasubandhu, he also cites the same views of the different masters on the scope of this cause.

In fact, he records two more (*loc. cit.*):

(1) Concerning the non-defiled non-defined five *skandha*-s, some masters maintain that five are the fruits of four (i.e., four are the homogeneous cause of five); [that is,] matter — being inferior in strength (勢力劣故) — is [only] the homogeneous cause of the four other aggregates.[40]

(2) According to some masters: matter on the one hand, and the four other aggregates on the other, are not mutually homogeneous cause. This is because matter is "inferior and of a different species (from the four mental aggregates)" (劣異類故).

This suggests that there were various interpretations in the Sarvāstivāda system on this cause, which were mostly tolerated. Of these views, Saṃghabhadra in fact criticizes only the last two cited above: the one related to the embryonic series and the Dārṣṭāntika view that there is no homogeneous cause among the *rūpa*-s.[41]

At the beginning of the entire discussion in this context, he defines this cause in the following words:

> Those that can nourish and produce the emanation (*niṣyanda*) fruits, whether remote or near, are called homogeneous causes. It is to be understood that this cause obtains in the case of similar *dharma*-s

with regard to similar *dharma*-s, not with regard to those of a different species.[42]

6.3.3. Universal cause (*sarvatraga-hetu*)

Like the homogeneous cause, this cause as well generates an emanation fruit. From this perspective, the universal cause may be considered to be a subset of the homogeneous causes, pertaining to the defiled *dharma*-s alone. There is homogeneity between this cause and its effect in terms of stage (sense sphere, etc.) and of moral species (both are defiled).

However, as the following passage shows, it is to be made a cause distinct from the homogeneous cause because there is no necessary homogeneity in terms of category of abandonability[43] (*nikāya*/*prakāra* — see § 12.6.2):

> The universal *dharma*-s arisen previously and belonging to a given stage are the universal causes of later defiled *dharma*-s belonging to their own stage. … On account of their being a cause applicable to all defiled *dharma*-s, they are established [as a cause] separate from the homogeneous causes and [also] because they are the cause of [defiled *dharma*-s] belonging to other categories as well, for, through their power, defilements belonging to categories different from theirs are produced.[44]

The MVŚ[45] enumerates different opinions as to which defilements constitute the universal causes:

> Some hold that all defilements are universal.
>
> Some hold that the defilements of the five categories of abandonability are all universal.
>
> Some hold that all the defilements abandonable by insight into unsatisfactoriness and its origin are universal.

Some hold that the defilements found in all the three spheres of existence are all universal.

Some hold that the defilements common to all the five categories of abandonability are universal, namely, ignorance, craving, hatred and conceit.

The Dārṣṭāntikas hold that the two defilements, i.e., ignorance (*avidyā*) and craving (*tṛṣṇā*), are universal. Their explanation is as follows: "The root of conditioned co-arising is said to be universal; ignorance is the root of the earlier part (*pūrvānta-koṭi*) of conditioned co-arising, and existence-craving (*bhava-tṛṣṇā*) is the root of the later part (*aparānta-koṭi*) of conditioned co-arising. Thus, they are universal."

The Vibhajyavādins hold that five are universal: ignorance, craving, view, conceit and thought (*citta*).

The Vaibhāṣika view is that three are universal: doubt (*vicikitsā*), view and ignorance, which are abandonable by insight into unsatisfactoriness, the cause of unsatisfactoriness, together with their conjoined and co-existent *dharma*-s.[46]

6.3.4. Retribution cause (*vipāka-hetu*)

This is the karmic cause. That is to say, it leads to a desirable or undesirable karmic retribution. The AKB explains the nature of this cause:

> The unskillful and skillful *dharma*-s are the retribution causes, as they are of the nature of retribution.
>
> Why do the neutral *dharma*-s not bring about retribution? Because they are weak, like rotten seeds.

> Why not the outflow-free [*dharma*-s]? Because they are not moistened by craving, like unmoistened intact seeds.
>
> [Why not those not belonging to any sphere?] Because, not belonging to any sphere, what kind of sphere-specific (*pratisaṃyukta* — bound [to a sphere]) retribution could they bring about?[47]

According to the Dārṣṭāntikas in the MVŚ, "there is no retribution cause apart from volition (*cetanā*), and no retribution fruit apart from sensation (*vedanā*)". According to others, such as the Mahāsāṃghikas, retribution causes and fruits are confined to thought and the thought-concomitants. Against these opinions, the Sarvāstivāda holds that retribution causes and fruits comprise all five *skandha*-s, that is, not only thought and the thought-concomitants but also the matter accompanying thought (*cittānuvṛttaka-rūpa*) and the conditionings disjoined from thought — the ideationless attainment (*asaṃjñī-samāpatti*), the cessation attainment (*nirodha-samāpatti*), all acquisitions which are *akuśala* and *kuśala-sāsrava*, and the accompanying characteristics of the conditioned (*saṃskṛta-lakṣaṇa*-s) — can constitute retribution causes.[48] The retributive *rūpa*-s are the bodily and vocal *karma* — both informative (*vijñapti*) and non-informative (*avijñapti*) (see *infra*, § 13.4). The ideationless attainment can effect the *asaṃjñika*, that is, it can result in an existence in the ideationless realm. However, the vital faculty (*jīvitendriya*), the group-homogeneity (*nikāya-sabhāga*) and the five material faculties pertaining therein are not its retributions, but those of the *karma* in the fourth *dhyāna*. Similarly, the cessation attainment can effect the four *skandha*-s of the sphere of neither ideation-nor-non-ideation (*naiva-saṃjñā-nāsaṃjñā-āyatana*) — excepting the vital faculty and the group-homogeneity therein which are exclusively karmic fruits — as its retributions.[49] Acquisition can effect the following as retributions: (a) matter — visual objects, sound, smell, taste; (b) thought and thought-concomitants — the three types of sensation (pleasant, unpleasant, neutral; (c) conditionings disjoined from thought — acquisition and the four characteristics of the conditioned.[50]

Vipāka-hetu ('retribution-cause') can be taken either as a genitive determinative compound (*tatpuruṣa*): *vipākasya hetuḥ*, i.e., the *vipāka* is the result of the process *vi-√pac*, or as a descriptive compound (*karmadhāraya*): *vipāka eva hetuḥ*: the retribution itself is the cause, i.e., the *vipāka* is that which is ripened (*vipacyate*).[51]

According to the Vaibhāṣikas: *vi* ('different') means *visadṛśa* ('dissimilar') — a *vipāka* is a *pāka* ('maturation') dissimilar from its cause. A retribution cause is never neutral, whereas its fruit is always neutral.[52] Saṃghabhadra explains that *vipāka* may refer to either the cause or effect aspect of the process of maturation:

> What is called *vipāka* may refer to a maturation (*pāka*) separate from the cause or distinct from the cause — these two [explanations] pertain to the effect [aspect]. Or rather, it may refer to the fact that the *karma* that has been done, on reaching the stage of the acquisition of the fruit, can be transformed into being capable of maturing — this [explanation] pertains to the cause [aspect of the process].[53]

6.3.5. Co-existent cause (*sahabhū-hetu*)

This is a new causal category innovated by the Sarvāstivāda. As we shall see (§§ 6.6 ff.), it is of central importance in the causal theory of the school. It became an indispensable doctrinal tool for the Yogācāra theory of cognition only (*vijñaptimātratā*) (§ 6.5).

> **MVŚ**: Question: What is the intrinsic nature of the co-existent cause? Answer: All the conditioned *dharma*-s... Question: What is the meaning of 'co-existent' (*sahabhū*)? Answer: 'Co-existent' means [i] 'not mutually separated (*avinā-bhāva*)', [ii] 'sharing the same effect',

[iii] 'mutually accordant with one another'. This co-existent cause is definitely found in the three periods of times and produces the virile effect (*puruṣakāra-phala*).[54]

AKB: The co-existent [causes] are those that are reciprocally [virile][55] effects… For example: the four Great Elements are co-existent [causes] mutually among themselves; so also, thought and the *dharma*-s that are thought-accompaniments (*cittānuvarttin*); so also the [four] characteristics of the conditioned and the characterized (*lakṣya*) [conditioned *dharma*]. In this way, the whole of the conditioned, where applicable (i.e., where a mutual causal relationship obtains) are co-existent causes. (Vasubandhu adds:) It is to be added that without being effects to each other, a *dharma* is the co-existent cause of its secondary characteristics (*anulakṣaṇa*) but not vice versa. … [The case of the co-existent cause] is like the staying in position of three sticks through their mutual strength/support — this establishes the causal relationship (*hetuphalabhāva*) of the co-existents.[56]

Ny: *The co-existent [causes] are those that are reciprocally virile effects*, on account of the fact that they can arise by virtue of mutual support … *For example: the four Great Elements are co-existent cause mutually among themselves,* … for it is only when the four different kinds of Great Elements assemble together that they can be efficacious in producing the derived matter (*upādāya rūpa*); *so also thought and the dharma-s which are thought-accompaniments; so also the [four] characteristics of the conditioned and the characterized [conditioned dharma]. In this way, the whole of the conditioned, where applicable (i.e., where a mutual causal relationship obtains) are co-existent causes*. (The italicized words are those also found in the AKB). Herein, the scope of the characteristics of the causes [as described by Vasubandhu] is too narrow — the thought-accompaniments and the characteristics [of the conditioned] should in each case be mentioned as co-existent causes amongst themselves. Thus, he should not have said that only those that are reciprocally the effect of one another are co-existent causes. A *dharma* and its secondary characteristics are not reciprocally effects, yet it is a [co-existent-]cause of the latter [although the latter are not its co-existent cause]. … Therefore, the characteristics [of this cause] should be explained thus: Those conditioned *dharma*-s that share the same effect can [also] be considered as co-existent causes; there is no fault [in explaining thus], as it is so explained in the fundamental treatises (*mūla-śāstra*)…[57]

Avatāra: The conditioned *dharma*-s that are fruits of one another or that together bring about a common fruit are named co-existent causes.[58]

6.3.6. Conjoined cause (*saṃprayuktaka-hetu*)

This cause pertains to the domain of the *citta-caitta-dharma*-s. Essentially, it may be considered to be a subset of the co-existent cause.

MVŚ: Question: What are the conjoined causes? Answer: *Dharma*-s that are thought and thought-concomitants. … Question: Why are thought and the thought-concomitants mutually conjoined causes to one another? Answer: Because they are reciprocally causes, arisen through their mutual strength, mutually induced, mutually nourished, mutually strengthened, mutually dependent. This is like two bundles of straw which stay in position through mutual dependence. [Likewise,] when many ropes are combined, a huge log can be dragged; and many people can cross a big river by joining hands together. Because conditioned *dharma*-s are weak in their intrinsic nature, they can accomplish their activities only through mutual dependence. If we were to ask sensation: 'Without ideation, can you [alone] sense/experience an object?' The answer would be: 'No.' The same questions [and answers] apply to the other thoughts and thought concomitants as well.[59]

AKB: The thought and thought-concomitants whose supporting basis is the same are conjoined causes to one another… Thus, the supporting basis of visual consciousness, which is the visual faculty of a given moment, is the very same supporting basis of the [thought-concomitants, i.e.,] sensation, etc., conjoined with it…[60]

Ny: This [conjoined] cause is established because thought and thought concomitants, being conjoined, accomplish the same deed by grasping the same object.[61]

Avatāra: The thought and thought-concomitants that are mutually conjoined with one another and that apprehend a common object are called conjoined causes.[62]

6.3.6.1. The distinction between the conjoined and co-existent causes

MVŚ: Question: What is the difference between the conjoined and the co-existent causes? Some say that there is no difference, as in one [and the same] moment, the sensation and ideation, etc., are both types of causes. Therefore, in this regard, one should say thus: Whichever are conjoined causes are also co-existent causes; some co-existent causes exist which are not conjoined causes, viz., the disjoined co-existent causes. Thus there are differences between the two causes… [Their differences]: conjoined causes have the sense of companionship; co-existent causes have the sense of having a common fruit. The first means having the same supporting basis, mode of understanding and object. The second means having the same production (*jāti*), deterioration (*jarā*), duration (*sthiti*), impermanence (*anityatā*), fruit, emanation and retribution. The first is like holding a stick; the second is like performing an action having held the stick. The first is like [a group of people] joining hands together; the second is like crossing a torrent having held hands together. The first means mutually accordant with one another; the second means not being mutually apart.[63]

AKB: Whatever is a conjoined cause is also a co-existent cause. In what sense then is it a co-existent cause and in what sense is it a conjoined cause? It is a co-existent cause in the sense of reciprocally being effects, like the case of fellow merchants traversing a road through their mutual strength. It is a conjoined cause in the sense of conjunction in terms of the fivefold equality,[64] like the case of these very merchants being engaged in the same activities of eating and drinking, etc.; even if one is lacking, they are not conjoined together.[65]

Ny: What is the difference between these two causes, i.e., the co-existent and the conjoined? To begin with, *dharma*-s that are conjoined causes are also co-existent causes. There exist *dharma*-s that are co-existent causes but not conjoined causes — viz., the [thought-]accompanying matter; *jāti*, etc.; the Great Elements. If a conjoined cause is also a co-existent cause, what, in this case, is the difference in significance between these two causes? It is not the case that the conjoined causes are none other than the co-existent causes, for these two causes differ in their significance. However, in the case where one and the same *dharma* is a conjoined cause as well as a co-existent cause, this is the difference in significance: conjoined causes signify 'not mutually apart'; co-existent causes signify 'having the same fruit'. Again, having the same production (*jāti*), duration (*sthiti*), etc., by virtue of the mutual strength — these are co-existent causes; grasping the same object by virtue of the mutual strength — these are conjoined causes. According to some masters: On account of the meaning of being reciprocally fruits, the co-existent causes are established; this is like the case of fellow merchants who, mutually supported, traverse a risky road together. On account of the meaning of the fivefold equality, the conjoined cause is established; this is like those same fellow merchants having the same experience, same activities of eating, etc. Herein, they are not conjoined even when one is missing, and thus is the fact of their being reciprocally causes universally established.[66]

> ***Avatāra***: The distinction between the conjoined cause and the co-existent cause [may be illustrated] by the example of a caravan of merchants: The merchants, by rendering mutual assistance to one another, are able to pass through a risky road — this is co-existent cause. They consume the same food and drinks — this is conjoined cause.[67]

6.4. Saṃghabhadra's defense of simultaneous causation

Of all the six causes, the co-existent cause is the most controversial. The case of this co-existent cause is the co-existent causality which best exemplifies what we may call, for want of a better English term, 'simultaneous causality' (see below, §§ 6.7.1, 6.7.2). Saṃghabhadra defends at great length the doctrine of simultaneous causation, as represented by this cause, against the Sautrāntika,[68] giving several explanations which are more articulate comparatively to those found in the earlier texts. An additional simile of the lamp in relation to its light is also given as an illustration of this category.[69] He begins his arguments with an examination of the nature of causality, invoking the Buddha's succinct statement of the principle of conditionality:

> This being, that exists. From the arising of this, that arises (*asmin satī'daṃ bhavati / asyo'tpādād idam utpadyate*).

Saṃghabhadra explains:

> Contrary to this are non-existence, non-arising. This is the general characteristic of causality. In [the Buddha's statement above], the first [sentence] illustrates the case of the conascent (*sahaja*, *sahajāta*) cause; the second further illustrates that of the previously-arisen (*agraja*, *pūrvaja*) cause.

In insisting that the co-existent cause should also include the meaning of 'sharing the same effect' besides that of 'being mutually effects',

Saṃghabhadra really has done no more than to keep in line with the MVŚ orthodoxy (cf. second meaning in § 6.3.5). Skandhila's **Abhidharmāvatāra*, another post-AKB Vaibhāṣika/Sarvāstivāda work, also mentions these two meanings explicitly:

> The conditioned *dharma*-s which are effects of one another or which together bring about a common effect are named co-existent causes — e.g., the Great Elements; the [conditioned *dharma*-s which are] characterized and the [four] conditioned characteristics; the thought and the thought-accompaniments. These are [in each case co-existent causes] for one another.[70]

Saṃghabhadra further articulates that in fact there are only three situations where such a simultaneous causality obtains:

> We do not concede that cause-effect relationship obtains reciprocally in all cases of the conascent: ... It obtains only [i] among those that share the same effect; or [ii] that are reciprocally effects; or [iii] where by the force of this, that *dharma* can arise. Such conascent [*dharma*-s] have a cause-effect relationship, [i.e., are co-existent causes].[71]

The third case is consistent with the definition of the virile effect — the effect corresponding to the co-existent cause (see infra, § 7.3.2.1). More generally:

> ...whatever are necessarily conascent, are necessarily cause one to another. ... although [*dharma*-s] may share the same cause of arising, those that are not reciprocally cause to one another do not necessarily arise together. [Conversely,] those that are necessarily conascent definitely arise with one another as reciprocal causes [exercising their causal functions at the time of their arising]. Accordingly, the conascent causes (including co-existent and conjoined causes) are universally established.[72]

This proposition may be seen as corresponding to the sense of necessary inseparability of *dharma*-s which are reciprocally co-existent causes given in the MVŚ (*supra*, § 6.3.5). This criterion, said to be laid down by the ancient logicians, representing the principle of inductive reasoning, is also invoked by the Vaibhāṣikas in the AKB in their dispute with the Sautrāntikas:

> For, according to the Logicians, this is the characteristic of a cause-effect [relationship]: When A exists or does not exist, B necessarily exists or does not exist; then A is the cause and B the effect (*etad dhi hetuhetumato lakṣaṇam ācakṣate haitukāḥ / yasya bhāvābhāvayoḥ yasya bhāvābhāvau niyamataḥ sa hetur itaro hetumān iti /*). Now in the case of the co-existent *dharma*-s, when one exists, all exist; when one does not exist, all do not exist. Thus, they are in a mutual cause-effect relationship.[73]

6.5. Explanations in the Yogācāra system

It is interesting to note that whereas the Sautrāntika — one of the precursors of the Mahāyāna Yogācāra — vehemently refuted the Vaibhāṣika doctrine of the co-existent causes, the Yogācāra takes it over together with its subset, the conjoined cause, without hesitation (see below, § 6.7.2). Thus, the *Abhidharma-samuccaya* of Asaṅga (traditionally the older brother of the author of the AKB) includes the notion under *pratyaya*-s which function by way of assistance/companionship (*sahāyataḥ*) and of common action (*saṃpratpattitaḥ*):[74]

> How [are *pratyaya*-s] by reason of companionship? Those *dharma*-s that arise in co-existence (*sahābhāvena*) not with any one of them lacking (*nānyatamavaikalyena*), such as the Elements (*bhūta*) and those derived from the Elements (*bhautika*). How are they by reason of common action? Those *dharma*-s that, being in co-existence, act together (*saṃpratipadyante*) on the object.

Sthiramati[75] comments as follows:

> The four Great Elements and *rūpa*-s, etc., derived from the Elements exist where possible, but not necessarily in all conglomerations. Thus, where [such a conglomeration] exists, it arises as a whole without [the members] being separated from one another. By way of the necessity of companionship, the co-existent cause is established. The mention of the Elements and those derived from the Elements is to be understood as a mere example; thought and the thought-concomitants [are also to be subsumed under this category] on account of the necessity of their mutual inseparability.
>
> [**Question**:] If so, there ought not to be the separate establishment of the conjoined cause since thought and the thought-concomitants are included under the co-existent causes.
>
> [**Answer:**] Although this is so, nevertheless [it is separately established] on account of a different signification: Those *dharma*-s that act on an object [necessarily] in co-existence and not with any one member lacking are established as conjoined causes by reason of their common action — not merely on account of their co-existence —as in the case of thought and the thought-concomitants.

In the **Mahāyāna-saṃgraha*, Asaṅga explains the *ālaya-vijñāna* and the *bīja* being mutually in a simultaneous causal relationship, giving the same examples as the Vaibhāṣikas.[76] For the Yogācāra, simultaneous causation is causality in the true sense:

> The *ālaya-vijñāna* and those defiled *dharma*-s are simultaneously cause to each other. How can [such a simultaneous causation] be observed? This is like the simultaneous arising of a flame and the burning of the wick being mutually [caused]. It is also like reed-bundles which, mutually supporting one another, [stand up] simultaneously without collapsing. The principle herein of mutual causation is to be understood likewise. Just as the *ālaya-vijñāna* serves as the cause for the defiled *dharma*-s, those defiled *dharma*-s likewise serve as the cause for the

> *ālaya-vijñāna*. It is only on such a basis [of simultaneous causation] that the *hetu-pratyaya*-s are established, for [apart from this], the other *hetu-pratyaya*-s are not apperceived (*na upalabhyante*).

In their commentaries on the above passage, both Vasubandhu[77] and Asvabhāva[78] state explicitly that this simultaneous causation refers to the co-existent cause. In the Chinese version of the *Vijñaptimātratā-siddhi*,[79] Dharmapāla also quotes the same passage in support of his view that there are also *bīja*-s which are newly engendered by the repeated perfuming (*vāsanā*) of the actual *dharma*. The same text,[80] again using the same similes, remarks further:

> The perfuming engenders the *bīja*; the *bīja* gives rise to manifestation (*samudācāra*), [namely, the actual *dharma*] — in the manner that a co-existent cause produces a virile fruit. The anterior *bīja* successively engenders a posterior *bīja* of the same species — in the manner that a homogeneous cause induces an emanation fruit. These two types [of causal processes] constitute causality (*hetu-pratyayatā*). Apart from these, other *dharma*-s are not *hetu-pratyaya*-s: If they happen to be called *hetu-pratyaya*-s, one should understand them as metaphorical expressions.

6.6. Summary of the notion of the co-existent cause given in the various sources

The definitions and examples given in the above sources (§ 6.3.5–6.3.6.1) are not always entirely distinct. Some are more or less identical, and sometimes what one source gives as examples of the co-existent cause, another would include under the conjoined cause. The variety in these descriptions suggests that there had been some effort on the part of the Sarvāstivādins to integrate various explanations passed down in their tradition over time. On the other hand, the near identical definitions seen in many cases, from sources stretching over several centuries (from the MVŚ to Ny), also indicate that the notions of the co-existent and conjoined causes must have been fairly well delineated and understood in their tradition. We may broadly classify these definitions or descriptions of the essential characteristics of co-existent/conjoined causes into three:

(1) In the sense that the conascent *dharma*-s are reciprocally causes, reciprocally (virile) effects,[81] mutually induced, arisen through mutual strength, necessarily conascent, etc. The very existence of one is necessarily dependent on the other.

(2) In the sense that the conascent *dharma*-s are mutually dependent and suitably coordinated and strengthened to give rise to a common effect or accomplish a common causal event simultaneous to them.

(3) In the sense that between the two conascent *dharma*-s, one is arisen necessarily through the strength of the other. Necessarily conascent *dharma*-s function as co-existent causes at the time of the arising of the *dharma*, i.e., in the future period. Thus, "all conditioned *dharma*-s have production (*jāti*) [— which exercises its function at the time when a *dharma* is arising], etc., as their co-existent causes".[82]

The former two senses may be said to be more specific to this causal category, attested in all the sources we have examined. The third, a more general sense, is logically deduced and made explicit by Saṃghabhadra.

The Yogācārins inherited the doctrine of simultaneous causation, even though, holding the standpoint of 'present only exist' as they do — as opposed to the tri-temporal existence — they must relegate the functioning of this causal principle exclusively to the present period of time.

6.7. The doctrinal importance of the co-existent cause for the Sarvāstivāda

6.7.1. The co-existent cause and Sarvāstivāda realism

The doctrine of simultaneous causation lends support to the Sarvāstivāda doctrine of direct perception which, in turn, again reinforced their doctrine of pluralistic realism. This is in contrast to the Sautrāntika theory of indirect perception which eventually paves the way for the idealistic Yogācāra theory of *vijñaptimātratā*. For the Sarvāstivādins, one can be absolutely certain about the existence of external objects because our five senses directly perceive them. Thus, within a single moment of visual perception, the visual faculty, the object and the corresponding visual consciousness all arise simultaneously. All three function as co-existent causes. This is, in fact, one of Saṃghabhadra's arguments for the co-existent cause:

> It contradicts the principle of 'conditioned co-arising' [to hold that there are no conascent causes]. Thus the *sūtra* says, 'Conditioned by the visual faculty and the visual object, there arises visual consciousness.' [If the visual faculty, the visual object and the visual consciousness were not simultaneous,] then the visual faculty and visual object produced in the preceding moment ought not to be the supporting basis and the perceptual object, [respectively,] for the visual consciousness of the succeeding moment, since, [in that case, the latter] exists and [the former are] non-existent. One cannot call an absolute non-existent (*atyantābhāva*) a supporting basis or a perceptual object. The same would apply here: At the time when the visual consciousness arises, the visual faculty and the visual object have already ceased. This would mean that without any conditions assisting, the visual consciousness arises by itself! This is due to the fact that non-existent *dharma*-s cannot serve as supporting basis, and that visual consciousness can take only a present object. If the visual faculty, the visual object and the visual consciousness do not arise simultaneously, it would entail that the visual faculty and visual objects do

> not serve as conditions for visual consciousness. Or, the auditory faculty and sound, etc., would also serve as conditions for visual consciousness, being equally unrelated to visual consciousness.[83]

But more importantly, this doctrine is indispensable for the fundamental thesis of *sarvāstitva*. Of the four major arguments put forward for the thesis — (a) *uktatvāt*, (b) *dvayāt*, (c) *sadviṣayāt*, (d) *phalāt*[84] — the first is simply an inference from the Buddha's mention of past and future objects. (c) and (d) are the only two logical arguments (*yuktitaḥ*), and (b) essentially has the same stress as (c), supported by the Buddha's own statement. (c) argues that since the object of any perception must be existent, the fact that the mind can think of past and future objects then proves the reality/existence of past and future *dharma*-s. (d) argues that past *dharma*-s must exist since a past *karma* is causally efficacious in generating a present *vipāka*. Now it must be noted that these two logical arguments cannot stand unless the simultaneous causality — in the sense that the cause and the effect must be existent at the same time — as exemplified by the *sahabhū-hetu* is conceded: Both require that the cause and the effect exist simultaneously. But it should be borne in mind that, in the Sarvāstivāda, "*existing* simultaneously" does not necessarily mean "*arising* simultaneously". When the cause and the effect do *arise* simultaneously — i.e., co-exist (*saha-bhū*) in the present moment — we have the case of the *sahabhū-hetu* (see § 6.7.2).

6.7.2. The co-existent cause as the only valid paradigm for causation

In Saṃghabhadra's argument above, the visual organ and object (causes) must be conascent with the visual perception (effect). A non-existent cause cannot be efficacious. In this case, all the three must exist at the present moment.

In general, if *A* causes *B*, both *A* and *B* must be existent at the same time — although they may belong to different time periods with respect to their own temporal frame of reference. That is: *A* may be past or present or future, and *B* may also be past or present or future — *but they must co-exist, although not necessarily be conascent*. To borrow Dharmatrāta's terminology, they are both existent, but not necessarily of the same 'mode of existence' (*bhāva*); or in Ghoṣaka's terminology, they do not necessarily have the same 'time-characteristic' (*cf.* § 5.2). Where *A* and *B* are necessarily conascent, i.e., both existing at the same *present* moment, we have the category known as the co-existent cause. In fact, in the Sarvāstivāda conception, all *dharma*-s in their essential nature have always been existent; it is only a matter of inducing their arising through causes and conditions. This is the fundamental principle underlining the Sarvāstivāda doctrine of causality (§ 6.2.2). Past and future *dharma*-s are also endowed with efficacies including that of actually giving an effect, although it is only a present *dharma* that has *kāritra* — the efficacy of establishing the specific causal relationship with the *dharma* to be produced as its effect.

We saw above that in arguing that the retribution fruit exists in the future period as well, Saṃghabhadra states that the establishment of *dharma*-s as causes is not dependent on their 'coursing in time', giving the examples of the co-existent and conjoined causes (*supra*, § 6.2.1). In that context, a question is raised: "Is it not the case that the establishment of the co-existent cause is relative to the middle time period (*adhvan*) [i.e., the present period]?" In the following reply, Saṃghabhadra makes an important clarification on the notion of the co-existent cause:

> This objection is unreasonable, for [such an establishment] is an implicit one (*neyārtha*) — [properly speaking,] the co-existent causes are so called on account of their existing at the same time (俱時有故); the meaning is that they are reciprocally cause and effect.[85]

Now, since for the Sarvāstivādins both the cause and the effect necessarily exist simultaneously, Saṃghabhadra's explanation here amounts to stating that in the final analysis, the co-existent cause is simply a special case of simultaneous causation obtaining among the necessarily conascent *dharma*-s. The co-existent cause then actually exemplifies the general case of simultaneous causation in which a distinct *A* generates a distinct *B* — both existing simultaneously. This fact can also be seen in the definition of the virile effect, the effect of the co-existent cause, which is essentially a general statement of causality:

> That [conditioned *dharma* (*B*)], which is born from the force of another (*A*), is the fruit [of that force (*A*) — a fruit] born of a virile action.[86]

It is no wonder that the Vaibhāṣikas exerted great effort in defending the validity of this causal category. Failure in this respect is tantamount to failure in establishing the Sarvāstivāda doctrine of causality as a whole — which, in an important way, is tantamount to failure in establishing the thesis of *sarvāstitva*.

The case of a homogeneous cause generating an emanation fruit as its own next moment of existence is an exception, as it involves not two ontologically distinct entities but simply the arising of a given entity itself in the next moment of its series.

The Yogācāra not only accepts the Sarvāstivāda position as regards causation, but is more explicit in stating that there is no other real causality outside that represented by the co-existent and conjoined causes.

6.8. Conclusion

The Sarvāstivāda is also known as the Hetuvāda probably owing to their special concern with the theory of causality. On the one hand, real entities (*dharma*-s) — the unconditioned being no exception — must be shown to be causal forces. On the other, the arising of and dynamic interplay among the conditioned *dharma*-s in phenomenal existence must be accounted for by an articulate theory of causes.

It is possible that the six-*hetu* doctrine was articulated in addition to the earlier four-*pratyaya* doctrine mainly because of the need to highlight the co-existent cause which exemplifies the school's fundamental principle of causality that cause and effect necessarily exist simultaneously, even though their modes (*bhāva*) of existence may differ — either past, present or future. Moreover, it corroborates importantly the thesis of *sarvāstitva*.

In the more specific or narrower sense, the co-existent causal relationship obtains where *dharma*-s are either reciprocally cause and effect to one another or together bring about a common effect. More generally, all necessarily conascent *dharma*-s are co-existent causes. For the Yogācārins who hold the 'present only exists' standpoint, this causal category becomes all the more important for their theory of perfuming. Accordingly, the *sahabhūhetu-puruṣakāraphala* causation came to be more explicitly emphasized by them as causality *par excellence*.

NOTES

[1] Ny, 416b–c.

[2] MVŚ, 79a–c.

[3] T 26, 773a, 920c–921a.

[4] T 49, 15b.

[5] MVŚ, 979c.

[6] MVŚ, 680c.

[7] MVŚ, 82a.

[8] Ny, 444a–444b.

[9] Ny, 448b.

[10] Ny, 447b.

[11] Ny, 621c–622a.

[12] Ny, 429a.

[13] Ny, 432a.

[14] *Cf.* TA(U-J), vol. I, 219.

[15] Ny, 431c.

[16] See AKB(C), T 29, 152c. The context here is the refutation of reality of the *pudgala* proposed by the Vātsīputrīya.

[17] MVŚ, 393c.

[18] *Ibid.*, 105c.

[19] *Ibid.*, 396a.

[20] *Ibid.*, 108c.

[21] *Ibid.*, 283b.

[22] MVŚ, 196c.

[23] Ny, 432b.

[24] AKB, 82: *saṃskṛtasya hi dharmasya svabhāvavarjyāḥ sarvadharmāḥ kāraṇahetuḥ / utpādaṃ prati* (note error in Pradhan's text) *avighnabhāvāvasthānāt //*

[25] MVŚ, 104a. Saṃghabhadra (Ny, 416c) quotes the same *sūtra* passage here to show that the *kāraṇa-hetu* is taught by the Buddha in the *sūtra*.

[26] MVŚ, 682c — no reason given for the denial.

[27] See AKB, 85.

[28] For the five categories of defilements, see *infra*, § 12.6.2.

[29] AKB, 85: *sadṛśā dharmāḥ sadṛśānāṃ dharmāṇāṃ sabhāgahetus tadyathā kuśalāḥ pañcaskandhāḥ kuśalānām anyonyaṃ... /* ***svanikāyabhuvaḥ*** *svo nikāyo bhūśca eṣāṃ ta ime svanikāyabhuvaḥ ... pūrvotpannāḥ paścimānām utpannānutpannānāṃ sabhāgahetuḥ / anāgatā naiva sabhāgahetuḥ /*

[30] Following Saṃghabhadra (Ny, 422a).

[31] Following Saṃghbadra (Ny, 422a): 有餘師言...

[32] The ten states in the development starting from the embryo to the post-embryo existence are: *kalala*, *arbuda*, *peśin*, *ghana*, *praśākhā*, *bāla*, *kumāra*, *yuvan*, *madhya* and *vṛddha*. (AKB, 130)

[33] This reason is given in Ny, 422a.

[34] Ny, 422a.

[35] AKB, 85.

[36] Ny, 416c.

[37] This passage is quoted in AKB(F), vol. I, 245, n. 4. La Vallée Poussin also gives the corresponding Pāli version: *Aṅguttara*, iii, 315.

[38] 於彼彼多隨尋伺, 即於彼彼心多趣入 ... *Cf.* M, i, 115: *yaṃ yad eva ... bhikkhu bahulaṃ anuvitakketi anuvicāreti tathā tathā nati hoti cetaso...*

[39] Ny, 416c.

[40] This view is not given in AKB, but it is recorded in AKB(C)

[41] Ny, 422a.

[42] Ny, 422a.

[43] AKB, 65: *yadi sarvatragahetor api samānaṃ phalaṃ kasmān na sabhāgahetor eveṣyate / yasmāt bhūmitaḥ kliṣṭatayā cāsya sādṛśyaṃ na tu prakārataḥ /*

[44] AKB, 89: *svabhūmikāḥ pūrvotpannāḥ sarvatragā dharmāḥ paścimānāṃ kliṣṭānāṃ dharmāṇaṃ sarvatraga-hetuḥ / ... kliṣṭadharma-sāmānyakāraṇatvenāyaṃ*

sabhāgahetuḥ pṛthak vyavasthāpyate / nikāyāntarīyāṇām api hetutvād eṣāṃ hi prabhāveṇānyanaikāyikā api kleśā upajāyante /

45 MVŚ, 90c.

46 *Cf.* also Ny, 416c.

47 AKB, 89: *akuśalāḥ kuśalāsravāśca dharmā vipākahetuḥ / vipākadharmatvāt / kasmādavyākṛtā dharmāḥ vipākaṃ na nirvarttayanti / durbalatvāt / pūtibījavat / kasmānnānāsravāḥ / tṛṣṇānabhiṣyanditatvāt / anabhiṣyanitasārabījavat / apratisaṃyuktā hi kiṃ pratisaṃyuktaṃ vipākam abhinirvarttayeyuḥ /* Also *cf.* MVŚ, 98b-c.

48 MVŚ, 96a–c.

49 Also *cf.* MVŚ, 615a–b.

50 MVŚ, 97a, 263c; for the meaning of *savipāka*, see MVŚ, 98c.

51 Ny, 427b.

52 AKB, 89; MVŚ, 264b, 741c, etc.

53 Ny, 427b.

54 MVŚ, 85b.

55 In Xuan Zang's translation of both the AKB (T 29, 30b) and Ny, the word *puruṣakāra-phala* is found. Paramārtha's translation (T 29, 188b) agrees with the Sanskrit which has only *phala*.

56 AKB, 83–85: *sahabhūr ye mithaḥphalāḥ / ... yathā ... catvāri mahābhūtāny anyonyaṃ sahabhūhetuḥ / cittaṃ cittānuvarttināṃ dharmāṇāṃ te'pi tasya / saṃskṛtalakṣaṇāni lakṣyasya so'pi teṣām / evaṃ kṛtvā sarvameva saṃskṛtaṃ sahabhūhetur yathāyogam / vinmāpi cānyonyaphalatvena dharmo'nulakṣaṇānāṃ sahabhūhetur na tāni tasyety upasaṃkhyātavyam ... tridaṇḍānyonyabalāvasthānavat ... sahabhuvāṃ hetuphalabhāvaḥ sidhyati //*

57 Ny, 417c.

58 *Entrance*, 142, § 5x.1.2.

59 MVŚ, 80a–b.

60 AKB, 88: *samāna āśrayo yeṣāṃ te cittacaittāḥ anyonyaṃ saṃprayuktaka hetuḥ / ... tadyathā ya eva cakṣurindriyakṣaṇaś cakṣurvijñānasyāśrayaḥ sa eva tatsaṃprayuktānāṃ vedanādīnām eva ... //*

61 *Ibid.*, 416c.

[62] *Entrance*, 142.

[63] MVŚ, 88b.

[64] The fivefold sameness or equality (*pañcadhā samatā*) — for the mental constituents to be said to be in conjunction — are: 1. they must be supported by the same sense organ (*āśraya-samatā*); 2. they must take the same object (*ālambana-samatā*); 3. they must have the same mode of activity (*ākāra-samatā*); 4. they must be simultaneous (*kāla-samatā*); 5. they must in each case be of a singular substance (*dravya-samatā*): in one *citta* is conjoined one *vedanā*, one *saṃjñā*, etc. (*cf.* AKB, 62; also *cf. Entrance*, 91, and note 301).

[65] AKB, 88: *yaḥ saṃprayuktakahetuḥ sahabhūheturapi saḥ / atha kenārthena sahabhūhetuḥ kena saṃprayuktakahetuḥ / anyonyaphalārthena sahabhūhetuḥ / saha sārthikānyonyabalamārgaprayoṇ(g)avat / pañcabhiḥ samatābhiḥ saṃprayoārthena saṃprayuktakahetuḥ / teṣām eva sārthikānāṃ samānānnapānādiparibhogakriyāprayo gavat / ekenāpi hi vinā sarveṇa na saṃprayujyante //*

[66] Ny, 425c.

[67] *Entrance*, 142.

[68] Ny, 417c–421c.

[69] We have discussed the controversy in Ny in detail in "The Sarvāstivāda Doctrine of Simultaneous Causality" (Numata Yehan Lecture on Buddhist Thoughts, University of Calgary, 2000. This was also subsequently published in *Journal of Buddhist Studies*, Vol. I, Colombo, 2003, 17 ff.). In this lecture we have given a detailed refutation of Kenneth K. Tanaka's claim that the *sahabhū-hetu* does not constitute a case of causation and that it "is not responsible for the production of *dharmas"* (*cf.* Kenneth K. Tanaka, "Simultaneous Relation (*Sahabhū-hetu*): A Study in Buddhist Theory of Causation", in *Journal of the International Association of Buddhist Studies*, Vol. 8, No. 1, 91–111).

[70] *Cf. Entrance*, 142.

[71] Ny, 419c.

[72] Ny, 420b.

[73] AKB, 84.

[74] *Abhidharma-samuccaya*, ed. Pradhan, P (Santiniketan, 1950), 28 f.

[75] *Abhidharma-samuccaya-bhāṣya*, ed. Tatia, N (Patna, 1976), 37. According to the Tibetan tradition (Tāranātha), Sthiramati studied both the *Abhidharmakośa-bhāṣya* and the *Abhidharma-samuccaya* under Vasubandhu.

[76] T no. 1594, 134c.

[77] T no. 1597, 328b.

[78] T no. 1598, 388b.

[79] T no. 1585, 8c.

[80] *Ibid.*, 10a.

[81] AKB, 96; also see Vy, 225.

[82] MVŚ, 82a–82b.

[83] *Ibid.*, 420c–421a.

[84] AKB, 295 f.; also *cf. supra*, § 3.3.1.

[85] Ny, 444b.

[86] AKB, 96. Saṃghabhadra (Ny, 436a) comments: "Herein, *puruṣa-kāra*, *puruṣa-bala*, *puruṣa-sāmarthya*, *puruṣa-śakti* — all these have the same meaning: As the efficacies (*gong-neng*) of *dharma*-s are like virile actions, they are called virile action (*puruṣakāra*); just as a strong man is called a lion because he is like a lion."

7. Theory of Causality II
The Four Conditions and the Five Fruits

7.1. Doctrine of the four conditions (*pratyaya*)

As we have noted above (*supra,* § 6.1), the doctrine of the four conditions preceded that of the six causes. The Sarvāstivāda asserts that the former were taught by the Buddha in the *sūtra-piṭaka*. Saṃghabhadra states that the efficacies of the conditions are in fact infinite, for the arising of *dharma*-s depends on the assemblage of numerous conditions, but that the Buddha mentioned only four in brief.[1] Among the extant Sarvāstivāda texts, it is in Devaśarman's *Vijñānakāya* (*ca.* 1st C.E.) that we first come across an elaborative exposition of the four conditions.[2] In a typically Abhidharmic manner, the conditions are discussed in relation to the six consciousnesses:

> There is the group (*kāya*) of six consciousnesses: visual, auditory, olfactory, gustatory, bodily and mental consciousnesses. Visual consciousness has four conditions: 1. condition qua cause (*hetu-pratyaya*), 2. equal-immediate condition (*samanantara-pratyaya*), 3. condition qua object (*ālambana-pratyaya*), 4. condition of dominance (*adhipati-pratyaya*).
>
> > Which are [its] conditions qua cause? Those *dharma*-s that are co-existent and conjoined with it.
> >
> > Which are [its] equal-immediate conditions? Those thought and thought-concomitant *dharma*-s immediately after (*samanantaram*) which such a visual consciousness has arisen (*utpanna*) [or] will arise (*utpatsyate*).
> >
> > What are [its] conditions qua objects? All the visibles.
> >
> > What are [its] conditions of dominance? All the *dharma*-s other than itself.
>
> These are said to be the four conditions for visual consciousness. …
>
> > Whose condition qua cause is such a visual consciousness? Those *dharma*-s that are co-existent and which are conjoined with it.
> >
> > Whose equal-immediate condition [is it]? Those thought and thought-concomitant *dharma*-s that have arisen or will arise immediately after the visual consciousness.
> >
> > Whose condition qua object [is it]? Those thought and thought-concomitants that take this [visual consciousness] as object.
> >
> > Whose condition of dominance [is it]? All *dharma*-s other than itself.

> Just as in the case of visual consciousness, likewise are those of auditory, olfactory, gustatory, bodily and mental consciousnesses.[3]

The following is another example from the text which better illustrates its method of exhaustive investigation. The discussion, under the section on the condition qua object, pertains to the possible types of temporal object that a visual consciousness can take:

> There is the group (*kāya*) of six consciousnesses: visual, auditory, olfactory, gustatory, bodily and mental consciousnesses. This group of six consciousnesses is either past, present or future.
>
> In the case of past visual consciousnesses:
>
> > Are there any that take a past, but not a future or present object?
> > Are there any that take a future, but not a past or present object?
> > Are there any that take a present, but not a past or future object?
> > Are there any that take a past or a present, but not a future object?
> > Are there any that take a future or a present, but not a past object?
> > Are there any that take a past or a future, but not a present object?
> > Are there any that take a past or a future or a present object?
>
> As in the case of past visual consciousnesses, the same [analysis is to be applied] in the cases of future and present visual consciousnesses.
>
> As in the case of visual consciousness, the same [analysis is to be applied] in those of auditory, olfactory, gustatory, bodily and mental consciousnesses.
>
> > All past visual consciousnesses take past objects; the other alternatives (*pāda*) are not available.
> > A future visual consciousness may take a past, future or present object.
> > All present visual consciousnesses take present objects; the other alternatives are not available.

> As in the case of visual consciousness, the same applies in those of auditory, olfactory, gustatory, bodily and mental consciousnesses.
>
> > All past, future and present mental consciousnesses should be said to take all *dharma*-s as objects.[4]

Not all Sarvāstivādins, however, would recognize the reality of the conditions. The MVŚ informs us that the early Dārṣṭāntikas and others[5] deny their reality. The Bhadānta too declares that they are unreal, being nothing more than terminologies conceptually designated by the Abhidharma masters. The MVŚ compilers defend the Ābhidharmika position:

> If it is held that the conditions are devoid of reality, then it would imply that all *dharma*-s are devoid of reality, since all four conditions completely subsume all *dharma*-s: The condition qua cause subsumes all conditioned *dharma*-s; the equal-immediate condition subsumes all past and present *dharma*-s other than the very last thought and thought-concomitant *dharma*-s of the past and present *arhat*-s. The condition qua object and the condition of dominance [each] subsumes the totality of *dharma*-s. …
>
> Moreover, if the conditions are unreal in nature, there would not be the possibility of transforming the three grades of wisdom. The inferior grade of wisdom will permanently be inferior; the medium grade permanently medium; the superior grade permanently superior. But the fact is that wisdom can change from being inferior to being medium, from being medium to being superior. Accordingly, the conditions must exist as real entities, for they are efficacious [in bringing about these changes]. …[6]

In regard to the mutual subsumption (*saṃgraha*) between the causes and the conditions, the MVŚ mentions two opinions:

> **Question**: Do the causes subsume the conditions, or do the conditions subsume the causes?

Answer: They mutually subsume each other, accordingly as the case may be: The first five causes constitute the condition qua cause; the efficient cause constitutes the other three conditions.

According to some: the conditions subsume the causes, but the causes do not subsume the conditions: The first five causes constitute condition qua cause; the efficient cause constitutes the condition of dominance; the immediate condition and the condition qua object are not subsumed by any cause.[7]

In regard to the arising and ceasing of a *dharma,* for the Sarvāstivāda Ābhidharmikas, both require causes and conditions. This is in contrast to the Dārṣṭāntika view that only arising, but not ceasing, requires causes and conditions.[8] But since the Sarvāstivāda holds that all *dharma*-s — causes and conditions included — are ever present, why do *dharma*-s not arise and cease incessantly? The MVŚ records several responses to this question:

The Venerable Vasumitra explains thus: "A *dharma* arises as a result of having assembled with one production (i.e., the disjoint conditioning *jāti*; see § 11.3.5); it ceases as a result of having assembled with one impermanence (i.e., the disjoint conditioning *anityatā*/*vyaya*; see § 11.3.5). [Each *dharma*] not assembling with two or more production and impermanence, how can *dharma*-s arise and cease incessantly?" He further explains thus: "Having arisen as a result of being assembled with causes and conditions, being submerged by a continuous series of moments that follow it is unable to re-arise. It is like the case of a person who, having fallen from a cliff, is further being continuously submerged by the mud falling from above. At the time, he cannot even move, not to speak of getting up.

According to the Bhadanta: the assembled causes and conditions being temporary, how can *dharma*-s arise and cease incessantly?

> Venerable Buddhadeva explains thus: "The activity of arising and ceasing of a *dharma* ought to occur only once in each case. If a *dharma* arises again and again, or ceases again and again, then it would not be having activity. Hence, *dharma*-s do not arise and cease incessantly."[9]

The first explanation above, by Vasumitra, represents the Vaibhāṣika view: In the arising of a *dharma*, the disjoint conditioning *jāti* must exercise its function. At the same time, it is equally emphasized that the ability of *jāti* in producing a *dharma* can be exercised only when an assemblage of causes and conditions, required for the arising of a the *dharma*, obtains.[10]

The MVŚ contains various other discussions on the four conditions. The following are two more examples:

> **Question**: Of these four conditions, which are superior, which are inferior?
>
> **Answer**: According to some: the condition qua cause is superior, the others are inferior, for it is when there is an increase in cause that arising or ceasing occurs.
>
> **According to some**: the equal-immediate condition is superior, the others are inferior, for it can give way to the gateway of the noble path.
>
> **According to some**: the condition qua cause is superior, the others are inferior, for it is the support for the [arising of] thought and thought-concomitants.
>
> **According to some**: the condition of dominance is superior, the others are inferior, for it does not hinder the arising and ceasing of *dharma*-s.
>
> **The correct position** (如是說者): All are superior, all are inferior, for the efficacies are distinctive….

Question: Following the deficiency of which condition does *parinirvāṇa* occur?

Answer: According to some: following that of the condition qua cause, for the cycle of *saṃsāra* is on account of the force of the condition qua cause; *saṃsāra* is abandoned when the condition qua cause is abandoned.

According to some: following that of the equal-immediate condition, for *parinirvāṇa* occurs upon the discontinuation of the last thought of an *arhat*.

According to some: following that of the condition qua object, for *parinirvāṇa* occurs when the *jñeya*-s (the objects of knowledge) do not generate the subsequent thought and thought-concomitant *dharma*-s.

According to some: following that of the condition of dominance; for after the last thought of an *arhat*, there is the complete extinction without there being any non-hindrance.

The correct position: *parinirvāṇa* occurs following the deficiency of the four conditions, for at the time of *parinirvāṇa*, the *arhat* attains *parinirvāṇa* without the *dharma*-s subsumable as the four conditions exercising any activity with regard to his serial continuity (*santati*).[11]

7.1.1. Condition qua cause (*hetu-pratyaya*)

This is the condition in its capacity as direct cause in the production of an effect — it is the cause functioning as the condition. In the example of the growth of a fruit plant: the condition qua cause is comparable to the seed. However, it is a common tenet of all schools of Buddhism that nothing is produced by a single cause (§ 2.4.3.1),[12] even though in the analysis of the causal complex, the main cause can be singled out. Of the six causes, all except the efficient cause are conditions qua cause.[13] Strictly speaking, however, some of the efficient causes should also come under this category if they make some positive contribution in the causal process. As we have seen above, this condition subsumes all the causes except the efficient cause. It comprises the totality of conditioned *dharma*-s.[14]

7.1.2. Immediate condition (*samanantara-pratyaya*)

A *citta* or *caitta* serves as a condition for the arising of the succeeding *citta* or *caitta*: It both gives way to and induces the arising of the next *citta-caitta* in the series. The AKB explains as follows:

> With the exception of the final [*citta-caitta*-s] of an *arhat*, the *citta-caitta*-s that have arisen are the equal-immediate conditions. This condition is equal as well as immediate, hence 'equal-immediate condition'... Why are the last *citta-caitta*-s of an *arhat* not equal-immediate conditions? Because there is no continuation of another *citta* [from them, i.e., they cannot 'drag out' or induce a subsequent fruit owing to the deficiency in the necessary conditions at that time].[15]

According to the Dārṣṭāntikas, this category also obtains among the material *dharma*-s, since the principle of the arising of the subsequent upon the ceasing of the precedent also applies — a preceding seed gives rise to a subsequent sprout; a flower gives rise to a fruit; etc.[16] Sthavira Śrīlāta, a Sautrāntika leader also holds a similar view.[17] The Sarvāstivādins, however, maintain that this homogeneous causality does not apply to the domain of matter, since there is no equality or sameness in the serial continuity of matter. According to the AKB, the Bhadanta concurs on this point with the Sarvāstivāda Ābhidharmikas.[18] "If a *dharma* is conjoined (*saṃprayuktaka*), has a supporting basis (*sāśraya*), has a mode of activity (*sākāra*), is alertive (*ābhogātmaka*) and has an object (*sālambana*), then it can be established as an equal-immediate condition. This is not the case with material *dharma*-s."[19] Moreover, Saṃghabhadra insists[20] that the notion of an equal-immediate condition necessarily entails that a subsequent thought moment can only arise upon the cessation of the preceding thought moment which thereby 'makes room' for the arising of the former.[21] Vasumitra characterizes this condition as follows: (i) giving way, (ii) being successive, (iii) giving activity, (iv) capable of generating a thought, (v) capable of inducing a thought, (vi) capable of alerting a thought, (v) capable of enabling the serial continuity of a thought. The view of the Ābhidharmikas is given in the MVŚ as follows:

> The characteristic of the equal-immediate condition consists of its enabling of the *dharma*-s that are having unique self-characteristics to arise immediately. The *dharma*-s having unique self-characteristics are the *caitta*-s, i.e., *vedanā*, *saṃjñā*, etc., and *citta*. Their self-characteristics are different individually; when they co-arise, there cannot be two [instances of them in each case].[22]

7.1.3. Condition qua object (*ālambana-pratyaya*)

According to the Sarvāstivāda, cognition is cognition of an object: A cognition cannot arise by itself, without taking an object. In fact, the very possibility of a cognition presupposes a real/existent as its object. (See *supra*, § 3.5.3.3). In this sense, the object serves as a condition for the cognition. As thought can take any object — the mind can think of anything — all *dharma*-s, i.e., *saṃskṛta* or *asaṃskṛta*, past, present or future, can become condition qua objects. Thus, "All *dharma*-s are objects [i.e., conditions qua objects], accordingly as the case applies: The visibles are the objects of visual consciousness and its concomitants. Sounds, of auditory consciousness, [etc.,]…"[23] Saṃghabhadra, speaking likewise, further explains why the totality of *dharma*-s are called conditions qua object:

> The condition qua object is none other than the totality of *dharma*-s. Outside the cognitive objects of thought and thought-concomitants,

> there is definitely no other *dharma* that can be apperceived (*upa-√labh*). That is to say, the totality of *dharma*-s is called condition qua object because thought and thought-concomitants hold onto (*ā-√lamb*) them for their arising. Because these very cognitive objects serve as the condition for their generation, they are called conditions qua object.[24]

That the nature of *ālambana-pratyaya*-s being objects of perception is determined — even when they are not being perceived (see *supra*, § 6.2.1) — may be considered as a definite assertion of objective realism on the part of the Sarvāstivādins.

7.1.4. Condition of dominance

This is the most comprehensive or generic condition, corresponding to efficient cause: It is whatever serves as a condition, either in the sense of directly contributing to the arising of a *dharma*, or indirectly through not hindering its arising. From the latter perspective, the unconditioned *dharma*-s — although transcending space and time altogether — are also said to serve as conditions of dominance. (See below, § 7.3.1; *cf. infra*, § 16.5.1). The AKB explains the meaning of the term:

> The condition of dominance is none other than the efficient cause. This condition is dominant [having the broadest scope], hence 'condition of dominance'. … Or rather, [it is so called] because it is the condition for the predominant [number of *dharma*-s]: All *dharma*-s are conditions of dominance of all the *saṃskṛta*-s, with the exception of themselves.[25]

7.1.5. A single dharma may function as all four conditions

The MVŚ[26] explains that the distinct functions of the four conditions may be found in a given *dharma*:

A thought or thought-concomitant of a given moment projects the arising of a similar thought or thought-concomitant — [this is] condition qua cause.

This same thought or thought-concomitant gives way to the thought or thought-concomitant of the next moment so that it can arise — [this is] equal-immediate condition.

This very one can serve as the object of cognition for the thought or thought-concomitant of the next moment — [this is] condition qua object.

This very one does not obstruct the arising of the thought or thought-concomitant of the next moment — [this is] condition of dominance.

In this case, the condition qua cause is like the seed-*dharma*. The equal-immediate condition is like a *dharma* that gives way (開導; 'gives way and guides'). The condition qua object is like a *dharma* walking-stick that supports. The condition of dominance is like a *dharma* that is non-obstructive.

7.2. Differences between a cause and a condition

The two terms, cause and condition, were used more or less synonymously in the *sūtra-piṭaka*. Even in the early canonical treatises of the Sarvāstivāda, the distinction was not articulated. In the MVŚ, however, we come across various well-defined distinctions between the two:

What are the differences between a cause and a condition? According to Venerable Vasumitra: There is no difference — a cause is a condition, a condition is a cause … He further explains: If when this existing that exists, then this is the cause as well as the condition of that…

> In addition: [what pertains to] the same species is a cause; what pertains to a different species is a condition, e.g., fire to fire, wheat to wheat.
>
> In addition: what is proximate is a cause; what is remote is a condition.
>
> In addition: what is unique is a cause; what is common is a condition. …
>
> In addition: what produces is a cause; what subsidiarily produces (隨能生) is a condition.
>
> In addition: what fosters its own series is a cause; what fosters another's series is a condition. …
>
> (Also *cf.* opinion of *apare* in the MVŚ, 663b: "*Adhipati-pratyaya*-s are either direct or indirect, close or remote, united or not united, arising here or arising in another. Those that are direct, close, united, arising here, are called *hetu*-s. Those that are indirect, remote, not united, arising in another, are called *pratyaya*-s.")
>
> Thus, we know that although a cause and a condition do not differ in respect of substance, there is a difference in significance: a cause signifies what is proximate, a condition signifies what is remote.[27]

Saṃghabhadra explains that in the case of both internal and external *dharma*-s — such as the fetal stages and the stages of plant growth, respectively — causes and conditions can be differentiated. As regards the fetal stage: *kalala* (first fetal stage), assisted by *vijñāna* (= *pratisandhi-citta*) in its capacity as a *cause*, produces the subsequent stages, *arbuda* (second stage), etc. Although it is not the case that *arbuda,* etc., are not dependent on *vijñāna*, the latter is not the *cause* on account of which the former are produced, for the two causal series — that of *vijñāna* and that of *arbuda,* etc. — are different. "But it is not that this *vijñāna* does not serve as the predominant *condition* for *arbuda,* etc., for [the principle of conditionality applies here —] this being, that exists; this not being, that does not exist."[28]

Other distinctions are also mentioned in the Ny, apparently acceptable to Saṃghabhadra:

> A cause is that which generates, a condition is that which fosters; the former is like the birth-mother, the latter, the foster mother.
>
> Further, a condition is that on account of the assistance of which a cause can generate and which fosters the series thus generated. For this reason, some say that a cause is singular, a condition is multiple — like the case of the seed in contrast to the manure, etc.
>
> Further, a cause is unshared in its function, a condition shares with other *dharma*-s — like in the case of visual perception, the eye in contrast to the visual object.
>
> Further, that the activity of which pertains to its own domain (作自事) is a cause, that the activity of which pertains to others' domain is a condition — like the case of the seed in contrast to the manure, etc.
>
> Further, that which induces the arising is a cause, that which sustains is a condition — like the case of the flower and the stalk.
>
> Further that which is near is a cause, that which is remote is a condition.
>
> Further what produces is a cause, what accomplishes is a condition.[29]

7.3. Five fruits (*phala*)

The Sarvāstivāda acknowledges five fruits: 1. disconnection fruit (*visaṃyoga-phala*), 2. virile fruit (*puruṣakāra-phala*), 3. fruit of predominance (*adhipati-phala*), 4. uniform-emanation fruit (*niṣyanda-phala*), 5. retribution fruit (*vipāka-phala*).[30]

7.3.1. Disconnection fruit (*visaṃyoga-phala*)

Disconnection means disconnection from defilements. This fruit refers to the cessation through deliberation (*pratisaṃkhyā-nirodha*). However, this is not in the sense that the unconditioned *pratisaṃkhyā-nirodha* (= *nirvāṇa*), transcending temporality as it does, can be produced as an effect through a space-time causal process. It is called a 'fruit' of disconnection only because it is acquired as a result of following the noble path — the path does not function as a cause as such, producing it as the effect; it only induces the arising of the acquisition (*prāpti*) of it. The AKB explains:

> Only the *saṃskṛta-dharma*-s have causes and fruits, an *asaṃskṛta* does not have them. Why? Because of the non-existence [in it] of the nature of the sixfold causes and of the fivefold fruits.
>
> Why is the [*ānantarya-mārga*] not conceded to be the efficient cause of disconnection? Because it is established [as a cause] on account of its being unobstructive to arising, and an *asaṃskṛta* has no arising.
>
> Of what then is it a fruit? How is it a fruit of the path? [It is considered a fruit of the path] because its acquisition is through the force of the [path].[31] (See below, § 7.3.2.2; cf. *infra*, § 16.3.2).

As Saṃghabhadra puts it, it is only in a special sense — in conformity with the *sūtra* usage of *śrāmāṇya-phala* and with conventional usage — that one can speak of the *pratisaṃkhyā-nirodha* as a fruit, without implying that it is causally produced; and as a "condition qua object" (*ālambana-pratyaya*), e.g., as an object of thought of a yogi, and *adhipati-pratyaya*, making an indirect contribution by merely not obstructing. In fact, "the way of establishing causes and effects among the *saṃskṛta*-s is not applicable to the case of the *asaṃskṛta*-s. Accordingly, a *pratisaṃkhyā-nirodha* is a cause which is without an effect, and an effect which is without a cause."[32]

7.3.2. Manly or virile fruit (*puruṣakāra-phala*)

7.3.2.1. Definition of virile fruit

This fruit has a rather wide scope. But it is particularly correlated to the co-existent cause and the conjoined cause. The AKB explains why it is termed 'virile':

> The co-existent and conjoined causes have the virile fruit. As the [action] is not separate from the very person [who does it], the virile action is the person himself. Its fruit is a virile fruit. What is this so-called virile action? That which is the activity (*kāritra*) of a *dharma*; [so called] because it is like a virile action.[33]

Also:

> That [conditioned *dharma*], which is born from the force of which, is the fruit [of that force — a fruit] born of a virile action.[34]

7.3.2.2. Four types of virile fruits

Saṃghabhadra distinguishes four types of virile fruits:

(1) conascent — produced by virtue of the *dharma*-s being simultaneously causes to one another;

(2) immediate — produced in the subsequent moment by virtue of the preceding thought as the cause, e.g., the *duḥkha-dharmajñāna*, produced by the *laukikāgra-dharma*-s;

(3) separated in time — produced immediately by virtue of successive causes in a series, e.g., a crop produced by a farmer etc.;

(4) not produced.

The fourth type refers to *nirvāṇa*,

because it is acquired, [not produced,] by the force of an *ānantarya-mārga*.

[Objection:] Since this is not produced, how can one call it a virile fruit produced by virtue of that?

[Answer:] It is observed that a thing acquired is also said to be produced. Thus, it is said 'I produced wealth', meaning 'I acquired wealth'.

When an *ānantarya-mārga* [— the moment of receptivity (*kṣānti*) in which defilements are being abandoned unhindered —] removes the *anuśaya*-s, the corresponding *pratisaṃkhyā-nirodha*-s are realized [in the next moment of definite knowledge (*jñāna*), called *vimukti-mārga*, in which the corresponding *prāpti*-s of *visaṃyoga* arise]. These *pratisaṃkhyā-nirodha*-s are called disconnection fruits as well as virile fruits.

When an *ānantarya-mārga* does not remove *anuśaya*-s, the corresponding *pratisaṃkhyā-nirodha*-s previously realized are realized again. Such *pratisaṃkhyā-nirodha*-s are not disconnection fruits; they are only virile fruits:

That is, when one who has not been detached from any craving pertaining to the sphere of sensuality, enters into the *darśana-mārga*, his *duḥkha-dharma-jñāna-kṣānti* removes ten *anuśaya*-s, and the [corresponding] *pratisaṃkhyā-nirodha*-s are realized. Such *pratisaṃkhyā-nirodha*-s are called disconnection fruits as well as virile fruits.

When one who has been detached from all cravings pertaining to the sphere of sensuality enters the *darśana-mārga*, his *duḥkha-dharma-jñāna-kṣānti* does not remove the *anuśaya*-s [involved], and the [corresponding] old *pratisaṃkhyā-nirodha*-s are realized [again]. Such *pratisaṃkhyā-nirodha*-s are not disconnection fruits since there already has been the disconnection; they are virile fruits for by virtue of this

> receptivity, other acquisitions [of these *pratisaṃkhyā-nirodha*-s are arisen], and they are realized again.
>
> When one who has been partly detached from the cravings pertaining to the sphere of sensuality enters the *darśana-mārga*, his *duḥkha-dharma-jñāna-kṣānti* removes some, but not others, among the ten *anuśaya*-s. Among the *pratisaṃkhyā-nirodha*-s realized, some are new, others are old, and they are respectively named as the two fruits or the one fruit.[35]

7.3.2.3. Virile action refers to the efficacy (功能) of a *dharma*

Saṃghabhadra objects to Vasubandhu's referring to *kāritra* as *puruṣakāra*: The implication of this usage is the proposition — which he says Vasubandhu should have made — that "it is called a virile fruit because they (the co-existent causes) together drag out a common fruit". This objection arises on account of the Vaibhāṣika definition of *kāritra* as *phala-ākarṣaṇa* (?) or *phala-ākṣepa*, i.e., the dragging out or projecting/inducing a fruit, as opposed to the actual 'giving' (*phala-dāna*) or producing a fruit. (See below, § 7.4). This would not be appropriate in the context of the present discussion of what causes *produce* what fruits.

Saṃghabhadra further asserts that such a proposition would entail that "there can only be virile fruits either immediately (*anantaram*) or sometime after the causes. They do not exist among the conascent. It is not possible that, among the conascent, all of them together acquire a common virile fruit for [a *dharma*] itself does not arise by virtue of itself. Nor can we say that each induces its fruit separately lest [the very definition be contradicted] that the co-existent causes do not share the same fruit." He then explains:

> Herein, *puruṣa-kāra, puruṣa-bala, puruṣa-sāmarthya* (士能), *puruṣa-śakti* (士之勢分) — all these have the same meaning: As the *efficacies* (功能) of

> *dharma*-s are like virile actions, they are called virile action (*puruṣakāra*); just as a strong man is called a lion because he is like a lion.[36]

7.3.2.4. Examples of virile fruits

The AKB gives the following as examples of virile fruits: The first *dhyāna* is the virile fruit of a *citta* which prepares it. A *citta* capable of magical transformation (*nirmāṇa-citta*) is the virile fruit of a pure *citta* in a *dhyāna*. An outflow-free *dharma*, e.g., *duḥkhe dharmajñāna-kṣānti*, can be the virile fruit of a *dharma* with outflow, e.g., the *laukikāgra-dharma*-s.[37]

7.3.3. Fruit of dominance (*adhipati-phala*)

This is the most generic type of fruit, correlated to the most generic type of cause, the efficient cause. In terms of the *karma* doctrine of the Sarvāstivāda, the fruits commonly shared by a collection of beings by virtue of their collective *karma*-s belong to this category. Thus, the whole universe with all its planets, mountains and oceans, etc., is the result — the fruit of predominance — of the collective *karma*-s of the totality of beings inhabiting therein. (See below, § 7.3.5; cf. *infra*, § 14.8).

AKB explains this fruit as follows:

> [The fruit of predominance] is a fruit born of the predominance of the [efficient cause].
>
> [The efficient cause] is established merely on account of its being non-obstructive — what predominance does it have? This fact itself [constitutes the predominance].
>
> Moreover, the efficient cause also has the nature of a contributive efficacy.

> Thus, [in this sense,] the ten *āyatana*-s [have predominance] with regard to the five sensory consciousnesses; the [collective] *karma*, with regard to the physical world. The auditory organ, etc., also have an [indirect] predominance, through a succession, with regard to the arising of visual consciousness, for having heard, there is, in a person, the arising of the desire to see. Other similar cases of this type of predominance are to be understood accordingly.[38]

As we have seen above, the virile fruit also has a very broad connotation. How does it differ from the fruit of predominance? The MVŚ explains:

> **Question**: What is the difference between a virile fruit and a fruit of predominance?
>
> **Answer**: That which is acquired through the exercise of an effort is a virile fruit. That which is acquired on account of non-obstruction is a fruit of predominance … Moreover, wealth is a virile fruit in respect of the doer, and a fruit of predominance in respect of the enjoyer. Thus the fruits [of a plant] are both virile fruits and fruits of predominance in respect of the planter; [but] only fruits of predominance in respect of the enjoyer…[39]

7.3.4. Equal-emanation fruit (*niṣyanda-phala*)

The Sanskrit word *niṣyanda* (*ni-√syand*) literally means 'flowing forth, issuing'. The notion is that of a fruit issued from a cause of a similar nature. Xuan Zang's translation of 等流 ('equal-flowing') is interpretive, but justifiable and meaningful, and our rendering echoes that (see above, § 7.1.2 for the explanation of its corresponding condition, i.e., *samanantara-pratyaya,* as 'equal and immediate'). *Avatāra*(T) defines it thus: *rgyu dang 'dra ba'i chos ni rgyu mthun pa shes bya'o /* — "A *dharma* which is similar to the cause is said to be 'cause-conforming'." This fruit is correlated to the homogeneous cause and the universal cause. The AKB explains why the latter is to be distinguished from the former:

> That *dharma* which is similar to the cause is an equal-emanation fruit, for instance, [those fruits similar to] the homogeneous and universal causes.
>
> If the universal [cause] also has the same fruit, why is it not conceded to be [a fruit] of the homogeneous cause, [i.e., why not call a universal cause 'a homogeneous cause']? Because its similarity is in terms of stage (*bhūmi*) and the nature of being defiled, but not of category [of abandonables].[40]

7.3.5. Retribution fruit (*vipāka-phala*)

This fruit, pertaining to sentient beings (*sattvākhyā*) only, correlates with the retribution cause. The causal relationship between this fruit and its cause pertains to the domain of *karma* which is twofold, personal and collective. Personal *karma* results in an individual retribution. Collective *karma*-s are actions done collectively by a group of beings, resulting in collective experiences. (See *infra*, § 14.8). Thus, the physical world — the *bhājana-loka* — inhabited by living beings is the result of the moral actions of the totality of beings. However, it is not named a retribution, which, by definition, is unique to the individual. Instead, such a collective result is considered as a fruit of predominance.

Being a result of a process of maturation (*vi-√pac*; *pac* meaning cook/mature), a retribution fruit is neither simultaneous with its cause nor produced immediately. The *Samabhedoparacaṇacakra*, however, records a view of the Mahāsāṃghika that "*karma* and *vipāka* can arise simultaneously".[41]

The retribution cause depends on the development or maturation of the series for the realization of its fruit.[42] Its moral nature is indefinable as being either *kuśala* or *akuśala*, i.e., it is non-defined (*avyākṛta*). Moreover, it is described as 'non-veiled/non-covered' (*anivṛta*), since it does not constitute a hindrance to the noble path. (See *supra*, § 2.4.3.2.1).

The AKB explains as follows:

> …retribution/maturation is a non-veiled-non-defined *dharma*, … pertaining to sentient beings, arising subsequent to a [morally] defined [*dharma* — its cause], for with respect to the retribution, a skillful or an unskillful *dharma* [as its cause] is [morally] defined on account of its definability. The retribution is that which arises from it subsequently, not simultaneously, not immediately. This is the characteristic of a retribution.
>
> Why is a non-sentient thing born of *karma* not [considered] a retribution? Because of its being common — for, another person also is similarly able to partake of it. [By definition,] however, a retribution is unique [to the person on account of whose *karma* it is the result], for it is not the case that another person experiences the retribution of the *karma* of some other person.
>
> Why does another person experience a fruit of predominance [which is also born of *karma*]? Because it is brought into being by a collective *karma*.[43]

7.4. The 'grasping' and 'giving' of a fruit

According to the Sarvāstivāda, a causal process resulting in the actualization of its effect involves the following two steps:[44]

(i) First, there must be the 'grasping of a fruit' (*phala-grahaṇa/ phala-pratigrahaṇa*). This step properly determines that the particular cause is causally related to its corresponding effect. Saṃghabhadra explains that 'grasping of a fruit' means 'inducing/projecting (*ā-√kṣip*) of the fruit'.[45] Yaśomitra also explains similarly:

> By '[the causes] grasp' is meant 'they project'. It means that they abide in the state of being a cause.[46]

(ii) When the effect so-determined actually arises, i.e., is made to enter into the present, it is called the 'giving of the fruit' (*phala-dāna*) by the cause.

All the six causes grasp their fruits in the present moment. It is this causal function of grasping a fruit, occurring only in the present moment, that is called the activity (*kāritra*) of a *dharma*.[47] For the Vaibhāṣikas, this activity of *dharma* of grasping or projecting its own fruit — causing the arising of its following moment in its serial continuity — uniquely defines its presentness. (See *supra*, § 5.5).

As for the giving of fruit: two causes — the co-existent and the conjoined causes — give their fruits only in their present moment. The homogeneous and universal causes give their fruits both in their present moment and when they are past. The retribution cause gives its fruit when it has become past.[48] It cannot do so in its present moment or the immediately subsequent moment, as the process of maturation requires a time lapse. (See above, § 7.3.5).

NOTES

[1] Ny, 445b.

[2] VKŚ, 547b ff. See also *supra*, § 4.1.2.1.

[3] T 26, 547b–c.

[4] T 26, 559b.

[5] MVŚ, 47b, 283a–b, 680b, 680c, 975a, 982b.

[6] MVŚ, 283b.

[7] MVŚ, 79a–b; same as that in the AKB; *cf.* chart in § 6.1.

[8] MVŚ, 105a–b.

[9] MVŚ, 105a.

[10] Ny, 411a; AKB, ii, stanza 46d.

[11] MVŚ, 703b.

[12] The same emphasis is also present in the Theravāda Abhidhamma. *Cf.* Vism, XVII: *paccaya-sāmaggiṃ paṭicca samaṃ phalānam uppādo* /

[13] AKB, 98: *kāraṇa-hetu-varjāḥ pañca hetavo hetu-pratyayaḥ* /

[14] PrŚ, 719a.

[15] AKB, 98: *arhataḥ paścimānapāsyotpannāś cittacaittāḥ samanantarapratyayaḥ / samaśca ayam anantaraśca pratyaya iti samanantara-pratyayaḥ / … kasmād arhataś caramāś cittacaittā na samanantarapratyayaḥ / anyacittāsaṃbandhanāt //* *Cf.* MVŚ, 50a; Ny, 443b–c.

[16] Ny, 445b.

[17] Ny, 447a.

[18] AKB, 98.

[19] MVŚ, 52a. Other reasons given by various masters for denying the existence of *samanantara-pratyaya*-s among matter are also given.

[20] Similarly in the MVŚ, 51a–b.

[21] Ny, 445b.

[22] MVŚ, 50b. Characterizations by other masters are also given therein.

[23] AKB, 100: ***ālambanaṃ sarvadharmāḥ*** [62c] /

yathā-yogaṃ cakṣur-vijñānasya sasaṃprayogasya rūpam / śrotra-vijñānasya śabdaḥ ... /

[24] Ny, 447b.

[25] AKB, 100: *ya eva kāraṇa-hetuḥ sa evādhipatipratyayaḥ / adhiko'yaṃ pratyaya ity adhipatipratyayaḥ / ... adhikasya vā pratyayaḥ / sarvaḥ sarvasya saṃskṛtasya svabhāvavarjyasya* //

[26] MVŚ, 109a.

[27] MVŚ, 109b–c.

[28] Ny, 409a.

[29] Ny, 449c–450a.

[30] MVŚ, 79a, 108c.

[31] AKB, 91: *saṃskṛtasyaiva dharmasya hetuphale bhavataḥ* /

nāsaṃskṛtasya te //55d//

kiṃ kāraṇam / ṣaḍvidha-hetv-asaṃbhavāt pañcavidha-phalāsaṃbhavāc ca / kasmāt mārgo visaṃyogasya kāraṇa-hetur neṣyate / yasmāt sa utpādāvighna-bhāvena vyavasthāpito na cāsaṃskṛtam utpattimat / kasyedānīṃ tatphalaṃ kathaṃ vā mārgasya phalam/ tadbalena prāpteḥ /

[32] Ny, 429a; *cf. infra,* § 16.3.

[33] AKB, 95: *sahabhū-saṃprayuktaka-hetvoḥ puruṣakāra-phalam / puruṣabhāvāyatirekāt puruṣakāraḥ puruṣa eva/ tasya phalaṃ pauruṣam / ko 'yaṃ puruṣakāro nāma/ yasya dharmasya yat kāritram / puruṣakāra iva hi puruṣakāraḥ* /

[34] AKB, 96: *yadbalājjāyate yattatphalaṃ puruṣakārajam* / See Vy, 225: *yad-balāj jāyate iti vistaraḥ / yasya balaṃ yad-balam iti ṣaṣthī-samāsaḥ / yasya balāj jāyate yat saṃskṛtaṃ tat phalaṃ tasya puruṣakārajam / puruṣakāraj jātaṃ puruṣakārajaṃ puruṣakāra-phalam ity arthaḥ* //

[35] Ny, 437a.

[36] Ny, 436a.

[37] AKB, 97.

[38] AKB, 94: *tasyādhipatijaṃ phalam / anāvaraṇabhāvamātreṇa avasthitasya kim ādhipatyam / etadeva/ aṅgībhāvo'pi cāsti kāraṇahetos tadyathā "pañcasu vijñānakāyeṣu daśānām āyatanānāṃ bhājanaloke ca karmāṇām / śrotrādīnām apy asti cakṣurvijñānotpattau pāraṃparyeṇa ādhipatyam / śrutvā draṣṭukāmatotpatter" ity evamādi yojyam //*

[39] MVŚ, 106c.

[40] AKB, 95: *hetor yaḥ sadṛśo dharmaḥ sa niṣyanda-phalam / tadyathā sabhāga-sarva traga-hetvoḥ / yadi sarvatraga-hetor api samānaṃ phalaṃ yasmān na sabhāga-hetor eveṣyate / yasmāt bhūmitaḥ kliṣṭatayā cāsya sādṛśyaṃ na tu prakārataḥ / yasya tu prakārato 'pi sādṛśyaṃ so 'bhyupagamyata eva sabhāga-hetuḥ //*

[41] T 49, 15c.

[42] AKB, 90.

[43] AKB, 95: *anivṛtāvyakṛto … dharmaḥ vipākaḥ …*

sattvākhyo vyākṛtodbhavaḥ [57b]/

kuśalākuśalaṃ hi vipākaṃ prati vyākaraṇād vyākṛtam / tasmād ya uttarakālaṃ bhavati na saha nāntaraṃ sa vipākaḥ / etad vipākasya lakṣaṇam / kasmād asattvākhyo'rthaḥ karmajo na vipākaḥ / sādhāraṇatvāt / anyo'pi hi tat tathaiva paribhoktuṃ samarthaḥ / asādharaṇas tu vipākaḥ / na hy anyakṛtasya karmaṇo'nyo vipākaṃ pratisaṃvedayate / adhipati-phalaṃ kasmāt pratisaṃvedayate / sādhāraṇa-karma-saṃbhūtatvāt //

[44] *Cf.* MVŚ, 98b.

[45] Ny, 437c.

[46] Vy, 226.

[47] Ny, 437c.

[48] MVŚ, 108c; AKB, 96 f.; Ny, 437c–438a — Saṃghabhadra here rejects an opinion recorded in the MVŚ (*loc. cit.*) that for the *kāraṇa-hetu*-s, both their grasping and giving of fruits can be in the present moment or when they are past.

8. The Category of Matter (*rūpa*)

8.1. General nature and definition of *rūpa*

At the early stage of *abhidharma* study, there did not seem to be much attempt at a formal definition of *rūpa*. This is most probably due to the fact that *rūpa* is one of the most matter-of-fact existents in the human experience. There was little need to elaborate on what *rūpa* was. However, the fundamental concern of *abhidharma* being the investigation of self-characteristic and intrinsic nature of the ultimate reals (*supra*, § 2.3.2.1), it was inevitable that the Ābhidharmikas eventually came to seek an articulate definition of this category.

8.1.1. Delimitation of the domain of *rūpa*

The definition of *rūpa* in the sense of matter is often given in the *sūtra* merely in the form of delimiting the domain of all that comes under this category. This practice is inherited by the *abhidharma* treatises. Thus, in explaining *rūpa-skandha*, the MVŚ quotes two such *sūtra* definitions:

> Question: What is *rūpa-skandha*?
>
> Answer: As it is said in the *sūtra*, 'All *rūpa*-s [comprise] the four Great Elements and those derived from the Great Elements.' Another *sūtra* says, 'What is *rūpa-skandha*? All those *rūpa*-s — past, future, present, internal, external, coarse, fine, inferior, superior, distant, near — all these grouped together into one heap is called the *rūpa-skandha*.'

In addition, however, the MVŚ gives its Ābhidharmika definition as follows:

> The Ābhidharmikas say thus: "What is *rūpa-skandha*? The ten [items in the] *rūpa-āyatana* and the *rūpa* subsumed under the *dharmāyatana*."[1]

The '*rūpa* subsumed under the *dharmāyatana*' is a special type of *rūpa* that is non-obstructive and invisible (*supra*, § 2.4.1.3.1, *infra*, § 13.7). Not all Sarvāstivāda masters, however, accept such a species of matter (*infra*, § 13.4.2.1).

8.1.2. Definition by the term *rūpaṇā*

However, there are also more articulate definitions. The AKB defines *rūpa* by the term *rūpaṇā* — which Xuan Zang renders as 'change-deteriorate' 變礙 — understood in the sense of being subject to deterioration or disintegration. The term is evidently linked etymologically to the root √*rup* (connected to √*lup*) — 'disturb', 'violate', 'break'. But *rūpaṇā* is also often implicitly linked to √*rūp*, a denominative root from the noun *rūpa*, in which case *rūpaṇā* means no more than 'the nature of being *rūpa*'. What this nature actually is, is then further articulated.

In its definition, the AKB quotes in support the *Saṃyuktāgama*:[2]

> It is repeatedly molested/broken, therefore, O *bhikṣu*-s, it is called the *rūpa-upādāna-skandha*. By what is it molested/broken? Touched by even the contact of the hand, it is molested/broken.[3]

The Chinese version of the SĀ[4] reads:

> That which is susceptible of being obstructed and decomposed (若可礙可分) is called *rūpa-upādāna-skandha*. It is obstructed by the fingers. It is touched by the hand, or stone, or stick, or knife, or coldness, or heat, or thirst, or hunger, or insects such as mosquitoes, or wind or rain — this is called resistance by touch. Thus, resistance is [the characteristic] of the *rūpa-upādana-skandha*.[5]

It is noteworthy that, in the *Saṃyukta-sūtra* quoted above, the oft-given definition of *rūpa* as that which is subject to resistance (*pratighāta*) and decomposition/disintegration was already found (see below). The AKB (*loc. cit.*) further quotes the following stanza from the *Arthavargīya*[6] to explain that 'is broken' means 'is oppressed/molested/disturbed' (*rūpyate bādhyata ityarthaḥ*):

> If, when desire is born in one who seeks sensual pleasure, those sensual pleasures do not abound, he is disturbed/molested (*rūpyate*) like being pierced by an arrow.
>
> And what oppression (*bādhanā*) does *rūpa* have? [An oppression] which is of the nature of change in arising.[7]

Yaśomitra observes that this question-and-answer is in anticipation of the question: "But how is *rūpa* oppressed?" — since *rūpa* is unlike a pleasure-seeking human:

> Thus it says, 'which is of the nature of change in arising'. This means: 'which is of the nature of being disfigured' (*vikriyotpādanā*).[8]

This apparently 'subjective' meaning is distinctly conveyed in Xuan Zang's translation of both *rūpyate* and *bādhyate* in this context as 惱壞, 'vexed(/molested)-broken'[9], and Yaśomitra here clearly seeks to explain away its subjective implication.

However, one may understand this as the Ābhidharmika attempt to relate *rūpyate* to the subjective sense encountered in the *sūtra*-s: This subjective sense becomes understood to refer to the human experience of *rūpa*: The *rūpa* that arises is that which is experienced by the human. Since it is of the nature of being subject to resistance and impermanent, it is mutated or disfigured as it arises — visibly so in contrast to other *dharma*-s — and therefore it is ultimately disturbing to the experiencer. In Saṃghabhadra's words, this characteristic of *rūpa* may be stated as that of being the cause of unpleasant sensation (*duḥkhavedanā-hetu*):

> Herein, why is matter-aggregate called matter? First of all, the Sugata's noble teaching states that matter is so called on account of the fact that it changes and deteriorates. The meaning of this statement is as follows: because it is the cause of unpleasant sensation, because it is obstructive, because it is subject to being transformed, it is said to change-deteriorate. On account of change-deterioration, it is called matter. 'It is the cause of unpleasant sensation' — this means that matter changes and deteriorates, and can generate unpleasant sensation, as is said in the *Arthavargīya*: ...[10]

8.1.2.1. *Rūpaṇā* interpreted as obstructiveness or resistance

The AKB[11] informs us that some Ābhidharmika masters interpret *rūpaṇā* as *pratighāta*, 'resistance', which means "the hindrance to the arising of another thing in its own location".[12] The MVŚ[13] quotes the Sarvāstivāda *ācārya* Vasumitra's explanation of what constitutes the characteristics of things having the nature or quality of *rūpa* (有色相):

> Those having (i) the nature of gradual accumulation, (ii) the nature of gradual disintegration, (iii) cognizable form-substance, (iv) cognizable location, (v) cognizable size, (vi) cognizable obstruction, (vii) cognizable offensiveness (*apakāra*), (viii) cognizable diminution or damage, (ix) cognizable addition, (x) the nature of the three kinds of *rūpa* — visible and obstructive, invisible and obstructive, invisible and non-obstructive, (xi) the nature of being brought here and taken away there, (xii) the nature of change-obstruction (*rūpaṇā*).

This characterization amounts to an elaboration on *rūpaṇā*. The characteristic given in (x) is most probably due to the consideration of the Sarvāstivāda tenet of the non-informative matter (*avijñapti*) — invisible and non-obstructive — as real entity. In brief, four distinctive features of *rūpa* stand out: (a) accumulative, (b) occupying space — obstructive, (c) visible, (d) susceptible to mutability.

8.1.3. Resistance and visibility highlighted as the two distinctive qualities

Vasumitra's characterization above can in fact be further narrowed down to two: visibility and resistance, for the susceptibility to accumulation, diminution and addition may be seen as derivable from the nature of *rūpa* as possessing mass — a fact which in turn may be characterized as resistance. It appears that the Ābhidharmikas gradually came to stress primarily these very two qualities of visibility (*sa-nidarśanatva*) and resistance (*sa-pratighātatva*). The susceptibility to mutability did not come to be stressed probably because it is a characteristic not confined to *rūpa* alone — all conditioned *dharma*-s are impermanent and subject to change.

Saṃghabhadra highlights them as constituting the distinctive nature of *rūpa*: Out of the ten items subsumed under *rūpa-āyatana*, the first one only is given the name *rūpa* as such on account of these two qualities most distinctive of *rūpa*:

> On account of it being obstructive, it deteriorates as soon as it is touched by the hand, etc., and on account of it being visible, one can indicate it as being located differently — here, there.[14]

These two qualities are further elaborated by Saṃghabhadra:

(i) On being visible or 'with-seeing':

> This is in two senses: 1. Matter is necessarily co-existent with seeing (*darśana*), hence said to be visible ('with-seeing', *sanidarśana*), for matter and the eye arise simultaneously; this is like [the sense of] 'with companion'. 2. Matter has indicatability, hence said to be visible, for it can be differently indicated as being here or being there;[15] this is like [the sense of] 'with-object' (*sa-ālambana*).[16]

(ii) On being resistant or 'with-resistance':

> Resistance means obstruction. 'This has the obstruction by that' (i.e., this is obstructed by that), hence it is said to be 'with-resistance'. Obstruction (*pratighāta*) is threefold: obstruction qua hindrance (*āvaraṇa-pratighāta*), obstruction qua object domain (*viṣaya-pratighāta*) and obstruction qua cognitive object (*ālambana-pratighāta*).[17]

An object domain (*viṣaya*) is to be distinguished from a cognitive object (*ālambana*): A *dharma*, *y*, is the object domain of another *dharma*, *x*, if *x* exercises its efficacy (seeing, etc.) in *y*. On the other hand, a cognitive object is a *dharma* grasped by a thought or thought-concomitant, (i.e., when the cognitive object is grasped, a consciousness is generated correspondingly to it).[18] Accordingly, whereas thought and thought-concomitants have both an object domain and a cognitive object, the sense faculties have only object domains.

Of the aforementioned threefold obstruction, it is the obstruction qua hindrance that is specifically referred to as a characteristic of matter. These three types of obstruction are explained as follows:

(1) Obstruction qua hindrance: When one material *dharma* occupies a location, another material *dharma* cannot arise in the same space. Two material *dharma*-s are mutually resistant or obstructive in this sense to each other.

(2) Obstruction qua object domain: When a sense faculty (e.g., the eye) meets with its corresponding object domain (e.g., a visible) and its efficacy (e.g., seeing) is exercised, then it is said to be obstructed by that object domain inasmuch as its sphere of vision is at that time confined to that object. An example is cited from the PjŚ: the eye of a fish is obstructed by encountering a visible in water, not on land; the eye of a human is obstructed by a visible on land, not in water.

(3) Obstruction qua cognitive object: When thought and thought-concomitants are so obstructed by — confined to — their cognitive objects.[19]

Like Saṃghabhadra, Yaśomitra highlights too "the nature of *rūpa* which is the indicatability of location: 'It is here, there'."[20] Saṃghabhadra argues that visibility as an intrinsic characteristic of the category of *rūpa* must apply to even the smallest unit — an atom. For, otherwise, it will forfeit its very intrinsic nature as *rūpa*. (See below, § 8.3.3).

Elsewhere, Saṃghabhadra also gives three defining characteristics of *rūpa*: (i) indicatability of location, (ii) susceptibility to deterioration through obstructive contact, (iii) *rūpa* by designation. The third characteristic pertains to the non-informative matter subsumed under the *dharmāyatana* rather than the *rūpāyatana*. "They are called *rūpa* by way of designation (*prajñapti*) in terms of *rūpa*: It is not the case that they can be designated apart from the bodily and vocal [*karma*-s] which are *rūpa* in nature and from which they are generated, for in the sphere of immateriality, this designation does not exist."[21]

Obviously, the third characteristic given by Saṃghabhadra above is intended to subsume the non-information *karma* as a special type of matter in spite of its being devoid of the first two characteristics (i.e., visibility and resistance). Besides the non-information matter which is unlike other matter that we encounter in phenomenal existence, the Sarvāstivāda concedes other types of special matter, such as that in the fine-material sphere and that of the intermediate beings (*antarābhava*); these kinds of matter are said to be transparent (*accha*). In fact, one reason that the faculty of suffering (*duḥkhendriya*) is absent in the beings of the fine-material sphere is that their bodies (*āśraya*) are constituted by transparent matter[22] on account of which they are not subject to being injured. We have also seen above that the sense faculties are said to comprise very subtle and perspicuous (*prasāda*) kinds of matter (cf. § 2.4.1.3.2) which are suprasensible (*atīndriya*), and their atoms, being transparent like crystal, are mutually non-obstructive.[23]

8.2. Primary and derived matter

Among the various definitions of a material (*rūpin*) *dharma* in the MVŚ, the following involves the notions of the 'Great Elements' and 'matter derived from the Great Elements':

> That *dharma* whose intrinsic nature consists of the four Great Elements or of that which is derived from the four Great Elements is called a material *dharma*. That *dharma* whose intrinsic nature does not consist of the four Great Elements or of that which is derived from the four Great Elements is called a non-material *dharma*.
>
> Furthermore, that *dharma* which has the Great Elements as its cause (*mahābhūta-hetuka*) and whose intrinsic nature consists of the derived matter is called a material *dharma*. That *dharma* which does not have the Great Elements as its cause and whose intrinsic nature does not consist of the derived matter is called a non-material *dharma*.[24]

In Sarvāstivāda Abhidharma, the totality of *rūpa-dharma*-s comprises (i) the primary matter comprising the four Great Elements (*mahābhūta*; 'Great Reals') — Earth (*pṛthivī*), Water (*ap*), Fire (*tejas*), Air (*vāyu*); (ii) 11 derived matter (*upādāya-rūpa*/*bhautika*)[25] — five sense-faculties (*indriya*), five corresponding objects (*artha*/*viṣaya*) and non-information matter (*avijñapti-rūpa*). The four Great Elements are also subsumed under the objects of touch (*spraṣṭavya*) together with other derived tangibles, because their functions can only be experienced through touch. They have the specific nature (*svabhāva*) of solidity (*khara*), humidity (*sneha*), heat (*uṣṇatā*) and mobility (*īraṇā*), respectively, and perform the functions of supporting (*dhṛti*), cohesion (*saṃgraha*), maturation (*pakti*) and extension (*vyūha*), respectively. The Sarvāstivāda acknowledges a total of 11 derived tangibles. The other seven are: smoothness (*ślakśṇatva*), coarseness (*karkaśatva*), heaviness (*gurutva*), lightness (*laghutva*), coldness (*śīta*), hunger (*jighatsā*) and thirst (*pipāsā*).

However, among the 'four great *ācārya*-s' of the Sarvāstivāda lineage, Buddhadeva holds that *rūpa* comprises the *mahābhūta*-s alone; the so-called derived *rūpa*-s are just specific types of *mahābhūta*-s (*mahābhūta-viśeṣa*). His conclusion is said to have been based on certain *sūtra* statements which speak, for instance, of the solidity within the fleshy eye as the internal Earth Element, the mobility within it as the internal Wind Element, etc.[26]

Dharmatrāta, while accepting the derived *rūpa*-s as real entities distinct from the Great Elements, denies the existence of the category of derived matter known as "matter subsumed under the *dharmāyatana*" — which amounts to the denial of the non-information matter. He further holds that the Great Elements alone are the tangibles; there are no derived tangibles.[27]

Saṃghabhadra informs us that the Sthavira Śrīlāta also denies the existence of the derived tangibles. For him they are nothing more than the specific configuration of the Great Elements. Thus, he argues, the so-called coldness is simply a designation for the state wherein the Heat Element becomes less or not predominant. Likewise, heaviness or lightness is simply a designation of the fact that there exists a bigger or smaller quantity of the Great Elements within a given form of matter. He offers another reason for his denial: these so-called derived tangibles are also cognizable by our eyes. That is to say: our eyes grasp, accordingly as the case may be, the shape, quantity, color or appearance of the Great Elements. They can also cognize things which are smooth or coarse. [28]

8.2.1. Explanation of the term *mahābhūta*

The MVŚ remarks that the compound *mahābhūta* is to be taken as a descriptive compound (*karmadhāraya samāsa*), as in the case of *mahābhūmi*, and *mahā-rājan,* etc.: they are both *mahā* and *bhūta*, hence named *mahābhūta*.[29] The *Avatāra* explains:

> They are called the Great Elements because of their being both great and having the nature of an Element (*bhūta*). Thus Space [although great], is not included among the Great Elements, *as by 'Element' one means the ability to produce its own fruit* (*svaphala*). They are said to be 'great' as they are found in all secondary matter. Thus, there are only four Great Elements because (i) there is no use for [any] more, and (ii) there will be inaptitude [with regard to the fulfillment of the four functions if any one of them is lacking]; as in the case of a couch [which has four and only four] legs.[30]

The sentence italicized above, potentially very informative in terms of doctrine, is, however, not found in the Tibetan version of *Avatāra*.[31] In the Vaibhāṣika doctrine, all conditioned *dharma*-s have this capability, and it is by virtue of this capability, technically called *kāritra*, that a conditioned *dharma* is distinguishable as being present, as opposed to being past or future (see *supra*, § 5.4). According to this explanation, Space is not a *bhūta* on account of its non-productivity. This is because, for the Sarvāstivāda, Space is an unconditioned which transcends causality in space-time. That 'Space' (虛空) in the above passage refers to the unconditioned *ākāśa* is clear from the fact that the Sarvāstivādin Ābhidharmikas sharply distinguish this from *ākāśa-dhātu* (空界) which is *rūpa* in nature.[32] In this same context, Vasumitra's explanation is that *ākāśa* is not one of the *mahābhūta*-s because it is devoid of their characteristics: increase, decrease; harm, benefit; gaining strength, waning — all characteristics of the conditioned. The Bhadanta's explanation[33] may be compared to that given by the compilers of the MVŚ themselves:

Bhadanta:

Space, although being great, is not *bhūta* in its nature as it is non-productive. The other *saṃskṛta dharma*-s [— other than the *mahābhūta*-s —] although capable of being considered as *bhūta*, are not great in their nature as their characteristics are not common [to all material *dharma*-s]. Thus, Space is not classified as *mahābhūta*.[34]

Compilers:

Question: Why are other *dharma*-s not called *mahābhūta*-s? Answer: Because the others do not have such characteristics as the *mahābhūta*-s. That is: because the unconditioned *dharma*-s are great but not *bhūta*; the other conditioned *dharma*-s are *bhūta* but are not great. Accordingly, these four alone receive the name *mahābhūta*-s.[35]

It can be seen that in Bhadanta's explanation, Space is clearly contrasted with the conditioned *dharma*-s; and the comparison with the compilers' own explanation bears out that Space, in all these explanations, refers to the unconditioned *ākāśa*. Accordingly, it can be concluded that *bhūtam,* in the compound *mahābhūta,* refers to the reals — the causally productive — in the domain of the conditioned. Among these, only those four reals are the 'Great Reals' because they alone form the indispensable basis for the arising of all the derived *rūpa*-s. Or rather, as the compilers here explain:

> *Bhūta* signifies that which can decrease or increase, harm or benefit, which arises and ceases. *Mahā* signifies that whose substance, characteristics, shape and quantity pervade everywhere, accomplishing great action.
>
> Question: How do these four accomplish great work?
>
> Answer: The great work consists in their being the supporting bases for the great masses of derived matter, causing them to disintegrate or to be formed. (*loc. cit.*)

8.2.2. Great Elements as *dhātu*-s

The Great Elements are also called *dhātu*-s in the sense of the ultimate source of genesis. Saṃghabhadra explains the significance of the term *dhātu* in this context, giving more than one sense of *bhūta*:

> [Question:] For what reasons are these Great Elements named *dhātu*?
>
> [Answer:] Because they are the place of origin of all *rūpa-dharma*-s. It is also from the Great Elements [themselves] that the Great Elements are produced. In the world, the places of origin are called *dhātu*-s; as for instance, the mines of gold, etc., are said to be the *dhātu*-s of gold, etc. Or, because they are the place of origin of various types of unsatisfactoriness (*duḥkha*), they are said to be *dhātu*; example as before. According to some: they are named *dhātu* because they sustain (√*dhṛ*) the self-characteristics of the Great Elements and secondary matter.[36]

8.2.3. Inseparability of the Great Elements

The four Great Elements exist inseparably from one another, being co-existent causes (*sahabhū-hetu*) one to another. Nevertheless, *rūpa*-

dharma-s are manifested and experienced in diverse forms because of the difference in intensity or substance of one or more of the four Elements. The MVŚ comments:[37]

> Question: From the predominance of what is there smoothness, etc., up to thirst?
>
> Some say: Smoothness, etc., [in each case,] is not due to the one-sided predominance of [any] *mahābhūta*. It is only owing to the *mahābhūta*-s being of different nature that the effect of smoothness, etc., up to thirst is produced.
>
> Other masters say: From the predominance of Water and Fire, there is smoothness. From the predominance of Earth and Wind, there is coarseness. From the predominance of Fire and Wind, there is lightness. From the predominance of Earth and Water there is heaviness … From the predominance of Water and Wind, there is coldness. From the predominance of Wind, there is hunger — because of the predominance of Wind, there is agitation causing the dissipation of food, inducing the hunger-tangible; the desire for food is thus produced. From the predominance of Fire, there is thirst — because of the predominance of Fire, there is oppression from heating up, causing the dissipation of what has been drunk and inducing the thirst-tangible; the desire for drink is thus produced.

But while the MVŚ here does not comment clearly which of the two views — predominance of substance, predominance of effect — represents the orthodox Vaibhāṣika standpoint, Saṃghabhadra[38] criticizes the Kośakāra for giving the latter view as the Vaibhāṣika view. According to Saṃghabhadra, the orthodox Vaibhāṣika view is that of predominance of substance.

Elsewhere, the MVŚ[39] explicitly affirms that in a given mass of *rūpa*, there can be a quantitative difference in the *mahābhūta*-s without contradicting the principle of their inseparability:

Question: Do the *mahābhūta*-s increase or decrease in substance (i.e., vary quantitatively)? … There is a fault in either case — if they increase or decrease, how can they be inseparable? For, if in a solid substance there are more atoms of Earth (*pṛthivī-paramāṇu*) and fewer of Water, Fire and Air, the Earth atoms quantitatively intermingled with Water etc., [accordingly as the case may be,] would be separated from the other Elements. [On the other hand,] if there is no increase or decrease, substances like water, stones, etc., ought not to differ in being solid, soft, etc.

Answer: One should say that there is increase or decrease in substance among the *mahābhūta*-s. … Although there is an increase or decrease, they are not separated, because together they perform a function by mutually supporting one another. Thus, in a solid substance, where the number of Earth atoms is greater than those of Water, Fire and Air, the Earth atoms are incapable of performing their functions in isolation from Water, etc. … It is like the case of many villages in which there is a collective management; there is a difference in the number of villagers [among the villages], yet [the villagers are in each case] mutually dependent and cannot be separated.

It is therefore clear that inseparability does not necessarily mean that the four Great Elements are juxtaposed. It means that the four always co-exist and are functionally interdependent. They are what the Sarvāstivādins call co-existent causes to one another. Their inseparability can be inferred from their specific characteristic and activity that can be observed in all material aggregates. Thus, in an aggregate of fluid, besides the obvious specific characteristic of the Water Element, there must also be the Earth Element without which ice cannot result when the weather is extremely cold, nor can a ship be supported; there must be the Fire Element without which the fluid would never become warm; there must be the Wind Element without which it would never move. Thus, the Sarvāstivāda maintains that despite their divergent characteristics, the four Great Elements always arise together:

> Question: The four Great Elements being opposed in their respective characteristic, how can they arise simultaneously unseparated?
>
> [Answer:] The Venerable Vasumitra explains thus: … it is not the case that what are different in characteristics are necessarily opposed to one another. Those which, while differing in characteristics are not mutually opposed, may arise together without being separated, just like the four Great Elements and smell, taste, touch, and colors such as blue, yellow etc.[40]

According to the Sautrāntika master, Śrīlāta, however:

> The Great Elements and the derived matter are mostly unseparated. But there are also some which are separated, such as the light of the sun, the moon, a lamp and a gem, as well as the fragrance, etc., that drifts apart from the flowers.[41]

8.2.4. Dependence of *upādāya-rūpa* on the Great Elements

All *rūpa*-s, except for the non-informative matter, are the fruits of karmic retribution. Although the so-called derived *rūpa*-s are already existing as ontological entities, their arising and functioning are dependent (*upādāya*) on the Great Elements. In this sense, the latter are said to be their cause: One set of the four Great Elements serves as the cause of an atom (*paramāṇu*) of the derived *rūpa* in a fivefold manner. The MVŚ[42] explains the sense of this dependence:

> Question: Is it in the sense of [having the *mahābhūta*-s as] cause, or in the sense of [having them as] conditions? …
>
> Answer: It should be said thus: it is in the sense of [having them as] cause.
>
> Question: These [*mahābhūta*-s], with regard to the derived matter, do not have [the functions of] any of the five causes [besides being efficient cause], so then how are they the cause?

> Answer: Although [the meaning of] any of the five causes, i.e., homogeneous cause, etc., is lacking, [the *mahābhūta*-s] are cause in five other senses: i.e., (i) generating cause (*janana-hetu*), (ii) reliance cause (*niśraya-hetu*), (iii) supportive cause (*pratiṣṭhā-hetu*), (iv) maintaining cause (*upastambha-hetu*), (v) development cause (*upabṛṃhaṇa-hetu*).

The AKB,[43] explaining in the same manner, defines each of these five causes: (i) because the derived *rūpa*-s arise from them, like a child from the parents; (ii) because they are influenced by them, like a pupil under a teacher; (iii) because they are supported by them; (iv) because they are their cause of non-interruption; (v) because they are their cause of development. Saṃghabhadra elaborates further:

> Although [the derived matter] arises simultaneously [with the Great Elements], the sense of causation is applicable here because it operates in accompaniment with (*anu-√vṛt*) [— i.e., it arises and ceases every moment together with — the Great Elements]; this is like the case of a sprout producing its shadow, or a lamp illuminating light.[44]
>
> [As a matter of fact,] although *dharma*-s are not non-existent since they already exist in their nature, their efficacies are accomplished in necessary dependence on the power of causes and conditions. For instance, it is not that the derived matter has not been existent as entities, but their efficacies are accomplished in necessary dependence on the Great Elements as cause.[45]

The MVŚ enumerates various differences between the Great Elements and the derived matter:

> The Ābhidharmika says: the Great Elements are invisible (*anidarśana*), the derived matter visible (*sanidarśana*) or invisible.
>
> The Great Elements are resistant (*sapratigha*), the derived matter resistant or non-resistant.

The Great Elements are with-outflow, the derived matter with-outflow or outflow-free.

The Great Elements are non-defined, the derived matter are skillful, unskillful, or non-defined.

The Great Elements pertain to the sense sphere (*kāmadhātu-pratisaṃyukta*), the derived matter pertains to the sense sphere, the fine-material sphere does not pertain to any sphere (*apratisaṃyukta*).

The Great Elements are of the nature of being neither-trainee-nor-non-trainee (*naivaśaikṣanāśaikṣa*), the derived matter is of the nature of trainee, non-trainee or neither-trainee-nor-non-trainee.

The Great Elements are abandonable through cultivation (*bhāvanāheya*), the derived matter is abandonable through cultivation or not to be abandoned (*aheya*).

The Great Elements are subsumed under the truths of satisfactoriness and the origin. The derived matter is subsumed under the truths of unsatisfactoriness, the origin and the path.

The Great Elements are without retribution (*avipāka*), the derived matter is with-retribution (*savipāka*) or without *vipāka*.

The Great Elements are non-defiled (*akliṣṭa*), the derived matter is defiled or non-defiled.

The Great Elements are not *karma*, the derived matter may or may not be *karma*.

Thus, the characteristics of the Great Elements differ in innumerable ways from those of the derived matter.[46]

8.3. 'Atomic' theory

Unlike the doctrine of the Great Elements, the Buddhist atomic theory is not discernible in the *sūtra*-s. It likely was taken over from outside the Buddhist schools — probably from the Vaiśeṣika. However, no Buddhists — including the Sarvāstivāda Ābhidharmikas — would conceive of atoms as being eternally immutable or permanent. Certain heretics (*tīrthakāra*) hold that the atoms, being eternal and immutable, remain when the universe dissolves. In contrast, the Sarvāstivādins teach that when the universe is destroyed by the three great calamities — through fire, water and wind — not even one atom can remain.[47] Atoms are in fact momentary (see Vasumitra's opinion below, § 8.3.5.2). They are not permanent (*nitya*) on account of their coursing through time. Only the *asaṃskṛta-dharma*-s are permanent, being beyond space and time. At least by the time of the MVŚ, the Buddhist Ābhidharmikas had already articulated the theory to a large extent in their own way. In addition, Buddhists — including the Ābhidharmikas — do not admit of any notion of quality inherent in a substance. The quality defines the ontological status of a real. For the Ābhidharmikas, a unique quality is in fact the real existent itself.

The term that we have roughly rendered as 'atom' here corresponds to *paramāṇnu*. However, at the outside, it should be borne in mind that the Vaibhāṣika notion of *paramāṇnu* is not entirely the same as the notion of atom in modern physics (see below).

The Vaibhāṣika concedes that an atom as the smallest unit of matter is known through mental analysis. This is called the 'conceptual atom' (假極微; **prajñapti-paramāṇu*). It is from this perspective that one could speak of *paramāṇu* as corresponding to the notion of 'atom'. Nevertheless, this does not mean that atoms exist only as concept. The conceptual is always based on the ultimately real, and this ultimately real atom is the intrinsic characteristic of matter (the visibles, etc.). While a single *paramāṇu* cannot be directly observed, a physical assemblage (和集; *he ji*) of them is known through direct perception (*pratyakṣa*).[48]

8.3.1. Descriptive definition of an 'atom'

The MVŚ gives a descriptive definition of an 'atom' as follows:

> An atom (*paramāṇu*) is the smallest *rūpa*. It cannot be cut, broken, penetrated; it cannot be taken up, abandoned, ridden on, stepped on, struck or dragged. It is neither long nor short, square nor round, regular nor irregular, convex nor concave. It has no smaller parts; it cannot be decomposed, cannot be seen, heard, smelled, touched. It is thus that the *paramāṇu* is said to be the finest (*sarva-sūkṣma*) of all *rūpa*-s.
>
> Seven of these *paramāṇu*-s constitute an *aṇu* — the finest among all *rūpa*-s perceivable by the eye and visual consciousness. [However,] this [*aṇu*] can be seen by only three types of eyes: 1. the *divya-cakṣus*, 2. the eye of a Universal Monarch (*cakravartin*), 3. the eye of a *bodhisattva* in his last birth. Seven *aṇu*-s constitute a *tāmra-rajas*. … Seven *tāmra-rajas*-s constitute an *ap-rajas* … Seven *ap-rajas*-s constitute a *śaśa-rajas*; … Seven *śaśa-rajas*-s constitute a *eḍaka-rajas* … Seven *eḍaka-rajas*-s constitute a *go-rajas* … Seven *go-rajas*-s constitute a *vātāyana-rajas* … [in this way, the whole universe is composed].[49]

This doctrine of the sevenfold incremental atomic agglomeration is also found in the AKB and Ny.[50] Saṃghabhadra defines the atom more succinctly:

> The finest part in a resistant matter which cannot be further divided is called a *paramāṇu*. That is, this *paramāṇu* cannot be further divided into many [parts] by means of another matter [or] the intellect (*buddhi*). This is then said to be the 'ultimately small' among matter. As there can be no further part, it is called the 'ultimately small'. In the same way, a *kṣaṇa* is the smallest [unit] of time; it cannot be further analyzed into half

> *kṣaṇa*-s. A multitude of such *paramāṇu*-s that are mutually combined and necessarily inseparable is called a *saṃghāta-paramāṇu.*[51]

From Saṃghabhadra's explanation above, we can therefore speak of two types of *paramāṇu*-s: 1. *paramāṇu* in the proper sense of the term — the smallest conceivable building block of matter. This is also called *dravya-paramāṇu*. 2. *saṃghāta-paramāṇu* in the sense of a molecule — the smallest unit of matter that can actually occur in the phenomenal world. (See below, § 8.3.4). Saṃghabhadra further says:

> The size of an atom can also be illustrated by examples. But it is not explained because it is known only by the Buddha. However, in order to define an *araṇya* ('forest dwelling', 'hermitage'), the [Sarvāstivāda] *Vinaya* says only that an agglomeration of seven atoms is called an *aṇu*, etc. …

8.3.2. Atoms of color and shape

Rūpa, in the sense of visible objects, is twofold, namely, color (*varṇa*) and shape (*saṃsthāna*). Corresponding to these two, there are individual atoms of colors (such as blue, etc.) and shapes (such as long etc.) even though they are not directly perceivable by the eye and visual consciousness. The Sarvāstivāda argues that if there were no individual atoms of color and shape, an agglomeration of atoms would not, for instance, become green or long.[52] The Sautrāntika, however, accepts the reality of color atoms only. For them, the so-called shape atoms are simply the color atoms arranged in various ways.

8.3.3. An aggregate of similar atoms as a real entity

It is not only that the ordinary human eye does not perceive the individual atoms which therefore individually cannot serve as the object of visual perception, but also an individual atom cannot serve as the supporting basis (*āśraya*) for visual consciousness:

> The five consciousnesses, visual, etc., have an agglomeration [of atoms] as their supporting basis and take an agglomeration [of atoms] as object. They have the resistant (*sapratigha*) as their basis and take the resistant as an object. They have a combination as their supporting basis and take a combination as an object.[53]

But does this mean that the *āyatana*-s are unreal, or that — as claimed by the Sautrāntika — direct perception is impossible? The Sarvāstivāda answers to both these questions are a definite "No." Although an individual atom is too feeble to function as a visual faculty, an agglomeration of atoms of the same kind will, in their collective and accumulative capacity, function as such.[54] Likewise, as Saṃghabhadra argues, although in the MVŚ the human eye is said to be unable to perceive an atom,[55] it does not mean that an atom is invisible in its intrinsic nature. It simply means that its visibility is virtually nil. An agglomeration of *rūpa* atoms comes to be directly perceivable.[56] The point here is that an agglomeration of atoms of the same type (和集) is also a real. This is in contrast to a unification of atoms (和合) — or for that matter various other *dharma*-s — of diverse species. Thus *rūpa* as a visual object is real, i.e., truly existent (*dravyato'sti*), whereas a combination of the five different *skandha*-s, imagined to be a 'person', is unreal.

8.3.4. The minimum octad as a molecule that arises

It is apparently after the period of the MVŚ that the Sarvāstivādins articulated a doctrine that, in the physical order, a minimum of eight substances (*aṣṭa-dravyaka*) — constituting the subtlest aggregate, *saṃghāta-paramāṇu* — are necessarily conascent in the sphere of sensuality: the four Great Elements, plus form, smell, taste and touch. This *saṃghāta-paramāṇu* ('atoms in aggregation') may be compared to the notion of a molecule, in contrast to *dravya-paramāṇu*, a single atom as a real entity. But it is sufficiently clear that this 'octad molecule' does not really mean a molecule comprising eight atoms. It represents the smallest unit of matter that can be cognized by us.

The octad molecule is the case of an agglomeration into the composition of which sound and the sense faculty do not enter. Where sound is produced, i.e., enters into the composition of the aggregate, one has a nonad molecule. Among the sense faculties, the *kāyendriya* is a nonad comprising the basic eight, plus a *paramāṇu* of *kāyendriya*.[57] This doctrine was not articulated in the MVŚ, although in a passage therein stating the possibility of the conascence of the four Great Elements and smell, taste, touch and color (see above, § 8.2.3), one might see the germ of the notion.

Vasubandhu expresses this requirement in the following line:

> *kāme 'ṣṭadravyako 'śabdaḥ paramāṇur anindriyaḥ /* [58]
>
> ("In Kāmadhātu, a *paramāṇu* which is without sound and sense faculty, consists of eight substances.")

In the prose, he explains that what is called *paramāṇu* (in the singular) in the stanza is the subtlest aggregate of matter that could be cognized (*sarvasūkṣmo hi rūpa-saṃghātaḥ paramāṇur ity ucyate / yato nānyataro vijñāyeta /*). That is, *paramāṇu* here does not refer to an individual atom, *dravya-paramāṇu*, but to a *saṃghāta-paramāṇu*.[59] Saṃghabhadra's explanation is similar:

> Among the resistant matter, the ultimately final part which cannot be subject to further division is called a *paramāṇu*. … Such *paramāṇu*-s,[60] when mutually combined and necessarily unseparated, are said to be a *saṃghāta-paramāṇu*. This, in the sense sphere, where sound and sense faculty are absent, arises as constituted of eight substances.[61]

Yaśomitra also explains that a *dravya-paramāṇu* is the *dravya* that is the smallest unit of *rūpa*.[62] This would mean that the smallest unit of matter that can actually arise in the empirical world consists of eight *dravya*-s — eight *dravya-paramāṇu*-s of which four are the Great Elements.

In accordance with the notion that an aggregate of real substances of the same species is also a real (§ 8.3.3), such a *saṃghāta-paramāṇu* is also a real existent in the absolute sense (*paramārtha-sat*).[63]

The author of the ADV is critical of Vasubandhu's interpretation of the word *paramāṇu* in the stanza. According to him, *paramāṇu* here actually designates the subtlest ultimate division of a material aggregate in phenomenal existence, i.e., the *dravya-paramāṇu*. "This, however, is inseparable from seven substances — this is the eighth [substance] arising unseparated from the four Great Elements and three kinds of derived matter, or from three [Great] Elements and four kinds of derived matter."[64] One would wish that the author of the ADV could be more elaborative in his explanation. But this explanation seems to mean that an 'atom' that can occur in the phenomenal world comprises at least eight substances. Such a notion of *paramāṇu*, then is quite different from the notion of atom in modern physics, and is more appropriately described as a kind of 'molecule'.

However, as criticized by their opponents, the Vaibhāṣikas' use of the term *dravya* here is ambiguous: Does it refer to an absolute real as an individual entity in itself, possessing an intrinsic characteristic, or as *āyatana*-s (i.e., *rūpa* as *rūpāyatana*, etc.) each possessing a distinctive common characteristic applicable to the type as a whole (e.g., all visibles are *rūpa*-s as a type — an *āyatana*)? The Vaibhāṣika answer is that the term is used in both senses: the four Great Elements as four *dravya*-s in the sense of individual entities; the four derived matter as four categories of *āyatana*-s.

The Vaibhāṣika notion of *paramāṇu,* as explained by the author the ADV, shows that *paramāṇu*-s are certainly not created identically. The nature of a *paramāṇu* will depend on the matter of which it is composed: an eye *paramāṇu* has the quality of eye; a *paramāṇu* of a visible has the quality of a visible; etc. Such a doctrine, in fact, seems to be quite in tune with the doctrine in the MVŚ concerning the relationship between a *paramāṇu* and the Great Elements. A question is posed as to whether from one set of four Great Elements is derived a single *paramāṇu* of derived matter, or numerous derived matter. The compilers of the MVŚ comment that from a single set of Great Elements, only a single *paramāṇu* of derived matter can be derived.[65] From this perspective, the doctrine that the smallest unit of matter occurring in nature comprises at least eight substances can be construed to mean that a *paramāṇu* comes into existence in the sense sphere when these eight material qualities come to be agglomerated.

8.3.5. Problems connected with the notion of atom

This divergence of interpretations concerning the term *aṣṭa-dravyaka* betrays a problem that had arisen from the way in which the Ābhidharmikas attempted, rather unsuccessfully it would seem, to synthesize two doctrines pertaining to matter — that of the *mahābhūta*-s which had an ancient root in the *sūtra-piṭaka*, and that of atoms coming subsequently from outside the Buddhist tradition. It would seem that at first the four *mahābhūta*-s were conceived of as being material qualities — Earth Element is solidity, etc. They are real entities qua material qualities. But when the atomic theory was introduced into the *abhidharma* system, the notion that matter is constituted of atoms and that *mahābhūta*-s exist as atoms came to be developed. This lead to a contradiction that seems to have been quietly left unsettled: On the one hand, the atomic theory requires that atoms are grouped as septuplets from which matter is derived. The smallest molecule, an *aṇu*, or *saṃghāta-paramāṇu*, consisting of just seven *paramāṇu*-s, is the smallest unit of matter that is perceivable — and even then not by an ordinary human being (see above, § 8.3.1). On the other hand, a new doctrine was then articulated that a molecule that can arise in the empirical world consists of a minimum of eight substances. Taking both doctrines into consideration, one commentarial opinion, in fact, arrives at 1,379 as the number of atoms that constitute a molecule of a visible![66] The contradiction, however, would not have necessarily arisen if the *mahābhūta*-s were conceived of as *dravya*-s in the sense of real material qualities — real forces — rather than atoms.

Apart from this, the very notion of an atom being the ultimately indivisible, impenetrable unit of matter devoid of extension gives rise to conceptual difficulties. The following are among some of the controversies.

8.3.5.1. The definition by *rūpaṇā*

The defining characteristics of *rūpa* do not exist in all *dharma*-s classified by the Sarvāstivāda as *rūpa*. The MVŚ:[67]

> Question: If to have the characteristic of *rūpaṇā* is to have the characteristic of *pratighāta* (變礙),[68] then the past and future [*dharma*-s], the atoms and *avijñapti* ought not to have the characteristic of *rūpa* since they have no *rūpaṇā*. And if they do not have the characteristic of *rūpa*, they ought not to be *rūpa* in their intrinsic nature.
>
> Answer: They are also *rūpa*-s since they acquire the characteristic of *rūpaṇā*: although a past *rūpa* is at the present moment without resistance, it has had resistance; although a future *rūpa* is at the present moment without resistance, it will have resistance; although each individual atom is without resistance, an aggregate of them has resistance; although an *avijñapti* is without resistance, its supporting basis (*āśraya*) — namely the four Great Elements — has resistance.

8.3.5.2. Are there intervening spaces between the atoms or do they touch one another?[69]

If two atoms touch one another, they do so either at a point of contact or in their totality. In either case, there is a problem: The former implies that an atom has parts or extension. The latter would result in two or more atoms coalescing into a single unit — in fact, the whole physical universe, in this case, ought to be the size of a single atom. On the other hand, if they do not touch one another at all, an agglomeration of atoms would fall into pieces when struck. Besides, how does one explain the possibility of sound being produced when two *rūpa*-s strike against each other?

The Vaibhāṣika position is that atoms do not touch. It is solely by the force of the Wind Element that atoms are held together. The production of sound, in fact, is possible precisely because atoms do not touch — for otherwise they would merge with the hand, etc., that strikes, and, there being no space in between, how can sound be produced?

Vasumitra explains that atoms cannot touch one another because they are momentary — the possibility of touch would imply that an atom can endure for more than one moment.[70]

Bhadanta Dharmatrāta explains that atoms are metaphorically said to touch one another when they are juxtaposed without an interval (*nirantara*).

Vasubandhu approves of this explanation, for if there should be any interval between atoms, what prevents other atoms from getting into it? This would then contradict the notion that atoms are impenetrable.[71]

Saṃghabhadra[72] also approves of Dharmatrāta's explanation. But this word, *nir-antara*, he says, cannot mean literally that there is absolutely no interval between two atoms, for in that case how are they not in touch? "The prefix *nis* signifies 'certitude': there certainly is an interval; just as *nirdahati* means 'it certainly burns'. Or, *nis* signifies 'absence': therein exists nothing of the size of an atom that intervenes. When atoms of the Great Elements which are *nir-antara* in this way arise close to one another, one says that they touch metaphorically."

The Vaibhāṣika position is a logical consequence of the doctrine that an atom has no spatial extension, and yet is aggregated with six other atoms in the six directions (see above § 8.3.1) — north, east, south, west, above and below — with the given atom at the centre. This may imply that an atom has at least six sides — a point seized upon by the Vijñānavādins in their refutation of the Ābhidharmika notion of atom.[73] To avoid this fallacy, atoms must be thought of as being aggregated in such a way that in between the atoms there must be gaps which are less than the size of a single atom.

In the MVŚ, there is a similar consideration as to whether there are gaps in an aggregate of the Great Elements. In either case, there is a fallacy: If there are gaps, how can the Great Elements be unseparated? If there are no gaps, why do they not coalesce into a unity? Two opinions are recorded: 1. There are gaps occupied by the space element (*ākāśa-dhātu*). Nevertheless, the four Elements are said to be unseparated because "the space elements can conceal themselves so that the substances are seen to be unseparated". 2. The Great Elements are juxtaposed without any intervening gaps. Nevertheless, they do not coalesce into one, "in the same manner that among the *skandha, āyatana, dhātu*, and the three periods of time, in spite of there being no gap in between, they [in each case] do not coalesce into one. Moreover, the Great Elements, etc., are each distinct in their intrinsic nature and functions, hence they do not coalesce into one."[74] The absence of comment by the compilers of the MVŚ here suggests that the earlier Sarvāstivādins were as yet undecided on this issue.

NOTES

[1] MVŚ, 383a. The second *sūtra* passage is also quoted in AKB, 13: *yad kiṃcid rūpam atītānāgata-pratyutpannam ādhyātmikaṃ bāhyaṃ vā audārikaṃ vā sūkṣmaṃ vā hīnaṃ vā praṇītaṃ vā yad vā dūre yad vā antike tat sarvam aikadhyam abhisaṃkṣipya rūpa-skandha iti saṃkhyāṃ gacchati /*

[2] *Cf.* T 2, 11b.

[3] AKB, 9: *rūpyate rūpyata iti bhikṣavas tasmād rūpopādānaskandha ity ucyate / kena rūpyate / pāṇisparśenāpi spṛṣṭo rūpyate /*

[4] T 2, *loc. cit.*

[5] *Cf.* S, iii, 86.

[6] *Cf.* T no. 198, 4, 175c; *Suttanipāta*, IV, *Aṭṭhakavagga* 1.2.

[7] AKB, 9.

[8] Vy, 34.

[9] See *Entrance*, 178, n. 285, n. 286.

[10] Ny, 337b.

[11] AKB, *loc. cit.*

[12] Vy, 34: *svadeśe parasyotpatti-pratibandhaḥ /*

[13] MVŚ, 389c–390a.

[14] Ny, 346b.

[15] *Cf.* AKB, 19: *sa hi śakyate nidarśayitum idam ihāmutra iti |*

[16] Ny, 348a.

[17] Ny, 348a.

[18] *Cf.* AKB, 19: *yasmin yasya kāritram sa tasya viṣayaḥ / yac cittacaittair gṛhyate tad ālambanam /* Xuan Zang translates *kāritra* here as *gong neng* (功能), efficacy, which is also the rendering in Ny in this context.

[19] AKB, 19 f.; Ny, 348a–b.

[20] Vy, 51: *idam ihāmutreti deśa-nidarśana-rūpaṇāt /*

[21] Ny, 540a

[22] AKB, 46: *duḥkhendriyaṃ nasty āśrayasyācchatvād…* /

[23] *Cf.* AKB, 5 f., 33: *na cānyo'nyam āvṛṇvanti sphaṭikavad acchatvāt* / This statement occurs in the description of atoms of the visual faculty. MVŚ (63a) has a similar description: "Because they are transparent/clear in nature, they do not mutually obstruct one another. That is to say, for such type of derived clear matter, even when a large number of them are accumulated together, there is no mutual obstruction. It is like the water in an autumn pond; on account of its clarity, even a needle that is dropped it into can be visible."

[24] MVŚ, 389c.

[25] MVŚ, 661c.

[26] MVŚ, 661c–662a

[27] MVŚ, 661c, 662b.

[28] For Śrīlāta's denial of the derived tangibles and Saṃghabhadra's refutation, see Ny, 352c ff.

[29] MVŚ, 663a

[30] *Cf.* Ny, 336b: "… There are only four Great Elements, no more, no less. The Vaibhāṣika says thus: If less [than four], there will be inaptitude; if more [than four], it will serve no purpose. Thus, there are only four, like the legs of a couch." The MVŚ, 663a records the same explanation, attributed to 'certain masters'.

[31] See *Entrance*, 169 f., n. 241.

[32] MVŚ, 388b; *cf. infra* § 16.5.1.

[33] However, the Bhadanta also seems to have denied the reality of unconditioned *ākāśa* (MVŚ, 949c). The Bhadanta in the MVŚ is often regarded by scholars to refer to Bhadanta Dharmatrāta, (e.g., Yin Shun in *Study*, 245 ff.). However, it has also been pointed out that where Xuan Zang's version of the MVŚ gives 'Bhadanta', the earlier translation (T no. 1546) gives 'Venerable 'Bhadanta' (尊者婆檀陀) or 'Venerable Buddhadeva' (尊者浮陀提婆, 尊者佛陀提婆). Moreover, we now also know that where the AKB (13) has simply 'Bhadanta', Xuan Zang in the AKB(C) inserts 'Dharmatrāta' (法救). Yaśomitra in that context objects to Bhagavadviśeṣa's identification of Bhadanta with Dharmatrāta and asserts that in the MVŚ, the one referred to simply as 'the Bhadanta' is a different master inclined toward the philosophy of the Sautrāntika (*sautrāntika-darśanāvalambin*), whereas the one explicitly named as 'Dharmatrāta' is a Sarvāstivāda

master (Vy, 44). Hence, there still seems to be much confusion yet to be cleared up in the identification of 'the Bhadanta' in the MVŚ.

[34] MVŚ, 662b–c. See also Ny, 336a.

[35] MVŚ, 663a.

[36] Ny, 335c.

[37] MVŚ, 665a.

[38] Ny, 355b.

[39] MVŚ, 682c–683a.

[40] MVŚ, 683b.

[41] Ny, 373a.

[42] MVŚ, 663a.

[43] AKB, 102 f.

[44] Ny, 452a.

[45] Ny, 440a.

[46] MVŚ, 665a.

[47] AKB, 189; also *cf.* MVŚ, 691a–b.

[48] Ny, 522a.

[49] MVŚ, 702a–b.

[50] AKB, 176: *rūpasyāpacīyamānasya paryantaḥ paramāṇuḥ / … etat paramāṇvādikaṃ saptaguṇottaraṃ veditavyam / sapta paramāṇavo 'ṇuḥ / saptāṇavo loharajaḥ / tāni saptābrajas tāni sapta… /* Also, Ny, 521c.

[51] Ny, 383c; SPrŚ, 799a.

[52] MVŚ, 64a–b.

[53] MVŚ, 63c.

[54] *Cf.* a similar argument by Vasubandhu for the reality of the *āyatana* in the AKB.

[55] MVŚ, 702a.

[56] Also cf. AKB, 189: *paramāṇvatīndriye 'pi samastānāṃ pratyakṣatvam.*

[57] AKB, 52 f.

[58] AKB, 52.

[59] Vy, 123: *sarva-sūkṣmo rūpa-saṃghātaḥ paramāṇur iti saṃghāta-paramāṇur na dravya-paramāṇūḥ / yatra hi pūrvāpara-bhāgo nāsti / tat sarva-rūpāpacitaṃ dravyaṃ dravya-paramāṇur itīṣyate / tasmād viśinaṣṭi 'saṃghātaḥ paramāṇur' iti /*

[60] Ny has 微 here which could correspond to *aṇu* rather than *paramāṇu.*

[61] Ny, 383c.

[62] Vy, 123.

[63] *Contra Katō*, 156.

[64] ADV, 65: *sarvasūkṣmaḥ khalu rūpasaṃskāropādānasaṃcaya-bhedaparyantaḥ paramāṇur iti prajñapyate / sa tu saptadravyāvinirbhāgī / caturbhir bhūtais tribhiś copādāyarūpais tribhir vā bhūtaiś caturbhiś copādāyarūpair avinirbhāgavarty asāv aṣṭama iti /*

[65] MVŚ, 663c. See also Kimura, T, 木村泰賢全集, Vol. V (Tokyo, 1968), 213 ff.

[66] See AKB(F), vol. 1, 148 f., note 1.

[67] MVŚ, 389c–390a.

[68] Xuan Zang sometimes uses this same rendering for *rūpaṇā.*

[69] MVŚ, 683c; AKB, 32 f.; Ny, 372a ff.

[70] MVŚ, 683c–684a.

[71] AKB, 33.

[72] Ny, 373b.

[73] Viṃś, 7.

[74] MVŚ, 683c–684a.

9. The Categories of Thought and Thought-concomitants (*citta-caitta*)

9.1. Definitions of *citta*, *manas* and *vijñāna*

Abhidharma Buddhism is sometimes considered as a form of depth psychology on account of its uniquely detailed analysis of the nature and function of the mind. This is in keeping with the emphasis of the supremacy of the mind in the Buddha's teachings — bondage in and liberation from *saṃsāra* are all fundamentally on account of our mind.

In contrast to Yogācāra idealism, Abhidharma Buddhism, as much as early Buddhism,[1] refers to the same mental reality by the three synonymous terms *citta*, *manas* and *vijñāna*.[2] However, whereas the Buddha explicitly stated that the mind or consciousness is no more than an empirical or functional reality that results from an assemblage of conditions,[3] the Sarvāstivāda Ābhidharmikas held that it is a real entity (*sad-dravya*). These three terms are distinguished only in terms of the different functional aspects of the mind that they represent: The mind is termed *citta* because it accumulates, *manas* because it thinks, *vijñāna* because it cognizes.[4] The AKB[5] records another distinction: *citta* because it is accumulated with the pure and impure elements; *manas* because it functions as the supporting basis (*tadevāśrayabhūta* — i.e., of the *citta* that succeeds it); *vijñāna* because it is supported (*āśritabhūta* — i.e., by *manas* for its arising). This amounts to saying that the *citta* that arises at the present moment is *vijñāna*.

The MVŚ[6] discusses the various distinctions:

> Question: What is the difference between the three — *citta*, *manas*, *vijñāna* — mentioned in the *sūtra*?
>
> [Answer:] There is the explanation that there is no difference — *citta* is none other than *manas*, *manas* is none other than *vijñāna*, for, although the three words are different, there is no difference in meaning …
>
> There is also the explanation that the three … are also differentiated: that is, the names themselves are different …
>
> Furthermore, there is a difference with respect to time (*adhvan*): what is past is called *manas*; what is future is called *citta*; what is present is called *vijñāna*.
>
> Furthermore, there is a difference with respect to designation (*prajñapti*): *citta* is designated among the *dhātu*-s; *manas*, among the *āyatana*-s; *vijñāna* among the *skandha*-s.
>
> Furthermore, there is a difference in terms of signification (*artha*): *citta* signifies 'clan' (*gotra*); *manas*, 'gateway of arising' (*āya-dvāra*), *vijñāna*, 'agglomeration'.

> Furthermore, there is a difference in terms of activity (*kriyā*): that of *citta* is far-going (*dūragama*) …; *manas*, fore-running (*pūrvaṅgama*) …; *vijñāna*, birth-relinking (*saṃdhāna/pratisaṃdhi*) …[7]
>
> Further, the activity of *citta* is being variegated (*citra*) …; *manas*, going towards (歸趣; *gati* (?)) …; *vijñāna*, cognition (*vi-√jñā*) …
>
> Furthermore, the activity of *citta* is increasing or nourishing (滋長; *saṃcitatva*); *manas*, thinking; *vijñāna*, cognizing.[8]
>
> According to Venerable Parśva: the activity of *citta* is increasing and severing; *manas*, thinking and contemplating, *vijñāna*, distinguishing and comprehending. Herein, it is to be understood that what increases is the with-outflow *citta*, what severs is the outflow-free *citta*; what thinks is the with-outflow *manas*, what contemplates is the outflow-free *manas*; what distinguishes is the with-outflow *vijñāna*, what comprehends is the outflow-free *vijñāna*.

9.2. Thought-concomitants (*caitta/caitasika*)

Citta can never arise by itself. It is always conascent with certain mental factors or concomitants known as *caitta*-s or *caitasika*-s each of which is a distinct real entity making a unique contribution to the perceptual process. What this means in simple terms is that a thought that arises is always one with a specific content and nature, one of doubt which is unskillful, etc., characterized by the *caitta*-s. The essential substance that remains if we abstract the particularized content is the *citta*. Likewise, these *caitta*-s — called the conjoined conditionings (*citta-saṃprayukta-saṃskārāḥ*) — are also always conascent with the *citta* and some other *caitta*-s. Accordingly, *citta* and *caitta*-s are in a reciprocal causal relationship — they are mutually conjoined causes (*saṃprayuktaka-hetu*), an exemplification of the co-existent cause (*sahabhū-hetu*).

9.3. Development of the theory of *caitasika*

9.3.1. Reference to *cetasika/caitasika* in the *nikāya/āgama*

In the *sūtra-piṭaka*, the term *caitasika* (Pāli: *cetasika*) occurs simply as an adjective: 'mental', 'pertaining to the mind'. This is used in contrast to *kāyika* which means 'bodily' or 'physical'.[9] There is therefore no indication of the abhidharmic theory of *caitasika* in *sūtra*-s. The earliest occurrence of the term *citta-cetasika* is to be found in *Paṭisambhidāmagga*,[10] a text which, although included in the *Khuddaka-nikāya*, is well known for its abhidhammic affiliation both in respect of style and content. In the *Milindapañha*,[11] a work around the latter part of the 2nd century B.C.E. (included by the Burmese tradition in the *Khuddaka-nikāya*), Nāgasena explains *nāma* — as opposed to *rūpa* — as the *citta-cetasikā dhammā*. Nevertheless, the Pāli *Anupada-sutta* (no correspondence in the Chinese *āgama*) enumerates — in the context of the meditative experience — the following *dhamma*-s which most likely serve as a source for the later Abhidharmic category of *cetasika/caitasika*: *vitakka*, *vicāra*, *pīti*, *sukha*, *cittekaggatā*, *phassa*, *vedanā*, *saññā*, *cetanā*, *chanda*, *adhimokkha*, *viriya*, *sati*, *upekkhā* and *manasikāra*.

There is, however, an occurrence in the *Citta-saṃyutta*[12] in which the term is used to refer to 'mental conditionings' (*citta-saṃkhārā*): Bhikkhu Kāmabhū explains to the householder Citta that *saññā* and *vedanā* are *cetasika*-s and bound up with *citta* (*citta-paṭibaddha*) which could suggest that the two *dhamma*-s are in some sense distinct from *citta*, although not necessarily having the same technical connotation as in the *abhidhamma/abhidharma* terminology. It is worth of note that the corresponding Chinese version[13] here likewise speaks of *saṃjñā* and *cetanā* as mental conditionings; they are "*caitasika*-s, based on *citta*, connected with *citta*" (想思是心數法，依於心，屬於心). Exactly the same description in the form of Dhammadinnā's explanation to Visākha is also found in the *Cuḷa-vedalla-sutta*.[14]

9.3.2. Development in the early *abhidharma* texts

At the outset, it must be borne in mind that certain developed features — in this case pertaining to *caitasika* — found in the extant versions (in Xuan Zang's translation) of an earlier text could well be a later interpolation or modification on the basis of a text or texts post-dating it. In the decidedly earlier canonical *abhidharma* texts — DSŚ, SgPŚ, PjŚ — where *caitasika* is clearly referred to as mental factors, their enumeration is characterized by a lack of systematization. Thus, in the DSŚ[15] a large number of *caitta*-s are simply enumerated together as "*dharma*-s" — apparently without any taxonomical consideration — to be abandoned completely (*atyantaṃ prahātavya*):

> At one time, the Bhagavat was staying at the Anāthapiṇḍada *ārāma*, in Jetavana in Śrāvasti. At that time, the Bhagavat told the *bhikṣu*-s: 'If you could completely abandon one *dharma*, I assure you that you would acquire non-return (*anāgāmitva*). One *dharma* — that is *rāga* — whoever can abandon it completely, I assure you that he would definitely acquire *anāgāmitva*. Likewise: *dveṣa*, *moha*, *krodha*, *upanāha*, *mrakṣa*, *pradāsa*, *īrṣyā*, *mātsarya*, *māyā*, *śāṭhya*, *āhrīkya*, *anapatrāpya*, *māna*, *atimāna*, *mānātimāna*, *asmimāna*, *abhimāna*, *ūnmāna*, *mithyāmāna*, *mada*, *pramāda*, …'

Then follows the commentarial explanation on each of the items: "What is *rāga*? It is the *rāga*, *saṃrāga* with regard to the sensual object…" In terms of the later systematization in Vasubandhu's *Pañcaskandhaprakaraṇa*,[16] *rāga*, *dveṣa/pratigha*, *moha/avidyā* and *māna* would come under the category *kleśāḥ*, and the underlined items under *upakleśāḥ*.

In the *Pañcavastuka* of Vasumitra's PrŚ,[17] while there is as yet no explicit classification, the manner in which the items are specifically enumerated under *caitasika-dharma*-s suggests an implicit taxonomical consideration influenced by the *sūtra*-s (in the order as in the text):

vedanā, *saṃjñā*, *cetanā*, *sparśa*, *manaskāra*, *chanda*, *adhimokṣa*, *smṛti*, *samādhi*, *prajñā*;
śraddhā, *vīrya*;
vitarka, *vicāra*;
apramāda, *pramāda*;
the *kuśala-mūla*-s, the *akuśala-mūla*-s, the *avyākṛta-mūla*-s;
all the *saṃyojana*-s, *bandhana*-s, *anuśaya*-s, *upakleśa*-s, *paryavasthāna*-s;
all that are *jñāna*-s, all that are *dṛṣṭi*-s, all that are *abhisamaya*-s;
and the other *dharma*-s of this kind conjoined with *citta*.

This enumeration represents the early stage of the development of the theory of *caitasika* in which no explicit grouping was done. However, as noted by Yin Shun:[18]

(i) The first ten items later came to be classified as the ten *mahābhūmika*-s. These were already enumerated as a group exemplifying the *saṃprayuktaka-hetu* in the JPŚ.[19]

(ii) *Śraddhā* and *vīrya* follow *smṛti*, *samādhi* and *prajñā* as the *pañcendriya*-s mentioned in the *sūtra*, and *vitarka* and *vicāra* are among the important *dhyāna-aṅga*-s — all being *caitta*-s discussed in the ancient doctrine of spiritual praxis.

(iii) The rest are enumerated as contrast between the *kuśala* and the *akuśala caitta*-s.

(iv) The *kleśa*-s to be abandoned are summarized as *saṃyojana*-s, etc., mentioned in the *sūtra*; the *prajñā*-s to be cultivated are summarized as "all that are *jñāna*-s…".

9.3.3. Further development in the later *abhidharma* texts

It was probably in the *Dhātukāya-śāstra* that the *caitta*-s were explicitly classified — for the first time — into eight classes totaling 55 *dharma*-s.[20] This text is closely related to the *Saptavastuka* which could have been a version of it that later came to be incorporated into the PrŚ.[21] The *Saptavastuka* gives the same classification, with the addition of ten more items grouped under *kuśala-mahābhūmika*-s. Yin Shun believes that this new class was taken over from the MVŚ.[22] In the MVŚ we see the development into seven classes totaling 58 *dharma*-s as follows:

I.	*mahābhūmika*	10
II.	*kleśa-mahābhūmika*	10
III.	*parītta-kleśa-bhūmika*	10
IV.	*kuśala-mahābhūmika*	10
V.	*akuśala-mahābhūmika*	5
VI.	*nivṛtāvyākṛta-mahābhūmika*	3
VII.	*anivṛtāvyākṛta-mahābhūmika*	10

But there are some repetitions. Thus, *avidyā* is enumerated in II, IV and V; *avidyā*, *styāna* and *auddhatya* in IV and V; all the ten in I are repeated in VII. The compilers of the MVŚ explain that the repetitions are intentional — for the sake of emphasis. Thus, whereas "*āhrīkya* and *anapatrāpya* are acquired only in all the *akuśala-citta*, hence called *akuśala-mahābhūmika-dharma*-s; *styāna* and *auddhatya*, subsumed under *kleśa* and *paryavasthāna*, are conjoined with all *akuśala-citta*-s and, at the same time, strongly obstruct *śamatha* and *vipaśyanā*; hence they are repeated under the *akuśala-bhūmika*. [Likewise,] *avidyā*, subsumed as one of the *anuśaya*-s, is conjoined with all *akuśala-citta*-s; hence it is repeated in the *akuśala-bhūmika*." If we omit these repetitions, the total comes to 43.

The MVŚ[23] explains each class as follows:

I. The universal *dharma*-s (*mahābhūmika*): *dharma*-s which exist in all types of *citta* — whether *kliṣṭa* or *akliṣṭa*; *sāsrava* or *anāsrava*; *kuśala*, *akuśala* or *avyākṛta;* bound to the three spheres of existence or not bound to any sphere; pertaining to the trainee (*śāikṣa*), to the non-trainee (*aśaikṣa*) or to neither;

abandonable by insight (*darśana-heya*), by cultivation (*bhāvanā-heya*) or not to be abandoned (*aheya*); in the mind-ground (*mano-bhūmi*) or in the first five groups of consciousness.

II. The universal *dharma*-s of defilement (*kleśa-mahābhūmika*): *dharma*-s which exist in all defiled *citta*-s — whether *akuśala* or *avyākṛta*; bound to any sphere of existence; abandonable by insight or cultivation; in the mind-ground or the first five groups of consciousness.

III. The defilements of restricted scope (*parītta-kleśa-bhūmika*): *dharma*-s which exist only in a small number of defiled *citta*-s, are abandonable by cultivation and exist in only the mind-ground; "when one arises there is necessarily not a second one, being mutually opposed".

IV. The universal skillful *dharma*-s (*kuśala-mahābhūmika*): *dharma*-s which exist in all *kuśala-citta*-s.

V. The universal unskillful *dharma*-s (*akuśala-mahābhūmika*): *dharma*-s which exist in all *akuśala-citta*-s.

VI. The universal veiled-non-defined *dharma*-s (*nivṛta-avyākṛta-mahābhūmika*): *dharma*-s which exist in all *nivṛta-avyākṛta-citta*-s — *citta* conjoined with the *satkāyadṛṣṭi* and *antagrahadṛṣṭi* pertaining to the *kāmāvacara*; *citta* conjoined with all the defilements pertaining to the *rūpa*- or *ārūpya-dhātu*; all *nivṛta-avyākṛta-citta*-s existing in the mind-ground or the first five groups of consciousness.

VII. The universal non-veiled-non-defined *dharma*-s (*anivṛta-avyākṛta-mahābhūmika*): *dharma*-s which exist in all *anivṛta-avyākṛta-citta*-s — whether bound to *kāma*-, *rūpa*- or *ārūpya-dhātu*; in the mind-ground or the first five groups of consciousness; whether retribution-born (*vipākaja*), pertaining to deportment (*airyapathika*), pertaining to arts and crafts (*śailpa-sthānika*) or supernormal power (lit. 'fruit of higher knowledge', *abhijñā-phala* = *nairmāṇika*). (For these four types of *dharma*, see also § 2.4.3.2.3)

9.3.4. Classic list in the AKB

The AKB enumerates a total of 46 *caitta*-s differentiated into six classes in the Sarvāstivāda system:

I.	*mahābhūmikā dharmāḥ*	10
II.	*kuśala-mahābhūmikā dharmāḥ*	10
III.	*kleśa-mahābhūmikā dharmāḥ*	6
IV.	*akuśala-mahābhūmikā dharmāḥ*	2
V.	*parītta-kleśa-bhūmikā dharmā*	10
VI.	*aniyatā dharmāḥ* (indeterminate *dharma*-s)	8

(See chart in § 2.4.2 for the items listed under each class).

This classification represents more or less the classic one adhered to by the Sarvāstivādins, although slight variants are to be noted. Thus, the post AKB *Avatāra*, apparently inheriting the tradition of the PrŚ, enumerates the *caitta*-s under *vedanā*, *saṃjñā* and *citta-saṃprayukta-saṃskāra*, in conformity with the five-*skandha* taxonomy.[24]

Below, we will discuss only the *mahābhūmika-dharma*-s on account of their importance as universals and comment on the *aniyata*-s on account of their ambiguous nature. Among the former, *prajñā* will be treated at considerable length as it is of fundamental importance for the *abhidharma* system. The definitions of the *caitta*-s given in the *Avatāra* are more or less identical with those given in the ADV whose author is an avowed Vaibhāṣika, and the reader is referred to this work for the rest of the *caitta*-s.[25]

9.3.4.1. Ten *mahābhūmika-dharma*-s[26]

The word *bhūmi* is explained as "the sphere of movement" (*gati-viṣaya*). The sphere of movement of a *dharma* is the *bhūmi* to which it belongs (*yo hi yasya gati-viṣayaḥ sa tasya bhūmir ity ucyate*). The ten *caitta*-s to be enumerated below are called "great *bhūmi*" *dharma*-s because they are always conascent with any *citta*. That is, they always exist in every moment of thought. They are the distinct forces which together make possible the operation of consciousness. However, within the early Sarvāstivāda lineage itself, the acceptance of the doctrine of the *mahābhūmika*-s is far from being unanimous. In the time of Saṃghabhadra, the Sautrāntika leader Śrīlāta asserts that there are only three *mahābhūmikadharma*-s — *vedanā*, *saṃjñā* and *cetanā*. (See below, § 9.5).

9.3.4.1.1. Sensation (*vedanā*) is that force which contributes to the mental ability of sensation or feeling. It is the threefold experience (*anubhāva*) of pleasurable, unpleasurable and neutral feelings produced by different psycho-physical states (*kāyacitta-avasthāviśeṣa*) born of the coming together of an object (which is, respectively, desirable, undesirable or neutral), the sense faculty and the corresponding consciousness. It is that which causes the consciousness of an unenlightened being to be always tainted with craving.[27]

9.3.4.1.2. Volition (*cetanā*) — That which causes the mind to be karmically creative (*citta-abhisaṃskāra*). It is the mental *karma*. The *Avatāra*[28] describes it thus: "It moves forth (*pra-√syand*) the thought." Saṃghabhadra's definition[29] runs: "*cetanā* is that which causes *citta* to do *kuśala*, *akuśala* and *avyākṛta* [*karma*], resulting in good, bad and neutral [*vipāka*]. On account of the existence of *cetanā*, the *citta* has the activity of moving forth with regard to the object. It is like a magnet, owing to the force of which iron can move forth."

9.3.4.1.3. Ideation (*saṃjñā*)

This contributes to the mental ability to form definite ideas or concepts. It is that which grasps the marks — 'male', 'female', etc. — of an object (*viṣaya-nimittodgraha*). Saṃghabhadra[30] defines it thus: "That which causes the determination and grasping of the diverse forms (*nimitta*) of male, female, etc., is named ideation." The definition in the *Avatāra*[31] says: "With regard to *rūpa* such as blue, yellow, ..., *dharma*-s such as males and females, etc. — it comprehends them, [in each case,] by conceptually combining together (*eka-√jñā*) their appearances (*nimitta*), names (*nāma*) and signification (*artha*). It is the cause of reasoning (*vitarka*) and investigation (*vicāra*)."[32]

9.3.4.1.4. Predilection (*chanda*)

This is the desire for action (*kartu-kāmatā*). The *Avatāra*[33] says: "It accords with vigor (*vīrya*), [arising from the thought]: 'I will make such and such an undertaking.'"[34] Thus, predilection or desire in this general sense is indispensable for the undertaking of any action — skillful or unskillful. The desire for the acquisition of skillful *dharma*-s, called *kuśala-dharma-cchanda*, is encouraged in the spiritual practitioners and is specifically distinguished from desire in the bad sense of greed (*rāga*) or craving (*tṛṣṇā*).[35]

9.3.4.1.5. Contact (*sparśa*)

This is the contact born of the coming together of the sense faculty, the object and the consciousness (*indriya-viṣaya-vijñāna-sannipātajā spṛṣṭiḥ*); it is also by virtue of this *dharma* that the three are in contact. "It has the characteristic of enlivening the *caitasika-dharma*-s."[36]

The early Sarvāstivādin Dārṣṭāntikas deny the reality of contact, citing the *sūtra* passage which speaks of the coming together of the three — the visual faculty, the visible and the visual consciousness — as contact. So also the Sautrāntika Śrīlāta.[37] The MVŚ compilers argue that contact is not the mere meeting of these three. They in fact serve as the conditions for the arising of a real entity called contact. Without the operation of this real force, the fact of contact among the three would be impossible.[38]

9.3.4.1.6. Understanding (*prajñā*)

This, defined as the investigation of *dharma*-s (*dharma-pravicaya*), is one of the most important *caitta*-s. For the Ābhidharmikas, "apart from *dharma-pravicaya* (= *prajñā*), there is no proper means for the appeasement of defilements on account of which the world wanders in the ocean of existence".[39] In its pure form, it is *abhidharma per se*.[40] The specific understanding that operates in the discernment of the four noble truths in the course of spiritual progress is called discriminative deliberation (/consideration) (*pratisaṃkhyā*).[41] It is through this that absolute cessation of a defilement, and finally *nirvāṇa* (= *pratisaṃkhyā-nirodha*), is acquired. In other words, when fully perfected, *prajñā* is the perfect wisdom of a Buddha. However, in its general functioning, it may be pure or impure, right or erroneous. Thus, all views, both right or false, are *prajñā* in their essential nature. Likewise, *asaṃprajanya*[42] and *akliṣṭa-ajñāna* (§ 10.4)[43] are also *prajñā*. *Prajñā* is in fact the *sine qua non* for the element of understanding in any perceptual process. Saṃghabhadra explains that, among the various *caitta*-s conjoined with a *citta*, it is *prajñā* alone that has the function of being aware.[44] It plays a predominant role in powering the mental capacity of conceptual discrimination. The definition in the *Avatāra*[45] is typically abhidharmic in emphasis:

> Understanding is the investigation (*pravicaya*) of *dharma*-s. It is the examination (*upalakṣaṇa*), as the case may be, of the following eight kinds of *dharma*-s: inclusion (*saṃgraha*), conjunction (*saṃprayoga*), endowment (*samanvāgama*), causes (*hetu*), conditions (*pratyaya*), fruitions (*phala*),

specific-characteristic (*sva-lakṣaṇa*), common-characteristic (*sāmānya-lakṣaṇa*).[46]

9.3.4.1.7. Mindfulness (*smṛti*)

This enables the mind to remember clearly the object (*cittasyārthābhilapanā*), to be mindful of what has been done, what is being done and what will be done.[47] The operation of this *caitta* becomes particularly important in the practice of meditation. Like *prajñā*, it too plays an important role in the functioning of conceptual discrimination (see *infra*, § 11).

9.3.4.1.8. Mental application (*manaskāra*)

This alerts (*ā-√bhuj*) the *citta* and directs it toward the object (*āvarjayati*). The *Avatāra* says: "It is also the holding in mind (*samanvāhāra*) of an object which has earlier been experienced (*pūrvānubhūta*)."[48]

There are said to be three types of *manaskāra*:

(1) *svalakṣaṇa-manaskāra* — such as the reflection that *rūpa* is characterized by the susceptibility of change and obstruction; *vedanā* is characterized by experience; etc.;

(2) *sāmānyalakṣaṇa-manaskāra* — such as the sixteen modes of activities (*ākāra*) in the process of *satyābhisamaya* (see § 11, § 16.2.2.1);

(3) *adhimokṣa-manaskāra* — such as the meditational practices of the contemplation on the impure and mindfulness of breathing, etc.

According to the opinion of the MVŚ compilers, an *ārya-mārga* (i.e., a spiritual attainment), may occur immediately after any of these three types of *manaskāra*, and, conversely, any of these three may occur immediately after an *ārya-mārga*.[49]

9.3.4.1.9. Determination (*adhimokṣa/adhimukti*)

This enables the mind to be determined and inclined toward an ascertained object (*niścite viṣaye*). The *Avatāra*[50] defines thus: "It is the affirmation (*avadhāraṇa*) with regard to an object, i.e., it enables one to be free from diffidence with regard to an object being perceived (*cittasya viṣayāpatisaṃkoca*)."

The commentary on the *Pañcaskandha-prakaraṇa*[51] comments that: "'[with regard to] the ascertained object' means with regard to the five *skandha*-s, etc.: In accordance with the Bhagavat's saying that "*rūpa* is like foam, *vedanā* is like a bubble, *saṃjñā* is like a mirage. *saṃskāra*-s are like a banana tree, *vijñāna* is like an illusory object"[52] — they are accordingly ascertained. Or rather, in accordance with the *svabhāva* belonging to the particular *dharma*-s, one accordingly gives rise to ascertainment. The meaning of ascertainment is affirmation (印持 = 印可; *avadhāraṇa*). It has the function of [enabling the mind] not to be misled or influenced by others." Saṃghabhadra[53] mentions the opinion of certain Sarvāstivāda masters: "*adhi* means dominance or sovereignty (增勝), *mokṣa* means liberation (解脱). This [*caitta*] enables the mind to operate freely, unobstructed, with regard to the object; like *adhiśīla*, etc."

9.3.4.1.9.1. Different nuances of *adhimokṣa*

Adhimokṣa is perhaps one of the most problematic terms to translate. Considering the various descriptions given in these *abhidharma* texts, however, it seems to include the following connotations (some of which are probably not entirely distinct from others):

- (i) affirmation/commitment/acceptance/approval;
- (ii) decisiveness/determination/resolve;
- (iii) conviction/faith;
- (iv) liking/inclination;
- (v) mental freedom resulting from the eradication of indecision;
- (vi) mental freedom resulting from detachment.

It may be noted that this term seems to bear some similarities particularly with *śraddhā* and *chanda*. Saṃghabhadra[54] explains the relationship among the three: "*śraddhā* is that which serves as the basis (*āśraya*) for *chanda* and an aid for *adhimokṣa*." The MVŚ[55] speaks of faith as being of two modes of activity or forms: faith in the form of acceptance/affirmation (信可), and faith in the form of liking/inclination (信樂). As regards *adhimokṣa* as liberation from defilement (vi), the MVŚ explains that

> with regard to all *dharma*-s, there are two types of liberation: one, unconditioned, viz., *pratisaṃkyā-nirodha*; two, conditioned, viz., *adhimokṣa*.
>
> (The conditioned *adhimokṣa* is only sovereignty over an object, not disjunction (*visaṃyoga*).)[56] This [*adhimokṣa*] is again two-fold: one, defiled, viz., improper (*mithyā*) *adhimokṣa*; two, non-defiled, viz., proper (*samyañc*) *adhimokṣa*.
>
> This [latter] is again two-fold: one, with-outflow, viz., those conjoined with the contemplation of the impure and mindfulness of breathing; two, outflow-free, viz., those conjoined with *duḥkha-dharma-jñāna-kṣānti* (see § 16), etc.[57]

The MVŚ also distinguishes between right *adhimokṣa* and right *mokṣa*: The former is the cause, the latter is the fruit. Further, the former pertains to the stage of preparation (*prayoga*), the latter, the stage of perfection.[58]

9.3.4.1.10. Concentration (*samādhi*)

Concentration, defined as "the one-pointedness of the mind",[59] enables the *citta* to remain focused on an object. The *Avatāra*[60] describes it thus:

> It controls the monkey-like *citta* so that it can operate (*vartate*) on a single object. The Vaibhāṣika says thus: "Just as a snake that is confined in a bamboo pipe does not move in a crooked manner, *citta*, when concentrated (*samāhita*), proceeds upright."

9.3.4.2. Indeterminate *caitta*-s

Among the extant *abhidharma* texts, the AKB was apparently the first to make an explicit mention of this class. In stanza 23c–d of chapter 2 of the AKB,[61] Vasubandhu states that "the *caitta*-s are of five types, in respect of the division into the *mahābhūmi*[-*ka*], etc." But at the end of the definitions of all the *caitta*-s of the five classes, he remarks that "there are also other [*caitta*-s] which are indeterminate (*aniyata*) — reasoning (*vitarka*), investigation (*vicāra*), regret (*kaukṛtya*), drowsiness (*middha*), etc."[62] Yaśomitra explains that they refer to "those which sometimes exist in a *kuśala-citta*, sometimes in an *akuśala-citta*, sometimes in an *avyākṛta-citta*.[63] Thus, regret can arise in either a *kuśala* or *akuśala citta*: In the former case, one regrets not having done a good action or having committed a bad action. In the latter case, one regrets not having done a bad action or having accomplished a good action.[64]

Yaśomitra further remarks that by the word "etc." in Vasubandhu's prose commentary, the following are to be included: (i) secondary *kleśa* (*upakleśa*) such as disgust (*arati*), yawning (*vijṛmbhikā*), exhaustion (*tandrī*), uneven consumption of food (*bhakte asamatā*) (these four together with *cetaso līnatva* occur in the AKB as the five nourishments (*āhāra*) of *styāna-middha*);[65] and (ii) *kleśa* such as *rāga*, etc. "These [*caitta*-s], *rāga*, etc., are indeterminate with regard to [their inclusion in] any of the five classes: They are not *mahābhūmika*-s because they are not found in all cases of mind; not *kuśala-mahābhūmika*-s because they are not connected with skillfulness (*kuśalatva-ayogāt*); not *kleśa-mahābhūmika*-s because they are not found in all cases of defiled thought — for *rāga* does not exist in a mind conjoined with *pratigha* (*sa-pratighe cetasi*) nor does *pratigha* exist in a mind conjoined with *rāga*."[66]

He further quotes a stanza by *ācārya* Vasumitra which states that eight *aniyata dharma*-s are recognized — *vitarka*, *vicāra*, *kaukṛtya*, *middha*, *pratigha*, *śakti* (= *rāga*), *māna* and *vicikitsā*. It is to be noted that Pu Guang, a prominent disciple of Xuan Zang, later followed this tradition and explained that the word "etc." in the AKB stanza subsumes *rāga*, *pratigha*, *māna* and *vicikitsā*.[67] However, Yaśomitra here objects to the number of eight, for "why are the *dṛṣṭi*, etc., not conceded as *aniyata* as well — since *mithyā-dṛṣṭi* does not arise in a *citta* conjoined with either *pratigha* or *vicikitsā*?"[68]

9.4. Sarvāstivāda doctrine of conjunction (*saṃprayoga*)

The doctrine that the *citta* and *caitta*-s always arise and operate in union is expressed by the notion of conjunction (*saṃprayoga*). However, the early Sarvāstivāda *ācārya*-s interpreted this notion differently.[69] For Vasumitra, *saṃprayoga* means mutually giving rise to each other and having the same basis (*āśraya*). For Dharmatrāta, it is companionship or association. The *vijñāna* and *caitta*-s are *saṃprayukta* only if they mutually accommodate each other, co-arise and take the same object. For Ghoṣaka, it refers to the sameness (*samatā*) of the *citta* and the *caitta*-s with regard to basis, object (*ālambana*), mode of activity (*ākāra*), and action (*kriyā*).

Eventually, a fivefold equality or sameness (*pañcadhā samatā*) among the *citta* and *caitta*-s came to be accepted as the standard requirements for the notion of conjunction:[70]

I. Same basis: both the *citta* and *caitta*-s must be supported by the same basis (*āśraya*), i.e., the sense organ.

II. Same object (*ālambana*): they must have the same object.

III. Same mode of activity (*ākāra*): the mode of apprehending the percept must be the same; thus, if the *citta* apprehends greenness the *caitta*-s too apprehend likewise. (See also § 10.8 for a further discussion on *ākāra*.)

IV. Same time (*kāla*): they must be conascent.

V. Same substance (*dravya*): in a given *citta* there is conjoined only one *vedanā* (either pleasurable, unpleasurable or neutral), one *saṃjñā* (either the idea of 'small' or 'big', or 'male' or 'female', etc.), etc.

As to whether a *citta* can be conjoined with another *citta*, the Vaibhāṣika answers in the negative: "A *citta* may be conjoined with the *caitta*-s; the *caitta*-s may also be conjoined with [other] *caitta*-s; the *caitta*-s again may be conjoined with a *citta*. There can be no conjunction (*saṃprayoga*) between one *citta* and another, as no two *citta*-s co-arise within one [and the same] person."[71]

9.5. Dārṣṭāntika and Sautrāntika Doctrine of successive arising

However, it is to be noted that in spite of the questionable attribution[72] of the meaning of 'companionship' to Dharmatrāta, he, in reality — together with other early Dārṣṭāntikas — asserts that the *citta-caitta*-s arise successively and not simultaneously, like a group of merchants who pass through a narrow road one by one.[73] For them, *saṃprayoga* means not simultaneous association but the association or 'companionship' of two mental *dharma*-s one immediately following the other without anything else in between the successive arising of the two.[74]

Thus, in the early Dārṣṭāntika perspective, when a *citta* is said to be conjoined with a *caitta* — say *sukhā vedanā* — what it means is that the thought that arises at this given moment is one of pleasurable feeling. A so-called *caitta* is not a real mental entity distinct from the *citta*; it is simply a specific state or mode of functioning of the mind itself. This is precisely the definition given by 'some other masters' (unnamed) in the AKB.[75] These are in fact the followers of the Dārṣṭāntika master Buddhadeva whose view, as given in the MVŚ,[76] is that there is no *caitta* apart from the *citta*. This argument of Buddhadeva is also recorded in the ADV.[77]

Dharmatrāta states that "the *citta-caitta*-s are [but] the specific modes of *cetanā* (*cetanā-viśeṣa*)".[78] This means that whatever one may choose to call it — *citta* or *caitta* — the mind arises specifically; mental activity as such being characterized by *cetanā* — 'consciousness', 'understanding'. As a matter of fact, *citta* (> *caitta*), *cetas* (> *caitasika*) and *cetanā* are all derived from the same root √*cit*, and *cetanā*, in a more general sense (than that of 'volition'), can mean 'understanding', 'consciousness', etc., thus referring to mental activity in a general sense. Understood in this way, then, Dharmatrāta's view is not so much different from Buddhadeva's. The only significant difference seems to be that whereas Buddhadeva would absolutely not allow any reality status of the *caitta*-s apart from *citta* itself, Dharmatrāta would view the *caitta*-s as being distinguishable from (hence not exactly identical with) the *citta*/*vijñāna* inasmuch as they belong to the different stages of mental activity subsequent to the initial arising of consciousness.

A modification of Dharmatrāta's doctrine is recorded in the AKB:

> According to some, sensation [arises] subsequently to contact (*sparśa*). First, there are the sense faculty and the object, then the consciousness. The coming together of these three is contact. From contact as the condition, sensation [arises] subsequently in the third moment.[79]

This doctrine is ascribed by the commentarial tradition to Śrīlāta.[80] The Ny explains his doctrine (quoted as "the Sthavira" in the Ny) as follows:

> There are only three *caitta*-s [i.e., *vedanā, saṃjñā, cetanā*].[81]

> The *saṃskāra-skandha* comprises *cetanā* alone — the *samskāra*-s, *manaskāra*, etc., all have *cetanā* as their intrinsic nature.[82]

Śrīlāta claims that he bases himself on the *sūtra* passage which says:

> Conditioned by the eye and the visibles, visual consciousness arises. The coming together of the three is contact (regarded as another distinct real *caitta* by the Sarvāstivāda). Born together are *vedanā*, *saṃjñā*, *cetanā*.[83]

The Vaibhāṣika capitalizes on the phrase 'born together' (*sahajāta*) in support of their doctrine of simultaneous arising of thought and thought-concomitants. The Sautrāntika, although equally leaning on this scriptural passage for their *caitta* doctrine, interprets 'born together' differently:

> 'Born together' does not mean 'born together with contact'. … This word 'together' has also been observed to mean 'immediately after' (*samanantaram*).[84]

That 'arising together' can be taken to mean 'arising one immediately after another', reminds us of the notion of *saṃprayoga* advocated by Dharmatrāta and others in the MVŚ. (See above).

The Pāli[85] version corresponding to the above-quoted sūtra passage does not contain the term *sahajāta* (*cakkhuṃ ca paṭicca rūpe ca uppajjati cakkhuviññāṇaṃ / tiṇṇaṃ saṅgati phasso / phassa-paccayā vedanā / vedanā-paccayā taṅhā / ayaṃ kho bhikkhave dukkhassa samudayo /*). This would lend support to the sequential model of the Dārṣṭāntika-Sautrāntika: *vijñāṇa* → *vedanā* → *saṃjñā* → *cetanā*. It is apparently on this basis that Śrīlāta acknowledges only the three *caitta*-s mentioned in the *sūtra* and regards all the so-called *caitta*-s other than *vedanā* and *saṃjñā* as merely *cetanā-viśeṣa*.

The **Satyasiddhi-śāstra* (SatŚ) too apparently inherits the early Dārṣṭāntika standpoint and repudiates the Sarvāstivāda doctrines of distinct *caitta*-s and *saṃprayoga*:

> *Vedanā*, *saṃjñā* and *saṃskāra*, etc., are the various names of the *citta*. For instance, [in the *sūtra,*] one and the same *smṛti* has five different names: *smṛty-upasthāna*, *smṛtīndriya*, *smṛti-bala*, *smṛti-bodhyaṅga* and *samyak-smṛti*; likewise for *vīrya*, etc. … Thus, the same *citta*, at different times, receives different names. Accordingly, we know that [the *caitta*-s] are none other than the *citta*…[86]

There are no conjoined *dharma*-s. Why? Because, there being no *caitta*-s, with what is the *citta* conjoined? Furthermore, the different characteristics, sensation, etc., cannot be simultaneous. Furthermore, cause and effect do not co-exist: Consciousness is the cause of ideation and other *dharma*-s, and these *dharma*-s should not exist simultaneously. Hence, we know that there is no *saṃprayoga*.[87]

9.6. Difference in functionality between *citta* and *caitta*-s

With the development of the doctrine of the *caitta*-s as entities distinct from but conascent with the *citta*, the functional distinctions between the two came to be articulated. *Citta* or *vijñāna* is the general discernment or apprehension with respect to each individual object.[88] This discernment is the mere grasping of the object itself, without apprehending any of its particularities. A *caitta*, on the other hand, apprehends the particularities of the object.[89] Thus, in a visual perception, the *citta*, i.e., visual consciousness in this case, can only apprehend a blue object. It is only in conjunction with the *caitta* called *saṃjñā*, whose function it is to categorize, and *prajñā* whose function it is to discriminatively conceptualize, that the mind apprehends specifically: "This is blue."

The AKB defines consciousness as follows:

> Consciousness is the cognition relative to each [object] (*vijñānaṃ prativijñaptiḥ*). The cognition (*vijñapti*), apperception (*upalabdhi*), relative to each object, is called the consciousness-aggregate.[90]

On this, Saṃghabhadra comments:

> 'Consciousness is cognition' in the sense that it grasps the characteristic of an object in a general manner. 'Cognition relative to each object' means that each [type of consciousness — visual, etc. —] grasps in a general manner the object specific to it [— *rūpa*, etc.]. That is, although numerous objects —

> *rūpa*, etc. — are present, visual consciousness grasps only *rūpa*, not *śabda*, etc.; only blue, etc., not 'It is blue', etc., or 'It is agreeable, not agreeable', etc., or 'a male, a female', etc., or 'a human, a post', etc., or 'It is a gain, loss', etc. The same applies to the other types of consciousness each of which grasps its specific object in a general manner.[91]

The *dharma* being cognized serves as a condition qua object, *ālambana-pratyaya*. That is, it is the indispensable condition for the generation of that consciousness which arises with an image (*pratibimba*; *gzugs brnyan*), as in the case of a sensory perception, or with a mode of understanding (*ākāra*), as in the case of a mental cognition (see § 7.1.3, § 10.7). The MVŚ[92] compares this *pratyaya* to things of the nature of supporting, such as a walking stick.

The ADV explains that while the *citta* is conascent with the *caitta*-s, it is distinguishable as the chief substance (*pradhāna-dravya*) inasmuch as it is the *citta* that grasps the mere object. The specifics pertaining to the object so apprehended are grasped simultaneously[93] by a *caitta* — *saṃjñā* ideates, *smṛti* recollects, *prajñā* examines, etc. The implication is that without the raw or general grasping of the object to begin with, there cannot be the specific functioning of the *caitta*-s. Accordingly, the *caitta*-s are functionally subordinate to and dependent on the *citta* which is like the governor (*rāja-sthānīya*) in relation to the governed. It is by the *citta* that the fundamental essence of a being (*mūla-sattva-dravya*) is designated.[94] That the *citta* is the chief is also to be understood from the fact that the unenlightened are attached to it — not to the *caitta*-s — as the *Ātman*.

Moreover, when a person is liberated, one speaks only of the *citta* being liberated even though it is at that moment being accompanied by *caitta*-s and *dharma*-s belonging to other *skandha*-s. This is once again because these accompanying *dharma*-s are all dependent on the *citta*, and, when the *citta* is pure, the other *skandha*-s too are likewise pure.[95] The ADV further invokes the scriptural authority: It is said in the *sūtra* that beings are defiled or purified on account of the defilement and purification of the *citta*.[96]

According to Xuan Zang's disciple,[97] there were four ancient schools or views on the functional relationship between the *citta* and the *caitta*-s:

I. The *citta* apprehends the general characteristic — *rūpa*, *śabda*, etc. — and a *caitta* apprehends the specific characteristic in keeping with its functional nature — agreeable, disagreeable, etc.; for, with regard to a given substance, there cannot be more than one apprehensional function at one time.

II. The function proper to the *citta* is the apprehension (正取) of the general characteristic; it can also apprehend the specific characteristics. The *caitta*-s each apprehend their corresponding characteristic but cannot apprehend the general characteristics. This is because the *citta* has greater strength but the *caitta* is weak, therefore the *caitta* can perform only one function.

III. The *caitta*-s each can properly apprehend their own characteristics and at the same time secondarily apprehend the general characteristics. The *citta* can only apprehend the general characteristics but not the specific characteristics. This is because the *citta* is like the 'king' in relation to the *caitta*-s: where the *citta* operates, it, being the king, is necessarily followed by the *caitta*-s which are its subordinates — i.e., the *caitta*-s also do what the king does. However, where the *caitta*-s go, the *citta* does not — the king does not follow the subordinates.

IV. Both *citta* and *caitta*-s apprehend both the general and specific characteristics. But the *citta* primarily apprehends the general characteristics and secondarily apprehends the specific characteristics; whereas the *caitta* primarily apprehends the specific characteristic in keeping with its own nature and also secondarily apprehends the general characteristics and the specific characteristics proper to other *caitta*-s.

9.7. Difference between the first five and the sixth consciousnesses

Although all six consciousnesses are equally consciousness in nature and are equally dependent on the object and the sense organ in their arising, they differ in the way they grasp objects. Firstly, mental consciousness can grasp objects pertaining to the three periods of time. In terms of species of objects, it can grasp all *dharma*-s, conditioned and unconditioned. In contrast, the five sensory consciousnesses can grasp only the present objects and only those specific to them, i.e., visual consciousness can grasp only *rūpa*, etc.

Another important difference is stated in the MVŚ as follows:

> The five sensory consciousness are exclusively without discrimination (*vikalpa*). The sixth consciousness may or may not have discrimination: When it occurs in meditation, it is always without discrimination. If it is not in meditation, there can be discrimination, for discrimination in the form of examination occurs universally with non-concentrated (*asamāhita*) mental consciousness.[98]

This difference involves the notion of the three types of discrimination:[99]

1. *Svabhāva-vikalpa* — discrimination which is in the very nature of consciousness itself. It is *vitarka* and *vicāra* — or *vitarka* according to Saṃghabhadra.[100]

2. *Anusmaraṇa-vikalpa*—discrimination in the form of recollection. It is the *smṛti* associated with mental consciousness.

3. *Abhinirūpaṇā-vikalpa* — discrimination in the form of examination. It is the non-concentrated *prajñā* pertaining to the mental sphere (*mano-bhūmi*).

The first five consciousnesses can have only *svabhāva-vikalpa*. Although they are also always associated with *smṛti* and *prajñā*, their functions of recollection and discrimination, respectively, are feeble therein.[101] Accordingly, although they can discriminate in a general manner the object proper to their specific domain — visual consciousness can know a *rūpa*, say, a blue color — it cannot know "This is blue".[102] In contrast, mental consciousness can have all the three types of distinctional functions. Sthiramati explains that the *prajñā* conjoined with a sensory consciousness is not named a *abhinirūpaṇā-vikalpa* on account of the fact that it does not take name as its object.[103]

On account of its superimpositional function, mental consciousness plays the key role in the *saṃsāra* process of defiling and purification. The MVŚ[104] speaks of six events uniquely distinguishing mental consciousness from the first five consciousnesses: 1. spiritual retrogression, 2. detachment from defilements, 3. death, 4. birth, 5. the cutting off of the skillful roots, 6. the relinking with the skillful roots which have been cut off.

As to whether, like mental consciousness, the sensory consciousnesses too can project *karma*, various opinions are recorded in the MVŚ:

> Herein, there are two kinds of origination (*samutthāna*): origination qua cause (*hetu-samutthāna*) and the moment-origination ([*tat*]*kṣaṇa-samutthāna*, i.e., origination at the very moment of the action). The origination qua cause is the [initial] propelling thought (*pravartakaṃ cittam*). The moment-origination is the subsequent propelling cause (*anuvartakaṃ cittam*).
>
> Question: Are the five sensory consciousnesses also capable of serving as both types of origination and project bodily and vocal *karma*-s?
>
> One opinion: The five sensory consciousnesses cannot project bodily and vocal *karma*-s because mental consciousness alone can serve as the [initial] propeller and subsequent propeller, causing the *karma* to come into the presence. The five sensory consciousnesses cannot serve as the

> [initial] propeller and subsequent propeller, causing the *karma* to come into the presence. …
>
> Another opinion: The five sensory consciousnesses can also project bodily and vocal *karma*-s because mental consciousness can serve as the [initial] propeller and subsequent propeller; the five sensory consciousnesses cannot serve as the [initial] propeller, but can serve as the subsequent propeller. …
>
> According to the Venerable Saṅghavasu (僧伽伐蘇): The five sensory consciousnesses can also project bodily and vocal *karma*-s, serving as the origination qua cause and the moment-origination. …
>
> The correct opinion (如是説者): The five sensory consciousnesses cannot serve as the origination qua cause to project bodily and vocal *karma*-s because mental consciousness can serve as the [initial] propeller and subsequent propeller for bodily and vocal *karma*-s; the five sensory consciousnesses can serve only as the subsequent propeller, but not the [initial] propeller.[105]

However, Saṃghabhadra argues that the sensory consciousnesses can be skillful, unskillful and non-defined (i.e., are not exclusively non-defined). They can therefore also generate defilements:

> [A sensory consciousness,] although staying for one thought moment in the object (*viṣaya*), is capable of grasping marks (*nimitta*); they are therefore morally definable. Thus, the *sūtra* says: "Having seen *rūpa*-s with the eyes, he does not grasp the marks [or] the subsidiary marks (*anuvyañjana*) (*sa cakṣuṣā rūpāṇi dṛṣṭvā na nimitta-grāhī bhavati / nānuvyañjana-grāhī*)."[106] Because the visible objects are grasped by two consciousnesses, there is first the arising of visual consciousness that grasps the marks of *rūpa*, then the arising of mental consciousness that grasps its subsidiary marks. Thus, the *sūtra* intends to show that because visual consciousness can grasp marks, it can also generate defilements.

> But if so, why is mental consciousness alone said to be discriminative (*vikalpaka*)?
>
> It should be understood that it is only on account of the force of discrimination that there come to be the various faults. … The sensory consciousnesses [are said to be without discrimination in the sense that they have no discrimination in the form of examination and recollection]; but it is always conjoined with the intrinsic discrimination….
>
> Sentient beings are of different natures; some with feeble defilements, others with strong defilements. For those with feeble defilements, there must first be the generation of false discrimination (虛妄分別; *abhūta-parikalpa*) before a defilement can come into play (*sam-ud-ā-√car*). For those with strong defilements, without depending on *vikalpa*, a defilement arises as soon as it accords with the object. Accordingly, there are cases where a defiled mental consciousness first arises, and other cases where another type of defiled consciousness first arises … Thus, the five sensory consciousnesses are of all the three moral natures.[107]

9.8. Original nature of thought

The question of the original nature of the *citta* was one of the major controversies in Abhidharma Buddhism. One major doctrine is that it is originally or intrinsically pure. This doctrine seems to have been originally connected with meditational practice, for in the context of the three-fold training, *śīla-samādhi-prajñā*, *samādhi* is also often given in the *sūtra* as *citta*. This is because meditational practice is seen as a process of removing the mental hindrances so that *prajñā* can, as it were, shine forth unobstructed. This seems to have inspired the doctrine of the original pure nature of *citta*.[108]

The Theravāda, which holds this doctrinal position, is apparently inspired by the following passage in the *Aṅguttara-nikāya*:

> This mind, O *bhikkhu*-s, is luminous (*pabhassara*). But it is defiled by adventitious defilements (*āgantuka upakkilesa*). The uninstructed worldling does not understand this as it really is; therefore for him there is no mental development.
>
> This mind, O *bhikkhu*-s, is luminous, and it is freed from adventitious defilements. The instructed worldling understands this as it really is; therefore for him there is mental development.[109]

The Pāli commentary identifies *citta* in this context as the *bhavaṅga-citta* — the *citta* in its intrinsic, neutral state (non-arising) — and interprets "luminous" as "pure/clean" (*pabhassaran ti paṇḍaraṃ parisuddhaṃ*).[110] Mental defilement and liberation do not pertain to the *bhavaṅga-citta* but to the phenomenal *citta* that arises from the *bhavaṅga-citta* at the stage of *javana*, i.e., the stage of karmic volition, skillful or unskillful.

The **Śāriputrābhidharma* also cites a very similar passage as the above-quoted *Aṅguttara* passage.[111]

From the *Samayabhedoparacana-cakra*, we learn that the Mahāsāṃghika too holds the same thesis.[112] The *Lakṣaṇānusāra* (隨相論) explains as follows:

> As the Mahāsāṃghika says: 'The nature of the mind of beings is originally pure; it is defiled by adventitious dusts (眾生心性本淨, 客塵所污). Pure — that is, the three roots of skillfulness. Beings from beginningless time possess adventitious dusts — that is, defilements. The defilements are the defilements of *anuśaya*, etc. The defilements of *anuśaya* are the three roots of unskillfulness.[113]

The Mahāsāṃghika explains that both the roots of skillfulness and unskillfulness are not conjoined with thought — they are potentialities of skillfulness and unskillfulness. (Note that this school has only *kuśala* and *akuśala*; no neutral *dharma*-s). The idea is that the unskillful defilements and thought-concomitants can be removed; the mind in correspondence with the skillful potential is said to be "the originally pure nature of the mind".

In the MVŚ, it is also recorded that the Vibhajyavādins too hold a similar view:

> Some hold that the nature of thought is originally pure, like the Vibhajyavādins. They say that the nature of thought is originally pure. On account of being defiled by adventitious defilements, it has an impure appearance. … They say that the essential nature of thought does not differ whether it is defiled or undefiled. That is, when the conjoined defilement has not been abandoned, it is called a defiled thought; when the conjoined defilement has been abandoned, it is called an undefiled thought. Just as a copper vessel, when the taint has not been removed, is called a tainted vessel, etc.; when the taint has been removed, a taintless vessel, etc. The same is true for thought.[114]

The Ny records the Vibhajyavāda view as follows:

> The Vibhajyvādins assert thus: It is only the thought having greed (*sarāga-citta*) that now gets liberated, like a vessel having becoming freed from the taint subsequently. It is like a crystal that shows different colors according to the specific color of its supporting basis, a different color arises. Likewise, when the pure thought is defiled by greed, etc., it is called [a thought] having greed, etc. Subsequently it again becomes liberated. The noble scriptures also say that the nature of thought is originally pure and at times is defiled by adventitious defilements.[115]

The MVŚ (110a) also informs that "those who hold the view of a single thought series" (一心相續論者) also maintain that the nature of thought remains the same whether defiled or not, and gives the similes of washing a cloth, refining gold, etc., which are also found in the *Aṅguttara nikāya*. (A, III, 100):

> Some hold that there is only the one *citta*, like those who hold the single serial continuity of *citta*. They assert thus: Whether a thought is with proclivities (*sānuśaya*) or without proclivities, its nature is not different. When the noble path arises, it is opposed to the defilement, not to the nature of *citta*; it [arises] in order to counteract the defilements, not *citta*. This is like the case of washing clothes, polishing a mirror, or refining gold, etc.; what it is opposed to are the taints, etc., not the clothes, etc. Likewise the noble path. … Although a difference exists at different times as to whether there is taint or no taint, etc., there is no difference in terms of nature. Likewise the case of *citta*.

Saṃghabhadra (Ny, 733a-b) rejects the positions of the Mahāsāṃghika and the Vibhājyavādins. He proposes that the *sūtra* statements cited by them must be properly interpreted. He explains the Sarvāstivāda position thus: when *citta* abides in its intrinsic nature, i.e., the neutral nature, it is necessarily pure — essentially agreeing with the Theravāda commentarial tradition. But when it abides in adventitious nature, it can be defiled:

> If they assert that *citta* has purity as its nature, and subsequently turns into being defiled at the stage of being conjoined with defilements, then it should have lost its intrinsic nature (*svabhāva*). Since it has lost its intrinsic nature, it should not be called *citta*. Thus, it should be asserted that *citta* is pure in its original nature and is, at times, defiled by adventitious defilements. If they keep their foolish faith and dare not to deny that this is *sūtra*, they should know that this *sūtra* contradicts reasoning and is thus an implicit teaching. … The *sūtra* … says so with the implicit reference to the original (*prakṛti*) and adventitious (*āgantuka*) nature [of *citta*]. That is, *citta* in its original nature is necessarily pure. A *citta* in its adventitious nature may be defiled. *Citta* in its original nature is the neutral *citta* which arises freely, being neither sorrowful nor joyful. The different species of sentient beings mostly abide in this *citta*, for it can exist in all situations. This *citta* is necessarily pure, being undefiled.

> The *citta* in its adventitious nature refers to the other *citta*-s. It is not the case that sentient beings mostly abide in it. All [types of *citta*] may not obtain in some situations, because those who have cut off their roots of skillfulness necessarily do not have skillful thoughts, because at the non-trainee (*arhat*) stage there is necessarily no defiled [*citta*], and because this *citta* may be defiled and not always pure. As it is said: The river water is intrinsically clear; there are times when it becomes turbid on account of the adventitious mud. In the same way, it is only with reference to a *citta* in its serial continuity that one speaks of it as being pure when it abides in its original nature; when it abides in the adventitious nature, it is conceded to be temporarily defiled.[116]

When this *citta* does not arise in conjunction with defilements, it is liberated. Thus, contrary to the Vibhajyavāda, the lustful (*sa-rāga*) *citta* cannot be liberated.

In a similar manner, the SatŚ speaks of the Buddha's teaching in this regard as being an expedient teaching:

> It is not that the nature of *citta* is not originally pure and becomes impure on account of the adventitious defilements. It is just that the Buddha, for the sake of those who think that *citta* is eternal, speaks of it as becoming impure when defiled by adventitious defilements. Again, for the sake of those lazy beings who, on hearing that *citta* is originally impure, think of its nature as being unalterable and thus do not generate pure *citta*-s, He speaks of it as being originally pure.[117]

NOTES

[1] *Cf.* S, ii, 95.

[2] PrŚ, 692b; MVŚ, 371a–b; etc. AKB, 61: ***cittaṃ mano 'tha vijñānam ekārtham*** / Also *cf. Entrance*, 141.

[3] M, i, 257: *aññatra paccayā natthi viññāṇassa sambhavo.*

[4] AKB, 61: *cinotīti cittam / manuta iti manaḥ / vijānātīti vijñānam /*

[5] AKB, *loc. cit.*

[6] MVŚ, 371a–b.

[7] *Cf.* DhsA, 112, on the description on *citta.*

[8] *Cf.* explanation in AKB cited above.

[9] *Cf.* D, ii, 306; M, iii, 287–8; etc.

[10] *Paṭisambhidāmagga*, 84.

[11] *Milindapañha*, 49.

[12] S, iv, 293.

[13] T 2, 150b.

[14] M, i, 301; also *cf. Paṭisambhidhāmagga*, I, 187.

[15] DSŚ, 494c.

[16] T 1612, 848a.

[17] PrŚ, 692c–694a.

[18] *Study*, 159.

[19] T 26, 920c.

[20] T 26, 614b.

[21] T 26, 689b f.; *cf. Study*, 162 ff.

[22] *Study*, 164; MVŚ, 220a–b.

[23] MVŚ, 220b–c.

[24] *Cf. Entrance*, 39 ff.

[25] *Entrance*, 93 ff.

[26] AKB, 54 ff.

[27] *Cf.* ADV, II, 69: *vedanā sukhādistrividho'nubhavaḥ / trividhaṃ saṃveditam iti paryāyaḥ / iṣṭāniṣṭobhayaviparīta-viṣayendriyavijñāna-sannipātajā dharma-yoniḥ kāya-cittāvasthā-viśeṣaḥ prahlādyupatāpī tadubhayaviparītaś ca tṛṣṇāhetur vedanety ucyate* / Also Cf. *Entrance*, 88.

[28] *Entrance*, 91.

[29] Ny, 384b.

[30] Ny, *loc. cit.*

[31] *Entrance*, 89.

[32] *Cf.* ADV II, 69: *nimitta-nāmārthaikyajñā saṃjñā vitarka-yoniḥ* / Also *Cf.* AKB, 10: *yāvan nīla-pītadīrgha-hrasva-strī-puruṣa-mitrāmitra-sukha-duḥkhādi-nimittodgrahaṇam asau saṃjñā-skandhaḥ* /

[33] *Entrance*, 92.

[34] *Cf.* ADV, 69: *chandaḥ kartukāmatā vīryāṅgabhūtaḥ* / Also *Siddhi*(C), 28a : "What is *chanda*? It has as its nature the aspiration for a desired object; and it serves as the basis for *vīrya*."

[35] *Cf.* AKB, 289.

[36] *Avatāra* — *cf. Entrance*, 92. Also, ADV, 69: *viṣayendriyavijñāna sannipātajā cittasya viṣayaspṛṣṭiḥ caitasikadharmo jīvanalakṣaṇaḥ sparśaḥ* /

[37] Ny, 384b.

[38] MVŚ, 760a.

[39] AKB, 2.

[40] AKB, *loc. cit.*; *cf.* § 1.2.

[41] AKB, 4 *yaḥ sāsravair dharmair visaṃyogaḥ pratisaṃkhyā-nirodhaḥ / duḥkhādīnām āryasatyānaṃ pratisaṃkhyānaṃ pratisaṃkhyā prajñā-viśesas tena prāpyo nirodhaḥ pratisaṃkhyā-nirodhaḥ* /

[42] MVŚ, 220a.

[43] Ny, 502a. See Dhammajoti, KL (1998a), 89 ff.

[44] Ny, 396a.

[45] *Entrance*, 93.

[46] *Cf.* ADV, 70: *dhiḥ prajñā dharma-saṃgrahādy-upalakṣaṇa-svabhāvā* /

[47] *Cf.* ADV, 69; *Entrance*, 92. AKB, 54: *smṛtir ālambana-asaṃpramoṣaḥ /*

[48] *Entrance*, 92. *Cf.* ADV (90): *cittasyābhogo manaskāraḥ pūrvānubhūtādisamanvāhāra-svarūpaḥ /*. Also Vy, 127 f.: *manaskāraś cetasa ābhoga iti. ālambane cetasa āvarjanam. avadhāraṇam ity arthaḥ /*. *Siddhi*(S) gives a similar definition, with an elaboration on *avadhāraṇa* — directing *citta* again and again on the same object: *manaskāraścetasa ābhogaḥ / ābhujanamābhogaḥ / ālambane yena cittamabhimukhīkriyate / sa punarālambane citta-dhāraṇakarmā / cittadhāraṇaṃ punas tatraivālambane punaḥ punaś cittasyāvarjanam...* Asm 6: *manaskāraḥ katamaḥ / cetasa ābhogaḥ / ālambana-citta-dhāraṇakarmakaḥ /*

[49] MVŚ, 53a–b, 422c–423a.

[50] *Entrance*, 92.

[51] T no. 1613, 851c.

[52] *Cf. Khandha Samyutta*, *Pupphavagga*, *sutta* no. 3.

[53] Ny, 384b.

[54] Ny, 391a.

[55] MVŚ, 26a.

[56] MVŚ, 172b.

[57] MVŚ, 147a, 172b, 524c, 757c, etc.

[58] MVŚ, 487b.

[59] AKB, 54: *samādhiś cittasyaikāgratā.*

[60] *Entrance*, 93.

[61] AKB, 45.

[62] AKB, 57.

[63] Vy, 132.

[64] *Cf.* AKB, 58.

[65] AKB, 318.

[66] Also cf. MVŚ, 243b, on the mutual exclusiveness of the two.

[67] T 41, 78b.

[68] Vy, *loc. cit.*

[69] MVŚ, 79c–81b, 270a–b.

[70] *Cf.* AKB, 62; MVŚ, 80c.

[71] *Ibid.*, 79c, 270a.

[72] *Cf. Study*, 255 ff.

[73] MVŚ, 79c, 270a, 493c, 745a, etc.

[74] Asm (33 f.) enumerates six types of *saṃprayoga*:

1. *saṃprayoga* in terms of non-separation (*avinirbhāga-saṃprayoga*),
2. *saṃprayoga* in terms of being mixed (*miśrībhāva-saṃprayoga*),
3. *saṃprayoga* in terms of conglomeration (*samavadhāna-saṃprayoga*),
4. *saṃprayoga* in terms of co-existence (*sahabhāva-saṃprayoga*),
5. *saṃprayoga* in terms of execution of duty (*kṛtyānusthāna-saṃprayoga*),
6. *saṃprayoga* in terms of concurrence (*saṃpratipatti-saṃprayoga*).

Among them, only the sixth type refers to the concurrence of thought and thought-concomitants with regard to the same object (*cittacaitasikānām ekasminn ālambane'nyonyaṃ saṃpratipattiḥ*). The fifth clearly admits of the sense of companionship and co-operation which do not necessarily demand the condition of simultaneity. (See also AsmB, 47).

[75] AKB, 440: *avasthāviśeṣo hi nāma cetasaś caitasiko bhavati /*

[76] MVŚ, 661c.

[77] ADV, 76: *kathaṃ puṇa(na)r idaṃ vijñāyate cittād arthāntarabhūtāś caitasikāḥ / cittam eva hi tadvedanādināmabhirvyapadiśyata ity evaṃ ceṣyamāne buddhasūtram anulomitaṃ bhavati / yad uktaṃ bhagavatā — "ṣaḍdhātur ayaṃ bhikṣavaḥ puruṣapudgalaḥ" ity atra vijñānadhātur evoktaḥ / tasmān nārthāntarabhūtāś caitasikā iti bhadantabuddhadevaḥ /*

[78] MVŚ, 8c.

[79] AKB, 145: *sparśād uttarakālaṃ vedanety apare / indriyārthau hi pūrvānto vijñānam / so'sau trayāṇāṃ saṃnipātaḥ sparśaḥ sparśapratyayāt paścād vedanā tṛtīye kṣaṇa iti /*

[80] Vy, 307: *sparśad uttarakālaṃ vedanety apar iti bhadānta-śrīlātaḥ /*; Ny, 387c; *Pūrṇavardhana, Abhidharmakośa-ṭīkā-lakṣaṇānusāriṇī*, Peking no. 5594, Vol. 17, 232, 336a: *gzhan dag na re reg ba'i og tu tshor ba 'byung ste zhe zer ba ni slob dpon dpal len te /*; etc.

[81] Ny, 388b.

[82] Ny, 339b.

[83] *Cf.* AKB, 146: *cakṣuḥ pratītya rūpāṇi cotpadyate cakṣurvijñānam / trayāṇāṃ saṃnipātaḥ sparśaḥ sahajātā vedanā saṃjñā cetaneti* / Also *cf.* SĀ, 72c, 87c.

[84] AKB, 146.

[85] S, ii, 72.

[86] T 32, 274c.

[87] T 32, 276b.

[88] AKB, 11: *viṣayaṃ viṣayaṃ prati vijñaptir upalabdhir vijñāna-skandha ity ucyate* /

[89] Vy, 38: *upalabdhir vastu-mātra-grahaṇaṃ vedanādayas tu caitasā viśeṣā viśeṣa-grahaṇa-rūpāḥ* / Also cf. *Entrance*, 140 f.

[90] AKB, 11: ***vijñānaṃ prativijñaptiḥ*** (16a) /

viṣayaṃ viṣayaṃ prati vijñaptir upalabdhir vijñāna-skandha ity ucyate /

[91] Ny, 342a.

[92] MVŚ, 109a, 284a, 285b; etc.

[93] See Saṃghabhadra's argument in Ny, 395b.

[94] *Cf. Entrance*, 141.

[95] MVŚ, 141b–c; Ny, 345b (Saṃghabhadra cites *sūtra*-s which stress consciousness/ thought as the chief essence of a being).

[96] ADV, 78: *vastūpalabdhi-mātraṃ hi cittaṃ tenopalabdhe vastuni saṃjñāsmaraṇe lakṣaṇānusmaraṇābhinirūpaṇādayo viśeṣāḥ saṃjñā-prajñā-smṛty-ādibhir gṛhyante … ātmābhiniveśād rājasthānīyatvāc ca* / … *uktaṃ hi bhagavatā citta-saṃkleśāt sattvāḥ saṃkliṣyante* / *citta-vyavadāna-hetor viśudhyante* /

[97] T 41, 26a–b.

[98] MVŚ, 374b.

[99] MVŚ, 219b; AKB, 22.

[100] Ny, 350b.

[101] Ny, *loc. cit.*

[102] See *supra* § 9.6.

[103] ZW, 236.

[104] MVŚ, 315b.

[105] MVŚ, 610a.

[106] This *sūtra* statement is also cited in Vy (81) in the "what sees" debate.

[107] T 29, 349a.

[108] See SĀ, T 2, 341c; Pāli, A, iii, 100. Cf. Yin Shun, *A Study of the Tathāgatagarbha* (Taipei, 1982), 67 ff.

[109] A, i, 10.

[110] *Manorathapūraṇī*, I, 60.

[111] T 28, 697b.

[112] T 50, 15b–c.

[113] T 32, 163b.

[114] MVŚ, 140b–c.

[115] Ny, 733a.

[116] Ny, 733b.

[117] T 32, 258b.

10. Theories of Knowledge

10.1. Sarvāstivāda realism: From epistemology to ontology

10.1.1. A real existent is established through experience (mundane or supramundane)

10.1.2. Realism expressed in the doctrine of defilements

10.1.3. Realism expressed in the doctrine of sensory perception

10.1.4. *Dharma*-s as knowables (*jñeya*)

10.2. Various modes of operation of *prajñā*

10.2.1. Understanding (*prajñā*)

10.2.2. Knowledge (*jñāna*)

10.2.3. Receptivity (*kṣānti*)

10.2.4. View (*dṛṣṭi*)

10.2.5. Correlation between understanding, view and knowledge (and receptivity)

10.3. Reflexive knowledge and omniscience (*sarvajñā*)

10.4. *Prajñā* of the Buddha and the two *yāna*-s

10.4.1. Inferior *prajñā* of the two *yāna*-s owing to *vāsanā* and *akliṣṭājñāna*

10.4.2. Examples of the inferiority of the two *yāna*-s' *prajñā*

10.4.3. *Kleśa-āvaraṇa*, *jñeya-āvaraṇa*, *vimokṣa-āvaraṇa* and *akliṣṭa-ajñāna*

10.4.4. Saṃghabhadra's distinctions: *kliṣṭa*- and *akliṣṭa-ajñāna*, and *vāsanā*

10.5. Instrument of perception

10.5.1. Four views on "what sees?"

10.5.2. The "eye sees" view of the Vaibhāṣika

10.5.3. The Sautrāntika position and Saṃghabhadra's defence of the Vaibhāṣika position

10.5.4. Role of consciousness in perception

10.6. Important Sarvāstivāda thought-concomitants involved in discriminative cognition

10.7. Ontological status of the objects of knowledge

10.7.1. Debate in the Ny on the ontological status of the object

10.8. Direct perception, *ākāra*, *sākāra-vijñānavāda, nirākāra-vijñānavāda* and the Sarvāstivāda

10.8.1 The notion of *ākāra* in the Sautrāntika and the Sarvāstivāda

10.8.2 Several *ākāra* on a given *ālambana*

10.1. Sarvāstivāda realism: From epistemology to ontology

In the preceding chapters (particularly chapters 2, 3, 6, 7 and 9) we have already discussed some aspects of the Sarvāstivāda theory of knowledge. In this chapter, we will offer some elaborations on what we have discussed earlier and also add other important epistemological doctrines that we have not covered so far.

10.1.1. A real existent is established through experience (mundane or supramundane)

Like all other forms of Buddhism, Sarvāstivāda Abhidharma is primarily concerned with the problem of knowledge: Given that we are bound to *saṃsāra* through ignorance (*avidyā*), how can we overcome the topsy-turvy way of cognizing things (*viparyāsa*) and acquire the liberating insight (*prajñā*) which sees things truly as they are (*yathābhūtam*)? With this central soteriological concern and starting from an epistemological investigation, the school arrives at a list of roughly 75 types of ultimate reals known as *dharma*-s. This central concern and fundamental methodology of investigation are summarily reflected in what the school underscores as Abhidharma in the absolute sense: i.e., pure *prajñā* defined as *dharma-pravicaya* (*supra*, §§ 1.2, 1.3).

A *dharma* — whether, physical, mental, neither physical nor mental, or even unconditioned — is a unique force, possessing a unique, intrinsic characteristic, that has impact on the human experience, and it is discovered by a valid means of knowledge (*pramāṇa*), either direct perception (including spiritual realization) or inference having its ultimate basis on direct experience (cf. *supra*, § 6.2.1) The absolute reality of *nirvāṇa* is establishable even though it is an unconditioned, for an *ārya* can experience it directly, and it moreover has impact on our thinking and aspiration (cf. *infra*, § 16.2.1, point 6). The Sarvāstivāda investigation into the absolute real leads to the conclusion that it is the universal principles directly realized by the *ārya*-s that constitute absolute truth (see *supra*, § 3.5.1). A metaphysical notion, like the Self (*ātman*) or the Person (*pudgala*), is not acceptable for the Sarvāstivāda as an ultimate real precisely because it cannot be cognized by any means of cognition or be experienced through the spiritual insight of the *ārya*-s.[1]

10.1.2. Realism expressed in the doctrine of defilements

In the Sarvāstivāda explanation of the cognitive process, it is the external object that affects the manner of our cognition. The force of the object domain is one of the three conditions that can generate defilements, the other two being the cause and the preparatory effort (*prayoga*).[2] Arguing against the Dārṣṭāntika stance that the object domains are unreal because pleasure and displeasure are all only due to the force of mental discrimination, Saṃghabhadra states:

> The advocates of logic (Yuktavādins = Sarvāstivādins) assert thus: "All object domains are real." … It is observed that with regard to the objects, defilements arise differently. … Because, although there is no difference in terms of the cause and the preparatory effort, the manifestation of defilement is observed to be different, we therefore know that the object

> domains are not unreal entities — the difference results from the force of the object domain.[3]

In the following discussion on the nature of the objects of defilement, the Sarvāstivāda Ābhidharmikas' stance of realism is once again clearly contrasted with the idealistic predilection of the Dārṣṭāntikas:

> The Ābhidharmikas state: "The object of bondage (*saṃyoga-vastu*) is real, the fetter which binds is also real. The Person is unreal."
>
> The Vātsīputrīya asserts: "The object of bondage is real, the fetter which binds is also real. The Person is also real."
>
> The Dārṣṭāntikas assert: "The fetter which binds is real, the object of bondage is unreal. The Person is also unreal."[4]

10.1.3. Realism expressed in the doctrine of sensory perception

The external world is perceived directly by our senses in spite of the Abhidharma doctrine of the momentariness of all conditioned *dharma*-s, thanks to the fact of co-existent causality (*supra*, § 6.7). In an experience of direct perception (*pratyakṣa*), whether sensory or mental, the perceptual object as the *ālambana-pratyaya* (*supra*, § 7.1.3) is actually the object out there existing at the very moment of the arising of the corresponding consciousness. It is a real entity, just as a single atom is a real.

Saṃghabhadra argues that a sensory consciousness necessarily takes a physical assemblage or agglomeration of atoms (*he ji* 和集; **saṃcaya*, **saṃghāta*,[5] **samasta*) as its object. What is directly perceived is just these atoms assembled together in a certain manner, not a conceptualized object such as a jug, etc. The jug *per se* is never perceived by the visual consciousness; only the *rūpa* as agglomerated atoms of color and shapes. This is direct perception which perceives only the intrinsic characteristic (*svalakṣaṇa*), i.e., the entity in itself. It is the succeeding mental consciousness, with its judgmental or calculative (*abhirūpaṇā*) and conceptualizing capability and using names, that it can cognize its common characteristic and determines that the object is a 'jug'. At this stage, it is no more an experience of direct perception but an inference. (See also *supra*, § 9.7). From the Sarvāstivāda perspective, if we cannot perceive the external object at the very moment when it is existing, then direct perception is impossible, which implies that inference too is impossible — and, finally, no true knowledge of the external is at all possible.

Saṃghabhadra rejects Śrīlāta's theory that the object of visual perception is a unified complex (*he he* 和合;[6] **sāmagrī*, **saṃghāta*) of atoms. He maintains that even an individual atom is in actual fact visible, even though its visibility is almost nil on account of its being very subtle for visual consciousness, which can grasp only a gross object (取境麤故). In fact, it is conceded that each individual atom, in its own right, actually serves as a perceptual object or a supporting basis. He argues that such a superimposed unity as proposed by Śrīlāta can only be grasped by *abhinirūpaṇā-vikalpa*. A sensory consciousness, lacking this capacity as it does, can take only an existent — not a conceptualized unity — as its object.[7] He further explains that a unified complex obtains where speech operates, as a result of the arising of an appellation (*adhivacana*) with regard to a multiplicity of *dharma*-s.[8] It is on account of its non-discriminative nature that visual consciousness is incapable of discerning the extremely subtle form of an atom; only those endowed with the power of excellent wisdom can do so. In any case, he says, atoms are always found assembled and thus are visible[9] (cf. *supra*, § 8.3).

While the MVŚ certainly states that an atom "cannot be seen by the eye",[10] it also explains, much like Saṃghabhadra, that this is not in the sense of an object not being of the intrinsic nature of an object. Thus, with regard to an atom of color or shape, the MVŚ says:

> There exists [an atom of green]; it is just that it is not grasped by visual consciousness. If a single atom is not green, an accumulation of numerous atoms cannot be green; likewise for yellow, etc. … .
>
> There exists [an atom of a long shape, etc.]; it is just that it is not grasped by visual consciousness. If a single atom is not long, etc., in shape, an accumulation of numerous atoms cannot be long, etc., in shape.
>
> Furthermore, there exist *rūpa*-s that are not visible on account of being extremely fine, not on account of being non-objects (*viṣaya*).[11]

10.1.4. *Dharma*-s as knowables (*jñeya*)

We may say that from the period of Abhidharma Buddhism onwards, the question of what constitutes the knowables (*jñeya*) becomes an increasingly important topic of investigation among the Buddhist schools. In the case of Sarvāstivāda, as we have seen above, all *dharma*-s, in the proper Abhidharmic sense of the term, exist and constitute objects of cognition and knowledge, the congizables and the knowables. The PrŚ explains what these knowables and cognizables (*vijñeya*) refer to:

> What are the knowable *dharma*-s? All *dharma*-s are known through the knowledges (*jñāna*) in accordance with the [specific] objects (*yathā-vastu*). How, moreover, is that? The knowledge of unsatisfactoriness (*duḥkha-jñāna*) knows unsatisfactoriness. The knowledge of origin knows origin. The knowledge of cessation knows cessation. The knowledge of the path knows the path. There is also the skillful conventional knowledge (*saṃvṛti-jñāna*) that knows unsatisfactoriness, origin, cessation, the path, as well as Space and cessation independent of deliberation (*apratisaṃkhyā-nirodha*). Hence it is said that all *dharma*-s are known through the knowledges in accordance with the [specific] objects. These are known as the knowable *dharma*-s.

> What are the cognizable *dharma*-s? All *dharma*-s are cognized through the consciousnesses in accordance with the [specific] objects. How, moreover, is that? Visual consciousness cognizes the visibles. Auditory consciousness cognizes sounds. Olfactory consciousness cognizes smells. Gustatory consciousness cognizes tastes. Bodily consciousness cognizes tangibles. Mental consciousness cognizes *dharma*-s; the eye, the visibles and visual consciousness; the ear, sounds and auditory consciousness; the nose, smells and olfactory consciousness; the tongue, tastes and gustatory consciousness; the body, tangibles and bodily consciousness. The mind, *dharma*-s and mental consciousness. Hence it is said that all *dharma*-s are cognized through the consciousnesses in accordance with the [specific] objects. These are known as the cognizable *dharma*-s.[12]

On "in accordance with the [specific] objects", the MVŚ comments that it means: in accordance with the (sphere) of activity (*gocara*?), with the object domain (*viṣaya*), with the cognitive object (*ālambana*).

Not all the masters in the MVŚ, Sarvāstivādins included, would agree with the orthodox Sarvāstivāda position. Some hold that "there are knowledges that do not take object domains as their cognitive objects, and there are object domains that are not the cognitive objects of knowledge".[13] Others assert that "there are knowledges that do not know what is to be known, and there are object domains to be known that are not knowable by knowledge".[14] The Venerable Pārśva explains in this way:

> Knowledge is so called because it knows.
>
> A *dharma* which is an object of [cognitive] activity, a cognitive object or object domain that is apprehended is called a knowable.
>
> Knowledge and the knowable are established in mutual relation to each other; hence there is no knowledge that does not know the knowable, nor is there any knowable that is not known by a knowledge.[15]

In the case of the Sarvāstivāda orthodoxy, the very possibility of a cognition necessarily implies the true ontological status of the object cognized (see also, § 3.5.3.3). All *dharma*-s are cognizable means all *dharma*-s exist truly. In arguing for the absolute reality of past and future *dharma*-s, Saṃghabhadra states:

> Just as a consideration of the knowables proves that merely relatively existent past and future *dharma*-s cannot become objects of knowledge (*jñeya*), just so, from various other considerations — of the abandonables and the realizables — one can prove, in each case, that the past and the future cannot be mere relative existents, for unreal *dharma*-s cannot be abandoned, etc.[16]

The very notion of *dharma*-s being *jñeya*-s spells out the fundamentally epistemological approach of the Sarvāstivāda orthodoxy in their *dharma-pravicaya*. Saṃghabhadra powerfully underscores this approach in his definition of an existent (*sat*):

> The characteristic of the existent (*sallakṣaṇa*) consists in it being capable of serving as an object domain generating cognition (*buddhi*).[17]

In brief: all ultimate reals — *dharma*-s — are knowable, cognizable. There can be no exception to this. And these knowables, cognizables, have their objective existence which affects our perception of not only the phenomenal world, but also the domain of the unconditioned. This is then truly an ontological commitment derived from an epistemological consideration.

10.2. Various modes of operation of *prajñā*

In the Sarvāstivāda system, knowledge (*jñāna*), view (*dṛṣṭi*), receptivity (*kṣānti*) and other related terminologies are used very articulately, even though they all have understanding (*prajñā*) as their intrinsic nature. In other words, *prajñā* as the faculty of understanding has different modes of operation according to which it receives the different appellations —*jñāna*, *dṛṣṭi*, etc. Moreover, unlike in other schools such as the Theravāda, *prajñā* may be skillful (*kuśala*), unskillful (*akuśala*), proper or right (*samyañc*), false or wrong (*mithyā*), with-outflow (*sāsrava*, 'impure'), outflow-free (*anāsrava*, 'pure'); etc. At the highest level, *prajñā* represents the Buddha's perfect wisdom.

With regard to *abhinirūpaṇā-vikalpa*, it is particularly the aspect of judgmental investigation of *prajñā*, represented by *saṃtīraṇa*, that characterizes its function. In this connection, we may note that in the *Dharma-saṃgraha*,[18] the three *vikalpa*-s (cf. § 9.7) are given as *anusmaraṇa*-, *saṃtīraṇa*- and *sahaja*-; with *saṃtīraṇa*- obviously corresponding to *abhinirūpaṇā*. When understanding displays its judgmental nature, *samtīraṇatva*, it is called a view.[19]

Prajñā can also function in other modes, resulting in receptivity (*kṣānti*) and knowledge (*jñāna*). The MVŚ discusses the various modalities of *prajñā* in detail, showing their interrelation in the form of a *catuṣkoṭi*.[20] These descriptions provide considerable amount of information, both positive and negative, on the Vaibhāṣika epistemological doctrines.

10.2.1. Understanding

As one of the ten universal thought-concomitants in the Vaibhāṣika system, it necessarily arises in any mental state. It is usually defined as the "discernment/examination of *dharma*-s (*dharma-pravicaya*)".[21] The MVŚ,[22] besides giving the usual description that it is "examination of *dharma*-s" and that it is found in all mental states, also defines it as the set of understanding conjoined with all the six forms of consciousness. (See also, *supra*, § 9.3.4.1.6).

10.2.2. Knowledge

In the MVŚ, it is recorded that some hold knowledge (*jnāna*) to be none other than consciousness (*vijñāna*):

> There are some who hold that *vijñāna* is just *jnāna*; only that [the former] is longer by one syllable, *vi-* (i.e., the prefix to *jñāna*).[23]

For the Sarvāstivāda, however, knowledge is not synonymous with consciousness (*vijñāna*). There indeed can be consciousness without knowledge in the proper sense. A total of ten knowledges are generally enumerated in their texts:

1. *Dharma*-knowledge (*dharma-jñāna*)

   The knowledge that realizes the truth pertaining to the nature of *dharma*-s — that they are unsatisfactory, etc. In the saṃsāric faring of the practitioner, this knowledge arises for the first time in the second moment of his entry into the direct insight (*abhisamaya*) into the four noble truths. That is, when he gains spiritual insight into the truth of unsatisfactoriness pertaining to the sense sphere. In the first moment that precedes, he has acquired the receptivity (*kṣānti*) to this knowledge; i.e., the ability to completely accept the truth even though its knowledge proper is not yet acquired. Following this moment, this knowledge refers to the knowledge of the *dharma*-s that arises by taking the four truths pertaining to the sense sphere as object (cf. *infra*, § 15.3).

2. Subsequent-knowledge (*anvaya-jñāna*)

   This knowledge is so called because it arises subsequently to the dharma-knowledge, and is similar to the latter, though generated by taking the four truths pertaining to the two higher spheres (*rūpa-* and *ārūpya-dhātu*-s) as object.

3. Knowledge of unsatisfactoriness (*duḥkha-jñāna*)

   This arises in the process of the direct insight by taking the truth of unsatisfactoriness as object. It is the counteragent for the defilements pertaining to this truth.

4. Knowledge of origin (*samudaya-jñāna*)

   This arises in the process of the direct insight by taking the truth of origin as object. It is the counteragent for the defilements pertaining to this truth.

5. Knowledge of cessation (*nirodha-jñāna*)

   This arises in the process of the direct insight by taking the truth of cessation as object. It is the counteragent for the defilements pertaining to this truth.

6. Knowledge of the path (*mārga-jñāna*)

   This arises in the process of the direct insight by taking the truth of the path as object. It is the counteragent for the defilements pertaining to this truth.

7. Conventional-knowledge (*saṃvṛti-jñāna*)

   This is the knowledge that arises taking conventional objects. It is therefore a with-outflow knowledge at the stage when the practitioner has not abandoned the defilements. Four subdivisions are enumerated:

   i. innate knowledge (*upapatti-pratilambhika*);
   ii. knowledge derived from listening to the teachings (*śruta-maya*);
   iii. knowledge derived from reflection (*cintā-maya*);
   iv. knowledge derived from cultivation (*bhāvanā-maya*).

8. Knowledge of the thoughts of another (*paracitta-jñāna*)

This knowledge knows the thought and thought-concomitants of another being. It arises with the support of the *dharma*-knowledge, the subsequent knowledge, the knowledge of the path and the conventional knowledge. Accordingly, it may be either outflow-free or with-outflow.

It does not arise with the support of the truths of unsatisfactoriness and origin because an outflow-free one does not know with-outflow thoughts. It does not arise with the support of the truth of cessation because the latter is unconditioned.

There are limitations to this knowledge: one at a lower stage (*bhūmi*) does not know a thought of a higher stage. One belonging to a weaker faculty does not know the mind of a higher faculty (e.g., one belonging to a *śraddhādhimukta* does not know the thoughts of a *dṛṣṭi-prāpta* — see § 15.3.2). One belonging to a lower spiritual fruition does not know the thoughts of a higher one. Since this knowledge takes a present thought as object, it cannot know the past and future thoughts of another. Finally, one subsumed under *dharma*-knowledge does not know a subsequent knowledge; one subsumed under subsequent knowledge does not know a *dharma*-knowledge.

9. Knowledge of exhaustion (*kṣaya-jñāna*)

This knowledge arises in a non-trainee (i.e., an *arhat*) who has abandoned the ninth (final) grade of the defilements abandonable by cultivation (*bhāvanā-heya*) at the stage of existence-peak (*bhavāgra*). It is an outflow-free knowledge conascent with the acquisition (*prāpti*) of the exhaustion of outflows (*āsrava-kṣaya*), in the form of the certainty (*niścaya*): "unsatisfactoriness has been fully known by me (*duḥkhaṃ me parijñātam*), the origin has been abandoned (*samudayaḥ prahīṇaḥ*), cessation has been realized (*nirodhaḥ sākṣātkṛtaḥ*), the path has been cultivated (*mārgo bhāvitaḥ*)".

10. Knowledge of non-arising (*anutpāda-jñāna*)[24]

    'Non-arising' refers to the acquisition of the cessation independent of deliberation of the efficacies of knowing, abandoning, realizing and cultivating with regard to the four truths. The outflow-free knowledge that knows this non-arising, conascent with the acquisition of the said cessation independent of deliberation, is called the knowledge of non-arising. It arises in the form: "unsatisfactoriness has been fully known by me; it is not to be known any more (*duḥkhaṃ me parijñātaṃ na punaḥ parijñeyam*); …the path has been cultivated by me, it is not to be cultivated any more (*mārgo bhāvito na punar bhāvitavyaḥ*)." It arises only in an *arhat* of sharp faculty (*tīkṣṇendriya*) who is not susceptible to retrogression (*aparihāṇa-dharman*).

The category of knowledge is described in the MVŚ as the set of all understanding conjoined with the first five forms of sensory consciousness, as well as all the understanding conjoined with mental consciousness excepting the pure receptivity (*anāsrava-kṣānti*).[25] The latter is excepted because it represents only a preliminary stage of receptivity, but not final, thorough and decisive knowledge, as regards the four noble truths. Here, we learn that knowledge must be full, ultimate, thorough knowing. Vasumitra offers a similar view. The Bhadanta (Dharmatrāta) requires that "it is only the thorough seeing of a thing that can be qualified as knowledge, while Vāṣpa says that knowledge is derived through repeated examination. These *ācārya*-s' explanations are apparently uncontested by the compilers.[26]

10.2.3. Receptivity

This represents the stage of understanding that precedes knowledge in the proper sense. At this stage, one sees a fact or a doctrine for the first time and is capable of being receptive to it even though one has not quite experienced it directly yet. Thus, at this stage of understanding, there is still the possibility of doubt. In the process of direct insight, it arises at the moment of the unhindered path (*ānantarya-mārga*) at which the defilement is being abandoned. The corresponding knowledge proper arises in the succeeding moment of the path of liberation (*vimukti-mārga*). (Also cf. § 11.3.1).

The following discussion highlights the differences between receptivity and knowledge:

> Question: Why are the outflow-free receptivities not knowledges?
>
> Answer: Because they have not had repeated examination on the domain which is seen. That is: From beginningless time, [the practitioner] has not seen the four noble truths with the outflow-free true insight; although he sees [them] now for the first time, he has not repeated the observation. Thus, [this insight] is not called a knowledge. For a knowledge is accomplished only when a homogeneous insight repeats the observation.[27]

10.2.4. View

The MVŚ states, as does the AKB, that only the eye and the understanding which is of the nature of judgment or decision, are views. They comprise the eye, the five false views, the worldly right view and the views of the trainees and non-trainees. For the Sarvāstivāda, it is the eye that sees; not consciousness, as held by the Vijñānavādins.[28] It is therefore included as a view on account of its function of seeing (*ālocana*) in spite of its being non-epistemic. A view — other than the case of the eye — is defined as that which has the nature of judgment or decision (*saṃtīrakatva*), which is also part of Vasumitra's definition which requires judgment and investigation.[29] Elsewhere,[30] four characteristics of view are given — seeing, judging, firm attachment, and penetrating into the objects of perception.

10.2.5. Correlation between understanding, view and knowledge (and receptivity)

The inter-relationship of the aforementioned categories can be summarized as follows:

1. Some views are not knowledges — viz., visual faculty and the pure receptivity.
2. Some knowledges are not views — viz., the understanding conjoined with the group of the first five forms of sensory consciousness (*pañca-vijñānakāya-samprayukta-prajñā*); knowledges of exhaustion (*kṣaya-jñāna*) and non-arising (*anutpāda-jñāna*); all impure understanding conjoined with mental consciousness (*sāsrava-mano-vijñāna-samprayukta-prajñā*), excepting the five false views (*mithyā-dṛṣṭi*) and the worldly right views (*laukikī samyak-dṛṣṭi*).
3. Some views are also knowledges — viz., the five false views; the worldly right view; all pure understanding, excepting the pure receptivity, the knowledges of exhaustion and of non-arising.
4. Some views are not understanding — viz., the visual faculty.
5. Some understanding are not views — viz., the understanding conjoined with the group of the first five forms of sensory consciousness; the knowledges of exhaustion and of non-arising; all impure understanding conjoined with mental consciousness, excepting the five false views and the worldly right views.

6. Some views are also understanding — viz., all pure understanding excepting the knowledges of exhaustion and of non-arising, the five false views, and the worldly right view.

7. All knowledges are also understanding.

8. Some understanding are not knowledges — viz., the pure receptivity (for it has insight into the four truths for the first time, and therefore cannot make decisive judgment).

This inter-relationship may be diagrammatically (not to the scale) represented as follows:

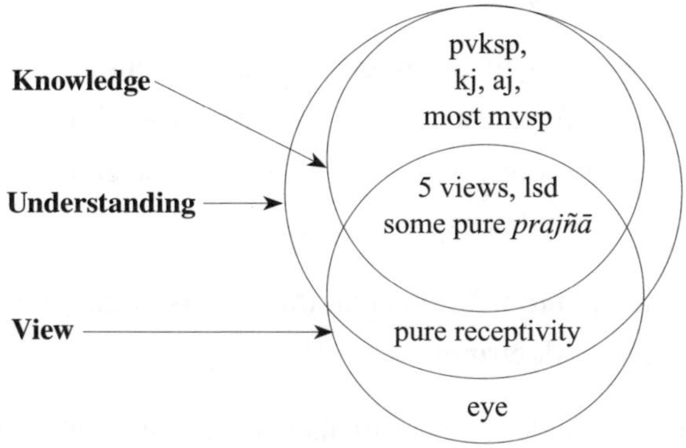

Diagram Text Abbreviations

pvksp = *pañcavijñākāya-samprayukta-prajñā*
kj = *kṣaya-jñāna*
aj = *anutpāda-jñāna*
mvsp = *manovijñāna-samprayukta-prajñā*
lsd = *laukikī samyag-dṛṣṭi*

These distinctions clarify that the eye is not a member of the set of understanding and therefore not knowledge, a subset of understanding. On the other hand, the understanding conjoined with the first five forms of sensory consciousness all fall within the set of knowledge. That is, the necessary condition for knowledge is understanding, defined as having the discerning/discrimination of mental objects as its nature. But this condition is not sufficient. Understanding becomes knowledge only when it is full, final, and decisive. Such a requirement in the Vaibhāṣika notion of knowledge may seem more demanding than that in our ordinary usage of the term. These distinctions and explanations in the MVŚ, together with the other sources given above, make it abundantly clear that for the Vaibhāṣika, visual consciousness, but not the eye as seeing (i.e., the seeing by the eye) is epistemic. In other words, the mere seeing by the eye is non-epistemic, whereas visual consciousness is "conscious seeing" and epistemic.

10.3. Reflexive knowledge and omniscience (*sarvajñā*)

Reflexive knowledge refers to the doctrine that a thought or thought concomitant *dharma*, in knowing a *dharma*, also knows itself. This doctrine seems to be connected with that of omniscience, and these two doctrines are therefore discussed together here.[31]

The *Samayabhedoparacaṇa* mentions that the Mahāsāṃghika holds the following Buddhological doctrine:

> [The Buddha,] in a single moment of thought, cognizes all *dharma*-s. With the *prajñā* conjoined with the single moment of thought, He knows all *dharma*-s.[32]

This means that, for the Mahāsāṃghika, both cognition and knowledge of all *dharma*-s — including thought and the knowledge itself — within a single moment is possible. Such a position is unacceptable to the Sarvāstivāda which holds that an intrinsic nature (i.e., a *dharma* in itself) cannot know itself. More generally, an intrinsic nature cannot exercise any efficacy on itself.

In Sarvāstivāda Abhidharma, the JPŚ already addresses this issue:

> Question: Is there a single knowledge that knows all *dharma*-s?
>
> Answer: No.

Question: If this knowledge generates [the understanding] that all *dharma*-s are without the Self, what does this knowledge not know?

Answer: It does not know itself (lit: the intrinsic nature) and the *dharma*-s that are conjoined or co-existent with it.

Question: Are there two thoughts that are mutually cause to each other?

Answer: No. Why? Because there is no *pudgala* who generates two thoughts simultaneously — i.e., not before, not after. …[33]

The MVŚ[34] cites the above passage and elaborates:

[This discussion] is for the purpose of refuting the tenets of others and elucidating those of our own. There are some who hold that the *citta-caitta-dharma*-s can cognize their own intrinsic natures (i.e., themselves), like the Mahāsāṃghika which asserts: "Because knowledge, etc., has cognition as its intrinsic nature, it can cognize both itself and others. This is just like the case of a lamp; because it has illumination as its intrinsic nature, it can illuminate both itself and others."

There are some, like the Dharmaguptaka which holds that the *citta-caitta-dharma*-s can cognize what are conjoined with them. It asserts thus: "*Prajñā* can cognize the sensation conjoined with it."

There are some, like the Mahīśāsaka, which holds that the *citta-caitta-dharma*-s can cognize what are co-existent with them. It asserts thus: "There are two types of *prajñā* which arise simultaneously: one is conjoined [with thought], the other not conjoined. The conjoined *prajñā* knows the unconjoined one; the unconjoined *prajñā* knows the conjoined one."

There are some, like the Vatsīputrīya, which holds that the *pudgala* can cognize *dharma*-s. It asserts thus: "It is the *pudgala* that knows *dharma*-s, not knowledge (*jñāna*)…"

The MVŚ comments that in the JPŚ passage cited above, the questions are posed by the Vibhajyavādins and the answers are those of the Yuktavādins (i.e., Sarvāstivādins) and then goes on to elaborate further:

> If the question is posed: … "[Among the ten knowledges,] is there one that knows all *dharma*-s?" The answer is: "Yes. The conventional knowledge."
>
> If with regard to this conventional knowledge, the question is posed: "Is there a case that within two moments [of thought], all *dharma*-s are known?" The answer is: "Yes. In the first moment, this knowledge knows all [the *dharma*-s] excepting itself and those that are conjoined or co-existent with it. In the second moment, it also knows [what has existed] in the first moment, [namely] itself as well as those *dharma*-s that were conjoined or co-existent with it." …
>
> Question: Why is it that an intrinsic nature does not know itself?
>
> Answer: Lest there be the fault of there being no difference between cause and effect, between that which does and that which is done, between the accomplisher and the accomplished, between the projector and the projected, between the producer and the produced, between the attribute and the attributed, between the propeller and the propelled, between the characteristics and the characterized, between the cognizer and the cognized. …
>
> *Dharma*-s do not relate to themselves. They can only serve as conditions for others (lit. for other-natures, *parabhāva*). Accordingly, an intrinsic nature does not know itself.[35]

It is therefore clear that reflexive knowledge is impossible for the Sarvāstivāda. Omniscience is possible; but it cannot be achieved within a single moment.

In later Indian treatises, the Sautrāntikas are described as holding the view of reflexive knowledge, denoted by the term *svasaṃvedana/svasaṃvitti* (also, *ātmasaṃvedana*) which means 'self-awareness'.[36] In the MVŚ, as we have seen, the doctrine is attributed to the Mahāsāṃghikas, but not to the Dārṣṭāntikas who were the forerunners of the Sautrāntikas. In the Ny, although there is no explicit attribution of such a theory under this term to the Sautrāntika-Dārṣṭāntikas, in a discussion on the latter's doctrine of direct perception, it is mentioned that they assert the simultaneous occurrence of *anubhava-pratyakṣa* and *buddhi-pratyakṣa*. That is to say, one has awareness of what one is directly sensing: "One has the awareness of a direct perception (現量覺; **pratyakṣa-buddhi*) with regard to one's own sensation."[37] This is clearly a doctrine of reflexive awareness. Śrīlāta argues there that unless this fact is accepted, we will not be able to account for the sense of vividness — as demanded by experience of direct perception — in the subsequent moment when one is completely convinced that "this is directly perceived by me" (*idaṃ me pratyakṣam iti*) (see below, § 10.8).

10.4. *Prajñā* of the Buddha and the two *yāna*-s

10.4.1. Inferior *prajñā* of the two *yāna*-s owing to *vāsanā* and *akliṣṭājñāna*

In the *Mūlapariyāya-sutta*, both an *arahant* and the Buddha are said to know each object of cognition truly as it is, and are therefore entirely free from any wrong conception. But whereas the *arahant* is described as "knowing perfectly" (*pariññātaṃ*), the Buddha is described as "knowing perfectly to the end" (*pariññātantaṃ*),[38] which clearly indicates a quantitative difference between the wisdom of an *arhant* and the Buddha. On this difference, the Pāli commentary explains:

> Whereas there is no difference between Buddha-s and *sāvaka*-s as regards the abandoning of defilements by the [four] paths, there is a difference as regards perfect understanding (*pariññā*).[39]

This means that although both an *arahant* and the Buddha are fully liberated through having removed all defilements, it is really only in the case of the Buddha that wisdom (*paññā*) is perfected. Such an explanation, given in the 5th–6th century Pāli commentary, represents a conscious working out of the much earlier feeling, on the part of the ancient Buddhists probably going back to the Buddha's time, of the superiority of the Buddha's supreme wisdom over that of the 'two-*yānā*-s', namely, the *arhat*-s and the *pratyeka-buddha*-s.

In the Pāli sub-commentaries (*ṭīkā*), it is explicitly stated that the Buddha alone is omniscient — not the *arhant*-s or the *paccekabuddha*-s. For it is only the Buddha who can completely abandon the defilements (*kilesa*) together with their traces (*vāsanā*);[40] and this effects — indeed it *is* — the abandoning of all hindrances to knowledge, or, more literally, hindrances to the knowables (*ñeyyāvaraṇa*).[41] As in the case of Sarvāstivāda Abhidharma (§ 10.1.4), these knowables are equated with all *dhamma*-s.[42] When this cognitive hindrance is removed, omniscience (*sabbaññutā*) is attained.

When we examine the literature of the northern Buddhists, we find very similar (and in many ways more elaborate) ramifications of these notions, through the Abhidharma texts to the Mahāyāna scriptures, where — their intra-diversities in doctrines not-withstanding — the inferiority of an *arhat*'s *prajñā,* in sharp contrast to the Buddha's perfect wisdom, is consistently exploited to the utmost.[43]

10.4.2. Examples of the inferiority of the two *yāna*-s' *prajñā*

The MVŚ, although offering no definition on the two key concepts, traces (*vāsanā*)[44] and non-defiled ignorance (*akliṣṭājñāna*), provides sufficient descriptions contrasting the *prajñā* of the Buddha with that of the two *yāna*-s, and a number of concrete examples. For instance, it tells us that even Śāriputra, the *śrāvaka* foremost in wisdom, is unable to know what happens in very remote times and places. Only the Buddha can know the infinite varieties of names of things; not the two *yāna*-s.[45] While both the Buddha and Śāriputra can correctly understand all that is subsumable under the 12 *āyatana*-s, the Buddha has both omniscience (*sarvajñā/sarvajñatā*) and 'wisdom of all modes' (*sarva-ākāra-jñāna/ sarvathā-jñāna*), and knows them with regard to both their common and intrinsic characteristics. Śāriputra has only *sarvajñā* which knows only their common characteristics.[46] A supreme-perfect Buddha (*anuttara-samyak-sambuddha*) alone, as a result of having absolutely abandoned all defiled (*kliṣṭa*) and non-defiled (*akliṣṭa*) ignorance (*ajñāna*), understands all knowables, both conventional and absolute.[47]

A supreme-perfect Buddha alone, having absolutely abandoned both types of ignorance, understands the diverse nature of the infinite number of beings and can benefit them accordingly.[48] No *śrāvaka* (i.e., 'disciple', referring in this context mainly to an *arhat*) or *pratyekabuddha* (privately enlightened Buddha) is able to know even the names of the various meditational attainments (*samāpatti*) that the Buddha enters into. No *śrāvaka* can know the *samāpatti* that a *pratyekabuddha* enters into. The *samāpatti*-s that Śāriputra enters into are not known by other *śrāvaka*-s. The *samāpatti*-s that Mahā Maudgalyāyana enters into are known only to Śāriputra, but not any other *śrāvaka*.[49]

The AKB[50] gives essentially very similar descriptions. It explains that the Buddha alone is called *sarvathā-sarvahatāndhakāra*, "he who has destroyed all darkness in every way". For, by virtue of the acquisition of the antidote to *ajñāna*, He has absolutely destroyed *ajñāna* with regard to all knowables in every way, so that it cannot arise anymore.[51] The *pratyekabuddha*-s and *śrāvaka*-s have also destroyed darkness with regard to all things (*sarvatra*), as they have removed the defiled delusion (*kliṣṭa-saṃmoha* = *kliṣṭa-ajñāna*), but they have not destroyed it in every way (*sarvathā*), because they have not removed the *akliṣṭa-ajñāna*. Accordingly, they still have this *akliṣṭa-ajñāna* with regard to things far remote in time and space, to the infinite categories of things, and to the unique spiritual qualities of the Buddha (*āveṇika-buddhadharma*).[52]

These descriptions are of a general nature and we therefore do not gain any further information on the concept than what we have already seen in the MVŚ. However, we may note that here the distinction between the Buddha and the two *yāna*-s is entirely based on whether or not the *akliṣṭa-ajñāna* is absolutely (*atyantam*) abandoned. No mention is made of *vāsanā*.

The Vy,[53] commenting on this AKB passage, states explicitly that "abandoning the *ajñāna* absolutely" means that there is no further manifestation (*samudācāra*) of them. This means that the *ajñāna* that can still manifest in the case of the *pratyekabuddha* and *śrāvaka* is the *akliṣṭa-ajñāna*. For, like the Buddha, they have already absolutely abandoned the defiled type.

The Vy[54] also offers some concrete examples which, like those in the MVŚ, include *ajñāna* with regard to mundane things as well as spiritual qualities:

(1) *Ajñāna* with regard to things far remote in space — Maudgalyāyana cannot know that his mother is in the far distant Mārīcī *lokadhātu*. The two *yāna*-s in fact cannot know visible matter composed of atoms which are extremely distant, or invisible, non-material things belonging to far away places on account of their being many world systems away.

(2) *Ajñāna* with regard to things or events extremely distant in time — Śāriputra fails to perceive the spiritual potential of a seeker for ordination, which has to be pointed out by the Buddha.

(3) *Ajñāna* with regard to the infinite divisions of things. This refers to things difficult to perceive, such as the divisions of spheres, planes of existence, types of birth (*yoni*) and rebirth (*upapatti*). "For, it has been said, the [generative] cause — in all its

various aspects — for even a single peacock feather is not to be known by those without *sarvajña*. This is because such knowledge [of a thing in all its modes/aspects] is the power of the Omniscient One."[55]

(4) *Ajñāna* with regard to the Buddha's qualities (the 18 *āveṇika dharma*-s, etc.), on account of their being extremely subtle and profound in nature (*svabhāva-parama-sūkṣmagambhīratvāt*) — Śāriputra does not know the Tathāgata's fivefold outflow-free *skandha*-s (*śīla, samādhi, prajñā, vimukti, vimukti-jñāna-darśana*).

10.4.3. *Kleśa-āvaraṇa*, *jñeya-āvaraṇa*, *vimokṣa-āvaraṇa* and *akliṣṭa-ajñāna*

In the definition of *vāsanā* given by the 5th century C.E. Dhammapāla in his *Udānaṭṭhakathā*, *vāsanā* is said to cease by the abandoning of *ñeyyāvaraṇa*.[56] In the northern tradition, the term *jñeya-āvaraṇa*, side by side with *kleśa-āvaraṇa*, is already attested — albeit only once — in the MVŚ:[57]

> All four [proper abandonments (*samyak-prahāṇa*)] have the meaning of abandonment (*prahāṇa*): The former two abandon the *kleśa-āvaraṇa*. The latter two abandon the *jñeya-āvaraṇa*; for, when the skillful *dharma*-s are practiced, *ajñāna* is abandoned.

The context suggests that spiritual practice aims at abandoning the two-fold hindrances: hindrance of defilements (*kleśa-āvaraṇa*) and hindrance of the knowables (*jñeya-āvaraṇa*). These removed, spiritual perfection is achieved. The term *jñeya-āvaraṇa* clearly indicates its cognitive significance: The Buddha's omniscience is achieved when this hindrance is overcome, and this hindrance is constituted of *akliṣṭa-ajñāna*. In the terminology of the Vaibhāṣika, the *akliṣṭa-ajñāna* is in fact the intrinsic nature (*svabhāva*) of *jñeya-āvaraṇa*.

In addition to *kleśa-āvaraṇa*, the hindrance that prevents the *arhat*-s and *pratyekabuddha*-s from achieving spiritual perfection like that of the supreme-perfect Buddha is also referred to as the 'liberation-hindrance' (*vimokṣa-āvaraṇa*). The MVŚ[58] explains why, when the 'liberation-hindrance' is abandoned on the cessation-attainment (*nirodha-samāpatti*), one is said to have "well done what is to be done":

> Question: Why is it that when one acquires the knowledge of exhaustion, one is said to have well done what is to be done?
>
> Answer: Some say that the nature of the liberation-hindrance is an inferior *ajñāna* (下無智). … [They] explain that when the Bhagavat acquired the knowledge of exhaustion, he had already abandoned all *ajñāna*-s and produced the *jñāna* which counteracts them. For this reason He is said to have abandoned the liberation-hindrance.

Saṃghabhadra insists that this liberation-hindrance must be a real entity — and it is none other than the *akliṣṭa-ajñāna*:

> What is this so called nature of liberation-hindrance? An *arhat*, having liberated his *citta*, seeks further liberation, in order to be liberated from the [liberation-]hindrance: In the liberations which are hindered, there exists an inferior *ajñāna* which is non-defiled non-defined and of the nature of hindering liberation. This is the nature of the liberation-hindrance. When one acquires detachment from a particular sphere (*dhātu*), one has abandoned it without any remainder, and liberation arises. However, it is only when it no longer is active (*sam-ud-ā-√car*) that one is said to have been liberated from it. …
>
> [This] explanation is a valid one. Because there must necessarily be some [real] *dharma* whose force is capable of hindering one from being at ease with regard to the meditation. Otherwise, why is he not at ease with regard to the meditation?[59]

10.4.4. Saṃghabhadra's distinctions: *kliṣṭa-* and *akliṣṭa-ajñāna*, and *vāsanā*

It is in the Ny[60] that we find articulated distinctions between *kliṣṭa-* and *akliṣṭa-ajñāna* on the one hand, and that between *akliṣṭa-ajñāna* and *vāsanā* on the other. Saṃghabhadra distinguishes the two types of *ajñāna* — *kliṣṭa* and *akliṣṭa* — as follows:

> (a) That, on account of which the foolish and the wise are differentiated, is *kliṣṭājñāna*. That, on account of which the foolish excels the wise with regard to certain objects of perception, is *akliṣṭājñāna*.
>
> (b) Furthermore, that, having abandoned which, there exists no difference between the Buddha and the two *yāna*-s, is the first type (*kliṣṭājñāna*). That, having been abandoned which, there exists a difference — in respect of re-arising (*samudācāra*) or otherwise — between the Buddha and the two *yāna*-s, is *akliṣṭājñāna*.
>
> (c) Furthermore, that on account of which one is deluded with regard to the intrinsic characteristic and common characteristic of things is *kliṣṭājñāna*. That on account of which one does not know truly the taste, force, maturity, virtues, magnitude, quantity, place, time, similarities, differences, etc., of *dharma*-s, is *akliṣṭājñāna*. This very *akliṣṭājñāna* is called *vāsanā*. …

Saṃghabhadra clarifies that *akliṣṭājñāna* is an inferior or blunt *prajñā*, one of the recognized universal *caitta*-s in the Sarvāstivāda scheme of classification. His explanations[61] are as follows:

> The understanding (*prajñā*) which does not strive diligently to understand the taste, force, maturity, etc., [of *dharma*-s], co-existing with *dharma*-s of other natures, serves as the cause for the arising of a subsequent similar understanding. This understanding again does not strive diligently to understand, becoming the cause for the arising of another understanding which does not strive diligently to understand. Such a successive cause-

> effect series from beginningless time gives rise to a tendency, acquired through practice. Thus, it is this inferior knowledge (*jñāna*) — induced [through a succession] by previous knowledges which repeatedly become accustomed to being incapable of understanding the objects' taste, etc. — that is called *akliṣṭājñāna*. Those very *citta-caitta*-s conascent with it are known collectively as *vāsanā*.

According to him then, *akliṣṭa-ajñāna* and *vāsanā* are not exactly one and the same thing, although they are intrinsically connected, being conascent. Moreover, it is clear in his explanation that *vāsanā*, being the collective name for a group of *citta-caitta*-s — i.e., the whole mental make-up in which *akliṣṭa-ajñāna* is a conascent member — is a mere concept and not a distinct, real entity.

10.5. Instrument of perception

10.5.1. Four views on "what sees?"

The question of what actually constitutes the instrument through which we come to acquire knowledge of the external world is one of the important epistemological issues among the Abhidharma schools. As regards the problem: "What sees?", the MVŚ[62] informs us that in addition to the Vaibhāṣika's own view, there are three others, which are all refuted :

> There are some who hold that visual consciousness sees, like Venerable Dharmatrāta.
>
> There are some who hold that the 'understanding' conjoined with visual consciousness sees, like Venerable Ghoṣaka.
>
> There are some who hold that the complex (*sāmagrī*) [of *citta-caitta*][63] sees, like the Dārṣṭāntika …
>
> Now, if visual consciousness sees, then consciousness should have

> the characteristic of seeing; since consciousness does not have this characteristic, the proposition is not acceptable.
>
> If the understanding conjoined with visual consciousness sees, the understanding conjoined with auditory consciousness should also hear sound; since understanding does not have this characteristic of hearing, the proposition is not acceptable.
>
> If it is the complex that sees visible forms, it follows that we should be able to see forms at all times, since a complex always exists; hence this proposition too is unacceptable.

This controversy, in a more elaborated form, is also found in the PVV (= *Pañcavastuka-vibhāṣā*)[64] by a certain Dharmatrāta, *ca*. 4th century C.E. Here, all four divergent views (i.e., including the Vaibhāṣika view) are also enumerated and then refuted, by a certain disputant. Another work of this Dharmatrāta, the **Abhidharma-hṛdaya-vyākhyā* (T no. 1552) contains an even more elaborate account of the controversy, the first part of which is very similar to that in the PVV. Vasubandhu (known to have substantially based his AKB on this work and Dharmaśrī's **Abhidharma-hṛdaya*, of which this work is a commentary/revision), the author of the ADV as well as Saṃghabhadra seem most likely to have consulted this text in their accounts on this controversy. The ADV differs from the *Pañcavastuka* mainly with regard to the notion of "the complex which is given as that of the eye, etc." (*cakṣurādisāmagrī paśyati*).[65]

10.5.2. The "eye sees" view of the Vaibhāṣika

The various sources[66] all explain that the Vaibhāṣika considers the eye as a view in the sense of seeing/perceiving, *ālocanārthena*. This is unlike the other views subsumed under *prajñā* which are views on account of their judgmental nature.[67] According to the Vaibhāṣika, the mere-seeing by the eye is, strictly speaking, non-epistemic, since the proper operation of *prajñā* is not involved — which is to say, in this instantaneous process there is no element of 'understanding', properly speaking. This is to be contrasted with the function of cognizing by the simultaneously arising visual consciousness and the discriminative function of the mental cognition (*mano-vijñāna*) induced in the subsequent moment.

In the context of explaining why the five sense faculties are called thus — that is, in each case an "*indriya*" which is said to denote *ādhipatya*, "supremacy/dominance" — Vasubandhu in the AKB differentiates the Vaibhāṣika and the Sautrāntika views: According to the Vaibhāṣika, the eye is an *indriya* because it exercises dominance in the seeing of visual forms, whereas for the Sautrāntika, the dominance is with regard to the apperception of its specific object (*svārthopalabdhi*).[68]

As far as the statement in the Sautrāntika proposition — "dominance in the perceiving of its specific object" — is concerned, the author of the ADV may be justified in remarking that it is not any different from the Vaibhāṣika view.[69] However, the different senses ascribed to the statement underscore their fundamentally different views as regards the perceptual process. For the Sautrāntika, it means that the dominance is with regard to consciousness (*vijñāne tu tayor ādhipatyam*), for the perceiving — as far as one can speak of a "perceiving agent" in a relative sense — is performed by visual consciousness, not by the visual faculty. There is in fact no "seeing of a visual form" or "hearing of a sound" apart from consciousness:[70] There can be no seeing of form apart from grasping (*grahaṇa*), and grasping is none other than consciousness.[71] In other words, in-as-much as the eye has dominance in the arising of visual consciousness, one could speak of its "seeing of a visual form". But this should really mean the "perceiving of a visual form by consciousness". And as the Dīpa-kāra (= author of the ADV) notes elsewhere, the mere seeing (*ālocana*) by the eye is vastly different from the apperceiving (*upalabdhi*) by consciousness.[72]

In the Ny, Saṃghabhadra argues vehemently that it is absolutely necessary for the function of seeing visible forms to belong uniquely to the visual organ. It is in fact, for that matter, absolutely necessary that each *dharma*, in the complex process of dependent origination, is able to exercise its specific function. Here we can better appreciate why Saṃghabhadra insists at such great length that it is the eye that sees. This absolute necessity, of course, stems from the central Vaibhāṣika conception that in the persistence of all *dharma*-s in the three periods of time, each and every *dharma* is a distinct *dharma* by virtue of its specific nature and function. Thus the MVŚ says:

> Question: How are the 12 *āyatana*-s to be established ?
>
> Answer: On the basis of the difference as regards intrinsic nature and activity. Although the 12 *āyatana*-s all pertain to the one personal existence, their 12 species of intrinsic natures and activities are different; they are not mutually commingled.[73]

Now, if the eye does not have a specific function — the only one of seeing visible forms — as mentioned in the *sūtra* (at least so from the Vaibhāṣika viewpoint) and confirmed in experience of the world — the eye as an *āyatana* or a unique *rūpa dharma* will fail to be established. By the same token, the specific nature and function of consciousness must be established and distinguished from those of the eye. The conditioned (*saṃskṛta*) *dharma*-s, however, are said to be "feeble in their *svabhāva*, not free, dependent on others, not capable of exercising their functions by themselves, and unable to accord with their own wishes".[74] The Vaibhāṣikas believe that they can remain as good Buddhists by explaining the causality of the functions of *dharma*-s in accordance with the Buddha's teaching of conditioned co-arising. But their theory of *sarvāstitva* logically requires that each function too must not only belong uniquely to a given *dharma*, it must also persist in time together with the *dharma*. Unlike the *dharma*'s substance, it can be brought into operation with the help of causes and conditions, but it is not anything new that comes into existence.

It is in accordance with such a Vaibhāṣika doctrine that Saṃghabhadra persistently seeks to establish that the seeing by the eye must properly belong to the eye (and hearing of sound must belong to the ear, etc.), even though at the same time its exercise needs the assistance of visual consciousness as a supporting condition.

10.5.3. The Sautrāntika position and Saṃghabhadra's defence of the Vaibhāṣika position

Toward the end of the debate in the AKB, the Sautrāntika ridicules the debaters for their attempt to "devour empty space":

> Are you not devouring empty space here! Conditioned by the visual organ and visible objects, visual consciousness arises. Therein, what is it that sees, and what is it that is seen? It is really devoid of any function (*nirvyāpāra*) — a mere play of *dharma*-s as cause and effect. Therein, in conformity with the wish of worldly conventional usage, it is said figuratively that "the eye sees", "consciousness cognizes". But [the wise ones] should not be attached to such figurative usages here. For, the Bhagavat has said, "One should not obstinately cling to regional usages, nor should one [unnecessarily] rush towards (/clash with) worldly notions."[75]

Saṃghabhadra retorts that it is in fact the Sautrāntika who is "trying to grab empty space"! He argues that the Buddhist principle of conditioned co-arising will in fact collapse altogether if the reality of the individually specific functions of the *dharma*-s — such as the seeing of visibles by the eye — is denied.

Saṃghabhadra further claims that the Sautrāntika has misunderstood what the Buddha means when He urges us "not to obstinately cling to regional linguistic usages nor to rush towards worldly notions". He argues that when the Buddha's advice is applied in the context of their debate, it means that the reality of the collective must be denied — this accords with absolute truth — but not that of the individual *dharma*'s function participating in the collective, complex process of conditioned co-arising. Denial of the latter amounts to a denial of the possibility of dependent origination *in toto*. The Vaibhāṣika position in this debate, he concludes, is in fact founded in accordance with this reasoning and stands firmly on both conventional and absolute truths: Following the Buddha's advice, in asserting that "the eye sees", it does not unnecessarily clash with the conventional point of view. By establishing that the eye — rather than a fictitious collective agent such as the Soul — has the unique, intrinsic function of seeing, it conforms to the absolute truth that while a collection of *dharma*-s as such is unreal, real *dharma*-s indeed exist, each being uniquely defined by its specific characteristic and function.[76]

10.5.4. Role of consciousness in perception

Saṃghabhadra articulates that consciousness is the cause for seeing, not the very entity that sees:

> The eye, sustained by the force of consciousness, gives rise to its specific activity. This is like the arising of the specific activity of fire with the support of the force of fuel.
>
> In fact, if the activity of seeing visible forms is a *dharma* produced by consciousness, then this activity ought to arise [even] when separated from the visual organ. The conascent *mahā-bhūta*-s, nourished by consciousness, are caused to produce the specific organ capable of seeing visible forms. Therefore, it is wrong to say that it is the supporting consciousness that sees.

> Will any wise one say: "Whatever causes and conditions give rise to cognition, the resulting cognition is none other than those very causes and conditions"? Consciousness is the cause, not the essence, of seeing.[77]

That is, in the simultaneous cause-effect relationship which obtains when visual consciousness, the eye, and other necessary conditions flash forth their individual functions in co-ordination to give rise to the seeing of a visible form, visual consciousness is a cause, not an effect (seeing). This is in contrast to the Sautrāntika view that visual consciousness — which is the seeing of the object — is an effect that is produced in the moment subsequent to that when the eye, the visible form, etc., were present.

In terms of intrinsic efficacy, the Vaibhāṣika maintains that whereas the eye sees, consciousness cognizes (*vijānāti*). But, what exactly does consciousness do in the perceptual process? In the AKB, Vasubandhu discusses this question:

> It is said in the *sūtra*, 'consciousness cognizes'. Herein what does consciousness do?
>
> It does nothing ... Although doing nothing, consciousness is said to cognize because of the obtaining of itself resembling [the object] (*sādṛśenātma-lābhād akurvad api kiṃcit*) — [i.e., with the object as its supporting condition, it simply arises as an effect resembling the object]. What is its resemblance [with the object]? This consists in having the form or aspect of that [object] (*tadākāratā*).[78]

Given the proper context — especially Vasubandhu's usage of the term *ākāra* (equated with the resemblance of the object) here — this doctrine, as some scholars like La Vallée Poussin[79] assert, can be considered a Sautrāntika one. Nevertheless, even the Vaibhāṣika would have no objection to the statement that consciousness in this process does nothing in particular. Saṃghabhadra too accepts that it is only with regard to the specific nature of *dharma* that one speaks in conventional terms of an agent, so as to refute the view that apart from consciousness there exists a real agent which is conscious; consciousness actually does nothing in the perceptual process:

> In what other situations does one see the reference of an agent as a conventional expression (*prajñapti*) to nothing more than the nature of a *dharma*? One sees in the world that people speak of a shadow as that which moves. In this case there is no movement; but when it arises in a different place in the following moment (*anantaram*), it is said to move. The same is true for the case of consciousness; when it arises serially with regard to a different object, it is said to be that which cognizes — i.e., it cognizes the object — even though there [really] is no action [on its part].[80]

10.6. Important Sarvāstivāda thought-concomitants involved in discriminative cognition

In accordance with the Sarvāstivāda doctrine of the *mahābhūmika caitta*-s, all the ten *caitta*-s so named are important in any process of cognition that is made possible thanks to their collective contribution. However, some among them, when functioning prominently, bring about the mental capacity of conceptual discrimination and hence the possibility of inferential knowledge. In a sensory perception which is the bare, generic awareness of the sense data, their functioning is not prominent. These thought concomitants are, in particular, *prajñā*, *smṛti* and also *saṃjñā* and the two *aniyata caitta*-s, *vitarka* and *vicāra*. *Prajñā* and *saṃjñā* are in fact respectively the main power supply for examination/deliberation (*abhinirūpaṇā*) and recollection (*anusmaraṇa*), respectively — the two *sine qua non* for a discriminative cognition (*vikalpa*) (§ 9.7). Saṃghabhadra explains why mental consciousness, in contrast to a sensory perception, can have the capacity of discriminative (*vikalpaka*) conceptualization:

> If a consciousness can, within a single moment, grasp objects belonging to numerous species and can, with regard to one given perceptual object, generate a stream of thoughts — a consciousness of such a nature is said to be discriminative. The five groups of *vijñāna*, on the other hand, grasp only present objects. No two moments [of thought] have the same perceptual object, for when the previous grasping of a perceptual object has ceased, there cannot be the arising of a repeated grasping [of the same object] by the consciousness in the second moment. Mental consciousness can take objects belonging to the three periods of time. [In this case,] a *dharma*, although having ceased, can still be its object, and a stream of thoughts can be generated with regard to the same object. For these reasons, only this [consciousness] is said to be discriminative. However, since the five *vijñāna-kāya*-s are always conjoined with *svabhāva-vikalpa*, they are also discriminative. The *sūtra*-s speak of them as being non-discriminative [only] in the sense of being without *anusmaraṇa*- and *abhirūpaṇa-vikalpa*-s.[81]

The involvement of the above-enumerated *caitta*-s may be summarized thus:[82] *saṃjñā* is the cause of *vitarka*, and *vitarka* is in turn the cause for the arising of a sensory consciousness. At this stage, there is a simple inquiry or searching on the mere object grasped, in the form "what is it?" Both schools, Sarvāstivāda and Sautrāntika, would agree that some kind of inarticulate mental inquiry is involved here.

The Sarvāstivāda perspective may be understood to conceive of this as a contribution coming from the conascent thought-concomitants, *saṃjñā*, *prajñā* and *smṛti* — all operating weakly — and *vitarka*. For the Sautrāntika, it is the thought itself operating in its gross state, represented by *vitarka,* which makes the inquiry in the form of an inarticulate murmur. At the same time, a sensory consciousness is said to be distinguished from mental consciousness by its lack of *abinirūpaṇā-vikalpa* on account of its not taking name (*nāma*) as is object. This must then mean that, for the Sarvāstivāda, in a sensory perception the "wind of *saṃjñā*" (*saṃjñāpavana*) is strong enough only for a rudimentary determination, in a generic manner, of the object as a thing in itself, but not for conceptualization based on judgment and association. The same must be said of the contribution from *prajñā*, *smṛti* and *vitarka*. *Vitarka*, although not subsumed as a universal thought-concomitant, is nonetheless always present at the arising of a sensory perception. It is in fact considered the latter's cause, evidently in the sense that it makes the main contribution in such a rudimentary discrimination as regards the object's appearance (*nimitta*) that constitutes the grasping of an object by a sensory consciousness.[83] At the stage of conceptual discrimination in a mental cognition with which *vicāra* accords, the "wind of *saṃjñā*" is sufficiently strong, and *prajñā* and *smṛti* operate prominently.[84]

10.7. Ontological status of the objects of knowledge

We have seen above that already in the VKŚ, Maudgalyāyana represents the Vibhajyavāda stance that there can be consciousness that takes a non-existent object (§ 4.1.2.1). Likewise, the Dārṣṭāntikas in the MVŚ maintain that the objects of defilements are unreal (§ 10.1). More generally, the early Dārṣṭāntikas as well as the Sautrāntika-Dārṣṭāntikas in the AKB, etc., hold that non-existent objects can also give rise to cognition.[85]

In contrast, for the Vaibhāṣika, all object domains are real existents; for "whatever does not fall outside the object-domain of [sensory] consciousnesses, visual, etc., exists truly".[86] "Whatever is conceptually real can only be the object domain of mental consciousness."[87] In the VKŚ, the main epistemological argument advanced for the central thesis of the tri-temporal existence of *dharma*-s is that, in conformity with the Buddha's teaching, consciousness necessarily has a perceptual object; the fact that we can be conscious of past and future objects proves that these objects exist truly.[88] The AKB inherits this as one of the four major arguments for *sarvāstitva* (*supra*, § 3.3.2).

Saṃghabhadra states succinctly that "the characteristic of an existent (*sal-lakṣaṇa*) is that it can serve as an object producing cognition (*buddhi*)". Accordingly, an object of knowledge is necessarily existent, even though it may exist truly (*dravyato 'sti*) or conceptually (*prajñaptito 'sti*).[89] (See also § 3.5.3 ff.). Stated otherwise, the possibility of knowing an object necessarily implies the true ontological status of the object.

10.7.1. Debate in the Ny on the ontological status of the object

In the Ny, there is a lengthy debate between the Vaibhāṣikas and the Sautrāntikas on the issue. The Sautrāntikas, represented by Śrīlāta, enumerate the following cases which they claim to represent examples of perception of non-existent objects:[90]

(a) The optical illusion of a fire-wheel (*alāta-cakra*) resulting from a whirling fire brand.

(b) The cognition of the non-existent Self (*ātman*).

(c) The meditational experiences, such as the all-pervasiveness of a meditational object (the so-called 'base of entirety', *kṛtsnāyatana*), e.g., a primary color, that results from resolute mental application (*adhimukti-manaskāra*).

(d) The view (*dṛṣṭi*) that has non-existence as its object, as mentioned in the *sūtra*.[91]

(e) The awareness of the non-existence of certain mental states such as craving, as spoken in the *sūtra*.

(f) Objects in a dream.

(g) The optical illusion of a double-moon, etc., resulting from ophthalmic disease.

(h) Knowing something that is non-existent.

(i) The cognition that takes as its object the prior non-existence (*prāg-abhāva*) of a sound.

As a general reply to the Sautrāntika claim, Saṃghabhadra invokes the scriptural authority that each of the six cases of cognition — visual, etc., up to mental — necessarily has two requisites: the sense faculty and the corresponding object. There is not a seventh type of cognition that is generated apart from the object, so that one can call it a cognition of non-existent object. In fact, if this could be the case, then a blind person ought to be able to see as much as one possessing eyes, there being no specifically requisite conditions that distinguish the two cases. Besides, non-existent *dharma*-s cannot be subsumed under any of the six types of objects taught in the *sūtra*-s. All the Vaibhāṣika arguments here are based on the main premise — which we have seen above — that whatever can serve as a perceptual object producing a cognition is an existent, although it may be real in the absolute sense or in the relative sense as a mental construction or concept. What is non-existent in the construction necessarily has as its basis something real. It is this latter basis that constitutes the actual object of the perception. An absolute non-existent (*atyantam asad*) has no function whatsoever and hence can never engender a consciousness. Thus, in the case of the perception of the unreal *pudgala*, the perceptual object is not the *pudgala* which is superimposed, but the five *skandha*-s which are real existents. The illusory perception of a double-moon has as its object the single moon; etc. In the same way, dreams, illusion, are actually recollections of real entities previously experienced — just that the element of imagination sets in, resulting in the superimposition on these real entities under certain influences such as mental sluggishness, etc. Likewise, the imagination of a fictitious thing such as the tortoise's hair (*kaurmasya romaḥ*) and a hare's horn (*śaśa-śṛṅga*) become possible because the rabbit, the horn, etc., have been experienced before. Even in the case of negations, their perception does not arise having absolute non-existents as objects. Thus, the perception of what we ordinarily regard as a pure abstraction, such as 'non-existence', too has a real object: the expression (*abhidhāna*) itself, which for the Vaibhāṣika is real, being word (*nāma*) which is a *viprayukta-saṃskāra-*

dharma. When the knowledge taking this as its object arises, it knows that the negated does not exist. In the case where one perceives a negation such as 'non-brahmin' (*abrāhmaṇa*), the knowledge arises with the expression and the expressed (*abhidheya*) as its objects; the expression itself negates *brāhmaṇa*, operating with regard to what is expressed by it — *kṣatriya*:

> When this knowledge first arises, by taking merely the expression as its object, it knows that the negated [i.e., *brāhmaṇa*,] does not exist. When it arises subsequently, it may also take the expressed [i.e., *kṣatriya,*] as its object and knows that what is negated does not exist in that.[92]

10.8. Direct perception, *ākāra*, *sākāra-vijñānavāda*, *nirākāra-vijñānavāda* and the Sarvāstivāda

In contrast to the Sautrāntika and Yogācāra, the Sarvāstivāda theory of knowledge is described in the Sanskrit texts[93] as *nir-ākāra-*(*vi*)*jñānavāda*: the theory that the external object is directly perceived without the need of any representational form in the consciousness. However, according to the tradition passed down by Xuan Zang,[94] among all the northern Buddhist schools it is only the Sāṃmitīya that really holds such a theory, since this school asserts that only mental *dharma*-s are momentary; external things can last longer than one moment. All other schools, including the Sarvāstivāda, would would therefore have to be included in the camp of *sākāra-vijñānavāda*. We know of course that the Theravāda school too holds that a *rūpa* lasts 16 moments (*citta-khaṇa*-s) longer than a *citta*, so that direct perception in the true sense becomes possible.[95] The confusion between these two traditional sources can only be cleared by examining the notion of *ākāra* explained differently in these schools.

10.8.1. The notion of *ākāra* in the Sautrāntika and the Sarvāstivāda

The Sautrāntika stance is that the *ākāra* corresponds exactly to the external object. It allows no possibility of a cognitive error in a genuine *pratyakṣa* experience. However, this *ākāra* is a resemblance (*sadṛśā*) constructed by the mind.

In the case of the Sarvāstivāda tradition, at the outset we note the information provided by the MVŚ that various Ābhidharmika masters — most probably Sarvāstivādins — give various interpretations to *ākāra*:

> Question: What is the intrinsic nature of the so-called *ākāra*?
>
> Answer: Its intrinsic nature is *prajñā*. Herein it should be understood thus:
>
> (i) *prajñā* is *ākāra*; it is also what cognizes with a form (*ākārayati*) and what is cognized with a form (*ākāryate*);
> (ii) the *citta-caitta-dharma*-s conjoined (*saṃprayukta*) with *prajñā*, while not being *ākāra*, are what cognize with a form as well as what are cognized with a form;
> (iii) those *viprayukta-saṃskāra*-s and other existent (*sat*) *dharma*-s, while being neither *ākāra* nor what cognize with a form, are what are cognized with a form.
>
> According to some: What is called *ākāra* has collectively all *citta-caitta-dharma*-s as its intrinsic nature. This theory would imply that all *citta-caitta*-s are *ākāra*, and what cognize with a form (*ākārayati*) and what are cognized with an *ākāra*. All the other *dharma*-s, while being neither *ākāra* nor what cognize with an *ākāra*, are what are cognized with an *ākāra*.
>
> According to some others: What is called *ākāra* has all *dharma*-s as its intrinsic nature. This theory would imply that the conjoined *dharma*-s are *ākāra*, as well as what cognize with a form and what are cognized with an *ākāra*. The disjoined *dharma*-s, while being *ākāra* as well as what are cognized with an *ākāra*, are not what cognize with an *ākāra*.

> Comment: It should be said that what is called *ākāra* has *prajñā* as its intrinsic nature, as given in the first explanation....
>
> Question: What is the meaning of *ākāra*?
>
> Answer: *Ākāra* means the operation in the manner of examination/ discernment (簡擇而轉; *pra-vi-√ci*) with regard to the nature of the object.[96]

From this, it is clear that the orthodox Sarvāstivāda view is that *prajñā* is *ākāra*, explained as the function of "operating investigatively with regard to the object". This is essentially the same as the definition given for *prajñā* as "the investigation of *dharma*-s" (*dharma-pravicaya*).[97] But this investigative operation may be correct or incorrect, skillful (*kuśala*) or unskillful (*akuśala*), sharp (*tīkṣṇa*) or blunt (*mṛdu*), with-outflow (*sāsrava*) or outflow-free (*anāsrava*). Thus, when one commits the cognitive error of mistaking a rope for a snake or an aggregate of five *skandha*-s for a *pudgala*, it is a case of "the *ākāra* being topsy-turvy" (*viparīta*); the *ālambana* is existent and not illusory — the rope or the *skandha*-s.[98] In brief, as stated by Saṃghabhadra: "Only a discriminative (*sa-vikalpaka*) consciousness is capable of grasping the specific characteristic of the object [in the form]: 'it is blue, not green', etc.".[99] Accordingly, in the Sarvāstivāda epistemology, the operation of *ākāra* pertains to the domain of mental consciousness, not to that of a sensory consciousness where *prajñā* cannot properly function (see *supra*, § 9.7). Moreover, it may or may not correspond exactly to the actual form of the external object.

10.8.2. Several *ākāra*-s on a given *ālambana*

That, according to the Sarvāstivāda, with regard to one and the same perceptual object there can be various *ākāra*-s, is clearly brought out in a consideration in the MVŚ on the question: "If one leaves behind an *ākāra*, does one also [leave behind] the perceptual object (*ālambana*)?" The answer to this is given as a four-fold alternative (*catuṣkoṭi*):

(I) There is a case where one leaves behind the *ākāra* but not the perceptual object: viz., a person contemplates a given characteristic with a given *ākāra*; without abandoning this characteristic, he further has another *ākāra* — e.g.: he takes the *rūpa-skandha* as his object and has the *ākāra* of impermanence, immediately after that, the *ākāra* of unsatisfactoriness of the *rūpa-skandha* arises before him…

(II) There is a case where one leaves behind the perceptual object but not the *ākāra*: viz., a person contemplates a given characteristic with a given *ākāra*; with this same *ākāra*, he further contemplates another characteristic — e.g.: he takes the *rūpa-skandha* as his object and has the *ākāra* of impermanence; immediately after that he takes the *vedanā-skandha* as object and the *ākāra* of impermanence arises before him…

(III) There is a case where one leaves behind the *ākāra* as well as the perceptual object: viz., a person contemplates a given characteristic with a given *ākāra*, he further contemplates another characteristic with another *ākāra* — e.g.: he takes the *rūpa-skandha* as his object and has the *ākāra* of impermanence; immediately after that he takes the *vedanā-skandha* as object and the *ākāra* of unsatisfactoriness arises before him…

(IV) There is a case where one leaves behind neither the *ākāra* nor the perceptual object: viz., a person contemplates a given characteristic with a given *ākāra*, and continues to do so for some time — e.g.: he takes the *rūpa-skandha* as his object and has the *ākāra* of impermanence in a serial continuity for some time.[100]

10.8.3. The 16 *ākāra*-s as *prajñā* and not 'images/aspects' of objects

The above passage also indicates the possibility of simultaneously having one and the same *ākāra* with regard to many and even all *dharma*-s, excepting the knowledge itself at that given moment, its conjuncts and co-existents, as when one contemplates that all *dharma*-s are devoid of a Self, etc.[101] In fact, the only case where the *ākāra* of an object corresponds exactly to the actual nature of the object is when the yogi acquires the *prajñā* qua true insight in the direct insight (*abhisamaya*) into the noble truths — he sees conditioned things truly as they are, in their aspects of being unsatisfactory, impermanent, etc. The contemplating yogi can see several aspects pertaining to a given object, each with a distinct and unconfounded *ākāra* — i.e., *prajñā*. Thus:

> With regard to each with-outflow object (*sāsrava-vastu*), if the knowledge operates by way of the four *ākāra*-s, [understanding it] as *duḥkha*, etc., it receives the name *duḥkha-jñāna*. If the knowledge operates by way of the four *ākāra*-s, [understanding it] as *samudaya*, etc., it receives the name *samudaya-jñāna*. Hence the *ākāra*-s of the *duḥkha*- and *samudaya-jñāna*-s are not mixed (雜; *miśra*), while the *ālambana*-s are mixed…[102]

This is clearly a case of mental exertion — mental application with regard to the common characteristics (*sāmānya-lakṣaṇa-manaskāra*).[103] It is for this reason that the 16 *ākāra*-s of the four noble truths — *duḥkhatā*, etc. — as direct perception of the *yogi* are said to be *prajñā* — the outflow-free or pure *prajñā*.[104] They clearly do not refer to images or 'aspects' of the objects, but are in the active sense of the mental function of understanding. These common-characteristics (*sāmānya-lakṣaṇa*) are the universal principles of all *dharma*-s intuited by spiritual insight pertaining to the absolute truth,[105] not universals abstractly constructed by the mind as in the case of mental inference.

10.8.4. *Ākāra*-s as *pratyakṣa-jñāna*.

The spiritual insight acquired in the process of direct insight is called a *dharma*-knowledge (*dharma-jñāna*) where it pertains to the sense-sphere and a subsequent-knowledge (*anvaya-jñāna*) where it pertains to the two upper spheres. Both are knowledges qua direct perception (*pratyakṣa-jñāna*).

Saṃghabhadra insists that the term *anvaya* does not imply that the subsequent-knowledges are *anumāna*, since in the *sūtra* both knowledges are equally spoken of as capable of seeing truly *duḥkha*, etc. Moreover, the *ārya-jñāna*-s cannot be inferential in nature, and no object pertaining to the *ārya-satya*-s can be realized by an inferential knowledge. He further argues that if the subsequent-knowledges are inferential, then there would not be even the *dharma*-knowledges having *nirodha* as object, since a *nirodha* is always non-empirical (*adṛśya*). But it is from the point of view of *indriyāśrita*- and *anubhāva-pratyakṣa* (see *infra*, § 10.8.8) that the objects of subsequent-knowledges are said to be non-empirical. And in that case there ought not to be even the *dharma*-knowledges of *nirodha* since a *nirodha* cannot be an object for these two *pratyakṣa*-s. From the point of view of *buddhi-pratyakṣa* (see *infra*, § 10.8.8), however, it is not true that the objects of subsequent-knowledges are those of inferential knowledges. "Hence, all determination of things truly as they are (實義決擇; **tattvārtha-viniścaya*), properly accomplished (如理所引; **yoga-vihita*), are *pratyakṣa-jñāna*-s."[106]

10.8.5. The Sarvāstivāda doctrine of sensory perception is *nirākāra-jñānavāda*

Accordingly, from the Sarvāstivāda perspective, a sensory perception is definitely without an *ākāra*. It is for this same reason that the MVŚ states that the *prajñā* conjoined with the five types of sensory consciousness is not *dṛṣṭi* although it is also a knowledge (*jñāna*):

(1) it does not have a keen or sharp (*tīkṣṇa*, *paṭu*) mode of activity (*ākāra*) and cannot penetrate deeply into the perceptual object;

(2) it cannot discriminate;

(3) it can have only the *svalakṣaṇa* but not the *sāmānya-lakṣaṇa,* as its perceptual object;

(4) it has only present objects, whereas a view can have *dharma*-s of all the three temporal periods, as well as the unconditioned, as objects;

(5) a view can grasp an object repeatedly, but this *prajñā* can only grasp an object in a single moment;

(6) unlike a view, it cannot cogitate and examine a perceptual object.[107]

These explanations are essentially a good description of the Sarvāstivāda notion of sensory direct perception. We may note here once again the unambiguous notion that where *prajñā* operates, *ākāra* does not denote the 'exact image/representation' of the *ālambana*.

The conclusion therefore is that, as far as sensory perception is concerned, the Xuan Zang tradition is not quite justified in grouping the Sarvāstivāda theory under *sa-ākāra-jñānavāda*. It is, properly speaking, *nirākāra-jñānavāda*.

10.8.6. The two aspects of the notion of *ākāra* according to Pu Guang

However, Pu Guang does speak of two aspects of the notion of *ākāra*: According to him, this notion connotes both a 'comprehending activity' (行解) and a representational image (影像; *ābhāsa*, *pratibimba*):

> 'Comprehending activity' refers to the difference in the comprehending activity of the *citta-caitta*-s when they grasp [respectively] the generic and

specific characteristics pertaining to an object. It refers to the difference in the activities of the *citta* and the *caitta*-s. This comprehending activity may generate a correct or wrong comprehension with regard to the object … *Ākāra* refers to the fact that the *citta-caitta*-s are clear by nature; as soon as they are confronted with an object, an image arises [in them] spontaneously without the need of any mental application — just as images appearing in a clear pond or mirror. … If one uses the term 'comprehending activity', only the difference in the activities of the *citta*, etc., is referred to. If one uses the term *ākāra*, it refers to two types [of *ākāra*]: (1) *ākāra* in the sense of an image, (2) *ākāra* in the sense of a comprehending activity…

Question: With reference to which of the two — the mode of understanding or the *ākāra* [in the sense of an image] — is it said that [the *citta-caitta*-s] have the same *ākāra* (*sākāra*)?[108]

Explanation: It is with reference to *ākāra* that they are said to have the same *ākāra*. The *citta-caitta-dharma*-s are clear by nature; as soon as they are confronted with a certain object, its form appears spontaneously. As they equally have this form, they are said to 'have the same *ākāra*'. Thus, the *Abhidharmāvatāra*, in its second fascicle, says:

> Just as visual consciousness, etc., are produced with eyes, etc., as their support, manifesting with an image of the object (義影像; **arthasya pratinidhi*, **arthābhāsā*), the visible, etc., and [thus] comprehend their respective objects.[109]

Accordingly, it is only from the point of view of *ākāra* [as the image of the object] that they are said to be having the same *ākāra* …

Question: From the point of view of which of the two — the comprehending activity or the *ākāra* [in the sense of an image] — is the perceiver so called?

Explanation: From the point of view of the latter, not the former: When the *citta*, etc., is confronted with the object, an image appears; in this sense [the

> *citta*, etc.,] is called the perceiver and the object is the perceived. This is because, when the *citta-caitta* perceive an object, they do not do so like a lamp-flame radiating its ray to reach an object or like a pair of pincers grasping an object.[110] It is from the perspective of the manifestation of the image that the perceiver and the perceived are so called.[111]

Pu Guang's explanation above shows that Xuan Zang's tradition describes the Sarvāstivāda theory as *sākāra* because (i) the conjoined *citta-caitta*-s are said to have the same *ākāra* that Pu Guang takes in the sense of the object's image; and (ii) the school speaks of a sensory consciousness arising with an image of the object. But, as we have observed, unlike the Sautrāntika, the Sarvāstivāda consistently equates *ākāra* with *prajñā*, so that only Pu Guang's interpretation of *ākāra* as 'comprehending activity' may be acceptable, even though at the same time, his exposition of the Sarvāstivāda theory here is otherwise basically correct. Moreover, it must be noted that the Chinese *Abhidharmāvatāra* passage cited by him uses the word 'image' (影像) which clearly means an image, and not 'mode of activity' (行相) which is Xuan Zang's usual rendering for *ākāra*. In the corresponding example given in the ADV (109) too, the word used is *pratinidhi* instead of *ākāra*. Since both texts are authored by orthodox Vaibhāṣika masters, it seems safe enough to surmise that in the Sarvāstivāda epistemological theory, the image arising in the sensory consciousness is not an *ākāra* — a mental construction by *prajñā* — but an image essentially belonging to the object, not the mind. And as Pu Guang says, it arises spontaneously like a reflection in a mirror: The reflection does not belong to the mirror which is always clear by nature.

Pu Guang's discussion on the meaning of *sākāra* above refers to the Sarvāstivāda tenet that the conjoined *citta-caitta*-s are all *sākāra* — having the same *ākāra* (see above). In another context, all mental *dharma*-s are also described as *sākāra*, 'with an *ākāra*'. But what this term means in this context becomes controversial.

10.8.7. The notion of *sākāra* as an attribute of *citta-caitta*-s

Vasubandhu raises the question in the AKB that since the *caitta prajñā* itself is *ākāra*, *sākāra* in this context would imply that *prajñā*, as a mental *dharma*, is conjoined with another *prajñā*, which is against the Ābhidharmika tenet.[112] He proposes to avoid this apparent contradiction by defining *ākāra* as the 'object-grasping-mode (*ālambana-grahaṇa-prakāra*) of all the *citta-caitta*-s'.[113] In this way, *prajñā* too as a *caitta* can be said to be 'with an *ākāra*'. Yaśomitra states that this is a Sautrāntika definition. However, if the sense of compound means a 'mode of understanding' in the perceptual process and not an image, then it is essentially Sarvāstivāda rather than Sautrāntika. Moreover, it is noteworthy that Vasubandhu here does not contest the MVŚ statement that *ākāra* is *prajñā* and, in fact, proceeds to conclude with the same threefold classification of *dharma*-s (*ākāra*, *ākārayati*, *ākāryate*) that we have seen in the MVŚ passage quoted above. This is, however, not to say that Vasubandhu's definition of *ākāra* is identical with that of the Sarvāstivāda. It is for this reason that Saṃghabhadra objects to it, demanding from Vasubandhu more articulation on his definition:

> Herein, the Sūtrakāra affiliates himself with another school and asserts thus: 'What is called *ākāra* is the object-grasping-mode of the *citta-caitta*-s'. This does not necessarily conform to logic. It must be considered what is meant by the 'object-grasping-mode':
>
> If it refers to the different modes/species of the form of the object, then the notion that all [*citta-caitta*-s] can assume the image-form (能像) [of the object] cannot be established at all, for an object has various forms, skillful, permanent, etc. Or rather, the *rūpa-dharma*-s are to be subsumed under *ākāra*, since *rūpa-dharma*-s can also assume the images of the forms of others.
>
> If it refers to the ability to grasp the specific characteristic of the object, then *ākāra* ought not to be possible for the five [sensory] consciousnesses,

> since they are not capable of grasping the specific characteristic of the object — since only a discriminative (*sa-vikalpaka*) consciousness is capable of grasping the specific characteristic of the object [in the form]: 'it is blue, not green', etc. However, this is not what is conceded [by his definition]. Hence [his definition] is logically invalid.[114]

Saṃghabhadra's objections confirm our surmise above that, for the Sarvāstivāda, *ākāra* does not mean the specific form or image of the object. It refers to the operation of *prajñā* at the stage of mental consciousness and is not applicable in the case of a sensory perception. After criticising Vasubandhu's definition, Saṃghabhadra then proceeds to claim that the Sarvāstivāda explanation is the correct one:

1. The *prajñā* which operates investigatively with regard to the object is said to be the *ākāra*.

2. All *citta-caitta-dharma*-s, including *prajñā*, are said to be 'those that cognize with a form', which is synonymous with 'those that grasp objects' — *prajñā* investigates the object, *vedanā* feels it, *saṃjñā* grasps its appearance, *vijñāna* becomes conscious of it, etc.[115]

3. All *dharma*-s, real or unreal, are equally said to be 'those that are cognized with a form'.

In other words, this explanation leads to the same threefold classification as given in the MVŚ which Saṃghabhadra, in fact, spells out explicitly in conclusion.[116]

10.8.8. Yogic direct perception of *sāmānya-lakṣaṇa* as a form of *sākāra-jñāna*

But although the Vaibhāṣika doctrine of sensory perception can legitimately be labelled as a form of *nirākāra-jñānavāda*, we have seen above that the *pratyakṣa* of the yogi is said to perceive *sāmānya-lakṣaṇa*.

This perspective is also discernible from the three types of *pratyakṣa* enumerated by Saṃghabhadra:

1. that which is dependent on the sense faculty (依根現量; *indriyāśrita-pratyakṣa*);
2. that which is experience (領納現量; *anubhāva-pratyakṣa*);
3. that which is discernment (覺了現量; **buddhi-pratyakṣa*).

The first refers to the direct grasping (*pratyakṣaṃ √grah?*), supported by the five sense faculties, of the five types of external objects, *rūpa*, etc. The second refers to the coming into the present of the *citta-caitta-dharma*-s, *vedanā*, *saṃjñā*, etc. The third refers to the direct realization (*sākṣāt-√kṛ*) of the specific or common characteristic (*sva-sāmānya-lakṣaṇa*) — accordingly as the case may be — of *dharma*-s.[117]

From this, it is clear that it is the visual consciousness, not the mere seeing by the eye, that is *indriya-pratyakṣa*.

The second type of *pratyakṣa* is intrinsically linked with the first in-as-much as these *caitta*-s become present at the first moment of the perceptual process together with visual consciousness, sensing and categorizing (albeit weakly), etc., on the very same object that is being grasped generically by visual consciousness.

The third type is mental consciousness that follows immediately from the first moment. It can still be considered a type of direct perception since it is a clear vivid perception directly induced by the immediately preceding sensory perception.[118] Saṃghabhadra's articulation, that the **buddhi-pratyakṣa* is the direct realization of either *svalakṣaṇa* or *sāmānya-lakṣaṇa* accordingly as the case may be, can be comprehended as follows: As long as the contribution from the conascent *caitta*-s is still weak, it too, like the preceding consciousness, can only apprehend the mere object, e.g., a blue color; it is therefore a grasping of *svalakṣaṇa*. But when the contribution is strong enough and it can apprehend, using name, "it is blue", etc., it is apprehending universals — e.g., *sāmānya-lakṣaṇa* (see § 9.7). This is, then, not a case of *pratyakṣa*. The mode of activity (*ākāra* = *prajñā*) that functions at this time can be erroneous. However, in the case of spiritual realization — 'realization-knowledge' (證智; *pratyakṣa-buddhi*, **pratyakṣa-jñāna*, *adhigama-jñāna*) — the meditator apprehends directly, truly as they are, the universal characteristics of all *dharma*-s. The modes of activity in this case differ not in the slightest from the true nature of the *dharma*-s being examined. This is a case of direct seeing or direct perception *par excellence* (真現量; **bhūta-pratyakṣa*, **tattva-pratyakṣa*)[119] — without any conceptualization, even though *sāmānya-lakṣaṇa* is involved. For this reason the Sarvāstivāda identifies the 16 *ākāra*-s pertaining to the four noble truths with *prajñā* — operating as spiritual insight. The MVŚ states that "outside the 16 *ākāra*-s, there is no other outflow-free *prajñā*". "The *prajñā*-s not subsumed under the 16 *ākāra*-s mostly discern *svalakṣaṇa*-s; the *prajñā*-s subsumed under the 16 *ākāra*-s discern only *sāmānya-lakṣaṇa*-s."[120]

Saṃghabhadra argues that *sahabhū* causality obtains in a sensory perception; the sensory faculty and the object as the causes and the sensory consciousness as the effect all arise in the same first moment. Moreover, *vedanā*, the instrumental force for *anubhāva*,[121] must be 'conjoined with' consciousness — which entails not only simultaneity, but also that both take the same object, etc.[122] In fact, a sensory consciousness necessarily has a present perceptual object, or it will not be possible for one to have the *pratyakṣa* experience. For, with regard to what is personally sensed, one experiences it and discerns it at different times. That is, the *anubhāva-pratyakṣa* and *buddhi-pratyakṣa* are not simultaneous. Discernment occurs at the state of recollection, taking the experience — the *vedanā* — that has just ceased as its object. Accordingly, "a sensation — pleasurable, etc. — must first be experienced by the *anubhāva-pratyakṣa* before a *pratyakṣa* discernment can arise having it as its perceptual object. Likewise, an external object must first be experienced by *indriyāśrita-pratyakṣa* before a *pratyakṣa* discernment can arise having it as the perceptual object, by virtue of the thrust of presentness."[123] This is consistent with the Sarvāstivāda view that the *citta-caitta-dharma*-s cannot discern themselves or those conjoined or coexist with them. (See above, § 10.4). Saṃghabhadra argues that since the Sautrāntika maintains that on account of causation being successive, an external object in the preceding moment has not been experienced directly (*pratyakṣam*), there can be no possibility of a subsequent discernment that is of the nature of *pratyakṣa*[124] — having the thrust of vividness and immediacy.

The Sautrāntika, on the other hand, argues that not mere recollection, but rather the simultaneity of the experiencing (*anubhāva*) and the discerning (*buddhi*) must be admitted to account for such an experience.[125] That is, unless one is self-aware of what one is presently cognizing or knowing — i.e., unless what is termed *sva-saṃvedana*[126] in later Buddhist logical texts is a fact — one cannot in the subsequent moment recollect as a *pratyakṣa* understanding in the manner: "I have experienced such a pleasure or pain."[127]

10.8.9. Summary

Its theory of simultaneous causality notwithstanding, the Sarvāstivāda school, too, holds that sensory perception as a *pratyakṣa* experience is fully accomplished only in the second moment on recollection. The reasoning is that the external object must first be experienced by the *indriyāśrita-pratyakṣa* before a *buddhi* — i.e., the *buddhi-pratyakṣa* — having that *pratyakṣa* as its *ālambana* can arise.

Both the Vaibhāṣika and the Sautrāntika seek to account for the sense of vividness and immediacy necessarily entailed in a *pratyakṣa* experience, albeit via somewhat different mechanism: The former relies on the principle of simultaneous causality in the perceptual act and on the conascence of the sensory consciousness with *vedanā* and the other *mahābhūmika-citta-caitta*-s. The latter, while rejecting simultaneous causality, maintain that in the *pratyakṣa* act, the experiencing (*anubhāva*) and the discerning (*buddhi*) are necessarily simultaneous — the perceptual act is intrinsically self-aware.

The Sarvāstivāda school, in its various texts, consistently equates *ākāra* with *prajñā*, both being defined as the investigative operation with regard to the perceptual object. (However, the sense of *ākāra* in the notion of *sākāra* as an attribute of the *citta-caitta-dharma*-s is treated differently.) This is in contrast to the Sautrāntika and Yogācāra for whom *ākāra* connotes both an image/representation and a mental understanding arising in the mind — with the difference that the Sautrāntika would regard it as a correspondent to an external existent. To this extent, therefore, it is inappropriate to describe the Sarvāstivāda theory of sensory perception — said to be non-discriminative on account of the weak functioning of *prajñā* therein — as *sākāra-jñānavāda*. On the other hand, we must note that the *pratyakṣa* of the yogi is said to perceive *sāmānya-lakṣaṇa*. This perspective is also discernible from the explanation of *buddhi-pratyakṣa*. This is the case of *satyābhisamaya*, in which the outflow-free *ākāra*-s perceived by the yogi are not conceptual understanding. They correspond truly and exactly to the *sāmānya-lakṣaṇa*-s as universal principles pertaining to the absolute truth (*paramārtha*). This perception is therefore also a *pratyakṣa* experience; in fact, *pratyakṣa par excellence* — and in-as-much as it involves *ākāra*-s, is describable as a form of *sākāra-jñāna*. *Prajñā* at this stage is truly non-discriminative/non-superimposing, although not in the Vijñānavādin sense of transcending the 'subject-object' dichotomy. This Sarvāstivāda notion that a practitioner endowed with true spiritual insight perceives reality through *ākāra*-s might well have influenced those members among the latter-day Yogācārins who opt for the view that even for those who have acquired the non-discriminative insight (*nirvikalpaka-jñāna*) too, knowledge is *sākāra*.[128]

NOTES

[1] *Cf.* AKB, 461: *kathaṃ punar idaṃ gamyate skandhasaṃtāna evedam ātmābhidhānaṃ vartate nānyasminn abhidheya iti / pratyakṣānumānābhāvāt / ye hi dharmāḥ santi teṣāṃ pratyakṣam upalabdhir bhavaty asaty antarāye /*

[2] MVŚ, 313c, 989c.

[3] Ny, 639b.

[4] MVŚ, 288a.

[5] For the possibility of this correspondence, see AKB, 176.

[6] *Cf. Viṃśikā vijñapti-mātra-siddhi* in Levi, S (ed.) *Vijñaptimātratāsiddhi Deux Traities de Vasbandhu* (Paris, 1925), 6, stanza 11: *na ca te saṃhatāḥ…*

[7] Ny, 351a–b.

[8] T 29, 788c.

[9] Ny, 350c–351c.

[10] MVŚ, 702a.

[11] MVŚ, 64a–b.

[12] T 26, 713c.

[13] MVŚ, 228b–c.

[14] MVŚ, 558b.

[15] MVŚ, 558b.

[16] Ny, 625a.

[17] Ny, 621c: 為境生覺是真有相.

[18] Müller, M, ed., *Dharma-saṃgraha* (Oxford, 1885), § 135.

[19] *Cf.* AKB, 29; Vy, 80.

[20] MVŚ, 489b ff.

[21] AKB, 54: *matiḥ prajñā dharmapravicayaḥ.* ADV, 70: *dhiḥ prajñā dharma-saṃgrahādyupalakṣaṇasvabhāvā.* Similar in *Prakaraṇa-śāstra* (T. 1542), *Saṅgītiparyāya-śāstra* (T. 1536), etc.

[22] MVŚ, 490b.

[23] MVŚ, 44a.

[24] *Cf.* MVŚ, 546b ff.; AKB, 394; ADV, 373. The MVŚ justifies the enumeration of eight knowledges (without *kṣaya-* and *anutpāda-*) in the JPŚ as conforming to the *sūtra*-s. See also, *Entrance*, 118, and note 443.

[25] MVŚ, 490b.

[26] MVŚ, 490b–c.

[27] MVŚ, 229a.

[28] 'Vijñānavādins' here does not necessarily refer to the Yogācāra. It refers to all those who hold that it is *vijñāna* that sees.

[29] MVŚ, 490c–491a.

[30] MVŚ, 744a.

[31] In the early discourses, the Buddha's wisdom (*prajñā*) is mainly described as the realization of the truth of conditioned co-arising (e.g., M, i, 167; Vin, i, 4 f.). This is further elaborated as the threefold knowledge (*trividyā*): 1. knowledge of former births (*pūrvanivāsānusmṛti-jñāna*), 2. knowledge of the disappearance and reappearance of beings (*cyutyupapāda-jñāna*), 3. knowledge of the exhaustion of the outflows (*āsravakṣaya-jñāna*). We further see the enumeration of the six-fold higher knowledges (*ṣaḍabhijñā*) which adds three more to this list: 4. psychic power (*ṛddhy-abhijñā*), 5. divine ear (*divya-śrota*) and 6. knowledge of the thoughts of another (*paracitta-jñāna*).

[32] T no. 2031, 15c.

[33] JPŚ, 919b. Note that 'cause' is used in the strict Sarvāstivāda sense as an efficacy pertaining to the same (here, the person's own) serial continuity.

[34] MVŚ, 42c–43a.

[35] Some masters provide the examples of a finger-tip not touching itself, a knife not cutting itself, etc. (MVŚ, 43a).

See also, Ny, 742a–b, where Saṃghabhadra states that the Ābhidharmikas take as a premise that intrinsic natures do not take themselves as their *ālambana*-s. They do not relate to themselves.

[36] E.g., Candrakīrti's *Madhyamakāvatāra*, 167; also see La Vallée Poussin (1925), 182, n. 2.

[37] Ny, 374c.

[38] M, I. 6.

[39] MA, 52: *buddhānañhi sāvakehi saddhiṃ kiñcāpi tena tena maggena kilesappahāne viseso natthi, pariññāya pana atthi.*

[40] *na hi bhagavantaṃ ṭhapetvā aññe saha vāsanāya kilese pahatuṃ sakkonti Visuddhimagga-mahāṭīkā*, 1.219; *Sāratthadīpanī-ṭīkā* 1.217.

[41] *Sīlakkhandavagga-abhinavaṭīkā* 1.4: *savāsanappahānañhi kilesānaṃ ñeyyāvaraṇap-pahānanti*

[42] *Dhammasaṅgaṇi-anuṭīkā, vīsatigāthāvaṇṇanā: dhamma-saddena ñeyyā visesitabbā … ñeyya-saddena dhammā visesitā…*

[43] The discussion under section § 10.4 is taken from my paper entitled: 'The Defects in the Arhat's Enlightenment — His *akliṣṭājñāna* and *vāsanā*' in *Bukkyo Kenkyu*, vol. XXVII (Hamamatsu, 1998), 65–98.

[44] For a further discussion on *vāsanā*, see *infra*, § 12.10.

[45] MVŚ, 74a.

[46] MVŚ, 382c–383a.

[47] MVŚ, 887b.

[48] MVŚ, 887b.

[49] MVŚ, 821.

[50] AKB, 1.

[51] *Loc. cit.*: *tac* (i.e., *ajñānam*) *ca bhagavato buddhasya pratipakṣalābhenātyantaṃ sarvathā sarvatra jñeye punaranutpattidharmatvād dhatam* /

[52] AKB, *loc. cit.*: *eṣāṃ buddhadharmeṣv ativiprakṛṣṭadeśakāleṣv artheṣu cānanta-prabhedeṣu bhavaty evākliṣṭam ajñānam* /

[53] Vy, 4.

[54] Vy, 5.

[55] *tathā hi āha: sarv'ākāraṃ kāraṇam ekasya mayūra-candrakasyāpi nāsarvajñair jñeyaṃ, sarvajña-balaṃ hi taj-jñānaṃ*. Also quoted in AKB, 474.

[56] UdA, 194: *kā panāyaṃ vāsanā nāma? yaṃ kilesarahitassāpi santāne appahīnakilesānaṃ samācārasadisasamācārahetubhūtaṃ, anādikālabhāvitehi kilesehi āhitaṃ sāmatthiya-mattaṃ, tathārūpā adhimuttîti vadanti. taṃ panetaṃ abhinīhārasampattiyā ñeyyāvaraṇap-pahānavasena yattha kilesā pahīnā, tattha bhagavato santāne natthi. yattha pana tathā kilesā na pahīnā tattha sāvakānaṃ paccekabuddhānañca santāne atthi, tato tathāgatova anāvaraṇañāṇadassano.*

[57] MVŚ, 724b.

[58] MVŚ, 780b.

[59] Ny, 724b.

[60] Ny, 501c–502a.

[61] Ny, 502a.

[62] MVŚ, 61c.

[63] *Cf. Pañcavastuka-vibhāṣā* quoted below.

[64] T no. 1555, 991b–c.

[65] ADV, 31 f.

[66] AKB, 30; ADV, 32; Vy, 80; Ny, 363c.

[67] *Cf.* Vy, 80: *rūpālocanārtheneti cakṣur na saṃtīrakatvena dṛṣṭi ... prajñā saṃtīrakatveneti darśitaṃ bhavati.*

[68] AKB, 39.

[69] ADV, 47.

[70] AKB, 39: *nāpi vijñānād rūpadarśanaṃ śabdaśravaṇaṃ vā 'sti /*

[71] Vy, 96: *nāpi vijñānād anyad rūpa-darśanaṃ śabda-śravaṇaṃ vā 'stīti / na rūpa-darśana-śabda-śravaṇaṃ grahaṇa-vyatiriktaṃ vicāryamānaṃ labhyate / grahaṇaṃ ca vijñānam eveti nānyad bhavati /*

[72] ADV, 32: *caksuḥ paśyati vijñānaṃ vijānāti svagocaram / ālocanopalabdhitvādviśeṣ aḥ sumahāṃstayoḥ //*

[73] MVŚ, 378c–379a.

[74] *Ibid.*, 283b.

[75] AKB, 31. In the last sentence, *nābhidhāvet* could also be rendered as 'not [unnecessarily] contravene (/find faults with)'. The Pāli (M, 139, *Araṇavibhaṅga-sutta*) has: *janpadaniruttiṃ nābhiveseyya samaññaṃ nātidhāveyyāti /*

Cf. YBŚ (T 30, 826b): "If one states that all conditionings comprise mere causes and effects at all times, absolutely without any experiencer or agent, then this is to be known as *śūnyatā* from the standpoint of absolute truth."

[76] Ny, 367c–368a. For a complete account of the whole debate based on AKB, Vy and Ny, see *Perception*, 30 ff.

[77] *Ibid.*, 364b.

[78] AKB, 473 f.

[79] *Siddhi*(F), 445.

[80] Ny, 342a; SPrŚ, 783c. Also *cf. Siddhi*(C), T 31, 39c: 識生時無實作用 ....

[81] T 29, 349a.

[82] For more details, see *Perception*, chapter 5.

[83] Saṃghabhadra (Ny, 349a) stresses that it is because a visual consciousness is also capable of grasping the appearance of a *rūpa* that it is also capable of generating defilements.

[84] *Cf.* ADV, 81: *kaḥ punarayaṃ vitarkaḥ ko vā vicāraḥ / vitarko nāma cittaudāryalakṣaṇaḥ saṃkalpadvitīyanāmā viṣayanimittaprakāravikalpī saṃjñāpavanoddhatavṛttiḥ audārikapañcavijñānakāyapravṛttihetuḥ / vicārastu cittasaukṣmyalakṣaṇo manovijñānapravṛttyanukūlaḥ* / Also, similar definitions on the two *caitta*-s in *Abhidharmāvatāra* (see *Entrance*, 93).

[85] MVŚ, 288a–b, 228b. For a fuller discussion of this stance of the Sautrāntika-Dārṣṭāntikas, see *Perception*, 8 ff.

[86] Ny, 472b. For this reason, Saṃghabhadra (*loc. cit.*) argues that since reflections in the mirror can be seen, they exist truly.

[87] Ny, 536a.

[88] VKŚ, 535a ff.

[89] Ny, 621c–622a. See also the definition given in **Satya-siddhi-śāstra*: "The mark of the existent consists in the fact that it is where cognition operates" (T 32, 254a: 知所行處, 名曰有相).

[90] Ny, 622a ff. Also cf. ADV, 271 ff.; **Satyasiddhi-śāstra*, T 32, 254a ff.

[91] The 幻網經 (*Māyā-jāla-sūtra*) corresponding to the *Brahma-jāla-sūtra* of the *Dīrgha-āgama.*

[92] Ny, 624a.

[93] E.g., SDS, 46, 368–371, which classifies the Buddhist schools in terms of *ākāravāda*.

[94] *Cf.* Pu Guang's commentary on AKB, T 41, 27a; Kuei Ji's commentary on *Siddhi*(C), T 43, 269c, 318a; etc.

[95] *Cf. Abhidhammatthasaṅgaha*, IV, 8.

[96] MVŚ, 408c–409a.

[97] *Cf.* AKB, 54: *matiḥ prajñā dharma-pravicayaḥ* / ADV, 70: *dhiḥ prajñā dharma-saṃgrahādy-upalakṣaṇa-svabhāvā* /; etc.

[98] MVŚ, 36a; Ny, 623b.

[99] Ny, 741b. See also *infra*.

[100] MVŚ, 929a.

[101] *Cf.* MVŚ, 45c, which states explicitly that the *ākāra* of this form is *prajñā*. The MVŚ (42c, 43a) explains that within two moments, one can come to acquire such a knowledge with regard to the totality of *dharma*-s.

[102] There are four *ākāra*-s for each truth: For *duḥkha-satya* — *duḥkhatā*, *śūnyatā*, *anityatā*, *nairātmya*; etc. See AKB, 343 (see also, *infra*, § 15.2.2.1).

[103] MVŚ, 53a. *Cf.* AKB, 108.

[104] *Cf.* AKB, 399: *kāśmīrāṇāṃ tāvat*

nāmalaḥ ṣoḍaśabhyo 'nya ākāraḥ

nāsty anāsravākāraḥ ṣoḍaśākāra-nirmuktaḥ / For the Vaibhāṣika tenet that the 16 *ākāra*-s are *prajñā*, see also AKB, 401.

[105] MVŚ, 399c–400a.

[106] Ny, 735c. Saṃghabhadra argues against an opinion held by certain masters that *anvaya* (類) here means comparison (比類): the comparison of facts not directly perceived with those that are directly perceived. It receives the name *anvaya-jñāna* as it is subsumed under inference (*anumāna*).

Vy, 542, explains *tad-anvaya* as *tad-dhetuka* — having the *dharma-jñāna* as cause — thus dissenting from the Vaibhāṣika view.

SatŚ, 245, too rejects the Sarvāstivāda definition above and declares his adherence to the *sūtra* when giving the same opinion thus: "The knowledge of the present *dharma* is named *dharma-jñāna*. As it is said in the *sūtra*, the Buddha told Ānanda, 'With regard to these *dharma*-s, see thus, know thus, penetrate thus. Know the past and future [*dharma*] also thus. The knowledge of the remaining — i.e., the past and future — *dharma*-s is named *anvaya-jñāna*. … *Dharma-jñāna* is *pratyakṣa-jñāna* (現智). Following this *dharma-jñāna* one deliberates and knows inferentially — this is called *anvaya-jñāna*."

[107] MVŚ, 490c.

[108] The Vaibhāṣika tenet is that *citta* and *caitta*-s co-arise necessarily. They are said to be conjoined (*saṃprayukta*).

[109] T 28, no. 1554, 987c. Tibetan version of *Abhidharmāvatāra*: *shes pa bzhin du don gyi tshul gyi gnas lta bu'i rnam par rang gi don khong du chud par byed pa* / — "Just like *jñāna* which causes the understanding of *svārtha* (*svārtha-pratyāyana*) in the form of a representation of the *artha*." *Cf.* ADV, 109: *jñānavat / tadyathā jñānaṃ cakṣurādīn hetūnapekṣyārthaṃ vibhāvayati* /; also, 111: *jñānavat / tadyathā jñānaṃ cakṣurādīn hetūnapekṣyārthaṃ vibhāvayati* /

[110] Pu Guang seems to have taken these two examples illustrating that consciousness simply arises with an image of the perceptual object from *Siddhi*(C) — *cf. Siddhi*(C), 93c; T 43 (Kuei Ji's commentary on *Siddhi*(C)), 493c–494a.

[111] T 41, 26b–c.

[112] *Cf.* MVŚ, 79c.

[113] *Cf.* AKB, 401: ***prajñākāraḥ /***

evaṃ tarhi prajñā sākārā na bhaviṣyati / prajñāntarāsaṃ[pra]yogāt / evaṃ tu yuktaṃ syāt / sarveṣāṃ citta-caittānām ālambana-grahaṇa-prakāra iti /

[114] Ny, 741b.

[115] Saṃghabhadra does seem to acknowledge that *sākāra* in this context needs interpretation to avoid the difficulty pointed out by Vasubandhu and he proposes a few of them (Ny, 741a–b). Besides the one he gives in the conclusion here, another one given before-hand is that the *citta-caitta*-s are all said to be *sākāra* because they equally — i.e., simultaneously — with *ākāra* (= *prajñā*) operate on the object. This is compared to the term *sāsrava*: An object being equal to the *āsrava* is said to be 'with *āsrava*' in the sense that it requires the same counteractive agent (*pratipakṣa*) as the *āsrava* itself.

[116] *Loc. cit.*

[117] T 29, 736a.

[118] *Cf.* Pu Guang's explanation in T 41, 135b.

[119] Saṃghabhadra (Ny, 684a) speaks of the insight arising in *satyābhisamaya* as the 真現量證智.

[120] MVŚ, 217a.

[121] *Cf.* AKB, 229: One making present a feeling is said to experience it — *saṃmukhīkurvaṃs tu tāṃ vedayata ity ucyate* /

[122] The two in conjunction satisfying the five-fold equality (*samatā*): *āśraya*, *ālambana*, *ākāra*, *kāla*, *dravya* (see AKB, 62). In this case of a sensory perception of course, the *ākāra* does not function prominently.

[123] Ny, 374c.

[124] Ny, 374c–375a.

[125] Ny, 374c.

[126] Candrakīrti criticizes this as a Sautrāntika doctrine. See La Vallée Poussin (ed.), *Madhyamakāvatāra* 167 f.

[127] Ny, 574c.

[128] The discussion on the Sarvāstivāda notion of *ākāra* and direct perception is extracted from my article, '*Ākāra* and Direct Perception: Vaibhāṣika versus Sautrāntika', in MORI, Sodo, ed., *Bukkyō Kenkyū* (Hamamatsu, 2007), vol. XXXV, 1 ff.

11. The Category of the Conditionings Disjoined from Thought (*citta-viprayukta-saṃskāra*)

11.1. Doctrinal evolution of the category

In comparison with the Sarvāstivāda and other northern schools, the doctrinal development in the Pāli canonical *abhidhamma* texts is more archaic and, in a way, more faithful to the doctrines of the *sutta*-s. Thus, with regard to the conditioned *dhamma*-s, the Theravādin Ābhidhammikas went no further than the dualism of mind and matter. The Northern canonical *abhidharma* texts, on the other hand, made distinct advance, formulating new doctrinal categories not traceable to the Buddha's teachings. One such important advancement was the category known as *citta-viprayukta-saṃskāra* — conditionings disjoined from thought. In some cases at least, they may be considered as laws of nature. In the doctrinally fully articulated form, they are real entities which are neither mental nor material in nature, which yet can operate on both domains. What is more, although themselves conditioned, two of them — *prāpti* and *aprāpti* — can operate on even the unconditioned *dharma*-s.

This category seems to have evolved in the process of the Ābhidharmika analysis of the *svalakṣaṇa* of *dharma*-s. The methodology of *saṃgraha* (*supra*, § 4) was applied to all *dharma*-s in respect of the taxonomical doublet — "*citta-saṃprayukta*" and "not *citta-saṃprayukta*": *dharma*-s that are conjoined with the mind and those that are not. Already in the **Śāriputrābhidharma* — one of the oldest extant northern *abhidharma* texts, known to have been based upon by several schools belonging the Sthaviravāda lineage — a distinction was made between these two classes of *dharma*-s which were said to constitute the *dharmāyatana*:

> *Dharmāyatana* is the one divisible into two portions — [*dharma*-s] which are either *citta-saṃprayukta* or *citta-viprayukta*.
>
> What is the [portion of the] *dharmāyatana* that is *citta-saṃprayukta*? Those pertaining to the *dharmāyatana* which are *caitasika* — *vedanā*, *saṃjñā*, etc., up to the *kleśa*.
>
> What is the [portion of the] *dharmāyatana* that is not *citta-saṃprayukta*? Those pertaining to the *dharmāyatana* which are not *caitasika* — *jāti*, etc., up to [the attainment] which is neither ideation nor non-ideation.[1]

We may note that this taxonomical doublet is actually one of the *mātṛkā*-s found in many early *abhidharma*. Items like *jāti*, etc., which later came to be included in the developed list of *citta-viprayukta-saṃskāra,* were enumerated among those "that are not *citta-saṃprayukta*". They were still not explicitly named elsewhere; on the basis of this doublet, **Śāriputrābhidharma* classifies the five *skandha*-s into those that are (i) *citta-saṃprayukta*, (ii) not *citta-saṃprayukta*, (iii) neither said to be *citta-saṃprayukta* or not *citta-saṃprayukta*, (iv) partly *citta-saṃprayukta* and partly not *citta-saṃprayukta*:

> Of the five *skandha*-s, how many are *citta-saṃprayukta*, how many are not *citta-saṃprayukta*?
>
> Two are *citta-saṃprayukta*. One is not *citta-saṃprayukta*. One is not said to be either *citta-saṃprayukta* or not *citta-saṃprayukta*. One contains two portions: either *citta-saṃprayukta* or not *citta-saṃprayukta*.
>
> What are the two which are *citta-saṃprayukta*? The *vedanā-skandha* and *saṃjñā-skandha*…
>
> What is the one which is not *citta-saṃprayukta*? The *rūpa-skandha*…
>
> What is the one which is not said to be *citta-saṃprayukta* or not *citta-saṃprayukta*? The *vijñāna-skandha*…
>
> What is the one which is of two portions — either *citta-saṃprayukta* or not *citta-saṃprayukta*? The *saṃskāra-skandha*…
>
> What is [the portion of the] *saṃskāra-skandha* which is not *citta-saṃprayukta*? That [portion of the] *saṃskāra-skandha* which is not *caitasika* — *jāti*, etc., up to *nirodha-samāpatti*.[2]

However, the **Śāriputrābhidharma* speaks only negatively of *saṃskāra*-s which are "not *citta-saṃprayukta*", and not positively of a category known as *citta-viprayukta-saṃskāra*. This kind of broad connotation given to the term "*dharma*-s which are not conjoined with *citta*" is found even in the later texts wherein *citta-viprayukta-saṃskāra* as a technical category is known to have been established. Thus, in the PrŚ we find:

> What are the *citta-viprayukta-dharma*-s? They are the *dharma*-s which are not *caitta*-s…, i.e., the *rūpa*-s, the *asaṃskṛta*-s, and the *citta-viprayukta-saṃskāra*-s.[3]

It was probably in the JPŚ that for the first time we saw the explicit establishment by the Sarvāstivādins of this category.[4] Thus, on the topic of *vipāka-hetu*, JPŚ speaks of "*rūpa*, *citta*, *caitasika-dharma*-s, *citta-viprayukta-saṃskāra*".[5] It also explains that the mental series of a sentient being in the *ārūpya-dhātu* proceeds (√*vṛt*) with "*jīvitendriya*, *nikāya-sabhāga* and other such *citta-viprayukta-saṃskāra*-s as its basis". In Vasumitra's *Pañcavastuka*,[6] the totality of *dharma*-s are explicitly classified into five categories:

> There are five [categories of] *dharma*-s: — (1) *rūpa*, (2) *citta*, (3) *caitasika*, (4) *citta-viprayukta-saṃskāra* and (5) *asaṃskṛta*. …
>
> What are the *citta-viprayukta-saṃskāra*-s? Those *dharma*-s that are not *citta-saṃprayukta*.
>
> Now what are these? *Prāpti, asaṃjñi-samāpatti, nirodha-samāpatti, āsaṃjñika, jīvitendriya, nikāya-sabhāga*, **upadhi-pratilambha*, **vastu-pratilambha*, **āyatana-pratilambha*, *jāti, sthiti, jarā, anityatā, nāma-kāya, pada-kāya*, *vyañjana-kāya*; and all other such *dharma*-s which are not *citta-saṃprayukta*. They are collectively named the *citta-viprayukta-saṃskāra*.

However, it must be noted that from the beginning, even within the broad Sarvāstivāda tradition itself, this newly articulated doctrinal category had not been unanimously accepted, either as regards their reality (as a *dravya* having a *svabhāva*) or as regards their total number. Thus, in the MVŚ, we find that Bhadanta Dharmatrāta[7] and the early Dārṣṭāntika *ācārya*-s[8] deny the reality of the whole *viprayukta-saṃskāraskandha*. Buddhadeva considers all the *saṃskṛta-dharma*-s to be subsumable under either the *mahābhūta*-s (as in the case of the *rūpa*) or *citta* (as in the case of the *citta-caitta*-s), which, of course, is tantamount to the denial of any such category as the *citta-viprayukta-dharma*-s which are conjoined neither with *rūpa* nor *citta*. Yet he seems to concede a relative reality to at least some of them, such as *prāpti*,[9] *jīvitendriya* and *nikāya-sabhāgatā*.[10]

In the JPŚ, we find neither clear definitions nor a definite list of them, but only scattered descriptions of *nikāya-sabhāgatā*, *jīvitendriya*, *jāti, sthiti, jarā, anityatā, pṛthagjanatva*[11] and *prāpti*.[12] In both the DSŚ and the PrŚ, we find 16 enumerated, and in the *Amṛtarasa-śāstra*, 17. It seems not until the *Abhidharmahṛdaya* that the number came to be more or less fixed at 14. The AKB too enumerates 14, as does the PrŚ whose list differs from the AKB one only in replacing *aprāpti* with *pṛthagjanatva*. Significantly, the *Avatāra* gives the same 14 as in the AKB, although in a different order.

But the number of these *viprayukta-saṃskāra*-s seems never to have become absolutely fixed at 14 in the Sarvāstivāda tradition.[13] Vasubandhu enumerates the 14 in a verse,[14] ending with *ca iti*. Yaśomitra comments:

> The word *ca* [in the verse] is for the purpose of indicating those *viprayukta*-s of a similar type that have not been [explicitly] mentioned, for *saṃghabheda*, etc., are conceded as *citta-viprayukta*-s existing as real entities. This is because of the mention in the *śāstra* 'and also those [*viprayukta*-s] of a similar type' (see PrŚ quoted above).[15]

Saṃghabhadra, commenting on *-ādayaś ceti* in the same context, says:

> *-ādaya* is meant to include *pada-kāya* and *vyañjana-kāya* as well as *sāmagrī* (和合性); *ca iti* indicates the *dharma*-s speculated by others which are none other than those of the previously [mentioned] categories: There are some who speculate that, apart from *prāpti,* etc., there exist such [intrinsic] natures as **skandha-prāpti,* etc.[16]

The MVŚ mentions *asāmagrī* as a *citta-viprayukta-saṃskāra,* and *Saṃghabheda* states that it is a force which operates to cause schism in the *saṅgha* has this as its intrinsic nature.[17] There are also certain other forces of operation which, in the opinions of the MVŚ compilers, are subsumable — in a general sense — under "other *dharma*-s of such types which are [*citta*-]*viprayukta"* (此即攝在，復有所餘如是類法不相應中). These include *mūrdha-patitatva* — a force which causes the falling from the spiritual attainment called *mūrdhan*; *parihāṇi* — retrogression from spiritual attainment; and *pṛthagjanatva* — a force obstructing the endowment of the *ārya-dharma*-s, thus rendering one an ordinary worldling. However, it is stated explicitly that they have certain *dharma*-s recognized in the Sarvāstivāda scheme of classification as their intrinsic natures. Thus, just as *saṃghabheda* is *asāmagrī* in its intrinsic nature, *mūrdha-patitatva*, *parihāṇi* and *pṛthagjanatva* have non-endowment (*asamanvāgama* = *aprāpti*) as their intrinsic nature.[18] Accordingly, they are acknowledged, not so much as real entities distinct from those *dharma*-s said to be their intrinsic nature, but simply as distinct modes of operation of the latter. This is much like the case that *jñāna*, *kṣānti*, *dṛṣṭi* and *akliṣṭa-ajñāna* are all distinct modes of operation of *prajñā* which constitutes their intrinsic nature in each case. They are as such not specifically enumerated as distinct *dharma*-s (apart from *prajñā*) in the Sarvāstivāda scheme of classification. It is, however, to be noted that in some Sarvāstivāda *abhidharma* texts such as the *Abhidharmahṛdaya* (AH),[19] the *Abhidharmahṛdaya Sūtra* (*AHS)[20] and the *Abhidharmahṛdayavyākhyā*,[21] *pṛthagjanatva* is enumerated in place of *aprāpti* under the category of *citta-viprayukta-saṃskāra*. This is probably on account of its importance in the Sarvāstivāda doctrine of spiritual progress. The AmRŚ enumerates *pṛthagjanatva* (凡夫性) at the end of its list.[22] The MVŚ records that, according to some masters, there is in a sentient being a certain mark (相 *nimitta*?) of the nature of *viprayukta-saṃskāra*. When the Buddha contemplates it, He is able to know the specific past karmic cause and future consequence of that being. It is not clear as to whether the compilers of the MVŚ accept such a *viprayukta-saṃskāra dharma*, since their rejection of this view is from the perspective that the Buddha does not require any inferential means to have such a knowledge.[23]

The ADV speaks of 13 in its verse[24] although, in its prose commentary, it actually explains the same 14 in the same order as in the AKB. All these post-AKB sources indicate that the Ābhidharmikas of this period did not fully agree as to the exact number of *dharma*-s to be included under the category of *citta-viprayukta-saṃskāra*. Indeed, this is the period when, challenged by severe criticism from the Sautrāntikas, particularly with regard to the reality of these *viprayukta-saṃskāra*-s, the Sarvāstivāda Ābhidharmikas felt tremendous pressure to give clear definitions and proofs of these *dharma*-s as real entities. The larger part of the controversies in the AKB is in fact concerned with this. Threatened by the serious objections posed by Vasubandhu in his AKB, the Ny, the SPrŚ and the ADV became all the more determined to defend their position against the Sautrāntikas. Saṃghabhadra devoted much space in both his works, invoking scriptural authority and applying logical arguments, to establishing their reality. The author of the ADV is just as determined and emphatic in this regard, explicitly declaring his intention to prove their *svabhāva*-s.[25] Skandhila too in his *Avatāra,* which is also post-AKB, in spite of his avowed intention to steer away from controversies, cannot help sharing the same concern — and it would seem — to the same degree.

11.2. Definition of *citta-viprayukta-saṃskāra* in later texts

It was in the post-AKB manuals that we find articulate definitions of the category itself and of the items enumerated under the category. Saṃghabhadra[26] explains that the three components (*citta-*, *viprayukta-*, *-saṃskāra*) together uniquely define *citta-viprayukta-saṃskāra* as a distinct doctrinal category in the fivefold category classification of *dharma*-s:

citta — to signify that like *citta*, these *dharma*-s are not *rūpa*;

viprayukta — to signify that the *caitta*-s, although also not of the nature of *rūpa*, are to be excluded as they are *saṃprayukta*;

saṃskāra — to signify that the *asaṃskṛta*-s, although not of the nature of *rūpa* and not *saṃprayukta* with *citta*, are also to be excluded.

Yaśomitra, in a similar manner, in explaining the doctrinal significance of each of the components of the term, differentiates this category from the other four:

> *Cittaviprayuktāḥ* — the word *citta* for the purpose of showing that they belong to the same type as *citta*: this means that like *citta*, they are disjoined from *citta*. And what is their sameness in type with *citta*? Inasmuch as they are not material for *rūpa*, in spite of the nature of being disjoined, does not obtain the name in respect of the nature of being *viprayukta* on the very account of it being *rūpa*. Or, their sameness in type with *citta* consists in their being of the nature of *nāma* in respect to the *nāma-rūpa* [distinction].
>
> The *caitta*-s are also of the same type as *citta*, but they are conjoined (*saṃprayukta*) with *citta* in respect to the object; the word *viprayukta* is for the purpose of distinguishing them [from the *caitta*-s].
>
> The *asaṃskṛta*-s are also of the same type as the [*viprayukta-saṃskāra*] in respect to their not taking any objects (*anālambanatvena*); the word *saṃskāra* is for the purpose of excluding the [*asaṃskṛta*-s which, being unconditioned, are not *saṃskāra*-s].[27]

11.3. Classic list in the AKB

The 14 enumerated in the AKB are:

1. *prāpti* (acquisition),
2. *aprāpti* (non-acquisition),
3. *nikāya-sabhāga* (group-homogeneity),
4. *āsaṃjñika* (ideationlessness),
5. *asaṃjñi-samāpatti* (ideationless attainment),
6. *nirodha-samāpatti* (cessation attainment),
7. *jīvitendriya* (vital faculty),
8. *jāti-lakṣaṇa* (production-characteristic),
9. *sthiti-lakṣaṇa* (duration-characteristic),
10. *jarā-lakṣaṇa* (deterioration-characteristic),
11. *anityatā-lakṣaṇa* (impermanence-characteristic),
12. *nāma-kāya* (word-group),
13. *pada-kāya* (phrase-group),
14. *vyañjana-kāya* (syllable-group).

Among these, *prāpti*, *aprāpti* and the four *lakṣaṇa*-s may be said to be the ones most important doctrinally. Accordingly, we shall devote more space to them in the explanations that follow:[28]

11.3.1. *Prāpti* and *aprāpti*

Prāpti is perhaps the most important *viprayukta-saṃskāra-dharma*, and this fact seems to be reflected by its leading position in the list. It is a force that links a *dharma* to a particular series (*santati/santāna*), i.e., the individual. *Aprāpti* is another real entity whose function and nature are just opposed to those of *prāpti*: It acts to ensure that a given *dharma* is delinked from the individual series.

As an illustration: when I have a certain jealousy in me, it is because, given the required assemblage of conditions for inducing the arising of this *dharma*, jealousy, a force called *prāpti* is also induced to arise at the same time, by virtue of which the jealousy comes to be linked to me. This force of *prāpti* will continue to link the jealousy to me from moment to moment — even at those times when my mind is not occupied with this defilement but with a skillful or non-defined thought — arising and ceasing in a serial continuity of its own. It is only when I am able to develop a sufficiently strong insight as the counteragent that it comes to be delinked from me: At this moment, there arises another *prāpti* of another *dharma*, the *prāpti* of the cessation (*nirodha*) of this defilement; and at the same time, the *aprāpti* of this defilement is also induced to arise, effecting the delinking. The cessation and the *aprāpti* together ensure that the defilement will not arise in me any more.

The ADV, the *Avatāra* and the Ny define *prāpti* as that which enables us to affirm that an individual is in possession of a particular *dharma*. The *Avatāra*:

> Acquisition is the cause (*kāraṇa*) that permits the affirmation: 'one is in possession of a certain *dharma*' (*dharmavat*). There are three kinds of *dharma*-s: pure (*śubha*), impure (*aśubha*) and non-defined (*avyākṛta*). … One who possesses [any of] these *dharma*-s is said to be 'in possession of that *dharma*'. The cause of certainty for such an assertion is named acquisition (*prāpti*), obtainment (*lābha*, *pratilābha*) and possession (*samanvāgama*).[29]

The case of *prāpti* exemplifies the doctrinal versatility of the *viprayukta-saṃskāra-dharma*-s. Being a force which is neither material nor mental itself, it can act on both types of *dharma*-s — and in the case of *prāpti*, even on the unconditioned. As the following explanation in the MVŚ shows, the particular species to which a *prāpti* belongs will depend on the *dharma* that is being acquired, and may be identical with or different from that of the *dharma*:

Question: Why is it that the species of the *prāpti* may be either identical with or different from that of the *dharma* acquired (*prāpta*)?

Answer: There are three types of *prāpti*: 1. the *prāpti* of a conditioned *dharma*; 2. the *prāpti* of a cessation through deliberation; 3. the *prāpti* of a cessation independent of deliberation.

(1) The particular species of the *prāpti* of a conditioned *dharma* is specified according to that of the *dharma* acquired. This is because a conditioned *dharma* possesses its activity that projects its own *prāpti*.

(2) The particular species of the *prāpti* of a cessation through deliberation is specified according to that of the path through which [the cessation] is realized (*sākṣāt-√kṛ*). This is because a cessation through deliberation, [being an unconditioned *dharma,*] does not possess its own activity. Its *prāpti* is projected through the force of the path at the time when [the practitioner] is seeking its realization.

(3) The particular species of the *prāpti* of a cessation independent of deliberation is specified according to the [practitioner's] own supporting basis (*āśraya*). This is because a cessation independent of deliberation does not possess its own activity that projects its own *prāpti*, and it is not sought through a path; it is in dependence on [the practitioner's] vital faculty (*jīvitendriya*) and group-homogeneity (*nikāya-sabhāga*) alone that its *prāpti* arises.[30]

The strength of the *prāpti* can also vary. Along the different stages of spiritual progress of the practitioner, the strength of the *prāpti* of a particular cessation of a defilement can come to be increased, even though the practitioner does not need to re-abandon the same defilement. At some critical junctures, a single *prāpti* can be strong enough to effect the collective abandonment of a large group of defilements.

For instance: at the 16th moment — the moment following the end of the 15 moments of direct insight — the practitioner acquires the fruit of stream entry (*srotaāpatti*), there arises a *prāpti* of the collective abandonment of all the defilements to be abandoned by the path of insight (*darśanamārga-praheya*).

As another example: when the practitioner abandons the last grade (the lower-lower grade) of defilement to be abandoned by cultivation (*bhāvanā-heya*), pertaining to the neither-ideation-nor-non-ideation sphere, he is completely liberated from all the hindrances pertaining to the triple spheres and the five categories of abandonability. At this very moment, the *prāpti* arising in him effects the collective acquisition of all the unconditioned *dharma*-s.[31]

Saṃghabhadra explains the function of *prāpti* in the distinctively Ābhidharmika manner:[32]

> … Since *bīja* [as maintained by the Sautrāntika] does not exist, we know that the *prāpti* as acknowledged [by us] definitely possesses a [distinct] function as it is the cause by virtue of which a *dharma* which has been acquired is not lost, and as it is the marker of the knowledge (*jñāna-cihna*) that "this belongs to that person" (*idam asyeti*). Since its [distinct] function is established, we know that it exists as a distinct entity. Thus, both the essential nature and function of the acknowledged *prāpti* are universally established (*prasiddha*).

His definition, quoted in the *Vyākhyā*,[33] thus emphasizes two aspects of its function which uniquely qualify it as an ontological entity: (1) *prāpti* — or rather its series — continues to bind an acquired *dharma* to the individual; (2) it makes possible the knowledge that a given *dharma* belongs to this person, and not another. Together, these two aspects help to account for the fact that, given the Sarvāstivāda scheme of distinct ontological entities (*dharma*-s) perpetually existing in their intrinsic nature throughout time and neither decreasing nor increasing, the same category of *dharma* — e.g., *rāga* or *śraddhā* or *prajñā* — can be said to be uniquely experienced or realized by a given individual.

The above explanation given by the Sarvāstivāda spells out the important role that *prāpti* plays in spiritual attainments. In the Sarvāstivāda perspective, the relationship between a transcendental absolute and the empirical is effected by *prāpti* which is a real force existing in its own right. On the path of spiritual progress, when one abandons (*pra-√hā*) a defilement, two final moments are involved: In the first moment, known as the unhindered path (*ānantarya-mārga*), the *prāpti* of the defilement is severed. In the second moment, known as path of liberation (*vimukti-mārga*), the *prāpti* of the corresponding cessation through deliberation (*pratisaṃkhyā-nirodha*) arises, and the practitioner is said to have realized the cessation (cf. *infra*, § 12.9.2, § 16.2.2).

Prāpti, in its articulate sense as one of the *viprayukta-saṃskāra*-s at a somewhat later stage — as opposed to the early stage when it was used in a general sense — may have originated out of a pragmatic concern of the Sarvāstivādins: It seems to have originally referred to the *prāpti* of *ārya-dharma*-s, on the basis of which the *ārya* can be properly distinguished from the *pṛthagjana*. This stage of development may have taken place shortly after the compilation of the JPŚ and before the MVŚ. The argument that the unreality of *samanvāgama* (= *prāpti*) entails the indistinguishability of an *ārya* and a *pṛthagjana* is already found in the MVŚ.[34] However, even in the later *abhidharma* texts like the AKB, the ADV, the Ny and the *Avatāra*, we can still sense this central concern which forms the chief argument for the necessary existence of *prāpti* as a real entity. Thus, the *Avatāra* gives the following as the only logical argument:

> If *prāpti* were non-existent, when *kleśa*-s like *rāga*, etc., arise, the *śaikṣa,* being without the *anāsrava-citta,* ought not to be an *ārya*. [Likewise,] when a *pṛthagjana* gives rise to a *kuśala* or an *avyākṛta-citta*, he ought to

> be at that moment said to be *vītarāga*. Moreover, there being no *prāpti* of *nirvāṇa* for the *ārya* and the *pṛthagjana*, both of them will be similar to each other and, therefore, both ought to be called *pṛthagjana* or *ārya*.[35]

That at the stage of its dogmatic finalization as a *citta-viprayukta-saṃskāra dharma*, *prāpti* has to do with spiritual attainment, can also be seen in the notion of *aprāpti*. This is said to be opposite to *prāpti*; and *pṛthagjanatva* is defined as the *aprāpti* of *ārya-dharma*-s. In this latter definition, the Vaibhāṣikas typically allowed themselves to be dictated by the dogma of the JPŚ. This is to such an extent that they had consistently and dogmatically to explain their assertion of *aprāpti* being never pure (*anāsrava*) as simply a Vaibhāṣika postulate — one that is a corollary of the JPŚ definition.

11.3.1.1. *Prāpti*, *pratilambha* (/*lābha*) and *samanvāgama*

It was at a relatively later stage that *prāpti* came to be defined generally as the *dharma* that effects the relation of any *dharma* to a living being (*santāna*). At this stage, two more terms, *pratilambha*/*lābha* (obtainment) and *samanvāgama* (endowment), then came to be distinguished in the explanation of *prāpti*. However, it is to be noted that even in the post-AKB manuals, they are still regarded as synonyms of *prāpti*, even though they are at the same time used to designate two different cases of the latter, as is clear from the above quotation from the *Avatāra*. The ADV too clearly states: "What is called *prāpti* is synonymously called 'endowment', 'obtainment'" (*prāptir nāma samanvāgamo lābha iti paryāyaḥ*). If this is to be considered an ambiguity, it is already so in the MVŚ: In fascicle 157[36] of this work, it quotes the *Prajñapti-śāstra* to show that *prāpti, samanvāgama* and *lābha* are synonyms "differing in sound but not in meaning".[37] But in fascicle 162[38] of the same work, seven differences between *prāpti* and *samanvāgama* are enumerated:

[I] Some say: the names themselves are different: one named *prāpti*, the other *samanvāgama*.

[II] Some say: the acquisition of what has not been acquired is named *prāpti*; the acquisition of what has already been acquired is *samanvāgama*.

[III] Some say: the acquisition at the very first instance is named *prāpti*; the subsequent repeated acquisition is named *samanvāgama*.

[IV] Some say: the possession (*sam-anu-ā-√gam*) of what has not been previously possessed is named *prāpti*; the possession of what has already been possessed is named *samanvāgama*.

[V] Some say: what did not previously belong to one, now belongs to one — this is named *prāpti*; what has already belonged to one now [continues to] belong to one — this is named *samanvāgama*.

[VI] Some say: the acquisition at the first instance is named *prāpti*; the non-relinquishment of what has already been acquired is named *samanvāgama*.

[VII] Some say: the initial obtaining (*pratilambha, lābha*) is named *prāpti*; the not-losing of what has already been acquired is named *samanvāgama*. Hence, whereas *prāpti* applies to the first moment, *samanvāgama* applies to both the first and subsequent moments.

From these different opinions recorded in the MVŚ, two basic forms of distinction between *prāpti* and *samanavāgama* are discernible: the first is based on the stage — first moment or subsequently — at which a given *dharma* comes to be acquired by the individual; the second focuses on the acquired *dharma* itself — whether it is acquired or possessed by the individual for the first time, or whether it is re-acquired or being continuously possessed subsequently.

Vasubandhu's distinction between *lābha, pratilambha* and *samanvāgama* in the AKB is based on [VI] and [VII] and essentially follows the first form inasmuch as the former is said to refer to the first moment of obtainment, whether or not the given *dharma* is acquired for the very first time or re-obtained after having been lost:

> Acquisition is of two types: the obtainment (*lābha* = *pratilambha*) of what has not been acquired or of what has been lost [and re-acquired], and the endowment (*samanvāgama*) with what has already been obtained. It is established that non-acquisition is the opposite.[39]

Saṃghabhadra's distinction, in contrast, is based on [II], and essentially follows the second form:

> Although *prāpti*, *lābha* and *samanvāgama* have the same meaning, these different names are given from different perspectives. There are two types of acquisition: that of what has not been previously acquired and that of what has already been previously acquired. The acquisition of what has not been acquired is called obtainment. The acquisition of what has been acquired previously is called endowment.
>
> Non-acquisition is to be understood as opposite to this: that of what has not been previously acquired and that of what has been acquired and lost. The non-acquisition of what has not been previously acquired is called non-obtainment (*apratilambha*). The non-acquisition of what has been lost is called non-endowment (*asamanvāgama*). Thus, *pṛthagjanatva* is called the non-obtainment of the *ārya-dharma*-s [since a *pṛthagjana* has never yet acquired any *ārya-dharma*].[40]

11.3.1.2. Temporal distinctions of *prāpti* and *aprāpti*

A *prāpti* may arise simultaneously (*sahaja*) with the acquired *dharma*; this is comparable to a shadow that follows the figure. It may arise prior (*agraja*) to the *dharma* to be acquired by an individual series;

this is comparable to the head bull (*vṛṣabha*) that leads the herd, since it conduces to the arising of the *dharma*. It may also arise subsequent (*paścātkālaja*) to the acquired *dharma*; this is comparable to a calf that follows the mother, since it remains after the acquired *dharma* has ceased.

The *Avatāra* gives examples of each kind:

> The first kind of *prāpti* is mostly like that of the non-veiled-non-defined *dharma*-s.
>
> The second kind is mostly like that of the skillful *dharma*-s of the sense sphere at the moment when one who has 'fallen' from a higher stage and is about to be reborn (*pratisaṃdhi*) in the sphere of sensuality.
>
> The third kind is mostly like that of the understanding (*prajñā*) produced by listening (*śrutamayī*), by reflection (*cintamayī*), etc., excluding the simultaneous acquisitions.
>
> Here, a brief commentary (*vibhāṣā*) [as to which *dharma*-s have which kinds of *prāpti*] is in order:
>
> The skillful and unskillful matter belonging to the sense sphere have simultaneous and posterior, but not anterior, *prāpti*.
>
> All non-veiled-non-defined *dharma*-s and veiled-non-defined information matter (*nivṛtāvyākṛta-vijñapti-rūpa*) have only simultaneous *prāpti*-s excluding the supernormal faculties of vision and audition (*cakṣurabhijñā*, *śrotābhijñā*) and the transformation-thought (*nirmāṇa-citta*) [which, being strong (*balavat*) and achieved through a special effort (*prayogaviśeṣa*), can have all three kinds of acquisition], and excluding a small part among the arts and crafts (*śailpa-sthānika*) and deportment (*airyāpathika*) which have been intensely practiced. They do not have anterior and posterior *prāpti* on account of their feebleness (*durbalatvāt*).

> All remaining *dharma*-s can have the posterior, anterior and simultaneous *prāpti*.[41]

The following discussion in the MVŚ on the fetters offers another illustration of the three types of *prāpti*:

> Those fetters that are present — do they bind now?
>
> Answer: Those fetters that are present, they bind now. That is, the present fetters necessarily have present *prāpti*-s. This is like the case of a shape and its shadow: the shadow is necessarily co-existent [with the shape].
>
> There are fetters that bind now, but they are not present. That is, fetters that are past or future which bind now: the past or future fetters have present *prāpti*. The past fetters are like the bull that leads the *prāpti*-s [which are like the calves]. The future fetters are like the calves that go behind the *prāpti*-s. Because their *prāpti*-s are present, they are said to bind now.[42]

The temporal distinctions of *prāpti* and *aprāpti* are also made from the observer's perspective, and in this way *dharma*-s of the three periods of time can in each case have three varieties of *prāpti* — past, present and future. This gives rise to a total of nine possible varieties: Thus, a *dharma* which is past from the observer's perspective can have a *prāpti* which — from the *dharma*'s own perspective — may be past, present or future, since the *prāpti* may be prior to, simultaneous with or subsequent to it. The same applies to a present and future *dharma*. However, not all *dharma*-s can have the threefold — prior-simultaneous-subsequent — *prāpti*-s. Thus, the *prāpti*-s of some *anivṛta-avyākṛta dharma*-s — e.g., those that are *vipākaja* and *rūpa* — can only be simultaneous: An individual does not acquire these *dharma*-s prior or subsequent to their arising. This is said to be due to the weakness of these *dharma*-s on account of their not being a result of an effort.[43] Moreover, the *prāpti*-s of the *asaṃskṛta-dharma*-s also cannot be subjected to this threefold distinction since they transcend the temporal process altogether.

As for *aprāpti*, only the past and future *dharma*-s can have *aprāpti* which are past, present or future. *Dharma*-s that are present from the individual's perspective can only be past or future. That is, there can be no *aprāpti* that is simultaneous with the *dharma* which is presently being acquired by the individual — a *dharma* that is presently being linked to the individual is not at the same time being delinked.

11.3.1.3. *Prāpti* and spiritual praxis

The Ābhidharmika recognition of the doctrinal importance of *prāpti* is discernible in the fact that it appears at the very top of the various lists — of both the *abhidharma* schools and the Yogācāra — subsequent to the stage when the category of *citta-viprayukta-saṃskāra* had been fully articulated doctrinally. For the Sarvāstivāda in particular, given their theory of *sarvāstitva*, *prāpti* had become a *sine qua non* for the mechanism of defilement as well as purification. A defilement as a real *dharma* exists always (*sarvadā asti*); it cannot be destroyed. But its linkage with the practitioner effected by the corresponding *prāpti* can be severed by interrupting the *prāpti*-series. Likewise, a pure *dharma* can only come to be possessed by the practitioner through the operation of a *prāpti* that effects the linkage (*infra*, § 12). *Prāpti*, although conditioned in itself but neither mental nor material in nature, in fact plays the indispensable role of relating the unconditioned to the conditioned. It is the *sine qua non* for person's experience of *nirvāṇa*. Moreover, *nirvāṇa* becomes a unique personal spiritual experience only by virtue of the *prāpti* that links the *nirvāṇa* to him (*infra*, § 16).

11.3.2. Group-homogeneity (*nikāya-sabhāga, sabhāgatā*)

This is a force which causes the mutual similarity among sentient beings. This is applicable only to sentient beings and what pertains to sentient beings. The AKB, the Ny and the SPrŚ speak of *sattva-sabhāgatā* and *dharma-sabhāgatā*. The former operates on sentient beings. The latter operates on the *dharma*-s pertaining to sentient beings, distinguishing them as the *skandha*, *āyatana* and *dhātu* which constitute the basis of the *sattva-sabhāgatā*.

There is no such force operating among non-sentient things.[44] Saṃghabhadra here points out that the Buddha has never spoken of such a non-sentient homogeneity. The reason is, according to him, that among non-sentient things, such as grass and trees, there are no such mutual similarities with regard to functionalities and inclinations as in the case of sentient beings. Moreover, it is because of sentient beings that grass, etc., comes to be produced. Furthermore, this *dharma* is generated only on account of previous *karma* and present active effort (*prayatna*), and both these factors are not found among the non-sentient.[45]

Both the ADV[46] and the Ny[47] inform us that *nikāya-sabhāgatā* is the term used in the Sarvāstivāda canonical *abhidharma* texts. Saṃghabhadra defines it as follows:[48]

> There is a distinct entity called *sabhāgatā*. It is the mutual similarity (*sādṛśya*) among sentient beings. The cause of similarity (*sābhāgya-kāraṇa*) among various species of sentient beings born in the same plane of existence (*gati*), with regard to the body (*śarīra*), shape (*saṃsthana*), the [specific] functionalities of the faculties (*indriya*), and food (*āhāra*), etc., as well as the cause for their mutually similar inclinations (*ruci*), is called *nikāya-sabhāga*.

Saṃghabhadra further stresses that *karma* alone cannot fully determine such similarities:

> Just as *karma*, the *citta* and the Great Elements are all the cause for the clear matter (*rūpa-prasāda*) [of which the sense organs are constituted], thus the body and shape, etc., are not caused by *karma* alone, for it is observed that the bodies and shapes [of sentient beings] are results projected (*ā-√kṣip*) by mutually similar *karma*, [and yet] there exist differences with regard to the faculties, functionalities and food, etc. If one says that such differences result from those in the completing *karma*-s (*paripūraka-karma*), it is not reasonable, for there can be bodies and shapes which are projected by similar projecting *karma* (*ākśepaka-karma*); it is on account of there being difference in the group-homogeneity that the functionalities become different. If the bodies and shapes, etc., are no more than the result of *karma*, then it would not be possible [for beings] to abandon or perform any function in accordance with their inclination. Herein, *sa* (homogeneity) because of the mutual similarities in physical appearances, functionalities and inclination. *Bhāga* means cause (*nimitta*). There is a distinct real entity that is the cause of this homogeneity, hence it is named *sabhāga*.

In the Sarvāstivāda doctrine of *karma*, one's existence is determined by two types of *karma*. (1) The projecting (*ākṣepaka*) *karma* which results in one's being born in a particular plane of existence (*infra*, § 13). This existence is designated principally by one's *nikāya-sabhāga* since "it is only when one acquires the *nikāya-sabhāga* that one is said to be born".[49] (2) A multiplicity of completing (*paripūraka*) *karma*-s which together determine the particularities of the existence so projected. *Nikāya-sabhāga* in acting along with the *paripūraka-karma*-s to work out these particularities, contributes to the similarities so described among members of the same species.

The AKB, ADV and *Avatāra* divide *nikāya-sabhāga* into the general (*abhinna*) and specific (*bhinna*) types. The *Avatāra*:[50]

The group-homogeneity is the cause for the similarities in striving and inclination among sentient beings (*sattvānāmekārtharuciḥ sādṛśyahetubhūta*). This is subdivided into two: (i) non-differentiated [or general] (*abhinna*), and (ii) differentiated [or particular] (*bhinna*).

In the first case, all sentient beings equally have self-attachment (*ātmasneha*), are similarly nourished by food, and have similar inclinations (*rati*) — this cause of sameness (*sāmya*) is named the [general] group-homogeneity. Each [sentient being] has within him his own group-homogeneity.

In the second case, sentient beings may belong to different spheres, stages, planes of existence, births, caste (*jāti*); they may be male, female, *upāsaka*, *bhikṣu*, trainee, non-trainee, etc. Within each being [of a given category], there is a *dharma* which is the distinguishing cause (*pratiniyama-hetu*) for the similarity in striving and inclination [among members of the same category]. This is named the group-homogeneity. If this were non-existent, there would be confusion in all the conventional usages (*lokavyavahāra*) such as *ārya*, non-*ārya*, etc.[51]

11.3.3. Ideationless attainment, cessation attainment and ideationlessness

The word *samāpatti* (< *sam-ā-√pad*) means attainment. In Buddhism, it means, in particular, the attainment of a meditational state. For the *abhidharma* scholiasts, it connotes an attainment in which there is complete evenness in mind and body — a connotation supposedly conveyed by the prefix *sam* taken in the sense of *samatā* ('evenness', 'equality'). Xuan Zang's rendering of this term as 等至 ('equal-attainment'/'equanimity-attainment') as well as 定 ('equipoise', 'evenness', 'stableness'), and the Tibetan *snyoms par 'jug par*, 'entering into evenness/equanimity', reflect this connotation. The ideationless attainment and cessation attainment are two meditational attainments in which there is completely no mental activity at all. But just as *nirvāṇa* is not a mere state of absence of *duḥkha* but a positive entity capable of absolutely hindering the further arising of all defilements (*infra,* § 16), likewise these two attainments too are real entities.

The ideationless attainment (*asaṃjñi-samāpatti*) is sought by an ordinary worldling who falsely conceives of the state of extinction of all ideation as liberation and of this attainment as its means. He enters into this by first resolving to extinguish all ideations. Saṃghabhadra explains that it is called thus "because it is on account of being disgusted with ideations that one enters into this *samāpatti*. The *pṛthagjana*-s are not capable of being disgusted with sensations (*vedanā*), for it is on account of being attached to sensations that they enter into *samāpatti*-s."[52]

This attainment is subsumed under the fourth *dhyāna*:

> When one has been detached with regard to the third but not to the fourth *dhyāna*, there is a disjoined *dharma*, named the ideationless attainment, [which can cause] the cessation of the thought and thought-concomitants of one in the stage of the fourth *dhyāna.*[53]

The cessation attainment (*nirodha-samāpatti*), also called the attainment of the cessation of sensation and ideation (***saṃjñā-vedita-nirodha-samāpatti***), belongs to the stage of existence-peak (*bhavāgra*); that is the stage of the fourth *ārūpya*, the neither-ideation-nor-non-ideation attainment (*naiva-saṃjñā-nāsaṃjñā-samapatti*), which is the highest stage of saṃsāric existence:

> When one has been detached with regard to the abode of no-thing-ness (*ākiṃcanyāyatana*), there is a disjoined *dharma* [which can cause] the cessation of the thought and thought-concomitants of one in [the stage of] the existence-peak. As it causes the even (*sama*) continuation of the Great Elements, it is named the cessation-attainment.[54]

An *ārya* who seeks to abide in tranquility and loathes distraction can enter into it. He does so by first applying his mind to the thought of appeasement, resolving to extinguish both ideation and sensation.[55] In fact, an ordinary worldling is incapable of this attainment, since he is incapable of transcending the defilements pertaining to the stage of existence-peak, which are abandonable by insight.[56] Not all *ārya*-s, however, can acquire this attainment at the time of acquiring the existence-peak — it has to be acquired through effort (*prayoga*). "It is only in the case of a Buddha Bhagavat [— who is absolutely free from all hindrances of meditational attainment (*samāpatty-āvaraṇa-vimukta*)[57] —] that its obtainment is said to be by [the mere fact of] detachment: At the very moment of obtaining the knowledge of exhaustion (*kṣaya-jñāna*), He is already capable of producing this attainment at will — the qualities (*guṇa*) of a Buddha are not through any exertion; they appear before Him as soon as He desires them — it is [in this sense] that He is said to have obtained it."[58]

The ideationlessness (*āsaṃjñika*) is the rebirth state of ideationlessness which is the retribution fruit of the ideationless attainment. Like the latter, it is not a mere state but a real force capable of causing the cessation of the thought and thought-concomitants of those born among the deities who are ideationless beings (*asaṃjñi-sattva*). It temporarily (*kālāntaraṃ*) prevents the arising of all mental activities, like a dam which prevents the flow of a river (*nadītoyasaṃnirodhavat*).[59] However, the ideationless attainment has only the ideationlessness and matter of those beings as its retribution. Their homogeneity and vital faculty are retributed by the fourth *dhyāna*, wherein thought exists, and the remaining aggregates (*skandha*) are retributed by both this attainment and the fourth *dhyāna*.[60] These ideationless beings dwell in the Ideationless Heaven which is an elevated abode in the Great-fruit (*bṛhatphala*) Heaven within the fourth *dhyāna*.[61] When mentation arises anew in them, they fall (*cyavante*) from their abode and are necessarily reborn in the sphere of sensuality, for those who are to be born in the Ideationless Heaven necessarily possess a *karma* retributable in the sphere of sensuality in the existence after the next (*aparaparyāya-vedanīya*), just as those who are to be born in the Uttarakuru necessarily possess a *karma* that will lead to rebirth in a heavenly plane of existence.[62]

11.3.4. Vital faculty (*jīvitendriya*)

The word 'faculty' (*indriya*) is said to denote sovereignty or dominance (*ādhipatya*).[63] The Sarvāstivāda acknowledges 22 faculties.[64] The MVŚ explains that the dominance of the vital faculty consists in (i) enabling one to assert that a being is in possession of the faculties (*sa-indriya*), (ii) sustaining the faculties.[65] The former implies that sentience is defined by the presence of the vital faculty; the latter, that it is the *sine qua non* for being alive as opposed to being dead. "A body possessing the faculties lives" (*sendriyaḥ kāyo jīvati*).[66] Thus presence of the vital faculty sufficiently defines a living sentient being. The MVŚ makes the clear distinction:

> *Dharma*-s possessing the faculty [— sentient —] and *dharma*-s devoid of the faculties [— non-sentient —] are different.[67]

This Buddhist view is contrasted with the Jaina doctrine that external things — water, plants, etc., — are also sentient, as the vital faculty exists in all, i.e., internal and external.[68]

The definition given in the canonical *abhidharma* texts is a simple one. Thus, the PrŚ:

> What is the vital faculty? The life principle (*āyus*) in the three spheres.[69]

The MVŚ quotes and follows this definition.[70] However, we can see already in this text the doctrine of this category in the process of development and elaboration on the one hand, and certain controversies relating to it on the other. First, in spite of its adoption of the definition from the PrŚ, the MVŚ quotes various opinions distinguishing the vital faculty conditioning (*jīvitendriya-saṃskāra*) and the life principle conditioning (*āyuḥsaṃskāra*), without making any comment.[71] Explaining the possibility of an *arhat*'s ability to willfully prolong or shorten his life, it records an opinion by 'some' that such a possibility is by virtue of an *arhat*'s mastery over the power of *samādhi*. With this, he transforms the momentum for the duration (*sthitikālāvedha*) of the *mahābhūta*-s of the faculties and projects, through his power of *samādhi,* a new momentum for the same. This amounts to saying that the vital faculty is a mere designation of the said momentum. The compilers of the MVŚ rejects this explanation and states that the vital faculty exists as a distinct entity which is not of the nature of the *mahābhūta*-s of the faculties.[72] Although itself neither material nor mental, the vital faculty can operate (*vṛt*) with either as its supporting basis. The question is asked as to why someone born in the sphere of sensuality can give rise to the cessation attainment, but not someone in the immaterial sphere. The MVŚ answers as follows:

> The vital faculty operates with two *dharma*-s as its supporting basis: 1. matter, 2. thought. This meditation is devoid of thought, having arisen by the cutting off of thoughts.
>
> When someone born in the sphere of sensuality gives rise to this meditation, the vital faculty operates with matter as its supporting basis even though thoughts have been cut off.
>
> When someone born in the immaterial sphere gives rise to this meditation, the vital faculty operates with thought as its supporting basis even though matter has been cut off.
>
> [However,] if someone born [in the immaterial sphere] were to give rise to this meditation — there being neither matter nor thought — the vital faculty would be interrupted in the absence of a supporting basis. The person should then be said to be dead and not in the state of meditation.[73]

These early doctrinal ramifications and controversies pertaining to the category are continued in later texts such as the AKB, the Ny[74] and the *Avatāra*. In the AKB, Vasubandhu gives a Sautrāntika notion of the vital faculty — similar to the one given by 'some' in the MVŚ quoted above: It is not a distinct entity (*dravyāntara*), but simply "the momentum of the duration of the group-homogeneity, [projected] by the *karma* in the three spheres of existence".[75] Saṃghabhadra reacts to this:

> That the life principle exists as a real entity has been proved in the section dealing with the faculties.[76] Here, we will merely question the Kośakāra thus: Where there are not the five internal *rūpāyatana*-s, projected by *karma*, there may sometimes not be the sixth *āyatana*, *manas,* projected by *karma* [which is morally non-defined (*avyākṛta*)] — that is, in the case where someone for a long time continuously gives rise to a *kliṣṭa vijñāna*, or *kuśala-sāsrava* or *anāsrava vijñāna* — there is no momentum (*āvedha*) which is a retribution projected by *karma*; what is there to be called the life principle? If there is in this case a karmic retribution which always exists uninterrupted from the moment of conception until death, then we may say that there is a momentum called vital faculty projected by *karma*, by virtue of which a being continues to exist during a determined period of time. But such a retribution force is not found in this case. How then can we say that the vital faculty exists herein? This being the case, what *dharma* is referred to as the momentum for the duration projected by *karma*? There being no [such] momentum for the duration projected, to whom then does the specified series belong? There being no such specified series, in what sense can it be claimed that the life principle is that which endures for as long as it is so determined [by the *karma*] to endure. …
>
> Hence the life principle which exists as a distinct entity, capable of supporting warmth (*ūṣma*) and consciousness, is called the vital faculty. This vital faculty does not operate with only the body as its supporting basis, since the vital faculty exists in the immaterial sphere. Nor does it

> operate with only thought as its supporting basis, since the vital faculty also exists in one who is in the state devoid of thought. If so, with what as the supporting basis does the vital faculty operate? Its operation has the projecting *karma* in a previous life and the group-homogeneity of the present life as its supporting basis.[77]

Skandhila and the author of the ADV likewise react to the Sautrāntika interpretation, defining and arguing in virtually identical terms:

> A [real entity] projected by previous *karma*, serving as the cause for the uninterrupted series of the six entrances (*āyatana*) [of the human personality], and forming the basis for the designation (*prajñapti*) of the four births and the five planes of existences — this is named the vital faculty. It is also called the life principle (*āyus*) … Apart from the vital faculty, there could be no other *dharma* of the nature of a faculty, found in all the three spheres (*traidhātukavyāpin*), continuing uninterrupted for a given period of existence and forming the basis for the designation of the four births and the five planes of existence.[78]

11.3.5. Four characteristics of the conditioned (*saṃskṛta-lakṣaṇa*)

These four characteristics — sometimes called the primary characteristics — are intrinsic to a conditioned *dharma*, operating on it so that it arises only to cease. A *dharma* possessing these four characteristics is said to be a conditioned *dharma*. The Vaibhāṣikas maintain that there are four of them even though the *sūtra* speaks of only three.[79] The apparent discrepancy is explained away as follows: Duration is the characteristic which supports the conditioned *dharma*-s making them stay and to which beings easily get attached. This is in contrast to the other three characteristics which cause the transitoriness of the conditioned *dharma*-s, helping them traverse through the three periods of time. Thus, in order that beings may get disgusted with the conditioned, the Buddha does not enumerate duration separately. The two characteristics, duration and change, are spoken of together as one, "just as *Śrī* [the goddess of prosperity] and *Kālakarṇī* [the goddess of bad luck]".[80]

(i) The **production-characteristic (*jāti-lakṣaṇa*)** enables a *dharma* to arise. The *Avatāra* explains that "the causes of production of *dharma*-s are twofold: (i) internal and (ii) external. The former is the production-characteristic and the latter comprises the six causes or the four conditions."[81]

Saṃghabhadra defines production-characteristic as follows:

> Herein, production is a distinct *dharma* which is the dominant cause of non-obstruction at the stage of arising of the *saṃskāra*-s; for it induces them, enabling them to arise. 'Inducing them' refers to the fact that at the time of their arising, this *dharma* serves as their dominant condition. While the arisings of the *saṃskṛta*-s are all called production (*jāti*), this name *jāti* is given solely from the point of view of its being the dominant cause of non-obstruction at the stage of the arising of the *saṃskāra*.[82]

The production-characteristic operates on the *dharma* that is about to arise, i.e., when it is in the future period. But it cannot operate alone;[83] and it is for this reason that the future *dharma*-s do not all arise at once. Saṃghabhadra elaborates on this:

> The production-characteristic serves as the conascent proximate cause (*āsanna-kāraṇa*) and produces the produced, i.e., the conditioned *dharma*-s. But [their production is not brought about by production-characteristic alone]; this must be assisted by the assemblage of the previous causes of their own species as well as other external conditions. This is just like the case of a seed and earth serving as distinctive cause and conditions (*hetupratyaya-viśeṣa*), [together] assisting the production of sprout, etc.[84]

(ii) The **duration-characteristic (*sthiti-lakṣaṇa*)** is the internal cause of a *dharma* which enables it to stay temporarily. It is "a distinct *dharma* which is the dominant cause of non-obstruction for the conditioned [*dharma*] that has been produced but not yet destroyed, to project its own fruit".[85] This means that duration is a necessary and, in fact, the dominant condition for a conditioned *dharma* to exercise its *kāritra*, defined by the Vaibhāṣika as the activity for projecting a *dharma*'s own emanation fruit (*niṣyanda-phala*).[86] This characteristic does not make a *dharma* stay long, as it operates at the time when the *dharma* is disappearing:

> [The *saṃskāra*-s] cannot be said to stay at the time when they have disappeared or when they are being produced, as [at these times] they are without *kāritra*. … . It is only at the time of disappearing that the *saṃskāra*-s possess the *kāritra* of *phalākṣepa*.[87]

(iii) The **deterioration(/decay)-characteristic (*jarā/anyathātva-lakṣaṇa*)** is the distinct internal force of a *dharma* which impairs (*vi-√han*) its activity of projecting fruit, rendering it incapable of further projecting another distinct fruit. It is "the cause for the *saṃskṛta* to be different in the subsequent [moment] from the previous [moment], in its continuation as a series".[88] It is argued that without the operation of this force a conditioned *dharma* will keep on projecting one distinct fruit after another *ad infinitum*. And if this would be the case, it ought not to be momentary (*kṣaṇika*) in nature, as we experience it.[89]

(iv) The **impermanence(/disappearance)-characteristic (*anityatā/vyaya-lakṣaṇa*)** is that internal force that causes a present *dharma* whose activity has been impaired by the deterioration-characteristic, to enter into the past. In other words, it makes the *dharma* impermanent.

11.3.5.1. Operation of the characteristics at different phases of the *dharma*'s arising

In the MVŚ, the Dārṣṭāntikas hold that the three characteristics represent three different stages of the existence of a *dharma*:

> There are some, such as the Dārṣṭāntikas, who hold that the three characteristics of the conditioned do not pertain to a single moment. They assert: "If there are the three characteristics within a single moment, then a *dharma* would be produced, deteriorate and vanish at one and the same time. But this is not reasonable, for they are mutually contradictory. It should be stated thus: production refers to the initial arising of a *dharma*; impermanence refers to its final disappearance; deterioration refers to the maturation [process] in between.[90]

In the AKB, the Sautrāntikas argue in a rather similar manner. They assert that these four characteristics are identical in substance with the conditioned *dharma*-s they characterize. For, if they exist as real entities apart from the latter, then a conditioned *dharma* should all, at the same time, be arising, staying, deteriorating and ceasing.[91]

The Vaibhāṣika replies that in fact this Sautrāntika proposition would entail that, just as the characterized and the characteristics are identical, the characteristics themselves should also not be mutually different. If so, *dharma*-s should be produced when they are actually disappearing, and should be disappearing when they are being produced. Or rather, they are never produced at all.[92]

Saṃghabhadra explains that the simultaneous existence of the characteristics does not result in the fallacy pointed out by the Sautrāntika-Dārṣṭāntikas:

> The four characteristics exercise their activities at different stages (*avasthā*): At the time when a *dharma* is arising, the *jāti-lakṣaṇa* exercises its activity. When [this *dharma*] has reached the stage of having arisen,

the three — *sthiti*, *jarā* and *vyaya* — exercise their respective activities at the same time. Thus, the four characteristics exercise their activities at different times and there is no fallacy that one and the same *dharma* arises, stays, deteriorates and ceases at the same time.[93]

11.3.5.2. Secondary characteristics (*anu-lakṣaṇa*)

These four primary characteristics, themselves being conditioned just as the *dharma*-s they characterize, possess four secondary characteristics (*anulakṣaṇa*), viz.: production-production (*jāti-jāti*), duration-duration (*sthiti-sthiti*) deterioration-deterioration (*jarā-jarā*) and impermanence-impermanence (*anityatā-anityatā*). This, however, does not lead to an infinite regression. Each of the four primary characteristics characterizes eight *dharma*-s, but each of the secondary characteristics can characterize only one *dharma*. As a matter of fact, when a *dharma* is produced, nine *dharma*-s co-arise — the *dharma* itself, the four primary characteristics and the four secondary characteristics. The primary characteristic, production, produces the other eight *dharma*-s, excluding itself. The secondary characteristic, production-production, produces only the primary production, owing to its weakness compared to the primary production. The same applies to each of the other primary characteristics, on the one hand, and the three corresponding secondary characteristics on the other.[94] The MVŚ gives a straightforward explanation as to why each *anulakṣaṇa* can operate on one *dharma* only (i.e., a primary characteristic), whereas each *mūla-lakṣaṇa* can operate on the eight *dharma*-s: "It is so by virtue of the very nature of *dharma*-s (*dharmatā*)."[95] According to Saṃghabhadra, this is "because of their difference in efficacy" (*vṛtti*/*vyāpāra*/*sāmarthya*).[96]

11.3.6. Word-group (*nāma-kāya*), phrase-group (*pada-kāya*) and syllable-group (*vyañjana-kāya*)

In the Sarvāstivāda conception, these three categories — which are synonyms respectively for name (*saṃjñā*), sentence (*vākya*) and phoneme (*akṣara*)[97]— are real forces that operate on words, phrases and syllables respectively, making meaningful human communication possible. The fact that these three are listed at the very end of the list of *viprayukta-saṃskāra*-s may suggest their being articulated and incorporated into the list at a relatively late stage. The development of this Sarvāstivādin doctrine seems to have been influenced by the contemporary Mīmaṃsakas and the Grammarians (Vaiyakaraṇa).[98] However, in this process, the Sarvāstivādins consciously steer clear of the Grammarian notion of the eternal sound, retaining the distinctive Buddhist emphasis of impermanence.

11.3.6.1 *Nāma* and the nature of *buddha-vacana*

As PS Jaini has observed, this Vaibhāṣika doctrine can be traced primarily to their speculation on the nature of *buddha-vacana*.[99] Yaśomitra quotes the following passages from the JPŚ on the nature of *buddha-vacana*:

> What is *buddha-vacana*? That which is the Tathāgata's speech, words, talk, voice, explanation, vocal-path, vocal sound, vocal action, vocal expression (*vagvijñapti*)...
>
> What is this *dharma* which has just been spoken of as *buddha-vacana*? The sequential arrangement, sequential establishment and sequential combination of the *nāma-kāya*, *pada-kāya* and *vyañjana-kāya*.[100]

The MVŚ explains the motives for the two passages: The first is given in order to prevent misconception of *buddha-vacana* (*buddha-vacana-saṃjñā*) with regard to what is in fact not *buddha-vacana*, and to show that what is spoken by the Buddha is true *buddha-vacana*.[101] Elaborating on this first passage, the compilers of the MVŚ state that *buddha-vacana* has vocal information (*vāg-vijñapti*) as its nature. The second passage quoted is said to be intended to show not the nature, but the function of *buddha-vacana*. The MVŚ also mentions here the opinion of some who assert that *buddha-vacana* has *nāma,* etc., as its nature. The compilers do not reject this view; instead, they interpret it as referring to vocal speech as the successive cause — speech (*vāk*) gives rise to *nāma*; *nāma* manifests the *artha*. However, properly speaking, it has *vāg-vijñapti* as its nature.[102]

Thus, in the MVŚ we see two views acceptable to the orthodox Sarvāstivādins, although the first is the preferred one. The same two views are also given in the AKB. There, Vasubandhu says that those who take speech as the nature of *buddha-vacana* subsume the Buddha's *dharma-skandha*-s under the *rūpa-skandha*; whereas those who take *nāma* as its nature subsume them under the *saṃskāra-skandha*.[103] According to Yaśomitra also, the Ābhidharmikas accept both views.[104] The author of the ADV also seems to accept both views; as he quotes an *āgama* passage which says that when the Buddha was alive, the *buddha-vacana* was of the nature of both *vāk* and *nāma*, and after His *Parinirvāṇa*, it is of the nature of *nāma* only.[105] Collett Cox, however, asserts that "Yaśomitra's interpretation of the position of the Ābhidharmikas conflicts with that offered by the **Mahāvibhāṣā* and Saṃghabhadra. For these two representatives of the Kāśmīra Sarvāstivāda-Vaibhāṣikas, the intrinsic nature of the Buddha's teaching is speech…"[106] But, as we have seen, the compilers of the MVŚ actually accept both interpretations. As to Saṃghabhadra's position in this regard, what he actually says is as follows:

> Some assert that *buddha-vacana* has *vāk* as its *svabhāva*. They assert that the *dharma-skandha*-s are all subsumed under the *rūpa-skandha*, for *vacana* has *śabda* as its *svabhāva*.

> Some assert that *buddha-vacana* has *nāma* as its *svabhāva*. They assert that the *dharma-skandha*-s are all subsumed under the *saṃskāra-skandha*, for *nāma* is of the nature of a *viprayukta-saṃskāra*. [Now,] *vāk* and *vacana* being synonyms, *vacana* may be conceded to be *vāk*; [but] *nāma* and *vāk* are distinct entities, so how is the [*buddha*-]*vacana* *nāma*? They explain thus: There must be *nāma* for it to be called *vacana*; hence the nature of *buddha-vacana* is none other than *nāma*. Why? It is called *buddha-vacana* because it conveys the *artha* truly; *nāma* can convey *artha*; hence *vacana* is *nāma*. Accordingly, *buddha-vacana* definitely has *nāma* as its *svabhāva*.[107]

It is clear from the above passage that Saṃghabhadra does not particularly hold that *buddha-vacana* is speech in nature nor does he object to either of the two views.

11.3.6.2 Further investigation into the nature and function of *nāma*

The consideration of the nature of *nāma*, etc., in the MVŚ has already gone beyond the preoccupation with the nature of *buddha-vacana*. On a discussion on "the group of multiple words" (*bahu-nāma-kāya*) in the JPŚ, the MVŚ[108] gives various views on its motives. These include:

(i) This discussion purports to analyze the meaning of the *sūtra*-s. "Thus, the *sūtra* says, 'O *bhikṣu*-s, from the time when the Tathāgatas appear in the world, the *nāma-pada-vyañjana-kāya*-s appear in the world.'[109] Although it says thus, it does not analyze what the *nāma-pada-vyañjana-kāya*-s are, this discussion here intends to analyze them."

(ii) It purports to dispel doubts in those who might think that while the author is skilled in meaning — there being the analysis of various meanings in the treatise — he might not be skilled in literary expression.

(iii) It is in order to refute the Dārṣṭāntikas and others, and the Śābdikas — the former deny the reality of the three categories, the latter hold that the three have *śabda* as their intrinsic nature. The author intends to show that *nāma-kāya*, etc., are real *dharma*-s, subsumed under the *viprayukta-saṃskāra-skandha*.

(iv-vi) ……

(vii) It purports to elucidate the nature of defilement and purification — the *nāma-kāya,* etc., is the root of that which elucidates these two.

From the way the MVŚ cites the *sūtra* passage which we quoted in the above paragraph, it is clear that the Sarvāstivādins consider *nāma,* etc., as impersonal, objective forces. This same passage is also cited by Skandhila and the author of the ADV. The latter, in fact, states that the *nāma-kāya*, etc., which conveys the *dhātu*, *āyatana* and *skandha*-s is *apuruṣeya* — not created by any individual.[110]

Skandhila argues for the Sarvāstivāda position that vocal sound (*vāk-śabda*) does not directly convey the object-referent (*artha*):

> Lest it be that when one utters the word (*nāma*) 'fire', one's mouth is immediately burnt.[111] Words like 'fire', etc., must rely on speech for their production. From the words, 'fire', etc., the object-referents, i.e., fire, etc., are then conveyed.

He further explains that

> by 'conveying' is meant producing in others a comprehension (*buddhi*) of the object-referent to be illumined (*dyotita*). It does not mean that [the word] unites with the object-referent.[112]

The author of the ADV explains in a very similar manner, summarizing as follows:

> A vocal sound operates on the word; the word expresses the object-referent (*vāṅ nāmni pravartate/nāmārthaṃ dyotayati*).[113]

Both masters similarly compare this to the perceptual process:

> Just as visual consciousness, etc., are produced with eye, etc., as their support, manifesting with an image of the object (*jñānavad arthasya pratinidhi-sthānīyāḥ*), the visible, etc., and [thus] comprehend their respective objects. The same applies to words, etc.[114] (See also § 10.8.2).

The Sautrāntikas maintain that *nāma* is none other than *śabda*. On this premise, it is argued that vocal sound cannot produce *nāma* which, according to the Sarvāstivādins, is a unitary, distinct, meaning-conveying entity: sounds, being *rūpa* and hence resistant, cannot be collocated; they must arise serially. It is unreasonable to say that the last moment of a vocal sound series creates the *nāma*, for in that case, the last sound alone would suffice for the conveying of the object-referent. The same difficulties are present if the Sarvāstivādins should argue that vocal sound produces the *vyañjana* which in turn produces the meaning-conveying *nāma*.[115] In reply, Saṃghabhadra first argues for *nāma* being distinct from sound:

> Sometimes one gets the sound but not the phoneme; sometimes one gets the phoneme but not the sound. Hence we know that they differ in substance.
>
> The first case is that of hearing the sound and not comprehending the *artha*: It is observed that some people listen to others' words vaguely and then ask, "what did you say?" It is all because they have not comprehended the syllables uttered. How then can one assert that the syllables are not different from the sound?
>
> The second case is that of comprehending the *artha* without hearing the sound: It is observed that some people, without hearing the actual words spoken by others, know what they are saying by watching the movement

of their lips, etc. This is all because they have comprehended the syllables uttered. This proves that the syllables must be different from the sounds.

Again, it is observed in the world that people recite *mantra* silently, hence we know that the syllables of a *mantra* differ from the sound of the *mantra*.

Again it is observed in the world that of two debaters whose articulation of the sound is similar, one loses and the other wins. This cause of losing and winning must exist separately from the sound.

Again as the objects (*viṣaya*) of the 'unhindered knowledge of *dharma*-s' (*dharma-pratisaṃvid*) and 'unhindered knowledge of etymological interpretation' (*nirukti-pratisaṃvid*)[116] are different, we know that the phonemes are distinct from sound.

Hence, [we may conclude from all this that] sound is merely the articulation of a language, and its form is not differentiated. The inflection therein must be made in dependence on *ka, ca, ṭa, ta, pa*, etc. The phoneme must be uttered by means of vocal sound. When the phonemes are joined together, *nāma* is produced. *Nāma* having been produced, it can illuminate the *artha*. Hence, we assert the following [causal] sequence: vocal sound gives rise to *nāma*; *nāma* illuminates *artha*. Therefore, it is universally established that *nāma* is different from *śabda*. It should be understood here that *śabda* is that which utters and *akṣara* is that which is uttered; *artha* is neither. Thus they are established without confusion.[117]

As to the Sautrāntika argument that sound arises serially and hence cannot create a unitary meaning-conveying *nāma*, Saṃghabhadra turns the opponents' argument against themselves: Given their Vibhajyavāda standpoint, the meaning of a word cannot be conveyed by a vocal sound series:

The objection [of the opponent in fact] harms his own tenet: "Given his assertion that past and future [*dharma*-s] are devoid of intrinsic nature, and [the fact] that preceding and succeeding moments of sound do not arise at once, how can the *vyañjana*, the *nāma*, the *pada* come to be accomplished?" If the preceding moments contribute to the succeeding ones successively, so that the last moment accomplishes [the production of] the *vyañjana*, *nāma* and *pada*, [respectively], then one ought to be able to understand the *artha* by listening merely to the last [sound].

Moreover, the past and the future being non-existent, there is no successive contribution — since there is always only the single [present] thought moment, how can there be successive contribution? There being no successive contribution, the preceding and succeeding moments are mutually alike. The last thought moment, being like the initial one, should not be able to convey [the *artha*]; and one listening to the last [sound] as if [listening to] the initial one, should not be able to understand the *artha*.

Hence, his assertion that sound comes to be able to convey the *artha* [through] the successive contribution of the preceding to the succeeding moments, cannot be established.[118]

Skandhila gives two succinct reasons for the logical necessity of establishing the ontological status of the three categories:

As sound is resistant and, as the eternal sound falsely held by the grammarians (*vaiyākaraṇena parikalpita*) cannot be established logically, there cannot be any *dharma* [such as sound], apart from these three — words, phrases and syllables — which are capable of conveying a corresponding object-referent.[119]

The disproof of sound as being permanent is a popular theme in Buddhist logical texts which hardly needs mentioning. The first reason that sound is resistant (*sa-pratigha*) should also be clear from Saṃghabhadra's arguments above: being resistant *rūpa*, sounds must arise in a series, and this entails all the unacceptable logical consequence as argued by Saṃghabhadra. Moreover, for the same reason, there cannot be a real collocation of sounds in a single moment that can constitute a unitary, discrete *dharma* called *nāma* capable of the unique function of conveying an object-referent. As the author of the ADV puts it, they cannot stand in unity like a bundle of *balvaja* grass possessing the collective strength contributed from the co-existent strands.[120] For the Sarvāstivāda, since *nāma* is not a mental *dharma* — as agreed upon even by the opponents — nor can it be a *rūpa* or a permanent *asaṃskṛta*, as a real force it must exist as a *viprayukta-saṃskāra*.

NOTES

[1] T 26, 528c.

[2] T 26, 547b.

[3] PrŚ, 714a.

[4] *Cf. Study*, 157.

[5] T 26, 920c.

[6] *Ca.* 100 B.C.E.; T 26, 692b.

[7] MVŚ, 730b.

[8] MVŚ, 198b.

[9] *Cf.* MVŚ, 316b.

[10] *Cf.* MVŚ, 97a.

[11] JPŚ, 929a.

[12] JPŚ, 1008a–b.

[13] In the Yogācāra works around this period (i.e., 4th and 5th centuries), we find 23 in *Abhidharma-samuccaya* and 24 (with the addition of *asāmagrī*) in T no. 1614.

[14] AKB, 35–36a.

[15] Vy, 142: *ca-śabda evaṃjātīyakānukta-viprayukta-pradarśanārthaḥ / saṃghabheda-prabhṛtayo hi dravyataś citta-viprayuktā iṣyante iti ye 'py evaṃjātīyakā iti śāstre 'py uktatvāt /*

[16] Ny, 396c.

[17] MVŚ, 313b.

[18] MVŚ, 27c, 313a, 231b.

[19] T 28 no. 1550, 830c.

[20] T 28 no. 1551, 866a.

[21] T 28 no. 1552, 943b.

[22] T 28, 970a.

[23] MVŚ, 51b.

[24] ADV, 85: *prāptyādayastu saṃskārā viprayuktāstrayodaśa /*

[25] ADV, *loc. cit.*

[26] Ny, 396c.

[27] Vy, 142 f.: *cittaviprayuktā iti citta-grahaṇam citta-samānajātīya-pradarśanārtham / cittam iva cittena ca viprayuktā ity arthaḥ / kiṃ ca teṣāṃ samānajātīyatam / yadarūpino 'mī bhavanti / rūpitvād eva hi viprayuktve'pi rūpaṃ na viprayuktve nāma labhate / yad vā'mīṣām nāma-rūpam iti nāmatvam tat teṣām cittena samānajātīyatvaṃ caittā api cittena tulyajātiyāḥ / te tu cittena sahā'lambane samprayuktās tad-viseṣaṇārthaṃ viprayuktagrahaṇam / asaṃskṛtam api tat-samāna-jātīyam / anālambanatveneti tat-parihārārthaṃ saṃskāra-grahaṇam /*

[28] AKB, 62:

> *viprayuktāstu saṃskārāḥ prāptyaprāptī sabhāgatā /*
> *āsaṁjñikaṃ samāpattī jīvitaṃ lakṣaṇāni ca // 35 //*
> *nāmakāyādayaśceti*

[29] *Cf. Entrance*, 126. ADV, 87: *prāpt(i)rnāma samanvāgamo lābha iti paryāyaḥ... / 'dharmavattā vyavasthitiḥ' / dharmāḥ khalu tridhā kuśa[lāḥ] ...*

[30] MVŚ, 801a.

[31] *Cf.* MVŚ, 141b.

[32] Ny, 398b.

[33] Vy, 148: *idam asyeti jñāna-cihnaṃ pratilābdha-dharmāvipraṇāśa-kāraṇaṃ ca prāptirity ācārya-saṃghabhadraḥ.*

[34] MVŚ, 796c.

[35] See *Entrance*, 126.

[36] MVŚ, 797a.

[37] MVŚ, 797a.

[38] MVŚ, 823a.

[39] AKB, 62: *dvividhā hi prāptir aprāptavihīnasya ca lābhaḥ pratilabdhena ca samanvāgamaḥ / viparyayād aprāptir iti siddham /*

[40] Ny, 396c.

[41] *Entrance*, 127f. Also *cf.* MVŚ, 311c which gives the following as the example of the *paścātkālaja-prāpti*: those fetters which although having been connected (*saṃyukta*) are not past, i.e., those future and present fetters whose *prāpti*-s are past.

[42] MVŚ, 312a–b.

[43] Vy, 152: *anabhisaṃskāravattvād durbalatvam /*

[44] SPrŚ, 805c; cf. AKB, 68.

[45] Ny, 400b.

[46] ADV, 89: *nikāya-sabhāga ity asya śāstra-saṃjñā /*

[47] Ny, 400a.

[48] Ny, *loc. cit.*

[49] Ny, 585b.

[50] *Entrance*, 134 f.

[51] *Cf.* a very similar passage in ADV, 89: *sabhāgatā nāma dravyam / sattvānām ekārtha-ruciḥ sādṛśyahetubhūtam / nikāya-sabhāga ity asya śāstra-saṃjñā / sā punar abhinnā bhinnā ca / abhinnā sarva-sattvānāṃ sattva-sabhāgatā / sā pratisattvaṃ sarveṣvātma-snehāhāra-rati-sāmyāt / bhinnā punas teṣām eva sattvānāṃ dhātu-bhūmi-gati-yoni-jāti-strī-puruṣopāsaka-bhikṣu-śaikṣāsaikṣādīnām ekārtha-rucitva-bheda-pratiniyama-hetuḥ / tasyāṃ khalv asatyāṃ sarvāryānārya-lokavyavahāra-saṃkara-doṣaḥ prasajyeta /*

Cf. a similar definition of Saṃghabhadra quoted in the Vy, 159: *śarīrendriya-saṃsthāna-ceṣṭāhārādi-sābhāgya-kāraṇam anyonyābhir abhisambandha-nimittaṃ ca sabhāgatety ācārya-saṃghabhadraḥ /* Also given in Ny, 400a: *sa* (homogeneity), because of the mutual similarities in physical appearances, functions (of the *indriya*) and desire; *bhāga* means cause (*nimitta*). There is a distinct real entity which is the cause of this homogeneity, hence it is named *sabhāga*.

Cf. also AKB, 67. AKB (*loc.cit.*) also speaks of *dharma-sabhāgatā* which does not seem to occur in any other extant Sarvāstivāda *śāstra* except Ny, 400b and SPrŚ, 805c.

[52] Ny, 401a.

[53] *Entrance*, 131.

[54] *Entrance*, 131. MVŚ, 775b: "Why is this *nirodha* called a *samāpatti*? It is called a *samāpatti* because, with regard to the *nirodha dharma*-s, there is no obstruction, no rejection; one experiences it at will and personally realizes it. For this reason the Bhagavat has said that [whereas] *nirodha* is momentary, *samāpatti* is continuous.

Question: A *samāpatti* is that which causes the thought to be even (*sama*). But in this case there is no mentation (*acitta*), how can it be named a *samāpatti*?

Answer: There are two kinds of *samāpatti*: (I) that which causes the thought to be even, (II) that which causes the *mahābhūta*-s to be even. Although the *asaṃjñi*- and *nirodha-samāpatti* interrupt the even-ness of mind, causing it not to continue, they induce the even-ness of *mahābhūta*-s, causing them to manifest. Hence they are called *samāpatti*-s."

55 Ny, 401b, 403a; MVŚ, 776a.

56 Ny, 401c; MVŚ, 780a. Skandhila explains that an *ārya* enters into it "in order to dwell in bliss in the present life" (*dṛṣṭa-dharma-sukha-vihārārtham*) and that a *pṛthagjana* cannot enter into it on account of his dread of it as annihilation (*Entrance*, 132). Saṃghabhadra ascribes this view to "some master", and rejects it. (Ny, *loc. cit.*).

57 Ny, 402a.

58 *Entrance*, 134; Ny, 401c–402a; *cf.* MVŚ, 780b.

59 AKB, 68; Ny, 400c; *Entrance*, 132.

60 Ny, 400c; MVŚ, 615a.

61 *Cf.* MVŚ, 784b.

62 Ny, 400c; *Entrance*, 133, ADV, 91.

63 AKB, 38: *kaḥ punar indriyārthaḥ / idi paramaiśvarye / tasya indantīti indriyāṇi / ata ādhipatyārtha indriyārthaḥ /* MVŚ, 730c, explains the word in eight senses of which the first is *ādhipatya*.

64 MVŚ, 728c; AKB, 40.

65 MVŚ, 731b. Another view gives four aspects of its dominance: (i) in connecting up with the *nikāya-sabhāga*, (ii) in sustaining the *nikāya-sabhāga,* (iii) in fostering the *nikāya-sabhāga*, (iv) in enabling the *nikāya-sabhāga* to continue uninterrupted.

66 AKB, 243.

67 MVŚ, 635a.

68 MVŚ, 729a.

69 PrŚ, 694a, 723a.

70 MVŚ, 657c, 732b.

71 MVŚ, 657c.

72 MVŚ, 657b.

73 MVŚ, 779b.

[74] Ny, 404b–c.

[75] AKB, 74: *na hi nāstīti brūmo na tu dravyāntaram / kiṃ tarhi / traidhātukena karmaṇā nikāya-sabhāgasya sthiti-kālāvedhaḥ /*

[76] Ny, 377c.

[77] Ny, 404c.

[78] For the full translation of these passages in *Avatāra*, see *Entrance*, 133f. *Cf.* almost identical description in ADV, 97: *uktaṃ hy abhidharme — "jīvitendriyaṃ katamat / traidhādhukam āyuḥ" iti / tat punaḥ 'gati-prajñapty-upādānaṃ' vipākaja-svabhāvatvāt / uktaṃ hi sūtre- "nirvṛtte vipāke nāraka iti samkhyāṃ gacchati / evaṃ yāvan naivasaṃjñā-nāsamjñāyatanopagasaṃkhyāṃ gacchati" iti / na cānyad indriyaṃ vipākajaṃ traidhātukavyāpy asti yajjanmaprabandhā'vicchedena vartamānaṃ gati-prajñapty-upādānaṃ syāt, anyatra jīvitendriyāt /*

[79] *Cf.* SĀ, 12, 21; A, i, 152.

[80] *Cf. Entrance*, 137. *Cf.* ADV, 104 f.: *... etāny eva vineyaprayojanavaśāt sūtre sthity-anyathātvam ekīkṛtya trīṇy uktāni /... tato bhagavatā 'nyathātvākhyayā jarayā sahoktā śrīr iva kālakarṇyānubaddhā saṃvegānukūlā bhaviṣytīty eṣo'rtha-[vi] ṣayo dṛśyate tasmāc catvāri /* Also cf. AKB, 75; MVŚ, 201a–c.

[81] *Entrance*, 136.

[82] Ny, 405c.

MVŚ (202c–203a): "Question: When the *saṃskṛta-dharma*-s arise, do they arise on account of the fact that they are in themselves of the nature of arising (體是生法故生), or on account of being joined with *jāti-lakṣaṇa*?

Answer: ... They arise on account of the fact that they are in themselves of the nature of arising... But, although they are in themselves of the nature of arising, they cannot arise without being joined with *jāti-lakṣaṇa*. ... At the time of their arising, *jāti-lakṣaṇa* is their dominant cause of production. Just as a destructible *dharma* is destroyed by a cause of destruction and an abandonable *dharma* is abandoned by a cause of abandonment, a producible *dharma* is produced by *jāti-lakṣaṇa*."

[83] *Cf.* AKB, 79: *nahi vinā hetupratyaya-sāmagryā jātir janikā bhavati /*

[84] Ny, 411a.

[85] Ny, 405c. Cf. MVŚ, 201c: "By the force of the *sthiti-lakṣaṇa*, the *saṃskāra*-s, having arisen, are capable of grasping their own fruit and of grasping the *ālambana*. By the force of *jarā* and *anityatā*, there is no more activity after one *kṣaṇa*. If the *sthiti-lakṣaṇa*

were non-existent, there ought not to be the cause-effect series of the *saṃskāra*-s, and the *citta-caitta dharma*-s ought not have any *ālambana*."

[86] Ny, 409c, etc.

[87] Ny, 411c. *Cf.* ADV, 105: *yadi hi dharmasya sthitir na syāt, tasyātmany avasthitasya hetvākhyaḥ śakti-prabhāva-viśeṣo na syāt / anityatāgra[sta]sya ca notpakti-śaktir ityataś ca kriyāṃ na kuryāt / kriyā'bhāvāt phalābhāvaḥ syāt / phalārthaścāyamārambh aḥ / tasmād āstikair nāstika-pakṣaṃ vikṣipya sthitiḥ pratigṛhyata iti siddham //*

[88] Ny, 405c.

[89] *Cf. Entrance*, 136.

[90] MVŚ, 200a.

[91] *Cf.* AKB, 78.

[92] *Cf. Entrance*, 137 f.

[93] SPrŚ, 810a–b. See also MVŚ, 200a.

[94] *Cf.* AKB, 76; *Entrance*, 138.

[95] MVŚ, 200c–201a.

[96] Ny, 406a–b.

[97] AKB, 80; *Entrance*, 139.

[98] See Jaini, PS, 'The Vaibhāṣika Theory of Words and Meanings', in Jaini, PS, ed., *Collected Papers on Buddhist Studies* (Delhi, 2001), 201 ff.; especially 211 ff.

[99] Jaini, PS, *op. cit.*, 202.

[100] Vy, 52: *tathā hi jñanaprasthāna uktam / katamad buddha-vacanam / tathāgatasya yā vāg vacanaṃ vyāhāro gīr niruktir vāk-patho vāg-ghoṣo vāk-karma vāg-vijñaptiḥ / .... punas tatraivānantaram uktaṃ buddha-vacanaṃ nāma ka eṣa dharmaḥ / nāma-kāya-pada-kāya-vyañjana-kāyānāṃ yā anupūrva-racanā anupūva-sthāpanā anupūrva-samāyoga iti /* See JPŚ, 981a–b.

[101] MVŚ, 658c, 659c.

[102] MVŚ, 659b.

[103] AKB, 17.

[104] Vy, 52.

[105] ADV, 11.

[106] Cox (1995), 162 f.

[107] Ny, 346c.

[108] MVŚ, 69c–70a.

[109] *Cf* ADV, 113: *uktaṃ hi bhagavatā / "tathāgatānām utpādān nāma-pada-vyañjana-kāyānām utpādo bhavati" / ... ye hy apauruṣeyā dhātv-āyatana-skandhādy-avadyotakās te prathamaṃ buddha-viṣayā eva /*; *Entrance,* 140.

[110] See previous note.

[111] *Cf.* MVŚ, 73a.

[112] See *Entrance*, 139.

[113] Also cf. AKB, 80; Ny, 413c.

[114] See *Entrance*, 139. *Cf.* ADV, 108 f.:

> ***vākchabdādhīnajanmānaḥ svārthapratyāyanakriyāḥ /***
>
> ***saṃjñādyaparanāmānastrayo nāmādayaḥ smṛtāḥ //***

viprayuktāḥ khalu nāmādayaḥ saṃskāra-skhanda-saṃgṛhītāḥ / vāk tu rūpa-skhandha-saṃgṛhītā vāg gīr niruktir ity arthaḥ / te ca tad-adhīnotpattayo nirukty-adhīnārtha-pravṛttayaś ca jñānavad arthasya pratinidhi-sthānīyāḥ / nirukti[ḥ] nāma saṃjñā / nārthānām ekasaṃjñatvāt / yathā tu cakṣur-vijñāna-kāyādayaḥ pañca-rūpādy-āyattavṛttayaḥ, tadvat te'pi 'vākchabdādhīnajanmānaḥ' / ataścoktam — "vāṅ nāmni pravartate, nāmārthaṃ dyotayati /" iti. Ibid., 111: *jñānavat / tad-yathā jñānaṃ cakṣurādīn hetūn apekṣyārthaṃ vibhāvayati, tadvan nāmādayo'pi ghoṣādīn hetūn apekṣyārthaṃ pratyāyayanti /*

[115] *Cf.* AKB, 81.

[116] *Cf.* AKB, 418 f.

[117] Ny, 413c.

[118] Ny, 415b.

[119] *Entrance*, 139.

[120] ADV, 110.

12. Defilements

12.1. The goal of spiritual praxis and the abandonment of defilement

It is sometimes stated that the goal of Buddhism is moral perfection — a state where all defilements are removed and complete purity is attained. In the Buddha's own discourses, the knowledge of the destruction of the outflows (*āsravakṣaya-jñāna*) is highlighted as a unique attribute of an *arhat*, so much so that the term *kṣīṇa-āsrava* — 'one who has exhausted the outflows' — came to be used as an epithet for an *arhat*. This fact is sometimes cited as evidence that for Early Buddhism, the final goal is the destruction of all defilements. It is further argued that the Ābhidharmika tradition follows this tradition.[1] However, it must be borne in mind that the Buddha himself stated most unambiguously that all his teachings have but one goal, the goal of liberation from or cessation of *duḥkha*. Statements such as: "*citta* is liberated from the outflows"[2] is to be understood as emphasizing the mental freedom from *duḥkha* in the absence of the disturbances from the defilements. The significance of defilement can be seen in the Buddhist emphasis of the meaning of 'defilement' or 'impurities' as indicated in the Sanskrit word *kleśa* which primarily means 'disturbance' or 'molest' (see below): *kleśa*-s are to be purged or abandoned as impurities because they afflict our mind. Apart from this, moral purity has no intrinsic value in itself for Buddhism. The abandonment of defilements, along with the transcendence of *karma*, serves as the means — not the end — of spiritual perfection. In any case, *nirvāṇa*, the *summun bonum* of Buddhism, is stated by the Ābhidharmikas as the absolute cessation of all *duḥkha*-s pertaining to the three spheres of existence.[3] As a matter of fact, it is more correct to say that for the Ābhidharmikas too, *prajñā* (= *dharma-pravicaya*) is the supreme means for the ending of *duḥkha*-s. The first chapter of the AKB states this explicitly: Beings wander in *saṃsāra* — hence experience *duḥkha* — on account of their defilements. *Abhidharma*, which in the highest sense is equated with the pure *prajñā*, constitutes the only means for the appeasement of defilements. This of course spells out, at the same time, the Ābhidharmika emphasis on the investigation of defilements.

The Ābhidharmika emphasis on the necessary dependence on insight for the overcoming of defilements is also underscored in their notion of two types of complete knowledge (*parijñā*) which they claim is a teaching in the *sūtra*-s — not only is the means of the abandonment emphasized as complete knowledge but the result, i.e., the abandonment itself, too, is called complete knowledge (see also, § 12.10.5):[4]

> The *sūtra*-s say that there are two types of complete knowledge: [1] complete knowledge qua knowledge (*jñāna-parijñā*) and [2] complete knowledge qua abandonment (*prahāṇa-parijñā*). …
>
> [1] What is complete knowledge qua knowledge? The knowledges (*jñāna*), seeing (*darśana*), wisdom (*vidyā*), discernment (*buddhi*), direct insight (*abhisamaya*) — these are called complete knowledges qua knowledge. … Knowledge is thus called because it counteracts ignorance (*ajñāna*). Seeing is thus called because it counteracts wrong views. Wisdom is thus called because it counteracts nescience (*avidyā*). Discernment is thus called because it counteracts wrong discernment. Direct insight is thus called because it counteracts wrong direct insight. …

[2] What is complete knowledge qua abandonment? It is the absolute abandonment (*atyanta-prahāṇa*) of greed, the absolute abandonment of hatred and delusion, the absolute abandonment of all defilements. …

Question: Complete knowledge is thus called because it knows the cognitive object completely. An abandonment does not have a cognitive object and the function of knowing completing. Why is it called a complete knowledge?

Answer: Because the abandonment is the result of knowledge, it is also called a complete knowledge. … What is called complete knowledge qua knowledge has knowledge as its intrinsic nature. What is called complete knowledge qua abandonment has abandonment as its intrinsic nature.[5]

The complete knowledge qua abandonment is subdivided into nine types: six abandonable by insight and three abandonable by cultivation:[6]

1. abandonment of the defilements abandonable by insight into the truths of unsatisfactoriness and origin, pertaining to the sense sphere;

2. abandonment of the defilements abandonable by insight into the truth of cessation, pertaining to the sense sphere;

3. abandonment of the defilements abandonable by insight into the truth of the path, pertaining to the sense sphere;

4. abandonment of the defilements abandonable by insight into the truths of unsatisfactoriness and origin, pertaining to the two higher spheres;

5. abandonment of the defilements abandonable by insight into the truth of cessation, pertaining to the two higher spheres;

6. abandonment of the defilements abandonable by insight into the truth of the path, pertaining to the two higher spheres;

7. abandonment of all defilements abandonable by cultivation pertaining to the sense sphere, called 'the five fetters pertaining to the lower portion' (§ 12.3.1);

8. abandonment of all defilements abandonable by cultivation pertaining to the fine-material sphere, called 'complete knowledge which is the exhaustion of the greed for matter' (*rūparāgakṣaya-parijñā*);

9. abandonment of all defilements abandonable by cultivation pertaining to the non-material sphere, called 'complete knowledge which is the complete end of all fetters' (*sarvasaṃyojana-paryādāna-parijñā*).

The rationale for the above nine-fold division is as follows:

(a) Under the defilements abandonable by insight, those connected with the truths of unsatisfactoriness and origin are grouped as complete knowledge because under these two truths, there are universal defilements (§ 12.6.2.2). Even when one has abandoned the universal defilements under the truth of unsatisfactoriness, one still cannot be freed from bondage as long as one has not also abandoned the universal defilements under the truth of origin. Hence only the complete abandonment of all defilements under both truths can qualify as a 'complete knowledge'.

(b) A complete knowledge is established separately for the abandonment of the defilements connected with the truth of cessation and the truth of the path, because the practitioner has already abandoned the universal defilements earlier when contemplating the truths of unsatisfactoriness and origin.

(c) With regard to the defilements pertaining to the two higher spheres, those abandonable by insight are grouped together as a single complete knowledge because the counteracting path is the same for the two higher spheres; in the case of defilements abandonable by cultivation, one complete knowledge each is established for the two higher spheres because the counteracting paths are different for the two higher spheres.

12.2. *Kleśa* and *anuśaya* as the generic terms for defilement

Many terms are used to denote defilements, characterizing their different functionalities and scope of operation. The two most generic terms, used as equivalents in the Sarvāstivāda system, are *kleśa* and *anuśaya*.

12.2.1. *Kleśa* (< √*kliś* 'afflict', 'molest')

This term is understood in the sense of 'defilement' or impurity. In the Buddhist usage, the corresponding past participle, *kliṣṭa*, means 'defiled', 'soiled'. However, the primary etymological sense of 'molest' or 'be vexed' is found in the early treatises[7] and continues to be emphasized even in the late *abhidharma* treatises. Thus, the *Avatāra* defines the term as follows:

> Defilements (*kleśa*) are thus named because they perturb and afflict (煩亂逼惱; *kliśnantīti kleśāḥ*) the psycho-physical series. (*Avatāra*(T): *de dag ni lus dang sems kyi rgyud nyon mongs par byed pas nyon mongs pa rnams zhes bya ste /*)[8]

The occurrence of this term is rare in the *sūtra-piṭaka*. Its use was historically preceded by that of ***upakleśa***, although subsequently the latter generally came to be understood as 'secondary defilements' — those which proceed from *kleśa*. At this later stage, it is explained that the *upakleśa*-s are also the *kleśa,* but they additionally include other defilements which are not called *kleśa*.[9] Examples of these secondary defilements are moral immodesty, avarice and restlessness which are said to be emanations (*niṣyanda*) from greed (*rāga*).[10]

The AKB enumerates a total of 19 secondary defilements — non-diligence (*pramāda*), slackness (*kauśīdya*), faithlessness (*āśraddhya*), torpor (*styāna*), restlessness (*auddhatya*), immodesty (*āhrīkya*), shamelessness (*anapatrāpya*), anger (*krodha*), enmity (*upanāha*), dissimulation (*śāṭhya*), jealousy (*īrṣya*), depravity (*pradāśa*), concealment (*mrakṣa*), avarice (*mātsarya*), deceptiveness (*māyā*), pride (*mada*), harmfulness (*vihiṃsā*), remorse (*kaukṛtya*) and drowsiness (*middha*). An examination of the defilements listed under the 75 *dharma*-s in § 2.4.2 will show that these 19 secondary defilements comprise all the defiled *dharma*-s and two of the indeterminate (*aniyata*) *dharma*-s, but exclude the primary defilements. The latter, represented by the terms *kleśa* and *anuśaya*, are six: greed (*rāga*), hostility (*pratigha*), conceit (*māna*), ignorance (*avidyā*), views (*dṛṣṭi*) and doubt (*vicikitsā*) (see below, § 12.6.1). This means that the totality of defilements can be considered as comprising the primary and secondary *kleśa*-s.

12.2.2. *Anuśaya*

Etymologically, *anuśaya* is derived from *anu* + √*śī* ('lie down', 'sleep'). In the Sarvāstivādin explanation, however, the chief meaning is 'to adhere and grow concordantly [with the object]'. The prefix *anu* connotes the tenacity of the defilement. The sense of *śī* is not taken to convey the notion of latency as in the case of some other schools but rather that of subtlety. An *anuśaya* is that which has or does *anuśayana,* i.e., the function of growing or intensifying in accord with an impure object. For example, greed, when it arises taking a with-outflow (*sāsrava)* object, it becomes intensified as a defilement of that nature; the object in this case conduces to such an intensification. In the AKB, following the PrŚ,[11] the following four meanings of *anuśaya* are attributed by the Sarvāstivāda:

1. *aṇu*: meaning 'fine', 'subtle' — A pseudo etymological interpretation of the prefix *anu* — stressing the difficulty in detecting the arising of the defilements which are subtle in nature.

2. *anu* + √*bandh* ('bind') — They 'bind along with' (*anu*-√*bandh*), i.e., they proceed together with the psycho-physical series (*saṃtati*), 'like the image of a bird moving in the sky (*khacara*) being followed by a fish moving in water (*jalacara*)'.[12] "It is extremely difficult to be separated from them… According to some: this means that their *prāpti*-s always follow along."[13]

3. *anu* + √*gam* or *anu* + √*saj* (Tibetan *rjes 'brel* suggests *anu*-√*saj*) — They follow along or adhere 'like the oil in sesame seeds or the grease in a morsel of food'.[14] Vasubandhu explains in the sense of *anu* + √*saj*: "they adhere through adhesion of their *prāpti*-s".[15] Saṃghabhadra: from beginningless time, one is followed along by the *prāpti*-s arising in one's serial continuity.[16]

4. *anu* + √*śī* — They grow or become intensified in accord with (*anu*-√*śī*): They become nourished from (a) the objects they take (*ālambanato 'nuśerate*) and from (b) the thought concomitants with which they are conjoined (*samprayogato 'nuśerate*).[17] Saṃghabhadra explains that the first way (a) is like the case of an enemy seeking a weak point; the second way (b) is like the case of a heated ball that heats up the water. Like a foster mother who causes the growth of an infant, both the object taken and the conjoined mental *dharma* cause the series of the defilement to grow and accumulate.[18]

Out of the four senses given above, the MVŚ gives only three, i.e., without that of *anu*-√*gam*. It attributes the explanation in terms of the four senses to the foreign masters.[19]

12.3. Other doctrinal terms denoting defilements

Apart from *kleśa* and *anuśaya*, other major doctrinal terms used to describe defilements are: 1. fetter (*saṃyojana*); 2. bondage (*bandhana*); 3. envelopment (*paryavasthāna*); 4. outflow (*āsrava*); 5. flood (*ogha*);

6. yoke (*yoga*); 7. clinging (*upādāna*); 8. corporeal tie (*kāya-grantha*); 9. hindrance (*nivaraṇa*).

12.3.1. Fetter — The MVŚ gives three meanings of *saṃyojana*: 'binding', 'union with *duḥkha*', and 'mixing with poison'. The first meaning is said to be derived from the *sūtra*.[20] The second, because the fetters of the sphere of sensuality unite beings with *duḥkha* in that sphere; likewise for those of the fine-material and immaterial spheres. The third, because the *ārya*-s are disgusted with even the best states of birth and with the with-outflow *dhyāna*-s, as with excellent food mixed with poison.[21]

There are nine fetters: lust (*anunaya*), hostility, conceit, ignorance, views, irrational adherence (*parāmarśa*), doubt, jealousy and avarice.[22] There is also the doctrine of the 'five fetters pertaining to the lower portion' (*pañca-avarabhāgīya*) — to the sphere of sensuality; and the 'five fetters pertaining to the higher portion' (*pañca-ūrdhvabhāgīya*) — to the fine-material and immaterial spheres. The former comprise: Self-view (*satkāya-dṛṣṭi*), irrational adherence to abstentions and vows (*śīla-vrata-parāmarśa*), doubt, sensual-desire (*kāmacchanda*), malice (*vyāpāda*). The MVŚ explains that these five are thus called because they "manifest in the lower sphere, are abandoned in the lower sphere, re-link (*prati-sam-√dhā*) birth in the lower sphere, grasp emanation and retributive fruits in the lower sphere".[23] The latter comprise: greed (*rāga*) arisen from the fine-material sphere, greed arisen from the immaterial sphere, restlessness, conceit and ignorance.[24]

12.3.2. Bondage — As is clear from the first meaning given to 'fetter' above, the nine fetters are also to be known as bondages. The *Avatāra*, apparently following the PrŚ,[25] states explicitly that this is the case. It, however, also gives three bondages mentioned in the *sūtra*: (i) the greed-bondage (*rāga-bandhana*) which comprises all greed, with the same characterization as for the lust-fetter; (ii) the hatred-bondage (*dveṣa-bandhana*), which comprises all hatred, with the same characterization as for the hostility-fetter; and (iii) the delusion-bondage (*moha-bandhana*), which comprises all delusion, with the same characterization as for the ignorance fetter.[26] This term stresses the aspect of defilement which is the binding of beings to the triple spheres of existence (see below § 12.4, the 15th function of *anuśaya*). Saṃghabhadra defines bondage as that which binds, "that is, it prevents one from going towards detachment".[27]

12.3.3. Envelopment — The Vaibhāṣika enumerates the following as ten envelopments: 1. torpor, 2. drowsiness, 3. restlessness, 4. remorse, 5. jealousy, 6. avarice, 7. immodesty, 8. shamelessness, 9. anger, 10. concealment. The PrŚ[28] enumerates only the first eight. These are called 'envelopments' as they envelop one's psycho-physical series.[29] Saṃghabhadra: "these ten bind sentient beings and place them in the prison of *saṃsāra*, hence they are called envelopments. Or rather, these ten serve as the causes giving rise to various evil actions, so that [beings] are retained in the evil planes of existence (*durgati*)."[30]

12.3.4. Outflow — This is an important term; all conditioned *dharma*-s are subsumable as being either with or without outflows (see *supra*, § 2). There are three kinds of outflows: sensuality-outflow (*kāmāsrava*), existence-outflow (*bhavāsrava*) and ignorance-outflow (*avidyāsrava*). Both the AKB and the *Avatāra* give three etymologies for *āsrava*: (i) they keep (*āsayanti*) beings in the three spheres of existence; (ii) they cause beings to flow around (*āsravanti*) between the highest state of existence (*bhavāgra*) and the lowest, the Avici hell;[31] (iii) they incessantly discharge (*kṣar*) inexhaustible impurities through the six wound-like entrances — the six sense faculties — of beings (*ṣadbhir āyatanavraṇāiḥ*).[32] Vasubandhu favors the Sautrāntika explanation: "They are *āsrava*-s because by them the mental series flows into the objects."[33] The MVŚ gives the following six meanings:

(i) keep/detain — they keep beings in the three spheres of existence;

(ii) moisten or soak — just as when seeds are soaked in a wet vessel, they give rise to sprouts, likewise the *karma*-seeds, when soaked in the *kleśa*-vessel, give rise to future existences;

(iii) discharge or ooze — just as water oozes from a spring, and milk from the breast, likewise the *āsrava*-s ooze from the six wounds of beings;

(iv) confine — just as when confined by others, one is unable to travel everywhere at will, likewise beings are confined by *kleśa*-s to move around the various *dhātu*-s, *gati*-s, and *yoni*-s, and are unable to move freely toward the *nirvāṇa-dhātu*;

(v) bewitch — just as when one is bewitched by a spirit, one says what should not be said, does what should not be done, and thinks what should not be thought, likewise beings, bewitched by the *kleśa*-s, give rise to evil corporeal, vocal and mental acts;

(vi) intoxicate — just as when one has consumed too much alcohol derived from roots, stems, branches, leaves, flowers, fruits, etc., one does not know what should or should not be done, one is immodest (*ahrī*), shameless (*anatrāpa*), topsy-turvy, and indulgent.

The Śabdavādins explain that *ā* means 'from here up to there', *srava* means 'flowing'. The *kleśa*-s are called *āsrava* because they carry beings adrift in *saṃsāra* up to *bhavāgra*.[34]

12.3.5. Flood — There are four floods: sensuality-flood (*kāmaugha*), existence-flood (*bhavaugha*), view-flood (*dṛṣṭyogha*) and ignorance-flood (*avidyaugha*). The MVŚ gives three meanings: the *kleśa*-s, etc., are called *ogha* because they cause beings to revolve in *saṃsāra* by (i) drifting them about, (ii) torrentially pouring onto them, (iii) submerging them (in the ocean of *saṃsāra*).[35]

12.3.6. Yoke — The same four given as floods are also called yokes, because they join (*śleṣayanti*)[36] or yoke (*yojayanti*)[37] beings onto various forms of *duḥkha*.[38]

12.3.7. Clinging — There are four clingings: sensuality-clinging (*kāmopādāna*), view-clinging (*dṛṣṭy-upādāna*), clinging to abstentions and vows (*śīla-vratopādāna*), and Soul-theory-clinging (*ātmavādopādana*). The *Avatāra* gives three meanings of the term: (i) 'fuel' (*indhana*) — because it enables the fire of *karma* to continue blazing and growing; (ii) 'forcefulness' (*paṭutva*) — because their mode of activity (*ākāra*) is very forceful or sharp;[39] (iii) 'envelopment' — just as a silk-worm within a cocoon envelops itself to death, likewise beings, enveloped by the four clingings, go around in *saṃsāra* losing their wisdom-life.[40]

12.3.8. Corporeal tie — This topic is not discussed in the AKB. The *Avatāra* enumerates four of them: bodily tie of covetousness (*abhidhyā-kāyagrantha*), bodily tie of malice (*vyāpāda-kāyagrantha*), bodily tie of irrational adherence to abstentions and vows (*śīlavrataparāmarśa-kāyagrantha*), and bodily tie of dogmatism (*idaṃsatyābhinirveśa-kāyagrantha*). Skandhila explains that "they are called *kāyagrantha* because they variously tie around sentient beings. The meaning is the complete entrapping of the [psycho-physical] complex (*kāya*) of beings."[41] The MVŚ enumerates the following four: the bodily tie of (i) sensual-desire (*kāmacchanda*), (ii) malice (*vyāpāda*), (iii) irrational adherence to abstentions and vows, (iv) the attachment 'this is real'; and gives two meanings of *grantha*: (a) corporeal bondage (*kāya-bandhana*), (b) rebirth-linking (*pratisaṃdhi*).[42]

12.3.9. Hindrance — There are five hindrances: (i) sensual-desire, (ii) malice, (iii) torpor-drowsiness (*styāna-middha*), (iv) restlessness-remorse (*auddhatya-kaukṛtya*) and doubt. These are found in the sphere of sensuality alone, as they are purely unskillful.[43] The *Avatāra* explains that they are called hindrances because they constitute the obstacles for the noble path, for detachment, and for the roots of skillfulness which are preparatory (*prāyogika*) for the two.[44] The MVŚ gives the following six meanings for *nivaraṇa*: obstructing, covering, breaking, ruining, (causing) to fall, (causing) to lie down.[45] It enumerates the same five hindrances, but states that ignorance constitutes the sixth:

> ...outside these five *nivaraṇa*-s, there is a sixth, i.e., *avidyā-nivaraṇa*, ... [But] although *avidyānuśaya* is also a *nivaraṇa*, it is not mentioned among the five *nivaraṇa*-s owing to its heaviness; the Bhagavat has designated it separately as the sixth *nivaraṇa*: *avidyā* is mentioned separately because it is heavy compared to the previous five *nivaraṇa*-s which are of equal strength.[46]

12.4. Defilements as the root of existence

In the *abhidharma* scheme of explanation, *duḥkha* results from *karma*, and *karma* arises from defilements. The AKB[47] declares that without the latter, *karma*-s are incapable of producing new existences. Accordingly, they are the root of existence (*mūlaṃ bhavasya*). From another perspective, all defilements arise on account of ignorance, and it is for this reason that it constitutes the first link (*nidāna*) in the twelvefold formula of conditioned co-arising (*pratītya-samutpāda*), even though there is no notion of the First Cause in Buddhism. (See *infra*, § 13). Accordingly, ignorance is also declared to be the root of all existences.[48]

In this context, ten functions that a defilement performs are listed. Saṃghabhadra adds six more:

> Why are the *anuśaya*-s capable of serving as the root of existence?
>
> This is because, when a defilement is arising, it performs 16 functions:

1. It makes firm its root, the counteragent (*pratipakṣa*) being distant. The root of a defilement is its *prāpti*.

2. It generates a weightiness of one's basis, for it brings about an inaptitude in one's basis for actions (*āśraya-dauṣṭhulyaṃ janayaty akarmaṇyat'āpādanāt*).

3. It establishes a series (*saṃtatim avasthāpayati*), for it enables itself to be produced continuously.

4. It accommodates its field (*kṣetram āpādayati*), for it makes the basis [— the person —] conducive to its abiding.

5. It loathes virtues, for its nature is opposed to the virtues (*guṇān dveṣṭi tad-virodhitvāt*).

6. It serves as the seat of reproach, for it projects bodily, vocal and mental *karma*-s which are reproached by the wise (*apavādānām āspadī-karoti vidvad-vigarhita-kāya-karmotthāpanāt*).

7. It engenders a poisonous emanation (*niṣyanda*), for it engenders the secondary defilements (*upakleśa*) which are like [— of a similar nature to —] itself.

8. It blocks the path of liberation, for it abandons drawing near to those who teach the true doctrine.[49]

9. It leads to *karma-bhava* (*karmabhavam abhinirharati*), for it induces the *karma* for new existence.

10. It gathers up its own requisites (*sva-saṃbhāraṃ parigṛhṇāti*), [i.e., its own causes,] for it repeatedly gathers up and gives rise to improper mental application (*ayoniśomanaskāra*).

11. It deludes one as regards the object of consciousness (*ālambane saṃmohayati*), for it harms the proper understanding of the person.

12. It plants the seeds of sufferings, for it can generate all forms of suffering in *saṃsāra* (*vividhānārtha-bījaṃ ropayati sarva-saṃsāra-vyasanānāṃ tat-prabhavatvāt*).

13. It conducts the stream of consciousness (*vijñānasroto namayati*), for it induces consciousness on the objects of rebirth.

14. It makes one go astray from what pertains to the good (*kuśalapakṣād vyutkramayati*), for it causes the falling away of the good *dharma*-s.

15. It amplifies its significance as bondage through preventing the surmounting of the sphere and stage to which it belongs (*bandhanārthaṃ spharati dhātvanatikrama-yogena*), for it nourishes the defiled spheres.

16. It brings together the undesirable of the world in the form of *ādhipatya-phala*, for, by virtue of this, there comes to be the deterioration of the external things (*ādhipatya-phalena lokasyāniṣṭam upasaṃharati tad-vegena bāhya-bhāva-vikār'āpatteḥ* /).[50]

12.5. Ābhidharmika investigation of defilements

If *anuśaya*-s, the root of existence, must be eliminated, how should one proceed to do so? The Ābhidharmika starting point is *dharma-pravicaya*, a thorough investigation into their nature. Saṃghabhadra enumerates the following as among the essential taxonomical topics — representing the different perspectives — for this examination:

1. Whether a given *anuśaya* is to be abandoned by insight (*darśana-praheya*) or by cultivation (*bhāvanā-praheya*).

2. Whether it pertains to one category (*prakāra*) of abandonability, or two, or three, or four, or all five — abandonable by insight into (i) *duḥkha*, (ii) origin of *duḥkha*, (iii) cessation of *duḥkha*, (iv) the *mārga* leading to the cessation, and (v) by the path of cultivation.

3. Whether it is a universal (*sarvatraga*) or non-universal defilement.

4. Whether it is universal with respect to its own sphere or to other spheres.

5. Whether it takes objects which are with-outflow (*sāsrava-ālambana*) or outflow-free (*anāsrava*).

6. Whether it takes objects which are conditioned (*saṃskṛta*) or unconditioned (*asaṃskṛta*).

7. How does it arise? [Three possible causes — *infra*, § 12.8.1].

8. How does it grow concordantly with the object (*anuśerate*)? [Two possible ways — § 12.8.2].

9. Whether it is abandoned by fully knowing the object (*pari-√jñā*) or by abandoning the object.

10. Whether it is abandoned by the absolute destruction of its accompaniments or on account of the purification of the series (*santati*) that constitutes the practitioner.

11. Whether it is conjoined or not conjoined with a particular *caitta*.

12. Whether, after having abandoned it, one is still liable or not liable to retrogression.

13. Whether it gives rise to an undesirable retribution (*aniṣṭa-vipāka*) or is completely without any retribution.

14. Whether it is an equal-immediate condition (*samanantara-pratyaya*) for a particular *caitta* or its object.

15. Whether or not it is abandoned as a result of its object being abandoned.

16. Whether, although it is abandoned in terms of its intrinsic nature, one is still bound to it on account of its object.

17. Whether it is a defilement that cannot exist in the stages of concentration (*samāhita-bhūmi*).

18. Whether it is a defilement that cannot be eliminated by a worldly path of counteraction.

19. Whether it pertains to the group of mental consciousness (*manovijñāna-kāya*) alone or to all six groups of consciousnesses.

20. Whether or not it can serve as the originating cause (*samutthāna-hetu*) for bodily and vocal *karma*.

21. Whether it can cause the cutting of the roots of skillfulness.

22. Whether it can cause the relinking with the roots of skillfulness [which have been cut].

23. Whether or not it is of the nature of speculation (*dṛṣṭi-svabhāva*).

24. Whether it is abandoned only when all its nine grades are abandoned or when only one grade is abandoned.

25. Whether it is abandonable either when one grade is abandoned or when all nine grades are abandoned.

26. Whether it comes to be endowed (*samanvāgata*) by an individual on account of a particular *dharma*.

27. Whether it does not come to be endowed (*asamanvāgata*) by an individual on account of a particular *dharma*.

28. Whether it comes to be conjoined (*saṃprayukta*) or not conjoined on account of a particular *dharma*

29. Whether there is a possibility of its manifestation in a particular stage.

30. Whether, although not yet abandoned, it does not manifest its activity.

31. Whether it is abandoned in the sphere of sensuality (*kāma-dhātu*) alone or in the upper spheres as well.

32. Whether or not there is the endowment of this as a fruit.

33. Whether or not it shares the same counteragent with another defilement.

In summary, Saṃghabhadra states:

> It is after having properly understood the nature of the *anuśaya*-s in this way that one can decisively eliminate them.[51]

12.6. Classification of defilements

12.6.1. Fundamental defilements

The fundamental defilements are six in number (see A below). However, *rāga* is divisible into *kāma-rāga*, i.e., greed with regard to the sphere of sensuality (*kāmadhātu*), and *bhava-rāga*, i.e., greed for the subtler forms of existence in the *rūpa*- and *ārūpya-dhātu*, giving a total of seven (see B below). In the third classification (see C below), *rāga* is taken as one, and *dṛṣṭi* is divided into five forms, giving a total of ten.

Among the views, *satkāya-dṛṣṭi* is the false view that the five *skandha*-s of grasping constituting the person is the real Self. The Vaibhāṣika explains *sat* to mean 'real/existent', and *kāya*, 'accumulation'. *Satkāya-dṛṣṭi,* therefore, refers to the view of a real Self superimposed on the impermanent *skandha*-s. Properly speaking, it is the view which falsely believes in the Self as well as that which pertains to the Self. Vasubandhu, however, presents the Sautrāntika view which interprets *sat* as 'perish'; accordingly, this view is the false belief with regard to the 'perishing accumulation' (*ātma-dṛṣṭir ātmīya-dṛṣṭir vā satkāya-dṛṣṭiḥ / sīdatīti sat / cayaḥ kāyaḥ saṃgātaḥ skandha ityarthaḥ /* — AKB, 281). The Tibetan rendering as *'jig tshogs la lta ba* reflects this interpretation.

Mithyā-dṛṣṭi is the false view which denies causal efficacy, the four noble truths, etc. This is an important defilement, for it alone is responsible for the cutting of the roots of skillfulness (*kuśalamūla-samuccheda*).[52]

One who harbors the *satkāya-dṛṣṭi* either thinks of the superimposed Self as being eternal or as susceptible to complete destruction at death — the view having these two extremes (*anta*) as objects is called *anta-grāha-dṛṣṭi*.

Dṛṣṭi-parāmarśa is the attachment to or esteeming of one's own views as being true and superior when, in fact, they are not. In particular, it refers to the obstinate attachment to the previous three views.

The fifth, *śīla-vrata-parāmarśa*, is the view expressed as irrational attachment to religious vows and observances by the heretics who undertake them as means for purification and liberation. An example of this is the belief that by immersing oneself in the Ganges, one will be cleansed of all sins.

(A) 6 kinds	**(B) 7 kinds**	**(C) 10 kinds**
1. *rāga* — greed	1. *kāmarāga* — sensual greed	1. *rāga*
	2. *bhavarāga* — existence-greed	
2. *pratigha* — hostility	3. *pratigha*	2. *pratigha*
3. *avidyā* — ignorance	4. *avidyā*	3. *avidyā*
4. *māna* — conceit	5. *māna*	4. *māna*
5. *vicikitsā* — doubt	6. *vicikitsā*	5. *vicikitsā*
6. *dṛṣṭi* — view	7. *dṛṣti*	6. *satkāyadṛṣti*
		7. *antagrāhadṛṣṭi*
		8. *mithyādṛṣti*
		9. *dṛṣti-parāmarśa*
		10. *śīla-vrata-parāmarśa*

12.6.2. Some important classifications

Of the various ways of classificatory topics mentioned above (§ 12.5), the more important ones are: (i) *darśana-heya-* and *bhāvanā-heya*; (ii) *sarvatraga* and *asarvatraga*; (iii) *sāsrava-ālambana* and *anāsrava-ālambana*; (iv) the five categories (*nikāya*) of abandonables — (1–4) by insight into *duḥkha*, *samudaya*, *nirodha*, *mārga*, and (5) by *bhāvanā* (cultivation).

12.6.2.1. *Darśana-heya* and *bhāvanā-heya kleśa*

When the cognitive object (*ālambana*) of a defilement can be abandoned by the mere insight into the four truths (*satyānāṃ darśana-mātreṇa prahāṇāt*), that defilement is said to be one 'abandonable by (the path of) insight' (*darśana-mārga-praheya*).[53] Otherwise, it belongs to the category called 'abandonable by (the path of) cultivation' (*bhāvanā-mārga-heya*), that is, by repeated practice. Of the total of ten defilements, the five views and doubts are cognitive in nature; they are thus abandoned once proper insight is gained. On the other hand, *rāga*, *pratigha*, *māna* and *avidyā* partake of both cognitive and affective nature; thus their manifestations are not entirely abandonable by insight alone. Hence these four in their affective aspects have to be further counteracted by the path of repeated practice or cultivation.

(a) *Darśanamārga-praheya* (abandonable by the path of insight)

Darśanamārga refers to the stage of 15 thought-moments of direct realization (*abhisamaya*) into the four noble truths, at the end of which — i.e., in the 16th moment — one becomes a *śrotaāpanna*. During these 15 moments, a total of 88 defilements are abandoned by insight into the four noble truths, as shown below:

In the sphere of sensuality:

Defilements	I. *duḥkha-darśana-heya*	II. *samudaya-darśana-heya*	III. *nirodha-darśana-heya*	IV. *mārga-darśana-heya*
1. *rāga*	✓	✓	✓	✓
2. *pratigha*	✓	✓	✓	✓
3. *māna*	✓	✓	✓	✓
4. *avidyā*	✓	✓	✓	✓
5. *vicikitsā*	✓	✓	✓	✓
6. *satkāyadṛṣti*	✓	-	-	-
7. *mithyādṛṣti*	✓	✓	✓	✓
8. *antagrāhadṛṣṭi*	✓	-	-	-
9. *dṛṣti-parāmarśa-d.*	✓	✓	✓	✓
10. *śīla-vrata-p.-d.*	✓	-	-	✓
	10	7	7	8

A total of 10 + 7 + 7 + 8 = 32 *kleśa*-s pertaining to the sphere of sensuality are abandoned.

Note that *satkāyadṛṣṭi* and *antagrāha-dṛṣṭi* are absent under *samudaya*. This is because *satkāyadṛṣṭi* arises with regard to the five-*skandha* complex constituting the human individual. That is, it arises on account of not understanding the *duḥkha-satya* which, for the Sarvāstivādins, is the five *skandha*-s of grasping in their fruit aspect.[54]

Since the arising of *antagrāha-dṛṣṭi* is dependent on *satkāya-dṛṣṭi*, it too is confined under *duḥkha-satya*.

Śīlavrata-parāmarśa is also an erroneous view regarding the psycho-physical complex — the type of view, for instance, which inclines one to torture the body or mind — hence it is included under *duḥkha-satya*. Since it is also the type of view which mistakes irrational extreme asceticism as the path of purification, it also arises with regard to the path, hence it is subsumable under *mārga-satya* as well.

In the two upper spheres:

In the fine-material sphere, the same scheme applies as in the sphere of sensuality, but excluding *pratigha*, because in both the two higher spheres of meditational experience the mind is free from *pratigha*, in all four categories of abandonables. Thus, a total of 9 + 6 + 6 + 7 = 28 defilements are abandoned in the *rūpadhātu.*

The same applies to the case of the immaterial sphere, giving again a total of 28 defilements which are abandoned.

This is how 88 (= 32 + 28 + 28) defilements come to be abandoned in the three spheres of existence by the *darśana-mārga*.

(b) *Bhāvanāmārga-praheya* (abandonable by the path of cultivation)

While the path of insight lasts for only 15 consecutive moments, the path of cultivation may last a whole life time or even more. The *śrota-āpanna* saint now embarks on a journey of repeated cultivation (*bhāvanā*) to elevate his insight (*prajñā*) for the purpose of counteracting the defilements that still remain. *Bhāvanā* means more than just 'meditation'. However it is clear that the most fundamental part of the *bhāvanā-mārga* is indeed meditation. Thus, *bhāvanāmayī prajñā* is also known as *samādhija-prajñā* — insight or understanding born of meditation. Although in a broader sense, *samādhi* connotes the perfect integration of all psychic energies, the main method employed to achieve that is still meditation. Therefore meditation is given a prominent role. Hence we can see an emphasis on meditation consistent in all Buddhist traditions. The Sarvāstivādins in fact assert that the Buddha's perfect wisdom — in contrast to that of an *arhat* — consists in the complete and absolute eradication of all defilements along with their subtle traces (*vāsanā*), and this happens only when the practitioner finally attains the *vajropama-samādhi*, whose strength (concentration) is comparable to that of a diamond that cuts through everything but cannot be cut by anything.

There are a total of ten defilements abandoned by the path of cultivation. These are innate and are really constituted by four of the fundamental defilements — *rāga*, *pratigha*, *māna* and *avidyā*. These ten defilements are intrinsically much more tenacious and resilient than the cognitively superimposed ones abandoned in the *darśana-mārga*, and therefore persistent efforts by cultivation are needed for them to be abandoned. Four pertain to the sphere of sensuality and three to each of the two upper spheres:

kāmadhātu:	*rāga* +	*pratigha* +	*avidyā* +	*māna*	= 4
rūpadhātu:	*rāga* +		*avidyā* +	*māna*	= 3
ārūpyadhātu:	*rāga* +		*avidyā* +	*māna*	= 3

12.6.2.2. Universal (*sarvatraga*) and non-universal (*asarvatraga*) defilements

This distinction is applicable to the defilements subsumed under the four noble truths. Among the 98 *anuśaya*-s, 11 are said to be 'universal', as they can move in all the five categories (*nikāya*) of abandonables pertaining to their own sphere (*dhātu*).

According to Saṃghabhadra, this means that: (i) they can take as objects all *dharma*-s belonging to the five categories in their own *dhātu*, (ii) they operate as *anuśaya* (*anuśerate* — have *anuśayana*) with regard to all of them, and (iii) serve as the cause for the production of defiled *dharma*-s in all five categories.[55]

There are 11, pertaining to the *duḥkha*- and *samudaya-satya*-s: seven under *duḥkha-darśana-heya* — *satkāyadṛṣṭi*, *antagrāha-dṛṣṭi*, *mithyā-dṛṣṭi*, *dṛṣṭi-parāmarśa*, *śīlavrata-parāmarśa*, *vicikitsā* and *avidyā*; four under *samudaya-darśana-heya* — *mithyādṛṣṭi*, *dṛṣṭi-parāmarśa*, *vicikitsā* and *avidyā*. Nine of them — excepting *satkāyadṛṣṭi* and *antagrāha-dṛṣṭi* — are universals also in the other spheres (*visabhāga-dhātu-sarvatraga*).

That is, they can also bear on an upper sphere. *Satkāyadṛṣṭi* and *antagrāhadṛṣṭi* are *sabhāga-dhātu-sarvartraga*, i.e., they are universal only in their own sphere.

All the remaining *anuśaya*-s are non-universal.

12.6.2.3. Defilements that take outflow-free objects (*anāsravālambana*) and those that take with-outflow objects (*sāsravālambana*)

The defilements abandonable by insight into cessation and the path are classifiable as (i) those taking outflow-free objects, and (ii) those taking with-outflow objects. The former comprise *mithyā-dṛṣṭi*, *vicikitsā* and *avidyā*. The latter comprise the rest of the *nirodha-darśana-praheya* and *māga-darśana-praheya* defilements. The former do not have *anuśayana* with regard to their objects which, being outflow-free, are not favorable to *anuśayana*. The latter have *anuśayana* only with regard to *dharma*-s of their own category in their own sphere by way of taking objects (*ālambanataḥ*).

12.7. Relationship between defilements and the mind

Various controversies arise among the different Abhidharma schools as regards the nature of the defilements. Among these, two are prominent:

(1) Are they conjoined with (*saṃprayukta*) or disjoined from (*viprayukta*) thought?

(2) Can a distinction be made between defilements in the latent, potential form and the manifested form?

These two issues are in some way connected.

As regards the first, if defilements are by nature disjoined from the mind, how can they affect the mind? On the other hand, if they are conjoined with the mind, how can there be liberation from them at all?

Already in the MVŚ, these two controversies are recorded, and there we can also discern a very developed, articulate understanding of *anuśaya*. We learn that the 'abrupt-abandonment *śramaṇa*-s' (頓斷沙門) hold that "when the *vajropama-samādhi* manifests, all the *darśana-heya* and *bhāvanā-heya* defilements pertaining to the three spheres of existence are abandoned at once. At all the stages prior to this, there can be only the suppression of the *paryavasthāna*-s; the *anuśaya*-s are not yet capable of being abandoned."[56] In this proposition, there seems to be an implicit distinction between *paryavasthāna* and *anuśaya*.

The same distinction is also implied in the Bhadanta's view that ordinary worldlings cannot abandon *anuśaya*-s; they can only suppress the *paryavasthāna*-s.[57] This distinction becomes explicit in another discussion centered on the possibility of the retrogression of an *arhat*:

> The Vibhajyavādins further say that *anuśaya* is the *bīja* of *paryavasthāna*. The *anuśaya* is *cittaviprayukta* in its intrinsic nature *svabhāva*). The *paryavasthāna* is *cittasaṃprayukta* in its intrinsic nature. *Paryavasthāna* arises from *anuśaya*. Retrogression results from the manifestation (*saṃmukhībhāva*) of *paryavasthāna*. The *arhat*-s have already abandoned the *anuśaya*-s; the *paryavasthāna*-s not arising, how can an *arhat* retrogress? Hence they (the Vibhajyavādins) assert that it is logical that there is no retrogression.[58]

The following points can be gleaned from the above passage:

1. There is a definite contrast between *anuśaya* and *paryavasthāna* on the part of some Ābhidharmikas — in this case the Vibhajyavādins.

2. An *anuśaya* is asserted here to be the seed of *paryavasthāna* — seeds in the sense of potentialities are not real, existent entities, hence are not conjoined with the mind.[59] The implication in this context is that *anuśaya* is so subtle that it, in its latent state, has not conjoined with the mind; but, in its active state, i.e., as *paryavasthāna*, it conjoins with the mind.

3. The Vibhajyavādin point of view is that: When there is no *anuśaya* there is no *paryavasthāna*. When there is no *paryavasthāna*, there is no retrogression.

In the AKB and the Ny, we see that the Dārṣṭāntika-Sautrāntikas advocate a doctrinal position similar to that of the Vibhajyavādins cited above, with the only difference that the *anuśaya*, in the form of seeds, are potentialities and, therefore, cannot be said to be either conjoined with or disjoined from thought. In the AKB, the controversy, between the Vaibhāṣika and the Sautrāntika, on the relationship between *anuśaya* and *paryavasthāna*, takes the form of a debate on how the compound *kāmarāga-anuśaya* ('sensual-greed-proclivity' of which sensual greed is the first component, proclivity, the second) is to be interpreted: Is it a determinative compound (*tatpuruṣa*) meaning 'the *anuśaya* of *kāmarāga*' as the Sautrāntika holds, or a descriptive compound (*karmadhāraya*) meaning 'the *anuśaya* is *kāmarāga* itself' as the Vaibhāṣika holds? The Vaibhāṣika opts for the second interpretation which accords with their tenet that there is no such thing as a latent defilement — defilement and *anuśaya* are just synonyms. Vasubandhu, however, supports the Sautrāntika view:

> [The interpretation] according to the Sautrāntikas is good. But what is [the interpretation] of the Sautrāntikas? It is: *kāmarāga-anuśaya* means the '*anuśaya* of *kāmarāga*'. And the *anuśaya*, not being a distinct entity (*dravyāntara*), [i.e., a real existent,] is neither conjoined with nor disjoined from [thought]. For, when asleep, the defilement is called *anuśaya*; when

awakened, it is called *paryavasthāna*. But what is its sleeping state (*prasupti*)? The continuity of its non-manifested seed-state. What is its awakening (*prabodha*)? The state when it is manifested. …[60]

Some scholars claim that this Dārṣṭāntika-Sautrāntika theory expounded in the AKB has its source in the *Yogācārabhūmi-śāstra* (YBŚ). However, we know that Aśvaghoṣa, a typical Dārṣṭāntika master[61] already cited in the MVŚ, and Kumāralāta, a Dārṣṭāntika leader of *ca.* late 2nd or early 3rd century C.E., already held some form of the seed theory.[62] And since these early Dārṣṭāntikas were the precursors of the Sautrāntikas, there is no need to assume that Vasubandhu had to borrow his account from the YBŚ.

The standpoint of the various schools as to whether the *anuśaya*-s are *cittaviprayukta* or *cittasaṃprayukta* may be summarized in the following chart.[63]

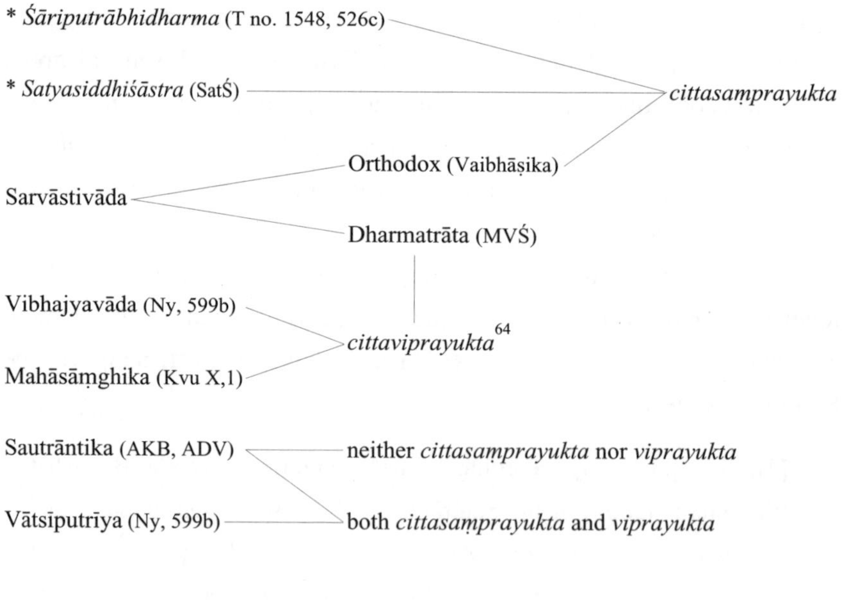

12.8. Operation of the defilements

In the Sarvāstivāda, *anuśaya* is merely a synonym for defilement and the concept of latency is not accepted. That is, *anuśaya* and *paryavasthāna* are synonymous. The term *anuśaya* is simply taken to denote the subtlety and tenacity of the defilements.[65]

12.8.1. How a defilement arises

The MVŚ informs us that, according to some heretics, the arising of a defilement is purely due to external stimuli — when the object exists, the defilement arises; when the former is destroyed, the latter does not arise. The Sarvāstivāda disagrees and proposes three reasons for the arising of defilements:[66]

1. On account of a cause (*hetu-balena*)

   This refers to the fact that the *anuśaya*-s in one's *saṃtāna* have not been completely known and abandoned (*aprahīṇa-aparijñāta*) — because their counteragents have not arisen, hence they can arise when the right conditions assemble.

2. On account of the object (*viṣaya-balena*)

   This refers to the external stimuli conducive to defilements coming into the field of one's experience (*pratyupasthita*, *ābhāsagata*) — as in the case of an *arhat* susceptible to retrogression.[67]

3. On account of preparatory effort (*prayoga-balena*)

   This refers specifically to improper mental application (*ayoniśo-manaskāra*).

Elsewhere in the MVŚ, Vasumitra explains that defilements can arise even for someone dwelling in a hermitage (*araṇya*). In this case, there is no influence from external object, but there are the forces of the cause

— the yet unabandoned *anuśaya* — and improper mental application within the hermit. On the other hand, even when in the presence of the cause and the object-stimulus, one may not generate defilement on account of the absence of improper application.[68]

12.8.2. How a defilement 'adheres and grows' (*anu-√śī*)

According to the Kaśmīrian masters, there are two ways by which a defilement grows/increases concordantly (*anuśete*), i.e., obtains a footing and growth (*pratiṣṭhāṃ labhate*, *puṣṭiṃ labhate*):

(I) by way of taking an object (*ālambanataḥ*): On account of taking a with-outflow object. "[The defilement] grows as a result of its attachment to the particular mode of activity (*ākāra*) arisen in respect to the object." When the object is outflow-free, *anuśayana* does not take place because it is not favorable to the growth of the defilement and hence there is no binding therein.

(II) by way of conjunction with a mental *dharma* (*saṃprayogataḥ*): The defilement 'adheres and grows' in concordance with the *dharma* with which it is conjoined, making the *dharma* have the same fault as itself. Thus, in the case of a *rāga* conjoined with a pleasurable sensation, the latter fuels the intensity of the former and the former also comes to have the aspect of greed; as a result, the whole mental complex (*citta-caitta*-s) becomes one of greed, i.e., a greedy mind.

According to the Western masters, the first mode of *anuśayana* is by way of bondage, the latter by way of companionship.[69]

12.8.2.1. Vasumitra's elaboration

In the same context, Vasumitra elaborates on this notion of 'adhering and growing':

1. Because of falling into an evil state of mind — just like a member of a group commits an evil and causes others in the group to fall into the same state of mind. In the same way, when one *anuśaya* arises, it causes the whole *citta-caitta* complex to be defiled. [Influence aspect]

2. Because it is like the heating of fire, e.g., a hot piece of iron is put into a vessel of water — both water and vessel become hot. In the same way, the whole *citta-caitta* complex becomes 'heated up' by the *anuśaya*. [Contamination aspect]

3. Because it is like smoke, etc. — when a garment is tainted by smoke and dust, etc., the whole garment becomes dirty. [Contamination aspect]

4. Because of it being reproachable — e.g., when one member of the *saṅgha* commits an offence, the whole *saṅgha* is reproached. Likewise, the presence of a single *anuśaya* renders the whole mental make-up reproachable.

The above constitute four reasons why one can speak of a defilement's adhering and growing by way of conjunction. The same also apply to the case of *anuśayana* by way of taking an object: That is, where an object causes an increase with regard to these four aspects, one says that the defilement adheres and grows therein.

12.8.2.2. Elaboration in the Ny

Concerning "*anuśayana* by way of taking an object", Saṃghabhadra explains this to mean that "the *anuśaya* adheres along and grows (隨住增長) in the (*sāsrava*) *dharma*, i.e., it binds concordantly and increases stagnation therein".[70] This is like the adherence of dust on a wet garment (*ārdra iva paṭe rajāṃsi saṃsthātum* [*utsahante*]), or the growth of seeds in an irrigated field. The *anuśaya*-s that take the *anāsrava dharma*-s

— *nirvāṇa* or the path — or a higher sphere (than the one to which they belong) as objects, do not operate in this mode, because these objects are not appropriated as the Self or what pertains to the Self either through Self-view (*ātmadṛṣṭi*) or craving (*tṛṣṇā*). As a matter of fact, the wish for the attainment of the pure *dharma*-s or a higher sphere is not a greed as such but a predilection or aspiration for the good (*kuśala-dharma-chanda*). Besides, the pure objects as well as the *dharma*-s belonging to a higher sphere are in nature opposed to the *anuśaya*-s that take them as objects, and hence not supportive of their growth. As such, the *anuśaya*-s cannot find a footing in them, just as the sole of a foot cannot stay when placed on a heated rock.[71]

The "*anuśayana* by way of conjunction" is elaborated as a threefold operation:[72]

1. inducing the *prāpti* [of the defilements];
2. obstructing the thought series (*citta-santati*);
3. serving as the homogeneous cause for the emanation of the subsequent moment in the series.

Saṃghabhadra also quotes the examples given by the *pūrvācārya*-s for the phenomena of *anuśayana*:[73]

(i) *saṃprayogataḥ* — Just as in an agglomeration of filth comprising excreta, water, mud, etc., the water and mud, etc., become filthy as a result of the excreta; by virtue of the water and mud, etc., the filthiness of the excreta too becomes more intense. Through mutual support, both become extremely loathsome. Likewise, in a mental agglomeration conjoined with defilements, the *citta-caitta*-s come to be defiled by virtue of the defilements; the latter too, by virtue of the former, become more intense. Through mutual support both become corrupted. The corruption gradually increasing in the series of this agglomeration, the accompaniments such as *jāti*, etc., also come to be defiled.

(ii) *ālambanataḥ* — Just as in a filthy place, the pigs and dogs sporting and sleeping therein are besmeared by excreta becoming all the more filthy; at the same time, due to the pigs and dogs, this filthy place becomes even more filthy. Likewise, a with out-flow (*sāsrava*) object belonging to its sphere manifests its nature as being with-outflow through the force of the defilement that takes it as its object; at the same time, this object is capable of operating in accord with the force of the defilement to cause the gradual intensification of three grades (strong-strong, etc.) of strength of this defilement.

(iii) The non-operation of *anuśayana* with regard to an outflow-free object — this is like the case of a slippery and spotlessly clean man who accidentally falls into an agglomeration of filth. Although in contact with the excreta, there is no increment of filth on his part. At the same time this man is incapable of increasing the filth of that agglomeration of filth. Likewise, although *dharma*-s which are outflow-free or which belong to a different sphere may at times be taken as objects by defilements, there is no mutual support for the increment of outflows therein. It is only by way of conjunction that there can be *anuśayana* with regard to such objects.

A further illustration, said to be by "some other" (*apare*), is also given: Just as, when wine is mixed with poison, its strength increases; at the same time, the power of the poison is also enhanced. Likewise, when a defilement takes a with-outflow object, the efficacies of both come to be enhanced through mutual support. On the other hand, when an effective medicine is placed inside a poison, it causes the diminution alone — not enhancement — of the efficacy of the poison. Likewise is the effect of an outflow-free object for a defilement. Accordingly, although false view (*mithyā-dṛṣṭi*) may arise when an outflow-free *dharma* is taken as an object, this false view does not have the strength to cut off the roots of skillfulness.[74]

12.9. Abandonment of defilements

12.9.1. Meaning of 'abandonment'

For the Sarvāstivādins, defilements cannot be 'destroyed' in an ontological sense since, like all other *dharma*-s, their *svabhāva*-s exist perpetually. Abandonment in the proper sense means the severing of the *prāpti* linking the defilement to the individual series. The MVŚ states that even past and future *anuśaya*-s are said to have the function of *anuśayana*, inasmuch as they, although without any present activity, can give rise to their *prāpti*-s that arise in the present, just as an extinguished fire can give rise to smoke even though it no longer arises in the present.[75] Therefore they too must be abandoned. Such an *anuśayana*, of course, does not entail 'adherence and growth' — a sense apparently articulated in a relatively later stage, despite the fact that Xuan Zang uses here the same standard rendering of '*sui zeng* 隨增'.

12.9.2. Role of *prāpti* in the abandonment of defilements

Whatever the original signification of *prāpti* might have been, when it came to be articulated as a *citta-viprayukta saṃskāra*, it became, for the Sarvāstivāda system, a *sine qua non* for the mechanism of defilement as well as purification. One is defiled by a defilement when it arises in oneself and comes to be connected with one's series by a conascent *prāpti*. When both this defilement and the *prāpti* come to cease — become past — in the next moment one continues to be defiled on account of one's continuous connection with this defilement which, although past, is still existent, effected by the homogeneous series of *prāpti* (a *niṣyanda*) perpetuated by the original *prāpti*. When one is finally freed from this defilement, it is not that one has made it extinct — the *svabhāva*-s of all *dharma*-s can never be destroyed. It is only that its linkage — *prāpti* — with oneself comes to be severed. This occurs when the counteracting path — i.e., the *ārya prajñā* — arises.

The MVŚ explains the role of *prāpti* in the abandonment of defilements as follows:

> When an *arhat* abandons the defilements, it is not that he renders them totally non-existent, for the [intrinsic] natures of past and future defilements continue to exist as realities. In the series [of the practitioner], when the path contradictory to the defilement has not appeared (*saṃmukhī-√bhū*), he is said to have not yet abandoned the defilement. When in the series, the path contradictory to the defilement has appeared, he abandons the *prāpti* of the *saṃyoga* and realizes the *prāpti* of *visaṃyoga*, and is [accordingly] not endowed with the defilement; he is then said to have abandoned the defilement. It should be explained thus: the cultivation of the noble path is an extra-ordinary event [in that], although it enables an *arhat* to abandon a defilement, it does not cause it to be non-existent. For this reason, the Venerable Ghoṣaka says: 'When a defilement does not operate in the person, it is said to have been abandoned [by the person]. It is not that [this abandonment] causes it to be totally non-existent.'[76]

Also:[77]

> It is not the case that when the noble paths are arisen, they cut off (abandon) the defilements like a knife cutting off a thing, [or] like a stone grinding incense. Rather, when the noble paths appear, they cause the cessation of the *samanvāgama-prāpti* (i.e., *prāpti* qua *samanvāgama*) of the defilements and the arising of the *asamanvāgama-prāpti* (i.e., the *asamanvāgama* which is *aprāpti*) of those defilements. At that time, one is said to have cut off/abandoned the defilements.

Indeed, without the intervention of *prāpti* which is in nature dissociated from the *citta-caitta*-s, it becomes impossible for a counteragent (*pratipakṣa*) to exercise its function on a defilement since the two are opposed in their moral nature. For the same reason, it is equally impossible for false view (*mithyā-dṛṣṭi*) to bring about the cutting off of the skillful roots (*kuśalamūla-samuccheda*), the two being unable to interact directly, as explained in the following passage:[78]

> Question: What is the meaning of the cutting off of the skillful roots?
>
> Answer: It is not like the case, in the world, of an axe, etc., cutting a tree, for *mithyā-dṛṣṭi* and the *kuśala* do not mutually come into contact [— the two being mental entities of opposed nature]. Rather, when *mithyā-dṛṣṭi* appears in [a person's] series, it causes the cessation of the *samanvāgama-prāpti* of the skillful roots and the arising of their *asamanvāgama-prāpti* — this is what is called 'cutting off'. If the *prāpti* of the skillful roots are non-existent, at that time the skillful roots are said to have been cut off.

More precisely, in abandoning a defilement, the ceasing of the *prāpti* of this defilement is followed by the arising of the *prāpti* of the disconnection (*visaṃyoga-prāpti*) with that defilement as well as the *aprāpti* of the same defilement; the latter is as important as the former since it ensures the disconnection with that defilement. The necessary co-operation of *prāpti* and *aprāpti* in this process is compared to the two successive actions contributing to the definite removal of a thief from the house — the throwing out of the thief immediately followed by the shutting of the door.[79] Two moments are therefore necessary in the Sarvāstivāda doctrine of the abandoning of a defilement:

> The first, known as the *ānantarya-mārga,* is the receptivity that actually 'cuts off' or abandons the defilement.
>
> The second, known as the *vimukti-mārga,* is knowledge proper which induces the *prāpti* of the fruit of disconnection — i.e., in this moment, the actual cessation (*pratisaṃkhyā-nirodha*) of the defilement is realized or acquired (*prāpta*).

The MVŚ[80] argues that if *asamanvāgama* (= *aprāpti*) were not a real entity (but merely a name as some masters assert), the cutting/abandoning of defilements cannot be spoken of (lit: conceptualized; *prajñapyate*):

For, when the noble paths arise, they do not cut off (or abandon) the defilements in the manner that a knife cuts off a thing or that a stone grinds a thing. They merely cut off the *prāpti* of connection (*saṃyoga*) [with the defilements] and realize (*sākṣāt-√kṛ*) the *prāpti* of disconnection, causing the arising of the *asamanvāgama* (= *aprāpti*) of the defilements. This is what is known as the cutting off of defilements.

12.9.2.1. An abandonment is done once for all

Once a particular counteracting path — an outflow-free knowledge — abandons a given defilement, it is done once and for all. There is no partial abandoning, and the abandonment is not repeated.[81] However, the *prāpti* of disjunction — i.e., the *pratisaṃkhyā-nirodha* — from the defilement can take place repeatedly.[82] This of course does not entail that a *nirodha*, which is unconditioned, can change qualitatively; only that the practitioner's attainment of it can be firmer and firmer or deeper and deeper as he progresses.

The afore-mentioned principle is summarized in the following line of a stanza in the AKB:

> Destruction [of a defilement] is at once. The obtainment of disjunction from them is again and again. (*sakṛt kṣayaḥ visaṃyogalābhas teṣāṃ punaḥ punaḥ*) (AKB, v, 63ab)[83]

Saṃghabhadra explains:[84]

> As a result of acquiring the unhindered path (*ānantarya-mārga*) pertaining to them, the defilements to be abandoned are completely abandoned at once. Apart from [the case of] retrogression, there can be no further abandonment subsequently. Once [a defilement] has been abandoned, any further abandonment becomes futile.

[On the other hand,] although the acquired disjunction (*visaṃyoga* = *nirodha*) does not become progressively superior following the paths [of advancement, *viśeṣa-mārga*], nevertheless as the paths advance, there can be the further arising of the *prāpti* which is superior. As the *prāpti* of disjunction is included in the path, when the path is relinquished or acquired, it too comes to be relinquished or acquired. Thus it is that there can be the repeated acquisition of the disjunctions.

12.9.3. Abandonment by the worldly path

The view of the 'abrupt-abandonment *śramaṇa*-s' quoted above (§ 12.7) implies that there is no possibility of an ordinary worldling abandoning any defilement. The Dārṣṭāntikas categorically assert that this is in fact the case. In his spiritual struggle, a worldling can only temporarily suppress his active *paryavasthāna*-s; the latent defilements have not been abandoned in an absolute manner (*atyantam*): by means of the worldly paths he hangs on to the first *dhyāna*, away from the attachment to the sphere of sensuality. In this way, gradually he hangs on up to the *naiva-saṃjñā-nāsaṃjñāyatana*, away from the attachment to the *ākiṃcanyāyatana* whence he cannot get away — there being no upper stage to hang on to. This is compared to an insect (or a man) climbing up a plant: it hangs onto an upper part leaving behind the lower part; but when it reaches the highest point, it necessarily retrogresses as there is nothing higher up to hang onto.[85]

As opposed to the Dārṣṭāntikas, however, the Sarvāstivādins maintain that a worldly path (*laukika-mārga*) entailing a with-outflow understanding is also capable of counteracting defilements of both types, those abandonable by insight and those abandonable by cultivation. As a matter of fact, even an *ārya* may occasionally make use of such a path.[86] Accordingly, when a *pṛthagjana* becomes an *ārya*, he does not need to again abandon the same defilements that he has earlier abandoned by the worldly path. Thus, if a practitioner has abandoned sufficient categories of defilements by the worldly paths prior to entering the *darśana-mārga*, he can skip the stage of stream-entry (*śrotaāpatti*) and plunge directly into that of either *sakṛdāgāmin* or *anāgāmin*.[87]

But there is some limitation: A *pṛthagjana* can abandon the *darśana-* and *bhāvanā-heya* defilements pertaining to all the spheres from *kāmadhātu* up to *naiva-saṃjñā-nāsaṃjñāyatana* only but not those pertaining to *bhavāgra* which are completely abandoned only when the *vajropama-samādhi* is produced.[88] Moreover, even if a worldling can abandon all the defilements that can possibly be abandoned by a worldly path of cultivation, he still remains a worldling. He must enter into the path of insight — into direct insight — in order to become an *ārya*. In other words, the worldly path of cultivation can only become effective by the path of insight: He does not have to abandon them again; but the disjunctions from these defilements that he has acquired by the worldly path must be re-acquired by means of the outflow-free knowledges in direct insight.[89]

The AKB states that all beings, *ārya*-s and *pṛthagjana*-s alike, are endowed with (*samanvāgata*) the *pratisaṃkhyā-nirodha*-s, excepting those who are *sakala-bandhana-ādikṣaṇastha*-s and the *sakala-bandhana-pṛthagjana*-s.[90] This is another expression of the tenet that even a *pṛthagjana* can acquire the cessation of defilements. A *sakala-bandhana-ādikṣaṇastha* is an *ārya* who has not yet abandoned any defilement — and hence is still 'bound with all bondages' — at the first moment (*duḥkhe dharma-jñāna-kṣānti*) of his entering the *darśana-mārga*;[91] a *sakala-bandhana-pṛthagjana* is a worldling who has not abandoned any of the nine categories of defilements pertaining to the sphere of sensuality by means of the worldly path.

12.9.3.1. Unhindered paths and paths of liberation of a worldling and an *ārya*

Although both worldlings and *ārya*-s can abandon defilements, there are differences concerning how their defilements are abandoned. Various views are found in the MVŚ:

> Question: When a worldling and an *ārya* gain detachment from the nine grades of defilement of a certain stage, by how many unhindered paths and paths of liberation do they acquire the detachment?
>
> According to some: A worldling is detached from the nine grades of defilement by only three unhindered paths and three paths of liberation. That is: he is detached from the three higher grades of defilement by the lower grade of the unhindered path and the path of liberation; he is detached from the three middle grades of defilement by the middle grade of the unhindered path and the path of liberation; he is detached from the three lower grades of defilement by the higher grade of the unhindered path and the path of liberation. The same applies in the case of an *ārya*.
>
> According to other masters: A worldling is detached from the nine grades of defilements all at once by one grade of the unhindered path and the path of liberation. An *ārya* is detached gradually from the nine grades of defilements by nine grades of the unhindered paths and the paths of liberation. Why? The path of a worldling is blunt, and cannot differentiate the cognizable and abandonables into nine grades. Thus, he abandons them all at once by one grade of the path. The path of an *ārya* is sharp and can properly differentiate the cognizable and abandonables into nine grades. Thus, he abandons them gradually by nine grades of the path.
>
> Comment: They should not explain thus. If they explain thus in order to show that a worldling is inferior to an *ārya*, they will end up showing the opposite — an *ārya* is inferior to a worldling. If a worldling is detached from the nine grades of defilement by a single grade of the path, and an

ārya is detached from the nine grades of defilement by nine grades of the path, is it not that an *ārya* is inferior to a worldling? This is like the case that one who, having taken a lot of poisons, can vomit them all out by taking just a little medicine — is it not wonderful? It should be explained thus: whether a worldling or an *ārya*, he is detached from nine grades of defilement by nine grades of the unhindered paths and the paths of liberation.

Question: If so, what is the difference between the case of a worldling and that of an *ārya*?

Answer: In the case of a worldling, by means of nine grades of the unhindered paths and the paths of liberation, he bundles together the fetters to be abandoned by insight and by cultivation into nine grades. Like the way of cutting grass, the different grades are abandoned all at once. In the case of an *ārya*, by means of a single unhindered path and a single path of liberation, he abandons the nine grades of defilements abandonable by insight all at once; by means of nine unhindered paths and nine paths of liberation, he abandons gradually the nine grades of defilement abandonable by cultivation. This is the difference between the case of a worldling and that of an *ārya*.[92]

12.9.4. Various synonyms in the process of gradual abandonment

There are as many abandonments as there are with-outflow objects,[93] and complete freedom from *duḥkha* must be gained by gradually and systematically abandoning the defilements and realizing the corresponding cessation (*nirodha*). Repudiating the view of the "abrupt-abandonment *śramaṇa*-s" (頓斷沙門) who hold the view that the *śrāmaṇya-phala* is acquired by "abrupt awakening" (頓覺), the MVŚ states that "there are 89 different stages in the abandonment of the defilements, for in all these stages there is the realization of *nirodha*".[94] Depending on the specific stage of progress at which a corresponding amount of defilements is abandoned:

The abandonment in its intrinsic nature [is given various names] — 'abandonment' (*prahāṇa*), 'disjunction' (*visaṃyoga*), 'cessation' (*nirodha*), 'truth' (*satya*), 'complete knowledge' (*parijñā*), 'fruit of the spiritual life' (*śrāmaṇya-phala*), 'sphere of *nirvāṇa* with a remnant of substratum' (*sopadhiśeṣa-nirvāṇa-dhātu*), and 'sphere of *nirvāṇa* without a remnant of substratum' (*nirupadhiśeṣa-nirvāṇa-dhātu*). These eight types [of synonyms] may or may not apply in full in the different stages. Thus, when the receptivity to the knowledge of *dharma* with regard to *duḥkha* (*duḥkhe dharma-jñāna-kṣānti*) ceases and the knowledge of *dharma* with regard to *duḥkha* arises, that abandonment acquired is called 'abandonment', 'disjunction', 'cessation', 'truth'; [but] it is not yet called 'complete knowledge', not yet called 'fruit of the spiritual life', not yet called 'sphere of *nirvāṇa* with a remnant of substratum', not yet called 'sphere of *nirvāṇa* without a remnant of substratum'… . [In this way, finally,] when [the practitioner] is dissociated from the ninth [— final —] grade of bond, the *vajropama-samādhi* (in which whatever defilements remaining are eradicated without any trace) having ceased and the *anutpāda-jñāna* having first arisen, that abandonment [of defilement] acquired receives [all the names except] 'sphere of *nirvāṇa* without a remnant of substratum'… When the *skandha*-s, *āyatana*-s and *dhātu*-s of an *arhat* cease and continue no further, and he has entered into the 'sphere of *nirvāṇa* without a remnant of substratum', [the abandonment receives all the names except] 'sphere of *nirvāṇa* with a remnant of substratum'.[95] (Cf. *infra*, § 16.2).

12.9.5. Methods of abandonment

Although it is often stated that a defilement is abandoned by a complete knowledge of its object, this is not the only method to abandon defilements. The Sarvāstivāda speaks of the following four methods — the first three for the defilements which are *darśana-heya*; the last, for those which are *bhāvanā-heya*:[96]

I ***ālambana-parijñāna***: Complete understanding of the nature of the object due to which the defilement arises. This is applicable to the following defilements: (a) those under *duḥkha-* and *samudaya-satya* that are *sabhāga-dhātv-ālambana* (= *sabhāga-dhātu-sarvatraga*); (b) those under *nirodha-* and *mārga-satya* that are *anāsrava-ālambana* — namely *mithyā-dṛṣṭi*, *vicikitsā* and *avidyā*.[97]

Thus, for example, greed under *duḥkha-satya*, with regard to a beautiful object: one must have complete knowledge of the aspects pertaining to *duḥkha-satya* — *duḥkha*, *anitya*, etc. — in order to abandon it. As another example: doubt, under *nirodha-satya*, with regard to *nirvāṇa*: when all the aspects pertaining to *nirodha-satya* — *nirodha*, *śānta*, etc. — are fully understood, doubt is removed.

II ***tadālambana-saṃkṣaya***: The destruction of a defilement which is the object of another defilement along with the destruction of the latter (the subject). This is applicable to the defilements under *duḥkha-* and *samudaya-satya-*s, which are *visabhāga-dhātv-ālambana* (= *visabhāga-dhātu-sarvatraga*). These are objects of the defilements that are *sabhāga-dhātv-ālambana*. When the latter are destroyed, they are also destroyed. Saṃghabhadra explains as follows:

> This refers to the *visabhāga-dhātvālambana* defilements pertaining to the sphere of sensuality. For, the *sabhāga-dhātv-ālambana* defilements pertaining to the sphere of sensuality which are *duḥkha-* and *samudaya-darśana-heya* take them as objects — these defilements serve as their support; when the support is abandoned, they are also abandoned accordingly. It is like a weak patient who stands with the help of some support; when the support is removed, he falls down accordingly. How can [these *sabhāga-dhātv-ālambana* defilements] serve as their support? Because these can serve as their causes.[98]

III ***ālambana-prahāṇa***: The abandonment of a defilement that takes as object another defilement by abandoning the latter — the object. This is applied to the *sāsrava-ālambana* defilements which are *nirodha-* and *mārga-darśana-heya*. These take the defilements which are *anāsrava-ālambana* (i.e., *mithyā-dṛṣṭi*, *vicikitsā*, *avidyā*) as object. "This is like a weak patient who walks with the help of a stick; when his stick is taken away, he falls down accordingly."[99] Example: When doubt (*vicikitsā*) with regard to the path is the object of *śīlavrata-parāmarśa* — when the doubt is removed, the irrational attachment to rites and observances will also vanish along with it.

IV ***pratipakṣodaya***: The abandonment of a defilement on account of the arising of its counteragent. This is specifically applied to the defilements that are *bhāvanā-heya*.

When one grade of a counteragent (e.g., weak-weak) opposed to one grade of defilement (e.g., strong-strong) arises, that grade of defilement is abandoned. However, as Saṃghabhadra explains,[100] it is also applicable to the *darśana-heya* defilements since their abandonment too results from the arising of their counteragents. Counteraction is fourfold:[101]

(i) A counteragent resulting in abandonment (*prahāṇa-pratipakṣa*). That is, a counteracting path which directly abandons the *prāpti*-s of the defilements. This is the unhindered path (*ānantarya-mārga*).

(ii) A counteragent that effects the maintenance (*ādhāra-pratipakṣa*) of the abandoning so obtained. That is, the noble path which first arises together with the *prāpti* of abandonment. This is the path of liberation (*vimukti-mārga*). By virtue of the fact that such a path maintains the *prāpti* of abandonment (i.e., the abandonment acquired is maintained; *tatprāpitaṃ prahāṇam ādhāryate*), the *prāpti*-s of the defilements become incapable of arising further.

(iii) A counteragent that results in distancing (*dūrībhāva-pratipakṣa*). That is, this counteractive path which causes the *prāpti* of the defilement that has been cut, to be more distant (*chinna-prāpti-dūrīkaraṇāt*), i.e., to be removed. This is the path of distinction (*viśeṣa-mārga*), thus called because it is the path arisen subsequent — as an advancement — to the path of liberation. Even the *jāti,* etc., which are conascent with its *prāpti* also receive the name 'paths', as they cause the increase in the series of those *prāpti*-s that are opposed to the *prāpti*-s of the defilements.

(iv) A counteragent that finds disgust (*vidūṣaṇā-pratipakṣa*). That is, the path by which the practitioner — seeing, from various perspectives, the faults in whichever sphere and stage where the counteragent arises — generates deep disgust. This is, in the main, the preparatory path (*prayoga-mārga*).[102]

Vasubandhu here proposes the following order as the correct one:[103]

(i) *vidūṣaṇā-pratipakṣa* constitutes the preparatory path (*prayoga-mārga*);

(ii) *prahāṇa-pratipakṣa* constitutes the whole of the unhindered path (*ānantarya-mārga*);

(iii) *ādhāra-pratipakṣa* constitutes the path of liberation (*vimukti-mārga*);

(iv) *dūrībhāva-pratipakṣa* constitutes the path of distinction (*viśeṣa-mārga*).

12.9.6. A defilement is abandoned through separation from its object

In the Ny[104] the question is raised: Through separation from what does the absolute abandonment of a defilement result? Is it from (i) its intrinsic nature (*svabhāvāt*), or (ii) its conjunction (*saṃprayogāt*)

— i.e., its conjoined (*saṃprayukta*) *dharma*-s such as sensations, etc., or (iii) its object (*ālambanāt*)?

(i) is not possible since the intrinsic nature can never be relinquished. (ii) also is impossible, for the conjoined *dharma*-s are mutually cause to one another (they constitute the *saṃprayuktaka-hetu*), and their nature of being (conjoined) causes will always remain. Moreover, a *citta* that becomes defiled as a result of (conjunction with) a given defilement will never become undefiled. Neither is (iii) possible: a *dharma* which is taken as an object by that defilement will always remain as its object.

The MVŚ explains the Sarvāstivāda position, which is that abandonment results from separation from the object:[105]

> One speaks of an *anuśaya* as being abandoned when, by the force of its counteragent, it will no longer give rise to any fault with regard to the object. This is like the case of a person restraining his son from further visits to a drinking house, a house of prostitution or a gambling house, etc. It is impossible that an *anuśaya* can be made to separate from its conjoined *dharma*-s.

In the Ny, Saṃghabhadra explains more elaborately:[106]

> The absolute abandonment of defilements definitely results from [separation from] their objects, for it is by the force of the complete knowledge (*ālambana-parijñāna-balena*) of the objects that the defilements are absolutely abandoned. …
>
> There are two types of objects of the *anuśaya*: *saṃyoga-vastu* (i.e., *sāsrava* objects) and *asaṃyoga-vastu* (i.e., *anāsrava* objects). The *prāpti*-s of the defilements that take the *saṃyoga-vastu*-s as objects and of those that are produced by the former type of defilements [but] not taking such objects, continue uninterruptedly in the present series of a sentient being even when his *citta* is presently non-defiled, constituting the effects and the causes of past and future defilements, [respectively]. Likewise are the *prāpti*-s of

those defilements that take the *asaṃyoga-vastu*-s as objects, and of those that do not take such objects and that are produced by these defilements, coming into activity following these defilements. By 'constituting the effects and the causes of past and future defilements' is meant: This *prāpti* existing at the present is the emanation (*niṣyanda*) effect of the past defilements — hence 'effect', and is the condition for the arising of future defilements — hence 'cause'.

But this *prāpti* is opposed to the coming into activity of the *prāpti* (both *prāpti* are plural in Xuan Zang's translation) which is the emanation from the *prahāṇa-pratipakṣa* for those [defilements] (*tat-prahāṇa-pratipakṣa-niṣyanda-prāpti-samavadhāna-viruddhā*), for it sustains (*ā-√dhā*) the past and future defilements that are acquired [by virtue of it], so that the defilements, on account of which object they are arisen, set into motion defilements which take other objects (*ato yen' ālambanenotpannāḥ kleśā any' ālambanān api kleśān pravartayanti*). When the emanations of the *prahāṇa-pratipakṣa* bearing on this object arise, the *prāpti* of the defilements is terminated. The acquired defilements, although still existing as entities, are said to be abandoned with respect to their objects on account of the absolute termination of the *prāpti* constituting their causes and effects. For, when a certain object has not been completely known, the *prāpti*-s — constituting the effects and causes of the past and future defilements — produced by the defilements which take this object and by the defilements produced by the force of these (former) defilements and taking other objects, arise uninterruptedly in the present series. When there is complete knowledge with regard to a certain object, the *prāpti* produced by the defilements does not continue any longer. Thus, it is known that the abandonment of a defilement definitely results from [the separation from] its object.[107]

It is to be noted that in the abandoning of a defilement, the counteracting noble path does not operate simultaneously with the defilement — the two being opposed in nature. Nevertheless, as a result of this path seeing the object in its aspects of being *duḥkha*, etc., the defilements bearing on this object are abandoned. The non-arising of the defilements results from the cessation of the *prāpti* constituting the effects and causes of defilements. Saṃghabhadra further illustrates this[108] by the example of a person bitten by a rat: Even when no fever or loss of consciousness is occurring, he is said to be a sick person on account of the presence of the poison which constitutes the causes for fever, etc. It is only by taking the *agada* medicine which counteracts the poison that he can be said to be free from the sickness. Although the *agada* and the sickness of fever, etc., are not present simultaneously in the body, the *agada* is said to eradicate the sickness since it is on account of its power that the poison within the body is eradicated so that fever, etc., do not arise any longer.

12.10. Traces (*vāsanā*) of the defilements and distinction between the wisdom of a Buddha and of an *arhat*[109]

12.10.1. Distinction between defilements and their traces (*vāsanā*)

We have seen that both the Pāli commentarial tradition and the northern Abhidharma tradition had come to emphasize the superiority of the Buddha's wisdom in contrast to that of the two *yāna*-s (the disciples and the *pratyeka-buddha*) (*supra*, § 10.4.1, § 10.4.4).

In the case of the Pāli tradition, this difference is accounted for mainly in terms of the notion of the distinction between *kilesa* and *vāsanā*. The Theravāda explanations on this distinction, however, are essentially the same as those in the Sarvāstivāda tradition, except that the Sarvāstivāda articulately connects the notion of *vāsanā* with that of the undefiled ignorance (§ 10.4). For both traditions, *vāsanā* constitutes the subtle traces that are left behind even after the defilements have been abandoned. Whereas a defilement is voluntary and kammically retributive, *vāsanā* is conceived of as being involuntary influences of past habits, morally neutral and non-retributive. A Buddha's superior wisdom is then accounted for by the doctrine that the Buddha alone can completely abandon the defilements together with their *vāsanā* (cf.: *na hi bhagavantaṃ ṭhapetvā aññe saha vāsanāya kilese pahatuṃ sakkonti*).[110] In the case of the Sarvāstivāda, it is said that the Buddha alone is completely freed from the non-defiled ignorance, and with this his *vāsanā* too is exhausted.

The following definition of *vāsanā*, given in the *Udānaṭṭhakathā,* is illustrative of such notions:

> And what is this so-called *vāsanā*? They say that it is a tendency of this nature: A mere potency in the continuum of even one who has removed the defilements, deposited by the defilements which have been practiced from beginningless time, and which have become the cause for behavior similar to the behavior of those who have not yet abandoned the defilements. This is not found in the Fortunate One's continuum where the defilements are abandoned by virtue of the abandoning of the knowable-hindrance on account of the 'perfection of resolution'. But where the defilements are not abandoned in this manner, it exists in the continua of the *sāvaka* and the *pacceka-budddha*. For this reason, it is only the Tathāgata who is unhindered in knowledge and vision.[111]

A Sarvāstivāda definition on *vāsanā*, given by Bhadanta Anantavarman, is found in the Vy:

> What is this so-called *vāsanā* of the *śrāvaka*-s? That specific potency which is a cause of distortion in bodily and vocal actions, existing in the thought of one who has previously committed a given act of defilement, created by that defilement, is called *vāsanā*. The *vāsanā* is a specific thought that is morally non-defined.[112]

Saṃghabhadra informs us of another definition given by "some ancient masters":

> There exists a distinct non-defiled *caitta* which is induced by the repeated practice of defiled and non-defiled *dharma*-s. It arises in the series of one who is not an omniscient, so that the *citta-caitta*-s do not operate freely. This is called *vāsanā*.[113]

These two Sarvāstivādin definitions, while agreeing in their essentials, are not entirely the same in detail. Anantavarman says that the *vāsanā* is a *citta-viśeṣa*, whereas the ancient masters say it is a *caitta-viśeṣa*. Moreover, the former speaks of them as being induced by defilements, whereas the latter, by both defiled and non-defiled *dharma*-s. Such a difference in relatively secondary points, however, does not necessarily amount to a contradiction between the two definitions.

12.10.2. Examples of *vāsanā* in the MVŚ

The MVŚ offers no formal definition of *vāsanā*. But there are sufficient descriptions of its visible effect on the *arhat*-s, from which we may derive a clear understanding of the Vaibhāṣika version of the notion which is essentially the same as what we read in the Pali *ṭīkā* (see § 12.10.1).

In the case of the Buddha, his *vāsanā* is completely abandoned, even though He occasionally uses words that may appear to be tainted with defilements — 'semblance of greed' (*rāga-sadṛśa*), 'semblance of hatred' (*dveṣa-sadṛśa*), 'semblance of delusion' (*moha-sadṛśa*), 'semblance of conceit' (*māna-sadṛśa*), etc.[114] To explain that these are not cases of *vāsanā*, — semblances and not actually defilements — the MVŚ compilers take pain to relate at length the *nidāna* for each of such episodes, showing that in such cases, the Buddha was actually consciously employing appropriate expedients to help the practitioners along.[115]

The case of the two *yāna*-s is quite different. Their acts resembling defilements are involuntary — and therefore morally non-defined; they are due to the conditioning of *vāsanā*. The two *yāna*-s are helpless against such "semblances of defilements". Étienne Lamotte, in one of his papers, gives examples of the *arhat*-s' *vāsanā,* although mainly from the Mahāyāna sources.[116] But there are many similar examples in the MVŚ.

> The most oft-cited one (by the Pali *ṭīkā* as well) is that of Pilindavatsa (Pali: Pilindavaccha), who by the force of his *vāsanā*, often calls others *vṛṣala* ("little man"). Thus, he shouts at the Ganga god: "O you *vṛṣala*! Stop the flow! I want to cross over." This is an example of *vāsanā* of hatred.[117]
>
> Ānanda has a "weakness" for the Śākya — he feels tender toward them. This is an example of *vāsanā* of greed (*loc. cit.*).
>
> Śāriputra throws away the medicine. This is an example of *vāsanā* of conceit.
>
> The Venerable Gavaṃpati always coughs before eating. He keeps on eating even knowing that he has not digested what has been eaten. This is an example of *vāsanā* of delusion (*loc. cit.*).
>
> Another example is given of an elephant who used to carry the Buddha's relic (*dhātu*) to Kāśmīra. By the merit of this, he was born a man and eventually became an *arhat*. When he was an elephant, he used to have merely one grain measure for his meal. After becoming an *arhat*, he continued to be able to fill himself up by eating merely one grain measure of food. This is a special *dharma* acquired by virtue of the *vāsanā* of his habit of eating as an elephant.[118]

12.10.3. Description in the AKB and the Vy

In the AKB, we find only two brief mentions of *vāsanā* in this sense, and these in the same chapter:[119]

(1) The 18 *āveṇika-dharma*-s of the Buddha are *āveṇika* (unique) because He has abandoned the defilements along with their *vāsanā* (*sa-vāsanam*).

(2) The Buddha's perfection as regards the abandoning of defilements (*prahāṇa-saṃpad*) is fourfold:

(I) He has abandoned all defilements (*sarvakleśa-prahāṇa*);
(II) He has abandoned them absolutely (*atyanta-prahāṇa*);
(III) He has abandoned them along with their *vāsanā* (*savāsanaprahāṇa*);
(IV) He has abandoned all hindrances to the attainment of *samādhi* (*sarva-samādhi-samāpattyāvaraṇaprahāṇa*).

For the Vaibhāṣika, the last (IV) aspect refers to the abandoning of *akliṣṭa-ajñāna*. (See *supra*, § 10.4.3).

12.10.4. *Vāsanā* and the two types of *ajñāna* in the Sarvāstivāda

The MVŚ distinguishes two kinds of false knowledges (*mithyā-jñāna*) — defiled and non-defiled:[120]

Question: What is this false knowledge?

Answer: This is the non-veiled-non-defined knowledge, to be abandoned by cultivation and pertaining to the sense sphere, and which has a false mode of understanding (邪行相, *mithyākāra*). Thus, it generates such thoughts as a man with regard to a post or a post with regard to a man, and of a path (*mārga*) with regard to a non-path (*amārga*), and a non-path with regard to a path…

> [As a matter of fact,] there are two kinds false knowledge: 1. defiled, 2. non-defiled. The defiled one is conjoined with nescience (*avidyā*), the non-defiled one, such as that which generates the thought of a man with regard to a post, is not.
>
> As for the defiled one, both the *śrāvaka*-s and the *pratyeka-buddha*-s can abandon it completely, as well as render it incapable of manifesting (*sam-ud-ā-√car*). As for the non-defiled one, although it can be completely abandoned by the *śrāvaka*-s and the *pratyeka-buddha*-s, it can still manifest in them.
>
> It is only in the case of the Tathāgata that it absolutely does not manifest any more, as He has permanently abandoned the defilements as well as the *vāsanā*-s. It is for this reason that He alone is called the Perfectly Completely Enlightened One (*samyak saṃbuddha*). The defiled false knowledge is a false knowledge from the absolute (*paramārtha*) standpoint. The non-defiled false knowledge is a false knowledge from the conventional (*saṃvṛti*) standpoint, not from the absolute standpoint, since it is not associated with the false *dharma*-s (*mithyā-dharma*) of defilement.

The non-defiled false view, which is here said to be a false view only from the conventional standpoint and not conjoined with those of defilement, is a mode of what is doctrinally articulated as the non-defiled ignorance. This passage also suggests the close relationship between this non-defiled ignorance and *vāsanā*, as it states that the Tathāgata, by permanently abandoning the defilements and the *vāsanā*-s, can render the non-defiled ignorance absolutely incapable of re-arising.

12.10.5. *Vāsanā*, non-defiled ignorance and perfect wisdom

When the knowable-hindrance (*jñeya-āvaraṇa*), the essence of which is the non-defiled ignorance (cf., § 10.4.3), is removed, omniscience is attained. For the Vaibhāṣika, this omniscience is not just a state of perfect wisdom. It represents a real, potent, counteractive force which arises at the time of attaining the supreme perfect enlightenment (*anuttarā samyak sambodhi*), counteracting the *vāsanā* and non-defiled ignorance. It is on account of this force that the defilement of the Buddha-to-be is utterly shattered without any trace.[121] In explaining why the Buddha's abandoning of defilement, unlike the two *yāna*-s', leaves no trace (*vāsanā*) behind, the MVŚ says:

> The wisdom fire of the *śrāvaka*-s and *pratyeka-buddha*-s is not fierce. [With it,] although the defilement is abandoned, the *vāsanā* remains. It is like the case of ordinary fire in the world: although it can consume a thing, it leaves behind ashes. The Buddha's wisdom is fierce; it consumes the defilement without leaving behind any *vāsanā*, like the fire at the end of time which consumes everything in its way leaving no ash behind.[122]

The function of perfect knowledge — in the spiritual sense or wisdom, as opposed to mere intellectual understanding — for the liberation from defilement is in fact a doctrine fundamental to Buddhism. As we have seen above, a term which emphasizes this is "complete knowledge" (§ 12.1); in the technical terminology of the Sarvāstivāda, the abandonment of defilement (*kleśa-prahāṇa*) is a fruit of knowledge (*jñāna-phala*).[123] The defilements, on account of which beings are bonded to *saṃsāra*, have their ultimate source in ignorance. Stated in terms of the doctrine of the two-fold ignorance, the defiled ignorance is the cognitive basis for defiled actions, and the non-defiled ignorance is that for actions which, although involuntary and not defiled in nature, bear resemblance to defiled actions and which prevent the totalistic vision of all knowables. While both *vāsanā* and non-defiled ignorance are differentiated from defilement, they are nonetheless intrinsically related to it. As we have seen (§ 10.4.4), Saṃghabhadra offers articulate explanations on the relationship between defilement on the one hand and non-defiled ignorance and *vāsanā* on the other.

The following discussion in the MVŚ explains that the comparatively inferior wisdom of the two *yāna*-s can be understood as due to the hindrance of *vāsanā* or non-defiled ignorance:

> Question: Why is it that the knowledge in the Tathāgata is designated as a power (*bala*), and not those in the *śrāvaka*-s and the *pratyekabuddha*-s ?
>
> Answer: A power is that which cannot be overcome and hindered. The knowledge in the *śrāvaka*-s and the *pratyekabuddha*-s can still be overcome by ignorance (*ajñāna*) and is hindered, hence it is not called a power. …
>
> Question: Since there is no difference in respect of the exhaustion of outflows (*āsrava-kṣaya*) among the three *yāna*-s, why is it that the knowledge of the exhaustion of the outflows (*āsrava-kṣaya-jñāna*) of the two *yāna*-s are not powers?
>
> Answer: The Buddha's knowledge of the exhaustion of the outflows is superior and sharp; those of the *śrāvaka*-s and the *pratyekabuddha*-s are no match for it. Although the [knowledge of the exhaustion of the outflows of the Buddha as well as those of the two *yāna*-s] can both exhaust the outflows, there is a difference in speed. This is like the case of two persons, each cutting down a tree. One is strong and uses a sharp axe, the other has inferior strength and uses a blunt axe. While each cuts down a tree, one does it faster than the other. For this reason, the Buddha's knowledge of the exhaustion of the outflows is designated as a power, not those of the two *yāna*-s. Furthermore, the knowledge of the two *yāna*-s is not called power even though it can exhaust the outflows, on account of the presence of *vāsanā*.[124]

12.10.6. Saṃghabhadra's explanation of *vāsanā*

On *vāsanā*, Saṃghabhadra[125] offers an explanation (cf. another explanation of his in § 10.4.4) according to which the mechanism whereby *vāsanā* results from defilement is somewhat complex:

At the stage when beings are still in possession of defilements, all their non-defiled *citta*-s, together with their series, are perfumed by defilements which intervene them, giving rise to impregnations (氣分, to be distinguished as a term from *vāsanā*, 習氣) which accord with the arising of defilements. Accordingly, special non-defiled *citta*-s and their retinue arise, operating in a manner similar to that of the [defilements]. They arise successively by virtue of the force of repeated conditioning, and for this reason those without faults [i.e., the *ārya-pudgala*-s] are still said to be in possession of *vāsanā*. In the case of the Omniscient One, it is permanently abandoned and does not manifest (*sam-ud-ā-√car*) any longer.

At the stage when one has already abandoned the [defilements] abandonable by insight, in the mental series which may be defiled or non-defiled, there remain habitual conditionings (習性) which accord with the arising of defilements. These are impregnations of defilements abandonable by insight. Among them, the defiled ones are called "nature/type" (類性) and are totally abandoned, without any possibility of manifesting, by the diamond-like (*vajropama*) path. Those that are non-defiled are called "*vāsanā* of defilements abandonable by insight". These are also abandoned by the same path; but they may or may not manifest, depending on the [practitioner's] faculty.

At the stage at which one has already abandoned the [defilements] abandonable by cultivation, it is only in the non-defiled mental series that there remain impregnations, acquired through practice, which accord with the arising of defilements. These are impregnations of defilements abandonable by cultivation and are called "*vāsanā* of defilements abandonable by cultivation". Being with-outflow, they have already been abandoned in the case of the non-trainee. But they may or may not manifest, depending on whether the [non-trainee's] faculty is superior or inferior. As the Bhagavat has acquired mastery over the *dharma*-s, such

> [*vāsanā*-s], just like the defilements, absolutely never manifest. It is for this reason that the Buddha alone is called the Skillful Series (*kuśala-santati*). On this very account, He has no lapses in his conduct and acquires the three *smṛty-upasthāna*-s and other unique *dharma*-s. It is a also on this very account that it is implicitly declared that the Buddha alone is said to be one who has acquired the fruition of non-trainee.

Saṃghabhadra's explanations may be considered to be more articulate regarding the dispositional forces induced by defilements. According to him, the impregnations or habitual conditioning forces induced by defilements may be defiled or non-defiled. But it is only the latter that is called *vāsanā*. This *vāsanā*-s is divisible into two types: (1) *vāsanā* of defilements which are abandonable by insight, (2) *vāsanā* of defilements which are abandonable by cultivation. The first type is abandoned by the diamond-like path. As for the second type, even though it has already been abandoned by an *arhat*, it may or may not manifest, depending on the faculty of the *arhat*. In the case of the Buddha, it can never manifest.

NOTES

[1] *Cf.* Cox (1992a), 67.

[2] *āsavehi cittaṃ vimuttam* — M, no. 112, 3, 30.

[3] E.g., Ny, 430b.

[4] In the Theravāda tradition, three types of *pariññā* are spoken of: *ñāta/ñāṇa-pariññā*, *pahāna-pariññā* and *tīraṇa-pariññā*. But these are found only in the exegetical literature.

[5] MVŚ, 175a–b.

[6] See MVŚ, 320c; AKB, 322 f.

[7] MVŚ, 244a, 417c (on *upakleśa*).

[8] *Entrance*, 108.

[9] E.g.: PrŚ, 693c; AKB, 312: *ye yāvat kleśā upakleśā api te* /

[10] AKB, 312.

[11] AKB, 308; PrŚ, 702a.

[12] *Cf.* MVŚ, 257a–b; ADV, 220; Ny, 641c.

[13] Ny, 641c.

[14] *Entrance*, 104.

[15] AKB, 308.

[16] Ny, 641c.

[17] *Entrance*, 104; AKB, 308; Ny, 641c.

[18] Ny, 641c.

[19] MVŚ, 257a–b; see also *Entrance*, Introduction § VII.

[20] *Cf. Saḷāyatana Saṃyutta, Samudda vagga* 5 and 6, (S 35, 191): "*seyyathāpi āvuso kālo ca balivaddo odāto ca balivaddo ekena dāmena vā yottena vā saṃyuttā assu … na kho āvuso kālo balivaddo odātassa balivaddassa saṃyojanaṃ, na pi odāto balivaddo kālassa balivaddassa saṃyojanaṃ, yena ca kho te ekena dāmena vā yottena vā saṃyuttā tam tattha saṃyojanam. evameva kho āvuso na cakkhu rūpānam saṃyojanam, na rūpā cakkhussa saṃyojanam yañ ca tadubhayam paṭicca uppajjati chandarāgo tam tattha saṃyojanam.*" This *sūtra* is quoted by both Skandhila (*cf. Entrance*, 102) and Saṃghabhadra (Ny, 642c) for the explanation of 'connection'.

[21] MVŚ, 237c.

[22] For item-wise explanations, see AKB, 309 ff.; *Entrance*, 97 ff.

[23] MVŚ, 252b.

[24] *Cf.* AKB, 310 f. Also see *infra*, § 16.

[25] PrŚ, 693b; so also Ny, 644b.

[26] *Entrance*, 102. Same three given in AKB, 311.

[27] Ny, 644b.

[28] PrŚ, 693c; AKB, 312.

[29] *Entrance*, 111.

[30] Ny, 646a.

[31] *Cf.* AKB, 308: *āsayanti saṃsāre āsravanti bhavāgrād yāvad avīciṃ ṣaḍbhir āyatanavraṇair ity āsravāḥ* / Also cf. ADV, 220: *ābhavāgram upādāya yāvad avīciṃ sravanti srāvayanti vā citta-santatim ity āsravāḥ* /

[32] AKB, 308; *Entrance*, 112 f.

[33] AKB, 308: *evaṃ tu sādhīyaḥ syād āsravaty ebhiḥ saṃtatir viṣayeṣv ity āsravāḥ* /

[34] MVŚ, 244a–b.

[35] MVŚ, 247a. *Cf. Entrance*, 113: "They are given the name floods as they make the good things of beings drift away, as does a flood." Also cf. AKB, 308: *harantīty oghāḥ* /

[36] AKB, 308.

[37] ADV, 220.

[38] *Cf. Entrance*, 113. Also cf. MVŚ, 247b.

[39] *Cf.* MVŚ, 247c — all three meanings in *Avatāra* are also among those given here in MVŚ.

[40] *Entrance*, 115.

[41] *Entrance*, 115, 215 notes 434 and 435.

[42] MVŚ, 248c.

[43] AKB, 318. *Cf. Entrance*, 115 f.

[44] *Entrance*, 115 f. Likewise, Ny, 648c; *cf.* MVŚ, 249c.

[45] MVŚ, 249c; the reason for the order of enumeration is also given (250c).

[46] MVŚ, 194c–195a. Anuruddha's *Abhidhammattha-saṃgaha* also adds *avijjā* as the sixth — see Bhikkhu Bodhi, ed., *A Comprehensive Manual of Abhidhamma* (Kandy,1993), 267.

[47] AKB, 277; Vy, 441.

[48] AKB, 306 f.

[49] Vy, 442: *satpathād udvartayati viparīta-daiśika-saṃsevā'bhimukhī-karaṇāt* — 'it causes one to leave the true path, for it makes one inclined toward associating with erroneous teachers'.

[50] Ny, 596a–b; The almost identical Sanskrit cited here given in Vy, 442, where the 16 functions are mentioned and attributed to 'another person': *ṣodaśety anyaḥ* /

[51] Ny, 596b.

[52] E.g., see MVŚ, 181c; AKB, 248: *kuśalamūlacchedas tu mithyādṛṣṭyā bhavaty adhimātraparipūrṇayā* /

[53] AKB, 280.

[54] AKB, 328: *phala-bhūtā upadāna-skandhā duḥkhasatyam* /

[55] Ny, 611a. Xuan Zang's translation of AKB (AKB(C), 101c) contains these same three reasons, which is a more elaborate explanation of *sarvatraga* than AKB, 286 f.

[56] MVŚ, 465c. Also see below, § 10.

[57] MVŚ, 264b.

[58] MVŚ, 313a.

[59] *Cf.* the Yogācāra doctrine — e.g., in **Mahāyāna-saṃgraha* (T 31, 134c), etc. — that the seeds as potentialities in the *ālayavijñāna* are morally non-defined; and when they are manifested (*sam-ud-ā-√car*), they can become either *kuśala* or *akuśala*.

[60] AKB, 278.

[61] See *Study*, 335 ff.

[62] See Dhammajoti, KL, 'Sarvāstivāda, Dārṣṭāntika and Yogācāra — Some Reflections on their Interrelation', in JCBSSL, Vol. IV, 190 ff.

[63] See Yin Shun, (1974a), 130.

[64] For the philosophical implications of these different standpoints, see Yin Shun, *op. cit.*, 129–137.

[65] *Cf.* Ny, 641c.

[66] MVŚ, 313c. The MVŚ here quotes the PrŚ which speaks of these three sources for the arising of a defilement (PrŚ, 702c). *Cf.* AKB, 305: *aprahīṇād anuśayād viṣayāt pratyupasthitāt / ayoniśo manaskārāt kleśaḥ saṃpūrṇakāraṇaḥ* / Also cf. MVŚ, 990a.

[67] AKB, 306.

[68] MVŚ, 989c.

[69] *Cf.* MVŚ, 112c–113a.

[70] Ny, 616b.

[71] *Loc. cit.*; cf. AKB, 289 f.

[72] Ny, 637c.

[73] Ny, 616b.

[74] Ny, 616c.

[75] MVŚ, 113a–b.

[76] MVŚ, 312c.

[77] MVŚ, 479c.

[78] MVŚ, 182b.

[79] MVŚ, 333c; AKB, 352; etc.

[80] MVŚ, 796c–797a; cf. 479c.

[81] AKB, 321: *sarveṣāṃ hi kleśānāṃ sakṛt kṣayaḥ / yasya yaḥ prahāṇa-mārgas tenaiva tasya kṣayaḥ /*

[82] AKB, 321: *visaṃyoga-lābhas teṣāṃ punaḥ punaḥ /*

[83] AKB, 321. Xuan Zang (AKB(C), 111c) renders the lines thus: "There is no repeated abandonment of defilements. [But] there is the repeated acquisition of [their] disconnection." (諸惑無再斷, 離繫有重得).

[84] Ny, 652a.

[85] MVŚ, 264c.

[86] MVŚ, 264b–c, 465a: 諸異生能斷欲界乃至無所有處見修所斷隨眠, 唯除有頂.

[87] *Cf.* AKB, 353 f. See also *infra*, § 15.7.

[88] MVŚ, 465a; 335a–c.

[89] It is perhaps from this perspective that the compilers seem to be able to tolerate the view of the Bhadanta that "it is not possible for a worldling to abandon the *anuśaya*; he can only suppress the envelopment (*paryavasthāna*)". The compilers' response is: "There is no harm in terms of reasoning if one explains thus."

[90] AKB, 62. MVŚ, 290a–b: One 'bound with all bondage' is so called because he can be bound by any of the five categories of abandonables (*kleśa*), and *dharma*-s of the five categories are all bound.

[91] *Cf.* MVŚ, 282c, 478b.

[92] MVŚ, 328c.

[93] AKB, 4: *yāvanti hi saṃyogadravyāṇi tāvanti visaṃyogadravyāṇi* /

[94] MVŚ, 465c.

[95] MVŚ, 321b–322b.

[96] MVŚ, 114b; AKB, 319; Vy, 498; Ny, 649c ff.

[97] AKB, 288: *nirodhadarśana-prahātavyās trayo 'nuśayā mithyā-dṛṣṭir vicikitsā 'vidyā ca tābhyāṃ saṃprayuktā 'veṇikī ca / mārgadarśana-prahātavyā apy eta eva trayaḥ / ity ete ṣaḍ anāsravālambanāḥ / śeṣāḥ sāsravālambanā iti siddham /*

[98] Ny, 650a.

[99] Ny, 650a.

[100] Ny, 650c.

[101] Ny, *loc. cit.*

[102] In AKB, 320, Vasubandhu argues that the sequential order of the four paths should be: (iv) → (i) → (ii) → (iii); *cf.* MVŚ, 114b.

[103] AKB, 320: *api tv eṣām iyam ānupūrvī sādhvī bhavet…* /

[104] Ny, 651a.

[105] MVŚ, 113b–c.

[106] Ny, 651a–b.

[107] Saṃghabhadra's explanation is quoted in Vy, 500: *atr' ācārya-saṃghabhadraḥ pariharati / ālambanāt kleśāḥ prahātavyāḥ / ālambana-parijñāna-balena hi kleśāḥ prahīyante / dvividhaṃ cānuśay' ālaṃbanaṃ saṃyoga-vastu asaṃyoga-vastu ca / tatra saṃyoga-vastu-viṣayāṇām anuśayānāṃ tad-anuśaya-balotpāditānāṃ a-tad-viṣayāṇām api pudgalasya santāne prāptir akliṣṭa-cittasyāpy avichedena pravartate / anāgatātīta-kleśa-hetu-phala-bhūtā / evam asaṃyoga-vastu-viṣayāṇām a-tad-viṣayāṇām api ca tad-viṣaya-kleśa-pṛṣṭha-samudācariṇāṃ kleśānāṃ prāptir veditavyā / sā hy anāgatānām*

utpattau pratyaya-gamanād dhetu-bhūtā bhavati / atītānāṃ ca niṣyanda-bhāvāt phala-bhūtā / sā ca tat-prahāṇa-pratipakṣa-niṣyanda-prāpti-samavadhāna-viruddhā / tad-ādhāritatvāt kleśānām / ato yen' ālambanenotpannāḥ kleśā any' ālambananān api kleśān pravartayanti / tad-ālambana-prahāṇa-pratipakṣa-niṣyandotpattau tat-prāpti-vigame te kleśās tad-ālambanā api santo hetu-phalāpakrāntāḥ prahīṇā ity ucyante / tad yasmād aparijñāte kasmiṃścit kleśa-viṣaye a-tad-viṣayāṇām api kleśānāṃ tad-viṣaya-kleśa-balena prāptir anāgatātīta-kleśa-hetu-phala-bhūtā santatau pravartate yathā vastu / tasmād ālambanāt kleśāḥ prahātavyā ity abhimatam iti /

[108] Ny, 651b.

[109] For a detailed discussion of this topic, see Dhammajoti, KL, (1998a), 65 ff.

[110] *Visuddhimagga-mahāṭīkā*, 1.219; *Sāratthadīpanī-ṭīkā,* 1.217.

[111] UdA 194: *kā panāyaṃ vāsanā nāma? yaṃ kilesarahitassāpi santāne appahīna-kilesānaṃ samācārasadisasamācārahetubhūtaṃ, anādikālabhāvitehi kilesehi āhitaṃ sāmatthiyamattaṃ, tathārūpā adhimuttîti vadanti. taṃ panetaṃ abhinīhārasampattiyā ñeyyāvara^appahānavasena yattha kilesā pahīnā, tattha bhagavato santāne natthi. yattha pana tathā kilesā na pahīnā tattha sāvakānaṃ paccekabuddhānañca santāne atthi, tato tathāgatova anāvaraṇañāṇadassano.*

[112] Vy, 647: *kaḥ punar iyaṃ vāsanā nāma śrāvakāṇām | yo hi yatkleśacaritaḥ pūrvaṃ tasya tatkṛtaḥkāyavākceṣṭāvikārahetusāmarthyaviśeṣaś citte vāsanety ucyate | avyākṛtaś cittaviśeṣo vāsaneti |*

[113] Ny, 502a.

[114] MVŚ, 77b.

[115] MVŚ, 77b–79a.

[116] Lamotte, E, 'Passions and Impregnations of the Passions in Buddhism', in *Buddhist Studies in Honour of I.B. Horner* (Holland, 1974), 92 f.

[117] MVŚ, 77a.

[118] MVŚ, 216a.

[119] AKB, vii, 414, 416.

[120] MVŚ, 42b.

[121] MVŚ, 780b. Also cf. SPrŚ (T no. 1563), 779a.

[122] MVŚ, 77c.

[123] MVŚ, 175b.

[124] MVŚ, 530c–531a; also *cf.* 158a.

[125] Ny, 502 a–b.

13. The Doctrine of *Karma*

13.1. Meaning and general nature of *karma*

The Sarvāstivāda Ābhidharmikas are quite aware of the profundity — and ultimately inconceivability — of certain teachings of the Buddha as verbalization of His perfect enlightenment. Among these is His doctrine of *karma*. The MVŚ goes so far as to declare that, of all the Buddha's discourses, those dealing with *karma* are the most profound. Likewise the *karmaskandha* among the eight *skandhaka*-s (discussed in the JPŚ); the power pertaining to *karma* among the Buddha's ten powers (*bala*); the inconceivability of *karma* among the four inconceivables[1] — apparently referring to the statement found in the *Aṅguttara* that the retribution of *karma* is inconceivable and not to be conceived.[2]

It should be noted at the very outset that the *karma* doctrine of the Sarvāstivāda is quite in keeping with the early Buddhist teaching that *karma* is neither fatalistic nor completely bound by mechanical rigidity. It is undoubtedly inspired by the Buddha's own doctrine on *karma* which is the Middle Way between absolute determination and absolute freedom, being in conformity with the universal principle of conditioned co-arising (*pratītya-samutpāda*).

The MVŚ gives a threefold meaning of the term *karma*:

(1) *karma* in the general sense of an action or deed (*kriyā*);

(2) *karma* as the ecclesiastical proceedings used for regulating the affairs of the sevenfold Buddhist community — *bhikṣu, bhikṣuṇī*, etc.;

(3) *karma* as a moral action on account of which the effect can be distinguished as desirable (*iṣṭa*) or undesirable (*aniṣṭa*).[3]

The third meaning refers to the moral action which principally — but not absolutely — determines the subsequent experiences of one's existence. It is to *karma* in this last sense that the doctrine here pertains. The MVŚ, however, also observes that people in the world generally apply the word *karma* to what is, in fact, its fruit (*karma-phala*).[4] In brief, *karma* in this last sense refers to the retribution causes (*vipāka-hetu*)[5] which effect a specific existence, either in their capacity as the principal projecting cause or as causes that assist in completing the specific details of the particular sentient existence. (See *infra*, § 14.5). The MVŚ explains more specifically that these retributive causes are called *karma* on account of their fundamental role in determining the various spheres (*dhātu*), planes (*gati*) and modes of birth (*yoni*) of a sentient being's existence and in differentiating the various types of persons (*pudgala*) with their various life-span, physical appearances, social status, etc.[6]

While all these retributive causes can be considered *karma* inasmuch as they contribute towards a being's rebirth, some are responsible for projecting a particular type of existence (e.g., human), and others contribute in terms of the specific details (e.g., the life span of the human, etc.) (§ 14.5); and among all the different types of karmic contribution, that from volition is the most predominant. It is from this perspective that sometimes *karma* is made to refer only to that which projects a specific existence and, at other times, it is only volition that is spoken of as *karma* in the proper sense. From this same perspective, it is stated, at yet other times, that it is not only *karma* alone that projects an existence. For instance, the AKB states:

> It is not *karma* alone which is the projector of a birth (*janman*).[7]

Citing the PrŚ, Saṃghabhadra explains that the conditionings disjoined from thought are not *karma*-s, articulately distinguishing what is *karma* in the proper sense from what, when co-existing and co-ordinating with *karma*, can also contribute as retributive *dharma*-s:

> These retribution causes are, in brief, of two types: 1. those which can project; 2. those which can complete.
>
> Now, the group-homogeneity and the vital faculty which are disjoined conditionings are exclusively the result of [karmic] projection (*ākṣipta*). How do we know? Because it is said in the *sūtra*. For instance, it is said in the *sūtra*: "*karma* is the cause of birth"; it is also said: "*karma* causes the saṃsāric cycle"; it is also said: "sentient beings are differentiated by the force of *karma*"; it is also said: "the inferior sphere (i.e., the sense sphere)

is projected by volition-*karma*". … It is also said in the PrŚ: "The vital faculties are the retribution of *karma*, because they are not *karma*-s. No disjoined conditioning is *karma*." …

It is only at the time when the *karma* is projecting the vital faculty and the homogeneity that those which are not karma [in the proper sense], when taking them as objects, can also incur the retribution. … The bodily and vocal *karma*-s which do not co-exist, [arising and ceasing together with it] (*cittānuvartin*), definitely cannot project the vital faculty and the homogeneity. Otherwise, both the scriptures and logical reasoning will be contradicted. For, the *sūtra* says that the inferior sphere is projected by volition. This means that the vital faculty and homogeneity belonging to the sense sphere existence is incurred by the mental *karma* alone, not by the bodily and vocal *karma*-s. …[8]

13.1.1. Three types of *karma* and the primary role of *cetanā*

As is clear from above, three types of *karma* are recognized in the Sarvāstivāda: mental, bodily and vocal. Correspondingly, *karma* is said to be established on a three-fold basis — in terms of originating cause (*samutthāna*), the mental *karma* is established; in terms of intrinsic nature, vocal *karma*; in terms of supporting basis (*āśraya*), bodily *karma*. This three-fold division of *karma* is also correlated with another three-fold signification of *karma*: It is *karma* because (i) it has efficacy (有作用), i.e., vocal *karma*, (ii) it entails movement, i.e., bodily action, even though there is no real movement as such, (iii) it is volitional (造作; *abhi-sam-√kṛ*), i.e., "mental *karma* which wills the two former actions".[9]

The MVŚ explains that *cetanā* comprises all that is mental *karma* — whether that which projects an existence (i.e., the group-homogeneity) or that which completes its specifics (cf. § 14.5); whether with-outflow or outflow-free; whether pertaining to the mind or to the five sensory consciousnesses — since all these *karma*-s have the characteristic of being volitional activities (*abhisaṃskāra*).[10] The notion of mental *karma* as the originating cause setting the other two types of *karma* into operation shows clearly that in spite of their insistence that *karma* comprises *cetanā*- as well as *cetayitvā-karma*, the Sarvāstivādins too assign the primary karmic role to *cetanā*. This emphasis is distinctively brought out in the following catechism in the MVŚ:

> Question: All with-outflow *dharma*-s, whether skillful or unskillful, are capable of effecting desirable or undesirable retribution fruits. Why is *cetanā* alone, and not other *dharma*-s, said to be capable of differentiating the desirable or undesirable fruits?
>
> Answer: It is so said because *cetanā* is most excellent [in this process]: *cetanā* has the most excellent strength in effecting a desirable or undesirable fruit.[11]

The JPŚ states that "all *dharma*-s (here referring to *prātimokṣa-saṃvara*; *cf.* § 13.5) are originated (*sam-ut-√sthā*) on account of thought, not that it is not on account of thought". Commenting on the statement, the MVŚ says:

> Herein it is shown that the bodily and vocal *karma*-s are originated on account of thought. There are two types of thought: [thought as] the propeller and [thought as] the subsequent propeller (§ 9.7). [The thought which serves as] the propeller projects the bodily and vocal *karma*-s; it arises before them. [The thought which serves as] the subsequent propeller assists the bodily and vocal *karma*-s; it arises together with them. Herein, it refers to [thought] as the propeller, not [thought] as the subsequent propeller.[12]

The MVŚ states that for the materialization of a future existence, one single *cetanā* generically projects it and many other *cetanā*-s then determine its specifics.[13] Saṃghabhadra, likewise, citing the *sūtra*-s and explaining the retributive causes in similar terms as the MVŚ, further articulates that it is mental *karma* — *cetanā* — that is to be regarded as *karma* in the proper or specific sense inasmuch as it is the prominent cause (勝因; **viśiṣṭa-hetu*) in projecting a sentient existence. Bodily and vocal *karma*-s, while also being part of the retributive causes, can only contribute as completing causes (see § 13.8.2). In fact, their contribution becomes possible only when the *cetanā karma* is exercising its function of projecting the particular sentient existence.[14] In stating that one *karma* projects one single existence, the story is related of Venerable Aniruddha who, by offering a single alms, projected several retributive fruits as a *deva* and as a human: This is possible not because one single *karma* of alms-giving projected several different existences, but because, when offering the alms, he had generated several streams of volition — several *karma*-s — corresponding to several future existences. (See *infra*, § 14.5). We must note here once again that the projecting *karma* is *cetanā*. Accordingly, we may justifiably speak of the Sarvāstivāda notion of *karma* in two senses: in the proper or narrower sense, *karma* refers specifically to *cetanā* — and the Sarvāstivāda doctrine here does not deviate from the standpoint of early Buddhism; in the broader sense, it refers to all that constitutes the retributive causes contributing to the retributive fruit. In this connection, we may note the explanation in Ny as to why the factor, *bhava*, in the twelve-fold formulation of dependent co-arising is not named *karma*: It is because *bhava* is the specific *karma* (*karma-viśeṣa*) which effects rebirth — all *karma*-s are not the cause for rebirth.[15]

13.1.2. The agent of *karma*

Given the Buddhist doctrines of impermanence — interpreted to its logical extreme as that of momentariness — and of non-substantiality (*nairātmya*), can it be said that the same person who incurs a *karma* experiences the effect himself? The MVŚ examines this question, and explains as follows:

(i) From a certain point of view it can be said so: Although the *skandha*-s, *āyatana*-s and *dhātu*-s of a being are different in each moment of their serial continuity, yet there is an overall integrity — each series is distinct from another.

(ii) From another point of view, it can be said that the doer and the experiencer are different — for instance, a being who has incurred a *karma* as a human, experiences its effect in a different plane of existence.

(iii) From yet another point of view, it can be said that no one incurs any *karma* and no one experiences the effect — for all *dharma*-s are without a Self, empty of a person (*pudgala*); all *karma*-s are "devoid of a doer and an experiencer, there being only the agglomeration of the conditionings which arise and cease [momentarily]".[16] Saṃghabhadra cites the following two lines of a stanza which he asserts are the Buddha's own words denying a truly, independently existing agent of *karma*:

> There is *karma*, there is *vipāka*;
> The doer is not apperceived (*na upalabhyate/na vidyate*).[17]

This, he says, nevertheless does not amount to the denial of agency in every sense. It denies only a really existent Self that leaves one group of *skandha*-s and continues with another group.

> It is for the sake of showing that the doers are none other than the conditionings (*saṃskāra*) themselves, constituting a serial continuity of causes and effects, that [the Buddha] says further: 'This being that comes to be; from the arising of this, that arises.' (*asmin satīdaṃ bhavati / asyo'tpādād idam utpadyate*)[18]

13.1.3. Defilements as the generating cause and supporting condition for *karma*

The Sarvāstivāda shares the basic Buddhist tenet that the unenlightened worldling experiences *duḥkha* in *saṃsāra* on account of his *karma*; and karma is generated because of defilements: defilement → *karma* → *duḥkha*. All *duḥkha* ceases when karma is transcended.

Defilements are not only the generating cause of *karma*. It is by virtue of defilements that *karma*-s accumulate (*upacayaṃ gacchanti* — see below), i.e., become necessarily productive of a retribution.[19] Without them, *karma*-s are incapable of effecting a new existence.[20] In fact, "It is not the case that an *arhat* does not have the indeterminate *karma*-s conducive to a rebirth. But on the account of the absence of the defilements, they become incapable of producing a rebirth."[21] That is, while *karma* is the direct cause for a retribution, it requires the defilements as the necessary supportive conditions for the process.

13.2. Classification of *karma*

Various classifications of *karma* are given in the Sarvāstivāda texts, among which the following are the main ones:

(1) volitional *karma* (*cetanā*) and *karma* subsequent to willing (*cetayitvā*);

(2) bodily, vocal and mental *karma*-s;

(3) informative (*vijñapti*) and non-informative (*avijñapti*) *karma*-s;

(4) skillful (*kuśala*), unskillful (*akuśala*) and morally neutral (*avyākṛta*) *karma*-s;

(5) *karma*-s which are with-outflow (*sāsrava*) and outflow-free (*anāsrava*) *karma*-s;

(6) (i) meritorious (*puṇya*) *karma* — skillful actions pertaining to the sphere of sensuality, (ii) non-meritorious (*apuṇya*) *karma* — unskillful actions pertaining to the sphere of sensuality, and (iii) immovable (*āneñjya*) *karma* — skillful actions pertaining to the upper spheres;

(7) (i) black (*kṛṇa*) *karma* yielding black retribution — impure (*aśubha*) action generating disagreeable (*amanojña*) retribution; (ii) white (*śukla*) *karma* yielding white retribution — action of *rūpa-dhātu* which is always pure (*śubham ekāntena*) generating agreeable (*manojña*) retribution; (iii) black-white *karma* yielding black-white retribution — pure action of *kāmadhātu*, being mixed with the impure, generating a mixed retribution; (iv) neither-black-nor-white *karma* yielding no retribution — outflow-free action which destroys the other three types of action;[22]

(8) *karma*-s conducive to pleasant experience (*sukha-vedanīya*), to unpleasant experience (*duḥkha-vedanīya*), to neither pleasant nor unpleasant (*aduḥkhāsukha-vedanīya*) experience;

(9) *karma*-s experiencible in this life (*dṛṣṭa-dharma-vedanīya*), *karma*-s experiencible in the next life (*upapadya-vedanīya*) and *karma*-s experiencible in a future life subsequent to the next (*apara-paryāya-vedanīya*);

(10) determinate (*niyata*) and indeterminate (*aniyata*) *karma* — e.g., a *karma* conducive to desirable (or to undesirable or neutral) experience is not necessarily retributed; but when it is actually retributed, it is necessarily experienced as a desirable retribution;[23]

(11) a *karma* that is done (*kṛta*) and one that is accumulated (*upacita*);

(12) projecting (*ākṣepaka*) and completing (*paripūraka*) *karma*-s.

13.3. Informative (*vijñapti*) and non-informative (*avijñapti*) *karma*

When one performs an action through body or speech, this action informs others of the corresponding mental state within. Accordingly, it is called an 'informative or information action'. Mental *karma* cannot by itself provide any information outside the mind. Thus, it does not have informative, and hence, non-informative *karma*. The following chart shows the correlation among the first three classifications given in § 13.2:

<table>
<tr><th>two-fold</th><th>three-fold</th><th>vijñapti/avijñapti</th></tr>
<tr><td>cetanā-karma</td><td>mental karma</td><td>no vijñapti or avijñapti</td></tr>
<tr><td rowspan="4">cetayitvā-karma</td><td rowspan="2">bodily karma</td><td>bodily vijñapti</td></tr>
<tr><td>bodily avijñapti</td></tr>
<tr><td rowspan="2">vocal karma</td><td>vocal vijñapti</td></tr>
<tr><td>vocal avijñapti</td></tr>
</table>

A bodily or vocal informative action may be preceded by a preparatory stage (*prayoga*) and followed by subsequent actions (*pṛṣṭham*) — actions consequential to the principal action. Thus, for the action of killing, it may be preceded by a series of preparatory actions — such as the volition to kill, followed by the detailed planning, buying a knife, sharpening it, etc., and finally stabbing the victim several times until he dies. At the very moment — at the very stroke — when the victim is actually killed, the doer has committed the transgression of killing. This action lasts only one moment. But simultaneous with the accomplishment of this principal action, an invisible karmic force is projected within the doer's body which continues to renew itself in a series. As this force is non-informing of the doer's mental state, it is called non-informative *karma* or non-information action. In terms of what is called a 'path of *karma*' (*infra*, § 13.6), the informative *karma* as well as the simultaneously arisen non-informative *karma* at the moment when the victim actually dies, constitute the 'principal (*maula*) path of *karma*'. From this point onward, all unskillful informative *karma*-s — such as skinning, cutting and eating the victim, etc. — and non-informative *karma*-s generated are called the subsequent actions.[24]

Each momentary member of the non-information-series is connected with the killer by the corresponding momentary member of the series of *prāpti* which is also simultaneously induced. In this way, by virtue of the *prāpti*-series, the killer continues to possess the non-informative *karma* — likewise, the volitional and informative *karma*-s. This *prāpti*-series can only be interrupted — and hence, the continuity of the karmic force brought to an end — by the actualization of the effect corresponding to the *karma* of killing.

13.4. Definition and intrinsic nature of informative and non-informative *karma*-s

13.4.1. Definition and nature of informative *karma*

There is a controversy as to what constitutes the intrinsic or essential nature of an informative *karma*.

The Sāṃmitīya asserts that it is movement (*gati*). For them, bodily movement can be real because, unlike the mental *dharma*-s, material things are not momentary.[25]

The ancient Dārṣṭāntika[26] as well as the Sautrāntika deny the ontological status of both the informative and non-informative *karma*-s. All *karma*-s are none other than volition: The *sūtra* reference to *cetanā* and *cetayitvā* *karma*-s corresponds to two types of volition. First, at the preparatory stage, the volition of intention (*saṃkalpa-cetanā*) arises. Next, a volition of action (*kriyā-cetanā*) arises, moving the body or emitting a speech — bodily or vocal action.[27]

For the Vaibhāṣika, *cetanā karma* is mental *karma* and *cetayitvā karma* comprises both informative and non-informative *karma*-s, all of which are real entities. Informative *karma* is of the nature of resistant (*sapratigha*) derived matter:

(i) A bodily informative *karma* is the specific bodily shape (*saṃsthāna-viśeṣa*) at the time of the accomplishment of the action. More precisely, it is the total number of shape-atoms (*saṃsthāna-paramāṇu*) of matter constituting the part of the body forming the basis of the action. This number varies as some actions are based on just a certain part of the body — as in the case of the snapping of the fingers, etc.; others are based on the whole body — such as worshipping the Buddha.[28]

(ii) A vocal informative *karma* is speech which again is matter, being articulated sound (*śabda*).

Saṃghabhadra argues that, if all *karma*-s are mere volition, then as soon as one produces a volition for patricide, one immediately has committed the mortal transgression. Should it be argued that this fallacy does not result, since one has not yet moved the body, it is then *ipso facto* established that bodily action exists apart from the volition. That is, it is only when the body moves that there is the bodily *karma* accomplishing the transgression of killing, etc. This is a bodily transgression, even though it is necessarily generated by an evil volition.[29] Saṃghabhadra, distinguishing the Vaibhāṣika from both the Sāṃmītīya as well as the Sautrāntika who asserts that the shape-atoms are merely specific arrangements of color atoms which alone are real, explains as follows:

> Within the body [of the doer], there exists a fruit of the four Great Elements arisen by a thought (*citta*) which is a specific shape capable of informing [others] of the thought. This is called bodily informative [matter].[30] That is, it is a fruit of the transient Great Elements of emanation (*anavasthāyi-naiṣyandika-mahābhūta*) born of a thought of preparation. It is the *saṃsthāna-rūpa* — a category of *rūpa* distinct from the *varṇa rūpa*-s — which serves as the cause for visual cognition and which eclipses the *saṃsthāna-rūpa*-s that are born of retribution (*vipākaja*) and that are

> of the nature of growth (*aupacayika*) [— the existing *saṃsthāna-rūpa*-s of the doer's body]. Such *saṃsthāna-rūpa*-s are called bodily informative [matter]. It is not the case that, as a result of such [*saṃsthāna-rūpa*-s] which are of the nature of being skillful, etc., those which are born of retribution and which are of the nature of growth come to be annihilated. This is like the case that, when the divine eye (*divya-cakṣus*) arises, the other faculties of vision and audition continue uninterrupted.[31]

The word 'transient' in the above definition is pointed at the Sāṃmitīya who holds that matter is not momentary; and the phrase 'a distinct category independent of other *varṇa-rūpa*-s' is intended to counteract the Sautrāntika view. We may note from the above explanation that (i) the *saṃsthāna-rūpa*-s constituting the bodily information matter are morally definable as skillful or unskillful; and that (ii) they are arisen by thought, or more correctly, a thought in conjunction with a specific volition (*cetanā-viśeṣa*). Herein we see the necessary relation of bodily and vocal *karma*-s with mental *karma*. It is for this reason that even the Vaibhāṣikas accept that if *karma*-s are to be classified from the view-point of their origination (*samutthāna*), it should be said that there is only one type of *karma* — since all *karma*-s are originated from volition.[32]

But although a mental *karma* — volition — is generally expressed through the agencies of the bodily and vocal *karma*, it does not mean that mental *karma* by itself cannot be retributive. The very fact that the retributive cause (*vipāka-hetu*) comprises *dharma*-s of all the five *skandha*-s — including thought and thought-concomitants — means that mental *karma* too conduces to karmic retribution. The MVŚ discusses the various cases of the "desired and undesired fruits effected by the three types of *karma*-s" — bodily, vocal and mental. Thus, there exists a situation where, "the vocal and mental *karma* do not effect their fruits of retribution in the manner a bodily *karma* does": This is the case "when there is restraint of the body, not speech, and at that moment one has a skillful or neutral thought; that is, the non-informative *karma* (*avijñapti*, *avijñapti-karma*)[33] projected by an unskillful bodily informative *karma* generated at the present moment co-arises (*anu-√vṛt*) [with thought], and the non-informative *karma* projected by a skillful vocal informative *karma* generated at the present or a previous moment co-arises [with thought]. At that very moment, a skillful or neutral thought arises — in this situation, the bodily *karma* effects an undesired retribution; the vocal *karma* effects a desired retribution. As for the mental *karma*, if it is generated by a skillful thought, it effects a desired retribution; if it is generated by a neutral thought, it effects neither a desired nor an undesired retribution."[34] There are also cases wherein, even without any bodily and vocal expression, bodily and vocal transgressions are incurred by virtue of the mental volition, e.g., the mental hatred (*manaḥ-pradoṣa*) of a *ṛṣi*, which can be fatal, and the silence, at the time of *poṣadha,* indicating acceptance.[35]

13.4.2. Definition and nature of non-informative *karma*

Vasubandhu defines non-informative matter in the AKB as follows:

> That serial continuity — pure or impure — which exists even in one whose thought is distracted (*vikṣipta*) or who is without thought (*acittaka*), and which is dependent on the Great Elements, is called the non-informative [matter].[36]

In the Ny, Saṃghabhadra objects to this definition:

> The Kośakāra is unable to describe the nature of the non-informative [matter] completely by this verse, for he says that the non-informative [matter] is a serial continuity (*anubandha*). His own commentary says: By serial continuity is meant a continuous series (*pravāha*). Now, [the *avijñapti* of] the first moment cannot be described as a series lest there be the fallacy of over-generalization (*atiprasaṅga*). Thus, his definition

> definitely excluded the non-informative [matter] of the first moment. Moreover, a series is unreal, and [to describe] the non-informative [matter] as unreal is contrary to the *abhidharma* tenets. Moreover, that which is projected by concentration (*samādhi*) does not continue as a series in the distracted and non-conscious states — it would then not be non-informative [matter]...[37]

He then gives the following verse definition which he claims to be free from such faults:

> That [morally] defined, non-resistant matter, which exists in the thought at the time of the action as well [as subsequently], which is of a dissimilar as well [as similar moral] species, and also in the thoughtless state — this is conceded as the non-informative [matter].[38]

In the SPrŚ[39] he replaces Vasubandhu's verse above with this, and explains each term in the prose commentary. With regard to *kṛte'pi*, he says: "*kṛte'pi* refers [by the word *api*] to those [*avijñapti*-s which are] apart from the action. Generally speaking, there are two kinds of *bhautika-rūpa*-s which are *apratigha*: the first kind arises in dependence on the *vijñapti*; the second on *citta*. Those which arise in dependence on *vijñapti* are further divisible into two kinds: those which co-exist with the action (i.e., the *vijñapti*) and those which exist after the action has ceased. The words *kṛte'pi* are given in order to include exhaustively these different kinds of *avijñapti*–s with their distinctive nature."[40]

Yaśomitra[41] quotes the above objection of Saṃghabhadra and refutes it: If what is called a series (*pravāha*) refers to many moments, then the first moment too amounts to a series, the word 'series' referring to the many moments beginning with the first moment. Moreover, if by 'a serial continuity' is meant 'that which continues' (*anubadhnātīty anubandhaḥ*), then grammatically — with the word having a final *a* suffix — a real entity is indicated. Accordingly, there is neither incompleteness in the definition nor any contradiction with the *abhidharma* treatises. On the other hand, even if by 'serial continuity' is meant '[the state of] serially continuing', expressing a flow (*anubandhanam anubandha iti sroto 'bhidhīyate*), there is still no fault since its reference is to matter.

In the Ny, Saṃghabhadra summarizes:

> In brief, the non-informative [matter] is that non-resistant skillful or unskillful matter which arises in dependence on a specific corporeal or vocal informative *karma*, and on a specific skillful or unskillful thought, etc.[42]

This definition may be compared with that given in the *Avatāra*:

> From a specific *vijñapti*, *citta* and [tetrad of] *mahābhūta*-s, there arises [in the actor] a continuous series of *kuśala* or *akuśala rūpa* which is non-cumulative and which persists in the states of sleep, wakefulness, distracted (*vikṣipta*) or non-distracted (*avikṣipta*) thought, or non-consciousness (*acittaka*). This is the characteristic of the non-informative [matter].[43]

13.4.2.1. Non-informative *karma* as matter

Although the non-information is invisible, non-resistant and non-spatialized,[44] it nevertheless is said to be of the nature of matter since its supporting basis (*āśraya*) — the four Great Elements — are resistant matter. This is comparable to the movement of a tree's shadow which follows that of the tree.[45] Vasubandhu likens this analogy to another supposedly Sarvāstivādin explanation that the non-informative *karma* is said to be *rūpa* because the informative *karma* from which it issues is *rūpa* in nature, and he objects to it.

Saṃghabhadra argues that it is, in fact, to be linked with the first interpretation: all non-informative *karma*-s, whether those in the *kāma-dhātu* which do not co-exist with thought or those which do (the *dhyāna-saṃvara* and *anāsrava-saṃvara*), are necessarily dependent on the Great Elements.[46] In the case of restraint (*saṃvara*), the MVŚ gives another reason: it is a *rūpa* "because it obstructs the arising of evil matter";[47] i.e., evil bodily and vocal actions which are matter in nature, for "it is universally acknowledged in the world that the guarding of bodily and vocal actions are said to be *śīla*"[48] — another explanation that can cover all categories of restraints.

Non-information is, however, subsumed as a special case under *dharmāyatana*, rather than *rūpāyatana*.[49] This subsumption is justified with the reference by the *Elephant-simile sūtra* to matter subsumed in the *dharmāyatana*.[50] From this subsumption, one can also see that while the orthodox Sarvāstivādins insist that the *avijñapti* is a subtle kind of matter for it to be capable of continuous interaction with the mind — as we shall see below that it is so meant to be — it is in this sense considered more akin to the thought concomitants. In a way, there is a doctrinal advantage regarding the non-informative *karma* as material rather than mental: if it is a mental *dharma* conjoined with thought, there would be the philosophical problem of its continuous co-existence with the thought series which is, at various stages, of various moral nature — skillful, unskillful, neutral. On the other hand, by postulating it as a material reality, the Sarvāstivādins fell into serious difficulties: it has to be considered so much of a special type of matter that it might as well — at least from the view-point of the critics — be treated as non-material. Besides, as the Sautrāntika argues, how can a material force be conceived of as being 'intelligent' — as a creative karmic force should be?[51] It is probably out of such consideration that Harivarman, a dissident Sautrāntika master — pointing out various faults in subsuming *avijñapti* as a *rūpa* — proposes in his SatŚ that it is a *dharma* disjoined from the mind *(citta-viprayukta)*.[52]

Orthodox Sarvāstivādins apart, some dissident masters within the fold of Sarvāstivāda itself — such as the early Dārṣṭāntika masters — also denied the reality of the non-informative matter.[53] Bhadanta Dharmatrāta denied the reality of the so-called *dharmāyatana-saṃgṛhīta-rūpa*,[54] while Buddhadeva, that of the derived matter.[55] This Dārṣṭāntika denial was inherited by the Sautrāntika.[56] It is also noteworthy that the DSŚ, one of the earliest Sarvāstivāda canonical *abhidharma* texts, also makes no mention of the *avijñapti* in all its discussion on matter. (See *supra*, § 4.1.1.1 f.).

13.4.3. Moral nature of informative and non-informative *karma*-s

Informative and non-informative matter — being karmic forces — must necessarily be either skillful or unskillful. A neutral informative action — being weak in nature — cannot generate a karmic force (i.e., non-informative *karma*). In this case, the moral nature of the informative and non-informative *karma*-s is endowed by that of the volition and the thought conjoined with the volition. The latter becomes skillful or unskillful by virtue of their conjunction (*samprayoga*) with a thought-concomitant of either nature — e.g., greed or moral shame (*hrī*). The informative *karma*, on the other hand, although being matter in nature, becomes morally defined by virtue of the morally defined volition that serves as the originating cause (*samutthāna*) for the informative *karma* which in turn defines the moral nature of the non-informative *karma* which it generates. (For *samutthānataḥ kuśala*/*akuśala*, see *supra*, § 2.4.3.2).

For the generation of a bodily or vocal action, two kinds of origination are spoken of:

(i) origination *qua* cause (*hetu-samutthāna*), i.e., the thought — more precisely the volition — which gives rise to the action; and

(ii) simultaneous origination (*tatkṣaṇa-samutthāna*), i.e., the thought that is simultaneous with the action and serving as its sustaining basis.[57]

Although the volition sets an action into motion, the action cannot actually take place without the latter. This is compared to an action projected by the volition "I shall go to that village". The actual action of going to that village cannot take place if the person dies immediately after the projection.[58]

As to whether the first five consciousnesses can also serve as these two types of origination, the MVŚ records diverse views. Some masters hold that mental consciousness alone can do so. Others assert that the first five consciousnesses also can generate bodily and vocal *karma*-s; however, they can only serve to sustaining the operation, whereas mental consciousness can be both the projecting cause (*pravṛtti-kāraṇa*) and the cause that sustains the operation (*anuvṛtti-kāraṇa*). Saṃghavasu maintains that the first consciousnesses can serve as both types of causes. The MVŚ compilers endorse the second opinion.[59] The AKB compares the first originating cause to the hand that propels a wheel to roll on the floor; on the other hand, it is only because of the floor — comparable to the 'simultaneous origination' — that serves to sustain the wheel at each moment that the actual rolling becomes possible.[60]

With regard to the Great Elements on which both the informative and non-informative *karma*-s depend (*upādāya*), it is explained that the non-informative *karma* is not derived from the same Great Elements forming the derivative basis for the informative *karma*. For, it is argued that the derived matter constituting the non-informative *karma* and that constituting the informative *karma* are different in nature — one is subtle, the other, gross. Accordingly, they must have different causes.[61] The informative *karma* is simultaneous with the Great Elements from which it is derived. As for the non-informative *karma* of the sphere of sensuality, in the first moment, it arises being derived from the simultaneous Great Elements. Subsequently, although having become past, the same Great Elements of the first moment continue to serve as the base of operation (*āśraya*) for the arising of the subsequent moments of the non-informative *karma* — they are the projecting cause. The Great Elements arising simultaneously with the non-informative *karma* in each subsequent moment in the doer's body serve as the support (*saṃniśraya*) of the non-informative *karma* — they are the sustaining cause of continuous operation. In other words, the Great Elements of the first moment are the origination *qua* cause, the simultaneously arising ones are the simultaneous origination. (See above).

13.5. Non-information as restraint, non-restraint and neither-restraint-nor-non-restraint[62]

The non-informative matter comprises the following three categories:

(i) restraint (*saṃvara*): divisible into (a) *prātimokṣa* restraint, i.e., restraint in respect of the Buddhist disciplinary codes, (b) meditation (*dhyāna*) restraint and (c) outflow-free (*anāsrava*) restraint,

(ii) non-restraint (*asaṃvara*),

(iii) neither-restraint-nor-non-restraint (*naivasaṃvara-nāsaṃvara*).

This third category does not refer to actions derived from a neutral mind, for all non-informative *karma*-s necessarily issue from a sufficiently strong intention, skillful or unskillful. Rather it refers to those karmic actions — comprising the majority of moral and immoral actions — that fall outside the first two categories. Thus, murder not for the sake of livelihood or not committed out of a vow-conditioned mentality, is an instance of this category.

(i) (a) The *prātimokṣa* restraint is further divided into eight: *bhikṣu* restraint, *bhikṣuṇī* restraint, *śikṣamānā* restraint, *śrāmaṇera* restraint, *śrāmaṇerī* restraint, *upāsaka* restraint, *upāsikā* restraint and *upavāsa* (/*upavāsastha*) restraint. These eight kinds of restraint belong (*pratisaṃyukta*) to the sphere of sensuality alone. The moral observances of the heretics (*bāhyaka*) do not constitute *prātimokṣa-saṃvara*. This is because they are undertaken with a view of some form of existence or another, conceived as real liberation (*vimokṣa*); such an undertaking does not lead to the absolute rejection of or release from evil.[63] The various disciplinary precepts may be differentiated as those pertaining to morality proper (*śīlāṅga*), being transgression in their intrinsic nature (*prakṛti-sāvadya*), and those which are precepts by way of prohibition (*pratikṣepaṇa-sāvadya*) or convention (*prajñapti*). Thus, in the case of the eight precepts observed by a lay Buddhist fortnightly, the first four — abstention from killing, stealing, unchastity, false speech — belong to the former category. The others belong to the latter category. Of the latter, abstention from intoxicants pertains to vigilance (*apramādāṅga*); the last three abstentions — from unseemly shows, etc., from wearing ornaments, from the use of high beds and seats — pertain to abstention (*viratyaṅga*) or observance of vows (*vratāṅga*).[64] When properly acquired, the *prātimokṣa-saṃvara* can act as a restraining force, helping the undertaker to avoid transgressing the precepts in the presence of conditions favorable for such transgression.[65] (See also § 13.5.1). The MVŚ explains that a skillful precept (= *saṃvara*) can counteract immorality (*dauśīlya*) by virtue of its being accompanied by an undertaking (*abhy-upagama*).[66]

(b) The meditation restraint is the non-informative matter co-existent (*anuvartaka*) with the concentrations (*samādhi*) of the fine-material sphere (*rūpa-dhātu*).

(c) The outflow-free restraint is that co-existent non-informative matter with the outflow-free concentrations (*anāsrava-samādhi*), not belonging to any of the three spheres.

(ii) Non-restraint is a serial continuity of unskillful non-informative matter arising in the following persons: butchers, hunters, robbers, prison-wardens, executioners (*vadhya-ghātaka*), etc.

(iii) The serial continuity of various skillful or unskillful non-informative matter generated by acts such as the following is of the category of "neither restraint nor non-restraint": the building of a *vihāra*, *stūpa* and *saṅghārāma*, etc., offering food and medicine, etc., to the Saṅgha, worshipping a *caitya*, singing religious hymns of praise; as well as striking (*tāḍana*), etc.

13.5.1. Acquisition and relinquishment of the non-informative matter

(i) (a) The *prātimokṣa* restraints are acquired by making vows to undertake them. The first seven kinds last until the end of one's life; the eighth, for one day and one night.

It is an emphatic Sarvāstivāda doctrine that *prātimokṣa-saṃvara* is not the mere abstention from a wrong doing — as maintained by the Sautrāntika.[67] Nor can it be acquired by a mere vowing. It is a distinct *dharma* (*dharmāntara*) with a distinctive nature (殊勝法性; **viśiṣṭo dharmatva*)[68] whose acquisition requires very specific conditions and ecclesiastical procedure. To begin with, the vows must be taken in front of a teacher whose utterances representing the vows are to be repeated word by word by the undertaker. This is called *paravijñāpana* — informing to and from another (*para*). However, the Vinaya hermeneutists (*vinaya-vaibhāṣika*) concede ten ways of acquiring full ordination, some of which — e.g., the self-ordination (*svayaṃbhūtvena*) by the Buddha and the *pratyekabuddha*-s — do not require a *vijñapti*. [69] In brief, it can be acquired only on account of either the force of an original resolution (*praṇidhāna*), or the complete perfection of intention (*āśaya*), or through the power of the Buddha. It is asserted that the principles involved in these various divergent cases of acquisition can only be properly understood by the Omniscient One.[70] In the case of the *upavāsa* restraint undertaken, the acandidate who repeats after the preceptor must be very humble, wearing no ornaments, and undertakes the complete set of eight precepts for one full day and night. It is only when all the requisite conditions are fulfilled that there arises the restraint as a distinct force endowed with the 'nature of restraint' (律儀性; **saṃvaratva*).[71] Because it is undertaken in this manner in front of a teacher, the undertaker can, through the force of moral shame (*apatrāpya*)[72] — the 'dominant influence of the world' (here, the teacher in front of whom he has made the commitment) — avoid transgression even in situations where his own moral modesty (*hrī*) is not operative.[73] On the other hand, when undertaken without fulfilling all the requirements, there can be "only the arising of good conduct (*sucarita*), not the acquisition of restraint.[74] Nevertheless, in order that [one's actions] will lead to desirable results, even such an undertaking should be done."[75] (See also *infra*, § 13.8.1).

The first seven *prātimokṣa* restraints are terminated by any of the following four conditions: (1) the willful giving up of the training that one has undertaken (*śikṣāpratyākhyāna*), (2) death (*mṛtyu*), (3) the cutting off of the three roots of skillfulness (*kuśalamūla-samuccheda*), and (4) the simultaneous arising of both the male and female sex organs (*ubhayavyañjanotpatti*, *dvivyañjanodaya*). The MVŚ tells us that, according to the Vinayadhara: "The time of the disappearance of the *Dharma* constitutes the fifth condition: at the time of the disappearance of the *Dharma*, all the *śikṣā*, *pravrajyā*, *upasaṃpad*, *sīmābandha*, and *karma-vācanā* completely cease. Therefore the *saṃvara* are also relinquished at that moment." The MVŚ compilers, while not rejecting this last condition straight-forwardly, offer their own interpretation.[76] According to Pu Guang, this condition is held by the Dharmagupta.[77] It is to be noted that this same condition is also enumerated as the fifth in the **Abhidharmahṛdaya*:[78] 1. giving up of the training, 2. transgression of *śīla*, 3. death, 4. when false views predominate, 5. when the *Dharma* vanishes. We may assume that this fifth condition is one well recognized by the Gandhārian/Foreign (*bahirdeśaka*) Sarvāstivāda masters. The eighth restraint is terminated by any of the aforesaid four conditions, or by the end of the night.

(b-c) The meditation restraint is acquired when the skillful thought is acquired upon entering into a meditation, and is terminated when it is relinquished upon one's exit from meditation. Likewise for the acquisition and termination of the outflow-free restraint which follows those of the outflow-free thought. These conditions are on account of the fact that these two categories of restraint are thought-accompaniments (*cittaparivartin/cittānuvartin/cittānuparivartin*).

(ii) The non-restraint is acquired by both doing (*kriyayā*) and willfully undertaking to do (*abhyupagamena*) an unskillful act. It is terminated by any of the following four conditions: (1) the undertaking of restraint, (2) death, (3) the simultaneous arising of both sex-organs, and (4) when the skillful thought of the fine-material sphere is acquired spontaneously (*dharmatā-prātilambhika*) when the world system is about to be destroyed, as under this situation, the skillful *dharma*-s are all intensified spontaneously.[79]

(iii) The category of neither restraint nor non-restraint is acquired by one of three ways: (1) by doing an action; as, for instance, with a pure and ardent thought one worships a *stūpa* with hymns; or, out of intense defilement, one strikes at other persons or things; (2) by a willful undertaking, as for instance when one vows thus: "I shall never eat before worshipping the Buddha"; (3) act of giving, as, for instance, building monasteries, making beds and seats (*śayanāsana*), putting up parks and making offerings to the *bhikṣu*-s, etc.; this non-informative matter is terminated when the originating thought (*samutthāna-citta*) and the material basis (*upadhi*) — the things offered — are completely destroyed.

What happens when one has acquired the non-information of restraint and then transgresses? According to the Sarvāstivāda masters outside

Kāśmīra, when a person abiding in the *prātimokṣa*-restraint transgresses against the restraint, he relinquishes the restraint and acquires the neither-restraint-nor-non-restraint — another karmically retributive force but having nothing to do with making a vow. If he, however, sincerely and properly repents, he then relinquishes the neither-restraint-nor-non-restraint and again re-acquires the restraint. According to the Kāśmīra masters: when the person transgresses against the restraint, he does not relinquish it, but acquires additionally the neither-restraint-nor-non-restraint. He is at that time said to be abiding in both the neither-restraint-nor-non-restraint as well as in restraint. If he sincerely and properly repents, he then relinquishes the neither-restraint-nor-non-restraint and is only said to be an abider in restraint (*saṃvarastha*). Both opinions are acceptable to the MVŚ compilers.[80]

13.6. Paths of *karma* (*karma-patha*)

The teaching of the ten paths of skillful and unskillful *karma* (*karma-patha*) have formed a major ethical guidance among the Buddhists from the Buddha's time. The Sarvāstivādins explain that these ten paths of *karma* are intended by the Buddha to include the most important skillful practices and the gravest unskillful practices.[81] The ten unskillful paths of *karma* are:

1. taking life (*prāṇātipāta*),
2. taking what is not given (*adattādāna*),
3. sexual misconduct (*kāma-mithyācāra*),
4. false speech (*mṛṣā-vāda*),
5. malicious speech (*paiśunya*),
6. harsh speech (*pāruṣya*),
7. frivolous speech (*saṃbhinna-pralāpa*),
8. covetousness (*abhidhyā*),
9. hatred (*vyāpāda*),
10. false view (*mithyā-dṛṣṭi*).[82]

The ten skillful ones are the opposites of these, i.e., abstention from killing, etc. These are skillful actions which are with-outflow, i.e., still conducive to rebirths in *saṃsāra*. The first three are bodily actions; the next four, vocal; and the last three, mental. The root-causes of the ten unskillful paths of *karma* are the roots of unskillfulness — greed (*lobha*), hatred (*dveṣa*) and delusion (*moha*): 1, 6 and 9 are achieved through hatred; 2, 3 and 8 through greed; 10 through delusion; 4, 5 and 7 through any one of the three roots.[83] Likewise, correspondingly, the ten skillful paths of *karma* are achieved through the three roots of skillfulness.[84]

It is emphasized that a mere conventional moral observation, without a dominant mental determination, is not a path of *karma*.[85] Conversely, if one harbors an evil intention of, say, disrupting the unity of a harmonious community — whether one succeeds or not, one commits the path of *karma* of malicious speech.[86] Each path of *karma* is divisible into nine grades — weak-weak (i.e., the lowest of nine grades), and so on, up to strong-strong (i.e., the highest of nine grades). (See *supra*, § 12). Thus, although murder leads to an undesirable rebirth, the particular plane of existence into which the murderer is going to be reborn will depend on the grade of gravity of the action.[87] The same applies to the other paths of *karma*. Among the ten unskillful ones, it is false view — which denies cause and effect — that cuts off the roots of skillfulness: The strong-strong root of skillfulness is cut off by the weak-weak false view — up to, the weak-weak root of skillfulness by the strong-strong false view.[88]

The paths of *karma* are called thus because they are the paths based on which the volition — *karma* — that originates them has its operation: "Because it operates as they operate; it moves as they move — it creates karmically (*saṃskaroti*) in conformity with their force… They are paths of *karma* because they are traversed by the volition: because the volition that originates the bodily and vocal *karma* operates through the latter as the object." They constitute the paths "through which the volition has its movement and operates to its accomplishment".[89] Thus, volition is not called a path of *karma*. "Just as the road traversed by the king is called the road of the king, and it is not the king; likewise it is called the path of *karma* because it is traversed by volition, and it is not volition."[90] Accordingly, among the ten paths of *karma*, the first seven are both *karma* — being bodily and vocal *karma* in nature, as well as paths of *karma* — being the paths for their originating volition. The last three mental ones are only paths of *karma* inasmuch as they serve as the paths for their conascent volition, but not *karma*.[91]

13.7. Rationale for the doctrine of non-informative *karma*

The MVŚ quotes the *sūtra* passage in which three types of *rūpa* are mentioned by the Buddha — visible and resistant (*sanidarśana-sapratigha*), invisible and resistant (*anidarśana-sapratigha*), invisible and non-resistant (*anidarśana-apratigha*).[92] The last is said to be alluding to the Sarvāstivāda category of non-information. Three logical arguments are also given:

(i) At the time when Ajātaśatru gave rise to the informative *karma* (*vijñapti-karma*) to kill his father, the latter had not died. When the latter actually died, the information *karma* had already become past. It is only on account of the subsequent non-information acquired through the force of the preceding informative action that he came to be 'touched' by the mortal transgression.

(ii) Likewise for the case of the heretical ascetic who killed Maudgalyāyana: when the latter attained *parinirvāṇa*, the previous informative *karma* of the killer had also faded into the past.[93]

(iii) If non-information were unreal, then there would be no legitimate establishment of the differences among those abiding in *saṃvara*, *asaṃvara*, and neither-*saṃvara*-nor-*asaṃvara*.[94]

Elsewhere, the MVŚ also mentions (more briefly than the AKB and Ny) the case of an action — say, murder — done through an emissary: at the time when the victim is actually killed by the emissary, the informative *karma* of the instigator is no more. Besides, this informative *karma* — vocal in nature — cannot be one that constitutes the principal act of killing. It is in fact only part of the preparation for the killing. There arises in him at this time, however, a non-informative *karma* of killing. It is this invisible karmic force at this present moment that causally effects the transgression of a murderer.[95]

In the AKB, eight reasons for the real existence of non-informative *karma* are offered:

(i) The *sūtra* speaks of three types of *rūpa*-s (= first reason in the MVŚ).

(ii) The Buddha speaks of outflow-free *rūpa*[96] — apart from the non-informative matter, there cannot be any *rūpa* which is invisible, non-resistant and outflow-free (in the case of the *anāsrava-saṃvara*).

(iii) The *sūtra* speaks of the incessant increase of merit in one who has performed a material meritorious action (*aupadhika-puṇya-kriyā*) — only by virtue of the non-informative karmic force could merit increase even when subsequently the donor's thought is unskillful or when he is in a thoughtless state.[97]

(iv) One who has an action done through an emissary would not be endowed with a *karma-patha* unless there exists the non-informative *karma* which constitutes the *karma-patha* itself. (See explanation below, § 13.8.2).

(v) The Buddha speaks of invisible and non-resistant matter which are subsumed in the *dharmāyatana* (see *supra*, § 13.4.2.1). He can only be alluding here to the non-informative matter.

(vi) One in meditation can only be endowed with these three — *samyag-vāc*, *samyak-karmānta* and *samyag-ājīva* — in the form of non-informative *karma*, for these three are incompatible with the state of concentration. Otherwise, there would not be the path comprising eight parts.

(vii) The non-informative matter must exist as the *prātimokṣa-saṃvara*; otherwise, there would not be anything on account of which the ordainee can still be called a *bhikṣu* or *bhikṣuṇī* when he or she later has a mental state different — unskillful or neutral — from that (a skillful one) in which the ordination vows were received (= (iii) in the MVŚ).

(viii) The *sūtra* speaks of the abstention (*virati*) from evil as a dike (*setu*) on account of its obstruction to the transgression of the precepts (*dauśīlya-vibandhatvāt*). Accordingly, this abstention — which is the non-informative matter — must be a real entity, or it would not have this obstructive efficacy.

This Sarvāstivāda doctrine of the non-informative *karma* is highly controversial among the various *abhidharma* schools. In the MVŚ, the Dārṣṭāntikas' standpoint is that "there is no retribution cause apart from volition; no retribution fruit apart from sensation".[98] They also agree with the Buddha's own teaching in stating that "the bodily, vocal and mental *karma*-s are all none other than *cetanā*".[99] Both these assertions constitute a refutation of the doctrine of the non-information *karma*. The Sarvāstivāda includes the non-information matter under the *dharmāyatana*, and speaks of it as 'the matter subsumed under the *dharmāyatana*' (*dharmāyatana-saṃgṛhīta-rūpa*). The Dārṣṭāntikas, as well as Dharmatrāta, deny that there is such a thing as 'matter subsumed under *dharmāyatana*',[100] which of course amounts to a denial of the non-information matter. A more direct repudiation is as follows:

> According to the Dārṣṭāntikas, the information and non-information *karma*-s are not existent entities. Why? If the information *karma* is an existent, then one can, with this as the basis, make the non-information [*karma*] an existent. But if the information *karma* is non-existent, how can it project the non-information, making it (the non-information *karma*) an existent?[101]

The Sautrāntikas, too, deny the real existence of the non-information matter. In the AKB, they are seen to be engaged in a lengthy debate with the Vaibhāṣika, repudiating all the eight reasons offered by Vaibhāṣika (see above) in detail.[102]

13.8. Role of the non-informative in the process of karmic retribution

It is arguable as to whether the Sarvāstivāda doctrine of the tri-temporal existence of the *dharma*-s alone suffices to ensure the continued existence of the efficacy of a *karma* that has become past. One of their major arguments for *sarvāstitva* is precisely that karmic retribution would be impossible if a past *dharma* ceases to be a real entity — possessing causal efficacy. Their doctrine of *phala-ākṣepa* and *phala-dāna* too could be seen to render any intermediary agent — such as the non-informative *karma* — futile for the preservation of karmic efficacy: At the very moment when a retributive cause arises, it determines the causal connection with the fruit-to-be; i.e., 'it grasps the fruit'. At a subsequent time, when the necessary conditions obtain, it, although past, can causally actualize the fruit by dragging it, as it were, out of the future into the present; i.e., 'it gives the fruit'. It might then be argued that the category of non-informative matter was not formulated for the *karma* doctrine, but for restraint. Such a conclusion becomes all the more tempting when one takes into consideration the notion that the non-information ceases at the time of the doer's death — or, in the case of *dhyāna*- and *anāsrava-saṃvara*, when he emerges from the meditation. What, then, can the karmic role of the non-information be when a fruit of retribution arises after one or more lives?

Moreover, as we have seen, in the causal process leading to retribution, it is the originating volition that is considered by the MVŚ to be the *karma* in the proper sense; the *avijñapti* (where it exists) constitutes the 'path of *karma*' — path "through which the volition has its movement and operates to its accomplishment". (*Supra*, § 13.6). Accordingly, one can speak of volition as *karma* in the proper or narrower sense; and of the corresponding *vijñapti*- and *avijñapti-karma*-s as karmic contributors — and, for that matter, also the associated *citta-caitta*-s and *viprayukta-saṃskāra*-s, all functioning as *vipāka-hetu*-s — as karmic causes only in a general sense.

Saṃghabhadra, too, consistent with the earlier Sarvāstivādins, emphasizes the primary and continuous karmic role of the originating volition (*infra*, § 13.8.2), in spite of the Sarvāstivādin insistence that *karma* comprises two categories, *cetanā* and the *cetayitvā*. The volition although past, is still existent and can subsequently give rise to the corresponding retribution fruit.

The Sautrāntika-Dārṣṭāntikas, as we have seen, deny the reality of both the information and non-information *karma*-s. They claim that their *karma* doctrine, known as the "seed theory", is in complete agreement with the causal principle governing the continuous process of growth from a seed into the final fruition: A seed, being momentary, does not directly give rise to the fruit. However, its causal efficacy for the fruition is continuously transmitted in the transformation of the series (*santati-pariṇāma*) progressively manifesting as seed, stem, branches, leaves, flowers, and finally fruit. Likewise, a *karma* — the volition — does not directly produce the retribution; but through a similar transformational series, the karmic efficacy is continuously transmitted, until finally —

when appropriate conditions obtain — the retribution is produced.[103] Such a theory then relies solely on volition as karma, and does away completely with the need of the doctrine of the information and non-information *karma*-s

Saṃghabhadra, however, claims that it is the Sarvāstivāda — rather than the Sautrāntika — doctrine of *karma* that can be said to accord with the causal principle of the sequential growth of a plant from its seed.[104] He faults the Sautrāntika theory: Even if one were, for the sake of argument, to grant the possible validity of this theory of a progressive transformational series, it is observed that in the case of the growth from a seed into its fruit, there cannot be any interruption in the process. But in the case of a thought-process that finally gives rise to an effect, there can be interruption — the person can have thoughts of different moral natures subsequent to the originating volition. He may also be in the states of *asaṃjñi-samāpatti* or *nirodha-samāpatti* in which there is the complete interruption of mental activity. Accordingly, the Sautrāntika, acknowledging only volition as *karma*, cannot account for a karmic series that continues uninterrupted until the final fruition. And since they hold the present-only-exists standpoint, it means that in such a case, the *karma* becomes extinct before any fruition can possibly take place. For the Ābhidharmikas holding the doctrine of tri-temporal existence, argues Saṃghabhadra, the causes of retribution can continue to exist in relation to the person until fruition on account of the acquisition-series. That is to say, although the originating volition — and for that matter the informative *karma* (where there is one), other accompanying thought-concomitants and disjoined *dharma*-s — has become past, it continues to exist and be karmically related to the personal series through the acquisition-series. When the appropriate conditions obtain, although past, it can still have the efficacy of giving fruit. This accords with the observed fact that a seed, although ceased, can still have its efficacy manifested in the final production of its fruit.[105]

The above discussion shows clearly that the Sarvāstivādins assign the primary karmic role to volition. What then precisely is the karmic role of the *avijñapti karma* where it exists, projected by the volition and the *vijñapti-karma*?

13.8.1. Clues from the MVŚ

To answer this question, we must not rely on the relatively later Sarvāstivāda texts alone, such as the AKB, Ny, *Avatāra*, etc. For these texts represent the later stage of development when the doctrine of non-information had come to be increasingly focused on the notion of restraint. Thus, in the case of a *bhikṣu* taking precepts from the preceptor, the non-information is emphasized as a force of restraint (in the case of *prātimokṣa-saṃvara*) that consequently arises in the former which legitimately defines his *bhikṣu*-hood. But this is an understandable development within the Saṅgha members — the Sarvāstivāda theorists — who found the notion of non-informative matter validly and conveniently applicable in this case. The preoccupation with the emphasis on restraint is particularly conspicuous in the post-AKB texts. Thus, the *Avatāra* classifies, as does the AKB, the *avijñapti* as *saṃvara*, *asaṃvara*, and *naivasaṃvaranāsaṃvara*, and gives the only logical argument for its reality that "it is by virtue of this [non-informative matter as *saṃvara*] that the status of a *bhikṣu,* etc., can be established. Were this non-existent, it would not be legitimately established that there exist *bhikṣu*-s, etc."[106] Saṃghabhadra's explanations, given summarily at the very end of his lengthy refutation of the Sautrāntika's objections to the eight reasons for the establishment of the *avijñapti*'s reality, could also give the same impression of this preoccupation:

> What does this non-informative [matter] refer to? It refers to abstention (*virati*). 'Abstention', 'non-doing', 'non-creating', 'non-informing' (*avijñapti*) — these are synonyms for one and the same entity. ...

> This non-informative matter is also called a *karma*, for it is produced [as a fruit of emanation] with the informative [*karma*] and the volition as its causes [and therefore has similar karmic nature]…[107]

Here, Saṃghabhadra speaks of the *avijñapti* as abstention (= restraint). But we must remember the context of this explanation: it is given in refutation of the Sautrāntika's claim that *saṃvara* is not a distinct entity but merely the non-doing of evil actions. In any case, as we shall see, Saṃghabhadra, like all Sarvāstivādins, does not confine *saṃvara* to the role of being a mere restraining force. To say that *saṃvara* (in the proper sense) is not *karma,* does not entail that it does not contribute at all to karmic retribution, but to emphasize that it is an emanation-fruit of the projecting *cetanā* and *vijñapti-karma*. But being such an emanation, it is necessarily of the nature of *karma* — albeit in the broader sense of the term— of being among the causes which contribute to karmic retribution. (See *infra*, § 13.8.2).

For better clues, we should therefore first turn to the MVŚ — compiled more than two centuries earlier than the AKB. Judging by the rationales offered therein, we may say that the doctrine of the non-informative matter seems to have been articulated to account for *both*

(1) the preservation of karmic efficacy as well as
(2) the ontological status of ordination restraint,

with the former probably as the initial problematization. At any rate, the same two concerns are also unmistakable even among the eight reasons offered in the AKB. It can be seen that, of the three logical reasons given in the AKB, two, i.e., (iv) and (vi), relate to the non-informative matter as karmic force, and one i.e., (vii) relates to the notion of *saṃvara* which is not explicitly karmic. The last reason, although in the form of scriptural authority, also interprets the non-informative matter as a restraining force. Moreover, as will be made clear below, although *saṃvara* is not explicitly mentioned as a karmic force in the context of ordination, it has indeed such a nature inasmuch as it is contributive to karmic retribution.

13.8.1.1. The emphasis of non-informative matter *qua prātimokṣa-saṃvara*

As for the emphasis of non-informative matter *qua prātimokṣa-saṃvara,* we may note the reasons given in the MVŚ as to why, of the three types of *saṃvara*, the *prātimokṣa-saṃvara* alone is used as the basis for differentiating the seven assemblies — *bhikṣu*, *bhikṣuṇī*, etc. The compilers' own explanation is as follows: The *prātimokṣa-saṃvara*-s, acquired progressively, establish the sevenfold assemblies progressively: (1) those who abstain from the four transgressions by nature (*prakṛtisāvadya*: from killing to false speech) and one transgression by convention (*prajñapti-sāvadya*, *pratikṣepaṇa-sāvadya*: drinking liquor) are the *upāsaka*-s; progressively up to: (6-7) those who abstain from all transgressions are the *bhikṣu*-s and *bhikṣuṇī*-s. This is then followed by an alternative explanation by 'some' (*kecit;* 有作是說):

> The *prātimokṣa-saṃvara*, from the first moment of its projection by the informative *karma*, is present at all times [in the ordainee who] is endowed (*samanvāgata*) with it: whether he is asleep, drunk, mentally derailed, fainted; whether he is having a volition or not; whether he is having a defiled or neutral thought, or is thoughtless (*acittaka*) — in all states it is present, existing as an uninterrupted serial continuity. Accordingly, it can form the basis for the distinctive establishment of the seven assemblies.[108]

This explanation, of course, is essentially the same as the major part of Vasubandhu's definition of the non-informative matter. (See above, § 13.4.2). But what is noteworthy is that it is only one of several explanations — not even the main one — endorsed by the MVŚ compilers whose own explanation does not allude to the ontological status of *saṃvara* as a form of *avijñapti*. Considering this endorsement as well as the third logical reason given by the compilers for the reality of the non-informative matter (see above, § 13.7), we may presume that such an explanation as offered by "some" must have already been an accepted one among the Sarvāstivādins around the time of the compilation of the MVŚ. But from our discussion above, we may also presume that there must subsequently have been a conscious shift of emphasis to the notion of the non-informative matter *qua prātimokṣa*-restraint.

13.8.1.1. The emphasis of non-informative matter as a karmic force

As for the emphasis on the non-informative matter as a karmic force, we may note, first of all, that the MVŚ speaks clearly of restraint-*karma* (律儀業; *saṃvara-karma*) as a distinctive *karma* (勝業; **viśiṣṭa-karma*) that gives rise to a fruit of restraint (律儀果; *saṃvara-phala*) which is a 'great fruit' (大果; *mahā-phala*).[109] As we have seen above, when the eight lay precepts are undertaken without fulfilling all the requisite conditions, what the undertaker has is good conduct (§ 13.5.1), and good conduct is certainly karmically retributive.

The MVŚ contains a discussion on such good conduct, in which a questioner elaborately cites two stories (*nidāna*) related by Venerable Kātyāyanīputra:

> (I) To certain butchers who said that they could not survive without practicing butchery during the day, the Venerable advised them to undertake the eight precepts at night. Doing accordingly, they were reborn as *preta*-s. In the day times they suffered by being repeatedly devoured by black dogs; but at night — because of their having undertaken the precepts — they were able to enjoy with their senses to the fullest, like the *deva*-s.
>
> (II) To certain prostitutes who complained that they could not abruptly forsake their old habit of prostitution at night, the Venerable

advised them to undertake the eight precepts during the day. Doing accordingly, they were reborn as *preta*-s, suffering during the day but enjoying like *deva*-s at night.

Now, will not these two stories contradict the doctrine that the *upavāsa* restraint must be undertaken for a full day and night? The answer is that such an undertaking — for less than a full day and night — "comes under 'good conduct'; they are not *saṃvara*. What was experienced by them [— the pleasurable part in the stories —] were the fruits of good conduct, not the fruits of *saṃvara*."

The MVŚ then proceeds to distinguish various types of undertaking of the *upavāsa-saṃvara*:

(i) wherein the fundamental *karma-patha* is pure but not the preliminary stages (*sāmantaka*);

(ii) wherein both are pure but there is the damage done by unskillful thoughts (*akuśala-vitarka*);

(iii) wherein both are pure and there is no damage done by unskillful thoughts, but there is no proper mindfulness of the Buddha, etc.;

(iv) wherein both are pure, there is no damage done by unskillful thoughts and there is also proper mindfulness, but no dedication (*pari-ṇāmana*) towards liberation;

(v) wherein it is as (iv), but there is the dedication. With reference to the first four types, the Buddha said that "the *saṃvara* undertaken by them, although being distinctive/excellent *karma*, does not yield great fruit".

It is only in the last case (i.e., (v) that "the *saṃvara* undertaken is a distinctive/excellent *karma* capable of yielding great fruit".[110] (See also above, § 13.5.1).

We are therefore given to understand that an abstention from killing, etc., qua *saṃvara* is not only a *karma* — a retributive good action — but has an additional, distinctive quality. The latter, which makes it at once a *saṃvara 'cum' karma* that is capable of yielding an 'excellent fruit', is the *saṃvaratva* (see *infra*), acquired through a definite ecclesiastical procedure within the context of a consciously committed monastic training and dedication to the Buddhist goal of liberation. This *saṃvaratva* also operates as a continuously restraining force within the undertaker until it is relinquished.

Next to be noted is that, of the three logical reasons given in the MVŚ, the first two clearly intend the non-information as the indispensable karmic agent: In both the examples given, it is at the time of the victim's death that the mortal transgression is established. There is the repeated emphasis in this context that "at that time the informative [*karma*] has already faded; it is on account of the subsequent non-informative [*karma*] acquired through the force of the previous informative [*karma*] that … [the transgressor] is touched by the mortal *karma*".[111] Such an emphasis prompts us to understand as follows: it is at this time that there occurs the sufficient causal determination of the fruit-to-be corresponding to the transgression. But at this time, the originating volition and the informative action have long become past. And while past *dharma*-s can have other causal functions (called *vyāpāra*, *vṛtti*, *kriyā*, *sāmarthya*, etc. — see *supra*, § 5.3), including that of 'giving the fruit', they cannot perform this causal function of helping to ensure the sufficiency of the causal determination. Even at their present moment, the simultaneously generated informative *karma*-s cannot 'grasp' or project the same retribution fruit together with the originating volition — not being mutually co-existent causes (*sahabhū-hetu*). This function therefore has to be done by a karmic force — a real entity — that is present. In this connection, we should note that the MVŚ, while stating that the retribution cause comprises all the five *skandha*-s

— the *rūpa-skandha*-s being informative and non-informative *karma*-s — also points out that the informative and the simultaneously generated non-informative *karma*-s have different retribution fruits: Not being mutually co-existent causes, these two cannot share the same fruit.[112] This would of course mean that the originating volition too does not have the same fruit as the non-informative *karma*. Saṃghabhadra's explanations are much the same. He also specifically rejects the view, held by some masters, that the thought and thought-concomitants and the informative and non-informative *karma*-s (unless these are *citta-parivartin*, as in the case in the *rūpa-dhātu,*) that originate in the same moment, collectively effect the same fruit. Saṃghabhadra further elaborates on karmic retribution pertaining to the sphere of sensuality:

> Sometimes one *skandha* serves as the retribution cause, collectively effecting a common fruit — namely, the morally defined acquisitions and their arising (*jāti*), etc.
>
> Sometimes two *skandha*-s serve as the retribution causes, collectively effecting a common fruit — namely, skillful and unskillful matter [i.e., the bodily and vocal *karma*-s] and arising, etc.
>
> Sometimes four *skandha*-s serve as the retribution causes, collectively effecting a common fruit — namely, skillful and unskillful thought and thought-concomitants and their arising, etc.[113]

It follows from the preceding discussion that, with reference to the two examples cited in the MVŚ, the informative *karma* at its present moment cannot function simultaneously together with its originating volition to project the retribution fruit; still less can it perform this function alone, being of the nature of a vocal instruction (see below) only. Neither can we conceive of the process of 'grasping' the same fruit as having taken place twice: first, by the originating volition when it arose, secondly by the non-informative *karma* arising at the time of the victim's death. The illogicality of a fruit being projected part by part is maintained consistently by the Sarvāstivādins.[114] This leaves us with only two options:

(i) either the originating volition or the subsequent non-informative *karma* — now endowed with the specific karmic nature by the previous volition — alone projects the retribution fruit;

(ii) first, the volition projects the fruit — a necessary, but not sufficient, first step; next, the non-informative *karma* sufficiently completes the causal determination.

Unfortunately, in both examples the causal role of the originating volition is not explicitly specified.

13.8.2. Clues from Saṃghabhadra

We saw above (§ 13.8.1) that Saṃghabhadra, concluding that *avijñapti* is a real entity, refers to it as abstention, etc., clearly equating *avijñapti* with *saṃvara*. Moreover, elsewhere, articulating on *avijñapti* as a completing *karma*, he likewise refers to it as abstention.[115] This seems to suggest that in Saṃghabhadra's mind, *saṃvara* represents the most important notion of *avijñapti*. And it is in this sense that one may be justified in speaking of an increasing emphasis on *saṃvara* in the Sarvāstivāda exposition of *avijñapti*.

However, Saṃghabhadra also definitely discusses the karmic role of the *avijñapti*. It is true that he states explicitly here that *avijñapti* is not *karma*, "but because it has *karma* as its cause, it also receives the name *karma*".[116] But this should not at all be understood to mean that *avijñapti* is not karmically contributive:

It means, first, that it is the emanation fruit of the originating causes, the volition and the *vijñapti*, which are considered as *karma*. Such a statement is quite consistent with the MVŚ orthodoxy.[117] It is also a common

Sarvāstivāda position that in a karmic retribution, it is only the volition involved that projects the individual's existence — his *nikāya-sabhāga* and *jīvitendriya*.[118] The only retributive causes involved — including the *avijñapti karma* — contribute only as completing causes.

Secondly, it means that an abstention is essentially a non-action — refraining from certain action; for this reason Saṃghabhadra concedes *avijñapti* could also be called a non-*karma*.

Further, while making *avijñapti* synonymous with 'abstention', 'non-doing', etc., he also argues in the same context that the Buddha himself speaks of *śīla* — abstention from evil actions — as *karma*, and that both the Grammarians and people in the world consider stages of non-activity such as sleeping and standing as actions (*karma*). Elsewhere, accepting the AKB exposition[119] that *prātimokṣa-saṃvara* has as its synonyms *śīla*, *sucarita*, *karma* and *saṃvara*, he explains as follows:

> It is called *sucarita* because it is praised by the wise, or because by practicing this, one acquires the *iṣṭa-phala*. It is called *karma* for it is action by nature (*kriyā-svabhāvatvāt karma*); because the shameful, by virtue of the *avijñapti*, do not commit evil, and thus there is the sense of action.[120]

Saṃghabhadra's explanations below, on the case cited above from the MVŚ concerning a murder committed through an emissary (*supra*, § 13.7), are helpful for an articulate Vaibhāṣika understanding of the precise karmic role of the non-informative *karma*:

> On account of the previous informative [*karma*] and the originating volition which served as the preparation, there still exists the unskillful acquisition (*akuśala-prāpti*) which continues to arise [in a series] even when the instigator subsequently generates skillful thoughts that continue for a long time. When the emissary accomplishes the action, [this preparation becomes] capable of projecting (*ā-√kṣip*) such a type

> of Great Elements and derived matter. This derived matter [— the non-informative *karma* —] that is generated is the principal *karma-patha*. That very previous informative [*karma*] and originating volition, at the time of their arising (their present moment), served as the cause that grasped the derived matter of this present moment as a fruit of emanation. At this very present moment when the non-informative matter is arising, they — existing as past [*dharma*-s] — can give the present fruit. It is only the volitional *karma* which was generated previously that served as the projecting cause (*ākṣepaka*) for the undesired fruit [i.e., the retribution of murder].
>
> The *karma-patha* [— the non-informative *karma* —] which is generated subsequently assists in completing (*paripūraka*), so that the fruit that has been projected will definitely arise in the future. …
>
> It is not the case that the force of projection alone can ensure that a future desired or undesired fruit will definitely arise. Apart from the instigator's volition which generates the informative [*karma*], in the case that subsequently a skillful thought continues [as a series] until the time when the emissary accomplishes the action, if the non-informative [*karma*] does not exist, there will not be any other *dharma* capable of assisting as the completing cause. The fruit would then not arise. If it is the case that the preparatory volition[121] alone can ensure the future arising of the fruit, without the need of a completing cause, then, in the event that the emissary subsequently does not commit the murder, the undesired fruit should still arise for the instigator [— which is inadmissible].[122]

Thus, according to Saṃghabhadra, in such a case:

(i) The preparation — comprising the initial volition and the informative *karma* — gives rise to the unskillful acquisition which continues as a series even when the subsequent mental states are skillful — e.g., the instigator may later become remorseful.[123] It is this series that continues to link up the unskillful volition with the instigator.

(ii) The initial volition and the informative *karma*, constituting this preparation, when they arise (i.e., at their present moment), first project or 'grasp' the fruit of emanation — the non-informative *karma* which is to arise when the murder is accomplished — and later actualize or 'give' this fruit at the time of the accomplishment of murder.

We should note here the important notion that the non-informative *karma* is not to be understood simply as a continuation of the momentary informative *karma*; it is generated "with the informative [*karma*] and the volition as its causes" (see above, § 13.8.1). We see the same notion in Saṃghabhadra's definition of non-informative matter: "The non-informative [matter] … arises in dependence on a specific corporeal or vocal informative *karma*, and on a specific skillful or unskillful thought, etc." (See above § 13.4.2). It is for this reason that Saṃghabhadra states that "the *avijñapti* has *karma* as its cause, and does not serve as the cause of *karma*".[124] It is for this same reason that it is endowed by the volitional *karma* with the specific karmic nature of murder, and not a mere invisible continuation of the vocal *karma* which, in this case, consists of an order to murder. In this way, the *karma* of murder is seen to involve the totality comprising the volitional, physical/vocal and non-informative contributions.

(iii) The non-informative *karma* is the principal *karma-patha* of killing. Its function is to assist as a completing cause, ensuring the future arising of the fruit of murder.[125]

(iv) It is only the initial *karma* of volition that projects this future undesired fruit of retribution.[126]

Point (iii) above accords with the general causal principle that a fruit, although projected by a projecting *karma*, can never arise in the absence of the completing *karma*.[127] This seems to mean that a future existence projected by a *karma* can only arise specifically — with the 'given' specified by the completing causes. This is reasonable since a personal existence comprises not only the *nikāya-sabhāga* and *jīvitendriya* projected by the projecting *karma* (volition), but also the body with the organs — comprising *rūpa*, *gandha*, *rasa* and *spraṣṭavya* — and with specific experiences as retributions derived from the completing *karma*-s. This is, in some respect, similar to the case that a thought always arises specifically — the specifics being contributed by the associated thought concomitants. The bodily and vocal *karma*-s effect, as their retribution fruits, "matter, thought and thought concomitants and conditionings disjoined from thought". But they cannot project a *nikāya-sabhāga* — an existence such as that in hell resulting from the *karma* of murder.

Elsewhere, Saṃghabhadra states that there are in fact two types of retribution cause — projecting and completing;[128] it accords with the *sūtra* to assign the volition — mental *karma* — to the former role and the non-informative *karma*-s to the latter.[129] Thus, according to some Sarvāstivāda masters, the 32 marks of a Great Man (*mahāpuruṣa*) are first projected by the volition which is the projecting *karma* of the *nikāya-sabhāga*; they are then completed by many volitions. "The 32 marks of a Great Man are the fruits of the completing *karma* of the *nikāya-sabhāga*, not that of the projecting *karma* of the *nikāya-sabhāga*." In this regard, the opinion of the MVŚ compilers is that 32 volitions project the 32 marks each of which is completed by many *karma*-s.[130] As another example, the MVŚ opines that the false view (*mithyā-dṛṣṭi*) that cuts off the roots of skillfulness can both project as well as complete a *nikāya-sabhāga*, for the reason that there is volitional *karma* conjoined with false view, and that these two share the same fruit.[131]

In other cases where the doer himself accomplishes the action with the informative *karma*, the informative *karma* so determined, plus the non-informative *karma* generated, constitute *karma* properly called. Thus, "if, with a thought of killing, one is actually depriving another's life, all the unskillful bodily informative *karma*-s and the simultaneous non-informative occurring at that very time, constitute the principal [path of *karma*] of killing".[132] Herein too, then, the karmic role of the non-informative *karma* is clearly acknowledged.

13.8.3. Non-informative *karma* as a medium of preservation of karmic force

One important question remains: After the fruit has been sufficiently determined, what is the use of the non-informative *karma* which is said to still continue until one's death unless it is beforehand relinquished through some causes? The answer lies in the tacit notion that a karmic force — unless relinquished — affects one's mind for as long as the mind exists. In the case of an ordination vow, the karmic force generated continues to show its effect in helping the ordainee to restrain himself. But this emphasis that came to be developed within the Saṅgha members must not be allowed to eclipse the karmic nature of the non-informative actions involved which are of a moral nature. In the case of a karmic action such as killing, its continuous effect is to be seen more explicitly in 'accumulating' (*upa-√ci*) the *karma*: that is, it continues to interact with the mind in various ways, as a result of which one may repeat similar actions, or rejoice in it, or feel remorseful about it (cf. § 13.5.1), etc. All these subsequent happenings will have consequences with respect to the actual karmic retribution: they may transform an indeterminate *karma* to be determinate — e.g., when there is rejoicing, etc.; or they may result in damaging the otherwise superior quality of the fruit — e.g., when the 'great fruit' to be of a *saṃvara-karma* is damaged by subsequent unskillful thoughts (see § 13.8.1); or intensify the sufferings in the retribution — e.g., when several mortal transgressions are committed after the first one; or even effectively expurgate or at least render harmless the effect of a grave transgression — e.g., through repentance (see *infra*, § 14.4).

Such an interaction presupposes a continuously present and active karmic agent — the *avijñapti* — through which the existing status of the karmic effect can be continuously modified. Above (§ 13.7), we have seen one of the arguments that the non-informative matter is the real force — the merit (*puṇya*) — that is said in the *sūtra* to increase incessantly in one who has done a meritorious action. In the case of a material giving, this merit increases by reason of the qualities of the recipients and of the benefits that they derive from the gifts (*guṇa-viśeṣād anugraha-viśeṣāc ca*). Saṃghabhadra explains that this increase is in the sense of the merit being transformed from a lower grade to a higher one, or becoming more in the serial continuation.[133]

13.8.4. Conclusion

From the discussion above, we may conclude that non-informative *karma*, as much as informative *karma*, is retributive. This is in fact what we should expect logically, since the very notion of *karma* implies retribution. In pristine clear terms, the MVŚ states that "the bodily and vocal *karma*-s refer to those two *karma*-s [comprising] the skillful and unskillful informative [*karma*-s] and the non-informative *karma*-s derived from the informative *karma*-s which are not co-existent with thought (*cittānuparivartin*) — *these definitely can effect retribution fruits*".[134] Moreover, as regards the *karma-patha*-s:

> Excepting sensual misconduct (*kāma-mithyā-cāra*), all the other principal (*maula*) *karma-patha*-s have necessarily non-informative, but not necessarily informative [*karma*]. If an action done by oneself is immediately accomplished, then it has informative *karma*. If it is done through another person, or if at the time of its accomplishment the informative [*karma*] has already ceased, then there is only non-informative [*karma*].
>
> For the case of sensual misconduct, there is also necessarily informative [*karma*]. At the preparatory stage, there is necessarily informative [*karma*],

> not necessarily non-informative [*karma*]... At the stage of subsequent action, there is necessarily non-informative [*karma*]; not necessarily informative [*karma*] — [the latter] exists if a [consecutive action] is done, not otherwise.[135]

All these, then, point clearly to the role of the non-informative *karma* as contributive to karmic retribution. Even after the series of a non-informative *karma* has ended — for example, when the person dies — as in the case of a past volition and informative *karma*, the non-informative *karma* too continues to be connected with the personal series (*santati*) by virtue of the continuous acquisition-series which ends only when the fruit is actualized. From Saṃghabhadra's explanation above, however, it would appear that it is still the originating volition that plays the primary karmic role; the role of the non-informative *karma* is a relatively limited one.

It is true that in the specific discussions on restraint — which occupy the larger part of the Sarvāstivāda exposition of *karma* — the non-informative *karma* is never explicitly stated to be karmically retributive. Nevertheless, in other contexts, we do find in the MVŚ the terms *saṃvara-karma*, *asaṃvara-karma*[136] and the explicit statement that bodily and vocal restraints are *karma*-s.[137] With regard to the seven non-mental paths of *karma*, restraint and non-restraint are explicitly made synonymous with *karma* and paths of *karma*. Thus,

> the seven principal skillful paths of *karma* — whether the informative [*karma*] or the non-informative [*karma*] arising in this same moment — each has seven significations: 1. morality (*śīla*), 2. good conduct (*sucarita*), 3. restraint (*saṃvara*), 4. *prātimokṣa*, 5. *prātimokṣa*-restraint, 6. *karma*, 7. path of *karma*. From this [moment] onward, the non-informative *karma*-s have only five significations — excluding *prātimokṣa* and path of *karma*. … .

Similarly for the seven non-mental principal unskillful paths of *karma*.[138] In the sphere of sensuality, all the ten skillful and unskillful paths of *karma* can be acquired. The skillful ones are subsumable either as restraint or neither-restraint-nor-non-restraint; the unskillful ones, non-restraint or neither-restraint-nor-non-restraint.[139]

Moreover, the category of non-informative matter which is neither-restraint-nor-non-restraint — vast in scope — comprises actions which are explicitly karmic in nature and which are more explicitly stated or understood as such. In such instances, the terms 'non-informative transgression' and 'non-informative *karma*' (*avijñapti-karma*) are a common-place. The following serves as a good illustration:

> Question: If with one preparation, a person simultaneously kills both his mother and another female, with regard to the mother, he acquires the non-informative transgression of killing (*prāṇātipāta-avadya*) and of an *ānantarya* (matricide), with regard to the other female, he acquires only the non-informative transgression of killing. …[140]

13.8.4.1. Summary

An examination of the rationale given in the MVŚ for the *avijñapti* doctrine — similarly reflected in the AKB and the Ny —suggests that it was probably first formulated out of a twofold consideration:

(i) There are situations — such as that of a murder committed through an emissary — in which an invisible force must be assumed, capable of preserving the karmic nature of the originating volition and serving as a completing cause to ensure the future arising of the retribution fruit.

(ii) The *avijñapti* as an invisible force — called 'restraint' or 'abstention' — preserving the essence of the ordination vows, serves as a legitimate cause for the distinction among the *bhikṣu*-s, *bhikṣuṇī*-s, etc.

From this, the contrasting categories called non-restraint and neither-restraint-nor-non-restraint, as well as the categories of meditation and pure restraints came to be elaborated. It would seem that the monastic *abhidharma* scholiasts gradually shifted their focus of discussion on the *avijñapti* as restraint and its related categories.

But this shift of emphasis has never obscured the nature of the *avijñapti* as a karmic force — as is evident from the AKB and the Ny. Both works, composed a couple of centuries after the MVŚ, still provide us with a clear picture of its karmic role, as follows:

(a) It is a retribution cause capable of karmic retribution, although its function is confined to be that of a completing — as opposed to a projecting — cause. This specific function is distinctly brought out by Saṃghabhadra.

(b) It preserves the karmic efficacy of the originating volition and the *vijñapti-karma* as a serial continuity with which the mind can interact in ways that modify its karmic existing status.

(c) This preservation, however, is a limited one, lasting at most till the end of one existence.

(d) Even after the *avijñapti* has been relinquished, the karmic efficacy that it represents — as well as those of the volitional and informative *karma*-s that have become past — continues to be linked with the personal series through the *prāpti*-series until the retribution fruit is actualized.

(e) Even where the *avijñapti* is conceptualized as a force of restraint, etc., its karmic function is still to be understood — as evidenced by terms like *saṃvara-karma* (律儀業), etc.

NOTES

[1] MVŚ, 586b.

[2] A, ii, 80: *kamma-vipāko bhikkhave acinteyyo na cintetabbo*; the other three inconceivables are: *buddhānāṃ buddhavisayo, jhāyissa jhānavisayo, loka-cintā. Cf. Milindapañha*, 189.

[3] MVŚ, 587b.

[4] MVŚ, 587a.

[5] For definition and nature of *vipāka-hetu*, *cf.* MVŚ, 98a–c. Also see *supra,* § 6.3.4.

[6] MVŚ, 102c.

[7] AKB, 258: *na ca kevalaṃ karmaivākṣepakaṃ janmanaḥ* /

[8] Ny, 427b–c.

[9] MVŚ, 578b–c.

[10] MVŚ, 216c.

[11] MVŚ, 217a.

[12] MVŚ, 975c.

[13] MVŚ, 604b: 一思總感，多思成滿. See also *infra*, § 14.5.

[14] Ny, 427b–c.

[15] Ny, 492a.

[16] MVŚ, 649b–c.

[17] *Cf. Visuddhimagga*, XVI, 90: *dukkham eva hi, na koci dukkhito / kārako na, kiriyā va vijjati / atthi nibbuti, na nibbuto pumā / maggam atthi, gamako na vijjati* // Also *cf.* Nāgārjuna's *Mūla-madhyamaka-kārikā*, VIII, especially stanzas 1 and 12.

[18] Ny, 485a.

[19] Vy, 441: *vipāka-dānāya niyatībhavanti.*

[20] AKB, 277: *tāni karmāṇy anuśaya-vaśād upacayaṃ gacchanti antareṇa cānuśayāt bhavābhinirvartane na samarthāni bhavanti.*

[21] Vy, 441: *na hy arhataḥ paunarbhavikāni karmāṇy aniyatāni na santi / anuśayābhāvāt tu punar-bhavābhinirvartane na samarthāni bhavanti /*

[22] See AKB, 234 f. The *sūtra*-s are cited as the basis of this classification — see *Aṅguttara*, ii, 230; *Dīgha*, iii, 230; T 1, 600a (*Madhyamāgama*); MVŚ, 589c; etc. (Other sources given in the AKB(F), 128, n. 6). The last category may in part be compared to the Theravāda notion of an *arahant*'s *kiriya(/kiriyā/kriyā)-citta*.

[23] *Cf.* Ny, 569a.

[24] *Cf.* MVŚ, 583b; AKB, 239. For the preparation of a skillful path of *karma*, *cf.* MVŚ, 595c.

[25] AKB, 192 f.

[26] MVŚ, 634b.

[27] AKB, 195.

[28] MVŚ, 635a.

[29] Ny, 527c–528a.

[30] Ny, 522a.

[31] Ny, 535c.

[32] MVŚ, 587b; AKB, 192.

[33] Xuan Zang in the AKB(C) translates *avijñapti* as both 'non-information' and 'non-information *karma*'.

[34] MVŚ, 614a–c.

[35] MVŚ, 617c.

[36] AKB, 8: *vikṣiptācittakasyāpi yo 'nubandhaḥ śubhāśubhaḥ / mahābhūtāny upādāya, sā hy avijñaptir ucyate //*

[37] Ny, 335b.

[38] Ny, 335c; Vy, 32: *kṛte 'pi visabhāge 'pi citte cittātyaye ca yat / vyākṛtāpratighaṃ rūpaṃ sā hy avijñaptir iṣyate //*

[39] SPrŚ, 781c–782a.

[40] SPrŚ, *loc. cit.*

[41] Vy, 30 ff.

[42] Ny, 335b.

[43] *Entrance*, 84, § 1.2.7.1.

[44] MVŚ, 395a.

[45] MVŚ, 390a; AKB, 9.

[46] Ny, 338a. Saṃghabhadra's explanation is justified by that in the MVŚ, 390a.

[47] MVŚ, 723c.

[48] *Loc. cit.*

[49] AKB, 196.

[50] *Dharmāyatana-saṃgṛhīta-rūpa* — Ny, 540b. *Cf.* T 2, 91c.

[51] *Cf.* AKB, 195 f.: *sā 'pi ca vijñaptiḥ satī tadākṣepe cetanāyā balaṃ nibhālayte / jaḍatvāt /*; Vy, 351: *sā 'pi ca vijñaptir bhavadīyā satī vidyamānā avijñapter ākṣepe utpādana-cetanāyā balaṃ sāmarthyaṃ nibhālayate apekṣate / kasmāt / jaḍatvād apaṭutvāc cetanā-balam antareṇa tām avijñaptiṃ janayituṃ na śaknoti / na hy asatyāṃ samādāna-cetanāyāṃ yadṛcchotpannā vijñaptir avijñaptiṃ janayati /*

[52] T 32, 290b.

[53] *Cf.* MVŚ, 383c.

[54] MVŚ, 662b.

[55] MVŚ, 661c, 730b.

[56] See AKB, 197 ff.

[57] MVŚ, 610a; AKB, 203.

[58] Vy, 364.

[59] MVŚ, 610a.

[60] AKB, 203.

[61] MVŚ, 684c: "The non-information generated by the information is of the nature of an emanation (*niṣyanda*); it is non-appropriated (*anupātta*) and belongs to a sentient being (*sattvākhyā*). The Great Elements from which it is derived are of the nature of emanation; they are appropriated (*upātta*) and belong to sentient beings."

[62] *Cf.* AKB, 205 ff.; *Avatāra*, 981a–b; *Entrance*, 84–87.

[63] AKB, 208: *na hi tad atyantaṃ pāpasya pratimokṣaṇāya saṃvartate.*

[64] MVŚ, 649a; AKB, 214.

[65] AKB, 205: *dauśīlya-prasarasya saṃvaraṇaṃ saṃrodhaḥ saṃvaraḥ* / *cf.* Ny, 552a.

[66] MVŚ, 623b.

[67] Ny, 543c. See also quotation from Ny in § 13.8.1.

[68] Ny, 539c.

[69] AKB, 212, Ny, 552a–b.

[70] Ny, 552b.

[71] Ny, 529c.

[72] For *hrī* and *apatrāpya*, see *Entrance*, § 4.5.14.

[73] *Cf.* Ny, 552a.

[74] See also, AKB, 213.

[75] Ny, 552a–b.

[76] MVŚ, 608c.

[77] T 41, 235c.

[78] T no. 1550, 814a

[79] *Cf.* AKB, 459; MVŚ, 779b.

[80] MVŚ, 623a–b.

[81] AKB, 238; cf. D, iii, 269; T 1, 437b; T 2, 274a.

[82] MVŚ, 583b ff.; AKB, 243 ff.

[83] MVŚ, 243a; AKB, 242.

[84] MVŚ, 582c.

[85] MVŚ, 103a–b.

[86] MVŚ, 583c, 584a.

[87] MVŚ, 243a. See § 14.2.

[88] AKB, 248: *tatsamutthānacetanāyās tān adhiṣṭhāya pravṛtteḥ* / AKB(C), 88c.

[89] MVŚ, 587c, 588a, 589a–b.

[90] MVŚ, 589a.

[91] MVŚ, 589b–c. *ibid.*, 587a: The Vibhajyavāda, in contrast, holds that the last three are *karma* in nature.

[92] *Cf.* D, iii, 217.

[93] Also *cf.* AKB, 238.

[94] MVŚ, 634c.

[95] *Cf.* MVŚ, 635a, 636c; AKB, 196, 238.

[96] *Cf.* T 2, 13b–c.

[97] AKB, 196 f.

[98] MVŚ, 96a.

[99] MVŚ, 587a.

[100] MVŚ, 383b.

[101] MVŚ, 634b.

[102] AKB, 196 ff.

[103] See AKB, 477: *naiva tu vayaṃ vinaṣṭāt karmaṇa āyatyāṃ phalotpattiṃ brūmaḥ / … tatsaṃtatipariṇāmaviśeṣād bījaphalavat / yathā bījāt phalam utpadyata ity ucyate / na ca tad vinaṣṭād bījād utpadyate / nāpy anantaram eva / … tatsaṃtati-pariṇāma-viśeṣād aṅkurakāṇḍapatrādi-kramaniṣpannāt puṣpāvasānāt /*

[104] Ny, 535b.

[105] Ny, 535a–b.

[106] See *Entrance*, 38.

[107] SPrŚ, 862a; also Ny, 543c. See below where Saṃghabhadra explains the *avijñapti* as a *niṣyanda-phala* generated by the originating volition and the *vijñapti*. (*Cf.* Vy, 356: *yathā vaibhāṣikāṇām avijñaptivādinām avijñaptiḥ karma-patha ity ākhyāyate / kārye kāraṇopacārāt / kāyika-vācikatvaṃ tu tat-kriyā-phalatvāt /* Also *cf.* MVŚ, 622c.

[108] MVŚ, 643c.

[109] MVŚ, 648a–b, 649c.

[110] MVŚ, 648a–b.

[111] MVŚ, 634c.

[112] MVŚ, 96b–c.

[113] Ny, 427c–428a; cf. MVŚ, 97b–c. The cases pertaining to the two spheres are also discussed.

[114] MVŚ, 604a, 887c; AKB, 258.

[115] Ny, 427c–428a: "…because multiple abstentions (遠離體) are generated by one *citta*…"; "The *vijñapti*-s consists of numerous *paramāṇu*-s. The *avijñapti*-s too consist of numerous abstention entities (遠離事; **virati-dravya*). Although [these numerous entities in each case] are necessarily conascent, they nevertheless have different fruits…"

[116] Ny, 544a.

[117] *Cf*, MVŚ, 622c. Also, MVŚ, 723c: "It should be understood that the mental *karma* is the cause projecting the *śīla* (= *saṃvara*). The very cause for *śīla* must not be called *śīla*, lest there be the fallacy of confounding the cause with the effect." Note also that in MVŚ (578c, 589a), AKB and Ny, *cetanā* is considered the *karma* in contrast to *karma-patha* — see *supra*, § 12.6.

[118] See for instance, MVŚ, 887c, where the role as projecting *karma* is ascribed to *cetanā*.

[119] AKB, 207.

[120] Ny, 549b.

[121] Judging from the context and from SPrŚ, 心 must be an error of 思.

[122] Ny, 543a; SPrŚ, 861c–862a.

[123] Ny, 542c.

[124] Ny, 544a.

[125] MVŚ, 96b.

[126] *Cf.* Ny, 542c27–28.

[127] *Cf.* Ny, 486c.

[128] Ny, 427b.

[129] Ny, 427c.

[130] MVŚ, 887c.

[131] MVŚ, 185a. For the discussion on the projecting and completing *karma*-s for the *nikāya-sabhāga*, also cf. MVŚ, 216c, 277a, 594a, 774a, 782c.

[132] *Cf.* MVŚ, 583b, etc.

[133] AKB, 197; Ny, 542b. However, note that in the case of one who acquires a restraint of a low grade with a generating thought of a low grade, there can be no increase in the sense of transforming the restraint to one of a higher grade in spite of subsequent moral efforts. The same principle applies to the other grades of both restraint and non-restraint — MVŚ, 607b–c.

[134] MVŚ, 96b. *Cf.* also MVŚ, 157c which says that the non-informative *karma* is to be known by going from the fruit into the cause; from the gross into the subtle…

[135] MVŚ, 635a.

[136] *Cf.* MVŚ, 649c, 650b, 651a, etc.

[137] MVŚ, 984c.

[138] MVŚ, 585c, 584a; cf. AKB, 207.

[139] MVŚ, 586b, 584b.

[140] MVŚ, 617c — various other instances abound. In this case, he of course also acquires the informative *karma* of killing — but this is with regard to matricide, as it is graver than the killing of another female (MVŚ, 619c; AKB, 263). See also the allusion to Ajātaśatru's *avijñapti-karma* above.

14. *Karma* and the Nature of its Retribution

14.1. Karmic retribution as a Middle Way doctrine

The Middle Way nature of the Sarvāstivāda doctrine of *karma* is especially conspicuous in their discussions on retribution. The way in which a given *karma* is to be retributed — the manner in which the 'doer' experiences it — is by no means absolutely fixed. For one thing, it depends on the spiritual status of the experiencer. The *Loṇa-phala sutta*[1] gives the example of the difference in the effect of a small amount of salt that is put into a cup of water and into the river.[2] It states explicitly that if the effect of a given *kamma* is necessarily to be experienced in an immutable manner, then the spiritual life would be in vain and there would be no possibility of the utter destruction of *dukkha*. In a similar vein, the AKB quotes the following stanza:[3]

> The ignorant, committing even a small evil goes below;
> The wise, although committing a great one, leaves behind the bad [abodes].
> A compacted [piece of] iron, although small, sinks into water;
> The same made into a bowl, although great, floats.[4]

This is likely an acceptable notion for the orthodox Sarvāstivādins since Saṃghabhadra also repeated the stanza in the Ny without any objection.[5]

14.2. Six causes affecting the gravity of a *karma*

The Sarvāstivāda teaches that given the same *karma* — e.g., killing — the gravity in terms of its retributive effect can vary depending on various factors. A *karma* can be divided into nine grades — low-low (i.e., the lightest), low-middle, etc., up to high-high (i.e., the most grave). According to the *Prajñapti-śāstra:*

> For the transgression of killing, the high-high grade leads to rebirth in Avīci hell [i.e., the lowest hell, with the greatest amount of sufferings incessantly]; the high-middle grade, to [rebirth in] Pratāpana Mahānaraka, …; the low-low grade, to [rebirth in] the planes of existence of the animals and *preta*-s.[6]

The causal factors influencing the retributive effect are said to be six:

(i) The subsequent actions (*pṛṣṭha*) following the principal action — the latter can become grave when, for instance, the subsequent actions contribute in such a way as to establish it as being necessarily retributed.

(ii) The nature of the 'field' (*kṣetra-viśeṣa*) — that is, the moral or spiritual status of the person with respect to whom the *karma* is incurred. Thus, among the five mortal transgressions (*ānantarya karma*),[7] the splitting of the Saṅgha is the most grave because it is the most excellent field of virtue; splitting the Saṅgha is ruining the Dharma Body (*dharma-śarīra*). Next is the shedding of a Buddha's blood, followed by the killing of an *arhat*, matricide and lastly patricide — a mother as a field is superior to a father because she has the kindness of nourishing and rearing the child. The AKB gives the example of a *bhikṣu* who was born as a female as a result of having insulted the Saṅgha as being women folk, even though the intention involved was weak.

(iii) The basis (*adhiṣṭhāna*) — that is, the deed itself (the *karma-patha*). Given the same factor of field, the deed itself can determine the relative gravity of the *karma*. Thus killing the parents is much graver than stealing from them.

(iv) The preparatory action (*prayoga*) leading to the principal action.

(v) Volition (*cetanā*) — the mental force through which the *karma-patha* comes to be accomplished.

(vi) The strength of the intention (*āśaya-viśeṣa*) involved. For this, the example is given of a eunuch who regained his masculinity as a result of having — with a strong intention (*tīvreṇ 'āśayena*) arising from the thought "I have such kind of suffering in losing my masculinity" — rescued bulls from being castrated.[8]

To these six, one may add another: the factor of the experience of the recipient of the action. This is clear from the way the Sarvāstivāda explains the *naiva-saṃvara-nāsaṃvara* type of *avijñapti*. Thus, when one offers some material gift, such as food, a monastery (*ārāma*), etc., to the *bhikṣu-saṅgha*, or offers medicine to the sick, etc., the merit increases in one according to both the excellence of virtues of the recipients as well as the benefits they derive from the offering.[9] Likewise, a factor that makes killing a grave transgression is the suffering that the victim undergoes.

An interesting question is raised in the MVŚ: Which transgression is the more grave — destroying the eggs of ants or killing a human who has cut off the roots of skillfulness? The opinion of the MVŚ compilers is that from the point of view of punishment, the latter is the more grave since the killer has thereby incurred an extreme transgression — the victim is a human. From the point of view of a path of *karma*, the former is the more grave since they are endowed with the skillful *dharma*-s. This means that karmically speaking, what matters most is the spiritual status of a sentient being: It is a very grave transgression indeed to interrupt the spiritual progress of any sentient being — be it as trifling as an ant![10]

14.3. Determinate and indeterminate *karma*

The *sūtra* was also said to have taught that there are certain *karma*-s which, although they ought to be retributed in the present life, are transformed to be retributed in the hells, and others which, although they ought to be retributed in the hells, are transformed to be retributed in the present life.[11] In this connection, the Sarvāstivāda notion of determinate (*niyata*) and indeterminate (*aniyata*) *karma* (see *supra*) is particularly noteworthy. The former comprises the three categories — 'experiencible in this life', 'experiencible in the next life', 'experiencible in a subsequent life'; their retribution is certain.[12] The latter may or may not be retributed. Saṃghabhadra explained the *aniyata-vedanīya-karma* as follows, clarifying in the process what is meant by a *karma* that is done (*kṛta*) but not accumulated (*upacita*):

> In what sense are they not necessarily retributed?
>
> The Bhagavat saw that there were certain types of *karma* which — on account of ethical conduct (*śīla*), or resolution, or the spiritual life (*brahmacarya*), or *samādhi*, or the power of knowledge (*jñāna-bala*) — are rendered fruitless or lightened, or moved into a different state. These are said to be indeterminate *karma*-s. In order to transform these *karma*-s, one should practice the spiritual life. Sentient beings have mostly these *karma*-s. However, when the *sūtra* says that there are certain *karma*-s which, although they ought to be retributed in the present life, are transformed to be retributed in the hells, it does not, in this context, refer to the *karma* to be experienced in this life. What it means is that there are *karma*-s which are not necessarily experienced. If one can vigorously cultivate the precepts

pertaining to the body, the thought (*citta*) and understanding (*prajñā*), these *karma*-s ought to be experienced in the human world. [However,] as a result of not cultivating the precepts pertaining to the body, the thought and understanding, one falls into *naraka* through these *karma*-s.

The *sūtra* also says that there are certain *karma*-s which, although they ought to be retributed in the hells, are transformed to be retributed in the present life. This too does not refer to the *karma*-s that are determinate with regard to the time [of retribution],[13] but to the indeterminate *karma*. The meaning is to be understood as above.

Alternatively, the meaning of the former *sūtra* reference is to be explained thus: There are *karma*-s which, although done, are not accumulated. If they are allowed to follow their own course, they would be retributed in the present life. If, [however,] one subsequently further commits *karma*-s that are retributable in the hells, nourishing the *karma* and causing it to be accumulated, one will proceed to experience it in the hells. Hence, the *sūtra* says that there are *karma*-s which one ought to experience presently among human beings, [but] which — as a result of one subsequently further committing *karma*-s retributable in the hells — are caused to be accumulated, transforming them to be retributed in the hells. Thus we know that the reference of the *sūtra* is to the indeterminate *karma*.[14]

The *sūtra* alluded by Saṃghabhadra here seems to be the *Salt-simile sūtra* corresponding to the Pāli *Loṇa-phala-sutta* (see above, § 14.1). The MVŚ cites this *sūtra* and explains its import thus: A person who — say — destroys a life, incurs a *karma* that can lead to the retribution of being born in hell. If this person does not vigorously practice the spiritual path and attain arhathood, he would indeed be born in hell. If, however, he can do so, he will be able to experience the hellish sufferings as the karmic consequence in his present human body. The MVŚ here quotes Vasumitra's opinion that such an experience is possible only in the case of an *arhat* whose body is perfumed by superior (*viśiṣṭa*) *samādhi* and *prajñā* — even the *śaikṣa*-s are incapable of doing so, let alone the *pṛthagjana*-s.[15]

Necessarily retributive *karma*-s other than the five mortal transgressions and the five quasi-mortal transgressions — defiling one's mother, defiling a female *arhat*, killing a predestined (*niyati-stha*) Bodhisattva, killing a trainee, stealing from the Saṅgha[16] — are transcended under three circumstances:

(i) When the practitioner passes from the stage of the summits to that of the receptivities (*kṣānti*) of the *nirvedha-bhāgīya*, he transcends the state of retribution of the *karma* retributable in the evil planes of existence.

(ii) When he is attaining non-returnership, he becomes detached from the sphere of sensuality; *karma*-s retributable in the sphere of sensuality — other than those to be retributed in the present life — are therefore transcended.

(iii) When he is attaining arhathood, he is definitely not going to have any more rebirths in any of the three spheres; the *karma*-s retributable in the *rūpa*- and *ārūpya-dhātu*-s — other than those to be retributed in the present life — are transcended.

The MVŚ and the AKB express these circumstances as those when the aforesaid corresponding *karma*-s, in each case, stand near the practitioner, as it were, obstructing him to the utmost (*vighnāyopatiṣṭhate*). The AKB compares the obstruction to that desperately made to the debtor by his creditors when he is about to leave the country. The MVŚ explains that it is as if the *karma*-s were to say:

> If you are able to enter into the state of the receptivities, you will definitely not be experiencing any births in the three evil planes of existence — in whose bodies then are we going to have the retributions?[17]

14.4. A *karma* that has been done, and one that has been accumulated

The distinction discussed by Saṃghabhadra above (§ 14.3), between an action that has been done (*kṛta*; *byas pa*; 造作) and one that has been accumulated (*upacita*; *bsags pa*; 增長), also represents an important aspect of the Sarvāstivāda doctrine of *karma*. These two terms occur juxtaposed in some of the Abhidharma works before the MVŚ, e.g., the SgPŚ,[18] the PrŚ[19] and the JPŚ,[20] but are not distinguished from each other or defined. In the MVŚ, elaborate distinctions are made between *karma*-s that are just done but not accumulated, and those that are both done and accumulated.[21]

We will follow the explanations given in the AKB[22] which are more concise than those in the MVŚ, supplementing with explanations and examples provided by the MVŚ where appropriate. According to the AKB, an action, although done, is not to be counted in terms of its effective karmic effect or of 'having been accumulated' under the following five conditions:

(i) If it is not done intentionally (i.e., not a *saṃcetanīya-karma*) or if it is done casually without having first involved the volition (i.e., not *cetayitvā*).[23]

(ii) If the number of actions which together are responsible for a particular rebirth are not completed. Thus, if one *karma* is responsible for a particular rebirth of a person, at the preparatory stage the *karma* is done, and at the stage of the completion it is both done and accumulated. If three *karma*-s are necessary for the person to effect the rebirth, then when he performs the first two, his *karma*-s are only done but not accumulated; when he further performs the third one, then his *karma*-s become both done and accumulated.[24]

An action is completed only by its consecutive (*pṛṣṭha*) action which comprises the moments of *avijñapti* projected by the principal action, e.g., killing, and other subsequent actions. One is in fact 'touched' (*spṛśyate*) by the transgression of killing on account of both the preparatory action (*prayoga*) and the achievement or completion of its result, i.e., the principal action of killing.[25] This applies even in the case of the five mortal transgressions. The MVŚ gives the following examples:

(a) There is preparation, but not accomplishment of the fruit — a certain person intending matricide mistakenly killed another woman thinking that she was his mother. Subsequently, while cleaning his knife by poking it into a heap of grain wherein the mother was hiding, the mother was hurt by the knife and died as a result. In this case, when the son did the preparation, the fruit was not accomplished; when the fruit was actually accomplished, there was no more preparation.

(b) There is accomplishment of the fruit, but no preparation — a certain person was holding his parents while passing through a dangerous path. Fearing that robbers would come, he forcibly pushed the parents forward. The parents fell down and died as a result.

In both examples, the person did not incur the mortal transgression.[26] In fact, one who prepares for the killing, without actually generating the killing, has the fruit of the preparatory action, but not the completion of this fruit.[27]

There are some other situations where one's killing does not actually incur the transgression of killing — e.g., when one causing the death of another, dies even before the victim's death. Since the killer dies before the accomplishment of the fruit (i.e., the principal action of killing), there is no subsequent *nikāya-sabhāga* to be endowed with (*samanvāgata*) that transgression.[28] But even the transgression of a preparation can be a very grave one — such as Devadatta's in his attempt to kill the Buddha, which amounts to a mortal transgression.[29] Saṃghabhadra explained that what is 'done' refers to the two together — preparatory and principal actions; what is accumulated refers to the consecutive actions.[30]

(iii) If there are no accompaniments (*parivāra*) — e.g., having committed an unskillful action, one does not rejoice in it.[31]

(iv) If it is followed by remorse (*vipratisāra*) or repentance through confession, etc., which is counteractive to its effect (*pratideśan'ādi-pratipakṣaḥ*).[32]

(v) If it is not necessarily retributed (*vipāka-dāne niyataṃ*).[33]

In brief, when a *karma* is said to be both done and accumulated, it means that it has been volitionally projected as well as accomplished, and it becomes necessarily retributive.[34]

Moreover, the MVŚ explains that whether a *karma* is accumulated or not also depends on the moral and spiritual status of the doer: thus, if an unskillful *karma* is done by having false views concerning cause and effect, it is both done and accumulated — hence necessarily retributed. Conversely, if this doer has, instead, the proper views in this regard, then the *karma* is only done but not accumulated.

Furthermore, having done such a *karma*, if the doer "can abandon, cast it away (*ut-√sṛj*) and relies on counteraction", or becomes remorseful, or does not "constantly recollect it", or does not "rejoice in it and dedicate (*pari-√nam*) it to the fruit", then it is not accumulated.[35] In this connection, the notion that *karma*-s can be destroyed by outflow-free *karma* (the neither-black-nor-white category) should also be noted (*supra*, § 13.2).

In terms of the distinction between 'grasping a fruit' (*phala-grahaṇa*) and the actual 'giving of a fruit' (*phala-dāna*) (§ 7.4), a *karma* which has both functions is both done and accumulated. If it has only the former function, it is said to be done but not accumulated. Bhadanta Dharmatrāta[36] expressed the same notion in different words:

> If a *karma* that has been done will — when an assemblage of conditions obtains — necessarily effect its fruit, it is said to be done as well as accumulated; otherwise it is only said to be done.[37]

The early Dārṣṭāntikas, who also belong to the general camp of the Sarvāstivāda, in fact had a doctrine that the effect of even the five mortal transgressions — the *ānantarya karma*-s — can be transformed:

> Question: Are the *karma*-s experiencible in this life (*dṛṣṭa-dharma-vedanīya karma*) necessarily retributed in the present life (*dṛṭe dharme*)? The same question for the *karma*-s experiencible in the next life (*upapadya-vedanīya karma*) and the *karma*-s experiencible in a future life subsequent to the next (*apara-paryāya-vedanīya karma*).
>
> The Dārṣṭāntikas hold that it is not necessarily so, for all *karma*-s are transformable — [all] up to the *ānantarya karma*-s are transformable.[38]
>
> Question: If so, why are they called *dṛṣṭa-dharma-vedanīya karma*-s, etc.?
>
> They explain thus: The *karma*-s retributable in this life do not necessarily have their fruits of retribution in the present life. [But] those which are retributed are necessarily retributed in this — and not another — existence; hence they are called *karma* retributable in the present life. The same applies for the *upapadya-vedanīya* and *apara-paryāya-vedanīya karma*-s.[39]

The above-mentioned doctrine of the Dārṣṭāntikas represents a denial of the *niyata karma*. This is in keeping with their doctrinal position which relegates the whole of *karma* and its retribution to the mental domain: "Apart from volition there is no retributive cause; apart from sensation there is no retribution fruit" (cf. § 6.3.4). Since, according to Buddhism, the mind can be trained and totally transformed, there is no reason to prevent the complete transformation of the karmic effect.

From the Vaibhāṣika perspective, karmic retribution is not determined by sensation alone; all the *dharma*-s subsumable as the retributive causes contribute to the determination. Saṃghabhadra,[40] for one, rejects this view of the transformability of all *karma*-s. He argues that if all *karma*-s were transformable, the Buddha would not have taught that there is determinate *karma*.

However, the AKB also speaks of the outflow-free *karma* as capable of destroying other *karma*-s.[41] It is further said that the wise, through a single thought of faith, can overcome an infinite heap of evil *karma*-s which are not of necessary retribution.[42] Such notions are once again quite in line with the early discourses. The *Saṃyutta-nikāya*,[43] for instance, also speaks of the transcendence of evil *kamma* (*pāpasa kammassa samatikkamo*) through abstention (*virati*) and meditation on loving-kindness (*mettā-bhāvanā*). The orthodox Sarvāstivāda too, while upholding the *niyata-karma* category, nevertheless would still accept the transformability of even such gravest evil through repentance — a doctrine that came to be developed in the Mahāyāna.[44]

The MVŚ relates the story of Mahādeva who committed four out of the five *ānantarya-karma*-s (excepting the shedding of a Buddha's blood):

> Having committed the third *ānantarya-karma*, by virtue of his not having cut off the roots of skillfulness, he gave rise to a deep sense of repentance and became restless. He was pondering as to how his grave transgressions could be expurgated. Later on, he learned that the Buddhist *śramaṇa*-s had a way to expurgate transgressions. Thereupon, he went to the *saṅghārāma* in *Kurkuṭa-vana*, outside the gate of which he saw a *bhikṣu* pacing up and down slowly and reciting the following *gāthā*:
>
>> If one has committed a grave transgression, [but later] cultivates the good for its expurgation, he is one who illuminates the world, like the moon set free from the cloud.[45]

Having heard this, he greatly rejoiced, realizing that by taking refuge in the Buddha's teachings the transgression can definitely be expurgated. (See also below, § 14.7, the case of a hungry ghost overcoming his karmic hindrance).[46]

The MVŚ explains how a moral practice (*śīla*) can counteract an immoral one (*dauśilya*):

> It is on account of the thought with which one makes the vow of undertaking (*abhyupagama-citta*) — serving as the assisting accompaniment (*saparivāra*) — that the immorality practiced from beginningless time comes to be relinquished upon the undertaking of the moral practice. This is like the long accumulated darkness in a room being banished on the arrival of a bright lamp. It is also like the case of one's long accustomed notion salt with regard to what is [actually] not salty being removed upon tasting salt. The same applies in the case of a moral practice counteracting an immorality. It is to be understood in the same manner that the path [as the counteragent] counteracts a defilement.[47]

14.5. Projecting and completing *karma*-s

According to the Sarvāstivāda, one, and only one, *karma* — in the one moment — projects one, and only one, *nikāya-sabhāga*, i.e., one existence.[48] Such a *karma* is called a projecting (*ākṣepaka*) *karma*. On the other hand, many *karma*-s are responsible for the specific experiences within the one existence — a person's life span, size, wealth or poverty, etc. These are called the completing or filling-up (*paripūraka*) *karma*-s. The example is given in the AKB of a painter who first paints the outline of a figure with one color and then fills in the details with various colors.[49]

In the MVŚ, the same example is given by some masters who opine that the completing *karma*-s follow the projecting *karma*. Other masters, however, assert that the order is reversed. The opinion of the MVŚ is that no hard and fast rule applies here — either type of *karma* can be incurred first.[50] In the case of a person who has committed more than one of the mortal transgressions, that are of the nature of being retributed immediately in the next existence, only the first one will project the next existence in hell; the others serve only as completing *karma*-s in that existence, causing more severe suffering to the doer.[51]

The statement that a single *karma* projects a *nikāya-sabhāga* does not contradict the Buddhist principle of causality that nothing is produced by a single cause but by an assemblage of causal factors. What is meant by this statement is that *karma* — the volition — is the principal cause. It is directly responsible for the arising of the *nikāya-sabhāga*. We have seen that the functioning of *karma* needs the assistance of the defilements (see below, § 14.6). In brief, a karmic force can take effect only when assisted by various conditions (*pratyaya*).[52] Moreover, it is explained that other retributive (*sa-vipāka*)[53] *dharma*-s co-existing with the *karma* — such as *vedanā*, etc. — also contribute to the projection.[54] It should also be understood that in a given existence, one can incur many projecting *karma*-s — not just one — each of which leads to a corresponding plane of existence in the future period.[55] (See also, § 13.1).

The Sarvāstivāda held that there is an intermediate existence (*antarā-bhava*) after death and before the next birth.[56] The projecting *karma* for an intermediate existence is said to be the same *karma* that projects the next existence (rebirth).[57] For this reason, an intermediate being has the form (*ākṛti*) of the future being to be born in the next birth.[58] According to the Ābhidharmikas, the *karma* for an intermediate existence, being of a very strong nature, cannot be transformed with regard to its sphere (*dhātu*) and plane of existence (*gati*).[59]

14.6. *Karma* in terms of *pratītya-samutpāda*[60]

The Middle Way position of the Sarvāstivāda *karma* doctrine — like those of other Buddhist schools — are also expressed in terms of the Buddha's teaching of conditioned co-arising (*pratītya-samutpāda*) comprising 12 links (*nidāna*). This is in conformity with the general Buddhist principle that nothing arises independent of conditions, thus avoiding the two extremes of eternalism (*śāśvata-vāda*) and annihilation (*uccheda-vāda*). The Sarvāstivāda stresses the 'embryological interpretation', distributing the 12 links over the three periods of existence as follows:

3 Periods	12 Links	Cause/Effect
past	1. ignorance (*avidyā*) 2. conditionings (*saṃskāra*)	past causes
present	3. consciousness (*vijñāna*) 4. psycho-physical complex (*nāma-rūpa*) 5. six entrances (*ṣaḍāyatana*) 6. contact (*sparśa*) 7. sensation (*vedanā*)	present effects
	8. craving (*tṛṣṇā*) 9. grasping (*upādāna*) 10. existence (*bhava*)	present causes
future	11. birth (*jāti*) 12. old-age-and-death (*jarā-maraṇa*)	future effects

The first two links, ignorance and conditionings, constitute the past karmic factors leading to a person's present existence as the result: Ignorance represents in a general manner all the defilements up to the very last thought of the past existence, since all these past defilements — whatever be their modes of operation — are necessarily conjoined with ignorance.[61] They all have ignorance as their cause.[62] Conditionings are all the past karmic formations driven by ignorance.

The third link, consciousness, is the relinking (*pratisaṃdhi*) consciousness that enters the mother's womb in the person's present rebirth.

The fourth link, the psycho-physical complex, represents the stage of embryonic development of which the completed development of the six sense faculties are represented by the fifth link, the six entrances (*ṣaḍāyatana*).

The sixth link, contact, represents the contact between the child's sense faculties and their objects.

The seventh link, sensation, represents the stage when the child can differentiate between different types of feelings.

At the stage of the seventh link, craving, the child has developed sexual awareness and craving (eighth link) for material things in general.

In the next stage, grasping (ninth link), intensified craving develops[63] and leads to strong clinging to the objects of craving.

The tenth link, existence, like the second link, is *karma* in nature. It subsumes all the present *karma*-s that — driven by the defilements of craving and grasping — project a future existence. The Ny explains why this link, although *karma* in nature, is not called *karma*:

> It is in order to show that this, being a cause that incurs a subsequent existence, is a distinctive type of *karma* (*karma-viśeṣa*); all *karma* is not a cause for the subsequent existence.[64]

The eleventh link, birth, represents the stage of the first relinking thought in the future birth. It is therefore similar to the third link of consciousness.

The last (i.e., twelfth) link, old-age-and-death, represents the stage of existence from the moment of the future rebirth till death. It is therefore similar to the four links of the present period — from psycho-physical complex to sensation.

These 12 links of conditioned co-arising are explained as the mutual conditioning among the three — defilement, *karma* and *duḥkha* — as follows:

(i) defilement generates *karma* — the conditionings have ignorance as their condition (*avidyā-pratyayāḥ saṃskārāḥ*);

(ii) *karma* generates *duḥkha* — consciousness has the conditionings as its conditions (*saṃskāra-pratyayaṃ vijñānam*);

(iii) *duḥkha* generates *duḥkha* — the psycho-physical complex has consciousness as its condition, and so on up to: sensation has contact as its condition (*vijñāna-pratyayaṃ nāma-rūpam … sparśa-pratyayā vedanā*);

(iv) *duḥkha* generates defilement — craving has sensation as its condition (*vedanā-pratyayā tṛṣṇā*);

(v) defilement generates defilement — grasping has craving as its condition (*tṛṣṇā-pratyayam upādānam*);

(vi) defilement generates *karma* — existence has grasping as its condition (*upādāna-pratyayo bhavaḥ*);

(vii) *karma* generates *duḥkha* — birth has existence as its condition (*bhava-pratyayā jātiḥ*);

(viii) *duḥkha* generates *duḥkha* — old-age-and-death has birth as its condition (*jāti-pratyayaṃ jarā-maraṇam*).[65]

The 12 links are also explained as being divisible into three parts:

(I) defilements: three links — ignorance as the past cause, craving and grasping as the causes for the future;

(II) *karma*: two links — conditionings as the past causes, and existence as the cause for the future;

(III) phenomenal bases (*vastu*), so called because they serve as the supporting bases (*āśraya*, *adhiṣṭhāna*) for the generation of defilements and *karma* — the remaining seven links.

These seven are the effects; the other five links are the causes.

The AKB[66] illustrates the mutual conditionality among these parts in a way similar to that given in the MVŚ for the defilement-*karma-duḥkha* triad:

(i) defilement from defilement;
(ii) *karma* from defilement;
(iii) phenomenal basis from *karma*;
(iv) phenomenal basis from phenomenal basis;
(v) defilement from phenomenal basis.

It follows from this mutual conditionality that ignorance — being a defilement and like craving and grasping — has as its cause either a defilement or a phenomenal basis; old-age-and-death — being a phenomenal basis and corresponding to links 4 to 7 — has as its fruit a phenomenal base or a defilement.[67]

The compilers of the MVŚ give another explanation: The cause of ignorance is improper mental application (*ayoniśo manaskāra*); the fruits of old-age-and-death are sorrow, lamentation, suffering, grief and despair (*śoka-parideva-duḥkha-daurmanasyopāyāsā*).[68] In brief, from *karma* are born the phenomena which, in turn, serve as the bases for the generation of further *karma*. And in this way, the twelve-link conditioned co-arising represents the endless cycle of saṃsāric existence, wherein neither ignorance is the first cause, nor old-age-and-death, the end.[69]

The Sarvāstivāda speaks of conditioned co-arising as being fourfold:

(i) momentary (*kṣaṇika*) — the 12 links being embraced within a single moment;

(ii) prolonged (*prākarṣika*) — extending over three periods of existence;
(iii) in states (*āvasthika*) — 12 states embracing the five *skandha*-s;
(iv) connected (*sāṃbandhika*) — through being causes and effects.[70]

The above 'embryonic' explanation is said to be the Buddha's explanation in terms of states, pertaining to sentient beings (*sattvākhya*); it is for the sake of eradicating delusion (*saṃmoha*) regarding the past, present and future.

The Ābhidharmikas also apply the principle of conditioned co-arising to external causality, thus covering both the sentient and the non-sentient. In the AKB, this extension of application is justified with the assertion that the teachings in the *sūtra*-s are intentional (*ābhiprāyika*), whereas those in the *abhidharma* are definitive (*lākṣaṇika*).[71] The MVŚ explains in a similar manner, asserting that application to both, the sentient and non-sentient — such as that in the PrS which speaks of conditioned co-arising as pertaining to all the conditioned *dharma*-s — represents the teaching at the level of absolute truth (*paramārtha*).[72]

However, the following comments given elsewhere in the MVŚ would seem to imply that some Ābhidharmikas themselves too hold that the Buddha himself at times applied the principle to the whole of phenomenal existence:

> For the sake of those to be transformed (*vineya*), the Fortunate One taught conditioned co-arising as being more or less:
>
> Sometimes he spoke of one conditioned co-arising — all the conditioned *dharma*-s are collectively called conditioned co-arising. Thus, it is said 'What is conditioned co-arising? All conditioned *dharma*-s.'
>
> Sometimes he spoke of conditioned co-arising as being two — cause and effect.

> Sometimes, he spoke of conditioned co-arising as being three — the three different periods of existence, or the [triad:] defilement, *karma* and phenomenal bases....[73]

14.7. Past *karma* of the *arhat*-s and the Buddha

What happens to the past *karma* of the *arhat*-s and the Buddha?

It would seem that even they cannot escape the consequences of those which are determinate. However, their moral and spiritual perfection are such that even the gravest past evil *karma* — such as the splitting of a *saṅgha* (*saṅgha-bheda*)[74] — can be made to be experienced in the present existence in such a way that finally no real harm is done. This then does not amount to a retribution as such.

The MVŚ states that an *ārya* does not have retribution of previous evil *karma*: He has necessarily experienced the retribution of the determinate *karma* before entering the noble path. As for the indeterminate *karma*-s, he has already transformed and extinguished them through the power of the noble path.[75] However, it is said that only an *arhat* can properly know his own previously incurred *karma*-s as to which are transformable and which are not. He transforms the former through the power of cultivation. As for the latter — of the completing type — he can induce them to be experienced in the present life, there being for him no more future existence.[76]

The MVŚ gives examples of evil *karma*-s which could not be averted by even the *arhat*-s. For instance, as a result of a previous evil *karma*, an *arhat* was imprisoned for a long time in the prison. The force of his evil *karma* was such that his disciples were made unaware of the imprisonment during all that time. It was only when this evil *karma* was exhausted that they could find out what had happened and requested the king to release their innocent teacher. On hearing the king's order to release the *śramaṇa* in prison, the *arhat* suddenly woke up as if from a dream and was able to rise up to the sky through his power.[77]

An example of a Buddha's non-transformable *karma* which therefore is necessarily retributed, is the event of Devadatta's splitting the Saṅgha. The MVŚ explains that the Buddha himself, having examined his own previous births by means of His proper knowledge, saw that, in a previous birth, innumerable *kalpa*-s ago, He had split the retinue of the *ṛṣi*-s. Seeing that the retribution of that *karma* was presently arising, He realized at the time that His Saṅgha was inevitably going to be split. Accordingly, He withdrew into His room and sat there silently as the schism was about to take place.[78]

Although the life-span of a sentient being is determined by the completing *karma*, both the Buddha and an *arhat* can extend or shorten their life span for the sake of benefiting sentient beings or the successful continuation of the Dispensation. Thus, through the power of the action of giving as well as that of *dhyāna*, an *arhat* can transform a *karma* conducive to the retribution of great wealth to that conducive to longevity, or *vice versa*.[79]

14.7.1. Can one's *karma* bear effect on another or be experienced by another?

Another allusion to the possibility of overcoming the serious effect of evil *karma* is found in a discussion on the hungry ghosts (*preta*), in the course of which the following case is examined: A person becomes a hungry ghost on account of his extreme miserliness. The resulting karmic hindrance that he experiences is such that he sees food as impurities and drink as blood, etc., thus being unable to consume either of them. His relatives then perform a meritorious act of making offerings to *śramaṇa*-s and *brāhmaṇa*-s on a large scale, with the wish that the meritorious action would help him become free from such sufferings. It is conceded that the hungry ghost would indeed acquire the *puṇya* (得其福).

But the question then arises as to whether this amounts to the case of transferring merit from one person to another — does it imply that the effect of a *karma* done by one person is experienced by another?

For the Mahāyānists, the answer would easily be in the affirmative.

The Sarvāstivādins, however, sticking to the early Buddhist teaching on *karma* that one reaps what one has sown, deny that such is the case. Their explanation, instead, is as follows: That person earlier created himself, through his miserliness, the karmic hindrance for the experience of food and drink. At the time of witnessing the meritorious act occurring in his own abode, he thought of the relatives and fellow villagers as if they were his very own family members and of their belongings as if they were his own. Thereupon, he greatly rejoiced in their merit and gave rise to faith and respect in the field of merit (*puṇya-kṣetra*), i.e., the religieux receiving the offerings.

> Realizing the merit of giving and the fault of miserliness, his volition conjoined with giving came to be accumulated, accomplishing the *dṛṣṭa-dharma-vedanīya-karma* and acquiring the *dṛṣṭa-dharma-phala*.[80]

Vasumitra explains the phenomenon thus:

> The fruit that he experiences now is projected by an earlier *karma*. The earlier *karma* is a hindrance which is removed by the present *karma* — hence there is no fallacy of a person experiencing the fruit of a *karma* done by another.

As a matter of fact, even if the person was born into a plane of existence other than that of the *preta*-s, he would still have been able to acquire the *puṇya* if he could likewise cause the volition conjoined with giving to be accumulated. And when this volition has accumulated, the person would experience the retribution of both requisites (getting food, clothings, houses, etc.) and a superior psycho-physical complex.[81]

There is another interesting discussion in the MVŚ that is relevant here: When the universe is at its last phase of existence, the human life-span is only ten years. However, those who can practice the ten skillful *karma-patha*-s will give birth to children with a life-span of 20. The question then arises: Does this not amount to that someone — the child — is experiencing the retribution of the *karma* of someone else — the mother? Dharmatrāta's explanation is interesting here:

> *Karma* and retribution fruit are individually fixed: A *karma* retributable as a 20-year life-span will effect a fruit of 20-year life-span, and so on up to, a *karma* retributable as a 80,000-year life-span will effect a fruit of 80,000-year life-span. However, on account of the parents' skillful *karma*-s, the child's *karma* [conducive to the retribution of a 20-year life-span] comes to be capable of giving fruit (*phala-dāna*): Although there is no way that someone can experience the fruit of someone else's *karma*; *karma*-s [of different individuals] can mutually serve as conditions in giving fruit.[82]

14.8. Man's *karma* and his environment, and collective *karma*

An individual's *karma* has repercussions not only for himself, but for the whole universe as well. All paths of *karma*, skillful or unskillful, are said to have a threefold result: fruit of retribution, fruit of emanation (*niṣyanda-phala*), and fruit of dominance (*adhipati-phala*). The ten paths of *karma* are in fact said to be established on account of these three fruits.[83]

For instance, for the path of *karma* of killing, practiced repeatedly:

(i) the fruit of retribution is rebirth in hell, among the animals or among the *preta*-s;

(ii) the fruit of emanation is a short life-span when the transgressor is subsequently reborn in the human world;

(iii) the fruit of dominance is the lack of vitality (*alpaujasa*) and non-durability of external things — such as plants, the planets, etc. Similarly for the other paths of *karma*.[84]

Whereas, of the three fruits, the first two are unique to the individual, the third is shared by all beings.

The case of the Universal Monarch's (*cakra-vartin*) sovereignty over all four continents is also illustrative: his personal mightiness is his fruit of retribution; things under his domination are his fruit of dominance — brought about by his past *karma* contributing to these objects for his personal enjoyment.[85]

The paths of *karma* are also said to be established on account of the fact that their prevalence, or otherwise, affects not only the person by way of retribution, but also visibly the external state of things. Thus, when the path of *karma* of the abstention from stealing prevails, all external things will not suffer any calamity or damages caused by frost, storm, etc. And when all ten skillful paths of *karma* prevail, this *Jambudvīpa* (ancient India) will witness four increases — of life-span, of sentient beings, of external items of utility and enjoyment (*pariṣkāra*), and of skillful *dharma*-s.[86] All these clearly imply that an individual's karmic action has both personal and collective aspects. The latter is what is called collective *karma*.

The Sarvāstivāda view — essentially in agreement with those of all Buddhists — is that the whole universe, with all its planets, mountains and oceans, etc., is the result — the fruit of dominance — of the collective *karma* of the totality of beings inhabiting therein.[87] It begins with the winds endowed with special power born of this collective *karma*.[88] The exhaustion of this collective *karma* brings about the dissolution of the universe through three great calamities — of fire, water and wind.[89] The fact that the *karma*-s of beings in this world are mixed — some good, some bad — accounts for the existence of beautiful and pleasant external things such as fragrant flowers, etc., on the one hand, and human bodies with all their impurities on the other. In the case of the gods (*deva*), their exclusively skillful *karma*-s result in the equal beauty of both their internal bodies and external objects of enjoyment.[90]

A question is raised: If the whole universe originates from the collective *karma* of all beings, why is it that when a person therein attains *parinirvāṇa*, there is no decrease in the external things resulting from the extinction of the *karma*-s of such a being? Vasumitra explains as follows:

> There would be decrease in those things that are virile fruits (*puruṣakāra-phala*) and proximate fruits of dominance [—fruits brought about personally and directly, and hence to be experienced personally]. [Mount] Sumeru, etc., are only the person's remote fruits of dominance [— he has only contributed to their arising indirectly and collectively along with other beings —] there is therefore no decrease in such cases.
>
> [Moreover,] Sumeru, etc., having arisen from the collective *karma* of all beings, would not become diminished even if among them [just] one single being remains, on account of their being sustained by his karmic force, how much more so when there are still innumerable beings who have not attained *parinirvāṇa*. …
>
> [Moreover,] even if innumerable beings have attained *parinirvāṇa* or have been born elsewhere, there are also innumerable beings who have come to be born in this universe; on account of the latter's karmic force, there is no decrease.[91]

NOTES

[1] A, i, 250; the Sarvāstivāda version is cited in MVŚ, 99b ff., as the *Salt-simile sūtra*, 鹽喻經 — see below.

[2] *Cf.* AKB(F), 1062, n. 219.

[3] AKB, 357.

[4] AKB, 357: *kṛtvābudho 'lpam api pāpam adhaḥ prayāti / kṛtvā budho mahad api prājahaty anartham / majjaty ayo 'lpam api vāriṇi saṃhataṃ hi / pātrīkṛtaṃ mahad api plavate tad eva /.*

[5] Ny, 694b.

[6] Quoted in MVŚ, 182b.

[7] *Cf.* MVŚ, 619a, etc.

[8] MVŚ, 620a–c; AKB, 232, 271; Vy, 394.

[9] See *supra*, § 13.8.3; AKB, 197; Ny, 542b.

[10] MVŚ, 184c.

[11] Ny, 569c; see passage quoted below.

[12] MVŚ, 593b.

[13] This is a rejection of the Dārṣṭāntika notion that there are *karma*-s which are determinate with regard to the time of retribution, but indeterminate with regard to retribution.

[14] Ny, 569c.

[15] MVŚ, 100a.

[16] AKB, 264.

[17] MVŚ, 276b–c. *Cf.* AKB, 265 — La Vallée Poussin's translation here is not in accord with the Sanskrit.

[18] E.g., T 28, 386b–c.

[19] T 26, 718a.

[20] T 26, 921b, etc.

[21] MVŚ, 125c. It states that according to some masters, the two terms do not signify any difference.

[22] AKB, 269, stanza 120, summarizes the five conditions under which a *karma* is said to have been accumulated:

> On account of [i] its being intentional, of [ii] its completion, of [iii] being without remorse and counteraction,
> Of [iv] accompaniments, and of [v] retribution, a *karma* is said to be accumulated.
> *saṃcetana-samāptibhyāṃ niṣkaukṛtya-vipakṣataḥ* /
> *parivārād vipākāc ca karmopacitam ucyate* //120//

[23] Cf. MVŚ, 125c.

[24] Cf. MVŚ, *loc. cit.*

[25] AKB, 239: *dvābhyāṃ hi kāraṇābhyāṃ prāṇātipātāvadyena spṛśyate prayogataḥ mṛte sati phala-paripūritaś ca* /

[26] MVŚ, 619a–b.

[27] Vy, 401: *prayogasya maulaḥ karma-pathaḥ phala-paripūriḥ* / *yo hi prayujyate maulaṃ karma-pathaṃ na janayati tasya prayoga-phalam asti* / *na tu phala-paripūriḥ* /

[28] MVŚ, 617c.

[29] *Cf.* AKB, 260.

[30] *Cf.* Ny, 569b.

[31] *Cf.* MVŚ, 126a.

[32] *Cf.* MVŚ, 126a; also see above where a *naiva-saṃvara-nāsaṃvara* — a retributive karmic force — is relinquished through sincere repentance, and through not doing in accordance with one's pledge, etc.

[33] AKB, 271 f.; Vy, 435; Ny, 569b; *cf.* MVŚ, 125c.

[34] *Cf.* MVŚ, 125b.

[35] *Cf.* MVŚ, 126a, 618a ff.

[36] MVŚ, 619a.

[37] *Cf.* MVŚ, 125c–126a, 618a–619a.

[38] *Cf.* MVŚ, 359b.

[39] MVŚ, 593b; Ny, 570b–571a.

[40] Ny, 570c–571a.

[41] AKB, 235.

[42] AKB, 416.

[43] S, iv, 317.

[44] *Cf.* Yin Shun, *Origin and Development of Early Mahāyāna Buddhism* 初期大乘佛教之起源與發展 (Taipei, 1981), 72.

[45] *Cf. Dhammapada*, 173; T no. 210, 562c.

[46] MVŚ, 511a.

[47] MVŚ, 623b.

[48] MVŚ, 99a–b; AKB, 258.

[49] AKB, 258.

[50] MVŚ, 98a, 887c.

[51] Ny, 578b; AKB, 261.

[52] *Cf.* Ny, 396a.

[53] MVŚ, 820c: Only the *akuśala* and the *kuśala-sāsrava dharma*-s are *sa-vipāka*, although their *vipāka-phala*-s may or may not be acquired.

[54] AKB, 259.

[55] *Cf.* AKB, 258; MVŚ, 99c.

[56] AKB, 120 ff.

[57] *Cf.* MVŚ, 356c ff.

[58] AKB, 123.

[59] MVŚ, 359b.

[60] MVŚ, 116b ff. — especially 122a–c; AKB, 131 ff.; Ny, 480c ff.

[61] *Cf.* MVŚ, 126a–b.

[62] Ny, 497a.

[63] Ny, 496c.

[64] Ny, 492a.

[65] MVŚ, 122b.

[66] AKB, 134 f.

[67] Ny, 497a.

[68] MVŚ, 121c; other explanations are also given (*ibid.*, 121c–122a; *cf.* AKB, 135).

[69] MVŚ, 122b; AKB, 134 f.; Ny, 496c–497a.

[70] MVŚ, 117c; AKB, 132 f.; Ny, 493b–494b.

[71] *Cf.* AKB, 133.

[72] MVŚ, 117b.

[73] MVŚ, 122a.

[74] MVŚ, 620c.

[75] MVŚ, 658b.

[76] MVŚ, 103c.

[77] MVŚ, 654c–655a, 655b.

[78] MVŚ, 603c.

[79] MVŚ, 656a–657c.

[80] MVŚ, 61a.

[81] MVŚ, 61a–b.

[82] MVŚ, 103a.

[83] MVŚ, 588c.

[84] MVŚ, 588c–589a; AKB, 253 f.

[85] MVŚ, 107a.

[86] *Cf.* MVŚ, 588a–c, 127c.

[87] MVŚ, 41b, 106c, 692c.

[88] AKB, 157 f., 189: *sattvānāṃ karmajaḥ prabhāva-viśiṣṭo vāyurbījam*. *Cf.* MVŚ, 691b; Ny, 216b.

[89] MVŚ, 690a ff.

[90] AKB, 192.

[91] MVŚ, 106c–107a.

15. The Path of Spiritual Progress

15.1. Doctrine of gradual enlightenment

The sixth chapter of the AḰB is devoted entirely to the discussion on the path and spiritual attainments and it enumerates and defines various paths.[1] Indeed, the study of the nature and functions of the various paths is an integral part of *abhidharma*. One of the four great Sarvāstivāda masters, Ghoṣaka, underscores this in his definition of *abhidharma*:

> For the seeker for liberation engaged in the proper practice, [*abhidharma*] can analyze what has not been understood: this is *duḥkha*; this is the cause

> of *duḥkha*; this is the cessation of *duḥkha*; this is the path leading to the cessation; this is the preparatory path (*prayoga-mārga*); this is the unhindered path (*ānantarya-mārga*); this is the path of liberation (*vimukti-mārga*); this is the path of advance (*viśeṣa-mārga*); this is the path of the candidate (*pratipannaka-mārga*); this is the acquisition of fruit. *Abhidharma* is so called because it can correctly analyze such meanings.[2] (See also, § 1.2).

For the Sarvāstivāda, the path of spiritual progress is a very long journey. It takes three *asaṃkhyeya-kalpa*-s for a practitioner to reach the state of perfect Buddhahood[3] practicing accumulatively the six perfections (*śīla*-, *dāna*-, *vīrya*-, *kṣānti-, dhyāna*- and *prajñā-pāramitā*) and tens of thousands of difficult practices on the way.[4] This long period of practice pertains, in fact, only to the stage of preparatory effort (*prayoga*).[5] The whole process is one of gradual progress, and the Sarvāstivāda doctrine is definitely not one of sudden enlightenment. The MVŚ records the Buddha's own statements in this regard:

> I remember that in the past, I have stated thus: 'There is no *śramaṇa* or *brāhmaṇa*, etc., in the past, present or future who can acquire knowledge and vision with regard to all *dharma*-s abruptly. If one says there is, [one is speaking of] an impossibility. One must first go through three *asaṃkhyeya-kalpa*-s, practicing tens of thousands of difficult practices, gradually perfecting the six *pāramitā*-s, in order that one can possess true knowledge and vision with regard to all *dharma*-s.[6]

The MVŚ records the view of some, such as the 'abrupt-abandonment *śramaṇa*-s', that defilements are abandoned all at once at the stage of the arising of the *vajropama-samādhi*; at all the previous stages there only can be the temporary suppression of the active *paryavasthāna*-s. Others, like the Dārṣṭāntikas and the Bhadanta, assert that ordinary worldlings cannot abandon any defilements at all. This is because only the *ārya*-s possess the noble (i.e., pure) *prajñā* with which alone the defilements can be abandoned (*cf.* § 12.9.3). For these various masters then one cannot properly speak of any spiritual progress through the worldly paths. The MVŚ states, in this connection, that it is in fact for the purpose of refuting such views that the two counteractions for the abandonment of defilements — the distinction between the path of insight (*darśana-mārga*) and the path of cultivation (*bhāvanā-mārga*) — are shown.[7] Each of the three spheres of existence has these two categories of defilements — *darśana-heya* and *bhāvanā-heya* — which must be totally eradicated, and this process takes place gradually. Like the Sarvāstivādins, these opponents also concede that there are four fruits of the spiritual life (*śrāmaṇya-phala*). However, they hold that the abandonment of the defilements can take place only at the time of *vajropama-samādhi*. The first three fruits can only suppress the defilements, inducing the *vajropama-samādhi*. Other opponents hold that direct insight into all four noble truths arises abruptly (see below, § 15.3.1). This view too is refuted in the same context by the Sarvāstivādins who argue that like the *bhāvanā-heya* defilements, the *darśana-heya* ones must also be abandoned gradually, not all at once.[8]

In brief, in the Sarvāstivāda system, the gradual path of spiritual progress begins at the stage when the practitioner is an ordinary worldling. When he becomes an *ārya*, he must continue to move up gradually. The gradual degrees of spiritual insight acquired on the whole path correspond to the gradual abandoning of defilements at the various stages. At the very final stage of the path of cultivation, the *vajropama-samādhi* arises and the practitioner cuts off whatever defilements remain. He then acquires a homogeneous acquisition of disjunction (*visaṃyoga-prāpti*) collectively with regard to the abandonment of all the defilements pertaining to the two categories in the three spheres, and he is said to have acquired the complete knowledge of the exhaustion of all fetters (*sarva-saṃyojana-paryādāna-parijñā*).[9] The end of the journey is when the knowledge of the absolute non-arising (*anutpāda-jñāna*) of all future defilements arises in him, and he is said to have attained *nirvāṇa*.

15.2. Preliminaries for the preparatory stage

The preparatory stage (*prayoga*), in the proper sense, comprises meditational practices. But, in keeping with the general Buddhist tradition, the whole spiritual path of the Sarvāstivāda is an integrated system of *śīla–samādhi–prajñā*. That is to say: meditational practices (*samādhi*) cannot be isolated from the total context of spiritual commitment and a life of ethical alignment that is, in general, in keeping with this commitment. Accordingly, there are preliminary preparations before one can even properly embark on those meditational practices.

Commenting on what the *sūtra* refers to in speaking of the "profound Abhidharma", the MVŚ states:

> In the absolute sense (*paramārtha*), the intrinsic nature of Abhidharma can only be the outflow-free faculty of understanding (*prajñendriya*). From this very perspective, those which bring about the excellent (*viśiṣṭa*) worldly 'understanding derived from cultivation' (*bhāvanā-mayī prajñā*) — namely, 'warmed-up', 'summits', 'receptivities' and the 'worldly supreme *dharma*-s' — can also be called Abhidharma on account of their ability to discern the four noble truths separately.
>
> Again from this very perspective, those that bring about the excellent 'understanding derived from reflection' (*cintāmayī prajñā*) — namely, contemplation on the impure, mindfulness of breathing, etc. — can also be called Abhidharma on account of their ability to discern the aggregates (*skandha*) separately and collectively.
>
> Again from this very perspective, those that bring about the excellent 'understanding derived from listening' (*śrutamayī prajñā*) — [namely,] the analysis and establishment of the intrinsic and common characteristics of *dharma*-s, destroying the delusion with regard to existent entities and cognitive objects (*ālambana*) — can also be called Abhidharma on account of the fact that they neither superimpose (*sam-ā-√ruh*) nor deny (*apa-√vad*) with regard to *dharma*-s.

> Again from this very perspective, those that bring about the excellent 'understanding derived from the abode of birth' (*upapatti-sthāna-prātilambhikā prajñā*) can also be called Abhidharma on account of their ability to operate (√*vṛt*) non-erroneously in receiving, bearing in mind, pondering and examining the12-limb (*dvādaśāṅga*) teaching of the *tripiṭaka*. ...[10]

The above explanations are in fact a statement of preparatory stages that lead to the attainment of perfect *prajñā* (= Abhidharma in the absolute sense). These stages are as follows:

Studying the Buddha's teaching with the support of the understanding derived from birth (*upapatti-prātilambhika-prajñā)*

⇓

Studying the Abhidharma — analyzing the characteristics of *dharma*-s (*śrutamayī prajñā*)

⇓

Meditations such as contemplation on the impure and mindfulness of breathing (*cintāmayī prajñā*)

⇓

'Warmed-up', 'summits', 'receptivities' and the 'worldly supreme *dharma*-s' (*bhāvanāmayī prajñā*)

⇓

Attainment of outflow-free *prajñā* (final destination)

A more comprehensive, although succinct, prescription for the steps leading to stream entry is given in the MVŚ as follows:

> These are the preliminary preparations for one [aiming at] the fruit of stream entry:
>
> At the beginning, because of his aspiration for the fruit of liberation, he diligently practices [i] generosity (*dāna*) and the pure precepts (*śīla*); [ii] the understanding derived from listening, [comprising] the contemplation of the impure, mindfulness of breathing and the foundations of mindfulness

(*smṛtyupasthāna*); and [iii] warmed-up, summits, receptivities and the worldly supreme dharma-s; and [then he enters into] [iv] the 15 moments of the path of insight (*darśana-mārga*). This is collectively said to be 'firmly on one's feet'.

The above prescription clearly includes the practice of skillful acts such as giving and ethical alignment.

Elsewhere, the MVŚ explains why there is no retrogression from stream entry and speaks of the foundation of the path of insight:

> Question: Why is there no one who retrogresses from stream entry?
>
> Answer: Because of the firmness of its foundation.
>
> What is the foundation?
>
> This comprises the [following practices] of the seeker for liberation: giving; ethical living; engagement in the works of the Buddha, Dharma and Saṅgha; attending on the old and the sick, recitation of the noble words and expounding them to others; proper mental application (*yoniso manaskāra*); the practice of the contemplation on the impure, mindfulness of breathing, the foundations of mindfulness, the contemplation of the three meanings (三義), skillfulness with regard to the seven abodes (七處善; **sapta-sthāna-kauśala*), warmed-up, summits, receptivities and the worldly supreme *dharma*-s.[11]

We have here the prescription of not only more skillful activities, both social and religious, such as attending on the sick and expounding the *Dharma*, but also the following two additional contemplative practices:[12]

(1) Contemplation of the three meanings, which refers to the sequential contemplation on the true meanings of the *skandha*-s, *āyatana*-s and *dhātu*-s.

(2) Skillfulness with regard to the seven abodes which is an examination of the five aggregates truly as they are, from seven perspectives. To take *rūpa* as an example: one examines *rūpa* itself as (i) fruit, and (ii) the causes from which it is generated. One further examines (iii) its cessation, (iv) the counteracting path leading to its cessation, (v) its enjoyable aspect (*āsvādana*) as an object of attachment, (vi) its loathsome aspect as a fault (*ādīnava*) to be avoided, and finally (vii) the transcendence of its attachment.

These two practices are not mentioned in the AKB. But their occurrence is already attested in the *Saṃyuktāgama*.[13]

The AKB prescribes the preliminaries as follows:[14]

(I) observance of the precepts (*śīlaṃ pālayati*);

(II) development of the proper understanding derived from listening (*śruta-mayī prajñā*) — studying and receiving instructions from teachers.

To ensure success in meditation, one must purify one's body and mind in three ways:

(i) physical withdrawal or distancing (*vyapakarṣa*) by dissociating from evil friends and cutting off unfavorable conditions, and mental withdrawal by eradicating unskillful thoughts (*akuśala-vitarka*);

(ii) practicing contentment and having few desires (*saṃtuṣṭiś ca alpecchatā ca*);

(iii) abiding in the four noble lineages (*ārya-vaṃśa*) — called thus because the noble ones are begotten from them (*āryāṇām ebhyaḥ prasavāt*) — which are non-greed in nature (*alobha*): [they are] (a-c) contentment with clothing, food, bed and seat, and (d) delight in the abandonment of defilements (= in the realization of cessation (*nirodha*)) and in the cultivation of the noble path (*prahāṇa-bhāvanā-ārāmatā*).[15]

15.3. Different stages of the path

The whole path leading to this final perfection is divided by the Sarvāstivādins into the seven stages of preparatory effort and four stages of spiritual fruits, as shown in the following chart:

7 *prayoga*	I. *śamatha* practices		*mokṣabhāgīya*
	II. *smṛtyupasthāna*-s (individually)	*vipaśyanā*	
	III. *smṛtyupasthāna*-s (collectively)		
	IV. *uṣmagata*		*nirvedhabhāgīya* (4 *kuśalamūla*)
	V. *mūrdhan*		
	VI. *kṣānti*		
	VII. *laukikāgradharma*		

4 *phala*	I. *śrotaāpatti*	*pratipannaka*	*darśana-mārga*
		phala	*bhāvanā-mārga*
	II. *sakṛdāgāmin*	*pratipannaka*	
		phala	
	III. *anāgāmin*	*pratipannaka*	
		phala	
	IV. *arhat*	*pratipannaka*	
		phala	*aśaikṣa-mārga*

From the chart above, one sees that the preparatory path comprises two portions:

(1) *mokṣa-bhāgīya*: those conducing, i.e., serving as causes, to liberation (= *nirvāṇa*);

(2) *nirvedha-bhāgīya*: those conducing to decisive distinction, i.e., to the arising of outflow-free knowledge.

In the AKB, the *nirvedha-bhāgīya* is also collectively called the four skillful roots, as they lead to the fruition of stream entry (*srotaāpatti*) which is the point of no return in the spiritual journey — the practitioner is henceforth destined for perfect liberation. It is the critical point at which a *pṛthagjana* becomes an *ārya*, never to retrogress to be a mundane worldling again. The MVŚ, however, speaks of both portions equally as being skillful roots[16] — in the sense of being seeds, and explains the two terms as follows:

> The *mokṣa-bhāgīya kuśala-mūla*-s: [the practitioner] plants the seeds that are decisive for liberation. On account of this decisiveness, he can attain *parinirvāṇa*.
>
> The *nirvedha-bhāgīya kuśala-mūla*-s: i.e., *uṣmagata*, *mūrdhan*, *kṣānti*, *laukikāgra-dharma.*[17]

15.3.1. *Mokṣa-bhāgīya*

The MVŚ[18] proceeds here to analyze the *mokṣa-bhāgīya* articulately:

(i) They have as their intrinsic nature (*svabhāva*) the threefold *karma* — bodily, vocal and mental — with the predominance of the mental.

(ii) They pertain to the mind ground (*mano-bhūmi*).

(iii) They are acquired through effort, not innate.

(iv) They are derived from *śruta-mayī* and *cintā-mayī*, not *bhāvanā-mayī prajñā*.

(v) They are produced only among human beings, only in those existing in *kāmadhātu* — not *rūpa-ārūpya-dhātu*-s; and only those in the three continents — not in the Uttarakuru-dvīpa.

(vi) They are planted (as seeds) only where the *Buddha-dharma* exists, hence only when a Buddha appears.

(vii) They are planted by both males and females.

(viii) They may arise as a result of the practice of giving, or of ethical observance, or of hearing (learning) the *Dharma* from others: One may plant these seeds of liberation by the mere giving of one lump (*piṇḍa*) of food or by the mere observance of the eight precepts (*upavasthā-śīla*), etc., provided the motivation is genuinely for liberation.

(ix) These can be planted only by those who have a strong aspiration for *nirvāṇa* and disgust for *saṃsāra*.

(x) Once they have been planted, it takes a minimum of three lives to attain liberation: in the first life the seeds are planted; in the second, they are matured; in the third, liberation is attained. But it may take many many *kalpa*-s (a) if the practitioner fails to give rise to the *nirvedha-bhāgīya*, or (b) if he, although having given rise to the *nirvedha-bhāgīya*, fails in the many *kalpa*-s that follow to give rise to *samyaktva-niyāma-avakramaṇa* (i.e., attain stream entry — see *infra*, § 15.4).

(xi) There are six progressively superior types (*gotra*) (see *infra* — on six types of *arhat*) of *mokṣa-bhāgīya*: (1) *parihāṇa-dharman* — those susceptible to retrogression; (2) *cetanā-dharman* — those capable of ending their existences at will; (3) *anurakṣaṇā-dharman* — those capable of protecting themselves from retrogression; (4) *sthitākampya* — those capable of abiding in their attainment without retrogressing, although they may not progress unless effort is exerted; (5) *prativedhanā-dharman* — those capable of penetrating the state of *arhat*; (6) *akopya-dharman* — those absolutely not susceptible to retrogression. Each preceding type is transformed progressively to the succeeding type.

(xii) The *śrāvaka*-type (*śrāvaka-gotra*) of *mokṣa-bhāgīya* is transformed, giving rise to those of the *pratyeka-buddha* and Buddha. The *pratyeka-buddha* type is transformed, giving rise to those of the *śrāvaka* and Buddha. The Buddha-type having been given rise to, there can be no further transformation as it is the strongest (*tīkṣṇa*, *tīvra*) type.

Those who have not planted the *kuśala-mūla*-s of *mokṣa-bhāgīya* are said to be stream-accordants (*anu-srota*); those who have done so, stream-discordants (*prati-srota*). "Stream" here refers to *saṃsāra*. For even if one should perform great meritorious actions, or master the *tripiṭaka*, or practice and have various meditational attainments and supernormal powers, etc., and obtain favorable states of rebirth, one would still have to experience *duḥkha* in *saṃsāra*. On the other hand, as a result of having planted the *kuśala-mūla*-s of *mokṣa-bhāgīya* at the preparatory stage,

> a person can be said to be abiding on the shore of *nirvāṇa*. [This is so] even if he should, on account of his defilements, subsequently commit various bodily, vocal or mental actions, or the *ānantarya-karma*-s, or cut off all *kuśala-mūla*-s to the extent that there exists in him not the slightest seed of white *dharma*-s, [even if he should] fall into the Avīci hells, undergoing various forms of suffering. This is on account of this person being destined to attain *parinirvāṇa*.[19] (However, he is not said to have entered *samyaktva-niyāma*).

Such being the spiritual significance of the *mokṣa-bhāgīya*, the meaning of the term should become obvious. It is said that it is better to be Devadatta who fell into the Avīci hell than to be Udraka-rāmaputra who was born into the *naiva-saṃjñā-nāsaṃjñā* heaven. For, although the former committed three of the *ānantarya-karma*-s and thereby cut off the *kuśala-mūla*-s, he will — on account of having acquired the *mokṣa-bhāgīya* — attain *pratyekabuddha-bodhi* at the time when human life can last 84,000 years, becoming a *tīkṣṇendriya* excelling even Śāriputra, etc. The latter did not plant the *mokṣa-bhāgīya*. Accordingly, in spite of his rebirth in the *bhavāgra*, he ended up in the evil planes of existence unable to gain liberation.[20]

15.3.1.1. *Śamatha* and *vipaśyanā*

The above emphasis on the critical importance of the *mokṣa-bhāgīya* for liberation also spells out the great significance of tranquility (*śamatha*) and insight (*vipaśyanā*) — of which the *mokṣa-bhāgīya* is comprised — as spiritual praxis.

The practitioner begins with the two *śamatha* practices of contemplation on the impure (*aśubha-bhāvanā*) and mindfulness of breathing (*ānāpānasmṛti*) which constitute the entrance[21] into spiritual cultivation proper. The former practice is the contemplation on the progressive deterioration of the body, and has the counteraction of greed as its aim. The latter comprises six aspects: counting, following, fixing, observing, modifying and purifying.[22] The MVŚ[23] calls these two meditational practices the two gateways of immortality (*amṛta-dvāra*), i.e., *nirvāṇa*.

In the Chinese commentary, the tranquility meditations are often collectively spoken of as the 'five-fold mental stilling' (五停心).[24] This is also the term that had been used in the various works of the great Tian Tai master, Zhi Yi (智顗; *ca*. 538–597).[25]

The corresponding Sanskrit term cannot be traced in the AKB or other related Indian Abhidharma texts in their original. In the MVŚ, the meditations under this group are mentioned in some places, but are not explicitly grouped together.[26] At one place in this text, it is stressed that "meditators rely mostly on the contemplation of the impurities as the gateway for entering into the noble path".[27] There, this contemplation is discussed at very great length,[28] and it is shown how, immediately after completing this contemplation, the meditator can sail into the *vipaśyanā* practice of the mindfulness on the body, etc.

But, as a specific group of tranquility practices, the five methods had probably developed at a fairly early stage. An early Chinese translation of the *Bodhisattva-bhūmi* (菩薩地持經; T 30, no. 1581) enumerates them as the five "gateways (/methods) for transcendence" (度門):

1. contemplation on the impure. 2. meditation on loving kindness (*maitrī*), 3. contemplation on conditioned co-arising, 4. contemplation on the division of the *dhātu*-s, 5. mindfulness of breathing.[29] In Buddhamitra's *Essential Methods of the Five-gateway Dhyāna-sūtra* (T 15, no. 619, 五門禪經要用法; 325c), the contemplation on the *dhātu*-s is replaced by the 'recollection on the Buddha' (*buddhānusmṛti*). These meditations are said to have been taught in consideration of the different personality types — those of the predominantly greedy type (*adhi-rāga*), those of the predominantly distracted type (*adhi-vitarka*), etc.:[30]

(1) contemplation on the impure — greedy type
(2) meditation on loving kindness — hateful type
(3) contemplation on conditioned co-arising — deluded type
(4) contemplation on the *dhātu*-s — conceited type
(5i) mindfulness of breathing — distracted type
(5ii) (recollection on the Buddha — those who are drowsy, have unwholesome thoughts, and are oppressed by object domains)

Having achieved tranquility, the practitioner then proceeds to the practice of insight comprising the fourfold application of mindfulness[31] on body (*kāya*), sensation (*vedanā*), ideations (*saṃjñā*) and *dharma*-s.[32] This is done in two ways: First, he contemplates the specific characteristics[33] of each of the four — the body is impure; sensations are unsatisfactory (*duḥkha*); ideations are impermanent; all *dharma*-s are without a Self.[34] He must also contemplate generally that the body, sensations, ideations and *dharma*-s are — in each case — like all conditioned *dharma*-s in being impure, unsatisfactory, impermanent and without a Self. Next, he contemplates collectively that all four — body, sensations, ideations and *dharma*-s — are equally impure, unsatisfactory, impermanent and without a Self.

It is to be noted that for the Sarvāstivādins, *śamatha* and *vipaśyanā* are not mutually exclusive practices, nor are they to be too sharply differentiated. It is an *abhidharma* doctrine that within one and the same thought there exists both *śamatha* and *vipaśyanā*.[35] Indeed, according to the Sarvāstivāda, *samādhi* and *prajñā* necessarily co-exist as two of the ten universal thought concomitants (see *supra*, § 9.3.4.1). The two types of practitioners are to be distinguished from the point of view of their preparatory stages:

> Those who mostly cultivate the provisions (*saṃbhāra*) of *śamatha* are those who, at the stage of preparatory effort, always delight in solitude and shun noisiness. They see the faults of socializing and constantly dwell in quiet places. When they enter into the noble path, they are called the *śamatha*-type of practitioner (*śamatha-carita*).
>
> Those who mostly cultivate the provisions of *vipaśyanā* are those who, at the stage of preparatory effort, always delight in studying and reflecting on the *tripiṭaka*. They repeatedly examine the specific and general characteristics of all *dharma*-s. When they enter into the noble path, they are called the *vipaśyanā*-type of practitioner (*vipaśyanā-carita*).[36]

Their mutual non-exclusiveness is also underscored in the various opinions given in the MVŚ[37] by different Ābhidharmika masters as to how many of the six aspects of mindfulness of breathing (§ 15.3.1.1) come under either *śamatha* or *vipaśyanā*: Some say the first three are *śamatha*, the last three *vipaśyanā*; others say the opposite. The compilers of the MVŚ remark that "there is no fixed rule here — all may come under *śamatha* or all may come under *vipaśyanā*".

One question here arises: Does one need to attain the *dhyāna*-s in order to acquire the pure *prajñā* which liberates us from *saṃsāra*? Does one in fact need to practice meditation at all?

From the Sarvāstivāda Ābhidharmika perspective, the answer is clearly 'yes'. It is stated that the four roots of skillfulness (i.e., the *mokṣabhāgīya*) can only be produced from the understanding derived from cultivation, not from those derived from reflection and listening.[38] In other words, at the preparatory stage leading to the actual attainment of warmed-up, etc., the practitioner necessarily depends on meditational practices.

It is further stated that the practitioner can acquire these roots only at the stages of the 'not-yet-arrived' (*anāgamya*), the intermediate meditation (*dhyānāntara*) and the four meditations (*dhyāna*).[39] This means that he must have acquired the degree of concentration of the 'not-yet arrived' stage. This stage is a 'neighborhood' (*sāmantaka*), i.e., a meditational state bordering the *dhyāna* stage proper into which its power of concentration is strong enough to lead. There is one such 'neighborhood' stage bordering each of the meditational attainments (*samāpatti*). Since there are eight meditational attainments — four *dhyāna*-s (also called the four 'fundamental or principal meditations', *maula-dhyāna*) of the fine-material sphere and four meditational attainments of the non-material sphere (*ārūpya*) — there are corresponding eight 'neighborhood' stages, the first of which, bordering the first *dhyāna*, is called the 'not-yet-arrived' stage.[40]

15.3.2. *Nirvedha-bhāgīya*

Penetration (*nirvedha*) here refers to insight — that is, the *ārya-mārga*. The AKB explains the term as follows:

> Penetrating (*vidha*) is in the sense of distinction (*vibhāga*). *Nir-vedhaḥ* means decisive distinction which is the noble path. For through it [— the noble path —] there is the abandonment of doubt and the distinction of the truths: 'This is *duḥkha*'; up to 'This is the path'. Its portion (*bhāga*) refers to one portion of the *darśana-mārga*. They are conducive to *nirvedha* (*nirvedha-bhāgīyāni*) because they are favorable to it on account of being its inducer. [41]

The *nirvedha-bhāgīya*-s comprise the warmed-up (*uṣmagata*), the summits (*mūrdhan*), the receptivities (*kṣānti*), and the worldly supreme *dharma*-s (*laukikāgra-dharma*); each serves as the *samanantara-pratyaya* for the succeeding one.[42] These four are also called

(1) "truth-coursing" (*satya-cāra* ?),
(2) "counteraction-cultivation" (*pratipakṣa-bhāvanā* ?),
(3) roots of skillfulness (*kuśala-mūla*):

(1) because they course through the four truths by means of the 16 modes of activities (*ākāra*); (2) because "for the sake of the *ārya-mārga*, one cultivates the body as a receptacle (*kāya-bhājana*), removing the impurities and inducing the *ārya-mārga*"; (3) because "these four constitute the very foundation and footing for the *ārya-mārga* and *nirvāṇa* which are the truly good (*paramārthena kuśala*)."[43] In terms of the threefold *prajñā* — *śruta-mayī*, *cintā-mayī* and *bhāvanā-mayī* — the *mokṣa-bhāgīya*-s are subsumed under *cintā-mayī prajñā*, while the *nirvedha-bhāgīya*-s under *bhāvanā-mayī prajñā*; both being induced by the *abhidharma* which, in its intrinsic nature, in the highest sense (*paramārthataḥ*) is the outflow-free *prajñā*.[44]

As to whether a *bodhisattva*, in the course of his previous existences has given rise to the *nirvedha-bhāgīya*-s, opinions differ among the Sarvāstivāda masters. The Vaibhāṣika view (*evaṃ tu varṇayanti*) is that within the one sitting of the fourth *dhyāna* of the present life, the *bodhisattva* gives rise to all the excellent *kuśala-mūla*-s from *aśuci-bhāvanā* up to *anutpāda-jñāna*.[45]

As in the case of the *mokṣa-bhāgīya*-s (*supra*, § 15.2.1), there are also six *gotra*-s of *nirvedha-bhāgīya*-s, each being progressively transformed into the succeeding superior type.[46] These are produced among humans of the three continents, excepting Uttarakuru-dvīpa, and among gods — of both sexes — of the sphere of sensuality, but not among beings of the three evil planes of existence. They can only be produced where one can enter into *samyaktva-niyāma*, and this is possible only where:

(i) both receptivity (*kṣānti*) and knowledge (*jñāna*) can be produced,
(ii) both the *dharma-jñāna* as well as the *anvaya-jñāna* can be produced,
(iii) there exist both the superior bodily basis (*āśraya*) and the experience of *duḥkha*.

In the other two spheres, only *kṣānti* and *anvaya-jñāna* can arise and there is no experience of *duḥkha*. Accordingly, the *nirvedha-bhāgīya*-s are not produced in the two upper spheres.[47]

15.3.2.1. Warmed-up (*uṣmagata*)

This is the first indication or the anticipation of the *anāsrava-jñāna*.

> As a result of the operation of knowledge on an object, there arises the warmth of the noble knowledge capable of burning the fuels of defilements. Hence, it is called 'warmed up'. This is like rubbing [two stones] to get fire — as a result of the mutual dependence of the lower and upper [stones], there arises the warmth of fire capable of burning fuels.
>
> Venerable Ghoṣaka explains: On account of seeking liberation, there arise the *kuśala-mūla*-s. They are the foresign for the arising of the sun of the noble path … [and] of the fire of the noble path; hence the name 'warmed-up'. This is like the case of smoke as the foresign preceding the arising of fire.[48]

This is a lengthy stage the practice of which is characterized by the three *prajñā*-s — *śruta-mayī*, *cintā-mayī* and *bhāvanā-mayī*. First, one begins with the cultivation of the *śruta-mayī prajñā* by learning from a teacher or studying the *tripiṭaka*. Then one realizes that all the *tripiṭaka* teachings can be summarized into the 18 *dhātu*-s, the 12 *āyatana*-s and the five *skandha*-s. One then proceeds — progressively seeking more and more concise teachings — to examine each of them, understanding in terms of terminology, specific characteristics and common characteristics. In this manner, one progresses to the practice of the four *smṛtyupasthāna*-s, and finally the repeated contemplation of the 16 *ākāra*-s of the four truths, pertaining to both the sphere of sensuality and the two upper spheres. *Ākāra* here means the mode of comprehending activity of the mind. This activity on an object results in a resemblance or reflection of the object in the mind — the 'mode'. The 16 *ākāra*-s are as follows:

(I) *duḥkha-satya* — impermanent (*anitya*), unsatisfactory (*duḥkha*), empty (*śūnya*) and soulless (*anātman*);

(II) *samudaya-satya* — cause (*hetu*), origin (*samudaya*), successive causation (*prabhava*) and condition (*pratyaya*);

(III) *nirodha-satya* — cessation (*nirodha*), calm (*śānta*), excellence (*praṇīta*) and escape (*niḥsaraṇa*);

(IV) *mārga-satya* — path (*mārga*), right method (*nyāya*), course of practice (*pratipatti*), conducive to exit (*nairyāṇika*).

This examination of the four noble truths, however, does not constitute direct spiritual insight; "it is like examining pictures through the veil of a silk-cloth". It is only up to this point that the practitioner has perfected the *śruta-mayī prajñā*.

> With this as the basis, he produces the *cintā-mayī prajñā*. Having perfected this, he next produces the *bhāvanā-mayī prajñā*. This is also called the 'warmed-up'. From warmed-up, the summits are produced. From summits, receptivity. From receptivity, the worldly supreme *dharma*-s. From worldly supreme *dharma*-s, the *darśana-mārga*. From *darśana-mārga*, the *bhāvanā-mārga*. From *bhāvanā-mārga*, the *aśaikṣa-mārga*. In this way, the *kuśala-mūla*-s are gradually fulfilled.[49]

The warmed-up may be lost through retrogression, or transcendence of sphere or stage, or loss of the *nikāya-sabhāga*. As a result, one may commit the *ānantarya-karma*-s, cut off the *kuśala-mūla*-s, and fall into the bad planes of existence. Nevertheless, it can serve as the decisive cause for the attainment of *nirvāṇa*. "One who has acquired the warmed-up is like a fish that has swallowed the fisherman's hook — [destined to be caught]; he is destined for the *nirvāṇa-dharma*."[50]

15.3.2.2. Summits (*mūrdhan*)

At this stage the practitioner continues to contemplate the 16 modes of activities of the four noble truths. But these roots receive another name on account of their excellence.[51] They are called summits/peaks because:

(i) They are the highest of the shakable skillful roots. At this stage, one can either proceed to the next stage or fall back to commit evils and be born in the *durgati*.[52]

(ii) They are like peaks, between the previous and the subsequent stages. This is like a person situated at the peak of a mountain: He does not remain for long — either, in the absence of any obstacle, he passes over this mountain to another mountain, or, in the presence of obstacles, he has to descend. The *nirvedha-bhāgīya*-s are twofold: retrogressible and non-retrogressible. Among the former, the inferior one is called "warmed up"; the superior, "summits". Among the latter, the inferior, "receptivity"; the superior, "worldly supreme dharma-s". It is also because these excel among the retrogressible *nirvedha-bhāgīya*-s that they are called 'summits'.[53]

Like the warmed-up, the summits may be lost through the same causes. As a result, one may commit the *ānantarya-karma*-s and fall into the bad planes of existence. However, these skillful roots excel the previous one in that even when the practitioner should fall to commit evil, he will never fall to the extent of having the skillful roots cut off.[54]

15.3.2.3. Receptivity (*kṣānti*)

Although all four *nirvedha-bhāgīya*-s are conducive to insight into the truth, receptivity accords with *satyābhisamaya* more so than the other three, hence this alone is said to be truth-accordant.[55] It is called receptivity "because of the greatest receptivity to the truths — on account of the non-regressibility [of this stage]":[56]

> At the stage of warmed-up, the truth is acceptable to one and pleases (*kṣamate rocate*) one weakly; at the stage of the summits, to a medium degree. Immediately after that, receptivity now arises because of the greatest receptivity to the truths. ... This is because receptivity does not retrogress, whereas there is the possibility of retrogression from the summits.[57]

Like the warmed-up and the summits, receptivity can be lost through the transcendence of sphere and stage or loss of the *nikāya-sabhāga*, not through retrogression. In fact, one who has acquired it can never retrogress from it, nor can he commit the *ānantarya-karma*-s or fall into the bad planes of existence.[58]

Receptivity is also threefold: weak, medium and strong. As in the case of the warmed-up and the summits, the weak and medium receptivities contemplate fully all 16 modes of activity of the four truths — four pertaining to the sphere of sensuality and four to the two higher spheres; in all, eight truths and 32 modes of activity. However, the strong receptivity contemplates only the truth of unsatisfactoriness pertaining to the sphere of sensuality. This is because, at the stage of contemplation of the medium receptivity, there begins a successive reduction of the higher modes of activity and spheres until finally, in the last two moments of the stage, the practitioner applies his mind to only two modes of activity — impermanence and unsatisfactoriness — of the sphere of sensuality.[59] The reason for being successively more restrictive in contemplation is so as to make the contemplation progressively more focused and thus more effective in inducing the outflow-free knowledge. The MVŚ[60] explains this with a simile: A wealthy man, unable to bring along all his possession to another country, changed them into money. Unhappy that the money was too much, he changed them into gold. Still unhappy that the gold pieces were too heavy, he changed them into expensive jewels. In this way, he was finally able to carry his possessions with him and travel freely.

In the very next moment when the strong receptivity comes into operation, the practitioner, in a single thought, contemplates only the unsatisfactoriness pertaining to the sphere of sensuality. At this stage, although the *darśana-heya* defilements are not yet abandoned, they are already successfully suppressed.

15.3.2.4. Worldly supreme *dharma*-s

Immediately following the last moment of the strong receptivity, the worldly supreme dharma-s arise, contemplating — like the strong receptivity — in one moment only the unsatisfactoriness pertaining to the sphere of sensuality. These *dharma*-s have as their intrinsic nature those *citta-caitta*-s which serve as the *samanantara-pratyaya* for the entrance into *samyaktva-niyāma* (i.e., *darśana-mārga*).[61] That is, with these as the *samanantara-pratyaya*, the practitioner relinquishes the nature of an ordinary worldling (*pṛthagjanatva* — see below, § 15.3.2) and acquires the nature of the noble (*āryatva*).

In the JPŚ[62] these are the first of the four *nirvedha-bhāgīya*-s to be discussed. The MVŚ attempts to justify this choice of order, giving elaborate explanations.

> These *citta-caitta*-s — [the last of an ordinary worldling] — in comparison to the other worldly *dharma*-s, are the best, the excellent, the senior, the chief, the superior, the wonderful; hence they are called the worldly supreme dharma-s.[63]

They are said to be excellent since they alone can open up the door of the noble path.[64] Moreover, they are said to be the best in comparison to the *śruta-mayī*; excellent, in comparison to the *śruta-mayī*; senior, in comparison to the *śamatha* and *vipaśyanā* practices; chief, in comparison to *uṣmagata*; superior, in comparison to *mūrdhan*; wonderful, in comparison to *kṣānti*. Various other explanations for these six attributes are given in the MVŚ.[65]

There is another view that the worldly supreme dharma-s have the five outflow-free faculties (*indriya*) — *śraddhā*, *vīrya*, *smṛti*, *samādhi*, *prajñā* — as their intrinsic nature. This view is attributed to either the old Ābhidharmika masters or the Vātsīputrīyas. The former in this way in order to refute the view of the Vibhajyavādins that these five faculties are necessarily outflow-free. By asserting in this way, the old Ābhidharmikas intend to show that these five faculties can also be with-outflow since they exist in an ordinary worldling. The Vātsīputrīyas hold that these five faculties are *kuśala* in their intrinsic nature (*svabhāvataḥ*), and all differences pertaining to the *ārya* are to be established on the basis of these five.[66]

The two Dārṣṭāntika masters, Dharmatrāta and Buddhadeva, also hold different views in this regard. For the former, all *citta-caitta*-s are simply specific states of *cetanā*; accordingly, the worldly supreme dharma-s have *cetanā* as their intrinsic nature. For the latter, the *citta-caitta*-s are none other than the *citta* itself; accordingly, the worldly supreme dharma-s have *citta* as their intrinsic nature.[67]

15.3.3. Summary

To sum up: the *nirvedha-bhāgīya* constitutes the *prajñā* derived from cultivation, and the *mokṣa-bhāgīya*, the *prajñā* derived from reflection. These two *prajñā*-s, together with that derived from hearing — which, in *abhidharma*, refers specifically to the study of the specific and common characteristics of *dharma*-s — in the preliminary stage, constitute the threefold impure or with-outflow *prajñā*. They are considered as *abhidharma* in the conventional sense, and we can discern here the reason for the Ābhidharmikas to be concerned with spiritual practices. These conventional *abhidharma*-s serve as the instruments for bringing about the out-flow-free *prajñā* which is *abhidharma* in the absolute sense[68] (see *supra*, § 1.2).

15.4 Direct realization (*abhisamaya*), path of insight (*darśana-mārga*) and stream entry (*srotaāpatti*)

In the stages of preparatory effort, contemplations on the truths were carried out with knowledges that are with-outflow (*sāsrava*). Immediately following the moment of the worldly supreme *dharma*-s, the practitioner is able to give rise to the outflow-free knowledges (*anāsrava-jñāna*) with which he again contemplates the 16 modes of activity of the four truths — those pertaining to the sphere of sensuality followed by those pertaining to the two upper spheres. The MVŚ explains why, for each of the modes of activity (*duḥkha*, etc.), the practitioner must first contemplate that pertaining to the sphere of sensuality, and then collectively that pertaining to the upper spheres:

(i) the former is grosser and more easily observed than the latter;
(ii) the sphere of sensuality is a non-concentrated stage, whereas the two upper spheres are both concentrated (*samāhita*) stages;

hence the practitioner must do the two contemplations separately.[69]

This contemplation is termed *abhisamaya* — direct realization — which is the direct spiritual insight into the truths. One of the Ābhidharmika definitions of *abhidharma* is that "it is that which directly realizes (*abhi-sam-√i*) and realizes (*sākṣāt-√kṛ*) the *dharma*-s". And Vasumitra explains that "*abhidharma* is that which can directly realize the four noble truths".[70] This process takes 16 thought moments the first 15 of which constitute the path of insight (*darśana-mārga*) and the 16th the beginning of the path of cultivation (*bhāvanā-mārga*).

Complete insight into each of the truths is achieved in two moments, called 'paths' on account of their having to be gone through. In the first moment, called the unhindered path (*ānantarya-mārga*), the outflow-free understanding that arises is called a receptivity (*kṣānti*) to knowledge, and with this, the defilements abandonable by insight into the particular truth are abandoned. In the following moment, called the path of liberation (*vimukti-mārga*), knowledge proper arises through the induction of which the acquisition (*prāpti*) of the cessation through deliberation (*pratisaṃkhyā-nirodha*) of the defilements arises.[71] In this way, for the whole contemplative process covering the sphere of sensuality followed by the two upper spheres, there arise eight receptivities and eight knowledges, all being *prajñā* in their intrinsic nature. This doctrine can be understood as follows: The abandoning of a defilement requires a sufficient degree of insight, represented by the notion of receptivity, into the true nature of things — unsatisfactory, impermanent, etc. When in the next moment the defilement which disturbs and sullies (two connotations of √*kliś*) the mind is no more, wisdom proper — a higher degree than receptivity — 'shines forth' as it were. Put differently, this can be seen as a corollary of the general Buddhist position that insight is the means as well as that which necessarily arises at the end — and in this sense the virtue *par excellence* — of spiritual praxis. In the Sarvāstivāda conception, the insight, designated as *jñāna*, that constitutes the very path of liberation is not just a mere state of mental clarity or cognitive perfection. It is a positive force having the efficacy of inducing the *prāpti* of *pratisaṃkhyā-nirodha*; which is to say, it serves as the necessary causal factor for the acquisition of the *nirodha*. The latter, being unconditioned, is not directly caused or directly produced by it; it is, however, acquired (*prāpta*) by virtue of the *prāpti* so induced by it. (See *infra*, § 16).

That the unhindered path and the path of liberation represent the indispensable functioning of insight in overcoming defilements and attaining cessation is also underscored by the doctrine of the three outflow-free cognitive faculties: *anājñātam-ājñāsyāmīndriya*, *ājñendriya* and *ājñātāvīndriya*. These three faculties, in their essential nature, are constituted of *manas*, *sukha*, *saumanasya*, *upekṣā*, *śraddhā*, *vīrya*, *smṛti*, *samādhi* and *prajñā*. These nine are said to be differentiated as the three distinctive faculties on account of the predominance that they exercise in the *darśana-mārga*, *bhāvanā-mārga* and *asaikṣa-mārga*, respectively: the *anājñātam-ājñāsyāmīndriya*, with regard to the cessation of the *darśana-heya* defilements; the *ājñendriya*, with regard to the cessation of the *bhāvanā-heya* defilements; the *ājñātāvīndriya*, with regard to the state of bliss in the present life (*dṛṣṭadharma-sukha-vihāra*) of an *arhat*.[72] In the acquisition of the fruit of stream entry, the *anājñātam-ājñāsyāmīndriya* functions as the inductor (*āvāhaka*) of the *visaṃyoga-prāpti*, and the *ājñendriya* functions as the support of this *prāpti*. The first constitutes the unhindered path; the second, the path of liberation. In the acquisition of the fruit of arhathood, the *ājñendriya* constitutes the unhindered path; the *ājñātāvīndriya*, the path of liberation.[73]

Vasubandhu explains that the *kṣānti*-s are called the *ānatarya-mārga*-s as they cannot be obstructed in the cutting of the *prāpti* of the *kleśa* (*kleśa-prāpti-vicchedaṃ pratyantarayitum aśakyatvāt*). The *jñāna*-s are called *vimukti-mārga*-s because in those who are thus liberated from the *prāpti*-s of these *kleśa*-s, they co-arise with the *visaṃyoga-prāpti*.[74] Saṃghabhadra criticizes:

> If so, the *vimukti-mārga* should also be named *ānantarya*, inasmuch as its co-nascence also cannot be obstructed. Rather, one should explain thus: it is called *ānantarya* because there exists no *antara* (nothing in between); *ānantarya* itself is the *mārga*, hence the name *ānantarya-mārga*. The meaning is that there is no *mārga* of the same species which can come in between, preventing it from becoming the condition for the [arising] of

the *vimukti-mārga*; for the *ānantarya-mārga* all last only one *kṣaṇa*, while the *vimukti-mārga* may continue as a series... [75]

In the contemplation of the four truths pertaining to the sphere of sensuality, the receptivities and knowledges are called *dharma-jñāna-kṣānti* and *dharma-jñāna* — the term *dharma* signifying the fact that the nature of *dharma*-s subsumable under the particular truth is seen for the first time.[76] Those pertaining to the two upper spheres are called *anvaya-jñāna-kṣānti* and *anvaya-jñāna*, the term *anvaya* — 'subsequent' or 'following' — signifying the fact that these truths are realized subsequently and in a similar manner to those pertaining to the sphere of sensuality.[77] Saṃghabhadra[78] insists that the *anvaya-jñāna* is not an inferential knowledge, but rather a direct one like *dharma-jñāna*.[79] The following chart summarizes the 16 moments of insight:[80]

The process of the direct insight into the four truths

darśana mārga (15 moments)

1. *duḥkhe dharmajñānakṣānti*
2. *duḥkhe dharmajñāna*
3. *duḥkhe anvayajñānakṣānti*
4. *duḥkhe anvayajñāna*
5. *samudaye dharmajñānakṣānti*
6. *samudaye dharmajñāna*
7. *samudaye anvayajñānakṣānti*
8. *samudaye anvayajñāna*
9. *duḥkhanirodhe dharmajñānakṣānti*
10. *duḥkhanirodhe dharmajñāna*
11. *duḥkhanirodhe anvayajñānakṣānti*
12. *duḥkhanirodhe anvayajñāna*
13. *duḥkhapratipakṣamārge dharmajñānakṣānti*
14. *duḥkhapratipakṣamārge dharmajñāna*
15. *duḥkhapratipakṣamārge anvayajñānakṣānti*

bhāvanā-mārga

16. *duḥkhapratipakṣamārge anvayajñāna*

(*Cf.* AKB, 350 f.)

15.4.1. *Satyābhisamaya* as a gradual process

The above process illustrates the Sarvāstivāda position that the direct realization into the truths is a gradual process. In support of this position, the MVŚ quotes a *sūtra* in which the Buddha is represented as stating to Anāthapiṇḍada (Pāli: Anāthapiṇḍika) explicitly that *satyābhisamaya* is a gradual process, like ascending a four-rung ladder.[81] This position is consistent with the Sarvāstivāda doctrine that defilements are abandoned gradually. In the AKB, Vasubandhu explains the rationale for the progressive sequence as follows:

> The discourse of the truths is in conformity with [the order of] direct realization. Now, what is the reason that the *abhisamaya* of these truths is in this way?
>
> For, that to which one is attached, by which one is oppressed, and from which liberation is sought — that very one, *duḥkha-satya*, at the stage of investigation is examined first.
>
> Afterwards, [proceeding to investigate:] "What is the cause of this (*duḥkha*)?" — the *samudaya-satya*. "What is the cessation of this?" — *nirodha-satya*. "What is the way of this?" — the *mārga-satya*.
>
> It is like having seen the disease, [there follows] the searching for its cause, its elimination and its medicine.[82]

However, other Buddhist schools disagree. The Mahāsāṃghika, Mahīśāsaka and Dharmaguptaka are known to hold that it is an abrupt process.[83] Thus, the Mahāsāṃghika states:

> Within the one moment of the knowledge pertaining to the direct realization [of the four noble truths] (*ekakṣaṇikābhisamayāntika-jñānena*), the differences in the various *ākāra*-s of the four noble truths are fully known (*parijñāta*).[84]

There was, however, a certain branch of the Mahāsāṃghika which held that there was a distinctive direct realization for each of the distinctive *ākāra* of the truths.[85]

According to Yaśomitra[86] the abrupt view belongs to the Dharmaguptakas, etc.; but according to Pu Guang,[87] the Mahāsāṃghikas, etc. The MVŚ mentions the Vibhajyavādins as among those holding the abrupt view:

> There are some who assert that the four noble truths are directly realized at once, such as the Vibhajyavādins. … They base themselves on the *sūtra*: The Bhagavat said, 'If, with regard to *duḥkha-satya*, there is no doubt, there is likewise no doubt with regard to the *samudaya-*, *nirodha-* and *mārga-satya*. Since doubt with regard to the four noble truths disappears at once, it is known that the direct realization is definitely abrupt and not gradual.[88]

The Bhadanta, while holding that the direct realization into the four truths is acquired gradually, held that at the first moment of gaining entry into *samyaktva-nyāma* (see below), one is said to have direct faith with regard to all the truths[89] [at once]:

> When one abides in the *duḥkha-dharma-jñāna*, if one does not acquire faith with regard to all four truths, one cannot be said to abide [therein]. This is like the case of one who takes an earthern vessel up a pavilion and then throws it onto the ground. When the vessel has not yet reached the ground, it can be said to be broken, even though it has [in fact] not yet been broken, on account of the fact that it is definitely about to be broken.[90]

The Theravāda also upholds the abrupt view. Buddhaghosa, in his *Visuddhimagga*, reasons as follows:

> In each of the four path-knowledges (*sotāpatti-magga*, etc.), [and] in that order, four functions— comprehension, abandonment, realization and practice — are exercised in one and the same moment. It follows that the four noble truths are fully realized in a single moment. Moreover, there is

the single realization of the four truths in the sense of trueness in 16 aspects: oppression (*pīḷana*), being compounded (*sankhata*), torment (*santāpa*) and change (*vipariṇāma*) pertaining to *dukkha-sacca*; accumulation (*āyūhana*), source (*nidāna*), connection (*saṃyoga*) and obstruction (*paḷibodha*) pertaining to *samudaya-sacca*; exit (*nissaraṇa*), separation (*viveka*), being uncompounded (*asaṅkhata*) and immortality (*amata*) pertaining to *nirodha-sacca*; leading out (*niyyāna*), cause (*hetu*), seeing (*dassana*) and dominance (*ādhipateyya*) pertaining to *magga-sacca*. This is compared to the simultaneous functions of the lamp:

> the lamp burning the wick — knowledge comprehending *dukkha*;
> the lamp dispelling darkness — knowledge abandoning *samudaya*;
> the lamp revealing light — knowledge developing the *magga*;
> the lamp consuming the oil — knowledge realizing *nirodha*.[91]

Although the Sarvāstivāda holds the gradual view, it too concedes a certain sense of abrupt realization. This school speaks of three types of *abhisamaya*:

(1) *darśanābhisamaya* (*abhisamaya* as *darśana*) — the direct clear realization of the four noble truths by pure *prajñā* alone;

(2) *ālambanābhisamaya* (*abhisamaya* of object) — this pure *prajñā* taking the same objects as its conjoined *dharma*-s;

(3) *kāryābhisamaya* (*abhisamaya* as enterprise) — this pure *prajñā*, the conjoined *dharma*-s sharing the same objects with it, and other conascent *dharma*-s such as *jāti* and other *viprayukta-saṃskāra*-s, etc., all participating in the same enterprise. The Sarvāstivādins would concede that it is permissible to speak of abrupt *abhisamaya* with regard to *kāryābhisamaya*: At the very moment of the direct realization into *duḥkha-satya*, there can be the abandoning of *samudaya*, the realization of *nirodha*, and the cultivation of *mārga*. This is so because at the time of

> the seeing of *duḥkha-satya*, there is the *kāryābhisamaya* with regard to the other three *satya*-s.[92]

An intermediate position between the 'abrupt view' and the 'gradual view' is given in the SatŚ. On the one hand, it states as follows:

> As a result of the insight into the *nirodha-satya*, one is said to be enlightened.[93]

Thus, when one truth is realized, complete insight into all the truths is obtained — a view similar to those of the Mahāsāṃghika and the Vibhajyavāda. On the other hand, the process that leads finally to the realization of *nirodha-satya* is a gradual one:

> The thought of concept (**prajñapti-citta*), the thought of *dharma* (**dharma-citta*), the thought of *śūnyatā* (**śūnyatā-citta*) — these three thoughts having ceased, it is called *nirodha-satya*.[94]

Initially, at the stage of developing the *śruta-mayī prajñā* and *cintā-mayī prajñā*, the practitioner eliminates the thought of *prajñapti* by realizing that concepts such as the *pudgala* and a vase, etc., exist only at the *saṃvṛti-satya* level and are without any ontological status from the absolute standpoint. But the *dharma*-s, such as *nirvāṇa* and the *skandha*-s are true existents. This is called the elimination of the *prajñapti-citta* by means of the *dharma-citta*.

Next, at the second stage, i.e., the stage of developing the *bhāvanā-mayī prajñā*, the practitioner further contemplates the *dharma*-s such as *nirvāṇa* and the five *skandha*-s. He then realizes that these *dharma*-s too, from the absolute standpoint, are non-existent — empty (*śūnya*). This is the elimination of the *dharma-citta* by means of the *śūnyatā-citta*:

> The five *skandha*-s too are in actual fact non-existent; they exist [only] from the standpoint of *saṃvṛti-satya*. … Moreover, as a result of the insight into the *nirodha-satya*, one is said to attain enlightenment (得道). Thus,

> we know that *nirodha* exists from the standpoint of *paramārtha-satya*, but not the *skandha*-s.[95]

Finally, at the third stage, one must eliminate even the thought of *śūnyatā*, i.e. "the thought taking *nirvāṇa* as its object".[96] It is only then that one perfectly realizes the *nirodha-satya*. Through further contemplation one now realizes that:

> [In the *anupadhiśeṣa-nirvāṇa*,] the *skandha*-s have ceased without any remainder — hence the name *nirvāṇa*. Herein, what is there that exists? … It is not that there is no *nirvāṇa*; only that there are no real *dharma*-s.[97]

In this way, one accomplishes the insight into the *nirodha-satya*.[98]

15.4.2. Entry into the certitude of perfection (*samyaktva-niyamāvakrānti*)

From the first moment of insight — the receptivity to the *dharma*-knowledge with regard to unsatisfactoriness (*duḥkhe dharma-jñāna-kṣānti*) — the practitioner becomes a noble one, an *ārya*, a term for the Buddhist saint. The AKB gives the popular etymology as *ārād yātaḥ* — 'has gone far':

> [The *ārya*-s are] those in whom the outflow-free path has arisen. They are *ārya*-s because they have gone far from the evil *dharma*-s on account of their obtaining the acquisition of absolute disconnection [from the defilements], for, being destined for the exhaustion of the defilements, they are destined for perfection (*samyaktva-niyatāḥ*).[99]

Prior to this critical point in his spiritual career, he has been an 'ordinary worldling'. The JPŚ defines the 'quality of an ordinary worldling' (*pṛthagjantva*) as the non-obtainment (= non-acquisition, *aprāpti*) of the *dharma*-s of the noble ones.[100] This non-obtainment is not just a mere abstract concept of negation; it is a *viprayukta-saṃskāra-dharma* — a real force — the efficacy of which is explained by Vasumitra as follows:

> It causes sentient beings to generate views of different types (*pṛthag-jāti*), defilements of different types, do *karma*-s of different types, experience fruits of different types and births of different types. Furthermore, it causes sentient beings to fall into different spheres, go to different planes of existence (*gati*), experience different births. Hence, it is called the quality of an ordinary worldling. …[101]

The MVŚ further explains that all *ārya*-s are called 'equal beings' (同生; *samāna-jana*?) because they attain the truth equally, see equally, are inclined equally. The ordinary worldlings are different from them — not having equality in the same manner as the *ārya*-s; hence they are called *pṛthagjana.*[102]

From the first moment of his entry into the *darśanaya-mārga* up to the 15th moment, this *ārya* is called the candidate for the fruit of stream-entry (*srotaāpatti-phala-pratipannaka*). He has now abandoned 88 defilements abandonable by insight (see *supra*, § 12.6.2.1 *a*). At the 16th moment, he is called the "abider in the fruit of stream entry" (*srotaāpatti-phala-stha*). He is destined to final liberation within a maximum of seven rebirths.[103] However, according to the Vaibhāṣikas, the stream-entrant is said to be reborn at most seven times in the sense that he will have seven births as a human, seven intermediate existences (*antarābhava*); likewise his births among the gods — a total of up to 28 existences.[104] The MVŚ explains the term stream entrant as follows:

> *Srotas* means the noble path; *ā-panna* means entered. He is called a stream entrant (*srotaāpana*) as he has entered the noble path.[105]

Two types of practitioners who enter the path of insight are distinguished: One with a weak faculty (*mṛdvindriya*) enters the path having first relied on faith in the teacher's teachings; the other, with a sharp faculty (*tīkṣṇendriya*), having first studied and understood the Buddha's teachings himself. In the first 15 moments of the path, the former is called a 'pursuer through faith' (*śraddhānusārin*); the latter, 'pursuer through the doctrines' (*dharmānusārin*).[106] At the 16th moment, the former is called 'one who is freed through predominance of faith' (*śraddhādhimukta*); the latter, 'one who has attained through views' (*dṛṣṭi-prāpta*):

> A liberated person with a predominance of faith is called *śraddhādhimukta*. It is not that he does not have any *prajñā* at all; but he is not illumined (i.e., made conspicuous) by that, hence he does not receive that name. One is a *dṛṣṭi-prāpta* from the fact of being illumined by views on account of the predominance of *prajñā*. It is not that he does not have any faith at all …
>
> Others, however, on the basis of etymology, explain thus: "A *śraddhādhimukta* is one freed from those abandonable by insight on account of the predominance of faith. A *dṛṣṭi-prāpta* is one who has attained the fruit on account of the predominance of views."[107]

The first receptivity is also explained as the entry into certitude (*niyama/niyāma/nyāma*), for it is the entry into the certitude of perfection (*samyaktva-niyamāvakrānti*). That is, from this point onward, the practitioner is destined for — i.e., will definitely attain — *nirvāṇa* (= *samyaktva*).[108] Xuan Zang's translation here — probably following a fanciful etymology of the variant *nyāma* as < *ni* + *āma* ('separation from the raw'; Tibetan: *skon med pa* — 'free from defects') given in the MVŚ[109] — corresponds additionally to the alternative term *samyaktva-nyāma*, rendered as 正性離生, 'perfection which is the separation from the raw':

> This is called 'entry into *samyaktva-nyāma*', and also 'entry into *samyaktva-niyāma*', for this is the first entry into *samyaktva-nyāma* as well as the first entry into *samyaktva-niyāma*. In the *sūtra*, *nirvāṇa* is called *samyaktva*. Or, *samyaktva* signifies the noble paths. 'Raw' (生 — *āma*) refers to the defilements or the immaturity of the [skillful] roots; the noble paths can go beyond them, hence 'separation from the raw'. The noble paths are

> said to be certitude on account of the fact that they can decisively lead to *nirvāṇa*, or that they can decisively discern the characteristics of the truths. Reaching this stage is said to be entry.[110]

Although an ordinary worldling who has obtained the *mokṣa-bhāgīya*-s will definitely attain *nirvāṇa* also, he is not said in the same way as having entered the certitude of perfection for he could still commit evil and fall into the category of being destined for evil-ness.[111] Moreover, unlike the stream entrant who will be reborn at the most seven times, the time of his attainment of *nirvāṇa* is unfixed. (See example of Devadatta, in § 15.2.1).

15.5. Non-retrogressibility of stream-entry[112]

The *darśana-mārga* is not retrogressible, for it is a path — process — which proceeds very swiftly, without being held back or prematurely interrupted. Just as one being carried forward by a rapid incapable of holding back, when the practitioner is on this path, he is being carried away by the great current of Dharma; there is no possibility of his going backward.

> Moreover, one retrogresses mostly on account of the manifestation of defilements; when one is within the *darśana-mārga*, there is no possibility of generating even a *kuśala-citta* that is with-outflow, let alone a *citta* of defilements. Hence there can be no retrogression.

Besides, retrogressibility in this case would entail the following fallacies:

> Having gained insight into the truths, one does not have the insight again; having attained the spiritual fruit, one does not attain it again; having directly realized, one does not directly realize it again; having entered into *samyaktva-nyāma*, one does not enter into it again; having become an *ārya*, one becomes an ordinary worldling again; having abided in the

> category of those destined for perfection (*samyaktva-niyata-rāśi*), one abides in the category of those who are not destined [for perfection or evilness (*mithyātva*)] again. ...[113]

In fact, the practitioner can fall from all the fruits excepting the first.[114] The Mahāsāṃghika, on the other hand, holds that a stream entrant is susceptible to retrogression. He is in fact said to be capable of committing all evils except the mortal transgressions (*ānantarya*).[115]

15.6. Path of cultivation (*bhāvanā-mārga*)

The word *bhāvanā*, often translated as 'meditation' is more literally — and also more correctly —'cultivation' or 'development' of the mind. It is, however, true that meditation constitutes the most important aspect of the process. But this 'meditation' must not be equated with *samādhi* as opposed to *vipaśyanā*. There is no indication in the Sarvāstivāda system that *darśana-mārga* refers to the latter, and *bhāvanā-mārga* — in contrast — to the former. The MVŚ states explicitly that, in truth, the two *mārga*-s are not separable from each other. The two are differentiated only on account of the fact that, while both *parijñā* and *apramāda* are present in both, in *darśana-mārga* the former predominates and is strong and in *bhāvanā-mārga*, the latter. Venerable Vasumitra explains that

> the defilements abandoned by the realization into the four truths cannot be distinguished as 'this is abandoned by insight', 'that is abandoned by cultivation'. However, what is abandoned (*prahīṇa*), cast aside (*pratiniḥ-sṛṣṭa*) and expurgated (*vyantī-bhūta*) by the power of insight is said to be abandonable by insight. Those [defilements] whose various grades come to be gradually thinned and finally abandoned completely as a result of practice, cultivation and repeated action (*āsevita-bhāvita-bahulīkṛta*) in accordance with the path that has been acquired are said to be abandonable by cultivation.[116]

The path of cultivation is the stage of repeated practice which begins at the 16th moment of *satyābhisamaya*. It is through this stage which may last a considerable period of time that all the tenacious defilements remaining after the *darśana-mārga* come to be gradually eradicated. These *bhavanā-heya* defilements comprise *rāga*, *pratigha*, *moha* and *māna* pertaining to the *kāmadhātu*; and three each — excluding *pratigha* which does not exist in a mind of meditation which is concentrated — in the two upper spheres. This gives a total of ten defilements (see chart in § 12.6.2.1 b). As these defilements are blunt by nature and hence difficult to detect and differentiate, they are collectively classified into nine grades on the basis of the degree of strength of their arising — weak (*mṛdu*), medium (*madhya*), strong (*adhimātra*); each again subdivided into weak, medium, strong — thus giving weak-weak, etc., up to strong-strong.[117] Whereas the *darśana-mārga* is a sharp or forceful *(tīvra, tīkṣṇa)* path which on arising cuts off all the nine grades (see below) of the defilements at once, the *bhāvanā-mārga* is not forceful, so that the nine grades are cut off gradually through repeated practice, one by one.

> This is like two knives, one sharp and one blunt, cutting the same thing; the sharp one cuts it at once, the blunt one gradually.[118]

The sequence of abandoning the defilements begins with the strong-strong grade in the *kāmadhātu* and ends with the weak-weak grade in the *bhavāgra bhūmi* of the *ārūpya-dhātu*. In this way, a total of 88 grades of defilements existing in the nine *bhūmi*-s — *kāma-dhātu*, the four *dhyāna*-s of the *rūpadhātu* and the four *ārūpya*-s of the *ārūpya-dhātu* — come to be successively eradicated. The strong-strong grade of defilements is abandoned by the weak-weak grade of the counteractive path. The reason for this is that the coarsest defilement is graded as the strong-strong and the subtlest, weak-weak. On the other hand, the most powerful counteragent is graded as the strong-strong, and the weakest is graded as weak-weak. Since the coarsest defilement is the easiest to counteract and the subtlest the most difficult; the weakest counteractive *jñāna* is utilized for the former, and the strongest, for the latter. The AKB explains this with two similes: the gross stain of a cloth is washed out first, and the subtlest, last; a great darkness is dispelled by a small light, and a small darkness by a great light.[119] As in the case of the *darśana-heya* defilements, the abandonment of each grade of the *bhāvanā-heya* defilements involves the unhindered path and the path of liberation. The difference is that in this case, the defilements are abandoned in the unhindered path by knowledge (*jñāna*), not receptivity.[120] At the final stage, when the practitioner abandons the weak-weak grade and arrives at its path of liberation, one enters into the path of the non-trainee (*aśaikṣa-mārga*) and becomes an *arhat*.

15.7. Attainment of the four fruits of the spiritual life

The four fruits have their origin in the *sūtra*-s. As explained above, according to the Sarvāstivāda, at the 16th moment of the *satyābhisamaya*, the practitioner attains the fruit of stream entry. He has abandoned all the 88 categories of defilements abandonable by insight. In the *sūtra*,[121] this attainment came to be associated with the overcoming of three fetters (*saṃyojana*) — *satkāya-dṛṣṭi* (Pāli; *sakkāya-diṭṭhi*), *śīla-vrata-parāmarśa* (Pāli: *sīlabbata-parāmāsa*) and *vicikitsā* (Pāli: *vicikicchā*). These three, together with *kāmacchanda* and *vyāpāda*, constitute the *avarabhāgīya* (Pāli: *orambhāgīya*). In this context, the Sarvāstivāda agrees with the Theravāda: The stream entrant has overcome only the first three *avarabhāgīya* fetters and must still overcome the last two as well as all the five *ūrdhva-bhāgīya* (Pāli: *uddhambhāgīya*) fetters — *rāga* pertaining to the two upper spheres, *auddhatya*, *māna* and *avidyā*.[122] However the AKB explanation here is not acceptable to Saṃghabhadra.[123]

In the path of cultivation, the practitioner who has overcome up to five grades of the defilements becomes a candidate for the fruit of once-returner. When he has abandoned the sixth grade, he attains the fruit of a once-returner (*sakṛdāgāmin*), so called because, having been born among the gods and returning once to the human world, he will have no further rebirth. In addition to being free from the first three *avarabhāgīya* fetters, he has now also weakened or thinned *rāga*, *pratigha* and *avidyā*.[124]

Having abandoned the seventh or eighth grade — or more strictly speaking, having reached the *ānantarya-mārga* of the ninth grade — he becomes a candidate for the fruit of a non-returner. Having completely abandoned the ninth grade and abiding in the *vimukti-mārga* of the ninth grade, he attains the fruit of a non-returner. He will no longer be reborn in the *kāmadhātu* since he has now abandoned all five *avarabhāgīya* fetters that bind one to the lower *dhātu*.[125] The non-returner who has realized the *nirodha-samāpatti* (= *saṃjñāvedita-nirodha-samāpatti*) is called a 'bodily witness' (*kāya-sākṣin*). He is so called because he has directly experienced the peace of this *samāpatti* through the basis of the body — there being no mentation — which is similar to *nirvāṇa*. This is the sharpest of all the faculties of non-returners.[126]

From the moment when the non-returner becomes detached from the first grade of the defilements pertaining to the first *dhyāna* up to the moment when he abandons the eighth grade of the defilements pertaining to *bhavāgra* — or more strictly, when he is in the *ānantarya-mārga* of the ninth grade of defilement of *bhavāgra* — he is a candidate for the fruit of arhathood. This unhindered path is the most powerful of all, capable of breaking all defilements whatsoever, and is accordingly called the *vajra*-like (*vajropama*) *samādhi*. When this ninth grade is completely abandoned, there arises in the practitioner the knowledge of the exhaustion of the outflows (*kṣaya-jñāna*). Immediately after this knowledge, if he becomes an *arhat*, if he is of the immovable (i.e., non-retrogressible) type in the *vimukti-mārga*, there arises in him the knowledge of the non-arising of outflows, for he has then absolutely abandoned all defilements along with their traces (*vāsanā*) and overcome the undefiled ignorance (*akliṣṭa-ajñāna — cf. supra*, § 12.10). Otherwise, if he is a retrogressible type, there arises in him the same knowledge of exhaustion or the perfect view of the non-trainee. An *arhat* is called a non-trainee, for he has completed all training.

15.8. Out-of-sequence attainments

The above account of the sequential attainment of the four fruits represents the stages of progress of an *ānupūrvaka* — one who progresses according to the regular order. He begins as a *sakala-bandhana*. As we have seen earlier (§ 12.9.3), however, the Sarvāstivāda maintains that an ordinary worldling can abandon defilements through the mundane paths, except those that pertain to the existence-peak (*bhavāgra*). Since spiritual progress results from the abandonment of defilements, it means that an ordinary worldling can make tremendous progress before he enters into the noble path, and when he does enter it, he can attain up to the stage of *anāgāmin-phala*.

The worldly path of cultivation is with-outflow. In making upward progress, an ordinary worldling practices it by contemplating six modes of activities:

In the mundane unhindered paths, he reflects on the lower spheres as being

1. coarse (*audārika*), or
2. unsatisfactory (*duḥkhila*), or
3. like a thick wall (*sthūlabhittika*).

In the paths of liberation, he sees the upper spheres as being

1. calm (*śānta*), or
2. excellent (*praṇīta*), or
3. escape (*niḥsaraṇa*).

In this way, by becoming disgusted with a lower sphere and finding delight in an upper sphere, he abandons the defilements pertaining to the former and moves up to the latter.[127] This method of practice, however, entails that he cannot abandon the defilements pertaining to the highest stage of existence, the *bhavāgra*, for there is no stage higher than it to contrast with in order to generate disgust. Accordingly, to complete his journey, he must rely finally on the outflow-free knowledge arising in *satyābhisamaya*.[128]

Before entering into the *darśana-mārga*, if the practitioner has not abandoned any *bhāvanā-heya* defilement pertaining to the sphere of sensuality through the worldly path, or has abandoned up to the fifth category only, he becomes a candidate for stream entry upon entering the *darśana-mārga*. However, if he has abandoned from six to eight categories, he thereupon skips to become a *sakṛdāgāmi-pratipannaka*. In the 16th moment, he abides in the fruit of *sakṛdāgāmin*. Such a practitioner is known as a *bhūyo-vītarāga* — 'one who has been much detached'. If the practitioner has become fully detached beforehand from the sphere of sensuality by having abandoned all the nine categories of defilement pertaining to it, or if he is detached with regard to the higher spheres by having additionally abandoned all nine categories of defilements pertaining to each of the stages of the fine-material sphere and the first three immaterial spheres — i.e., up to the stage of the *ākiñcanyāyatana* — he skips to become an *anāgāmi-pratipannaka* upon entering the *darśana-mārga*, and an *anāgāmin* in the following moment.

15.9. Retrogressibility of an *arhat*

It is an *abhidharma* controversy as to whether an *arhat* is retrogressible or not. For the Vibhajyavādins, his retrogression is impossible:

> When a vase has been broken, there remain only the broken pieces; it can no further be a vase. The case of an *arhat* ought to be the same — having

> crushed the defilements with the *vajropama-samādhi*, he ought not to give rise to the defilements again and retrogress. Just as, a log having been burnt, there remain only the ashes, it does not become a log any more. The same should be true for the *arhat* — having burnt the defilements with the fire of the outflow-free knowledge, he ought not give rise to the defilements again and retrogress.[129]

The Mahāsāṃghika is also known to hold a similar view.[130] So too, the Sautrāntika whose view is endorsed by Vasubandhu in the AKB.[131] According to the Sarvāstivāda, however, an *arhat* who has started as a *śraddhānusārin* is still susceptible to retrogression. He is said to be one circumstantially liberated (*samaya-vimukta*). His realization of *samāpatti* is also dependent on circumstances (*samaya*). The MVŚ quotes the *sūtra* as teaching that there are five reasons for the retrogression of such an *arhat*:

(1) having too many undertakings;

(2) indulgence in conceptual proliferation (*prapañca*);

(3) being fond of quarrel;

(4) being fond of traveling afar;

(5) being constantly sick.

> Moreover, the *sūtra* mentions an *arhat* named Gautika, a *samaya-vimukta* who had retrogressed six times. At the seventh time, fearing that he might again retrogress, he killed himself with a knife and attained *parinirvāṇa*.[132]

In contrast, one who has started as a *dharmānusārin* is not retrogressible. He is said to be non-circumstantially liberated (*asamaya-vimukta*) and is called 'one liberated through wisdom' (*prajñā-vimukta*). If, additionally, he has also overcome the hindrance to *samāpatti* and can enter into the *nirodha-samāpatti* at will, he is said to be 'liberated doubly' (*ubhayobhāga-vimukta*). In all, six types of *arhat*-s are distinguished:

(1) *parihāṇa-dharman* — those susceptible to retrogression;

(2) *cetanā-dharman* — those who can end their existences at will;

(3) *anurakṣaṇā-dharman* — those who can preserve themselves by constantly guarding against the loss of what has been acquired;

(4) *sthitākampya* — those who remain stable in their stage of attainment, with neither progress nor retrogression;

(5) *prativedhanā-dharman* — those capable of penetrating the state of the *akopya-dharman arhat* which they can attain quickly;

(6) *akopya-dharman* — 'the unshakable ones' — those not susceptible to retrogression. The first five are *samaya-vimukta*-s, the last *asamaya-vimukta*-s.[133]

NOTES

[1] AKB, 391.

[2] MVŚ, 4b; see *supra*, § 1.2.

[3] MVŚ, 70a, 85a, 315c, etc.

[4] MVŚ, 428b: *śrāvaka-bodhi* requires only 60 *kalpa*-s of *prayoga*; *pratyekabuddha*, 100 *kalpa*-s.

[5] MVŚ, 154a, 157c, 159a, 210b, etc.

[6] MVŚ, 327c.

[7] *Cf.* MVŚ, 264b–c, 465c; see also *supra*, § 12.7, § 12.9.3.

[8] MVŚ, 264c–265a.

[9] MVŚ, 317a.

[10] MVŚ, 3a-b.

[11] MVŚ, 933c.

[12] See JPŚ, 964b; MVŚ, 560b, etc.

[13] See SĀ, T 2, 10a–11c.

[14] AKB, 334 ff.

[15] AKB, 335 f.; MVŚ, 906c ff.

[16] MVŚ, 34c–35a speaks of three types of *kuśala-mūla*-s: *puṇya-bhāgīya*, *mokṣa-bhāgīya* and *nirvedha-bhāgīya*. The first are the seeds of good rebirths as human and *deva.*

[17] MVŚ, 35a.

[18] MVŚ, 35a–b.

[19] MVŚ, 885b–c.

[20] MVŚ, 885b–886a.

[21] AKB, 337.

[22] AKB, 339 f.; MVŚ, 134c.

[23] MVŚ, 384b, 662c, etc.

[24] E.g.: Pu Guang's commentary on the AKB, T 41, 339b; etc.

[25] E.g.: T 46, no. 1918, 557c–558a, 564a–b; T no. 1916; T no. 1911, 35c; etc.

[26] E.g., MVŚ, 410a.

[27] MVŚ, 205a.

[28] MVŚ, 205a–208c.

[29] T 30, 905b. Also *cf.* YBŚ, T 30, 427b, 458a-b, which enumerates them and also explains their respective counteracting functions, but without assigning to them a collective name.

[30] *Cf.* AKB, 337.

[31] *smṛty-upasthāna* — MVŚ, 936c ff., AKB, 341 ff.

[32] All *dharma*-s other than body, sensation and ideation. MVŚ, 937a: mental objects — other than the *vedanā-skandha* — subsumed under the *dharmāyatana*.

[33] *svalakṣaṇa* = *svabhāva* — AKB, 341.

[34] MVŚ, 938a: This fourfold mindfulness is for counteracting the four corresponding topsy-turvy-ness (*viparyāsa*).

[35] MVŚ, 148a.

[36] MVŚ, 148a.

[37] MVŚ, 135b.

[38] AKB, 346: *tac caitac caturvidham api nirvedhabhāgīyam*

bhāvanāmayam /

na śrutacintāmayam /

[39] AKB, 346.

[40] See AKB, 447 f.

[41] AKB, 346: *nirvedhabhāgīyāni ko 'rthaḥ / vidha vibhāge / niścito vedho nirvedhaḥ āryamārgas tena vicikitsā-prahāṇāt satyānāṃ ca vibhajanād idaṃ duḥkham ayaṃ yāvāt mārga iti / tasya bhāgo darśanamārgaikadeśaḥ / tasya āvāhakatvena hitatvān nirvedhabhāgīyāni /*

[42] MVŚ, 30a.

[43] MVŚ, 29c–30a.

[44] MVŚ, 3b.

[45] MVŚ, 33a–b.

[46] MVŚ, 33b.

[47] MVŚ, 33c.

[48] MVŚ, 28a.

[49] MVŚ, 34c.

[50] MVŚ, 30b.

[51] AKB, 344: *yādṛśā ūṣmāṇas catuḥsatyālambanāḥ ṣoḍaśākārāś ca / utkṛṣṭataratvāt tu nāmāntaram /*

[52] AKB, 344: *cala-kuśalamūlamūrdhatvāt mūrdhānaḥ / ebhyo hi pāto 'tikramo vā /* Vy, 532: *mūrdha-śabdo 'yaṃ prakarṣa-paryanta-vācī / tathā hi loke vaktāro bhavanti / mūrdha-gatā khalv asya śrīr iti … mūrdhabhyaḥ pātaḥ parihāṇiḥ / atikramo vā kṣānti-saṃmukhī-bhāvo vā / mūrdhnāṃ calatvāt /*

[53] MVŚ, 25c; Vy, 532: *dve hi kuśala-mūle cale / uṣmagata-mūrdha-lakṣaṇe parhāṇi-saṃbhāvāt / dve acale kṣānti-laukikāgra-dharma-lakṣaṇe viparyayāt / tatra tayor yan mṛdu tad uṣmagatam / yad adhimātraṃ te mūrdhānaḥ / acalayor api yan mṛdu sā kṣāntiḥ / yad adhimātraṃ te laukikāgra-dharmāḥ /*

[54] MVŚ, 30b.

[55] MVŚ, 24a ff.: various reasons given for the epithet; also *cf.* MVŚ, 223c.

[56] AKB, 344: *adhimātra-satya-kṣamaṇād aparihāṇitaḥ /*

[57] Vy, 533: *adhimātra-satya-kṣamaṇād iti / uṣmagatāvasthāyaṃ mṛdu satyaṃ kṣamate rocate / mūrdhāvasthāyāṃ madhyaṃ tad-anantaram idānīm adhimātra-satya-kṣamaṇāt kṣāntir utpadyate / … yasmāt kṣāntir na parihīyate / mūrdhabhyas tu parihīyata ity asti saṃbhavaḥ /*

[58] MVŚ, 30b–c.

[59] AKB, 344: *agradharma-saṃśleṣād asau kāmāvacara-duḥkhālambanaiva / ata evoṣmagatādīnāṃ traidhātuka-duḥkhādyālambanatva-siddhir niyamāvacanāt / yadā kila rūpārūpya-pratipakṣādīnām ekaika-satyākārālambanāpahrāsena yāvat kāmāvacaram eva duḥkhaṃ dvābhyāṃ kṣaṇābhyāṃ manasikaroty eṣā sarvaiva madhyā kṣāntir yadaikam eva kṣaṇaṃ tadādhimātreti /*; MVŚ, 25a–b.

[60] MVŚ, 25b.

[61] MVŚ, 7b.

[62] JPŚ, 918a ff.

[63] MVŚ, 5a ff.

[64] MVŚ, 11b. *Cf.* AKB, 345: *sarva-laukikaśreṭhatvād iti laukikāgradharmāḥ / vinā sabhāga-hetunā mārgasya tat-puruṣakāreṇākarṣaṇāt /*

[65] MVŚ, 11b–12a.

[66] MVŚ, 7b–8b.

[67] MVŚ, 8c — refuted by the Vaibhāṣika.

[68] MVŚ, 3b.

[69] MVŚ, 16a — other explanations are also given.

[70] MVŚ, 4a–b.

[71] According to the Kāśmīra Sarvāstivādins: "The *ānantarya-mārga*-s can abandon the *kleśa*-s, because they block the *prāpti*-s of the *kleśa*-s so that they do not continue; they can also realize the *nirodha*-s, because they induce the *visaṃyoga-prāpti*-s so that they may arise. The *vimukti-mārga*-s are only said to realize *nirodha*-s, as they appear together with the *visaṃyoga-prāpti*-s." (MVŚ, 465c)

[72] AKB, 40. For further explanation of these three *indriya*-s, see AKB, 42, 49.

[73] AKB, 49.

[74] AKB, 352.

[75] Ny, 690a.

[76] AKB, 350: *prathamato dharmatattva-jñānād dharma-jñānam*. Vy, 542: *ādito duḥkh' ādi-dharma-tattva-jñānād ity arthaḥ /* See also *Entrance*, 217 f., n. 446.

[77] AKB: *tadanvayād ūrdhvaṃ duḥkhālambanam anvaya-jñānam / tathaivānugamanād /* AKB(C): "It is called 'species' (類) because this knowledge, bearing on the subsequent object, is similar to the preceding one, for the subsequent one realizes the object in accordance with (/following) the preceding one." Vy, 542 explains *tad-anvayatvāt* as *tad-dhetukatvāt* ('having that (i.e., *dharma-jñāna*) as its cause').

[78] Ny, 735c.

[79] See *Entrance*, 219, n. 447.

[80] See IAKB, I, xxxx.

[81] MVŚ, 265a, 522a–b.

[82] AKB, 328.

[83] See *Entrance*, 224, n. 468; also *cf.* T 32, 257b.

[84] T 49, 15c.

[85] T 49, 16a.

[86] Vy, 542: *ārya-dharmagupta-prabhṛtayaḥ /*

[87] T 41, 351c.

[88] MVŚ, 533a.

[89] I take 寶 to be an error for 實 in the text.

[90] MVŚ, 533b.

[91] *Cf.* Vism, 593.

[92] AKB, 351; AKB(C), 121c–122a; MVŚ, 732c, 16b.

[93] T 32, 257b.

[94] T 32, 251b; see *Studies*, 586,

[95] T 32, 333b.

[96] T 32, 333c

[97] *Ibid.*, 368c–369a.

[98] See Yin Shun, *Study*, 586 ff.

[99] AKB, 157: *āryāḥ katame / yeṣām anāsravo mārga utpannaḥ / ārād yātāḥ pāpakebhyo dharmebhya ity āryāḥ / ātyantika-visaṃyoga-prāptilābhāt / ete hi kleśa-kṣaye niyatatvāt samyaktva-niyatāḥ /* See below for the notion of *samyaktva-niyāma-avakrānti.*

[100] JPŚ, 928c; *cf.* MVŚ, 232b. See also *supra*, § 11.3.1.

[101] MVŚ, 231c.

[102] MVŚ, 232a–b.

[103] AKB,355: *akṣīṇabhāvanāheyaḥ phalasthaḥ saptakṛtparaḥ /*

[104] AKB, 356.

[105] MVŚ, 240a. *Cf.* AKB, 356: *nirvāṇasroto hi mārgas tena tatra gamanāt / tadasāv āpanna āgataḥ prāpta iti srotaāpannaḥ /*

[106] Vy, 548.

[107] Vy, 549: *śraddhā'dhiko muktaḥ śraddhā'dhimukta iti kṛtvā / na tu tasya prajñā naivāsti / tayā na tu prabhāvita iti na tan nāma labhate / prajñā'dhikatvena dṛṣṭi-prabhāvitatvāt dṛṣṭi-prāptaḥ / na tu tasya śraddhā nāsti … apare tu punar nairukta-vidhim ālambya vyācakṣate / śraddh'ādhipatyena darśana-heyebho muktaḥ śraddhā'dhimuktaḥ / dṛṣṭy-ādhipatyena prāpta-phalo dṛṣṭi-prāpta iti /*

108 He is therefore said to be abiding in the class (*rāśi*) of those destined for *samyaktva*. *Cf.* MVŚ, 140b.

109 MVŚ, 12a. which gives various interpretations. The grammarians (*śābdika*-s) explain as follows: The term is *niyāma-avakrānti*; *yāma* also signifies going (< *yā*); *ni* signifies 'to prevent' and also has the sense of 'not'. The *yogācārya*-s, having acquired the noble path, will never go to the *gati*-s of the *asat-puruṣa*. Thus the noble path is also called *niyāma*.

110 AKB(C), 121b.

111 *Cf.* MVŚ, 140b.

112 *Cf.* MVŚ, 265a ff.

113 MVŚ, 22c.

114 *Cf.* AKB, 157, for the three classes (*rāśi*) of beings: Those in the *samyatva-niyata-rāśi* are destined for *nirvāṇa*; *mithyātva*, for rebirths in the evil destinies (*gati*); *aniyata*; non-destined or non-fixed as regard either. *Cf.* MVŚ, 22c, 316b; AKB, 374 f., for other arguments for the non-retrogressibility of the *darśana-mārga*.

115 T 49, 15c.

116 MVŚ, 276a–c.

117 AKB, 355.

118 MVŚ, 267a–b.

119 AKB, 355.

120 MVŚ, 267b.

121 E.g., S, v, 356–357.

122 AKB, 356.

123 Ny, 694a.

124 AKB, 358: *devāt gatvā sakṛn manuṣyalokāgamanāt sakṛdāgāmī / pareṇa janmābhāvāt / rāgadveṣamohānāṃ ca tanutvād ity ucyate / mṛdu-prakārāvaśeṣatvāt /*

125 AKB, 358 ff.; five types of *anāgāmin* who attain *nirvāṇa* in the *rūpadhātu* are mentioned and explained herein: *antarā-parinirvāyin*, *upapadya-parinirvāyin*, *sābhisaṃskāra-parinirvāyin*, *anabhisaṃskāra-parinirvāyin*, and *ūrdhvasrotas*. Including the type who, being detached from the *rūpa-dhātu*, is reborn in the *ārūpyadhātu* where he attains *nirvāṇa* — i.e., the *ārūpyaga* — the total number of *anāgāmin*-s becomes six. Also *cf.* A, iv 70, 380; S, v, 201; *Puggalapaññatti*, 16–17, 70; Vism, 677.

[126] AKB, 363.

[127] *Cf.* AKB, 368.

[128] *Cf.* AKB, 353 f.

[129] MVŚ, 312b.

[130] T 49, 15c; T 41, 375a.

[131] AKB, 375.

[132] MVŚ, 312b.

[133] AKB, 372 ff.; MVŚ, 315b.

16. The Unconditioned (*asaṃskṛta*) *Dharma*-s

16.1. Three unconditioned *dharma*-s of the Sarvāstivāda

The orthodox Sarvāstivādins teach that there are three categories of unconditioned *dharma*-s:

1. cessation through deliberation (*pratisaṃkhyā-nirodha*);
2. cessation independent of deliberation (*apratisaṃkhyā-nirodha*);
3. Space (*ākāśa*).

In the Sarvāstivāda perspective, the unconditioned domain — excepting Space — just like the conditioned domain, is pluralistic.

1. The cessations through deliberation refers to the cessation of defilements acquired through the process of discriminative or deliberative effort. There are as many *pratisaṃkhyā-nirodha*-s as there are impure (*sāsrava*; 'with-outflow') *dharma*-s.[1] This is the most

important unconditioned category, representing as it does, the goal of Buddhist praxis. In some schools, such as the Theravāda, this is the only unconditioned. Accordingly, among the three kinds of the unconditioned of the Sarvāstivāda, we will be dealing with this at considerably greater length below.

2. The cessations independent of deliberation are those acquired simply on account of the deficiency in the required assemblage of conditions for the particular *dharma*-s. They are so called because they are independent of any deliberative effort. The quantity of this category is even greater than that of the cessations through deliberation, being as numerous as the conditioned *dharma*-s.[2]

3. Space is that ontological entity by virtue of which resistant things can be accommodated. It is to be distinguished from the 'element of space' which is space in the ordinary case, such as that found in a window.

16.1.1. The controversial nature of the unconditioned *dharma*-s.

Various schools have different conceptions of the unconditioned and disagree as to the ontological status of these *dharma*-s.

In the Sarvāstivāda conception, an unconditioned is:

1. that which transcends arising and ceasing,
2. an ontologically real possessing a unique efficacy — albeit not causal efficacy obtaining in the temporal process.

The Mahāsāmghika upholds the criterion that the notion of an unconditioned entails that which remains unchanged eternally and, from this perspective, includes *pratītya-samutpāda* and the *ārya-mārga*, representing the eternal principles of causality and liberation respectively, as among the nine unconditioned *dharma*-s:

1. *pratisaṃkhyā-nirodha;*
2. *apratisaṃkhyā-nirodha;*
3. *ākāśa;*
4. *ākāśānantyāyatana;*
5. *vijñānānantyāyatana;*
6. *ākiñcanyāyatana;*
7. *naiva-saṃjñā-nāsaṃjñāyatana;*
8. *pratītya-samutpādatva;*
9. *ārya-mārgatva.*[3]

For the Sautrāntika, the unconditioned is simply a concept (*prajñapti*) of that which is opposed to the conditioned.

> All the unconditioned are non-entities (*sarvam evāsaṃskṛtam adravyam*), for they do not exist as distinct existents (*bhāvāntara*) like *rūpa*, *vedanā*, etc.[4]

Thus, *nirvāṇa* is nothing more than the absolute absence of *duḥkha*. Accordingly, this school categorically denies the reality of all unconditioned *dharma*-s.

Even within the Sarvāstivāda school itself, opinions differ as regards the ontological status of these unconditioned *dharma*-s. It appears that at the early stages, the Sarvāstivāda did not elaborate on the ontological status of the *asaṃskṛta dharma*-s. In the JPŚ, the canonical text upheld as the supreme authority by the orthodox Sarvāstivādins, one finds only the mention of *pratisaṃkhyā-nirodha* and *apratisaṃkhyā-nirodha*, but not *ākāśa*. In the MVŚ, the various *ācārya*-s hold contradictory views. Thus, Buddhadeva accepts the realities of all three;[5] the Bhadanta (= Dharmatrāta?)[6] denies the reality of *ākāśa*; the Dārṣṭāntika denies the ontological status of all three.[7] Probably in response to the denial by the Dārṣṭāntika and the Sautrāntika, in the post AKB period there had consistently been an additional requirement in the definition of 'Sarvāstivāda': A Sarvāstivādin must accept not only the tri-temporal existence of *dharma*, but also the reality of all three kinds of *asaṃskṛta*.[8]

The controversial nature of these unconditioned *dharma*-s is also evident in Saṃghabhadra's repeated accusation of the Sautrāntika as siding with the followers of the 'sky-flower' (空花; *ākāśa-puṣpa*) doctrine — apparently referring to the Śūnyatā-vāda prevailing at the time — obstinately denying the *svabhāva* of all *dharma*-s.[9]

16.1.2. Sarvāstivāda conception of the unconditioned

In its aspect of being a dependently co-arisen existent, a conditioned *dharma* is called a *saṃskṛta* — 'compounded', 'co-produced', 'conditioned'. In its other aspect of being a causally productive force, it is also called a *saṃskāra* — 'conditioning' or 'conditioning force'.

In direct contrast, the *asaṃskṛta*-s are neither produced by causes and conditions, nor are they causally productive of other *dharma*-s. Saṃghabhadra argues, however, that their reality cannot be denied simply on the ground that they are neither causes nor effects — the Sautrāntika, for one, accepts causality of past and future *dharma*-s but not their reality.[10] (See also below, § 16.2.1).

The AKB states that the *asaṃskṛta*-s are not subsumable under the *skandha* taxonomy, since "*skandha*" means a heap (*rāśi*), and, unlike *rūpa,* etc., the *asaṃskṛta*-s do not form separate heaps of "past *asaṃskṛta*-s", "present *asaṃskṛta*-s", etc.[11] In Sthiramati's **Tattvārthā*, a question is raised:

> If the *asaṃskṛta*-s are not real entities, it is reasonable that they do not form a *skandha*. Since they are asserted [by the Sarvāstivāda] to be existents, why is it not conceded that a plurality of them agglomerate as a heap — an *asaṃskṛta-skandha*?[12]

Sthiramati explains :

> There are two significations of a heap: (i) When those that exist separately in various locations are gathered together in one place, one calls it a heap.

(ii) When tri-temporal *dharma*-s are grouped together through our faculty of understanding (*prajñā*) into groups each pertaining to one temporal period, one calls these [groups] heaps. Now, as the *asamskṛta dharma*-s have neither of these two significations, how can they be called heaps?[13]

Thus, the essential characteristic of the *asaṃskṛta dharma*-s is that they are neither temporalized nor spatialized. This, however, does not mean that they are not distinctly individuated; rather, they exist as a plurality of real entities (*dravya*). Being beyond the space-time dimension, they can neither arise nor cease, and accordingly are not directly involved in any causal process.[14] Only the past and present *saṃskṛta dharma*-s have the functions of 'grasping a fruit' (*phala-grahaṇa/phala-ākṣepa*) and 'giving a fruit' (*phala-dāna*) (*cf. supra*, § 7.4). These two functions are lacking in the future *saṃskṛta dharma*-s as well as in the *asaṃskṛta dharma*-s. Nevertheless, the unconditioned *dharma*-s, qua *dharma*-s, are real forces and can have an impact on human existence, even though, as Saṃghabhadra puts it, the way of establishing causes and effects among the *saṃskṛta*-s is not applicable to the case of the *asaṃskṛta*-s. (See below, § 16.2).

16.2. Cessation through deliberation

In the Sarvāstivāda, the better known term *nirvāṇa* is synonymous with *pratisaṃkhyā-nirodha*. The latter is defined as a disjunction (*visaṃyoga*) from the impure (*sāsrava*; 'with outflow') *dharma*-s acquired through the process of discrimination/deliberation (*pratisaṃkhyāna*) which is a specific pure *prajñā*.[15] Sthiramati explains that this specific *prajñā* refers to that in the *ānantarya-mārga* (see below) when the acquisition (*prāpti*) of defilement is abandoned, subsequent to which *pratisaṃkhyā-nirodha* is realized (*sākṣāt-kṛta*)[16] or acquired (*prāpyate*). The MVŚ[17] enumerates as many as 14 synonyms for *pratisaṃkhyā-nirodha,* together with various interpretations for each of them:

(1) Nirvāṇa;
(2) Dissimilar (不同類; *asabhāga*);
(3) Non-agglomerated (非聚 *arāśi*?; *asamudaya*?);
(4) Non-manifest (非顯; *avarṇa*);
(5) Most Excellent (*parama*);
(6) Penetration (通達; *prativedha,*);
(7) Arhat;
(8) Non-intimate (不親近; *asaṃṣṛṣṭa*);
(9) Non-cultivated (*asevita*, *abhāvita*);
(10) Lovable (*abhipreta*, *ramaṇīya*);
(11) Proximate (*antika*, *āsanna*);
(12) Wonderful (*praṇīta*);
(13) Exit (*niḥsaraṇa*).

The first and foremost, *nirvāṇa*, is explained in four senses:

(i) the absolute exit (*nir*) from all *gati* (*vana*);

(ii) the absolute absence (*nir*) of karma and of defilements —bad smell (*durgandha* = *vana*) and impurities;

(iii) the absolute exit (*nir*) from all the forests (*vana*) of *skandha*-s with their three fires and three characteristics;

(iv) the non-(*nir*-)weaving (*vāna*) of the fabric — *vipāka-phala* — of saṃsāric existence.

Elsewhere, the MVŚ gives ten meanings of *nirvāṇa,* most of which are covered by the above four senses; the other senses that could be considered additional are: 'without further existence', 'freedom from bondage' and 'transcendence of all saṃsāric sufferings'.[18] Thus, *nirvāṇa* as the *summum bonum* of Buddhism is the *pratisaṃkhyā-nirodha* which is acquired at the final moment of enlightenment as a result of which all defilements — and hence all *duḥkha* — pertaining to the three spheres of existence have ceased absolutely, and saṃsāric existence is totally transcended. The MVŚ also speaks of this specifically in terms of the abandonment of defilement, the corresponding *jñāna* arisen and the path-structure as follows:

> When [the practitioner] is dissociated from the ninth (i.e., final) grade of bond, the *vajropama-samādhi* (in which whatever defilements remaining are eradicated without any trace) having ceased and the *anutpāda-jñāna* having first arisen, that abandonment [of defilement] acquired is called 'abandonment' (*prahāṇa*), 'disjunction' (*visaṃyoga*), 'cessation' (*nirodha*), 'truth' (*satya*), 'complete knowledge' (*parijñā*), i.e., the complete knowledge that [refers to] the destruction of all bonds, 'fruit of the spiritual life' (*śrāmaṇya-phala*), i.e., the *arhat-phala*, and 'the sphere of *nirvāṇa* with a remnant of substratum' (*sopadhi-śeṣa-nirvāṇa-dhātu*). … When the *skandha*-s, *āyatana*-s and *dhātu*-s of an *arhat* cease and do not continue any longer, [he enters] into the sphere of *nirvāṇa* without a remnant of substratum (*nirupadhi-śeṣa-nirvāṇa-dhātu*).[19]

Accordingly, one can speak only of the non-trainee's disjunction from defiled *dharma*-s as *nirvāṇa-dhātu*:

> The disjunction acquired by an ordinary worldling … is not subsumable as either of the two types of *nirvāṇa-dhātu*… It should only be called an abandonment, a disjunction, a cessation, a truth (*satya*). It is not to be called a complete knowledge (*parijñā*), or a *śrāmanya-phala*, or a *sopadhi-śeṣa-nirvāṇa-dhātu*, or a *nirupadhi-śeṣa-nirvāṇa-dhātu*.
>
> The disjunction acquired by a trainee is called an abandonment, a disjunction, a cessation, a truth; at some stage called a complete knowledge and at some stage not so called; at some stage called a *śrāmaṇya-phala* and at some stage not so called. It is not called a *sopadhi-śeṣa-nirvāṇa-dhātu* or a *nirupadhi-śeṣa-nirvāṇa-dhātu*.
>
> The disjunction acquired by a non-trainee is called an abandonment, a disjunction, a cessation, a truth, a complete knowledge, a *śrāmaṇya-phala*.

> At some stage it is called a *sopadhi-śeṣa-nirvāṇa-dhātu*; at some stage it is called a *nirupadhi-śeṣa-nirvāṇa-dhātu*.[20]

As the following discussion in the MVŚ sums up, while on the one hand each abandonment of defilement can be spoken of as a *nirvāṇa*, on the other hand, this term is in actual fact reserved for the perfect attainment of an *arhat*:

> Question: The abandonment of any [defiled] *dharma* such as *satkāya-dṛṣṭi* is *nirvāṇa*, why does it herein speak only of the absolute abandonment of greed (*rāga*) and so on up to the absolute abandonment of all defilements?
>
> Answer: Although the abandonment of each and every [defiled] *dharma* is *nirvāṇa*, herein it speaks only of the "perfect *nirvāṇa*". ... Furthermore, the name *nirvāṇa* is [reserved] exclusively for the stage of the non-trainee. The stage of the trainee being yet incomplete, it is not called *nirvāṇa*.[21]

As unconditioned *dharma*-s, the *pratisaṃkhyā-nirodha*-s are not causes or conditions in the proper sense. Hence they cannot be said to have fruits (*sa-phala*). Nevertheless, in conformity with the *sūtra* tradition which speaks of *śrāmāṇya-phala* and conventional usage, it is permissible to call *pratisaṃkhyā-nirodha* a "fruit of disjunction" (*visaṃyoga-phala*) without implying that it is causally produced, and it is also permissible to consider them as a "condition qua object" (*ālambana-pratyaya*) — e.g., as an object of thought of a yogi, and *adhipati-pratyaya* — making an indirect contribution by merely not obstructing.[22] According to the Sarvāstivāda:

> The way of establishing causes and effects among the *saṃskṛta*-s is not applicable to the case of the *asaṃskṛta*-s. Accordingly, a *pratisaṃkhyā-nirodha* is a cause which is without an effect, and an effect which is without a cause.[23]

16.2.1. Proof of the reality of *nirvāṇa*

For the Sarvāstivāda, *nirvāṇa* or *pratisaṃkhyā-nirodha* is a distinct positive entity (*dravyāntara*) — an ontologically real force that is acquired by the practitioner when a given defilement is completely abandoned.[24] In fact, this real force acts to ensure that the *prāpti* of the defilement so abandoned will absolutely not be able to arise any more.[25] Skandhila's definition clearly brings out this dynamic function:

> The cessation through deliberation is that which causes the non-production of *duḥkha* — [a real entity which is a positive presence]: like a dike holding back the water or a screen blocking the wind.[26]

The following are the main Vaibhāṣika arguments for its reality (Ny, 430a–434b):

1. The *sūtra* says, "Among all *dharma*-s — those which are *saṃskṛta*-s or those which are *asaṃskṛta*-s — detachment is supreme."[27] Here the *asaṃskṛta*-s are mentioned — in the plural — as among the *dharma*-s, and therefore cannot be non-existent. Those that are non-existent do not have the nature of *dharma*.

> How can a non-existent be said to be supreme among the non-existents? It is observed empirically that among *dharma*-s which have their self-characteristics (*svalakṣaṇa*), some are said to be superior, others inferior. Thus *nirvāṇa*-s definitely exist as distinct entities which sustain their self-characteristics and hence are called *dharma*-s. (*Cf. svalakṣaṇa-dhāraṇād dharmaḥ* / AKB, 2).

2. The essences and functions of *rūpa*, *vedanā*, etc., which exist as a series, are empirically observable. Those of *nirvāṇa,* which do not exist as a series, are subtle and difficult to perceive. Nevertheless, when as a result of diligent contemplative practices the *bhāvanā-mayī prajñā* arises in the practitioner, the true essential nature and function of *nirvāṇa* are realized by him. Indeed, at the moment when he comes

out from the contemplation, he exclaims: "Wonderful is *nirvāṇa*, it is cessation (*nirodha*), calmed (*śānta*), excellent (*praṇīta*) and exit (*niḥsaraṇa*)." These specific characteristics of *nirvāṇa* which are experientially verifiable by the practitioner prove their very existence as real entities. In fact, characteristic and essential nature are one and the same thing. We may also note here the MVŚ doctrine that what pertains to the absolute truth (*paramārtha*) is the universal principles directly cognized (*abhi-sam-√i)* by the *ārya*.

3. There are certain *sūtra*-s which explicitly say that *nirvāṇa* exists. Thus, a *sūtra* says:

> O monks! there is definitely the unborn. If this were not, there would not be an end to birth-death and *duḥkha*. As there is the unborn… (*cf. Itivuttaka*, 43).

Also:

> "There is an abode (*sthāna*), an exit"; "I see that there truly is the real category (*padārtha*) of *asaṃskṛta*, namely *nirvāṇa*"; "It is called *nirodha* on account of the *nirodha* of the five aggregates of grasping"; "There are three *dhātu*-s — *nirvāṇa-dhātu, saṃskṛta-dhātu, asaṃskṛta-dhātu*"; "There is a *nirodha-dhātu*"; "There is the born (*jāta*), there is the unborn (*ajāta*)"; "There is the *ārya-satya* of *duḥkha-nirodha*"; "I know directly the abode of security (*kṣemāyatana, kṣema-gati*)"; etc.

The Sautrāntika and others, of course, deny that these *sūtra* statements constitute proof of *nirvāṇa* as a real entity. Thus, "There is the unborn" refers not to a real entity, but simply to the discontinuity of the birth (*janmāpravṛtti*) of existents; it means simply: "there is the cutting off of the series of the born". Saṃghabhadra replies that it is only when the unborn is conceded to be a distinct real entity that it is meaningful to say "there *is*". Besides, if there were no such entity, the Buddha should have simply said "there is the discontinuity of the born". Moreover, before the path has arisen, there is no 'cutting off of the series'; when the path is arisen, there is; again there is not, when an *ārya* retrogresses in giving rise to defilements — thus the cutting off of a series should not be *asaṃskṛta*. To show its unreality, the Sautrāntika also cites the simile in the *sūtra* which likens *nirvāṇa* to the extinction of the flame of a lamp. The Vaibhāṣika, however, argues that this simile does not contradict their view-point: The extinction referred therein is the *anityatā-lakṣaṇa* which exists as a real *viprayukta-saṃskāra dharma*, distinct from the flame. Besides, this simile is made with reference to the time of entering into the *nirupadhiśeṣa-nirvāṇa* when all remaining *upadhi*-s are completely cut off.

4. The Sautrāntika and some *abhidharma* masters concede that *nirvāṇa* exists, but only as a relatively real (*prajñaptisat*). The Sarvāstivāda argues that if it is conceded to exist, it must be accepted to exist as an absolutely real (*dravya-sat*, *paramārtha-sat*), for a real supporting basis — on which *nirvāṇa* is designated as a relatively real — cannot be found.

The *saṃskāra*-s cannot serve as this basis for designating *nirvāṇa* as their cessation, for in this case, *nirvāṇa*, like its basis, would have to be a thing whose nature is to be abandoned, defiled, with outflow and impermanent — completely contradictory to the nature of *nirvāṇa*. Moreover, logically speaking, the *saṃskāra*-s being opposed in nature to *nirvāṇa*, cannot be the basis of the latter: there has never been a relatively real *dharma* that is opposed in nature to its very supporting basis, as in the case of light and darkness. Furthermore, since *nirvāṇa* is conceded to be the cessation of the *saṃskāra*-s, the latter cannot serve as the basis — it is not observed that light has darkness (its extinction) as the basis. Besides, it is also illogical in view of the fact that when the *saṃskāra*-s are existing, there is no cessation: a person who is non-detached, as long as he is still having defilements like greed, etc., cannot be said to have the cessation of these defilements. It is only when the defilements no longer exist in him that he realizes *nirvāṇa*.

Conclusion: If *nirvāṇa* has any reality, it must be a real entity in itself, not a mere designation derived from any basis. (*Cf.* the last argument to that employed in the Ny (624c ff.) in establishing that the past and future *dharma*-s are not just designations on the basis of the real present *dharma*-s. Also *cf.* ADV, 278).

5. Some assert that *nirvāṇa* is unreal because a knowledge (*jñāna*) necessarily has an object, and for them the *prajñā* which perceives *nirvāṇa* (*nirvāṇālambanā prajñā*) has name (*nāman*) as its object. Saṃghabhadra refutes this, pointing out that it would lead to the consequence of *mithyā-dṛṣṭi* and *samyag-dṛṣṭi* being mutually accomplishing:

> A *samyag-dṛṣṭi* comprehending *nirvāṇa* as being *śānta* and *nitya* would become a *dṛṣṭy-upādāna*, since all names are impermanent. A *mithyā-dṛṣṭi* vilifying *nirvāṇa* as being impermanent in nature would become a *samyag-dṛṣṭi*, since it would be an understanding in conformity to reality. Those who hold that *nirvāṇa* is devoid of any essential reality would never concede that name is a non-existent; those who hold that *nirvāṇa* has an essential nature would never concede that name itself is *nirvāṇa*.

6. If *nirvāṇa* were not a real entity, how can the receptive beings give rise to delight in *nirvāṇa* and disgust towards *saṃsāra* — there cannot be inferiority or superiority among non-existents. Moreover, it would mean that the Buddha had been deluding the receptive beings, for he would have been speaking of the non-existents in the same manner that he spoke of the existents. A further implication would be that a view that denies the reality of *nirvāṇa* would be a *samyag-dṛṣṭi*. (*Cf.* following argument).

In this argument, there is an implicit stress that *nirvāṇa*, as much as the conditioned *dharma*-s, are real forces which can have impact on the mental stream of sentient beings. It is cognizable (*vijñeya*), even though ordinary worldlings cannot cognize it truly as it is (*yathābhūtam*). This point is also brought out from the following discussion in the VKŚ:

> Can a thought pertaining to the sense sphere (*kāmadhātu-pratisaṃyukta-citta*) … cognize the *dharma*-s which do not pertain to any sphere (*apratisaṃyukta*) — [namely, the outflow-free *dharma*-s]?
>
> Answer: Yes, it can. That is: with regard to cessation, it may [cognize it] as cessation, calm, excellence and escape (the four *ākāra*-s of the truth of cessation — § 15.2.2.1). With regard to the path, it may [cognize it] as path, right method, course of practice and being conducive to exit (four *ākāra*-s of the truth of the path). … It may be a cognition of the nature of doubt, or of delusion, or of being generated from proper reasoning (*yoga-vihita*), or of being generated from improper reasoning (*ayoga-vihita*).[28]

7. The opponents argue: The Buddha explicitly states in the *sūtra* that "all" *dharma*-s are comprised in the 12 *āyatana*-s (*Saṃyutta-nikāya*, iv, 13), and also that these 12 *āyatana*-s are *sa-prapañca* and *anitya*. Now, if *nirvāṇa* is a real existent and is permanent, the Buddha would have distinguished it from the 12 *āyatana*-s. Saṃghabhadra answers: In the same context, the Buddha further speaks of all the 12 *āyatana*-s as being with-burning (*sa-dāha*) — i.e., having the heat of defilement. Now, surely the *ārya-mārga* is included in the 12 *āyatana*-s and yet it is certainly devoid of the burning of greed, etc. Why then does the Buddha not distinguish it from the other *dharma*-s? Thus, it must be understood that the Buddha in this context refers to the 12 *āyatana*-s which are with outflow. Hence the opponents, by quoting the above *sūtra* cannot establish the unreality of *nirvāṇa*.

8. When *duḥkha* is ceased, a *pratisaṃkhyā-nirodha* — distinct from *duḥkha* and *mārga* — is acquired. It is this that is called *nirvāṇa* (432c). If there were no *nirodha* that exists as a real entity, then an *arhat* ought to have defilements and one at the *śaikṣa* stage ought to have been freed from defilements, since the moment (known as *vimukti mārga*) following that at which the *prāpti* of the defilement is abandoned (known as *ānantarya-mārga*) would not be different. In fact, it is this

real entity arising at the following moment that functions as a force absolutely preventing the *prāpti* of the defilement so abandoned from linking up the defilement with the individual series (*saṃtati*). That is, *pratisaṃkhyā-nirodha* is not a mere concept; it is a real force that absolutely prevents the re-arising of the defilement.

9. *Nirvāṇa*, if unreal, could not have been subsumed as one of the noble truths — the *nirodha-satya* — a non-existent cannot be predicated as 'true' or 'false'. An *ārya*, in his *abhisamaya*, sees truly all four truths. Now since *prajñā* cannot arise with regard to a non-existent object (this is the articulated position of the Vaibhāṣika[29]), it would be topsy-turvy to say that an *ārya* sees a non-existent object. Moreover, with regard to a non-existent which absolutely defies all verbal qualifications, how can the *ārya*, in his spiritual realization, say: "*This* is cessation of *duḥkha*"? It is observed in the world that the demonstratives 'this' and 'that' are applicable only to existent things. Furthermore, all this will amount to the denial of the existence of the third truth. Besides, if *duḥkha-nirodha* signifies the mere absence of *duḥkha*, there need only be the mention of *duḥkha-nirodha-gāminī-pratipat* (the fourth truth) — the mention of *mārga-satya* suffices to indicate the absence of *duḥkha* that it counteracts. If it does not result in the absence of *duḥkha*, why is it said to be a counteractive path?

16.2.2. *Pratisaṃkhyā-nirodha*, *prāpti*, and spiritual liberation

The proposition that there are as many *pratisaṃkhyā-nirodha*-s as there are objects of junction (*saṃyogavastu*),[30] i.e., attachment on account of our defilement, is consistent with the Sarvāstivāda view that spiritual liberation is a gradual process dependent on the gradual abandoning of defilements. It is argued: If there is only one single *pratisaṃkhyā-nirodha* or *nirvāṇa*, then at the time when the practitioner first gains insight into *duḥkha-satya* and thereby realizes the *pratisaṃkhyā-*

nirodha of the corresponding defilement, he would have at the same time realized the cessation of all defilements. Consequently it would be futile for him to further cultivate the counteraction of the remaining defilements.[31]

The same proposition also entails that all sentient beings realize a common *nirodha* corresponding to the particular defilement. But this raises important questions as recorded in the MVŚ: when sentient beings realize *pratisaṃkhyā-nirodha*, (i) do they together realize a common one or (ii) do they individually realize a different (i.e., identical but distinct) one in each case? In the former case why is *nirvāṇa* said to be the unique (*asādhāraṇa*) Dharma? Moreover, when one sentient being realizes *nirvāṇa,* [then] all beings should also acquire it at the same time, which entails that liberation comes about automatically without any effort! On the other hand, if each sentient being realizes a different *nirodha*, why is *nirvāṇa* said to be non-similar (*asabhāga*). Furthermore, how, in that case, is one to understand the *sūtra* statement that liberation of the *tathāgata* and that of the others are not different?[32] The MVŚ compilers' answer is that

> when sentient beings realize *pratisaṃkhyā-nirodha*, they realize a common one. However, although *nirvāṇa* is in actual fact common as an entity, it is said to be non-common in respect to its *prāpti* since the *visaṃyoga-prāpti* arises separately in the series of each individual. (*loc. cit.*)

It is only when the *prāpti* of *nirvāṇa* arises in a particular individual that he is said to have acquired/attained *nirvāṇa*.[33]

The above explanation given by the Sarvāstivāda spells out the important role that *prāpti* plays in spiritual attainments. Any religion or philosophy that posits a transcendental absolute needs to account for the way in which the empirical is related to the transcendental. In the Sarvāstivāda perspective, the relationship is effected by *prāpti*, a real force existing in its own right, which connects a *dharma* to a given series. The *dharma* then is one possessed by that particular individual. In abandoning a defilement, two final moments are involved: In the first moment known as *ānantarya-mārga*, the *prāpti* of the defilement is severed. In the second moment, known as *vimukti mārga*, the *prāpti* of the corresponding *pratisaṃkhyā-nirodha* arises, and the practitioner is said to have realized the *nirodha*.

The notion of *prāpti* is also invoked to explain away the apparent contradiction involved in stating that the *nirvāṇa* is a *phala* — *visaṃyoga-phala* — although it is not causally produced by the spiritual path. Saṃghabhadra explains:

> Worldlings collectively sanction the name *phala* with regard to the accomplishment through effort of what has been longed for. Death is most distressful for human beings; accordingly it is deathlessness (*amṛta* = *nirvāṇa*) that human beings most long for. What is so longed for, when realized through the efficacy of the path, is called a *phala*. It is said to be without a cause (*ahetuka*) since the path is not any of the six causes for the *asaṃskṛta pratisaṃkhyā-nirodha* to be acquired. *Pratisaṃkhyā-nirodha* is not a *phala* [causally] produced by the path (the *ānantarya-mārga*); it is a *phala* realized by virtue of it. The path is not a generating cause for the *pratisaṃkhyā-nirodha*; it is a cause of realization.[34] Hence, between the two — the path and the *nirodha* — one cannot definitely speak of a cause-effect relationship or otherwise. … [As a matter of fact, the *prāpti* of the *nirodha* could be considered the *phala* of the path,] since the path is the homogeneous cause (*sabhāga-hetu*) — or also said to be the co-existent cause (*sahabhū-hetu*) — for the *prāpti* of the *nirodha*. Nevertheless, this is not the *phala* directly sought after by the *ārya*. It is with the *nirodha* to be acquired in mind that the *ārya* practices the *ārya-mārga*. Accordingly, the specific *phala* of the path is none other than the acquired *nirodha*; not the *prāpti* of *nirodha*, since it is not for the sake of the *saṃskṛta*-s that an *ārya* practices the *ārya-mārga*.[35]

In this connection the Sautrāntika raises a question (Ny, 432c): What cause is there to ensure that a specific *prāpti* is linked to a specific *nirodha*? — What ensures that one acquires a particular *pratisaṃkhyā-nirodha* and not another one? Saṃghabhadra replies that there is in fact no need for a specifying cause: by the power of one *mārga*, the defilements cease *en bloc* and the disjunction is acquired *en bloc*. Or, it is the very nature of things (*dharmatā*) that that which acquires (i.e., the *mārga*) and that which is acquired (i.e., the *visaṃyoga*) are specifically related. Or, it is the path by which the defilement is abandoned (*prahāṇa-mārga*) that is the specifying cause, for it is by virtue of the path that the arising of the acquisition of disjunction is induced — the *nirodha* of the defilements to be abandoned by a specific path cannot be acquired through a different path.

A further question:

> There is a plurality of *pratisaṃkhyā-nirodha*-s acquired through one and the same *prahāṇa-mārga* — what specifying cause is there to enable us to say this is [the *pratisaṃkhyā-nirodha*] of *rāga*, this of *dveṣa*, etc.?

To this, Saṃghabhadra answers similarly:

> All the [defilements] to be ceased, constituting a given category, are abandoned through a single path; the disjunctions acquired having the same *prāpti*, what need is there for a specifying cause? Or, as mentioned before, by virtue of the nature of things, the relation is not confused: From the beginning, there exists — between *rāga*, etc., and the [corresponding] *nirodha* — a specific, non-confused relation by virtue of the nature of things. Since at the time when the *prahāṇa-mārga* arises, the [*pratisaṃkhyā-nirodha*-s] are acquired *en bloc*, there is nothing wrong even if there is no specifying cause.

16.2.3. Sautrāntika conception of *nirvāṇa*

By way of contrast, we may here outline the Sautrāntika conception which Saṃghabhadra vehemently repudiates. The Sautrāntika (and others) maintain that *nirvāṇa* is a mere concept referring to the absence of *duḥkha*[36] on account of the absolute non-arising or abandoning of defilements due to the absence of the defilement-seeds (*kleśa-bīja*).[37] For them, *pratisaṃkhyā-nirodha* is "the non-arising — by virtue of the force of *pratisaṃkhyā* — of [any] other proclivity at the time of the cessation of the arisen proclivities and of birth".[38] The acquisition of *nirvāṇa* is explained as the acquisition of a personal basis (*āśraya* = *skandha-saṃtati*) absolutely opposed (*atyanta-viruddha*) to the defilements that would arise and to future existence.[39]

In the AKB, the Sautrāntika — in a similar manner — explains *prāpti* as a mere concept. There the Vaibhāṣika argues that *prāpti* must be a real entity without which one would not be able to differentiate an *ārya* from a *pṛthagjana*: an *ārya*, even when he possesses worldly thoughts at times, is different from a *pṛthagjana* because he has the *prāpti* of the *ārya dharma*-s. The Sautrāntika, however, argues that the validity of the distinction does not require such an ontological entity called *prāpti*. The distinction is made in terms of the difference in the personal basis: The whole personal basis of an *ārya*, as a result of his spiritual attainment, is totally transformed (*parāvṛtta)* to be pure, fully purged of all potencies (*bīja*) for defilements. As such, there will absolutely be no further arising of any defilement for him. Such an *ārya* is said to have abandoned the defilements.[40]

Saṃghabhadra refutes the Sautrāntika conception (Ny, 430a ff.):

(i) The *pratisaṃkhyā-nirodha* thus defined does not differ from the non-arising owing to the deficiency in conditions.

(ii) Spiritual cultivation would be in vain, since there can also be non-arising without the *ārya-mārga*.

(iii) The *dharma*-s destined not to arise are like those that have become past, unable to re-arise — even when their seeds have not been abandoned — why then the need to cultivate the path? In the Sarvāstivāda system which holds that *pratisaṃkhyā-nirodha*-s are realized separately through the gradual abandoning of the defilement and *duḥkha* pertaining to the three periods of time, *dharma*-s which cannot arise — owing to *apratisaṃkhyā-nirodha* having been acquired — still need to be abandoned through further cultivation, as their *prāpti* obstructs *nirvāṇa*.

(iv) If *nirvāṇa* is merely a non-arising, how can one speak of acquiring it? It is not logical to answer that, through the acquisition of the counteraction (*pratipakṣa*), there is the realization of a transformed personal basis as described above. For then, at the very moment when one first acquires the *ārya-mārga*, one ought to have acquired *nirvāṇa* of the defilements counteracted by the path, since at this very moment one would have acquired such a personal basis. The practitioner abiding subsequently in the *śaikṣa-mārga* would have already become an *aśaikṣa*. This would render any further cultivation futile. The Sautrāntika tries in vain to avoid this consequence by saying that such a personal basis is not acquired until one has absolutely abandoned the seeds of defilements, and that this occurs only after the arising of the *ānantarya-mārga*. For in that case, the seeds of defilements, not being opposed to the *āryamārga* of the first moment, ought to be likewise unopposed to those of the subsequent moments — which means that an *aśaikṣa* would have defilements! This fallacy cannot be avoided by the Sautrāntika which teaches that the seeds of defilements are merely the transformation of the series (*saṃtati-pariṇāma*) serving as the supporting basis of the defilement, and that *nirvāṇa* is merely the non-arising of defilement. Given this teaching, what distinct *dharma*-s are there that are opposed to which *dharma-s* and that are unopposed to which *dharma*-s? The Sarvāstivāda doctrine is free from this fallacy, for it teaches that *prāpti*-s are distinct entities in themselves. They are unopposed to the *kṣānti* at which moment the defilement is abandoned, and opposed to the *jñāna* at which subsequent moment the *prāpti* of disjunction arises: the *jñāna* arises at the same time as the *prāpti* of disjunction which is opposed to the *prāpti* of the defilements. Furthermore, when the *ārya-mārga* of the moment is about to arise, the body of the worldling (*pṛthagjana-kāya*) is about to perish; when the former arises, the latter is relinquished. What distinct seeds of defilements apart from this body are there which are said to be unopposed to the first *ārya-mārga* but become opposed to the subsequent ones — the paths being not different?[41]

16.2.4. Summary of the investigation of *pratisaṃkhyā-nirodha*

In the Sarvāstivāda perspective, there are as many *nirvāṇa*-s or *pratisaṃkhyā-nirodha*-s as there are impure *dharma*-s. These are ontologically distinct real entities. Their reality is not even dependent on the criterion of causal efficacy in the space-time dimension but on the fact that they can impact on the mental streams of beings. Each *nirvāṇa* — via *prāpti* — acts to ensure the absolute non-arising of the defilement counteracted by the *ārya-mārga* by virtue of which the *prāpti* of the *nirvāṇa* is induced, and each is experiencible by the *ārya* as having distinct characteristics.

Nirvāṇa in the sense of the ultimate spiritual realization of the Buddhist practitioner refers to the *pratisaṃkhyā-nirodha* realized when all the *kleśa*-s and *duḥkha*-s pertaining to the three periods of time are completely abandoned (Ny, 430b). Although all practitioners acquire the same *nirvāṇa* corresponding to a given impure *dharma*, each individual's experience of *nirvāṇa* is unique by virtue of the *prāpti* that links the *nirvāṇa* to him. *Prāpti* — although conditioned in itself but neither mental nor material in nature — in fact plays the important role of relating the unconditioned to the conditioned. It is the *sine qua non* for man's experience of *nirvāṇa*.

It is not difficult to understand why Saṃghabhadra's arguments for the reality of *nirvāṇa* — totally transcending the space-time dimension as it does — are not always cogent. Some obviously are contingent upon the Sarvāstivāda postulates and presuppositions. Ultimately, apart from some scriptural passages in their favor, the Sarvāstivādins cannot but appeal to the authority of spiritual insight:

> Its self-nature can be personally realized only by the *ārya*. This much, although, can be said: There exists a distinct entity which is permanent and skillful. That is called a disjunction and a *pratisaṃkhyā-nirodha*.[42]

16.3. Cessation independent of deliberation

Among the three unconditioned *dharma*-s, the reality of the *apratisaṃkhyā-nirodha* and *ākāśa* is especially contentious.[43] Unlike the cessation through deliberation, the cessation independent of deliberation is not of the nature of disjunction from a defiled *dharma*. The MVŚ defines this category as follows:

> It is called a cessation independent of deliberation because it is not acquired through deliberative understanding, not being its effect. Furthermore, it is so called because it is not acquired through deliberation by means of exclusive effort, preparation or exertion. Furthermore, … because its acquisition does not require the repeated ascertaining of *duḥkha*, etc. …
>
> It is [acquired] on account of the deficiency in conditions (*pratyaya-vaikalyāt*). Thus, when one is focused [on an object] in one direction, all the other objects — *rūpa*, *śabda*, *gandha*, *rasa and spraṣṭavya* — in the other directions cease. The thought and thought-concomitants that would have taken these objects do not arise absolutely (*atyantam*), do not arise owing to the deficiency in conditions. On account of this non-arising, the *apratisaṃkhyā-nirodha* [of these thought and thought-concomitants] is acquired.[44]

The Sautrāntika maintains that this cessation is nothing more than a notion designating the deficiency in conditions.[45] In Ny, Saṃghabhadra argues against this, emphatically making the point that the *apratisaṃkhyā-nirodha* is a real entity capable of obstructing absolutely the arising of the *dharma*-s concerned:

> The deficiency in *pratyaya* is merely a non-existence of *pratyaya*. A non-existent *dharma* is incapable of obstructing an existent: When later the necessary *pratyaya*-s happen to assemble together, what *dharma* will there be that is capable of preventing [the said *dharma*, which failed to arise earlier on,] from arising again? Yet it is impossible for a *dharma* which abides among the un-arisen (*anutpanna*) *dharma*-s to still arise later. Hence there must exist [a real *dharma*] capable of obstructing the *pratyaya*-s absolutely. It is not the mere deficiency in *pratyaya*-s that causes the absolute non-arising.[46]

This positive description by Saṃghabhadra is considered a 'neo-Sarvāstivāda' doctrine by many scholars. However, such a positive emphasis is already found in the MVŚ:

> This *apratisaṃkhyā-nirodha* is only acquired with regard to the *anutpatti-dharma*-s of the future period. Why? This *nirodha* is originally meant for obstructing absolutely a *saṃskṛta dharma*'s arising. The *prāpti* of this [*nirodha*] arises upon the non-arising of the said *dharma* [which has been thus obstructed].[47]

Skandhila too explicitly emphasizes this cessation as a real force. Having given a very similar definition to that in the MVŚ quoted above, he adds:

> The deficiency in the [necessary] conditions is also due to the force of this cessation. Hence, there definitely exists a real entity named 'cessation independent of deliberation'.[48]

16.3.1. Distinction between *pratisaṃkhyā-nirodha*, *apratisaṃkhyā-nirodha* and *anityatā-nirodha*

Skandhila further argues for the reality of this category by distinguishing it from cessation as *pratisaṃkkhyā-nirodha* and as impermanence:

> The Bhagavat has said: "If, at that moment the pleasurable sensation appears, the other two sensations [— unpleasurable and neutral —] cease." Now, what can this cessation be apart from the [cessation independent of deliberation], since it definitely is not [the cessation of] impermanence or the cessation through deliberation? Again, it is said in the *sūtra*, "O *bhikṣu*-s, if one attains stream-entry, one has exhausted [rebirths in] hells, the infernal regions and the animal region. The exhaustion here refers to the cessation independent of deliberation, since at the moment one has not acquired the cessation through deliberation for the retributive *dharma*-s."[49]

Such an articulate and valid distinction is important for the Sarvāstivādins, as it amounts to the establishment of the three *nirodha*-s as discrete ontological entities. Saṃghabhadra makes the same distinction, citing the same *sūtra* passage and arguing similarly:

> Moreover, cessation and exhaustion are two different names of the same substance. The *sūtra* says that a *srotaāpanna* exhausts [existence in] the three *durgati*-s. Therefore, we know that there is a distinct entity which is the *apratisaṃkhyā-nirodha*, as this exhaustion definitely cannot be included under other *nirodha*-s: The *sūtra* says:
>
> > A *srotaāpanna* has already exhausted [existence in] hells, has already exhausted [existence in] the animal realm, has already exhausted [existence in] the hungry-ghost realm. …
>
> Now, it is not the case that he is already capable of abandoning the *durgati*-s, since he has not yet been detached (*vīta-rāga*) with regard to the *kāmadhātu*, and the *durgati*-s are said to be abandoned only when one

> has completely been detached from *kāma-rāga*. … . Nor does the word 'exhaustion' here refer to the *anityatā-nirodha*, since what is exhausted is all as yet unproduced. Hence, it is proved that there definitely exists a distinct *dharma* named *apratisaṃkhyā-nirodha*. As a result of this *dharma* being acquired, the *durgati*-s are made absolutely incapable of being produced.[50]

The distinction between the three cessations already occurs in the JPŚ.[51] The MVŚ quotes this distinction and elaborately differentiates the *pratisaṃkhyā-nirodha* from the other two in distinctively abhidharmic terms:

In contrast to the other two, the *pratisaṃkhyā-nirodha*-s are not only a *nirodha*; they entail the disjunction from defilements and the acquiring of the corresponding acquisitions of the disjunction.[52] They are also the liberation (*vimukti*) from, and the subduing (*damana*, *viṣkambhana*), abandoning (*prahāṇa*) and transcending (*samatikrama*) of, defilements. They are acquired with regard to the impure *dharma*-s of the three periods of time, whereas the *apratisaṃkhyā-nirodha*-s are acquired with regard to the future non-arising conditioned *dharma*-s. The *anityatā-nirodha*-s operate on all of the present *dharma*-s.

In terms of moral species, the first (i.e., the *pratisaṃkhyā-nirodha*-s) are *kuśala* and so are their *prāpti*-s; the second (i.e., the *apratisaṃkhyā-nirodha*-s) are *avyākṛta*, and so are their *prāpti*-s; the third (i.e., the *anityatā-nirodha*-s) can be any of the three species, and so are their *prāpti*-s.

The first are *anāsrava* and their *prāpti*-s are either *sāsrava* or *anāsrava*; the second are *anāsrava*, and their *prāpti*-s are *sāsrava* only; the third can be either *sāsrava* or *anāsrava*, and so are their *prāpti*-s.

The first are not bound to any sphere of existence (*apratisaṃyukta*) and their *prāpti*-s may be bound to *rūpa-dhātu* or *ārūpya-dhātu* or unbound;

the second are unbound, and their *prāpti*-s are bound to the three spheres only; the third may be bound to the three spheres or unbound, and so are their *prāpti*-s.

The first are *naiva-śaikṣa-nāśaikṣa* and their *prāpti*-s *maybe śaikṣa*, *aśaikṣa* or *naiva-śaikṣa-nāśaikṣa*; the second are *naiva-śaikṣa-nāśaikṣa,* and so are their *prāpti*-s; the third can be any of the three types, and so are their *prāpti*-s.

The first are not to be abandoned (*aheya*) and their *prāpti*-s are either to be abandoned by cultivation (*bhāvanā-heya*) or not to be abandoned; the second are not to be abandoned, and their *prāpti*-s are to be abandoned by cultivation only; the third can be any of the three types, and so are their *prāpti*-s.

The first and the second are both non-defiled (*akliṣṭa*), and so are their *prāpti*-s; the third may be either defiled or non-defiled, and so are their *prāpti*-s. (Likewise for the characterization in terms of *sāvadyatva/ anavadyatva* and *parihāṇi/aparihāṇi*).

The first are without retribution (*avipāka*) and their *prāpti*-s are either with or without retribution; the second are without retribution, and so are their *prāpti*-s; the third can be of either type, and so are their *prāpti*-s.

The first are *mārga-phala*-s and their *prāpti*-s may be either *mārga*-s and *mārga-phala*-s or neither *mārga*-s nor *mārga-phala*-s; the second are neither *mārga*-s nor *mārga-phala*-s, and their *prāpti*-s are both; the third are either, or both, or neither, and so are their *prāpti*-s.

The first are subsumed under *nirodha-satya* and their *prāpti*-s are subsumed under the other three *satya*-s; the second are not subsumed under the *satya*-s, and their *prāpti*-s are subsumed under two *satya*-s, namely *duḥkha*- and *samudaya-satya*; the third are subsumed under three *satya*-s excepting the *nirodha-satya*, and so are their *prāpti*-s.[53]

16.4. Space

The ontological status of the unconditioned Space is also highly controversial among the *abhidharma* schools. It is noteworthy that even in the *Jñānaprasthāna-śāstra*, the canonical Sarvāsitivāda *abhidharma* text upheld by the Vaibhāṣika as the supreme authority, only the two *nirodha*-s are mentioned, but not *ākāśa*. In the MVŚ, some of the Sarvāstivāda *ācārya*-s, such as Dharmatrāta, while accepting the reality of the first two *asaṃskṛta*-s, deny that of *ākāśa* (§ 16.1.1). It is therefore possible that this category came to be regarded as one of the three unconditioned at a relatively later stage by the orthodox Sarvāstivādins. The latter maintain that the unconditioned Space is not to be confounded with the conditioned space-element (*ākāśa-dhātu*) which is the cavity of the door, mouth, etc, and of the nature of *rūpa* — more specifically of the nature of light and darkness (*āloka-tamaḥ-svabhāva*), as what we perceive in such cavities is light or darkness.[54]

16.4.1. Arguments in the MVŚ

The MVŚ gives the Ābhidharmika definition of the space-element and distinguishes the two as follows:

> The Ābhidharmikas assert thus: What is the space element? It is the *agha-sāmantaka rūpa*. By *agha* is meant agglomerated [matter] (*citasthaṃ rūpam*), i.e., a wall, etc. There exists a matter that is proximate to it, called *agha-rūpa*.[55] Such space as found in the wall, in the forest, in the leaves, in the windows, among the fingers — they are called the space-elements. …
>
> What is the difference between Space and the space-element? Space is not matter; the space-element is matter. Space is invisible (*anidarśana*); the space-element is visible. Space is resistant (*sapratigha*); space-element is non-resistant (*apratigha*). Space is outflow-free; the space-element is with-outflow. Space is unconditioned; the space-element is conditioned.[56]

Vasumitra argues that the existence of Space as a real entity is not only inferable from the *sūtra*-s; it can be known through direct perception (*pratyakṣa-pramāṇa*):

> (i) If Space does not exist, all existent things ought not be able to find accommodation. Since it is observed that things are accommodated in various places, one knows that Space exists.
>
> (ii) One knows its existence by observing that there are places for going, coming and gathering; These activities would not be possible without Space as the accommodative cause (*hetu*). That is, Space is efficacious.
>
> (iii) Obstructive things are seen to occupy space — if Space does not exist, they cannot be accommodated.
>
> (iv) In the absence of Space, there ought to be obstruction everywhere; the fact that some places are observed to be non-obstructive proves its existence.[57]

The MVŚ explains that, although the reality of Space is established from the fact of it being efficacious, it is not to be understood that it has any activity (*zuo yong*; 作用), since it is unconditioned. It means that it can serve as a dominant condition (*adhipati-pratyaya*), making an indirect contribution by way of non-obstruction (see *supra*, § 7.1.4):

> The *asaṃskṛta ā*
>
> *kāśa* has no activity. Nevertheless, it can serve as the proximate *adhipati-pratyaya* for the various *ākāśa-dhātu*-s. These various *ākāśa-dhātu*-s can serve as the proximate *adhipati-pratyaya* for the various *mahābhūta*-s. These various *mahābhūta*-s can serve as the proximate *adhipati-pratyaya* for the resistant (*sapratigha*) derived matter (*upādāya rūpa*). These resistant derived matters can serve as the proximate *adhipati-pratyaya* for the various *citta-caitta-dharma*-s.

> If Space were non-existent, such a successive causal sequence cannot be established. Hence the intrinsic nature and characteristic of Space exist, lest there be such a fallacy; they must not be denied.[58]

16.4.2. Arguments by Saṃghabhadra

Vasubandhu presents the Sautrāntika view that Space is unreal: It is merely the absence of tangible things (*spraṣṭavyābhāva-mātra*) — people in darkness say that there is space when they do not encounter any obstacles.[59] Saṃghabhadra informs us that the Sautrāntika master Sthavira Śrīlāta and all the other Dārṣṭāntika masters hold the view that the space-element is nothing apart from Space; but Space does not exist as a real entity, hence the space-element too is unreal.[60] Skandhila invokes scriptural authority and applies logical arguments to establish the reality of Space.[61]

Saṃghabhadra too argues at length against the Sautrāntika and others. His main argument is that *ākāśa* has an empirically observable intrinsic characteristic (*lakṣaṇa*), and this unique characteristic points to its existence as a distinct entity. Or rather, its effect is observable, and one can therefore infer the existence of the cause from that of the effect.[62] To conclude this chapter, we will give his lengthy argument below which reads very much like a commentary on the corresponding passage in Skandhila's *Avatāra*:

> As to their statement '*ākāśa* is merely the absence of *spraṣṭavya*', we also accept that *ākāśa* is the absence of *spraṣṭavya*, as *ākāśa* has no tangibility. [But] what *hetu* have you to prove your statement that *ākāśa* is merely the absence of *spraṣṭavya* and does not exist as a separate *dravya*?
>
> We have already proved that when people in darkness do not encounter any resistant object, they say that it is *ākāśa*. Is not this *hetu* sufficient to prove its non-existence?

One cannot by this *hetu* alone prove that *ākāśa* is definitely non-existent: They say only that it is *ākāśa*, not an obstacle. How do we know that they speak of the absence of *spraṣṭavya* alone as *ākāśa*? People in the world, for instance, say: "this is *sukha*, not *duḥkha*". Now, how can it be that the absence of *duḥkha* alone is said to be *sukha*?

You might argue: "No, it is a false analogy — the activities of the two *vedanā*-s, *duḥkha* and *sukha*, being harmful and beneficial respectively, are distinct. [On the other hand], *ākāśa*, not accomplishing anything at all, cannot be perceived like *sukha*." [But] if so, the above *hetu* given by you would be useless, since now you are proving the non-existence of *ākāśa* by the assertion that it absolutely accomplishes nothing.

Now, one definitely cannot take as necessary *hetu* that the absence of obstruction is said to be *ākāśa*, to prove that *ākāśa* is nothing but the absence of *spraṣṭavya*. Thus, the Kośakāra (i.e., Vasubandhu) here has no *hetu* capable of proving that *ākāśa* is definitely non-existent.

Moreover, the *sūtra* says that the unconditioned *ākāśa* accomplishes something; therefore it is not incomparable to *sukha*: Thus, the Bhagavat says, "Wind is supported by *ākāśa*; it has no activity, has a support, and is not appropriated by the thought."

Moreover, the *rūpa*, light, is the *lakṣaṇa* of *ākāśa*, hence we know that *ākāśa* exists as a real entity. Thus the *sūtra* says, "...Nevertheless, Space becomes manifest by reason of light." Hence the *lakṣaṇa* of Space, i.e., light, is decisively shown. It is for this reason that the *sūtra* goes on to say these words: The Buddha first says that Wind is supported by *ākāśa*; subsequently He says that *ākāśa* is without support. This is so that the *brāhmaṇa* [to whom the Buddha is speaking] would not harbor such doubt: "Now the Bhagavat has said that the Wind was supported by *ākāśa*. But how can one prove that *ākāśa* [really] exists?" In order to dispel his doubt, the Buddha goes on to say those words. If *ākāśa* were non-existent, what [is manifested] by reason of light? Light is material (*rūpin*), visible (*sanirdarśana*) and resistant (*sapratigha*); if there is no *ākāśa*, by what can it be accommodated? Therefore when the Bhagavat says: "Nevertheless, Space becomes manifest by reason of light", it shows that light, a *rūpa*, can serve as the truly-existent *lakṣaṇa* of *ākāśa*. The Sthavira [Śrīlāta], however, not comprehending the import of this *sūtra*, replies thus: "If *ākāśa* becomes manifest by reason of light, it ought to be included as a *rūpa-dharma*." How does he arrive at such a conclusion?

Moreover, *ākāśa* ought to exist as a real entity, because it is described in the *sūtra* just as thought (*citta*) is: Thus, the *sūtra* says: '*ākāśa* is immaterial, invisible and non-resistant. By what can it be supported?' Now there cannot be such words of differentiation with regard to [absolutely non-existent things as] the *ātman* or the horn of the hare, etc.

As to this, he explains that those words are uttered in direct response to the [*brāḥmaṇa*'s] question. Just as when the *sūtra* says: "Well subdue the *ātman*, the *ātman* is the support." But if those words were indeed uttered in direct response to the question, [the Buddha] should not have spoken thus; He should simply have said: "O *brāḥmaṇa*, *ākāśa* is without a substance, by what can it be supported?" Moreover, He should not have said: "Nevertheless, *ākāśa* becomes manifest by reason of light." The *pūrvānta* is not spoken of as being discernible; the doer of an action is not spoken of as apperceivable (*upa-√labh*) — and yet these are to be known as direct replies which accord with truth. If, with regard to a non-existent, one speaks in the manner of speaking of an existent, then it becomes meaningless (*anartha*) speech. Moreover, the example cited cannot serve as a proof, as the *ātman* to be subdued refers to thought (*citta*) — this has been considered in detail [earlier] (*ibid*., 260c; *cf*. also AKB(C), 39a) when discussing the meaning of *ādhyātmika*. If the words 'immaterial', etc., do not have a [corresponding] real object (*artha*), how can the example cited be valid? [Thought is also described as being immaterial, etc.]

Furthermore, as regards the Sthavira's assertion: "If *ākāśa* had any real substance at all, it would be eternal and hence the resistant *rūpa*-s would never be produced; or rather, one ought to subsume it as a *saṃskṛta*, as do the Vātsīputrīya-s." This is an assertion made without careful consideration, because [the *ākāśa*] imagined by him indeed cannot accommodate other resistant *rūpa*-s. It is not the case that the *ākāśa dravya* can be obstructed by other resistant *rūpa*-s so that it must give way to other *rūpa*-s being produced — which would imply that it is impermanent. On the other hand, because *ākāśa* is accommodative by nature and not *rūpa* by nature, it does not have to give way. [But] the *ākāśa-dhātu*, being an obstructible *rūpa*, necessarily gives way when other *rūpa*-s are being produced. That is to say: the *ākāśa-dhātu* is a fine *rūpa*; although not obstructing others, it is obstructed by others, and is so classifiable as impermanent and *saṃskṛta*. *Ākāśa* has the *lakṣaṇa* of being neither obstructive to others nor being obstructible by others, at the time when *rūpa-dharma*-s are being produced. How can it be classified as impermanent and *saṃskṛta*? As *ākāśa* co-exists harmoniously with *rūpa*, it does not arise or perish at the different stages [of the *rūpa*-s].

As to the fact that there is resistance in the wall, etc., it is because there are resistant *rūpa*-s in it which obstruct others. This is not the case with the unconditioned *ākāśa* since there is no [resistant *rūpa*] therein. The *ākāśa-dhātu rūpa* is fine and light and cannot obstruct others; as soon as it is excluded through being obstructed by other gross *rūpa*-s, it gives way. Such is the nature of *sapratigha rūpa*-s: When a given space is occupied by one, it cannot be occupied by another. The *ākāśa* differs from the *ākāśa-dhātu* in being *apratigha*; how can it be considered as impermanent like the latter.

Moreover, as regards his assertion: 'If *ākāśa* exists as a real substance, it ought to become *saṃskṛta*, as this does not differ from the *ākāśa-dhātu*.' This is an empty assertion without any truth, for the Bhagavat Himself says that they differ: Thus the *sūtra* says: "*ākāśa* is immaterial, invisible and non-resistant". It also says: "when one is detached with regards to *rūpa*-s, the *ākāśa-dhātu* is abandoned together with the four [*mahābhūta*-s; the *vijñāna-dhātu* is not said to be abandoned]" (also cited in *ibid.*, 347b). Now, if *ākāśa-dhātu* does not differ from *ākāśa,* which is immaterial, invisible and non-resistant, it ought also to be the same. It ought to be, like *vijñāna-dhātu*, said to be abandoned when one is detached with regard to the *ārūpya-dhātu*. Moreover, the *sūtra* says: "the *ākāśa-dhātu* accomplishes the *vyavahāra-puruṣa*"; and also says: "Nevertheless *ākāśa* becomes manifest by reason of light." Now, if *ākāśa-dhātu* is none other than *ākāśa*, and light is none other than *ākāśa-dhātu*, then would the *sūtra* not be saying [in effect]: "Nevertheless, light becomes manifest by reason of light"? Hence we know there is a difference [between the two].

Moreover the *sūtra* says: "Among all *dharma*-s, whether the conditioned ones or the unconditioned ones, detachment (*vairāgya*) is supreme." In this *sūtra*, *dharma*-s are said to be of two kinds; the unconditioned ones being *dharma*-s cannot be said to be non-existent, as without *dravya*, they ought not be of the nature of *dharma*-s. The words, 'the unconditioned ones' show that they comprise many *dravya*-s; therefore, there must be *ākāśa* and *apratisaṃkhyā-nirodha*-s from which one can be detached before they may be described in pluralistic terms, as apart from these there is no other *asaṃskṛta*. Hence this *ākāśa-dhātu* is not identical with *ākāśa*. The Sthavira, without reflection, asserts that the two are not different.

There are other *ācārya*-s who assert: "*Ākāśa* does not exist as a distinct *dravya*; for it is with regard to the absence of resistant *rūpa* that one gives rise to the idea (*buddhi*) of space." Their assertion is illogical. In fact, it is by this very *hetu* that one can prove that *ākāśa* exists as a distinct *dravya*: This is because there exists, at a location different from that occupied by the resistant *rūpa*, a distinct *ākāśa* that serves as the *ālambana* for the *buddhi* of space, and because where there is no *ālambana*, *buddhi* cannot arise. Hence their assertion is mere empty words. Furthermore, [by the same token,] one can also say: 'There exists no resistant *rūpa* as a distinct *dravya*, for the *buddhi* of *rūpa* arises where there is no space.' Yet this cannot prove the non-existence of *rūpa*. Hence, they are unable to prove, [in this manner,] that *ākāśa* does not exist.

Should they say that *rūpa*-s, possessing a [distinct] naure (有體; i.e., existing as a real entity), are cognizable, then the same ought to be true of *ākāśa*, for it can be cognized through inference: Just as *cakṣus*, etc., although not cognizable through direct perception (*pratyakṣa*), are known to possess a [distinct] nature through inference (*anumāna*) from the fact that they possess efficacies (有用). Likewise, as *ākāśa* too possesses efficacy — as mentioned above — one knows through inference that it possesses a [distinct] nature. Hence it is known that *ākāśa* has a distinct real nature (i.e., exists as a real entity).[63]

NOTES

[1] MVŚ, 162a; AKB, 4.

[2] MVŚ, 164.

[3] T 49, 15c.

[4] AKB, 92.

[5] MVŚ, 662a.

[6] MVŚ, 388c.

[7] *Cf. Entrance*, 16, 33, 59, 161 f.

[8] *Cf. Entrance*, 261 f.

[9] E.g., Ny, 432b.

[10] Ny, 433b.

[11] AKB, 14; *cf.* AsmB, 17.

[12] ZW, 188.

[13] ZW, 188.

[14] MVŚ, 105c–106a, gives various reasons why the *asaṃskṛta-dharma*-s are devoid of causes and effects.

[15] AKB, 4: *yaḥ sāsravair dharmair visaṃyogaḥ sa pratisaṃkhyā-nirodhaḥ / duḥkhādīnām āryasatyānāṃ pratisaṃkhyānāṃ pratisaṃkhyā prajñāviśeṣas tena prāpyo nirodhaḥ pratisaṃkhyā-nirodhaḥ / Cf.* also same definition in MVŚ, 161a.

[16] TA(U, J), II, 231.

[17] MVŚ, 163a–164b.

[18] MVŚ, 147b.

[19] MVŚ, 322a–b.

[20] MVŚ, 168b–c.

[21] MVŚ, 147b.

[22] Ny, 428c.

[23] Ny, 429a.

[24] MVŚ, 432c.

[25] *Cf.* TA(U-J), I, 219.

[26] *Entrance*, 146.

[27] *Cf. Aṅguttara-nikāya*, ii, 34; etc.

[28] VKŚ, 560a-b.

[29] Saṃghabhadra defines an existent (*sat*) as that which can serve as an object for the arising of *buddhi* (Ny, 621c–622a).

[30] *Cf.* AKB, 4: *yāvanti hi saṃyogadravyāṇi tāvanti visaṃyogadravyāṇi* /

[31] AKB, 4: *anyathā hi duḥkhadarśanaheya-kleśa-nirodha-sākṣātkaraṇāt sarvakleśa-nirodha-sākṣātkriyā prasajyeta* /; *cf.* MVŚ, 161c–162a.

[32] MVŚ, 162a–b.

[33] MVŚ, 162b.

[34] MVŚ, 108c: "The fruit of liberation is realized (*sākṣātkṛta*) by the path, not acquired by a cause."

[35] MVŚ, 428c; cf. MVŚ, 341a; AKB, 91 f.

[36] *Cf.* a similar view by 'some' in MVŚ, 177b.

[37] Ny, 430b.

[38] AKB, 92: *utpannānuśaya-janma-nirodhe pratisaṃkhyābalenānyasyānutpādaḥ prati-saṃkhyānirodhaḥ* /

[39] Ny, 431a.

[40] AKB, 63: *āśraya-viśeṣād etat sidhyati / āśrayo hi sa āryāṇāṃ darśanabhāvanāmārga-sāmarthyāt tathā parāvṛtto bhavati yathā na punas tatpraheyāṇāṃ kleśānāṃ prarohasamartho bhavati / ato 'gnidagdhavrīhivad abījībhūte āśraye kleśānāṃ prahīṇa-kleśa ity ucyate* / *Cf.* also the contrasting views (*bīja* and *prāpti*) in ADV, 166.

[41] Similar definitions of *prahāṇa* and *nirvāṇa* — with Mahāyāna overtones — in Asm, 62; AsmB., 42; *Siddhi*(S) (commentary on last 2 stanzas); etc.

[42] AKB. 92: *āryaireva tatsvabhāvaḥ pratyātmavedyaḥ / etāvattu śakyate vaktuṃ nityaṃ kuśalaṃ cāsti dravyāntaram / tadvisaṃyogaścocyate pratisaṃkhyā-nirodhaśceti* /

[43] It is interesting to note that the Theravāda *Nettipakaraṇa* also includes both *paṭisaṅkhā-nirodha* and *appaṭisaṅga-nirodha* as among a list of ten *nirodha*-s (*Nettipakaraṇa*, 87).

[44] MVŚ, 164b. *Cf.* AKB, 4:

utpādātyantavighno'nyo nirodho'pratisaṃkhyayā //6//

anāgatānāṃ dharmāṇām utpādasyātyantavighnabhūto visaṃyogād yo'nyo nirodhaḥ so'pratisaṃkhyānirodhaḥ / na hy asau pratisaṃkhyayā labhyate / kiṃ tarhi / pratyayavaikalyāt / yathaikarūpavyāsaktacakṣur manaso yāni rūpāṇi śabda-gandha-rasa-spraṣṭavyāni cātyayante / Also *cf. Entrance*, 148.

[45] *Cf.* Ny, 429a.

[46] Ny, 434b.

[47] MVŚ, 164b–c. See *Study*, 703 f.

[48] *Entrance*, 148.

[49] *Entrance*, 149.

[50] Ny, 435a.

[51] JPS, 923b.

[52] MVŚ, 161a.

[53] MVŚ, 161b–c.

[54] *Cf.* AKB, 18.

[55] AKB, 18, explains the Sarvāstivāda notion of *the agha-sāmantakaṃ rūpam* as follows: *aghaṃ kila citasthaṃ rūpam / atyarthaṃ ghātāt / tasya tat sāmantakam iti /*

Vy, 57, comments: *aghaṃ kila citasthaṃ rūpam iti citasthaṃ saṃghātastham / atyarthaṃ hanti hanyate ceti aghaṃ nairuktena vidhinā / atyartha-śabdasya a-kār'ādeśaḥ kṛto hanteś ca gh'ādeśaḥ / tasya tat sāmantakam iti tasyāghasya kuḍy'ādikasya sāmantakaṃ samīpastham / tad apekṣya vyavasthāpitam ity arthaḥ /* I.e., the etymology given here for *agha* is: *a* = *atyartham*; *gha* = *hanti*.

[56] MVŚ, 388b.

[57] MVŚ, 388c.

[58] MVŚ, 389a.

[59] AKB, 92.

[60] Ny, 347b.

[61] *Entrance*, 145.

[62] Ny, 347b.

[63] Ny, 429a–430a.

SELECT BIBLIOGRAPHY

I. PRIMARY SOURCES

1. *Abhidhammatthasaṅgaho.* Ed., Kosambi, D (Saranath, 1941).
2. *Abhidhammāvatāra.* Ed., Buddhadatta, AP. PTS (London, 1915).
3. *Abhidharmadīpa with Vibhāṣā-prabhāvṛtti.* Ed., Jaini, PS (Patna, 1959).
4. *Abhidharmakośa-bhāṣya of Vasubandhu.* Chapter I. Ed., Ejima, Y (Tokyo, 1989).
5. *Abhidharmakośabhāṣya of Vasubandhu.* Chapter IX: *Ātmavādapratiṣedha.* Ed., Lee, CL (Tokyo, 2005).
7. *Abhidharmakośabhāṣyam of Vasubandhu.* Ed., Pradhan, P (Patna, 1975).
6. *Abhidharmakośakārikā of Vasubandhu.* Ed., Gokhale, GV, JRAS. Vol. 22 (Bombay, 1946).
8. *Abhidharmakośaṭīkālakṣaṇānusāriṇī* (*chos mngon pa'i mdzod kyi 'grel bshad mtshan nyid kyi rjes su 'brang ba zhes bya ba*) of Pūrṇavardhana. Peking no. 5597
9. *Abhidharmakośa-vyākhyā (Sphuṭārthā) of Yaśomitra.* Ed.,Wogihara, U (Tokyo, 1932–36).
10. *Abhidharmasamuccaya and Abhidarmasamuccayabhāṣya.* Vol. I–III (Shiga, 2003).
11. *Abhidharmasamuccaya of Asaṅga.* Ed., Pradhan, P (Santiniketana, 1950).
12. *Abhidharmasamuccayabhāṣya.* Ed., Tatia, N (Patna, 1976).
13. *Aṅguttara-nikāya.* Ed., Morris, R, and Hardy, E. PTS (London, 1885–1900).
14. *Arthaviniścaya Sūtra and its Commentary Nibandhana.* Tr., Samtani, NH (Berkeley, 2002).
15. *Arthaviniścaya-sūtra-nibandhana.* Ed., Samtati, NH (Patna, 1971).
16. *Dhammasaṅgani.* Ed., Mūller, E. PTS (London, 1885).
17. *Dhātu Kathā Pakaraṇa and Its Commentary.* Ed., Gooneratne, ER. PTS (London, 1892).
18. *Dīghanikāya.* Vol. I–III. Ed., Rhys Davids, TW and Carpenter, JE. PTS (London, 1889–1910).
19. *Dukapaṭṭhāna.* Ed., Rhys Davids, CAF. PTS (London, 1906).

20. *Jñānabinduprakaraṇa of Yaśovijaya.* Ed., Saṅghavi, S, Singh Jain Series 16 (Calcutta, 1942).

21. *Kathāvatthu.* Ed., Taylor, AC. PTS (London, 1894–1897).

22. *Kathāvatthuppakaraṇa Aṭṭhakathā.* Ed., Minayeff, J. PTS (London, 1889); 1–22.

23. *Majjhima-nikāya, I–IV.* Ed., Trencker V, Chalmers R, Mrs. Rhys Davids. PTS (London, 1888–1925).

24. *Milindapañha, Being dialogues between king Milinda and the Buddhist sage Nāgasena.* Trenckner, V. PTS (London, 1890).

25. *Nyāyabindutīkā* (of Dharmottara), Bib. Bud. VII. Indian reprint (Delhi, 1992).

26. *Paṭisambhidāmagga.* Ed., Taylor, AC. PTS (London. 1979).

27. **Prakaraṇābhidharmāvatāra* (*rab tu byed pa chos mngon pa la 'jug pa zhes bya ba*). (Tohoku no. 4098, Peking no. 5599). Tr., by Jinamitra, Dānaśīla and Ye-shes-sde.

28. *Puggalapaññati.* Ed., Morris, R. PTS (London, 1883).

29. *Saṃyutta-nikāya.* Vols. I–VI. Ed., Feer, L. PTS (London, 1884–1904).

30. **Sāra-samuccaya-nāma-abhidharmāvatāra-ṭīkā* (*chos mngon pa la 'jug pa rgya cher 'grel pa snying po kun las btus pa zhes bya ba*). (Tohoku no.4097, Peking no. 5598). Tr. by Jinamitra, Dānaśīla and Ye-shes-sde.

31. *Sarva-darśana-saṃgraha.* Mainkar, TG (Poona, 1978)

32. *Sphuṭārthābhidharmakośavyākhyā of Yaśomitra.* Ed., Wogihara, U (Tokyo, 1971).

33. *Sum cu pa'i 'grel pa* (*Tibetan version of Sthiramati's Triṃśikābhāṣya*). Ed., Teramoto E (Kyoto, 1932).

34. *Tarkabhāṣā of Mokṣākara Gupta.* Ed., Embar Krishnamacharya (Baroda, 1942).

35. **Tattvārthā* (*chos mngon pa'i mdsod kyi bzhad pa'i rgya cher 'grel pa don gyi de kho na nyid zhes bya ba*) by Sthiramati. Tr., by Dharmapālabhadra (Peking no. 5875).

36. *Tattvasaṃgraha of Śāntarakṣita with Pañjikā of Kamalaśīla.* Vol. I–II, Gaekwad's Oriental Series, vols. xxx–xxxi (Baroda, 1926).

37. *Tattvasaṅgraha of Ācārya Shāntarakṣita with the Commentary 'Pañjikā' of Shri Kamalashīla.* Ed., Dwarikadas Shastri, Swami (Varanasi, 1982).

38. *Tibetan Tripiṭaka, Peking Edition.* Ed., Suzuki, DT (Tokyo-Kyoto, 1957).

39. *Vibhaṅga, being the second book of the Abhidhamma Piṭaka.* Ed., Rhys Davids, CAF. PTS (London, 1904).

40. *Vijñaptimātratāsiddhi — Deux Traites de Vasubandhu.* Ed., Lévi, S (Paris 1925).

41. *Visuddhimagga* of Buddhaghosa. Ed., Warren and Kosmbi. Harvard Oriental Series (1950).

42. *Yamaka, being the sixth book of the Abhidhamma Piṭaka.* Ed., Rhys Davids, CAF. PTS (London, 1911–1913).

43. *Yogācārabhūmi* (*Sanskrithandschriften aus den Turfanfunden*). Ed., Waldschmidt, E (1965).

44.	長阿含經	T no. 1	tr., Buddhayaśas and Zu Fo Nian.
45.	中阿含經	T no. 26	tr., Saṃghadeva.
46.	雜阿含經	T no. 99	tr., Guṇabhadra.
47.	增一阿含經	T no. 125	tr., Saṃghadeva.
48.	大智度論	T no. 1509	tr., Kumārajīva.
49.	阿毗達磨集異門足論	T no. 1536	tr., Xuan Zang.
50.	阿毗達磨法蘊足論	T no. 1537	tr., Xuan Zang.
51.	施設論	T no. 1538	tr., Dharmapāla *et. al.*
52.	阿毗達磨識身足論	T no. 1539	tr., Xuan Zang.
53.	阿毗達磨界身足論	T no. 1540	tr., Xuan Zang.
54.	衆事分阿毗曇論	T no. 1541	tr., Guṇabhadra *et. al.*
55.	阿毗達磨品類足論	T no. 1542	tr., Xuan Zang.
56.	阿毗曇八犍度論	T no. 1543	tr., Saṅghadeva *et. al.*
57.	阿毗達磨發智論	T no. 1544	tr., Xuan Zang.
58.	阿毗達磨大毗婆沙論	T no. 1545	tr., Xuan Zang.
59.	阿毗曇毗婆沙論	T no. 1546	tr., Buddhavarman & Daotai.
60.	鞞婆沙論	T no. 1547	tr., Saṅghabhūti.

61.	舍利弗阿毗曇論	T no. 1548	tr., Dharmyaśas *et. al.*
62.	阿毗曇心論	T no. 1550	tr., Saṃghadeva *et. al.*
63.	阿毗曇心論經	T no. 1551	tr., Narendrayaśas.
64.	雜阿毗曇心論	T no. 1552	tr., Saṅghavarman.
65.	阿毗達磨甘露味論	T no. 1553	tr., unknown.
66.	入阿毗達磨論	T no. 1554	tr., Xuan Zang.
67.	五事毗婆沙論	T no. 1555	tr., Xuan Zang.
68.	薩婆多宗五事論	T no. 1556	tr., Fa Cheng.
69.	阿毗曇五法行經	T no. 1557	tr., An Shi Gao.
70.	阿毗達磨俱舍論	T no. 1558	tr., Xuan Zang.
71.	阿毗達磨俱舍釋論	T no. 1559	tr., Paramārtha.
72.	阿毗達磨順正理論	T no. 1562	tr., Xuan Zang.
73.	阿毗達磨藏顯宗論	T no. 1563	tr., Xuan Zang.
74.	瑜伽師地論	T no. 1579	tr., Xuan Zang.
75.	成唯識論	T no. 1585	tr., Xuan Zang.
76.	阿毗達磨集論	T no. 1605	tr., Xuan Zang.
77.	阿毘達磨雜集論	T no. 1606	tr., Xuan Zang.
78.	大乘成業論	T no. 1609	tr., Xuan Zang.
79.	五蘊論	T no. 1612	tr., Xuan Zang.
80.	廣五蘊論	T no. 1613	tr., Xuan Zang.
81.	成實論	T no. 1646	tr., Kumārajīva.
82.	異部宗輪論	T no. 2031	tr., Xuan Zang.
83.	大唐西域記	T no. 2087	by Xuan Zang.

II. SECONDARY SOURCES

84. *Abhidharma and Indian Thought.* (2000). Published by the Committee for the Felicitation of Professor Doctor Junsho Kato's Sixieth Birthday. Tokyo.

85. Aiyaswami Sastri, N (1978). *Satyasiddhiśāstra of Harivarman.* Vol. 2. Baroda.

86. Armelin, I (1978) *Le Coeur de la loi suprême. Traité de Fa cheng. Abhidharmahṛdayaśāstra de Dharmaśrī.* Paris.

87. Aung, Shwe Zan and Rhys Davids, CAF (1910). *Compendium of Philosophy* (*Abhidhammattha Saṅgaho*). PTS; London.

88. —— (1915). *Points of Controversy or subjects of discourse: being a translation of the Kathāvatthu from the Abhidhammapiṭaka.* PTS, London.

89. Bagchi, P.Ch (1927). *Le canon bouddhique en Chine.* Paris.

90. Balasooriya, S., *et. al.* (1980). *Buddhist Studies in Honour of Walpola Rahula.* London.

91. Bareau, A (1950). 'Les Origines du *Śāriputrābhidharmaśāstra*." In: *Muséon* 63, nos. 1–2; 69–95.

92. —— (1951). *Dhammasaṅgaṇi* – thèse complémentaire présentée a la faculté des lettres de l'université de Paris. Centre de documentation Universitaire, Paris.

93. ——(1952). "Les sectes bouddhiques du Petit Véhicule et leurs Abhidharmapiṭaka." In: *Bulletin de l'École Française d'Extrême-Orient,* XLIV; 1–11.

94. —— (1955). *Les sectes bouddhiques du Petit Véhicule.* Paris.

95. —— (1956). "Trois traités sur les sectes bouddhiques attribués à Vasumitra." In: *Journal Asiatique,* CCXLIV; 167–191.

96. Bhikshu Thich Thien Chau (1999). *The Literature of the Personalists of Early Buddhism.* Delhi.

97. Broeck, José van den (1977). *La Saveur de l'immortel* (*A-pi-t'an Kan Lu Wei Lun*). Louvain.

98. Bu-ston. (1931–1932). *History of Buddhism.* Tr. by Obermiller, E. Heidelberg.

99. Cox, C (1988). "On the Possibility of a Non-existent Object of Consciousness: Sarvāstivādin and Dārṣṭāntika Theories." In: *Journal of the International Association of Buddhist Studies,* Vol. 11, no.1; 31–87.

100. —— (1992). "Attainment through Abandonment: the Sarvāstivādin Path of Removing Defilements." In: *Paths to Liberation – The Mārga and its Transformation in Buddhist Thought.* Honolulu; 63–105.

101. —— (1995). *Disputed Dharmas – Early Buddhist Theories on Existence – An Annotated Translation of the Section on Factors Dissociated from Thought from Saṃghabhadra's Nyāyānusāra.* Tokyo.

102. Deleanu, Florin (2006). *The Chapter on the Mundane Path (Laukikamārga) in the Śrāvakabhūmi*. Vol. I–II. Tokyo.

103. Demiéville, P (1931-1932). "L'origine des Sectes Bouddhiques d'après Paramārtha." In: *MCB*, vol. I; 15–64.

104. —— (1951). "A propos du Concile de Vaiśālī." In: *T'oung Pao,* vol. 40; 239–296.

105. —— (1961). "Un fragment sanskrit de I'Abhidharma des Sarvāstivādin." In: *Journal Asiatique,* CCXLIX; 461–465.

106. Dhammajoti, KL (1998a). "The Defects in the Arhat's Enlightenment: His *Akliṣṭa-ajñāna* and *Vāsanā*." In: *Bukkyō Kenkyū*, vol. XXVII. Hamamatsu; 65–98.

107. —— (1998b). *Entrance into the Supreme Doctrine (Skandhila's Abhidharmāvatāra)*. Colombo.

108. —— (2000). "The Sarvāstivāda Doctrine of Simultaneous Causality." *Numata Yehan Lecture on Buddhist Thoughts*. University of Calgary.

109. —— (2002a). "*Sahabhūhetu*, causality and *sarvāstitva*." In: *Arcanā*. Colombo.

110. —— (2002b). "Sarvāstivādin conception of *Nirvāṇa*." In: *Buddhist and Indian Studies in Honour of Professor Sodo Mori.* Tokyo; 335–348.

111. —— (2003). "Karmic role of the *avijñapti* of the Sarvāstivāda." In: *Buddhist Studies*, vol. XXVII. Hamamatsu; 69–90.

112. —— (2004a). *Abhidharma Doctrine and Controversy on Perception*. Colombo.

113. —— (2005a)."Logic in the *Abhidharma-mahāvibhāṣā*." In: *JCBSSL,* vol. II. Colombo; 180–197.

114. ——(2005b). "Abhidharma and Upadeśa." In: *JCBSSL,* vol III. Colombo; 112–125.

115. —— (2006). "Sarvāstivāda, Dārṣṭāntika, Sautrāntika and Yogācāra — Some Reflections on Their Interrelation." In: *JCBSSL,* vol. IV. Colombo; 184–212.

116. —— (2007a). "*Ākāra* and Direct Perception: Vaibhāṣika versus Sautrāntika." In: *Bukkyō Kenkyū*. Hamamatsu; 1–34.

117. —— (2007b). "The *Citta-caitta* Doctrine of Śrīlāta." In: *JCBSSL*, vol. V

118. Dietz, S (1984). *Fragmente des Dharmaskandha – Ein Abhidharma-text in Sanskrit aus Gilgit.*

119. —— (1989) "A Brief Survey on the Sanskrit Fragments of the Lokaprajñaptiśāstra." In: *Annual Memoirs of the Otani University Shin Buddhist Comprehensive Research Institute,* VII; 79–86.

120. Edgerton, F (1953). *Buddhist Hybrid Sanskrit Grammer and Dictionary.* New Haven.

121. Enomoto, F (1994). "A Note on Kashmir as Referred to in Chinese Literature: Ji-bin." In: *A Study of the Nīlamata – Aspect of Hinduism in Ancient Kashmir.* Kyōto; 357–365.

122. —— (1996). "A Sanskrit Fragment from the *Vibhāṣā* Discovered in Eastern Turkestan." In: *Sanskrit-Texte aus dem buddhistischen Kanon: Neuentdeckungen und Neueditionen* III; 135–143.

123. Frauwallner, E (1951). *On the Date of the Buddhist Master of the Law, Vasubandhu.* Rome.

124. —— (1995). *Studies in Abhidharma Literature and the Origins of Buddhist Philosophical Systems.* Eng. tr. by Sophie Francis Kidd under the supervision of Ernst Steinkellner. New York.

125. Fukuhara, R (1965). *Ubu Abidatsumaronsho no Hattatsu.* Kyoto.

126. —— (1972). *A Study on Shitai Ron.* Kyoto.

127. Funanashi, I and Lu Cheng (1961). "Abhidharmakośa-śāstra." In: *EnB,* vol. I, fasc. 1; 57–63.

128. Hirakawa, A (1974). *Indo Bukkyō shi.* 2 vols. Tokyo.

129. —— (1975). 仏教にわける法の研究. Tokyo.

130. —— (1977). *Buddhist Chinese-Sanskrit Dictionary,* vol. I & II. Tokyo.

131. —— (1980). "The Meaning of 'Dharma' and 'Abhidharma'." In: *Indianisme et Bouddhisme: Mélanges offerts à Mgr Étienne Lamotte.* Louvain; 159–175.

132. —— (1990). *A History of Indian Buddhism – from Śākyamuni to Early Mahāyāna.* Honolulu.

133. Hirakawa, A., *et. al.* (1973). *Index to the Abhidharmakośabhāśya – Part I: Sanskrit-Tibetan-Chinese.* Tokyo.

134. —— (1977). *Index to the Abhidharmakośabhāśya – Part II: Chinese-Sanskrit.* Tokyo.

135. —— (1978). *Index to the Abhidharmakośabhāśya – Part III: Tibetan-Sanskrit.* Tokyo.

136. Hofinger, M (1946). *Étude sur le concile de Vaiśālī*. Bibliothèque du Muséon, vol. 20.

137. Hurvitz, L (1977). "Paths to Salvation in the *Jñānaprasthāna*." In: *Studies in Indo-Asian Art and Culture,* V; 77–102

138. —— (1977). "The Abhidharma on the 'Four Aids' to Penetration'." In: *Buddhist Thought and Cilivization – Essays in Honour of Herbert, V. Guenther on his Sixtieth Birthday*. Ed., Kawamura, LS. and Scott, K. California.

139. Imanishi, J (1975). *Fragmente des Abhidharmaprakaraṇabhāṣya in Text and Übersetzung* (*Abhidharmatexte in Sanskrit aus den Turfanfunden II*).

140. Jaini, PS (1952). "The Sautrāntika-theory of Bīja." In: *BSOAS*, vol. XXII, part 2; 236–249.

141. —— (1958). "On the Theory of Two Vasubandhu." In: *BSOAS*, vol. XXI, part 1; 48–53.

142. —— (1959a). "Origin and Development of the *Viprayuktasaṃskāra*." In: *BSOAS*, vol. XXIII, part 3; 531–547.

143. —— (1959b). "The Vaibhāṣika Theory of Words and Meanings." In: Jaini, PS. Ed., *Collected Papers on Buddhist Studies*. Delhi; 201–217.

144. Jong, JW de (1979a). "L'auteur de I'Abhidharmadīpa." In: *Buddhist Studies by J.W. de Jong*. Ed., Gregory Schopen. Berkeley; 115–117.

145. —— (1979b). "Review of Abhidharmadīpa with Vibhāṣāprabhāvṛtti, critically edited with notes and introduction by Padmanabh S. Jaini." In: *Buddhist Studies by J.W. de Jong*. Ed., Gregory Schopen. Berkeley; 609–611.

146. —— (1979c). "Les Sūtrapiṭaka des Sarvāstivādin et des Mūlasarvāstivādin." In: *Buddhist Studies by J.W. de Jong*. Ed., Gregory Schopen. Berkeley; 229 –236.

147. Kajiyama, Y (1977) "Realism of the Sarvāstivāda School." In: *Buddhist Thought and Civilization – Essays in Honour of Herbert V. Guenther on his Sixtieth Birthday*. Ed., Kawamura, LS and Scott, K. California.

148. —— (1985). *An introduction to Buddhist Philosophy — An Annotated Translation of the Translation of the Tarkabhāṣā of Mokṣākaragupta*. Tokyo.

149. Karunadasa, Y (1967). *Buddhist Analysis of Matter*. Colombo.

150. —— (1983). "Vibhajyavāda versus Sarvāstivāda: the Buddhist Controversy on Time." In: *Kalyāni: Journal of Humanities and Social Sciences of the University of Kelaniya (Sri Lanka),* vol. II. Colombo; 1–28.

151. —— (1985). "The Buddhist Theory of Double Truth." In: *Kalyāni: Journal of Humanities and Social Sciences of the University of Kelaniya (Sri Lanka),* vol. III & IV. Colombo; 23–55.

152. —— (1987). "The Abhidhamma Theory of Paññatti: The Category of the Nominal and the Conceptual." In: *Professor N.A. Jayawickrama Felicitalion Volume.* Colombo; 20–50.

153. —— (1996). "The Dhamma Theory – Philosophical Cornerstone of the Abhidhamma ." In: *The Wheel Publication*, no. 412/413. Kandy.

154. Katō, J (1980). "Notes sur les deux maîtres bouddhiques Kumāralāta et Śrīlāta." In: *Indianisme et Bouddhisme: Mélanges offerts à Mgr Étienne Lamotte*; 197–213.

155. —— (1989). *Kyōryōbu no Kenkyū.* Tokyo.

156. Kimura, T (1937). *Abidatsumaron no Kenkyū*. Vol. 6 of *Kimura Taiken Zenshū,* 木村泰賢全集,第六卷.Tokyo.

157. —— (1968). Vol. 5 of *Kimura Taiken Zenshū,* 木村泰賢全集, 第五卷. Tokyo.

158. Kudara, K (1982) "Uiguru yaku Abidatsumajunshōriron shōhon." In: *Bukkyōgaku kenkyū*, 38; 1–27.

159. Lama Chimpa, *et.* Chattopadhyaya, A (1970). *Tāranātha's History of Buddhism in India.* Delhi.

160. La Vallée Poussin, L., de (1905). "Les deux premiers conciles." In: *Le Muséon,* vol. VI; 213–323.

161. —— (1908). "The Buddhist Councils." In: *The Indian Antiquary,* vol. XXXVII; 1–18 and 86–106.

162. —— (1910). "The 'Five Points' of Mahādeva and the Kathāvatthu." In: *JRAS*; 413–423.

163. —— (1913). *Théorie des douze Causes, Bouddhisme, Études et Matériaux.* London.

164. —— (1918). *Vasubandhu et Yaçomitra, Troisième chapitre de l'Abhidharmakoça Kārikā, Bhāṣya et Vyākhyā, Avec une analyse de la Lokaprajñapti et de la Kāraṇaprajñapti de Maudgalyāyana.* London; 326–350.

165. —— (1922). "Notes bouddhiques II, Le Vijñānakāya et le Kathāvatthu." In: *Académie royale de Belgique, Bulletin de la classe des lettres, 5e série,* VIII, no. 11; 516–520.

166. —— (1923-1931). *L'Abhidharmakośa de Vasubandhu*. Vol. I–VI. Paris.

167. —— (1925a). "Cosmologie Bouddhique." In: *Études asiatiques oubliées à l'occasion de 25e anniversaire de l'École Française d'Extrême-Orient,* vol. 1. Paris; 295–350.

168. —— (1925b) "La controverse du temps et du *pudgala* dans le *Vijñānakāya*." In: *Études asiatiques oubliées à l'occasion de 25e anniversaire de l'École Française d'Extrême-Orient,* vol. 1. Paris; 343–376.

169. —— (1925c). *Bouddhisme – opinions sur l'histoire de la dogmatique.* Paris.

170. —— (1928). *Vijñaptimatratāsiddhi,* vol. I–II. Paris.

171. —— (1930). "Documents d'Abhidharma: Texts relatifs au nirvāṇa et aux asaṃskṛtas en général I–II." In: *Bulletin de l'École Française d'Extrême-Orient,* 30; 1–28; 247–298.

172. —— (1931-1932). "Documents d'Abhidharma." In: *MCB,* I; 65–121.

173. —— (1936-1937). "Documents d'Abhidharma – la Controverse du Temps; les deux, les quatre, les trois vérités." In: *MCB,* V; 1–187.

174. Lamotte, E (1958). *Histoire du bouddhisme indien des origines à l'ère Śaka.* Louvain.

175. —— (1970). *Le Traité de la grande vertu de sagesse de Nāgārjuna* (*Ma hāprajñāpāramitāśāstra*). Vol. I–V. Louvain.

176. Lévi, S (1932). "Note sur des manuscrits sanscrits provenant de Bāmiyān (Afghanistan) et de Gilgit (Cachemire)." In: *Journal Asiatique*; 1–45.

177. Lu Cheng (1986). *Collected Works on Buddhist Studies by Lu Cheng*, 5 volumes. Beijing.

178. Masuda, J (1925). "Origin and Doctrines of Early Indian Buddhist Schools." In: *Asia Major,* vol. II; 1–78

179. Matsuda, K (1986). *'Newly Identified Sanskrit Fragments of the Dharmaskandha in the Gilgit Manuscripts'.* Kyoto.

180. Maung Tin (1920). *The Expositor* (*Aṭṭhasālinī*). Revised and Ed., Mrs Rhys Davids, PTS. London.

181. McGovern, WM (1923). *A Manual of Buddhist Philosophy.* Vol. I. London.

182. Mejor, M (1989–1990). “The Problem of two Vasubandhus Reconsidered.” In: *Indologica Taurinensia,* vol. XV–XVI; 175–183.

183. Mitomo, K (1978). “Abidarumadīpa sakusha ni taisuru ni, san no mondai.” *Indogaku Bukkyōgaku kenkyū* 27, no. 1; 221–225.

184. —— (1979). “Abidarumadīpa gōhon no kentō (ichi).” *Bukkyōgaku* 7; 65–93.

185. —— (1966). “Sharihotsuabidonron ni tsuite.” In: *Kanakura Hakushi koki kinen ronbunshū: Indogaku Bukkyōgaku ronshū.* Kyōto; 109–134.

186. Mizuno, K (1978). *The Buddhist Theories of citta-caitta.* Tokyo; (in Japanese).

187. Mochizuki, Sh (1960–1963). *Bukkyō Daijiten.* Tokyo.

188. Mookerjee, S (1935). *The Buddhist Philosophy of Universal Flux.*Calcutta.

189. Nakamura, H (1980). *Indian Buddhism – A Survey with Bibliographical Notes.* Tokyo.

190. Ñāṇamoḷi (1956). *The Path of Purification* (*Visuddhimagga*). Colombo.

191. Nishi, K (1975). 阿毘達磨佛教の研究. Tokyo.

192. Nyāyaponika (1952). *Abhidhamma Studies.* Colombo.

193. Nyāyatiloka (1952). *Guide through the Abhidhammapitaka.* Colombo.

194. Pandeya, R (1975). “Fragments from Buddhist Texts.” In: *Buddhist Studies in India.* Delhi; 137–183.

195. Pelliot, P (1930). “Les stances d’introduction de l’Abhidharmahṛdayaśāstra de Dharmatrāta.” In: *Journal Asiatique,* CCXVII; 267–274.

196. Prasad, HS (1991). *Essays on Time in Buddhism.* Delhi.

197. Pruden, LM (1988). Eng. tr. of *L’Abhidharmakośa de Vasubandhu Vols. I–VI by La Vallée Poussin, Louis de.* Berkeley.

198. —— (1988). Eng. tr. of *Le Traite de la Demonstration de ’Acte (Karmasiddhiprakaraṇa) by Lamotte, E.* Berkeley.

199. Przyluski, J (1931). “Sautrāntika et Dārṣṭāntika.” In: *Rocznik Orjentalistyczny*; vol. VIII. Paris; 14–24.

200. —— (1940). “Dārṣṭāntika, Sautrāntika and Sarvāstivādin.” In: *IHQ,* vol. XVI, 2; 246–54.

201. Rahder, J (1931–1932). “Le *satkāyadṛṣṭi* d’après Vibhāṣā, 8.” In: *MCB*; 227–239.

202. Rahula, Walpola (1984). "Pāli as a Language for Transmitting an Authentic Religious Tradition." In: *Buddhist Studies in Honour of Hammalava Saddhatissa.* Colombo; 211–218.

203. Renou, L and Filliozat, J (1985). *L'Inde classique – manual des études indiennes,* vol. I–II. Paris.

204. Rhys Davids, CAF (1900). *A Buddhist Manual of Psychological Ethics, being a translation of the Dhamma-Saṅgaṇi.* London.

205. Rhys Davids, TW (1892). "Kathāvatthu." In: *JRAS*; 1–37.

206. Rockhill, WW (1884). *The Life of the Buddha and the Early History of His Order.* London.

206. Ryose, WR. (1986). "The Position of the Abhidharmahṛdaya in the7Historical Development of Sarvāstivāda Thought." In: *Abhidharma Research Institute.* Tokyo; 1–16.

208. Sakaki, R (1916). *Mahāvyutpatti.* 梵藏和漢四譯對校翻譯名義大集 Vols. I–II. Tokyo.

209. Sakamoto, Y (1981). *Abidatsuma no Kenkyū.* Tokyo.

210. Sakuma, HS (1996). *Sanskrit Word-Index to the Abhidharmasamuccaya bhāṣyam.* Ed., Tatia, N. Tokyo.

211. Sakurabe, H (1960). "Abhidharmāvatāra by an Unidentified Author." In: *Nava Nālanda Mahāvihāra Research Publication,* vol. II; 359–370.

212. —— (1969). *Kusharon no Kenkyū.* Tokyo.

213. —— (1975). "Nyūabidatsumaron. (Chibetto bun yori no wayaku)." In: *Hajime Sakurabe, Bukkyo go no kenkyū.* Kyoto; 121–177.

214. Sakurable, H, *et.al.* (2004). 倶舎論の原典研究. Tokyo.

215. Sasaki, G (1958). *Abidatsuma shisō kenkyū.* Tokyo.

216. —— (1992). *Linguistic Approach to Buddhist Thought.* Delhi.

217. Schmithausen, Lambert (2007). *Ālayavijñāna, On the Origin and the Early Development of a Central Concept of Yogācāra Philosophy,* 2 Vols. Tokyo.

218. Shogaito, M (1991). *Studies in the Uighur Version of the Abhidharmakośabhāṣya-ṭīkā Tattvārthā.* Vol. I. Kyoto.

219. Shoten, H (2002). *Early Buddhism and Abhidharma Thought.* Japan.

220. Stcherbatsky, Th (1923). *The Conception of Buddhist Nirvāṇa.* Leningrad.

221. —— (1970). *The Central Conception of Buddhism and the Meaning of the Word 'Dharma'*. Delhi.

222. —— (1976). *The Soul Theory of the Buddhist* (*Translation of the 9th chapter of the Tibetan version of the Abhidharmakośabhāṣyam*). Delhi.

223. —— (1993). *Buddhist Logic*, vol. I & II, Indian Edition. Delhi,.

224. Yamaguchi, S (1941). 無と有との對論. Tokyo.

225. Tabata, T (1982). "Junshōriron ni okeru kyōju." In: *Indogaku Bukkyōgaku Kenkyū* 31, no. 1; 316–319.

226. Taisho University (1998). *Śrāvakabhūmi*. Revised Sanskrit Text and Japanese Translation. Tokyo.

227. Takakusu, J (1904-1905). "On the Abhidharma Literature of the Sarvāstivādins." In: *Journal of the Pali Text Society*, London; 67–146.

228. —— (1905b). "The Works of Saṃghabhadra, an Opponent of Vasubandhu." In: *JRAS,* XXXVII; 158–159.

229. Takasaki, J (1965). "Remarks on the Sanskrit Fragments of the *Abhidharmadharmaskandha-pādaśāstra*." In: *Indogaku Bukkyōgaku kenkyū* 13, no. 1; 411–403

230. Tatia, N (1960). "Sarvāstivāda." In: *Nava Nālandā Mahāvihāra Research Publication*, vol. II; 75–138.

231. Tekin, S (1970). *Abhidharmakośa-bhāṣya-ṭikā Tattvārtha-nāma. The Uigur Translation of Sthiramati's Commentary on Vasubandhu's Abhidharma-kośa-śāstra.* New York.

232. Ui, H (1979). 瑜伽論研究. Tokyo.

233. Van Den Broeck, J (1977). *La saveur de l'immortel* (*A-p'i-t'an Kan Lu Wei Lun) – La version chinoise de l'Amṛtarasa de Ghoṣaka.* Louvain.

234. Van Velthem, M (1977). *Le traité de la descente dans la profonde loi* (*Abhidharmāvatāraśāstra*) *de l'arhat Skandhila*. Louvain.

235. Venkataramanan, K (1953). "*Sāmmitīyanikāya Śāstra.*" In: *Visva Bharati Annals* V; 153–243.

236. Waldschmidt, E (1980). "Central Asian Sūtra Fragments and their Relation to the Chinese Āgamas." In: *Die Sprache der ältesten buddhistischen Überlieferung* (*The Language of the Earliest Buddhist Tradition*)*;* 136–174.

237. Watanabe, B (1954). *Ubu abidatsuma ron no kenkyū.* Tokyo.

238. Watanabe, F (1984). "A Study of the Saṃskāra Chapter in Saṃyukt ābhidharmasāraśāstra." In: *Buddhist Studies in Honour of Hammalava Saddhatissa.* Colombo; 238–248

239. Watters, T (1904). *On Yuan Chwang's Travels in India.* Vol. I–II. London.

240. Willemen, C, *et. al.* (1998). *Sarvāstivāda Buddhist Scholasticism.* Leiden.

241. Winternitz, M (1933). *A History of Indian Literature.* Vol. II. Calcutta.

242. Yin Shun (1968). 說一切有部為主論書與論師之研究 (*A Study of the Śāstras and Ācāryas of the Sarvāstivāda and Other Schools*). Taipei.

243. —— (1972) 攝大乘論講記. Reprint. Taipei.

244. ——. (1974a). 唯識學探源. (*An Investigation into the Source of the Vijñaptimātratā Philosophy*) Reprint. Taipei.

245. —— (1974b). 性空學探源. Reprint. Taipei.

246. —— (1974c). 佛法概論. Reprint. Taipei.

247. —— (1978). 印度之佛教. Reprint. Taipei.

248. —— (1987). 空之探究. Reprint. Taipei.

249. —— (1989). 印度佛教思想史. Taipei.

250. Yoshimoto, S (1982). *Abidaruma shisō.* Kyoto.

251. Yuyama, A (1987) "Remarks on the Kōkiji Fragment of the Lokaprajñapti." In: *India and the Ancient World, Trade and Culture before A.D. 650.* Ed., Gilbert Pollet; 215–227.

Sanskrit-English Glossary

(ordered according to the Roman alphabets)

ābhāsa — Appearance; representational image.

ābhāsagata — Appeared; coming into the field of one's experience.

abhāvita — Non-cultivated, one of the 14 synonyms for ***pratisaṃkhyā-nirodha*** in the MVŚ.

abhidhāna — Expression.

abhidharma — Envisaging ***Dharma***; supreme (***uttama***) doctrines. It is so explained because Abhidharma leads us to be face to face with (i.e.. direct realization of) ***Nirvāṇa***, or to the true insight into the characteristics of ***dharma***-s. In the highest sense, Abhidharma is pure ***prajñā***.

abhidharma-kathā — A solemn dialogue on the ***dharma*** (between ***bhikṣu***-s).

abhidheya — The expressed.

abhidhyā — Covetousness.

abhijñā — Higher knowledge; super normal power.

abhinirūpaṇā — Examination, judgemental investigation.

abhinirūpaṇā-vikalpa — Discrimination in the form of examination.

abhinna — Undifferentiated, general.

ābhiprāyika — With implicit intention.

abhipreta — Intended; Lovable/Inclined Toward, one of the 14 synonyms for ***pratisaṃkhyā-nirodha*** in the MVŚ.

abhisamaya — Direct comprehension/realization (of the four noble truths).

abhisaṃskāra — Volitional action (often implying a karmic significance); wilful preparation.

ābhogatmaka — Alertive in nature.

abhyupagama — Commitment, undertaking.

abhyupagama-citta — The thought with which one makes the vow of undertaking.

acittaka — 'Thoughtless', without any mental activity (as in the cessation meditation).

adattādāna — Taking what is not given.

adatta-phala — That which has not yet given fruit.

adbhuta-dharma — A wonderful occurrence.

ādhāra-pratipakṣa — Counteragent that effects the maintenance of the abandonment so obtained.

adhigama — Realization.

adhimātra — Strong (grade).

adhimokṣa — Resolve, inclination.

adhimukti — Inclination → ***adhimokṣa.***

adhimukti-manaskāra — Mental application of resolve.

adhipati-phala — Fruit of (pre)dominance.

adhipati-pratyaya — Dominant condition.

ādhipatya — Sovereignty, dominance.

ādhipatya-pratyaya — → ***adhipati-pratyaya***.

adhṣiṭhāna — Support, basis.

adhvan — Time.

adhvan-saṃcāra — Coursing in time.

ādhyātmika — Internal.

adhyavasāya — Determination, conceptual judgement.

ādīnava — Distress; the unpleasant aspect.

adṛśya — 'Invisible'; non-empirical.

aduḥkāsukha — Neither pleasant or unpleasant.

adveṣa — Non-hatred.

agada — Free from disease/affliction; a type of medicine that counteracts poison.

āgama — Traditional or canonical texts; scriptural authority.

agha — That which is exceedingly obstructive (*a* = *atyartham*, 'exceedingly'; *gha* = *hanti* 'strike/obstruct'; *atyarthaṃ hanti hanyate ceti agham*); i.e., agglomerated, obstructive matter.

agha-sāmantaka-rūpa — Matter that is proximate to ***agha*** (agglomerated matter); i.e., the space element.

agraja — Previously arisen.

āhāra — Food.

ahetuka — Without a cause.

aheya — Not to be abandoned (the outflow-free ***dharma***-s).

āhrīkya — Non-modesty.

airyāpathika — Pertaining to deportment.

aiśvarya — Sovereignty, freedom.

ajāta — The unborn.

ajñāna — Ignorance. There are two kinds: ***kliṣṭa*** and ***akliṣṭa***.

ājñātāvīndriya — The 'having fully known' faculty; the last of three outflow-free cognitive faculties. It exercises predominance with regard to the state of bliss in the present. In the acquisition of the ***arhat***-fruit, it constitutes the path of liberation. → ***anājñātam-ājñāsyāmīndriya.***

ājñendriya — The second of three outflow-free faculties. It exercises predominance with regard to cessation of ***bhāvanā-heya*** defilements. In the acquisition of the fruit of stream entry, it functions as the support of the ***visaṃyoga-prāpti***, and constitutes the path of liberation. In the acquisition of the ***arhat***-fruit, it constitutes the immediate path. → ***anājñātam-ājñāsyāmīndriya.***

ākāra — Mode of activity. The Sarvāstivāda explains this as ***prajñā***, that is, the particular mode of understanding that arises in the mind when an object is cognized. With regard to the four noble truths, there are four for each truth. There are, for ***duḥkha-satya***: ***anitya***, ***duḥkha***, ***śūnya***, ***anātman***; for ***samudaya-satya***: ***hetu***, ***samudaya***, ***prabhava***, ***pratyaya***; for ***nirodha-satya***: ***nirodha***, ***śānta***, ***praṇīta***, ***niḥsaraṇa***; for ***mārga-satya***: ***mārga***, ***nyāya***, ***pratipatti***, ***nairyāṇika***.

ākāra-samatā — Sameness in mode of activity. → ***pañcadhā samatā***.

ākāśa — Space, an unconditioned ***dharma***.

ākāśa-dhātu — Space element; to be distinguished from the unconditioned ***ākāśa***. → ***agha-sāmantaka-rūpa.***

ākāśānantyāyatana — The abode/sphere of infinite space; the first of four meditation attainments pertaining to the immaterial sphere. → ***samāpatti*** , ***ārūpya-dhātu***.

ākāśa-puṣpa — Sky-flower (referring to something absolutely non-existent).

ākiṃcanyāyatana — The abode/sphere of nothingness; the third of four meditation attainments pertaining to the immaterial sphere. → ***samāpatti***, ***ārūpya-dhātu***.

akliṣṭa-ajñāna — Non-defiled ignorance. This ignorance has nothing to do with defilements, and can be fully eliminated only in a ***buddha***.

akopya-dharman — 'Of the nature of being unshakable'. The highest type of ***arhat*** who is absolutely not susceptible to retrogression.

akṣara — Phoneme; one of the conditionings disjoined from thought. → ***viprayukta-saṃskāra***.

ākṣepa — Projection.

ākṣepaka-karma — Projecting ***karma*** (as opposed to ***paripūraka-karma***); ***karma*** responsible for determining the specific type of sentient existence into which one is reborn.

akuśala-mahābhūmika dharma — Universal unskilful/unwholesome ***dharma***-s.

akuśala-mūla — Unskilful roots.

akuśala-vitarka — Unskilful reasoning.

ālambana — Cognitive object.

ālambanābhisamaya — One of three types of direct realization. It refers to the fact of the pure ***prajñā*** taking the same objects as its conjoined ***dharma***-s in the process of direct realization. → ***abhisamaya***.

ālambana-pratighāta — Obstruction qua cognitive object. → ***pratighāta***.

ālambana-pratyaya — Condition qua object, one of the four ***pratyaya***-s.

ālambana-samatā — Sameness of cognitive object (one of five conditions for two mental ***dharma***-s to be said to be conjoined). → ***pañcadhā samatā***.

ālambanato 'nuśete — (A defilement) grows concordantly by taking a ***sāsrava*** object.

alāta-cakra — Fire-wheel.

ālaya-vijñāna — Store consciousness (of the Yogācāra system).

alobha — Non-greed.

ālocana — Perceiving, reflecting.

āloka — Light.

alpaujasa — Lack of vitality.

alpecchatā — Having few desires.

amala — Taintless, pure.

amanojña — Disagreeable.

amoha — Non-delusion.

amṛta-dvāra — Gateway to immortality (i.e. to ***Nirvāṇa***), referring to ***ānāpāna-(anu)smṛti*** and ***aśubhānusmṛti/aśucyanusmṛti***.

anāgāmin — Non-returner.

anāgāmin pratipannaka — Candidate of the fruit of non-returner.

anājñātam-ājñāsyāmīndriya — The 'I shall know what has not been known' faculty; the first of three outflow-free cognitive faculties which are: ***anājñātam-ājñāsyāmīndriya***, ***ājñendriya*** and ***ājñātāvīndriya***. These three faculties, in their essential nature, are constituted of ***manas***, ***sukha***, ***saumanasya***, ***upekṣā***, ***śraddhā***, ***vīrya***, ***smṛti***, ***samādhi*** and ***prajñā***. These nine are differentiated as the three distinctive faculties on account of the predominance that they exercise in the ***darśana-mārga***, ***bhāvanā-mārga*** and ***asaikṣa-mārga***, respectively. The ***anājñātam-ājñāsyāmīndriya*** exercises predominance with regard to the cessation of the ***darśana-heya*** defilements. In the acquisition of the fruit of stream entry, it functions as the inductor (***āvāhaka***) of the ***visaṃyoga-prāpti***, and constitutes the path of liberation.

anālambana — (Consciousness) having no cognitive object.

ānantarya karma — (The five) mortal transgression: patricide, matricide, killing an ***arhat***, causing the a buddha's bleeding, splitting the ***Saṅgha***.

ānantarya-mārga — Unhindered path. The moment of abandoning a defilement. Immediately after this is the path of liberation.

ānāpānasmṛti — Mindfulness of breathing.

anapatrāpya — Shamelessness.

anāsrava — Outflow-free ('pure' in the sense that such a ***dharma*** does not conduce to the saṃsāric process). → ***sāsrava***.

anāsrava-jñāna — Outflow-free knowledge.

anāsrava-saṃvara — Outflow-free restraint.

andhakāra-phala — Fruit of darkness/ignorance.

āneñjya — Immovable.

aṅga — Limb, part.

anidarśana — Invisible.

anidarśana-apratigha — Invisible and non-resistant.

aniṣṭa-vipāka — Undesirable retribution.

anityatā — Impermanence.

anityatā-anityatā — 'Impermanence-impermanence', one of four ***anulakṣaṇa***-s of the conditioned ***dharma***-s. Its function is to cause the perishing of ***anityatā-/vyaya-lakṣaṇa***. → ***anulakṣaṇa***.

anityatā-lakṣaṇa — 'Impermanence-characteristic', a ***viprayukta-saṃskāra-dharma*** that causes the perishing of a conditioned ***dharma***. One of four characteristics (***lakṣaṇa***) of the conditioned ***dharma***-s. → ***saṃskṛta-lakṣaṇa***.

anivṛta-avyākṛta — Non-veiled-non-defined. A ***dharma*** that is both morally non-defined and non-obstructive to the noble path.

aniyata dharma— Indeterminate ***dharma***. A category of ***dharma***-s whose nature (skilful, unskilful; etc.) cannot be determined.

aniyata karma — Indeterminate ***karma***. A ***karma*** that is not necessarily retributed.

antagrāhadṛṣti — A view grasping the two extremes: existence, non-existence.

antarā-bhava — Intermediate existence.

antika — Proximate, one of the 14 synonyms for ***pratisaṃkhyā-nirodha*** in the MVŚ.

aṇu — Fine, subtle. In the Sarvāstivāda atomic theory, seven ***paramāṇu***-s constitute an ***aṇu***. It is the finest among all ***rūpa***-s perceivable by the eye and visual consciousness; and even then by only three types of eye: 1. the ***divya-cakṣus***, 2. the eye of a ***cakravartin***, 3. the eye of a ***bodhisattva*** in his last birth.

anubandha — Series, continuity.

anubhava-pratyakṣa — Direct perception qua experience, one of three types of direct perception. → ***pratyakṣa***.

anudhātu — 'Subsidiary element', a term similar in significance to ***bīja*** (seed), used by Śrīlāta.

anulakṣaṇa — Secondary characteristic (of the conditioned ***dharma***-s). There are four: ***jāti-jāti***, ***sthiti-sthiti***, ***jarā-jarā***, ***anityatā-anityatā*** (***/vyaya-vyaya***). Each ***saṃskṛta-dharma*** is momentary thanks to the operation of the ***saṃskṛta-lakṣaṇa-s***, and each of these is in turn rendered momentary thanks to the operation of the four ***anulakṣaṇa***-s.

anumāna — Inference.

anunaya — Lust.

anupadhiśeṣa-nirvāṇa — ***Nirvāṇa*** without substratum.

anuprasaṅga — A subsidiary topic or digression from the main topic under discussion.

anupūrvaka — One who progresses according to the regular order.

anurakṣaṇā-dharman — Of the nature of being capable of protecting oneself from retrogression.

anuṣaṅga — → ***anuprasaṅga***.

anuśaya — Proclivity. For the Sarvāstivāda, it is one of the synonyms for ***kleśa*** (defilement), signifying its subtle nature. For the Sautrāntika and others, it is a latent defilement, the seed of the ***paryavasthāna***.

anuśayana — The act of adherence and growth.

anuśerate — (A defilement) adheres and grows concordantly (with an with-outflow object).

anusmaraṇa-vikalpa — Discrimination in the form of recollection; one of three forms of discrimination. → ***vikalpa***.

anu-srota — Stream-accordants, those who have not planted the skilful roots of ***mokṣa-bhāgīya***.

anutpāda — Non-arising.

anutpāda-jñāna — Knowledge of non-arising (of all defilements).

anupātta — Non-appropriated (by a being's ***citta-caitta***-s); i.e., sensitive (***rūpa***).

anuttarā samyak-saṃbodhi — Supreme Perfect Enlightenment (of a ***buddha***).

anuvartaka — Operating in accompaniment with; subsequent propeller.

anvaya-jñāna — Subsequent knowledge. It is a spiritual insight similar in nature to ***dharma-jñāna*** and acquired subsequently to it, while one is gaining insight into a noble truth pertaining to the ***rūpa***- and ***ārūpya-dhātu***-s.

anvaya-jñāna-kṣānti — Receptivity to the subsequent knowledge.

anyathānyathātva — Buddhadeva's explanation on temporality: a dharma is said to be future, present or past relative to that which precedes and/or that which succeeds.

ap — Water (one of four Great Elements).

apakāra — Harm, injury.

apara-paryāya-vedanīya karma — ***Karma***-s whose retribution is experiencible in a future life subsequent to the next.

apatrāpya — Shamefulness.

aparijñāta — Have not been completely known.

aprahīṇa — Have not been abandoned.

apramāda — Diligence, heedfulness.

apramādāṅga — (Pertaining to) the section of vigilance; this refers to the abstention from intoxicants.

apramāṇa — Immeasurable. There are four: ***maitrī***, ***karuṇā***, ***muditā***, ***upekṣā***.

aprāpti — Non-acquisition, one of the ***viprayukta-saṃskāra-dharma***-s. It is a force opposite in nature to ***prāpti***, and serves to severe the link of a ***dharma*** from the serial continuity of the sentient being.

apratigha — Non-resistant.

apratilambha — Non-obtainment.

apratisaṃkhyā-nirodha — Cessation independent of deliberation, one of the three types of ***asaṃskṛta-dharma***-s. It is a cessation acquired not through any effort of deliberation, but due to the deficiency in ***pratyaya***-s. But like a ***pratisaṃkhyā-nirodha***, it is also not a mere absence, but a positive force preventing the arising of the ***dharma*** which has ceased.

apratisaṃyukta — Not bound or yoked (i.e., not pertaining to any sphere of existence). This refers to the ***anāsrava dharma***-s.

apratyakṣa — Indirect perception.

apuṇya — A non-meritorious deed.

ārāma — A monastery.

araṇya — An hermitage dwelling.

arāśi — Non-agglomerated, one of the 14 synonyms for ***pratisaṃkhyā-nirodha*** in the MVŚ.

arati — Disgust, non-delight.

arbuda — The second stage in the foetal development.

arhat — 'A Worthy One', epithet for one who has achieved the highest spiritual attainment.

arhat pratipannaka — Candidate for the fruition of ***arhat***.

artha — Object-referent; meaning; purpose (There are many other meanings).

artha-kriyā-samartha — Efficacious for a purposeful action.

artha-pratisaṃvid — Unhindered knowledge with regard to meaning. One of four types of ***pratisaṃvid***: ***dharma-***, ***artha-***, ***nirukti-***, and ***pratibhāna-***.

artha-svarūpa — The object in its unique nature.

arthasya pratinidhi — Image or representation of the external object.

arthaviniścaya — Determination or ascertainment of meaning.

arūpi-dharma-s — Immaterial ***dharma***-s.

arūpin — Immaterial.

ārūpya — Immateriality. It also stands for the ***ārūpya-dhātu***.

ārūpya-dhātu — The sphere of immateriality. This is subdivided into four progressive stages (***bhūmi***): 1. ***ākāśānantyāyatana***, 2. ***vijñānāntyāyatana***, 3. ***ākiṃcanyāyatana***; 4. ***naivasaṃjñā-nāsaṃjñāyatana***.

ārūpya-dhātu-pratisaṃyukta — Pertaining to the sphere of immateriality.

ārūpyāvacara-pratisaṃyukta — Same as ***ārūpya-dhātu-pratisaṃyukta.***

ārya — Noble; also a term for one who has become a Buddhist saint (who has attained one of the eight stages of spiritual attainment, and hence no more a ***pṛthagjana***).

ārya-jñāna — Noble (i.e., ***anāsrava***) knowledge.

ārya-mārga — Noble path.

ārya-mārgatva — The (universal) nature of the ***ārya-mārga***; one of the unconditioned ***dharma***-s of some schools.

ārya-satya — Noble truth. There are four: ***duḥkha***, ***samudaya***, ***nirodha***, ***mārga***.

āryāṣṭāṅgika-mārga — The noble eightfold-path. It comprises: ***samyag-dṛṣṭi***, ***samyak-saṃkalpa***, ***samyag-vāk***, ***samyak-karmānta***, ***samyag-ājīva***, ***samyag-vyāyāma***, ***samyak-smṛti***, ***samyak-samādhi***.

ārya-vaṃśa — Noble linage.

asabhāga — Non-similar. Also, 'Dissimilar', one of the 14 synonyms for ***pratisaṃkhyā-nirodha*** in the MVŚ.

asad-ālambana — (Consciousness) taking a non-existent object.

asādhāraṇa — Unique.

asad-viṣayaṃ jñānam — Knowledge whose object-domain is non-existent.

aśaikṣa — Non-trainee; an epithet for an ***arhat***, because he has completed all training.

aśaikṣa-mārga — Path of the non-trainee.

asāmagrī — Non-harmony. It is mentioned in the MVŚ as a ***viprayukta-saṃskāra***, a force that causes schism in the ***Saṃgha***.

asamanvāgama — Non-endowment.

asamaya-vimukta — Non-circumstantially liberated.

āsaṃjñika — Ideationlessness, one of the ***viprayukta-saṃskāra***-s. This force causes the rebirth state of the ideationless attainment.

asaṃjñi-samāpatti — Ideationless attainment, one of the ***viprayukta-saṃskāra***-s. This is sought by the heretics who misconstrue that such a state is final liberation.

asaṃjñi-sattva — Ideationless beings.

asaṃkhyeya-kalpa-s — Incalculable aeons.

asaṃprajanya — Lack of proper discernment.

asaṃskṛta — Unconditioned. There are three categories of unconditioned ***dharma***-s: ***pratisaṃkhyā-nirodha***, ***apratisaṃkhyā-nirodha***, ***ākāśā***.

asaṃsṛṣṭa — Non-intimate, one of the 14 synonyms for ***pratisaṃkhyā-nirodha*** in the MVŚ.

asaṃvara — Non-restraint.

asaṃvara-karma — Non-restraint action.

asaṃyoga-vastu — Object without binding.

āsanna — Proximate, one of the 14 synonyms for ***pratisaṃkhyā-nirodha*** in the MVŚ.

āsanna-kāraṇa — The co-nascent proximate cause.

asarvatraga-kleśa — Non-universal defilement.

asattvākhya — Non-sentient, not pertaining to sentient beings.

āśaya — Intention.

āśaya-vipanna — Evil intention.

āśaya-viśeṣa — A specific type of intention.

asevita — Non-cultivated, one of the 14 synonyms for ***pratisaṃkhyā-nirodha*** in the

MVŚ.

āsevita-bhāvita-bahulīkṛta — Well practiced, cultivated and repeatedly done.

asmimāna — Self-conceit.

āśraddhya — Lack of faith.

āsrava — Outflow, a synonym of ***kleśa***.

āsravakṣaya-jñāna — The knowledge of the destruction of the outflows.

āśraya — Supporting basis.

āśraya-samatā — Sameness in respect of the supporting basis.

aṣṭadravyaka — Comprising eight substances.

astitva — Existence.

aśubha — Impure.

aśubha-bhāvanā — Contemplation on the impure.

aśucyanusmṛti — Recollection of the impure.

āsvādana — Tasting, enjoying; the enjoyable aspect.

atiprasaṅga — Over-generalization.

ātmavādopādana — Soul-theory-clinging.

atyantābhāva — An absolute non-existent.

atyantaṃ pra-hātavya — To be abandoned completely/absolutely.

atyanta-viruddha — Absolutely opposed.

audārika — Coarse.

auddhatya — Restlessness.

auddhatya-kaukṛtya — Restlessness-remorse.

aupacārika — Metaphorical.

aupacayika — Of the nature of growth.

aupadhika-puṇya-kriyā — A material meritorious action.

avadāna — One of the ***dvādaśāṅga-dharma-pravacana***. It is in the form of a simile or story clarifying or demonstrating the truth of a certain doctrinal point.

avadhāraṇa — Affirmation, emphasis.

avadya — 'Not praise-worthy', vice, transgression.

avara-bhāgīya — Pertaining to the lower section. — ***pañca-avara-bhāgīya.***

āvaraṇa — Obstruction, hindrance.

āvaraṇa-pratighātā — Obstruction qua hindrance. → ***pratighāta***.

avarṇa — Non-manifest, one of the 14 synonyms for ***pratisaṃkhyā-nirodha*** in the MVŚ.

avasthā — State, position.

avasthā-anyathātva — 'Difference in state'; Vasumitra's explanation on temporality: A

dharma in a given temporal state is termed future, present or past accordingly.

āvasthika pratītya-samutpāda — Conditioned co-arising in (twelve) states.

avayava — Part. It is also a synonym of ***svabhāva***.

avetya-prasāda — Faith/conviction (***prasāda***) based on insight.

avidyā — Ignorance, nescience.

avidyāsrava — Ignorance-outflow.

avidyaugha — Ignorance-flood.

avihiṃsā — Harmlessness.

avijñapti — Non-information.

avijñapti-karma — Non-informative action.

avijñapti-rūpa — Non-informative matter.

avikṣipta — Non-distracted.

avinā-bhāva — Being not mutually separated.

avinirbhāga — Non-separation.

aviparīta — Non-topsy-turvy, non-erroneous.

avyākṛta — (Morally) non-defined.

avyākṛta-mūla — Non-defined root.

āya-dvāra — Gateway of arising.

āyatana — Entrance, abode. There are 12: six internal faculties (from ***cakṣus*** to ***manas***) and the six corresponding object domains (from ***rūpa*** to ***dharma***).

āyatana-pratilambha — Obtainment of abode.

ayoniśo manaskāra — Improper mental application.

ayukta — Unreasonable, not logical.

āyus — Life principle.

bahirdeśaka — Foreign/outside masters (those outside Kāśmīra).

bahu-dhātu — Multiple elements.

bahu-nāma-kāya — Group of multiple words.

bāhya — External.

bala — Power.

balavat — Strong.

bandhana — Bondage. It is a also a synonym for ***kleśa***.

bhājana-loka — 'Receptacle world'; i.e., the physical world.

bhautika — 'Derived from the ***mahā-bhūta***-s' = ***bhāutika-rūpa***.

bhāutika-rūpa — Derived matter. Same as ***upādāya rūpa***.

bhāva-anyathātva — 'Difference in mode of existence/being'; Dharmatrāta's explanation on temporality: A ***dharma*** is said to be future, present or past according to its mode of existence.

bhavāgra — Existence-peak.

bhāvanā-mārga — Path of cultivation.

bhāvanā-mārga-heya — (Defilements) abandonable by repeated cultivation.

bhāvanā-mayī-prajñā — Understanding derived from cultivation.

bhavāsrava — Existence-outflow.

bhavaugha — Existence-flood.

bhedābheda — Non-difference in difference.

bhinna — Differentiated, specific.

bhikṣu — A fully ordained male member of the ***Saṅgha***.

bhikṣuṇī — A fully ordained female member of the ***Saṅgha***.

bhūmi — Stage.

bhūta-pratyakṣa — 'True direct perception', direct perception par excellence.

bhūyo-vītarāga — 'One who has been much detached'; a practitioner who, before entering into the ***darśanamārga***, has already abandoned (through the worldly path) the defilements abandonable by cultivation, from six to eight categories.

bīja — Seed.

bodhi — Enlightenment, awakening.

bodhipakṣya-dharma — ***Dharma***-s conducive to Enlightenment. There are 37: four ***smṛtyupasthāna***-s, four ***samyak pradhāna***-s, four ***ṛddhipāda***-s, five ***indriya***-s, five ***bala***-s, seven ***bodhyaṅga***-s, eight ***āryāṣṭāṅgika-mārga***-s.

bodhyaṅga — Enlightenment-factors. There are seven: ***smṛti***, ***dharma***-(***pra***)***vicaya***, ***vīrya***, ***prīti***, ***praśrabdhi***, ***samādhi***, ***upekṣā.***

brahma-carya — 'Brahma-faring', the spiritual life.

bṛhatphala — Great-fruit [Heaven].

Buddha-vacana — Words of the Buddha.

buddhi — Intellect, perception.

buddhi-pratyakṣa — Direct perception qua discernment.

caitasika — Thought-concomitant.

caitta — Same as ***caitasika.***

cakṣur-abhijñā — Supernormal power of vision,

cakṣur-indriya — Visual faculty.

cakṣus — Eye.

cakra-vartin — 'Wheel-wielding', Universal Monarch.

catuṣ-koṭi — 'Four-cornered' (alternative), tetralemma.

cetanā — Volition.

cetanā dharman — Of the nature of being capable of ending existence at will.

cetanā-viśeṣa — A specific type of volition.

cetayitvā-karma — ***Karma*** subsequent to willing.

chanda — Predilection, desire.

cintā-mayī prajñā — Understanding derived from reflection.

citastham rūpa — Agglomerated matter.

citra — Variegated.

citta — Thought.

cittānuparivartin — Accompanying thought; thought-accompaniment.

cittānuvartin — Same as ***cittānuparivartin.***

cittaviprayukta-saṃskāra — Conditionings disjoined from thought.

damana — Subduing, taming.

dāna-śīla-aviruddha — Unopposed to giving and precept.

darśana — Seeing, insight, vision.

darśanābhisamaya — Direct realization in respect of the seeing of the four noble truths by pure ***prajñā*** alone.

darśana-heya — (Defilements) abandonable by insight.

darśana-mārga — Path of insight.

dauśīlya — 'Bad behaviour', immorality, transgression of precepts.

dauśīlya-vibandhatva — Obstruction to the transgression of precepts.

dharma — (1) An ultimate factor of existence, defined as "that which sustains its specific characteristic". (2) Mental objects.

dharma-jñāna — The spiritual insight into the true nature of ***dharma***-s, derived for the first time in one's **saṃsāric** existence, in the direct realization of ***duḥkha-satya*** pertaining to the ***kāma-dhātu***.

dharmānusārin — Pursuer through ***dharma.***

dharma-pratisaṃvid — Unhindered knowledge with regard to ***dharma***, one of four types of ***pratisaṃvid*** → ***artha-pratisaṃvid***.

dharma-pravicaya — Investigation/examination of ***dharma***-s.

dharma-sabhāgatā — Homogeneity among ***dharma***-s.

dharma-śarīra — ***Dharma*** Body.

dharmatā — Nature of ***dharma***; nature of things.

dharmatā-prātilambhika — Obtained spontaneously (acquired in accordance with the nature of things).

dharmāyatana — The ***dharma***-abode, the ***āyatana*** corresponding to ***manas*** in the twelve-***āyatana*** classification.

dharmāyatana-saṃgṛhīta-rūpa — Matter subsumed under the ***dharmāyatana***. This refers to the ***avijñapti-rūpa***.

dhātu — Element (also explained as "source of origin"); sphere.

dhṛti — Supporting, sustaining.

dhyāna — Meditation, reflection. Only the first four ***samāpatti***-s pertaining to the ***rūpa-dhātu*** can be called ***dhyāna***, because in these four meditations, ***śamatha*** and ***vipaśyanā*** exist evenly.

dhyāna-saṃvara — Meditation-restraint; one type of ***avijñapti***.

divya-cakṣus— Divine eye.

dravya — Substance; a real entity.

dravyāntara — A distinct entity.

dravya-paramāṇu — Atom as a single entity.

dravya-samatā — Sameness in respect of being a singular substance, one of the five conditions for two mental factors to be said to be in conjunction (***saṃprayukta***).

dravyasat — Existent as a real entity; absolutely real.

dṛṣṭa-dharma-phala — Fruit experienced in the present life.

dṛṣṭa-dharma-sukha-vihāra — State of bliss in the present life.

dṛṣṭa-dharma-vedanīya-karma — ***Karma*** experiencible in this life.

dṛṣṭānta — Example, simile.

dṛṣṭe dharme — In the present existence.

dṛṣṭi-parāmarśa — Clinging to one's views as the only true ones.

dṛṣṭi-prāpta — One who has attained through views.

dṛṣṭyogha — View-flood.

dṛṣṭy-upādāna — View-clinging.

duḥkha — Unpleasant; painful; unsatisfactory; pain; unsatisfactoriness.

duḥkha-darśana-heya — (Defilements) abandonable by insight into unsatisfactoriness.

duḥkha-satya — The noble truth of unsatisfactoriness.

duḥkhatā — The fact of unsatisfactoriness.

duḥkha-vedanīya — Experiencible as being unsatisfactory; unpleasant/unsatisfactory experience.

duḥkhe anvaya-jñāna — Subsequent-knowledge with regard to ***duḥkha*** pertaining to It is a spiritual insight similar in nature, and acquired subsequently to the ***duḥkhe dharma-jñāna***.

dūragama — Far-going.

durgati — Unfortunate plane of existence.

dūrībhāva-pratipakṣa — Counteragent which results in distancing (from the ***prāpti*** of the defilement).

dvādaśāṅga — 'Twelve-limb', twelve-fold (classification).

dvādaśāṅga-dharma-pravacana — The twelve-fold classification of the Words of the [Buddha]***Dharma***: 1. ***sūtra***, 2. ***geya***, 3.***vyākaraṇa***, 4. ***gāthā***, 5. ***udāna***, 6. ***nidāna***, 7. ***avadāna***, 8. ***itivṛttaka/ityuktaka***, 9. ***jātaka***, 10. ***vaipulya***, 11. ***abhuta-dharma***, 12. ***upadeśa***.

dyotita — Illuminated, elucidated, clearly shown.

eḍaka-rajas — 'Ram-dust'. The size of seven ***śaśa-rajas***-s.

ekaṃśena — Categorically.

ekottara — One-incremental.

gahana — A dense forest.

gandha — Smell.

gandha-artha — Olfactory object.

gāthā — A stanza.

gati — Plane of existence.

geya — 'To be sung', the second of the ***dvādaśāṅga-dharma-pravacana***. It Originally referred to the an ***uddāna*** (summary) verse mnemonically summarizing the names of the (ten) preceding ***sūtra***-s during the first Council. It has subsequently come to denote a repetition verse summarizing what has been said in the preceding prose.

ghrāṇa — Nose.

ghrāṇa-indriya — Olfactory faculty.

go-rajas — 'Cow-dust', the size of seven ***eḍaka-rajas***.

gotra — Clan.

grāhaka — Grasper (subject).

grāhya — The 'graspable', the grasped (the 'object').

grāhyatā — The essence of being a 'graspable/object'

guṇa — Virtue, benefit.

gurutva — Heaviness.

haituka — Logician.

hetu — Cause, reason. There are six causes: ***kāraṇa-hetu***, ***sabhāga-hetu***, ***sarvatrga-hetu***, ***sahabhū-hetu***, ***saṃprayuktaka-hetu***, ***vipāka-hetu***.

hetu-jñāna — Knowledge of the cause.

hetu-kauśalya — Skillfulness with regard to cause.

hetu-phala-bhāva — The state of cause-effect, causal relationship.

hetu-phala-mātra — Mere cause and effect.

hetu-pratyaya — Condition qua cause.

hetu-samutthāna — Origination qua cause.

hrī — Modesty.

idaṃsatyābhinirveśa-kāyagrantha — Corporeal tie of dogmatism.

indhana — Fuel.

indriya — Faculty, organ.

indriya-pratyakṣa — Direct perception dependent on a sense faculty.

īraṇā — Mobility.

īrṣyā — Jealousy.

īryāpatha — Deportment.

itivṛttaka — "Of the form, 'it happened thus'", one of the ***dvādaśāṅga-dharma-pravacana***. It assumes the form of the narration of a past event.

ityuktaka — "Of the form, 'it was said thus'". Same as ***itivṛttaka***.

jaḍa — Dull, inanimate, unintelligent.

janana-hetu — Generating cause. One of a set of five ***hetu***-s: ***janana-hetu***), ***niśraya-hetu***, ***pratiṣṭhā-hetu***, ***upastambha-hetu***), ***upabṛṃhaṇa-hetu***.

janmāpravṛtti — Non-proceeding of birth, discontinuity of birth.

jarā-jarā — 'Deterioration-deterioration', one of the four ***anulakṣaṇa***-s. It function is to cause the deterioaration of ***jārā***.

jarā-lakṣaṇa — Deterioration-characteristic, a ***viprayukta-saṃskāra-dharma*** that causes the decay of a conditioned ***dharma***. → ***saṃskṛta-lakṣaṇa***.

jātaka — Birth stories (of the Buddha as a ***bodhisattva***).

jāti-jāti — 'Production-production', one of the ***anulakṣaṇa***-s. It function is to generate ***jāti***. → ***anulakṣaṇa***.

jāti-lakṣaṇa — Production-characteristic, a ***viprayukta-saṃskāra-dharma*** that causes the arising of a conditioned ***dharma***. → ***saṃskṛta-lakṣaṇa***.

jighatsā — Hunger.

jihvā — Tongue.

jihvā-indriya — Gustatory faculty.

jīvitendriya — Vital faculty.

jñāna — Knowledge.

jñāna-ākāra — Knowledge-form.

jñāna-bala — Power of knowledge.

jñeya — 'Knowable', object of knowledge.

jñeyāvaraṇa — Knowable-hindrance . Only a buddha can overcome this, in addition to overcoming the defilement-hindrance (***kleśāvaraṇa***).

kāla — Time.

kalala — The first foetal stage.

kāla-samatā — Sameness in respect of time. One of the five conditions for ***saṃprayoga***.

kalpanā — Conceptualization.

kāmacchanda — Sensual-desire.

kāma-dhātu-pratisaṃyukta — Pertaining (lit.: 'bound/yoked') to the sphere of sensuality.

kāma-mithyā-cāra — Sensual misconduct.

kāmāsrava — Sensuality-outflow.

kāmaugha — Sensuality-flood.

kāmavacara-pratisaṃyukta — Same as ***kāma-dhātu-pratisaṃyukta.***

kāmopādāna — Sensuality-clinging.

kāraṇa — Cause, reason, instrument.

kāraṇa-hetu — Efficient cause.

kāraṇa prajñapti — 'Designation/teaching on cause', name of a chapter in the PjŚ.

kārikā — Stanza.

kāritra — Activity. For the Vaibhāṣika, the activity belongs only to a present ***dharma***; it is its efficacy of projecting its own fruit (existence) in the next moment of its serial continuity.

karkaśatva — Coarseness.

karma — Action, deed. In the specifically Buddhist sense, it primarily means a morally skilful or unskilful action which determines specifically the manner of future existence of the doer.

karmadhāraya samāsa — Determinative compound.

karma-patha — Paths of ***karma***; the principal actions (usually given as ten) done through body, speech and mind.

karma-prajñapti — 'Designation/teaching' on ***karma***', name of a chapter in the PjŚ.

karma-vācanā — Speech such as announcement made during an ecclesiastical proceeding in a Saṅgha meeting.

karuṇā — Compassion.

kāryābhisamaya — direct comprehension of the practice performed

kaukṛtya — Remorse. It can be either positive or negative: remorse after having done a good action is negative; that after having done a bad action is positive.

kaurmasya roma — The tortoise's hair, a simile for something absolutely non-existent.

kauśīdya — Slackness, laziness.

kāya — Body; group.

kāya-bhājana — Body as a receptacle.

kāyacitta-avasthāviśeṣa — A distinctive psychophysical state.

kāya-grantha — Corporeal tie, a synonym for ***kleśa***.

kāya-indriya — Tangible faculty.

khara — Solidity.

kleśa — defilement.

kleśa-bīja — Defilement seed.

kleśamahābhūmika dharma — Universal ***dharma***-s of defilement.

kleśa-prahāṇa — Abandonment of defilement. This is not the destruction of defilement (as no ***dharma*** can be destroyed as such), but rather the severing of the ***prāpti*** from the serial continutity of the individual.

kleśāvaraṇa — Defilement-hindrance. → ***āvaraṇa***.

kliṣṭa — Defiled. This includes both what is ***akuśala*** and what is ***nivṛtāyākṛta***.

kliṣṭa-ajñāna — Defiled ignorance. This is ignorance connected with defilement. It is overcome in the ***arhat*** and the ***pratyeka-buddha*** as well as the ***samyak-saṃbuddha***.

kriyā — Action, activity (not in the specific sense of ***kāritra***).

kṛṇa karma — A black ***karma***; one that yields a black (i.e. disagreeable) retribution.

krodha — Anger.

kṛta — Done.

kṛtnāyatana — Base of entirety.

kṣaṇa — Moment; the shortest unit of time.

kṣaṇika — Momentary.

kṣaṇika pratītya-samutpāda — One of the fourfold interpretation of the Sarvāstivāda. This interpretation is that the 12 links of conditioned co-arising are embraced within a single moment.

kṣānti — Receptivity. Two major meanings: (i) The cognitive ability to fully accept a truth/doctrine in advance, even before one has actually acquired the ***jñāna*** proper of that truth/doctrine. It is the moment immediately preceding that ***jñāna***. (ii) The third spiritual attainment in the ***prayoga*** stage known as the four ***nirvedha-bhāgīya***-s.

kṣatriya — The warrior class; the second of the four major castes in the Hindu system.

kṣaya-jñāna — Knowledge of exhaustion (of the ***āsrava***).

kṣema — Security; also a synonym for Nirvāṇa.

kṣetra-viśeṣa — Distinctive field (of merit).

kṣīna-āsrava — One who has exhausted the outflows, an epithet for an ***arhat***.

kṣudra-vastuka — Minor/miscellaneous matter.

kuśala — Wholesome, skilful.

kuśala-dharma-chanda — Aspiration/desire for the good.

kuśalamahābhūmika dharma — Universal skilful ***dharma***-s.

kuśala-mūla — Roots of skilfulness.

kuśalamūla-samuccheda — Cutting off of the skilful roots.

laghutva — Lightness.

lajjā — Shamefulness

lakṣaṇa — Characteristic.

lakṣaṇa-anyathātva — 'Difference in characteristic'; Ghoṣaka's explanation on temporality: a ***dharma*** is future, present or past depending on the temporal characteristic of which it is in possession.

lākṣaṇika — Definitive.

lakṣya — The characterized.

laukika — Mundane, worldly.

laukikāgra dharma — The worldly supreme ***dharma***. The fourth ***nirvedha-bhāgīya***-s belonging to the ***prayoga*** stage immediately after which one enters into the ***darśana-mārga***.

laukika-mārga — Mundane path.

laukikī-samyak-dṛṣṭi — Worldly right view.

loka-prajñapti — 'Designation/teaching on of the world', a chapter in the PjŚ.

lokavyavahāra — Conventional usages in the world.

lokottara-jñāna — Transcendental knowledge.

mada — Pride.

madhya — Middle, medium.

mahābhūmika dharma — Universal ***dharma.***

mahābhūta — Great Element.

mahā-karuṇā — Great compassion.

mahāphala — Great fruit.

mahāpuruṣa — Great Man.

mahā-rājan — Great king.

maitrī — Love, loving kindness.

maitrī-bhāvanā — Meditation on loving-kindness

māna — Conceit.

manaḥ-pradoṣa — Mental hatred.

manas — Mind.

manaskāra (also: ***manasikāra***) — Mental application, attention.

mānātimāna — Extreme conceit.

mano-bhūmi — Mental sphere, mental stage.

manojña — Mentally agreeable.

mārga — Path.

mārga-darśana-heya — (Defilements) abandonable through insight into the path leading to cessation of ***duḥkha***.

mārga-jñana — Knowledge of the path.

mārga-satya — noble truth of the path leading to the cessation of ***duḥkha***.

mātṛkā — Matrix, a list summarily enumerating topics to be elaborated upon.

mātsarya — Avarice.

māyā — Deceptiveness, illusion.

middha — Drowsiness, sleep.

miśra — Mixed.

mithyā — Wrong, false.

mithyā-dṛṣṭi — False view.

mithyā-jñāna — False knowledge.

moha — Delusion.

mokṣabhāgīya — Preparatory efforts (***prayoga***) conducing to liberation. They essentially comprise ***śamatha*** and ***vipaśyanā*** meditational practices.

mrakṣa — Concealment.

mṛdu — Blunt, weak.

mṛdvindriya — Weak faculty.

mṛṣā-vāda— False speech.

mṛtyu — Death.

muditā — Sympathetic joy.

mūla — Fundamental, primary, basic.

mūla-lakṣaṇa — The (four) primary characteristics.

mūrdhan — Summits, the second stage of the ***nirvedha-bhāgīya.***

nairātmya — Soullessness, the fact of there being no Self; non-substantiality.

nairmāṇika — Transformational; pertaining to the psychic ability to transform.

nairyāṇika — Conducive to exit; one of the four ***ākāra***-s of the ***mārga-satya***.

naiva-śaikṣa-nāśaikṣa — Pertaining to neither the trainee or the non-trainee.

naivasaṃjñā-nāsaṃjñāyatana — The sphere of neither-ideation-nor-non-ideation', the fourth of the ***ārūpya-samāpatti***. — ***samāpatti***, ***ārūpya-dhātu.***

nāma-kāya — Word-group; one of the ***viprayukta-saṃskāra***-s.

naraka — Hell.

nāstitva — Non-existence.

nendriya — Not of the nature of a faculty.

neyārtha — (A doctrine) whose meaning is yet to be fully drawn out; implicit (teaching).

nidāna — Introduction; source; link.

niḥsaraṇa — Escape; Exit, one of the 14 synonyms for ***pratisaṃkhyā-nirodha*** in the MVŚ.

nikāya-sabhāga — Group homogeneity, one of the ***viprayukta-saṃskāra***-s.

nimitta — Mark, sign; cause.

nirantara — Without an interval.

nirdeśa — Exposition, discourse.

nirmāṇa-citta — Transformation-thought.

nirodha — Cessation.

nirodha-darśana-heya — (Defilements) abandonable through insight into the ***nirodha-satya***.

nirodha-jñāna — Knowledge of cessation.

nirodha-samāpatti — Cessation-attainment, a meditational attainment in which all mental activities come to cease.

nirodha-satya — noble truth of the cessation of ***duḥkha***.

nirukti-pratisaṃvid — Unhindered knowledge with regard to etymology, one of the four types of ***pratisaṃvid***. → ***artha-pratisaṃvid.***

nirupadhiśeṣa-nirvāṇa — ***Nirvāṇa*** without a remnant of substratum.

nirupadhiśeṣa-nirvāṇa-dhātu — The sphere of ***nirvāṇa*** without a remnant of substratum.

nirvāṇa — The goal of the Buddhist spiritual life, explained in Buddhism as the extinction/blowing out of the fire of ***rāga dveṣa*** and ***moha***. It is the state of perfect bliss, and transcedence of all ***duḥkha*** and births. In Sarvāstiv**ā**da, this is not a mere absence of ***duḥkha***, but a positive entity acquired when a defilement is abandoned, which serves to prevent the further arising of the defilement. It is a synonym for ***pratisaṃkhyā-nirodha***.

nirvāṇālambanā prajñā — wisdom (understanding in the highest form) having ***nirvāṇa*** as its object.

nirvāṇa-dhātu — Sphere of ***nirvāṇa.***

nirvedha — Penetration, decisive distinction.

nirvedha-bhāgīya — Preparatory efforts conducing to decisive distinction: i.e., to the arising of outflow-free knowledge. These are also called the skilful roots; there are four: ***uṣmagata***, ***mūrdhan***, ***kṣānti***, ***laukikāgra-dharma***.

niśraya-hetu — Reliance cause, one of a set of five causes. → ***janana-hetu***.

niṣyanda — Emanation.

niṣyanda-phala — Uniform-emanation fruit.

nītārtha — (A doctrine) whose meaning has been fully drawn out ; explicit. → ***neyārtha***.

nivaraṇa — Hindrance

nivṛta-avyākrta — Veiled-non-defined; i.e., morally non-defined but still obstructive to the spiritual path.

nivṛtāvyākṛta-vijñapti-rūpa — veiled-non-defined information matter

nivṛtti — Reversing/stopping of the ***saṃsāric*** process.

niyama — Principle, a fixed rule.

niyata karma — Determinate ***karma.***

nyāya — Logic, right method. It is also one of the ***ākāra*** of ***mārga-satya***.

ogha — Flood.

pāda — Foot; a line, a (fourth) part.

pada-kāya — Phrase-group, one of the ***viprayukta-saṃskāra***.

padārtha — (Real) category.

paiśunya — Malicious speech.

pāka — Cooking, maturation.

pakti — Cooking, maturing.

pañca-avara-bhāgīya — 'Five fetters pertaining to the lower portion', i.e., to the ***kāma-dhātu***. They comprise: ***satkāya-dṛṣṭi***, ***śīla-vrata-parāmarśa***, ***vicikitsā***, ***kāmacchanda*** and ***vyāpāda***.

pañcadhā samatā — The fivefold sameness or equality the fulfilment of which two mental factors are said to be conjoined (***saṃprayukta***).

pañca-nikāya — Five categories of abandonables: (1)-(4) those abandonable by insight into ***duḥkha***, ***samudaya***, ***nirodha***, ***mārga***, and (5) by ***bhāvanā***.

pañca-ūrdhva-bhāgīya — The 'five (***saṃyojana***-s) pertaining to the upper portion'; i.e., to the ***rūpa***- and ***ārūpya-dhātu***-s. They comprise: ***rāga*** arisen from ***rūpa-dhātu***, ***rāga*** arisen from ***ārūpya-dhātu***, ***auddhatya***, ***māna*** and ***avidyā***.

pañcavastuka — 'Comprising five things/categories', an important chapter of the PrŚ dealing with the five categories of ***dharma***-s: ***rūpa***, ***citta***, ***caitasika***, ***citta-viprayukta-saṃskāra*** and ***asaṃskṛta***.

pañca-vijñāna-kāya — The group five (sensory) consciousnesses.

paracitta-jñāna — Knowledge of another's mind.

para-kṛta — Done by others, other-caused.

parama — Highest. Also, 'Most Excellent', one of the 14 synonyms for ***pratisaṃkhyā-nirodha*** in the MVŚ.

paramāṇu — 'The extremely fine', an atom. The MVŚ defines it thus: "A ***paramāṇu*** is the smallest ***rūpa***. It cannot be cut, broken, penetrated. … It is neither long nor short … . It has no smaller parts; it cannot be decomposed … It is … the finest (***sarva-sūkṣma***) of all ***rūpa***-s."

parāmarśa — (Irrational) adherence.

paramārtha — Highest sense; an absolute real.

paramārtha-sat — Absolutely real, existent from the ultimate standpoint.

paramārtha-satya — Absolute truth.

parāvṛtta — Transformed.

paravijñāpana — Informing to or from others.

parihāṇa-dharman — Of the nature of being susceptible to retrogression.

parihāṇi— Retrogression (from spiritual attainment).

parijñā — Complete knowledge.

pariṇāma — Transformation.

parinirvāṇa — Complete, final ***Nirvāṇa***; i.e., the final passing away of an ***arhat*** or buddha.

paripūraka-karma — Completing ***karma***; ***karma*** that contributes to specific details of a given type of existence (human, etc.) determined by an ***ākṣepaka karma***.

pariṣkāra — Utensils.

parīttakleśabhūmikā dharmāḥ— Subsidiary universal ***dharma***-s of defilement.

parivāra — Retinue, accompaniment.

pāruṣya — Harsh speech.

paryavasthāna — Envelopment. For the Sautrāntika and some other schools, this represents the manifested (as opposed to latent) defilement. → ***anuśaya***.

paryāya — Synonyms, alternatives, doctrinal perspective.

paścātkālaja — That which arises subsequently.

paścāt-pādaka — That which accords with the latter (and not the former) alternative.

pāścātya — Western masters, the Sarvāstivāda masters living west (around the Gandhāra region) of Kaśmīra.

paṭutva — Forcefulness.

phala — Fruit.

phala-ākarṣaṇa — The dragging out of a fruit (out of its existence in the future temporal period).

phala-dāna — The actual giving of the fruit (as opposed to ***phalākṣepa/phala-parigrahaṇa***).

phalākṣepa — Projection of the fruit; i.e. the causal determination that a particular ***dharma***, ***y***, will be the corresponding fruit of a present ***dharma***, ***x***. Each ***dharma***, at the present moment, and only at the present moment, can project its own fruit (i.e., can have this activity of yielding its own next moment of existence in its serial continuity. → ***kāritra***).

phala-pratigrahaṇa — 'Grasping of the fruit'; i.e., acquiring, in the present moment, the causal efficiency for a ***dharma***'s effect. → ***phalākṣepa.***

pipāsā — Thirst.

prabhā — Radiance.

prabhava — Source, origin, cause, production. As one of the ***ākāra*** of ***samudaya-satya***, it means production or successive causation.

pradāśa — Depravity.

pradhāna-dravya — Chief substance/essence.

prahāṇa — Abandonment.

prahāṇa-bhāvanā-ārāmatā — Delight in the cultivation of abandonment (of defilements).

prahāṇa-mārga — Path of abandonment.

prahāṇa-pratipakṣa — Counteragent resulting in abandonment (of defilements).

prajñā — Understanding, wisdom.

prajñā-indriya — Faculty of understanding.

prajñapti — Designation, concept, convention, teaching, arrangement.

prajñapti-sat — Conceptually existent, relatively real.

prajñapti-sāvadya — An offence or transgression by way of convention (***prajñapti***); e.g., drinking liquor.

prajñaptitaḥ sat — → ***prajñapti-sat***.

prajñā-vimukta — Liberated through understanding/wisdom. This refers to te type f arhat who, through ***prajñā***, overcomes the ***kleśāvaraṇa*** and becomes liberated.

prākarṣika-pratītya-samutpāda — One of the fourfold Sarvāstivādin interpretation of the conditioned co-arising. According to this interpretation, conditioned co-arising extends over (***prākarṣika***) three periods (past, present, future) of existence.

prakṛti-sāvadya — A transgression which is an offence in its intrinsic nature; e.g., killing.

pramāda — Non-diligence, heedlessness.

pramāṇa — A valid means of knowledge.

prāṇātipāta — Taking of life.

praṇidhāna — Resolution, past vow.

praṇidhi-jñāna — Knowledge that is produced in accordance with the particular manner of the practitioner's former resolution to have the knowledge.

praṇidhi-jñāna-samādhi — The meditation, in accordance with the strength of which, the particular ***praṇidhi-jñāna*** is produced.

praṇīta — Excellent, wonderful. Also, one of the 14 synonyms for ***pratisaṃkhyā-nirodha*** in the MVŚ.

prapañca — Conceptual proliferation.

prāpti — Acquisition, a ***viprayukta-saṃskāra*** which links (establishes a relationship with) a ***dharma*** to a sentient being.

prasāda — 1. Faith, freedom from doubt. 2. Clarity, translucence, sensitivity (said of the sense faculties).

prasāda-rūpa — Translucent, sensitive matter.

prasaṅga — Attachment; consequence.

prasiddha — Bilaterally or universally established.

praśrabdhi — Calm.

prati-bimba — Image.

pratideśan'ādi-pratipakṣaḥ — Counteractive effect by way of confession, etc.

pratigha — Hostility.

pratighāta — Obstruction. Three types of pratighāta are: ***āvaraṇa***-, ***viṣaya***- and ***ālambana***-.

pratikṣepaṇa-sāvadya — A transgression that is by way of prohibition.

pratilābha — Obtainment.

pratilambha — → ***pratilābha.***

prātimokṣa-saṃvara — Restraint (as an ***avijñapti-karma***) in the form of undertaking ordination vows.

pratiniḥsṛṣṭa— Cast aside.

pratiniyama-hetu — Distinguishing/specifying cause.

prati-pad — Path (leading to ***Nirvāṇa***); a synonym for ***mārga***.

pratipakṣa — Counteragent.

pratipakṣa bhāvanā — Counteraction-cultivation.

pratipakṣodaya — (Abandonment of defilement on) arising of its counteragent.

pratipannaka — Candidate of a spiritual fruit on the path of spiritual progress.

pratipatti — Course of practice.

pratisaṃdhi — Relinking.

pratisaṃkhyā-nirodha — Cessation through deliberation. → ***nirvāṇa***.

pratisaṃvid — Unhindered knowledge. → ***dharma- pratisaṃvid.***

pratisamyukta — Connected with, pertaining to.

pratiśaraṇa — Reliance, refuge.

prati-srota — 'Stream-discordant', one who has planted the skilful roots of ***mokṣa-bhāgīya***. Stream (***srotas***) refers to ***saṃsāra***.

pratiṣṭhā-hetu— Supporting cause, one of a set of five ***hetu***-s. → ***janana-hetu***.

pratītya-samutpāda — Conditioned co-arising.

pratītya-samutpādatva — The fact/principle of ***pratītya-samutpāda***, one of the nine unconditioned ***dharma***-s of some schools.

prativedha — Penetration, one of the 14 synonyms for ***pratisaṃkhyā-nirodha*** in the MVŚ.

prativedhanā-dharman — ***prayoga***-s that are capable of penetrating the state of ***arhat.***

prativijñapti — Discernment/cognition with regard to an object

pratyakṣa — Direct perception.

pratyakṣa-buddhi — A perception that is a ***pratyakṣa***.

pratyakṣa-pramāṇa — The valid means of knowledge, which is direct perception.

pratyaya — Condition. There are four: ***hetu***-, ***ālambana***-, ***samanantara***-, ***adhipati***-.

pratyaya-kauśalya — Skill with regard to condition.

pratyupasthita — Coming into the field of one's experience; appearing right in front.

pravāhaḥ — A continuity.

pravartaka — (Initial) propeller.

pravrajyā — 'Going forth', leaving the home life.

pravṛtti — Process; the ***saṃsāric*** process.

prayoga — Preparatory effort.

prayoga-avasthā — The stage of ***prayoga.***

prayoga-mārga — The preparatory path.

prayogaviśeṣa — A special or distinctive effort.

prāyogika — Derived from preparatory effort.

premā — Affection.

preta — Hungry ghost.

prītīndriya — The faculty of joy.

pṛṣṭha — Subsequent.

pṛthagjana — A worldling (one who has not yet become an ***ārya***).

pṛthagjanatva — The quality of a worldling; sometimes listed as a ***viprayukta-saṃskāra***.

pṛthivī — Earth; also the Earth element, one of the ***mahābhūta***-s.

pudgala — Person.

pudgala-vāda — The doctrine of the Vātsīputrīya and its branches that there exists a ineffable 'person' which is neither identical nor different from the five ***skandha***-s.

puṇya — Merit, meritorious action.

puṇya-kṣetra — Field of merit.

puruṣa — A man.

puruṣakāra-phala — Manly/virile fruit.

pūrvācārya — Ancient master.

pūrvaṅgama — Fore-running.

pūrvānubhūta — Experienced before.

****pūrvānudhātu*** — Subsidiary elements that has been accumulated from the past; a term used by Śrīlāta in his version of the ***bīja*** theory.

pūrva-pādaka — That which accords with the former (and not the latter) alternative.

rāga — Greed.

rāja-sthānīya — Governor.

ramaṇīya — Lovable, one of the 14 synonyms for ***pratisaṃkhyā-nirodha*** in the MVŚ.

rasa — Taste.

rasa-artha — Gustatory object.

rāśi — Heap.

ṛddhipāda — Bases of (supernormal) power.

ruci — Inclination.

rūpa — Matter.

rūpa-artha — Visual object.

rūpa-dhātu-pratisaṃyukta — Pertaining to the sphere of fine-materiality.

rūpaṇā — The characteristic of ***rūpa*** (primarily: obstructiveness and resistance).

rūpāvacara-pratisaṃyukta — Pertaining to the fine material sphere.

rūpi-dharma-s — Material ***dharma***-s.

rūpin — Material, having a particular form or figure.

śabda — Sound.

śabda-artha — Auditory object.

sabhāga — Homogenous, similar.

sabhāga-dhātu-sarvatraga — (Defilements) that are aid to be 'universal' (***sarvatraga***) in that they move in all the five category (***nikāya***) of abandonables pertaining to their own sphere (***dhātu***).

sabhāga-hetu — Homogeneous cause. One of six causes.

sabhāgatā — Group-homogeneity; one of the ***viprayukta-saṃskāra***-s.

sābhāgya-kāraṇa — Cause of similarity.

sa-dāha — Having the heat (of defilement).

ṣaḍ-āyatana — The six entrances/abodes.

saddharma — The True Doctrine (of the Buddha).

sādṛśya — Resemblance.

sahabhū-hetu — Co-existent cause; one of six causes. → ***hetu***.

sahaja (/***sahajāta***) — Conascent, born together.

sahāya — Companion.

śaikṣa — Trainee, referring to the ***ārya***-s who are not ***arhat***-s; pertaining to the trainee.

śaikṣa-mārga — path of trainee

śailpa-sthānika — Arts and crafts.

sa-indriya — Possessing of the faculties.

sakala-bandhana — A worldling who has not abandoned any defilements through the mundane path before becoming an ***ārya***.

sākāra — (1) Having a mode of activity; this refers to the fact that all ***citta-caitta-dharma***-s can cognize an object. (2) having the same mode of activity, one of the conditions for ***saṃprayoga***. → ***pañcadhā samatā***.

sākāra-jñāna-vāda — The theory that knowledge necessarily possesses an image of its object.

sākāra-vijñāna-vāda — Same as ***sākāra-jñāna-vāda***.

sakṛdāgāmin — Once-returner.

sakṛdāgāmin pratipannaka — Candidate for the fruit of a once-returner.

sākṣāt — Directly, face-to-face

sākṣāt-karaṇa — Realization.

śakti — Power, potency.

sālambana — 'Having a cognitive object'; a descriptive term for all mental factors, since they all necessarily take an object in arising.

sallakṣaṇa — Characteristic of the existent.

samādhi — Concentration.

samādhi-bhāvanā — Cultivation of concentration.

samādhija-prajñā — Understanding/wisdom derived from concentration.

sāmagrī — Harmony.

samāhita-bhūmi — 'Concentrated stage', the stage of concentration.

samanantara-pratyaya — Equal-immediate condition, one of the four ***pratyaya***-s. It serves as the support for, and gives way to, the arising of the immediately succeeding ***dharma*** in the serial continuity.

sāmantaka — Neighbouring. In the context of meditation, this refers to the stage neighbouring a meditational attainment. → ***samāpatti***.

samanvāgama — Endowment. One is said to have an endowment of a ***dharma*** when one, having acquired the ***dharma***, continues to possess it.

samanvāgama-asamanvāgama-kauśalya — (An Ābhidharmika's) skilfulness with regard to endowment and non-endowment.

samanvāhāra — Holding in mind (of a previously experienced object).

sāmānya-lakṣaṇa — Common characteristic.

sāmānyalakṣaṇa-kauśalya — (An Ābhidharmika's) skilfulness with regard to common characteristics.

samāpatty-āvaraṇa-vimukta — Liberated from all hindrances to meditational attainment.

sāmarthya — Capability, potency.

śamatha — Calm, tranquility. As a meditation practice, it is distinct from (though not opposed to) ***vipaśyanā***.

śamatha bhāvanā — Tranquility cultivation/meditation.

śamatha-carita — The tranquillity type (of practitioner).

śamatha vipaśyanā — Tranquility and insight.

samatikrama — Transcending, transcendance.

samāpatti — Attainment. In particular, it refers to the nine meditation attainment: four ***dhyāna***-s pertaining to the ***rūpa-dhātu***, four ***ārūpya samāpatti***-s, and ***nirodha-samāpatti***.

sāṃbandhika pratītya-samutpāda — One of the fourfold interpretation of the Sarvāstivāda on conditioned co-arising. This interpretation is that the 12 links of conditioned co-arising are connected (***sāṃbandhika***) through being causes and effects.

saṃbhāra — Requisite, provision (needed on the spiritual journey).

saṃbhinna-pralāpa — Frivolous speech.

saṃcetanīya-karma — A deed that is done intentionally

saṃcitatva — The fact of being accumulated.

saṃdhāna — (Birth-)relinking; a descriptive term for ***vijñāna***. Same as ***pratisaṃdhi***.

saṃghāta-paramāṇu — Atoms in agglomeration, akin to the modern conception of a molecule.

saṃgraha — (1) Mutual subsumption, inclusion, subordination. (2) Cohesion.

saṃgraha-asaṃgraha-kauśalya — (An Ābhidharmika's) skilfulness with regard to subsumption, non-subsumption.

saṃjñā — Ideation.

saṃjñāpavana — 'Wind of ***saṃjñā***'.

saṃjñā-vedita-nirodha-samāpatti — (Meditation) attainment of cessation of sensation and ideation. Same as ***nirodha-samāpatti***.

saṃkalpa cetanā — Volition of intention.

saṃmoha — Delusion.

saṃmukhībhāva — Coming into direct presence, becoming face-to-face.

saṃnipāta — Coming together, assemblage.

saṃniśraya — Support.

saṃprayoga — Association, conjunction. Mental ***dharma***-s are said to be in conjunction in accordance with the five-fold equality. → ***pañcadhā samatā***.

saṃprayogato 'nuśete — (A defilement) adheres and grows through the process of conjunction with the object.

saṃprayoga-viprayoga-kauśalya — (An Ābhidharmika's) skilfulness with regard to conjunction, disjunction.

saṃprayukta — Conjoined, associated. → ***pañcadhā samatā.***

saṃprayuktaka-hetu — Conjoined cause; one of six ***hetu***-s. The ***citta-caitta***-s, when arising together, are conjoined causes.

saṃsāra — The cycle of births and death.

saṃskāra — Conditionings, conditioning forces.

saṃskṛta — Conditioned, compounded.

saṃskṛta-lakṣaṇa — 'Characteristic of the conditioned'. There are four of the them, of the nature of ***viprayukta-saṃsāra***: ***jāti***, ***sthiti***, ***jarā***, ***anityatā/vyaya***. Together, they render a conditioned ***dharma*** momentary (***kṣaṇika***).

saṃsthāna — Shape.

saṃtati (***/santati***) — Serial continuity.

saṃtati-pariṇāma-viśeṣa — A distinctive transformation of the serial continuity.

saṃtīraṇa — Judgement, judgemental decision.

saṃtuṣṭi — Contentment.

samudācāra — Manifestation, coming into play.

samudaya — Origin.

samudaya-darśana-heya — (defilements) abandonable through insight into the ***samudaya-satya***.

samudaya-jñāna — Knowledge of the origin (of ***duḥkha***).

samudaya-satya — Noble truth of the origin (of ***duḥkha***).

samutthāna-citta — Originating thought.

samutthāna-hetu — Originating cause.

saṃvara — Restraint.

saṃvara-karma — Restraint qua (***avijñapti***) ***karma***.

saṃvarastha — Abiding in restraint (i.e., possessing restraint).

saṃvṛti-jñāna — Conventional knowledge .

saṃvṛti-saṃjñā — Conventional notion.

saṃvṛti-satya — Conventional truth.

samyag-ājīva — Proper livelihood. One aspect of the ***āryāṣṭāṅgika-mārga***.

samyag-dṛṣṭi — Proper views. One aspect of the ***āryāṣṭāṅgika-mārga***.

samyag-vāc — Proper speech. One aspect of the ***āryāṣṭāṅgika-mārga***.

samyag-vyāyāma — Proper Vigor. One aspect of the ***āryāṣṭāṅgika-mārga***.

samyak-karmānta — Proper action. One aspect of the ***āryāṣṭāṅgika-mārga***.

samyak-pradhāna — Proper effort. Same as ***samyag-vyāyāma.***

samyak-samādhi — Proper concentration. One aspect of the ***āryāṣṭāṅgika-mārga***.

samyak-saṃkalpa — Proper thinking. One aspect of the ***āryāṣṭāṅgika-mārga***.

samyak-smṛti — Proper mindfulness. One aspect of the ***āryāṣṭāṅgika-mārga***.

samyaktva-niyāma — Certitude of Perfection (i.e. of ***Nirvāṇa***).

samyaktva-niyāma-avakramaṇa — Entering into ***samyaktva-nyāma***; i.e., attaining stream entry.

samyaktva-niyamāvakrānti — Same as ***samyaktva-niyāma-avakramaṇa.***

samyaktva-nyāma — Perfection that is the separation from the raw; i.e., from defilements or the immaturity of the skilful roots.

saṃyoga — Connection, conjunction.

saṃyoga-vastu — Object of conjunction.

saṃyojana — Fetter. It is also a synonym for ***kleśa***.

saṅgha — The monastic community

sanidarśana — Visible.

śānta — Calmed.

santāna — Same as ***santati/saṃtati***.

santāpa — Torment.

santati-pariṇāma — (Progressive) transformation of a serial continuity.

saparivāra — Together with the retinue.

sapratigha — Resistant.

sārūpya — Co-ordination.

sarvadā asti — All exists; i.e. ***dharma***-s always (***sarvadā***) exist, whether future, present or past.

sarvahatāndhakāra — One who has destroyed all darkness (/ignorance).

sarva-saṃyojana-paryādāna-parijñā — Complete knowledge of the exhaustion of all fetters.

sarvāstitva — The fact of 'all exists', tri-temporal existence (of all ***dharma***-s).

Sarvāstivāda — A follower of the ***sarvāstitva*** doctrine.

sarva-sūkṣma — The finest.

sarvathā-sarvahatāndhakāra — One who has destroyed darkness in all ways; i.e., a buddha (who has overcome both ***kliṣṭa*** and ***akliṣṭājñāna***).

sarvatraga — 'Going everywhere', universal.

sarvatraga-hetu — Universal cause. One of six ***hetu***-s.

śaśa-rajas — 'Rabbit-dust', the size of seven ***ap-rajas***.

śaśa-śṛṅga — Horn of a hare; a simile for something which is an absolute non-existent.

sāsrava — With-outflow. A with-outflow object is one by taking which the defilement adheres to it and grows. It is also one whose effect is to retain us in ***saṃsāra***.

sāśraya — 'Having a supporting basis', a descriptive term for the ***citta-caitta-dharma***-s.

śāstra— A treatise.

śāśvata-vāda — The theory of eternalism.

śāṭhya — Dissimulation.

satkāya-dṛṣṭi — Self-view.

satpuruṣa — The 'True Man'.

sattva — Sentient being.

sattvākhya — Pertaining to sentient beings.

satya — Truth.

satyābhisamaya — Direct realisation of the (four noble) truths.

Sautrāntika — Follower of an important school "who take the ***sūtra*** as the authority, not the ***śāstra***."

sāvayava — Having a part.

sa-vipāka — Retributive.

śikṣā — Training.

śikṣamānā — "Learning', 'training'; a female member of the Saṅgha who is under prabation for the ***bhikṣuṇī*** ordination.

śikṣāpada — Training factors.

śīla — Morality, precept.

śīlāṅga — The section of ***śīla***.

śīla-vrata-parāmarśa — (Irrational) adherence to abstentions and vows.

śīla-vratopādāna — Clinging to abstentions and vows.

sīmā-bandha — The bond of boundary.

śīta — Cold.

skandha — Aggregates, explained as 'heap' (***rāśi***). There are five aggregates: ***rūpa***, ***vedanā***, ***saṃjñā***, ***saṃskāra***, ***vijñāna***.

ślakśṇatva — Smoothness.

smṛti — Memory, recollection.

smṛtyupasthāna — Base of mindfulness. There are four: ***kāya***-, ***vedanā***-, ***citta***- and ***dharma***-.

sneha — Humidity, adhesion.

sopadhiśeṣa-nirvāṇa-dhātu — Sphere of ***Nirvāṇa*** with a remnant of substratum.

sparśa — Contact, touch.

spraṣṭavya — Tangible.

śraddhā — Faith.

śraddhādhimukta — (One who) is freed through predominance of faith.

śraddhānusārin — Pursuer through faith.

śrāmaṇera — A male novice member of the Saṅgha who has not yet received the Higher Ordination.

śrāmaṇerī — A female novice member of the Saṅgha who has not yet received the Higher Ordination.

śrāmaṇya-phala — Fruit of the spiritual life; spiritual attainment.

śrāvaka — 'Listener', a disciple of teh Buddha.

srotaāpanna — Stream entrant.

srotaāpatti phala — Fruit of stream entry.

srotaāpatti-phala-stha — Abiding in the fruit of stream entry.

srotaāpatti pratipannaka — Candidate for the fruit of stream entry.

śrotābhijñā — Supernormal power of audition.

śrotra — Ear.

śrotra-indriya — Auditory faculty.

śruta-cintā-bhāvanā-may, contemplation and cultivation.

śruta-mayī-prajñā — Understanding derived from listening.

sthāna — Abode, place.

sthitākampya — (Those) abiding in their attainment without retrogressing, although they may not progress unless effort is exerted.

sthitikālāvedha — Momentum for the duration.

sthiti-lakṣaṇa — Duration-characteristic, a ***viprayukta-saṃskāra-dharma*** that causes the momentary duration of a conditioned ***dharma***. → ***saṃskṛta-lakṣaṇa***.

sthiti-sthiti — 'Duration-duration', one of the four ***anulakṣaṇa***-s. Its function is to cause the momentary duration of ***sthiti*** . → ***anulakṣaṇa***.

sthūlabhittika — Like a thick wall.

styāna — Torpor.

styāna-middha — Torpor-drowsiness.

sucarita — Good conduct.

sugati — Fortunate plane of existence.

sukha-vedanīya — Conducive to pleasant experience.

sukhendriya — Faculty of happiness.

śukla karma — A white (***śukla***) ***karma*** yielding white retribution: the action of ***rūpa-dhātu***, which is always pure (***śubham ekāntena***) generating agreeable (***manojña***) retribution.

śūnyatā — Emptiness.

śūnyatā-citta — The thought of the nature of ***śūnyatā*** (as a concept).

sūtra — (1) A discourse by the Buddha. (2) A concise discourse; the first of the ***dvādaśāṅga-dharma-pravacana.***

sūtraviśeṣa — A specific type of ***sūtra.***

svabhāva — Intrinsic nature.

svabhāva-vikalpa — Discrimination which is the very nature of consciousness itself.

svalakṣaṇa — Specific characteristic (unique to a ***dharma***).

svalakṣaṇa-kauśalya — (An Ābhidharmika's) skilfulness with regard to specific characteristics (of ***dharma***-s).

svaphalākṣepa-kāritra — The activity which is the projection of a (***dharma***'s) own fruit. This is the definition of ***kāritra***.

svarūpa — Essential nature.

sva-saṃbhāraṃ parigṛhṇāti — (An ***anuśaya***) gathers up to its own requisites (i.e., its own causes). This is in the sense that it repeatedly gathers up and gives rise to improper mental application (***ayoniśo manaskāra***).

sva-saṃvedana — Reflexive knowledge/awareness.

svayaṃ-kṛta — Self-done, self-caused.

tadālambana-kleśa-prahāṇa — The abandonment of a kleśa which takes a particular (***kuśala*** or an ***avyākṛta dharma*** as) object. When this happens, the ***dharma*** which is the object is also said to be abandoned since at that time the ***dharma*** comes to be disconnected.

tāmra-rajas (/***loha-rajas***) — 'Copper dust'; the size of seven ***aṇu***-s.

tandrī — Exhaustion.

tarkābhimāna — Conceit in logical skill.

tatkṣaṇa-samutthāna — Moment-origination; i.e., origination at the very moment of the action.

tatsabhāga — 'Similar to that (which is presently active, although this itself is non-active)', a 'facsimile'. E.g. An eye in darkness which does not exercise its function of seeing is a ***tatsabhāga*** eye.

tattva — Reality, suchness.

tejas — Fire; also, one of the four ***mahābhūta***-s.

tīkṣṇa — Sharp.

tīkṣṇendriya — Sharp faculty.

tīrthakāra — Heretics

tīvra — Strong, intense.

traidhātukavyāpin — Pervading in all three spheres.

ubhayabhāga-vimukta — 'Doubly liberated'. An ***arhat*** is so called when he overcomes both the ***kleśāvaraṇa*** and ***vimokṣāvaraṇa***. Besides being ***prajñā-vimukta***, he is also freed from all meditation-hindrance.

uccheda-vāda — Theory of annihilation.

udāna — 'Breathing out', inspirational verses said to be uttered spontaneously by the Buddha; one of the ***dvādaśāṅga-dharma-pravacana***.

upabṛṃhaṇa-hetu — Development cause; one of a set of five ***hetu***-s. → ***janana-hetu***.

upacita — Accumulated.

upādāna — Clinging.

upādāya — Dependent on, derived.

upādāya rūpa — Derived matter.

upadeśa — 'Teaching', 'elaborative exposition'; the last member of the ***dvādaśāṅga-dharma-pravacana***. In a specific sense, it is synonymous with Abhidharma. In Saṃghabhadra's words, "***upadeśa*** refers to the non-erroneous revealing, answering of objections and ascertainment, of the preceding [eleven] members [of the ***dvādaśāṅga-dharma-pravacana***]".

upadhi — Material basis, substratum.

upakleśa — Secondary defilement.

upanāha — Enmity.

upapadya-vedanīya-karma — ***Karma***-s experiencible in the next life.

upāsaka — A male lay Buddhist.

upasaṃpad — 'Completion'; the higher ordination for one who has joined the Saṅgha.

upāsikā — A female lay Buddhist.

upastambha-hetu — Maintaining cause; one of a set of five causes. → ***janana-hetu***.

upātta — Appropriated (by the ***citta-caitta***-s); i.e., sensitive (***rūpa***).

upavāsa-saṃvara — Restraint undertaken for one full day and a night.

upekṣā — Equanimity.

upekṣendriya — The faculty of equanimity.

ūrdhva-bhāgīya — (Fetters) pertaining to the upper portion. → ***pañca-ūrdhva-bhāgīya.***

ūṣma — Warmth.

uṣmagata — Warmed-up, the first attainment in the ***nirvedha-bhāgīya*** of the ***prayoga*** stage.

uṣṇatā — Heat.

uttama — Supreme, highest.

vag-vijñapti — Vocal expression; the information karma of speech.

Vaibhāṣika — A Sarvāstivādin who takes the ***Abhidharma-mahāvibhāṣā*** as the authority.

vaipulya — 'Development', one of the ***dvādaśāṅga-dharma-pravacana***. → ***vaitulya***.

vairāgya — Detachment.

vaitulya — Unmatchability. As a technical term, it is said by the Vaibhāṣika to be synonymous with ***vaipulya*** and ***vaidalya*** (Pāli: ***vedalla***).

vajropama-samādhi — 'Diamond-like concentration', so called because, like a diamond that can cut through all things, it is the last stage in the abandonment of defilement; whatever defilements that have remained are all abandoned in this ***samādhi***.

vāk — Speech.

vākya — Sentence.

varga — A separate part/division, a chapter.

varṇa — Color.

vāsanā — Trace, perfuming.

vastu — Thing, base, reason.

vātāyana-rajas — Dust in the wind passage.

vāyu — Air.

vedanā — Sensation, feeling.

Vibhajyavāda — A school of thought doctrinally opposed to the Sarvāstivāda. It holds that the present ***dharma***-s alone exist. However, some among them, like the followers of the Kāśyapīya, concede that the past karma that have not yet given fruit (***adatta-phala***) can also be said to exist.

vibhaṅga — Analysis, exposition.

vibhāṣā — Commentary.

vicāra — Investigation.

vicikitsā — Doubt.

vidūṣaṇā-pratipakṣa — A counteragent which generates disgust.

vihiṃsā — Harmfulness.

vijñāna — Consciousness.

vijñāna-dhātu — The consciousness element.

vijñānānantyāyatana — The sphere of infinite consciousness, the second of four ***ārūpya samāpatti***-s. →***samāpatti, ārūpya-dhātu.***

vijñapti-karma — Informative ***karma.*** This refers to the bodily and vocal ***karma***-s that are 'informing', i.e., indicative of the mental state of the doer.

vijñaptimātratā — The Yogācāra doctrine of 'cognition-only'.

vijñeya — Cognizable.

vikalpa — Discrimination, conceptualization.

vikriyotpādanā — The nature of change (being disfigured) in arising.

vikṣipta — Distracted.

vimokṣa-mārga — Path of liberation. (= ***vimukti-mārga***)

vimokṣāvaraṇa — Hindrance of liberation. To attain perfect liberation, an ***arhat*** must overcome this hindrance besides the ***kleśāvaraṇa***. → ***ubhayabhāga-vimukta***.

vimukti-mārga — Same as ***vimokṣa-mārga.***

vineya — Those to be transformed/guided.

vipāka-hetu — Retributive cause.

vipāka-phala — Retribution fruit.

vipariṇāma — Change.

viparīta — Being topsy-turvy, turned upside down.

vipaśyanā bhāvanā — Insight cultivation/meditation.

vipaśyanā-carita — The insight-meditation type of practitioner.

vipratisāra — Remorse.

viprayukta-saṃskāra — Conditionings disjoined from thought. These ***dharma***-s are neither material nor mental.

viratyaṅga — The section of abstention.

vīrya — Vigor.

visabhāga-dhātv-ālambana — (Defilements) which take objects pertaining to other spheres (than that to which it belongs).

visadṛśa — Different, dissimilar.

visaṃyoga — Disjunction.

visaṃyoga-phala — Fruit of disjunction; i.e. ***pratisaṃkhyā-nirodha***.

visaṃyoga-prāpti — Acquisition of disjunction.

viṣaya — Object-domain.

viṣaya-pratighāta — Obstruction qua object-domain. → ***pratighāta***.

viśeṣa — Difference, distinction, special, specific.

viśeṣa-mārga — Path of advance/distinction.

viśiṣṭa — Distinct, special,

viśiṣṭa-karma — Distinctive ***karma.***

viṣkambhana — Subduing.

vīta-rāga — Detached.

vitarka — Reasoning.

viveka — Separation.

vratāṅga — The section of observation of vows.

vṛtti — Operation, action.

vyākaraṇa — Explanation, prediction (a later acquired meaning). Also, the third of the ***vādaśāṅga-dharma-pravacana***.

vyañjana-kāya — The syllable-group, one of the ***viprayukta-saṃskāra***-s.

vyantībhūta — Expurgated.

vyāpāda — Malice.

vyapakarṣa — Physical withdrawal.

vyāpāra — Function, operation.

vyatireka — The principle of difference(/exclusion).

vyaya-vyaya — 'Disappearance-disappearance'. Same as ***anityatā-anityatā***. → ***anulakṣaṇa***.

vyūha — Extension, distribution, arrangement.

yāna — Vehicle.

yathābhūtam — Truly, truly as it is.

yoga — Yoke.

yoni — Mode of birth.

yukti — Logical argument, logic.

Index

Corrigenda

Page	Line		Read
xi	13	*Abhidharma-mahā-vibhāṣa-śāstra*	*Abhidharma-mahā-vibhāṣā-śāstra*
xi	21	*Saṃyuktagāma,* 雜阿含, T no. 98	*Saṃyuktāgama,* 雜阿含, T no. 99
4	24	*Mahā-koṭṭhila*	*Mahā-koṭṭhita*
6	17	*sikhataṃ*	*sikkhataṃ*
13	21	is taught is taught by the Master	is taught by the Master
24	19	(*cf. infra,* § 15.2.2.1)	(*cf. infra,* § 15.3.2.1)
32	12	*Abhidharmāṃṛta*	*Abhidharmāmṛta*
53	5	*ṣadbhir āyatanavranāiḥ*	*ṣaḍbhir āyatanavranaiḥ*
106	26	*Madhyamāgama* (T 1, no. 181)	*Madhyamāgama* (T 1, no. 26)
259	21	*paramāṇnu*	*paramāṇu*
385	22	*samanavāgama*	*samanvāgama*
387	13	*cintamayī*	*cintāmayī*
403	11	Mīmaṃsakas	Mīmāṃsakas
403	11	Vaiyakaraṇa	Vaiyākaraṇa
403	20	*vagvijñapti*	*vāgvijñapti*
436	1	*saṃgātaḥ*	*saṃghātaḥ*
465	4	*kilese pahatuṃ sakkonti*	*kilese pahātuṃ sakkonti*
476	15	*upadāna-skandhā*	*upādāna-skandhā*
488	6	*kṛṇa*	*kṛṣṇa*
515	8	13.8.1.1.	13.8.1.2.
546	12	*pāpasa*	*pāpassa*
595	12	*darśanaya-mārga*	*darśana-mārga*
637	4	*prāpti-s maybe śaikṣa*	*prāpti*-s may be *śaikṣa*
639	19	The *asaṃskṛta ā* ...	The *asaṃskṛta ākāśa* has no activity ...
663	23	*ābhogatmaka*	*ābhogātmaka*
664	8	*adhṣiṭhāna*	*adhiṣṭhāna*
670	25	*ākāśā*	*ākāśa*
671	32	*āvaraṇa-pratighātā*	*āvaraṇa-pratighāta*
672	34	*bhāutika-rūpa*	*bhautika-rūpa*
676	29	*sarvatrga-hetu*	*sarvatraga-hetu*
679	14	*kṛṇa karma*	*kṛṣṇa karma*
694	7	*śruta-cintā-bhāvanā-may,*	[delete entry]
698	20	*vādaśāṅga*	*dvādaśāṅga*